*The Lord's Dominion*
*The History of Canadian Methodism*

*The Lord's Dominion* describes the development of mainstream Canadian Methodism, from its earliest days to its incorporation into the United Church of Canada in 1925. Neil Semple looks at the ways in which the church evolved to take its part in the crusade to Christianize the world and to meet the complex needs of Canadian Protestants, especially as it faced the challenges of the twentieth century.

Semple covers virtually every aspect of Canadian Methodism. He examines early-nineteenth-century efforts to evangelize pioneer British North America and the revivalistic activities so important to the mid-nineteenth-century years. He documents Methodists' missionary work both overseas and in Canada among aboriginal peoples and immigrants and analyses the Methodist contribution to Canadian education and the leadership the church provided for the expansion of the role of women in society. He also assesses the spiritual and social dimensions of evangelical religion in the personal lives of Methodists, addressing such issues as prohibition, prostitution, the importance of the family, and changing attitudes towards children in Methodist doctrine and Canada in general.

Semple argues that Methodism evolved into the most Canadian of all the churches, helping to break down the geographic, political, economic, ethnic, and social divisions that confounded national unity. Although the Methodist Church did not achieve the universality it aspired to, Semple concludes that it succeeded in defining the religious, political, and social agenda for the Protestant component of Canada, providing a powerful legacy of service to humanity and to God.

NEIL SEMPLE is currently working on a biography of Samuel S. Nelles, president of Victoria College.

McGILL-QUEEN'S STUDIES IN THE HISTORY
OF RELIGION
*G.A. Rawlyk, Editor*

Volumes in this series have been supported by the
Jackman Foundation of Toronto.

# The Lord's Dominion

## *The History of Canadian Methodism*

NEIL SEMPLE

McGill-Queen's University Press
Montreal & Kingston • London • Buffalo

*To Robert Semple (1914–1990), a Christian gentleman*

© McGill-Queen's University Press 1996
ISBN 0-7735-1367-1 (cloth)
ISBN 0-7735-1400-7 (paper)

Legal deposit third quarter 1996
Bibliothèque nationale du Québec

Printed in Canada on acid-free paper

McGill-Queen's University Press is grateful to the Canada Council for support of its publishing program.

**Canadian Cataloguing in Publication Data**

Semple, Neil, 1949–
    The Lord's dominion: the history of Canadian Methodism
    (McGill-Queen's studies in the history of religion; 21)
    Includes bibliographical references and index.
    ISBN 0-7735-1367-1 (bound)
    ISBN 0-7735-1400-7 (pbk.)
    1. Methodist Church of Canada – History. 2. Methodist Church – Canada –
    History. I. Title. II. Series.
    BX8251.S44 1996    287'.0971    C95-920976-X

Maps reprinted courtesy of Rosemary Gagan, from *A Sensitive Independence: Canadian Methodist Women in Canada and the Orient, 1881–1925* (Montreal: McGill-Queen's Univ. Press, 1992).

This book was typeset by Typo Litho Composition Inc. in 10/12 Baskerville.

# Contents

FIGURE

TABLES

MAPS

# Acknowledgments

One of the sincere pleasures associated with writing this book is the opportunity it provides for acknowledging the great debt I owe to so many individuals. After I have worked for a quarter of a century in the fields of Canadian social, urban, and religious history, much of my gratitude can only be expressed by a sincere thank-you to all who for lack of space must remain nameless. Only a small part of their academic influence is reflected in the reference notes accompanying this text. I hope to be able to thank them individually in the future.

More directly, only those intimately associated with the long history of the Jackman Methodist History Project can truly appreciate the contribution provided by its supervisory committee: Ramsay Cook, Jean Dryden, Goldwin S. French, John Webster Grant, Glenn Lucas, George Rawlyk, William Westfall, and Father Edward Jackman. They have always been willing to take time from their own busy careers, and their unequalled knowledge, sympathy, and patience have significantly improved the value of this study. The chairman of the committee, Goldwin French, deserves particular credit for his ongoing assistance with the innumerable details associated with publishing. The two anonymous external readers have likewise conscientiously evaluated and elevated the study. Together they have saved me from many errors of fact and interpretation; those that remain are my own responsibility.

Much of the early research for this book was carried on assiduously by Peter James, Michael Owen, Mary Pat Reilly, and Katherine Ridout. Their dedicated and meticulous work has been invaluable in recreating Methodism's rich heritage. As always, the United Church Archives at Victoria University in Toronto remains among the best research centres in the country. My debt to Jean Dryden, the archivist, and to her past and present staff of Ruth Wilson, Karen Banner, Joy Boggs, Cori Gaughan, Grace Griffiths, Alex Hutchinson, Tim Hutchinson, Grima Kaszap, Jim Lewis, Ian Mason, Molly O'Reilly, Laurel Parsons, Rick Stapleton, Alex Thomson, and Ken Wilson is enormous. They have been tireless in their assistance. I am also pleased in this context to acknowledge the aid of former archivists Mary Ann Tyler and especially Glenn Lucas, who struggled to build the archives and helped generations of researchers. At the same time, the United Church's regional archives across the country have provided much additional information to demonstrate the diversity, cohesion, and vitality of the Methodist church.

I would also like to thank Dr Eva Kushner, former president of Victoria University, and her successor, Dr Roseann Runte, for providing me with a home at the university in which to write this book. The faculty at both Victoria College and Emmanuel College have been unstinting in their moral and intellectual support for this project. They have provided a stimulating and enlightened community all too rare in these days of the anonymous modern university.

Philip Cercone and Joan McGilvray at McGill-Queen's University Press have done their usual fine job in producing *The Lord's Dominion*, and I was extremely fortunate to have Elizabeth Hulse copyedit the final manuscript. She has significantly improved the style, tone, and form of the book.

No book is written in a vacuum, and I would like to take this opportunity to record publicly my thanks to the many friends who have kept my spirits and enthusiasm high, and especially to my family, without whose help and encouragement this book would never have been finished. In dedicating it to my father, Robert Semple, I only inadequately recognize my debt to his quiet and gentlemanly leadership.

Finally, I would like to pay a special tribute to Father Edward Jackman, O.P., and the Jackman Foundation for their generous financial support. More than money, however, Father Jackman's interest and sympathetic understanding have sustained this project and many others as well. I hope this book will provide a small signpost to his Christian service.

*The Lord's Dominion*

# Introduction

When the fathers of the Canadian confederation searched for an appropriate designation for their new country, they found it in the biblical term "dominion." The Dominion of Canada appeared indeed to reflect the hope of Psalm 72 – "He shall have dominion also from sea to sea" – as well as the Old Testament prophet's claim for the Messiah: "and his dominion shall be from sea even to sea, and from the river even to the ends of the earth."[1] No group of Canadians prayed more vigorously than the Methodists that Canada would truly become the Lord's dominion and a Christian model for the entire world. Canadian Methodists intended to spread evangelical Christianity throughout the length and breadth of the country and to build Canada into the site of Christ's earthly kingdom. In fact, they had struggled to advance God's kingdom in British North America from the beginning of their work in the late eighteenth century; they shared John Wesley's mission to spread scriptural holiness throughout the land and to make disciples of all nations.

From its inception, Methodism had hoped to encompass everyone in its fellowship. In Canada it saw its destiny as supplying the spiritual and moral component of national life. Theologically, Methodism was founded on the assumption that salvation was universally available; there were no specially elect. Individuals consciously chose to accept or reject Christ's atoning grace. In this shared experience of salvation, everyone was equal. In fact, the world was only meaningfully divided between the saved and the damned. Hence Methodism helped to break down the secular barriers of class, race, sex, and ethnicity and to meld all people into one community. In addition, it remained a social religion; it did not attempt to hive its members off in utopian experiments or to fix itself in one time or place. It never wished to succumb to the pressures of secular life, but neither was it willing to remove itself from the world in which it found itself.

This book is a history of mainstream Canadian Methodism. It is designed to provide the interested general reader with basic factual information regarding the growth and influence of Canadian Methodism from its origin in England in the early eighteenth century until it merged into the United Church of Canada in 1925. Because of the breadth of this topic, the study touches only lightly on the more important elements of this story. Little attempt has been made to delve into church operations at the local level or to study particular individuals or congregations. However, the book will provide a broad institutional and intellectual context for those attempting to understand the more particular aspects of church life. It should also supply an essential starting-point for those interested in pursuing research on some component of Methodist or general Canadian church history. Rather than exhausting any topic, this history of Canadian Methodism may well suggest areas for further research and provide the core sources on which to base that work.

This monograph follows a thematic approach within a general chronological order and divides into two nearly discrete sections at about the middle of the nineteenth century. Beginning with John Wesley and the emergence of a "People Called Methodists" in Britain and the United States, the two sources of Methodist operations in British North America, the study moves quickly to the pioneering work in what is now Canada. The following chapters chronicle the emerging institution in Atlantic and central Canada to the middle of the nineteenth century and assess the early missions to native Canadians. At the same time, they explore the personal and social dimensions of Methodism and its attempt to create a deeply spiritual and moral Canadian society. Particular attention is given to the Methodists' use of mass evangelism to stimulate these goals and "revive" Protestantism in the country.

The second part of the book begins with an introduction to the growth and consolidation of Canadian Methodism. No longer an earnest body of converts striving to sustain a heroic mission to a pioneer society, it developed into a diverse and complex social institution and in 1884 emerged as the largest Protestant denomination in Canada. The following chapters explore in more detail the evolution and transformations taking place in the Methodist church as it attempted to sustain a relevant mission to Canadians. For Methodists, no element in this transformation was more important than education, and the book briefly discusses Methodist primary, secondary, and university education and analyses the training of the Methodist ministry, especially as it was forced to absorb the new approaches and knowledge introduced by Darwinian science and higher criticism. A brief survey of the Methodist mission operations follows. In attempting to fulfil its mandate to evangelize and build a Protestant nation, while working to mould Canadians into a just and moral people, the denomination gave high priority to mission work, particularly across western Canada and to new immigrants. By the 1870s, the Methodist church was also sufficiently large to join in the international crusade to evangelize the non-Christian world, and it developed missions in Japan and later China.

However, the role of the church was not merely to expand its own horizons, but more importantly, to create a moral social order and to promote God's kingdom on earth. The church assumed the right to inculcate in Canadian society its essentially middle-class value system in order to create a just and humane nation. By the end of the nineteenth century, young people

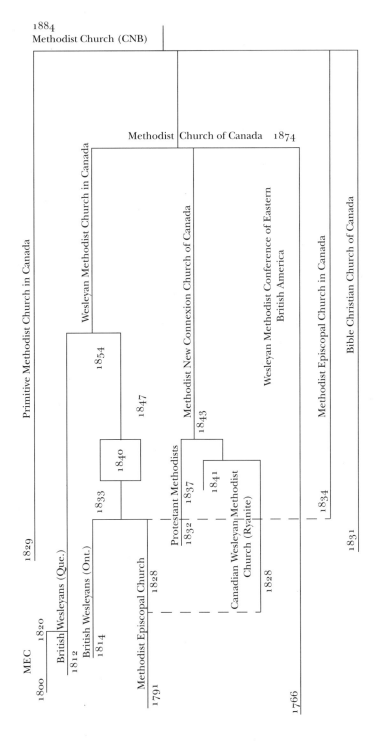

Figure 1
Methodist reorganizations in Canada

had become crucial in this task, both as subjects to be shaped and as allies in the struggle. In addition, the Methodist church had become a mature, national institution that occupied a leadership role in assisting Canadians to overcome the many challenges of the early twentieth century. Finally, however, Methodism refused to be confined by narrow denominational boundaries. To fulfil its perceived destiny as Canada's national church, it actively sought ecumenical cooperation and ultimately union with other like-minded Protestants. It believed little of importance still divided the mainstream Protestant churches. The last part of the study focuses on this church-union movement.

Since the book deals primarily with the mainstream Methodist connexions in Canada, it is important from the outset to understand their shifting ecclesiastical relationships, which culminated in interdenominational union in 1925. The accompanying chart should also provide a useful guide for understanding the rather complex reorganizations within Methodism; the issues involved in such restructuring will be dealt with more fully in subsequent chapters. The different connexions represented groups that emerged in Britain or the United States and emigrated to British North America during the eighteenth and nineteenth centuries. They would require most of the nineteenth century to work out their own destiny in Canada.

Beginning with Laurence Coughlan in 1766, Wesleyan missionaries from Britain ministered to the Protestant Irish and English settlers in Newfoundland. William Black, a Yorkshire Methodist raised in Nova Scotia, started evangelizing the Maritimes in 1781 and after the formation of the American *Methodist Episcopal Church* at Christmas 1784, received limited assistance from that quarter. A Nova Scotia district was organized in 1786, but after 1800 the region was supervised by the British Wesleyans. Newfoundland became a separate district in 1815, and later Bermuda was added to the Nova Scotia district. It was in turn divided into the Nova Scotia and New Brunswick districts in 1826, and the British Wesleyans subsequently subdivided the Nova Scotia district as membership grew. Finally, in 1855 the Wesleyans established the semi-autonomous *Wesleyan Methodist Conference of Eastern British America*.

In Upper Canada, the Methodist Episcopal Church commenced formal missionary work among the recent immigrants in 1791 under the ministry of William Losee. The region was soon organized as a district, first of the New York and later of the Genesee Conference. In 1824 it became the *Canada Conference of the Methodist Episcopal Church* and four years was set apart as the *Methodist Episcopal Church in Canada*. Most of the members of this church joined in 1833 with the much smaller British Wesleyan connexion to form the *Wesleyan Methodist Church in Canada*. The British and Canadian factions of this church briefly separated in 1840 but reunited seven years later. The members who had remained out of the 1833 union formed themselves into a continuing *Methodist Episcopal Church in Canada* in 1834, which expanded to become the second largest Methodist church in the country.

The Methodists in Lower Canada had relied on their own laity for leadership until the American Episcopal Methodists began sending missionaries in 1800. British Wesleyan missionaries competed in the region from the

War of 1812 until the Americans agreed to withdraw in 1820. The Wesleyans of Lower Canada amalgamated in 1854 with the Wesleyan Methodist Church in Canada. The same year the church acquired control of the British Wesleyan missions in the northwest, originally begun in 1840. The first broader union occurred in 1874, when the Wesleyan Methodist Church in Canada joined with the Wesleyan Methodist Conference of Eastern British America, and together they united with the *Methodist New Connexion Church of Canada.*

The Methodist New Connexion was itself an amalgamation of several smaller groups. The British New Connexion missionary John Addyman first came to Lower Canada in 1837. Three years later he visited Upper Canada and made official contact with the local *Canadian Wesleyan Methodist Church,* a different group from the Wesleyan Methodist Church in Canada. The Canadian Wesleyan Methodist Church was a faction under the leadership of Henry Ryan that had separated in 1828 from the original Methodist Episcopal Church in Canada. In 1841 it united with the New Connexion to form the *Canadian Wesleyan Methodist New Connexion Church.* Two years later the church absorbed the remnants of the *Methodist Protestant Church* in the Eastern Townships of Lower Canada. This offshoot of the American Methodist Protestant Church, which had begun sending missionaries to the area in 1832, was in serious decline. Addyman had served its main circuit in 1837 because it could not attract ministers from its own denomination. The combined church retained the name Wesleyan, despite the opposition of the New Connexion, until 1865, when it officially became the Methodist New Connexion Church of Canada.

The *Methodist Church of Canada,* formed by the 1874 union, led the amalgamation of the mainstream Methodists ten years later. At that time, it united with the Methodist Episcopal Church in Canada, the *Bible Christian Church of Canada,* and the *Primitive Methodist Church in Canada* to form the *Methodist Church* (Canada, Newfoundland, Bermuda).

The Primitive Methodist Church in Canada had been first organized in 1829 as a mission under the British Tunstall circuit. Limited to what is now Ontario, it gained district status in 1843 and became a separate conference in 1854. Like the New Connexion and the Primitive Methodist Church, the Bible Christian Church had begun as a breakaway movement from the Wesleyans in Britain. The Bible Christian Church of Canada had evolved out of missions to Prince Edward Island and Upper Canada begun in 1831. The stronger Upper Canadian operations developed into a conference in 1855 and united with the weak Prince Edward Island missions ten years later.

With the union of 1884, the Methodist Church became the largest Protestant denomination in Canada and had a substantial following in Newfoundland and Bermuda. Among the Methodist connexions, only the *British Methodist Episcopal Church* (an offshoot of the *African Methodist Episcopal Church,*) the German-speaking *Evangelical Association* and *United Brethren in Christ,* and the Canadian branch of the American *Free Methodist Church* remained out of the union. The Methodist Church united with the *Congregational Union of Canada* and the *Presbyterian Church in Canada* in 1925 to form *The United Church of Canada.*

I hope this information will help the reader understand the institutional development of Methodism which is discussed throughout the book. This study analyses the structural changes, infrastructure, and self-established values and goals, and concentrates on the role of the church leadership in establishing these priorities and setting the agenda for the general membership. Such an approach is perhaps more appropriate for the Methodist church than for the other large Protestant denominations since it was a highly centralized institution; decisions made by relatively few clerical and lay leaders tended to guide the whole connexion. At the same time, these individuals usually controlled the newspapers and the boards and committees that implemented policy. Moreover, in this study the social and political questions raised are those that interested the denomination, and they are assessed from the Methodist perspective. Unfortunately, taking this point of view means that the relationship of Methodism and the Methodist church to the broad range of issues facing secular Canadian society occupies little space. Nevertheless, the book should provide useful information for those interested in determining how Methodists reacted to specific social, intellectual, and political questions.

Methodism was never static or monolithic, and due attention is given to dissent within the Methodist structures and to the internal tensions that promoted change and kept the church from becoming rigid or mechanistic. As a denomination, it promoted a spiritual and moral fellowship among its members and demanded responsible social behaviour. But Methodism remained influential and vital because it was constantly prepared to transform its outward self to serve more effectively what it perceived to be the demands of contemporary society. Although it attempted to remain constant in essential matters of faith and belief, it was prepared to deal pragmatically with daily social issues in Canada. This approach was at least partially based on the church's belief in a humane and joyful religious experience and its optimistic trust in the future progress of the world.

This study focuses on the institutional development of the Methodist church, but that evolution cannot properly be separated from Methodism as a spiritual and social movement that transcended its institutional structures. The book therefore also explores the ideas and beliefs that undergirded the denomination and shaped its individual members. Methodism believed in the necessity of a personal experience of conversion and a rebirth to a life in Jesus Christ as Lord and Saviour. This rebirth was to be followed by the constant quest for a sanctified life totally committed to the love of God and humankind. Methodism in all its personal and social dimensions remained profoundly dedicated to the whole range of elements that composed spiritual and moral Christianity. Everything belonged to God; there should be no division between the sacred and secular in the world. Thus Methodism endeavoured to assist everyone ultimately to achieve heaven and to transform all of society into heaven on earth. Only then would the world truly become the Lord's dominion.

# 1 The Origins of Methodism

Methodism usually dates its birth to May 24, 1738, at Aldersgate in London. On that day John Wesley's religious conversion was confirmed as he felt his "heart strangely warmed."[1] He joyfully reported the event to his brother Charles, who had a similar, but more private conversion at about the same time. These experiences were the culmination of a long quest for personal redemption dating from at least their university days. The two Wesleys and several like-minded friends had sought salvation through the so-called Holy Club, which they had formed at Oxford over the winter of 1729–30. John had also attempted to establish a group for mutual spiritual improvement during his brief sojourn in Georgia between 1735 and 1737. Over the same decade, a number of independent evangelical groups committed to revival had been formed in England, and it was to the Fetter Lane Society at Aldersgate, under the leadership of the Moravians Peter Böhler and James Hutton, that he turned for spiritual nourishment.[2] However, even after his experience there, Wesley continued to face severe crises of faith and to search for the means of strengthening his relationship with God. His long and difficult struggle would serve as a vital example for future generations of Methodists undergoing similar battles.

John Wesley had been born at the rectory in Epworth on June 28, 1703, and Charles on December 18, 1707, two of nineteen children born to Samuel and Susanna Annesley Wesley. Their father was the high-church rector of Epworth. His frequent absences in London at church convocation meetings meant that the children received most of their early training from their mother, and throughout her life she remained a constant and effective counsellor. In a true sense, she was the mother of Methodism, uniting in herself strict discipline, a keen sense of mission and divine purpose, and a sound knowledge of Anglican and Reformed theology and history. She taught John that he had been set apart for "a divinely appointed task" and later encouraged him to accept innovations that would advance the cause of religious revival.[3] The family was the natural source of mutual support for the Wesleys, to which they turned when troubled or in need of advice. Although both John and Charles were self-reliant and enterprising, and at times even combative, they instinctively relied on each other.

John proceeded from intense home study to London's Charterhouse School and in 1720 to Christ Church College at Oxford. He was ordained deacon in the Church of England in 1725. A year later he became a fellow of Lincoln College. He received his MA in 1727, was ordained priest the following year, and in 1729 became lecturer in Greek and moderator of the daily philosophical disputations at the college. Between the summer of 1727 and the fall of 1729 he divided his time between Oxford and Epworth, where he assisted his father. Charles followed his brother to Christ Church in 1726 after studying at Westminster School in London, where another brother, Samuel, was a teacher. He was ordained into the Anglican ministry in 1735.[4]

After returning to Oxford in November 1729, John joined Charles in the Holy Club and soon assumed leadership among the three or four penitent scholars seeking a closer relationship with God by studying the Bible and other important works. In particular, John Wesley found the writings of the prominent Anglican nonjuror William Law, with their emphasis on inward holiness through self-discipline and practical Christianity, to be an invaluable guide. Sceptical outsiders who witnessed these men's constant attendance at worship and their acts of charity and social service had given the club its name. It gradually grew to include a number of like-minded students, among them George Whitefield, but internal discipline diminished after the Wesleys left college life to fulfil their clerical obligations.

In 1735 they accepted positions with an expedition to the newly formed colony of Georgia. John went as chaplain, with a special, but unrealized charge to work with native Americans, and Charles served rather ineffectively as secretary to the colony's founder, General James Oglethorpe, and its management committee. The expedition turned into a fiasco for the Wesleys; Charles returned to England after only six months, and a disheartened John followed in disgrace in 1737.[5] Quickly, however, John renewed his quest for personal salvation, strengthened by continual study and his association with the pietistic Moravians. He even visited Count Ludwig von Zinzendorf's settlement in Germany during a European tour. But the Moravians' introspective pietism was too narrow for Wesley's pragmatic and catholic mind, and he soon developed his own brand of evangelicalism. After his conversion in 1738, he took over leadership of the Fetter Lane Society and became influential in various Anglican religious groups. The following year he organized the first Wesleyan society, and it became the nucleus of the Wesleyan connexion.[6]

As preacher, writer, editor, and supervisor, John Wesley was unsurpassed among eighteenth-century religious leaders. His success was a reflection of his brilliant mind, broad theological understanding, disciplined work habits, and immense energy, but most especially of his complex character. He embodied the assurance, even pride, of his combined high Anglican and Dissenting heritage, and to it he added the prestige of a serious scholar and a pragmatic patience in organizing and carrying out his designs. In the religious sphere, he was never afraid either to promote tradition or to initiate revolutionary change; he was secure in his own ability and faith. Keenly aware of his singular role in society, Wesley conveyed a sense of authority to everyone he met. His complex make-up was also demonstrated by his social and political views. He remained an intensely conservative advocate of order and authority and a critic of the anarchistic and democratic impulses of his age. Yet he constantly condemned the evil and immorality he witnessed throughout Britain and criticized the social and economic system that had permitted them. Since he was later used by Methodists to legitimize their actions, his multifaceted character created a dynamic tension in the movement he founded.[7]

Charles Wesley shared most of his brother's traits. But he was more temperamental and less well organized, and he always remained a reluctant evangelist. Although he cooperated closely with John and shared the preaching and the physical hardship, especially during the early years, his major contribution was the nearly nine thousand hymns and sacred poems that he wrote for the movement. They embody the essential Methodist doctrines, creed, and liturgy. At a time when few people could read, these hymns provided spiritual guidance and gained the movement a popular appeal through their heartfelt expression of religious emotions.[8]

Despite the Wesleys' essential role in the beginnings of Methodism, they did not operate in a vacuum. In fact, George Whitefield was considered the leading Methodist during the movement's formative years, and the term "Methodist" predates both him and the Wesleys.[9] Born on December 16, 1714, the youngest of seven children, Whitefield was raised primarily by his mother, who owned and operated the Bell Inn in Gloucester. Following a period of indifferent study at the local parish school, he entered Pembroke College at Oxford in 1732. After years of loneliness and alienation, he became convinced of the need for a new birth in 1735 and two years later began preaching this message. Whitefield joined the Holy Club, and in early 1738 he replaced John Wesley as chaplain in Georgia. He was eventually ordained in 1739, after his return from Georgia, in part through the exertions of the Countess of Huntingdon. He would remain devoted to her and her Calvinist Methodist movement thereafter. Although most Anglican pulpits were closed to him, he never lost his earnest zeal or energy. With the Welsh preacher Howell Harris, he introduced open-air preaching to Methodism and persuaded the Wesleys to adopt the practice. During its early years, Whitefield was Methodism's most famous preacher. His "passionate temperament, bell-like voice, gifts of mimicry, dynamic gestures and uninhibited speech," together with his ability to get along with people, made him immensely popular among supporters and earned him vitriolic abuse from critics. Through his passionate theatricality, as well as his compelling message, he became the model for popular preachers of his day.[10]

In the course of seven tours of America, ending with his death at Newburyport, Massachusetts, in 1770, Whitefield played a key role in the first Great Awakening and planted the roots of Methodism in North America. By transcending denominational loyalties through his blending of Calvinist and Anglican beliefs with a dynamic experiential religion, he offered a welcome

Susanna Annesley Wesley (1669–1742). Mother of John and Charles Wesley and a major influence on Methodism's early development. (UCA, Artifact Collection: Prints, Oversize 1)

George Whitefield (1714–70). Great Calvinist Methodist evangelist in Britain and the American colonies. (UCA, P7112N)

John Wesley (1703–91). Principal founder of Methodism. (UCA, Artifact Collection: Prints, Oversize 1)

Charles Wesley (1707–88). Wrote nearly 9,000 hymns and sacred poems for Methodism. (UCA, Artifact Collection: Prints, Oversize 1)

alternative to both harsh puritanism and religious formalism in America. By the end of his life, his personal popularity, his example of sacrifice and service, and his evocation of an embryonic nationalism had helped to define evangelicalism on the continent. The laity he converted, together with the lay preachers he encouraged, kept the evangelical revival alive for a generation.[11]

Whitefield and John Wesley complemented each other. Wesley moved systematically to build up secure societies in strategic locations and to provide a written theological foundation for the movement. Through his published sermons, journals, and other writings, by translating and publishing critical theological works, and perhaps most essentially, through his constant correspondence, he kept close personal control over the expanding work. Conversely, Whitefield disliked study and refused to be distracted by organizational work or the development of a new denomination. He travelled constantly, arousing and exhorting those in need of salvation. He left behind revived individuals but little permanent structure to encourage the troubled or nurture the reborn. Although Whitefield and Wesley would openly dispute the theological underpinnings of the Methodist revival, they retained a strong mutual respect. Even after 1739, when they separated over the question of predestination, they continued to recognize each other's talents. Until his death in 1770, Whitefield preached Calvinist views of election; the Wesleys, on the other hand, built their movement on Arminian principles. These derived from the teachings of the Dutch theologian Jacobus Arminius (1560–1609), who had denounced the restrictive nature of predestination and stressed the universal availability of God's saving grace and human beings' responsibility to seek salvation and entire sanctification or complete holiness. However, Whitefield preferred preaching to theological disputes and refused to become entangled in evangelical rivalries.[12]

Together the Wesleys and Whitefield created a vast revival in religion. None the less, they were not prepared to abandon their Anglican orders, break up the Church of England, or create competing denominations. Their purpose was always to revitalize the Church of England, stimulate its spiritual influence, and make it the essential forum for personal and national regeneration. John Wesley was perhaps more successful in fulfilling such goals in the Church of Ireland. At least initially, therefore, Methodism represented a counter-reformation within the established Anglican church. In its attacks on deism and formalism, it found a ready clientele among the spiritually moribund members of eighteenth-century society, many of whom were unconsciously seeking a more profoundly spiritual and ethical Christianity.[13]

## DOCTRINE

John Wesley's enduring strength was as a "folk" theologian who could explain complex Christian doctrines to ordinary people and overcome such traditional disjunctions as faith and good works or reason and revelation in theology. Unlike Calvin and other Protestant leaders, he never sought to establish a comprehensive theological standard; rather, he hoped to reinvigorate religion for the general population. Although constant in essential articles of faith, he tolerated a myriad of opinions on secondary matters and was hazy or even contradictory on such questions as the function of the sacraments. This lack of clarity has led critics to dismiss his contributions to systematic theology, but it does not diminish his importance as a Christian thinker, his success in transforming religious belief, or his ability to communicate the power of the Bible.[14]

Wesley expounded his doctrines principally in his *Sermons on Several Occasions*, published originally in four volumes between 1746 and 1760, his printed *Journal*, and the *Minutes of Conferences*. These were reinforced by his essays, correspondence, revisions of traditional Anglican standards, and his fifty-volume *A Christian Library*. He accepted the fall of humanity through Adam and its complete depravity, degeneration, and sinfulness, which culminated in spiritual and physical death. None the less, he believed that common sense and the recognized notions of civil government, as well as natural law and God's ultimate benevolence, would be violated if humanity were to suffer eternal damnation solely because of Adam's guilt. The individual could be justly punished only for personal, not imputed, sinfulness. Wesley taught that, by virtue of Christ's atonement, "fallen humanity has lost much, but not all the freedom that belonged to Adam." Christ awakened a "prevenient" grace, identified by some as conscience, which allowed human beings to choose between right and wrong. If they were not saved, it was because "they do not *will* to be saved."[15] Therefore the individual remained a moral agent who was obliged consciously to accept or reject God's omnipresent grace – to choose damnation or salvation.

It must be added that for Wesley, humankind could not redeem itself. Only God's grace could save totally undeserving humanity; only God could justify, that is, make acceptable. But God had repeatedly promised, through Christ's new covenant, that all who had faith and humbly sought grace would be saved.[16] The Scriptures clearly promised that this grace was universally available. The notion that only a few preordained elect had been chosen for salvation was, to Wesley, logically and scripturally absurd. The many biblical injunctions to save the world and to live a holy life and love one's neighbour contradicted such narrow views of salvation. Wesley went so far as to claim that these Calvinist doctrines of election were placed in the path of human salvation by the devil.[17]

Rebirth was only the first step: "conversion was the beginning and was accompanied by an inner assurance of God's love, while the end was Christian Perfection, the growth of Spiritual holiness." Christian perfection, entire sanctification, and complete holiness were synonymous terms for "a state of grace characterized by a heart cleansed from sin and filled with a perfect love" of both God and humanity.[18] The quest for this spiritual condition was the central feature of Methodism. While never claiming complete holiness for himself, John Wesley believed it could be achieved, often as an instantaneous transformation after a period of gradual spiritual growth made possible by following the appointed means of grace, living in perfect love, and performing good works. But achieving entire sanctification was a process of continual struggle, not a single, final act.[19]

Wesley was careful to admonish his followers not to allow universal salvation to become the basis of unscriptural license, since it could lead to the self-delusion of antinomianism.[20] He denounced the assumption that once an individual was saved, sin could no longer be committed. Humanity could too easily fall back into damnation. In fact, salvation was a constant pilgrimage through dangerous territory, not a state of permanent safety. It demanded refraining from all sin, continual holy living, and the observance of God's commandments. Even if entire sanctification was achieved, a believer could still sin, even unintentionally, could still revert to perdition, and therefore could still require Christ's atonement. On earth there was no complete safety from sin; that was reserved for heaven.

What then was a Methodist? In Wesley's own words, "A Methodist is one who has 'the love of God shed abroad in his heart by the Holy Ghost given unto him'; one who 'loves the Lord God with all his heart, and with all his soul, and with all his mind, and with all his strength.' God is the joy of his heart, and the desire of his soul."[21] Methodists did not withdraw behind peculiarities of speech or dress, nor did they differentiate their community by narrowly defined scriptural doctrine. They accepted all the fundamental Protestant beliefs and desired simply to keep God's commandments. They were recognized by their deep spiritual fervour, hard work, and sobriety and the extent of their charitable acts. Methodism never desired to create an isolated utopian community; while avoiding contamination by the world's evils, Christians were always to be in the world. Methodism was a vital, expanding fellowship embracing all who "wished to flee from the wrath to come."[22]

Wesley developed his doctrines from four bases of authority – Scripture, tradition, reason, and experience – collectively known as the Wesleyan quadrilateral. Substantial debate continues among Methodist historians and theologians over the relative weight of these sources in Wesley's writings, but it is agreed that he drew from each as the situation demanded. Nineteenth-century Romanticism and twentieth-century fundamentalism tended to accentuate experience and Scripture, but all four were complementary and mutually sustaining components of his theology.[23]

A well-read biblical scholar, Wesley turned instinctively to Scripture in order to develop and substantiate his beliefs. At the same time, when it was silent, he relied on the writings of the early church fathers, believing that because of their proximity to biblical times, they could enlighten scriptural intentions. For him, tradition included the scholarship of the ancient Orthodox and western churches from all the preceding centuries. He was determined to prevent Methodism from becoming narrow or falling into heretical traps and was truly catholic in his use of historical and theological sources.[24]

Moreover, Wesley lived in the Age of Reason and was familiar with the great writings of the period. He demanded that belief be logical and rational. Reason did not necessarily produce faith, but faith without reason led to a fanaticism that he deplored. According to some of the most liberated minds of the era, God had created an ordered world and set it in logical motion. Science appeared to confirm this perception, and philosophers defended it. Natural law became the foundation of intellectual endeavour. In religious terms, this view attacked the legitimacy of orthodoxy and church dogma, but it emphasized rational restraint and balance as the most perfect expression of the proper functioning of society. A deistic humanism emerged which prized freedom and realism, as well as decorum. Individual worth was enhanced at the expense of traditional restraint since it was the enlightened individual who must reasonably test all things by the operation of experience on the mind.[25]

Although Wesley operated in this milieu and stressed both rationality and individualism as essential to sound religious growth, he also drew upon his own conversion and the example of others throughout Christian history in acknowledging experience as the ultimate test of rebirth. Methodism was a religion of the heart as well as the head; only when spirituality was sensed could it be truly understood. Here, Wesley built on John Locke's perception of experience as complementary to, rather than competing with, reason. "Wesley could not avoid rationalism's focus on the human mind and the knowing person as the place where religion must demonstrate its authority. Locke's experiential epistemology provided a structure within which Wesley could do justice both to divine initiative and human involvement in the knowing process."[26] According to Locke, ideas were not innate; they were formed on the basis of evidence gathered by the senses. Reason reflected on experience.

To Locke's physical senses, which in themselves could not discern the spiritual attributes or presence of God, Wesley added "spiritual senses" which permitted the individual to know the things of God. Although God had endowed everyone with these extraordinary senses, they had been dulled by the Fall and nearly obliterated by sinful conduct. Religion's task was to sharpen them so that God's ubiquitous grace could be recognized and received. This understanding gave rational support for experience as a legitimate source of religious authority. However, to Wesley and his eighteenth-century colleagues, experience was not a subjective "feeling" on the part of the seeker; rather, it was "evidence of the real world, the impress made on our senses ... Thus the content of experience is basically not subjective but the self-disclosure of a Reality that stands over against us, the evidence of God's being toward us ... Rather than producing the experience the subject is fundamentally modified by it."[27]

This concept was critical; the individual not only sensed an external experience, but in fact was transformed by it. It was not sufficient to recognize God's presence; experience created a new person who thus became an agent of God's love. Those who had truly experienced conversion were reborn. They were made new persons who could act only to further God's work both in their own lives and in the world around them.[28] This latter element strengthened the ethical dimensions of Methodism and made good works a sign of conversion and a basis for future growth in grace. The quest for earthly perfection was ongoing, and good works, when they proceeded from the true convert, furthered this end.

Wesley's understanding of experience must not be confused with irrational "enthusiasm," so anathema to eighteenth-century religious and secular leaders. He was always conscious of the excesses that enthusiasm could generate and was initially shocked at overly emotional responses to his preaching. Emotion was itself legitimate, but he warned that enthusiasts were too often fooled by a false sense of salvation or failed to live holy lives. Some mistakenly felt that God gave them special powers or intervened in their lives in trivial ways. They therefore believed that they were not obliged to participate in the divinely appointed means of grace. Emotion was a legitimate by-product of experience only when it confirmed and augmented, not irrationally dominated, true rational experience. Wesley came to accept that emotion was as much a part of human nature as reason, and if God chose to use it, he could not deny the beneficial results. Nevertheless, it must be carefully monitored and controlled.[29]

In his use of the quadrilateral, Wesley was empirical and pragmatic, drawing on the requisite source of authority as his perception of the situation demanded. However, his contribution to Protestantism went well beyond theology. In fact, it was perhaps in the realm of worship that his true genius emerged. He blended elements of Anglican liturgy with the freedom of Reformed practice. His emphasis on the sacraments, especially the Eucharist, and on sound and spiritual preaching, both reinvigorated the religious services of the Church of England and gave special cohesion to Methodist worship. Wesley continued to follow the Book of Common Prayer because he believed the Anglican service was the most scriptural and the most beautiful in existence. However, though he was hesitant to modify Anglican practice, his acceptance of limited extemporaneous prayer, lay preaching, and congregational singing of the new hymns of Charles Wesley and Isaac Watts added a freshness and an immediacy to worship. Together, they created a warm, joyful, sincere, and spontaneous fellowship well designed to promote the personal quest for salvation.[30]

### ORGANIZATION

During John Wesley's lifetime, the Methodist connexion witnessed impressive numerical growth, the introduction of numerous innovative practices, a shift away from the Church of England, and the beginnings of a worldwide spread of the movement. From its first society in 1739, membership rose to 31,340 in 1771, 44,417 ten years later, and 72,476 at Wesley's death in 1791. In that year, some 312 preachers worked for the Methodist cause in Britain. These numbers do not include adherents or ministers in other denominations who sympathized with Methodist revivalism. The Wesleyan church reached its greatest relative strength in Britain in 1840, when it represented about 4.5 per cent of the adult population.[31]

Although the Wesleys constantly promoted Anglican worship and means of grace, it early became apparent that new measures and a well-defined organization would be critical for maintaining discipline and spiritual growth in the Methodist fellowship. In 1738, before he had established his first society, John Wesley drew up basic rules for his followers. Anyone who "wished to flee from the wrath to come" was welcome. A "society" was simply "a company of men [and women] having the form and seeking the power of godliness, united in order to pray together, to receive the word of exhortation, and to watch over one another in love, that they may help each other to work out their salvation."[32] The rules demanded regular and punctual attendance and a confession of faults and triumphs. In 1743, noticing a decline in discipline and the appearance of un-Methodist activities, Wesley developed more elaborate rules for his United Societies. Not only was regular attendance at society and class meetings expected, so too was attendance at church services, and all were enjoined to private prayer and fasting. Members must avoid evil: drunkenness, swearing, quarrelling, litigation, usury, lawbreaking, vain attire, and immoral entertainments. They were also to be charitable, assist the distressed, and help others to find salvation.[33]

For members who had been reborn and were making a commitment to advance in grace, Wesley developed an intimate and spiritually intense group called a "band." Begun in 1738, the band was open only to spiritually advanced members, and in Britain it remained the core element of the quasi-congregation that the society eventually became. Four years later Wesley also developed the "class meeting" to furnish a similarly small gathering for all adherents who were seeking salvation. It was originally designed as a convenient means of raising money, but it quickly took on the function of a group confessional, stimulating self-examination and advancing the quest for salvation and entire sanctification. In North America, where the band seldom developed and was never popular, the class meeting became the essential and distinguishing institution of Methodism. Assembled weekly under the supervision of a mature Christian leader, it held the society together and sometimes even served as a surrogate family for lonely individuals who joined the fellowship. As mission operations expanded into newer areas, the class meeting often predated the arrival of the itinerant preacher or the formation of regular worship services, and thus it acted as a crucial advance base for church work.

It also functioned as a training ground for exhorters, lay preachers, and even itinerant ministers. Since attendance and participation in prayer, singing, and testimony at the class meeting were compulsory for all members of the connexion, the class leader could wield powerful disciplinary control by dropping backsliders or others who failed to follow Methodist strictures. More important, however, the leader helped those attending to reach that point of decision leading ultimately to conversion and a new life. Belonging to a class was the only means of joining the Wesleyan connexion.[34] Furthermore, the class and its leader provided critical links between the general membership and the local and itinerating preachers.

Although the class meeting was the germ cell and the local society was the focus of public worship, Methodism was first and foremost a connexion, not a group of quasi-independent congregations. Each society or appointment was bound into a circuit, with a superintendent itinerant minister as spiritual guide and an appointed lay leadership of class leaders and stewards to handle administrative duties. Each circuit had a quarterly conference composed of local preachers, class leaders, and stewards who met to oversee the circuit's work. Beginning in the early nineteenth century, circuits were grouped into districts under a chairman, who supervised relations among the local circuits.

The districts were bound together into annual conferences, which met to set general policy, station preachers, review and revise the Discipline, oversee the spiritual welfare of the connexion, and represent the church to the world at large. Conference

measured time; it defined space; it established the social boundaries, particularly among the preachers; it provided order and structure; it gave, only if implicitly, ecclesial expression to Methodism; and it fostered Methodist spirituality ... It was a family of preachers headed and governed by John Wesley; it was a monastic-like order held together by affection, by common rules, by a shared mission and by watchfulness of each member over one another; it was a brotherhood of religious aspiration and song; it was a quasi-professional society which concerned itself with the reception, training, credentialing, monitoring and deployment of Wesley's lay preachers; it was a community of preachers whose commitment to the cause and one another competed with all other relationships.[35]

Conference provided spiritual and social refreshment before the delegates returned to their often lonely and disheartening ministerial travels.

In order to intensify spiritual progress, Wesley also inaugurated the "love feast" as an intimate gathering of members for confession and spiritual nurture. The love feast revived the *agape,* or communal meal of the Eucharist, in the early Christian church. Bread and water were distributed as an expression of mutual fellowship. Lasting for about an hour before public worship, these extremely popular "feasts of love" exerted a powerful influence on Methodist spirituality. Although attempts were sometimes made to restrict attendance to members in good standing or to those with notes of admission, many non-members were induced to join Methodist class meetings after participating in the love feast.[36]

Prayer meetings were also powerful sources of nourishment for Methodist societies. Small groups of members and adherents could gather together between regular worship services, with or without clerical leadership, and communicate directly with God. On special occasions, "covenant" and "watch-night" services also provided valuable opportunities for spiritual growth. In fact, mutual support and stimulation to salvation and holiness were central features of all these social "means of grace." They gave vital expression to Methodism's evangelistic mission to both the saved and the unconverted. One of the great strengths of the movement was the fact that the intimacy and power of these small fellowship meetings were reproduced in the regular preaching services.[37]

Beyond Wesley's structures and means of grace, his movement owed much of its success to his ability to recognize and draw on the vast reservoir of talent, energy, and spirituality residing in the laity. Often people were searching for personal salvation and a meaningful religion even before he and his ordained associates commenced operations. The laity opened their homes to his preachers and organized the local community for worship. They built chapels to house the growing number of adherents and protected the embryonic movement from church and government proscription. It was the laity who withstood ridicule and sometimes mob violence after the preachers had departed. In particular, women supplied a disproportionate leadership in organizing classes and prayer groups, building connexional facilities, and sharing the vision of a new world in Christ. Through word and example, unordained men and women spread Wesley's message of salvation and entire sanctification throughout Britain and carried it as part of their precious luggage when they emigrated. They became true Christian evangelists, encouraging family and friends to abandon evil and to join the Methodist community.

Many of the more talented men and women became official exhorters who assisted the preachers in expounding the need for an immediate, personal commitment to God and creating a kinship of believers. After gaining practice and being tested as to their "gifts and graces," particularly to show that their exhorting was being blessed with victories, some became lay preachers. In the absence of Wesley and his ordained colleagues, these lay preachers carried the Wesleyan revival across the country and beyond. Originally, he had opposed the use of unordained preachers, but in 1740, on the advice of his mother and after witnessing for himself the God-given power of Thomas Maxwell, he adopted this important agency. Although Maxwell and other lay preachers would sometimes disrupt the Methodist movement, Wesley continued to advocate a dynamic role for a lay ministry.[38]

After further hesitation, he even welcomed the un-Anglican innovation of women preachers. Other religious groups had sponsored preaching by women, but the practice had generally fallen into disrepute. However, again on his mother's advice and early example and influenced by the rational arguments and the accomplishments of gifted women themselves, Wesley encouraged their work. Several factors inherent in Methodism contributed to leadership by women. The movement minimized scriptural injunctions and cultural limitations on their roles. Women shared the same vital Christian experience and achieved the same level of Christian perfection. God's grace recognized no differences between the sexes and guaranteed the spiritual equality of women. Even though Methodism denied the social equality of men and women, its emphasis on salvation and morality fitted religion into well-established women's spheres. Family nurture, charity, and moral reform were pre-eminently women's concerns, and it was advantageous that they pursue these issues outside the confines of the home.[39]

Whether his preachers were men or women, Wesley constantly provided them with counsel, support, and supervision. He advised them to be punctual and solemn, to aim their preaching at their specific audience, and to follow closely the biblical text they had selected. They were to avoid unofficial hymns and awkward or affected language or gestures, as well as excessive "allegorizing or spiritualizing." They were simply to preach Christ crucified, resisting overly detailed biblical interpretation, for which they were generally unprepared. Preachers were also enjoined to assist one another in following these precepts and in holding faithfully to Methodist doctrine and discipline.[40]

Methodist preachers – ordained or lay – were generally denied the use of Anglican churches. They therefore followed the Wesleys' example and preached in any available house or public building and even in the open air.

Their commission was to seek all who were lost, including those who failed to attend regular church services. Ultimately, field preaching became an integral part of Methodist practice by virtue of its spectacular success in drawing large audiences and converting sinners to Christ and the Methodist cause.

John Wesley's various innovations quickly brought Methodism into conflict with authorities in the established church and with its secular allies, who suspected schismatic and potentially revolutionary activities. Methodists dismissed such opposition as the actions of a corrupt institution that misunderstood and feared any change which might undermine it. However, from the Church of England's perspective, Methodism obviously represented a major schism in the traditional order and authority so critical for an established church.[41] For instance, although John Wesley avowed three orders of ministry – bishop, priest, and deacon – as both scriptural and apostolic, he claimed that it was "shockingly absurd" to suggest that the Reformed churches did not belong to the true church of Christ because they had abandoned this formulation. To many devout Anglicans this view appeared a serious contradiction.

Furthermore, in 1747 Wesley wrote, "We will obey the rules and governors of the Church whenever we can consistently with our duty to God. Whenever we cannot, we quietly obey God rather than men."[42] He denied the authority of the Church of England to limit his right to preach whenever and wherever he pleased on the grounds that he had been ordained a fellow of Lincoln College rather than a parish priest. Wesley, not the church, interpreted God's will. Anyone daring to oppose Methodist discipline or doctrine in such a fashion would have been condemned and expelled. Despite his claim to be a loyal Anglican, his actions eventually created a Methodist fellowship that weakened loyalties to the Anglican communion, divided congregations, and undermined its authority and power. The abuses within the Church of England during the eighteenth century were well known, but disharmony between priest and parishioners was not always the fault of the priest. Arrogance, pride, and presumption were traits among Wesley's followers as well.

In fact, some Methodists advocated a complete separation from the Church of England and the creation of a distinct denomination. Several leading Methodists, including Charles Wesley, feared that his brother might sanction such action, and they denounced any step that appeared to move Methodism out of the Anglican fold. Under Charles's persuasion, John published *Reasons Against a Separation from the Church of England* in 1758. It argued that ties with the established church were the best means to avoid dissension, divided affections, and a weakening of the work of conversion and reformation. Separation would force the Methodist laity and the ordained Anglican clergy to choose between the two fellowships. Such a split would waste the time, energy, and human resources vitally needed in the great work of revival. None the less, separatist sentiment remained just below the surface during the lives of John and Charles Wesley.[43]

In spite of his often-repeated concern for unity within the Church of England, by 1784 John Wesley was prepared to take actions that seriously threatened this relationship. Without church sanction, he assumed the authority, though not the title, of a bishop and ordained ministers for work in North America. He even appointed Thomas Coke as superintendent of this work, with the authority to ordain and consecrate others in the name of Methodism. Soon after, he ordained preachers for Scotland and even for England. Charles Wesley, with many other Methodists, believed that such ordination meant de facto separation from the Anglican church. The fact that in Britain the break with the Church of England was gradual and evolutionary and only took place long after John Wesley's death does not diminish the schismatic nature of eighteenth-century Methodism.[44]

## AMERICAN BEGINNINGS

John Wesley would probably not have ordained any ministers had not the situation in North America demanded it. The British colonies there represented a quite different world for him. Although the Church of England was established in some colonies, it had never gained the status or power it held in England, and most Americans had no desire to enter its communion. Instead, a multitude of denominations competed for members, especially in the immediate aftermath of the American Revolution, when the Anglican church was unable to fulfil its traditional ecclesiastical functions in the new republic and was often perceived as the church of the enemy. If Methodism was to survive and prosper here, it needed to break its ties with Britain and the Church of England and create an independent church. By so doing, Methodists hoped to avoid being tarred by the brush of disloyalty while offering a familiar fellowship to both evangelical Anglicans and other receptive individuals.

With regard to overseas mission work in general, Wesley's position was ambivalent. On the one hand, he confidently and energetically encouraged the proposition of missionary expansion. His belief that "all the world is my parish" and his commitment to "make disciples of all nations" were elaborations of the fundamental scriptural injunction that "calleth all men everywhere to repent."[45] Activity outside of Britain was also reinforced by Methodism's doctrine of universal salvation, which made mission work inevitable. It was impossible to confine the revival within narrow geographical or political boundaries.

However, despite this support in principle, Wesley was always preoccupied with fund-raising and with organizing and supervising the work of his domestic societies. There was never sufficient financial support or human resources to meet the demands of the existing Methodist connexion, and much work remained to be done in evangelizing Britain. He firmly believed that there was no sense beginning a mission without the means to consolidate and maintain it. Therefore, Wesley acted as a restraining influence on men such as Thomas Coke, who developed several ambitious, but premature schemes to spread Methodism to the so-called heathen world, and the expansion of the movement to the Channel Islands, the West Indies, and America was slow and cautious.

In a minor way, John Wesley's work in Georgia had been the first Methodist mission in North America. More important, George Whitefield's seven preaching tours had aroused Americans and laid the foundation for a Methodist fellowship.[46] The first formal societies were organized during the 1760s by expatriate lay leaders, especially from Ireland. Robert Strawbridge, a fiery farmer-preacher from County Leitrim, organized meetings at his home in Maryland in 1766 and carried on a travelling ministry from Pennsylvania to Virginia. Barbara Heck and Philip Embury, German-speaking Irish Palatines, formed a class in New York City at about the same time, and Laurence Coughlan, a converted Irish Catholic, served Methodist-style congregations in Newfoundland beginning in 1766. Other societies arose in New York, New Jersey, and Maryland through the influence of Captain Thomas Webb, the barrack master at Albany.[47] The movement spread quickly throughout the region from Georgia to New York and even into the originally hostile New England colonies. The societies that came into being, despite being isolated from one another and lacking an ordained ministry, began a rudimentary spiritual fellowship based on their members' religious training in England and Ireland and drew in adherents from among those awakened by evangelical preachers in the colonies.

In 1769 John Wesley finally answered the repeated American pleas for assistance by sending Joseph Pilmore and Richard Boardman, together with £50, to help consolidate the Methodist work. Between that year and 1774 four pairs of itinerant missionaries travelled to America. Among these, Francis Asbury, who arrived in 1771 with Richard Wright, was by far the most important in providing leadership to the American movement. He had been born near Birmingham in 1745, the son of a small farmer, and had received only a rudimentary education. Convinced of the need for repentance and rebirth after reading sermons by, among others, George Whitefield, he began preaching locally in 1762 while an apprentice in an ironworks. Wesley appointed him to his first circuit as a probationer four years later. Asbury eventually itinerated on five different circuits before volunteering for service in North America at the age of twenty-six.

Despite being only an adequate speaker and plagued by chronic poor health, Asbury quickly emerged as the dominant personality in American Methodism. He strongly disapproved of the settled ministry favoured by Pilmore and Boardman, and through his tremendous energy and determination and his indomitable spirit, he forced the other ministers to follow his itinerating routine. Throughout his long career, Asbury never had a permanent home; he travelled nearly constantly from Georgia to New England, followed the new settlers across the Appalachian Mountains into the western territories, and even visited what is now Canada. He died in Richmond, Virginia, on his way to the 1816 General Conference at Baltimore. By his example and through direct supervision, he established a model ministry that greatly facilitated missionary expansion into new regions. At the same time, he oversaw the creation of a strong connexional organization based on his understanding of Wesley's rules and intentions, but adapted to suit the different circumstances in America.[48]

These preachers also followed the British example and established a Conference in 1773 to help regulate and expand the Methodist cause. They vested it with governing powers and in so doing created a tension between later bishops and Conference over which should direct the connexion's work.[49] The War of

Independence precluded the arrival of new British preachers and resulted in the loss of both itinerants and members. Some returned to Britain or emigrated with other loyalists to British North America. But most, including Asbury, simply retired temporarily from the travelling ministry, although they continued to work quietly in more circumscribed areas. Despite these losses and the fear of persecution because of suspected disloyalty to the republican cause, overall membership expanded during this period. By 1783, eighty preachers, mostly Americans, oversaw a reported membership of 13,740 on thirty-nine circuits.[50]

Perhaps more significant, the Methodist movement became "Americanized" as it developed its own native-born ministry and increasingly identified itself with the aspirations of the emerging nation. It became apparent that the American connexion would no longer submit meekly to British control, nor would it continue its links with the discredited Church of England in America.[51] Many Methodists had been converted from non-Anglican traditions and felt no sympathy or loyalty to the Church of England. In 1779 the Virginia Conference, in the absence of Asbury who was still in semi-retirement, moved to ordain its own clergy and establish a distinct denomination. This decision threatened to split the southern Methodists from their more traditional northern co-religionists, who opposed such action. At the Conference the following year, Asbury was able to convince the southerners to postpone the decision until Wesley's judgment could be sought. Simultaneously, Asbury impressed upon him the seriousness and urgency of the matter.[52]

With these developments in mind, and with the status of the Anglican church in America in serious doubt, Wesley took the dramatic step of ordaining Thomas Coke as superintendent of the American connexion, with power to consecrate Francis Asbury as co-general superintendent. Born into a locally prominent, middle-class family in south Wales in 1747, Coke had entered Jesus College, Oxford, in 1764 and been ordained in the Church of England in 1772. Although he considered himself a dutiful Anglican, he was dismissed from his parish at South Petherton five years later because of his Methodist inclinations, and he joined the Wesleyans. Short and round-faced, but sturdy and intelligent, with a disarming smile and an amiable personality, by the 1780s he was Wesley's chief lieutenant. After his leader's death in 1791, he became the dominant voice in British Methodism. Between 1784 and 1804, Coke made nine short visits to the United States, helping to provide continuity between British and American Methodism and settling internal disputes over the respective powers of Bishop Asbury and the General Conference established in 1792. However, he was needed in Britain and was never able or willing to supply more than token supervision for the Methodist Episcopal Church in America. Although he and Asbury respected each other, they disagreed on the best strategy for expansion, and Asbury was not prepared to relinquish his control to a visiting Englishman. Coke's major interest was Methodist overseas missions, particularly to non-Christian lands, and he supervised that work until his death in 1814 on board a ship bound for India.[53]

At the time of Coke's appointment, Wesley also ordained Thomas Vasey and Richard Whatcoat, and the three arrived in the United States in time for the

Baltimore Conference at Christmas 1784. This gathering accepted Wesley's doctrinal standards and elected Coke and Asbury as its superintendents, actions that both confirmed Wesley's judgment and supreme authority and also demonstrated Conference's own right and power to act independently. As well, it organized the local connexion into the Methodist Episcopal Church, the first independent Methodist denomination in the world. The Conference also ordained its first clergy, formalized its doctrines, discipline, and liturgy, and defined its future mission.[54] The new church would be not merely a schism of the Church of England, but a distinct denomination with its own terms of association, beliefs, and goals. Equally critical for its pursuit of scriptural holiness, the church would function on a connexional basis, not as a congeries of local congregations. It was to be highly centralized in its annual and general conferences and its episcopal office. Rather than being transmuted on the frontier, it would bring the more remote areas of the country into a carefully disciplined, all-encompassing, Protestant culture that transformed the lives of everyone it seriously touched.[55] The Methodist Episcopal Church, particularly under the leadership of Francis Asbury, remodelled the doctrines and discipline of Wesley in order to promote an indigenous revival in pioneer America. With its greater emphasis on "experience" and with an independent institutional structure, it carried forward Wesley's dream of reforming the continent.[56]

Despite the church's adaptation to conditions in North America, however, Wesley and his successors retained significant doctrinal authority and moral suasion. At least until Wesley's death in 1791, even Asbury acknowledged the importance of British precedent in preventing the movement from losing its form and unity, and the American connexion remained essentially true to Wesley's Methodism.[57] Methodists everywhere were one people; they shared the same heritage, the same emphasis on spiritual revival, the same doctrines of salvation and grace, and the same mission to evangelize the world. Tensions would always exist between British and American Methodism, but these were family disputes that only reflected different strategies for enhancing the welfare of the common movement.

Throughout the world, Methodism would create a fellowship of believers, a bond which challenged traditional divisions of class, race, ethnicity, and even family. In the United States, it tended to merge its vast energy with the nationalistic goals and republican principles of the young country, and it played a vital role in shaping the nation's cultural, intellectual, and social priorities.[58] Methodism became a critical element in the evolution of the American people. But its pragmatic theology and practical message made it adaptable to diverse conditions and cultures. In essentials, it knew no political or geographic boundaries. By the end of the eighteenth century, the maturing Methodist institutions in Britain and in the United States were both ready and anxious to spread their influence into the newly defined territories of British North America.

## 2 The Early Mission to British North America

Infused with a dedication to Wesley's spiritual revival, a belief in the need for sanctified living, and a keen sense of evangelistic expansion, British and American Methodism undertook to meet the religious needs of the remaining British colonies in North America. As the essentials of Methodism were transmitted to this new world, with its multicultural stock and its diverse religious background, the broadly assumed understandings of the movement had to be clarified and modified to suit local needs.[1] In British America, supervision by Wesley and his successors was at best difficult. Because of the distances and the isolated nature of settlement, local conditions could not be easily monitored or local experimentation curbed. The British authorities never truly appreciated the physical and psychological hardships faced by either the settlers or the Methodist missionaries. Moreover, Methodism had to contend with Anglicanism and the Reformed tradition of Presbyterians and Baptists on the one hand and with paganism, irreligion, and scepticism on the other. Denominations that were even more experiential than Methodism also challenged its mission to evangelize the region.

The movement was also disadvantaged because it lacked access to the colonial power élites, who viewed it with disdain and at times overt hostility. The Church of England and, to a lesser extent, the Church of Scotland could rely on a respectful hearing and at least moral, if not financial, support from the colonial governments, but Methodism had to depend on voluntary contributions either from its parent bodies or from the local constituents. The latter were generally ill served, impoverished, and unfamiliar with the rather novel notion that members should pay for church services. It was only unswerving dedication to the cause of evangelical spirituality and an anxiety over the loss of any soul that drove missionaries to venture into the wilderness of North America.

NEWFOUNDLAND

Within the future Dominion of Canada, the first Methodist mission began in the fishing outports of Newfoundland with the arrival of Laurence Coughlan at Conception Bay in 1766. An Irish convert from Roman Catholicism, Coughlan had served as a Wesleyan travelling lay preacher in England and Ireland from 1755 to 1764. He left the connexion after Wesley refused to accept his ordination at the hands of the notorious Greek émigré Bishop Erasmus, but he retained his commitment to what he believed was Wesleyan evangelicalism. He was ordained by the bishops of Lincoln and Chester through the permission of the bishop of London in early 1766 and left immediately to serve the settlers at Conception Bay. By the end of the year, he was again in England, where he received £50 and the sanction of the Anglican Society for the Propagation of the Gospel to continue his work in Newfoundland.[2]

For the most part, he was met by a populace resolutely uninterested in religion, "while oppression, violence, profanity and licentiousness were practised without check."[3] Except at St John's and Trinity Bay, where there were Anglican ministers, the islanders lacked Protestant spiritual guidance. Even when a few were disposed to Methodism, effective pastoral oversight was all but impossible because the settlements were small and isolated. However, after nearly two years of familiarizing the population with the rudiments of religion, Coughlan was able to report some success in 1768: "At length God was pleased to bless my endeavours in a very wonderful manner ... The word was now like fire, or like a hammer that breaketh the rock in pieces. It was indeed quick and powerful, sharper than a two-edged sword. Under every sermon and exhortation, some were cut to the heart, and others rejoiced in loud songs of praise."[4] Small societies sprang up in Carbonear, Harbour Grace, and Old Perlican, and a chapel was erected at Blackhead in 1769. During the revival, communicant membership rose, according to Coughlan, from about eighty to nearly two hundred. When he returned to Britain, primarily because of the opposition of local merchants, he believed that he had laid a firm foundation for Methodism on the island.[5]

But Coughlan's success was short-lived. Although he was a stirring preacher, his unbending moral standards and, more importantly, his over enthusiastic approach gained him only a limited following. Theologically he was closer to George Whitefield and the Countess of Huntingdon than to the Wesleys. Despite the fact that he established a few class meetings that would prove vital for the survival of an embryonic society, his revival converts were rarely permanent. Coughlan relied more on emotional response than on a sound doctrine of grace, and his failure to appreciate the need for organized structures made disintegration almost inevitable after the flame of revival had died down.[6]

However, it was perhaps too much to expect that any eighteenth-century Methodist preacher would possess a mature sense of church organization. Certainly, the early failure of Methodism in Newfoundland was not Coughlan's alone. As late as 1813, Richard Taylor complained from Carbonear, "There has never been anything like system acted upon since the first labourers came out ... The people in general are as ignorant of our rules as if nothing of the kind existed."[7] Coughlan was not unique in failing to develop a systematic plan for his mission, and no solitary preacher could hope to furnish regular pastoral care to his scattered flock.

After Coughlan's departure, the cause was overseen by lay leaders, including Thomas Pottle at Carbonear, Arthur Tomey and John Stretton at Harbour Grace, and John Hoskins at Old Perlican. Without the authority of an ordained minister and faced with increasingly hostile Anglican mercantile and government factions, they were constantly frustrated in their work. When John McGeary arrived as Coughlan's first ordained replacement in 1785, he found fifteen members and only a faint memory of the past revival. Although he provided some stability, he never developed cordial relations with the independent-minded lay leaders, and the fundamental problems remained.[8]

McGeary resided in Newfoundland until 1791, and during his final months he witnessed a new revival led by the visiting superintendent of the Nova Scotia district, William Black. Black arrived at Carbonear on August 11, 1791. Over the following month he preached at Port de Grave, Bay Roberts, Harbour Grace, Carbonear, Freshwater, and Blackhead. In addition to the two hundred converts he reported, he organized proper class meetings, appointed leaders, deeded property to the connexion, and attempted to explain Methodist doctrines and rules to the societies. Although Black's visit was of critical importance at the time, it failed to provide the impetus for a permanent, well-organized mission. After his departure and McGeary's a few months later, Newfoundland again lacked Methodist clerical supervision, and membership soon declined sharply.[9]

In 1794 George Smith arrived to succeed McGeary, and over the following two decades a succession of missionaries gradually rebuilt the Methodist presence. William Thoresby joined Smith in 1796 and remained for two years; James Bulpit served from 1799 to 1806; John Remington worked alone from 1806 until 1808, after which he was supported by William Ellis and Samuel McDowell. The three expanded the work from Conception Bay to Bonavista and Trinity. William Ward served Bonavista from 1810 until he drowned in 1812; Richard Taylor worked for two years at Carbonear, beginning in 1812; and Sampson Busby replaced McDowell in 1813.[10] Of these, only Ellis made Newfoundland his permanent home; the remainder left after their short tours of duty were completed.

Moreover, no native Newfoundlanders were brought into the Methodist itinerant ranks. The lack of long-term service and local manpower were symptoms of the serious malaise facing the Methodist movement on the island. These problems were aggravated by the fact that many of the missionaries added teaching or other secular work to their preaching in order to supplement their meagre incomes. Such activity prevented full-time evangelistic labours. In addition to irregular religious services, discipline was generally lax, and Wesley's rules were only indifferently followed by the adherents. The work was further weakened by the failure to institute an itinerating ministry. Instead, they followed the settled plan favoured by the Anglicans.[11] Under these conditions, progress was slow and erratic, and little missionary work was attempted in the remoter settlements.

Although Methodist membership had reached about 500 in 1797, it stood at only 340 seventeen years later. The intervening period had seen peaks and valleys, but the cause was never strong. No missionary was serving St John's, the single important centre on the island. The only real progress was the construction of churches at Harbour Grace, Carbonear, Lower Island Cove, and Old Perlican by 1799.[12] In fact, the future of Methodism looked bleak until the reorganization of the British missionary operations. In 1815 Newfoundland became a district directly responsible to the British Conference, and plans were instituted to expand missionary work from Conception Bay. In the same year, a minister was stationed in St John's and a church was opened there. In 1816 the British Conference assigned six new missionaries to the reorganized circuits of Harbour Grace, Western Bay, Trinity Harbour, Fortune Bay, and Hant's Harbour. These circuits supplemented the existing ones in St John's, Carbonear, Blackhead, Island Cove and Perlican, Port de Grave, and Bonavista. From this period, Methodism expanded under the double impetus of greater financial support from Britain and increased local prosperity resulting from a temporary increase in the price of cod.

This boom was short-lived, however; a depression set in by 1818, and British assistance significantly diminished after 1820.[13] Despite its head start, the story of early Methodism in Newfoundland typifies much of the general history of the island. Both were plagued by isolation and poverty. Methodism in the colony suffered from "isolation without supervision, from emotionalism without doctrinal foundation, from evangelism without sound faith or sufficient discipline."[14] Without substantial external ministerial and financial support, it was sustained for long periods only by a dedicated laity and by private worship and prayer. Nevertheless, both Methodism and Newfoundland contained strong-willed and determined people. Once evangelized, Newfoundlanders demonstrated a resilient private resourcefulness and a deep spirituality, and Methodism provided an effective moral structure to community life.

### THE MARITIMES

Methodism in Nova Scotia, New Brunswick, and Prince Edward Island initially faced many of the same problems. By the beginning of the American Revolution, the large colony of Nova Scotia had contained nearly 20,000 people, settled in pockets around the coast and up the Annapolis Valley. The Protestant population included a small, but powerful Anglican presence, especially in the military and commercial centre of Halifax; Irish and Scottish Presbyterians, German Lutherans, particularly in the Lunenburg area; and Yorkshire English, some with Methodist backgrounds, along the Chignecto Isthmus. However, over 60 per cent of the Protestants shared a New England Congregational heritage. They retained strong ties of kinship and commerce, as well as religion, with their former homes.[15]

The immigrants from Yorkshire would provide an embryonic leadership and core membership, but it was vital for Methodist prosperity to attract these former New Englanders to the cause. Internally, Congregationalism, both before and during the American Revolution, was being torn apart and reordered as it sought a relevant meaning and mission from its religious traditions. Externally, it was being transformed by succeeding waves of religious revival as the fire of George Whitefield's and Jonathan Edwards's Great Awakening was rekindled by the New Light evangelism of Henry Alline and his associates. Alline was a native New Englander who charismatically preached salvation by faith alone. He believed the individual should be guided by the universally available inner light of personal experience. During the tumultuous period from 1776 until his death in 1784, he preached his "free will" gospel across the region and permanently altered its religious outlook.[16] Methodism, it seemed, might most reasonably look to those affected by Alline for converts and stalwart members.

None the less, the Yorkshire settlers, supplemented by transient support from the Halifax garrison, were the base of Methodist operations. These settlers had arrived during the early 1770s and furnished a seed-bed of members requiring only dynamic leadership to blossom into organized societies. The story of Methodism in the Maritimes really began with impromptu gatherings and spiritual awakenings in the homes of some of these pioneers. Through the ministry of William Black, it developed into a recognizable connexion. Black, who would later gain the affectionate, but unofficial sobriquet of "bishop," had been born in 1760 at Huddersfield, Yorkshire, and had settled with his family on a farm near Amherst in 1775. He was converted in 1779 at a revival service held at his neighbour's house and immediately began his career by exhorting and leading prayer meetings.[17]

Two years later, when he reached legal age, he left the farm and began preaching and organizing societies "on the Methodist plan" throughout the Maritimes. Black first preached in Halifax in 1782, and he described the town as "a stupid set of people few of whom seem to care for their souls."[18] Within two years, however, the town was receiving three services on Sunday and one every other night of the week. Initially, Black and Alline complemented each other in evangelizing Nova Scotia, and Black was considered Alline's equal in power and effectiveness. He loved to exhort and preach; he convinced hundreds of the joy of experiential religion and the certain damnation of those who did not achieve a conversion experience. However, he denounced the Allinite doctrine of the perseverance of the saints as antinomianism and eventually sought to make the Methodist revival more respectable and conservative in accordance with the British Wesleyan model. Despite his leading role, Black realized that he was inadequately prepared as an evangelist; the connexion required effective, ordained itinerants. John Wesley responded in 1783 to Black's request for missionaries by agreeing to seek volunteers.[19]

At about the same time, the Maritimes were inundated by some 35,000 Loyalists fleeing the newly independent United States. Coming mostly from the middle and southern colonies, they quickly dispersed over the region, especially in what became New Brunswick in 1784. These new arrivals immediately altered the religious, social, and political fabric of the Maritimes. Although they represented a great variety of religious affiliations, including Methodist, they were united in their criticism of American republicanism, and it was apparent that within "this embryonic society the Church of England was designed to become the principal ideological instrument of loyalty and the conservative principle."[20] Nevertheless, it was equally clear that the Church of England could not remould totally either the existing or the newcomer society to its own image. The region was too susceptible to the emotional evangelism that was transforming traditional denominational loyalties, or as one Anglican minister put it, he was "unable to cope with the ignorant people of the outstations who easily succumb to the novel doctrines of wild sectaries."[21]

By 1784, therefore, the religious condition of the Maritimes was both fluid and chaotic. The long period of social disintegration and alienation had shorn the people of the region of their secure doctrines and ecclesiastical anchors. As well, with the death of Henry Alline that year, there was a vacuum in the leadership of the ongoing evangelical revival. William Black felt confident that Methodism could take over this work if suitable preachers could be found. On Wesley's advice, he attended the famous Christmas Conference at Baltimore in 1784 to plead Nova Scotia's case to the newly created Methodist Episcopal Church. In response, the Conference appointed its first foreign missionaries, Freeborn Garrettson and James O. Cromwell, to work in the British territory.[22] Eastern British America was never formally linked to American Methodism, but it evolved a working relationship and gained ministerial support from this quarter until it became affiliated with the British missionary operations in 1800.

Cromwell and Garrettson arrived in Halifax in February 1785, and Cromwell proceeded to Shelburne, where his work was rather limited. He suffered from poor health and returned to the United States after two years. Garrettson also left the province in 1787, but his style and oratory marked him as a true successor to Henry Alline. He was a powerful, charismatic preacher obsessed with the need to spread scriptural holiness throughout the land. Born in 1752 into a wealthy slave-owning Maryland family, he had renounced his early Anglicanism as well as slavery when he was reborn and converted to Methodism in 1775. He began preaching the following year and was finally ordained at the Baltimore Conference of 1784. After his service in Nova Scotia, he spearheaded the mission operations in New York and Upper Canada. His marriage into one of New York's most prominent families gave him immediate access to many influential members of the establishment. While in Nova Scotia, he used Halifax as a base until May 1785, and he was able to so increase the membership that Philip Marchington, a wealthy merchant, built a private chapel for Methodist services the following year. When Marchington closed its doors because he was expelled from the society, the congregation built Zoar chapel in 1792. After May 1785 Garrettson began a series of preaching engagements in Windsor, Cornwallis, and the surrounding areas. Over the following two years, he visited nearly all the existing Nova Scotia societies, organized new classes in several smaller centres, and strongly supported the use of Wesley's new *Sunday Service for the Use of Methodists*. On his departure, there were about 600 members in Methodist societies out of a total Nova Scotia population of about 30,000.[23] This impressive figure should have meant that Methodism had reached the critical mass sufficient to generate its own success; but the work lagged after Garrettson left.

Like so many evangelists before him, he had been more anxious to save souls than to create an organization for loyal, disciplined Methodists. As a result, his ecumenical preaching reinvigorated the New Light movement by "providing it with a coterie of new, young, energetic and remarkably gifted leaders."[24] Along with their Maritime supporters, they preferred the evangelical Calvinism more reminiscent of their Congregational heritage. Indeed, a modern historian has noted, "It was ironic that a staunch Arminian Methodist from the United States would be involved in the transformation of Alline's 'Free Will' anti-Calvinist Nova Scotia 'ecumenical movement' into what was destined to become, among other things, a 'closed' Baptist Calvinist Church."[25] Garrettson also strengthened a small, yet very vociferous antinomian group in the region. Nevertheless, he maintained close personal and intellectual links with conservative American Anglican clergy.

What did the failure to attract the former New England Congregationalists mean for Methodism? On the simplest level, the leadership lost control of the powerful regional movement. Black and his associates were unable to sustain the spiritual fire on their own. Even where the converts were prepared to accept revival preaching, they would not abide the rigid connexional discipline. Methodism's strict moral code clashed with the coarse social behaviour of the pioneers, particularly those tainted with the antinomian notion that once an individual was saved, sin was no longer possible.[26] The Methodist response was to hold fast to its rules, stress respectability, and condemn the excessive enthusiasm of its more experiential competitors. Maritime Methodism throughout its history was strongly influenced by the British model of dutiful filial relations with the Church of England, non-involvement in radical politics, and a disapproval of uncontrolled enthusiasm and emotional revival services. These attitudes further alienated it from the contemporary pattern of evangelical religion without making the expected gains among the more respectable Anglican or ethnic communions.[27]

Black was finally ordained in 1789 and after the short and unsuccessful administration of James Wray, became superintendent of the Maritime connexion, a position he held until his retirement in 1812. He attempted to organize a society on Cape Breton Island in 1789 and visited Newfoundland in 1791, but lasting progress was rare.[28] He was never fully able to impress the population with the importance of Methodist discipline. Robert Cooney, a prominent Wesleyan missionary, recorded in his autobiography, "The peculiarities of Methodism are rather distasteful to many people. The doctrines are received in almost every instance, but the administration is regarded with suspicion and aversion. It is too particular; a little too strident; it has not enough of the democratic element in it ... Methodism seems too evangelical – too pure for the generality of the people ... It denounces usury, smuggling and extortion."[29]

During this period, membership growth was sporadic and transitory. In 1793 William Jessop wrote from Halifax, "We had powerful meetings and great shouts in the [military] Camp, which still continues in a greater or lesser degree," and James Boyd at Horton exalted, "I bless the Lord, the Ark is moving forward in this place ... Between 30 & 40 have Joy'd [*sic*] the Society the last quarter: and Sinners everyday come flocking home to God." But four years later Thomas Martin, also from Halifax, claimed, "Nothing but revelling, Swearing and drunkenness with every other Diabolical Scene reigns Predominant here."[30]

The work failed to prosper even in the Cumberland region, Black's original home and the heartland of Methodism. In 1804 he reported to the British missionary authorities, "On the Cumberland circuit ... we have two or three chapels, and about 90 members in Society. Of the state of this people I never think but with grief and pain ... There were about 200 persons who met together in class ... But alas! the Enemy of God and man came and sowed tares; the tares of antinomian doctrines amongst us ... The spirit of holy love, and godly fear, has been gradually declining almost ever since."[31] In the three provinces combined, Methodism reported only 914 members in 1804. Four years later Black again discussed the Cumberland circuit. "Presently, after I left they had two Baptist preachers amongst them who were very violent against the Methodists. The Baptists are the most growing connexion in the country."[32] He added that the societies at Liverpool and Saint John were also declining in membership.

This pattern continued until at least the middle of the War of 1812. Although the war tended to bring economic prosperity to the region, it also disrupted church services and put a strain on the strict Methodist moral code and disciplined living. A great many Maritimers profited by smuggling, privateering, and other wartime activities. The war also raised for a few the spectre of disloyalty, especially in isolated fishing villages. James Priestly, the Methodist preacher in Annapolis, felt obliged "to exhort the people to be piously loyal to their God and then there will be no doubt but that they will be loyal to their King. The fear of God is closely, may I not say, inseparably connected with loyalty to our king and country."[33] Interestingly, the only area where membership increased was along the New Brunswick border with Maine, where Duncan McColl continued to serve both sides. In Halifax, Cumberland, and the Annapolis Valley, Methodism remained weak and disorganized.

While competition, particularly from the other evangelical churches, hurt Methodism in the Maritime provinces, its failure rested more fundamentally on its own internal disabilities. During its first thirty years in the region, there were never sufficient ministers. With the departure of Garrettson and Cromwell, William Grandin was the only ordained Methodist in the Maritimes for two years. He arrived in 1786 and served various circuits for the following thirteen years. John Mann, who came from the United States in 1783, was ordained in 1789, the same year as Black, and his brother James served for nine years before his ordination in 1795. To these must be added McColl, who settled and began preaching in St Stephen in 1785 and who, although ordained in 1795, never itinerated. Although he built up a relatively strong local society, he tended to run it as his own community. William Jessop and James Wray arrived in 1788, but Wray lasted only until 1791, and Jessop itinerated intermittently until 1795. Thomas Whitehead was stationed in the region in 1789 but stayed only four years. By 1790 the whole Maritime region contained only four ordained ministers and 510 members.[34]

Over the following decades, the pattern of short visits by American and British preachers continued. In 1791 Abraham Bishop, James Boyd, John Cooper, William Ealey, Benjamin Fisher, and John Regan were sent to the Maritimes from the United States. Except for Cooper, who itinerated irregularly until 1803, none served more than three years and most left dispirited and financially distressed.[35] The men who followed averaged about two years' service. With such a ministry it was impossible to achieve permanent progress; the connexion was only held together by dedicated local preachers and class leaders, and even these were in short supply.

In 1800 Black persuaded the British Conference to take direct responsibility for the Maritime mission. It sent out James Lowry, William Bennett, Joshua Marsden, and Thomas Olivant. The most notable of these was Bennett, who served the region until his retirement in 1821 and succeeded Black as superintendent in 1812. Even with this new battery of workers and the additions made over the first part of the nineteenth century, the shortage of ministers continued and was only somewhat alleviated after 1813, when the Maritimes became a district in the British Conference, and after 1816, when the British missionary work was reorganized.[36]

However, a shortage of ministers was only part of the problem; no nineteenth-century denomination ever had sufficient for its needs. The quality of the work performed and of the administration in general was equally responsible for the lack of growth. Both the British authorities and the local leaders supplied ineffective supervision and discipline. This was perhaps most evident in the stationing of the missionaries. Black and his successor, Bennett, never carried the requisite authority or personal influence to administer the connexion effectively. Each missionary felt entitled to decide for himself where and how to serve. After 1786 appointments were made by a local conference of ministers, but these decisions were altered by whim, weather, or local preferences. Ministers were often late in arriving at new circuits or served other societies instead. When these factors were coupled with the short terms of service, illness, and natural impediments, local congregations faced long gaps in ministerial service. As a result, congregational independence was enhanced and connexional loyalty diminished, especially among those who already shared a heritage of congregational control from their earlier links to New England Congregationalism, and effective planning or missionary expansion was further hampered.[37]

The missionaries also often failed to follow directions from the superintendent or to accept connexional discipline. In some instances, drunken and disobedient missionaries not only greatly embarrassed Methodism, but also made it impossible to enforce the connexion's rules among the general laity. James Bulpit served Prince Edward Island from 1807 until 1814 yet was constantly being cited for insobriety and disobedience. His negative influence on the island was still visible a decade later.[38] His was an extreme case, but there were enough others to reflect badly on the whole church.

Methodism was further weakened by the failure to institute a sound itinerant system. As was the case in Newfoundland, the Maritime missionaries were far more interested in a settled, than an itinerating, ministry. Black himself tended to remain close to Halifax unless his supervising tours took him farther afield.

Bennett, it was claimed, spent as much time working his farm as itinerating. Most notably, however, McColl served only the St Stephen area during his long and relatively accomplished ministerial career. When a society was well established, this type of ministry had the advantage of permitting intensive pastoral care, but at best a minister's strengths were not shared with the rest of the connexion. When a society was weak, a settled ministry limited the connexion's ability to expand into outlying districts and undermined connexionalism by binding local loyalties to the minister. If his services or character came under attack, it often split the community, limited the ability to discipline, and drove dissatisfied members to other denominations. Bulpit would likely have been removed earlier and with less disruption if he had not developed a personal following and if he had been properly supervised during his career.[39]

Closely allied to the problem of local supervision was the lack of direction from the parent authorities. The American church leaders had quickly lost interest in the region. They could not afford to send sufficient resources and were not prepared to monitor the Maritime operations. The distance and time involved also precluded effective direction from England. As well, the English missionary work from 1791 to 1813 was the special province of Thomas Coke, and he was more interested in evangelizing the non-Christian world than in dealing with British America. Despite his many visits to North America, he never came to the northern British colonies. Through neglect, he permitted significant local autonomy to develop while limiting British missionary and financial support.

The missionary operations were also undermined by a weak financial system. In particular, the voluntary principle was never satisfactorily implemented in the region. Accustomed to the long tradition in Britain of a state-supported church, the impoverished settlers were never generous with their contributions. And the Wesleyan leadership was itself not deeply committed to the principle. Ironically, the long-term welfare of the connexion was probably equally hurt when British missionary grants largely precluded the need for local contributions. Missionaries consistently overdrew their accounts and spent money injudiciously. Buildings were erected without local resources, and these became too difficult for weak congregations to sustain. The missionaries' sense of evangelism was often diminished since they did not need to relate to the priorities of their members or to expand membership in order to receive their pay. When the depression set in after the War of 1812 and British resources were at least temporarily reduced, the Maritime church had only a poorly developed system of voluntary support. Even when prosperity returned, finances remained a considerable worry.[40]

At least as critical, the connexion failed to develop a native-born ministry. Up to 1820, no Maritimer was ordained into the Methodist itinerancy. Imported missionaries usually saw the work as only a temporary stage in their careers, and even William Black was anxious to "return" to England.[41] Few of these missionaries became truly acclimatized to the Maritimes or were able to appreciate the region's cultural identity. Their heads and hearts were too often elsewhere. Moreover, without the financial and psychological support of family and friends, they were significantly disadvantaged in their labours; they were separated from the kinship network so vital for the life of the Methodist church.

Although Methodism did grow in the Maritimes, it failed to gain control of the wider evangelical movement. The Baptists took over those most susceptible to experimental religion, and Methodism made no significant inroads among the Presbyterians, Anglicans, or Lutherans. In a sense, it was caught between these two religious poles. By seeking to appeal to one group, it antagonized and alienated the other and failed to provide a suitable fellowship for either. By 1827 Methodists represented only 7.6 per cent of the Nova Scotia population; of the 142,548 people in the province, 42,060 were Presbyterians, 31,199 Anglicans, 31,882 Roman Catholics, 19,848 Baptists, 2,970 Lutherans, 5,042 undesignated, and only 9,567 Methodists.[42] The proportion was slightly higher in Prince Edward Island and New Brunswick; nevertheless, Methodism's share of the population failed to expand significantly over the remainder of the century.

In its defence, however, is the fact that large denominational gains were perhaps unrealistic. The Methodist movement in Britain and North America was never able to make significant advances among Presbyterians, especially those with strong ethnic and economic links with Scotland. In the Maritimes, the religious affiliation of Anglicans during this period was also reinforced by powerful economic and political ties and by bonds of loyalty to the British empire. Finally, despite their long-term residency in the colonies, the expatriate New Englanders were still too closely tied to their former homeland and to its Calvinist, Congregational heritage to accept readily the connexionalism and Arminianism of the British Wesleyan church. Although Methodism was unable to capture the majority of immigrants to the region or to dominate its evangelical movement, for its members it provided a warm and active fellowship. In particular, it played an important role in introducing Christian principles to many of the economically and socially dispossessed in the region. In serving its traditional English and Irish clientele, the Methodist church was determined to create a mature ecclesiastical institution to support its evangelical community.

## LOWER CANADA

Methodism in what is now Ontario and Quebec also predated the arrival of an organized connexion or itinerant ministry. It resulted from the yearnings of individuals for a vital spiritual fellowship. The societies that emerged were initially held together by the tenacity and dedication of a few lay leaders, by men and women who commenced the work and then sought ordained assistance. The Methodism that arrived was part of the massive missionary activity from the United States and Britain, and many of its early developments mirrored those of co-religionists in the Maritimes. In other respects, however, Upper and Lower Canada presented different obstacles and new opportunities for the young connexion.

In Lower Canada the first "missionaries" were attached to the various British regiments garrisoning the province after 1760. The first recorded class leader was John Tuffy, who had been a local preacher under John Wesley and

Thomas Coke (1747–1814). Co-general superintendant of American Methodism and successor to the Wesleys in British Wesleyan Methodism. (UCA, Album 78.129C/OS, #1)

Jabez Bunting (1779–1858). Autocratic, conservative successor to Coke as leader of British Wesleyan Methodism. (UCA, Album 78.129C/OS, #1)

William Black (1760–1834). Driving force in early Methodism in Altantic Canada. (UCAMa)

Samuel Coate. Innovator and builder of Methodism in Lower Canada. (UCA, Album 78.105C/OS)

who served in the Quartermaster's Department at Quebec in the 1780s. He preached to both a military and a civilian Methodist audience. Although others continued this practice, most Methodists in the town joined the Protestant services held for a time in the so-called Jesuit Barracks.[43]

Beginning about 1800 with the American Methodist Conference's agreement to send missionaries, the Methodists at Quebec began meeting separately. A procession of American ministers, including Joseph Sawyer, Samuel Merwin, Thomas Madden, Nathan Bangs, and Samuel Coate, paid short, haphazard, and frustratingly unrewarding visits. Bangs, who served the circuit for part of 1806, recorded, "It seemed impossible to bear up under my trials. I could endure opposition, and had been tested in this respect; but to see no result of my labors; to be simply let alone by the great population around me seemed insupportable ... My money expended, and fearing the cause represented would be disgraced by my failure, I could only hide myself in God."[44] The society was too small to support an ordained minister. Although Quebec was regularly listed on the New York Conference rolls from 1804 and was part of the Lower Canada district formed in 1806, no minister stayed in the town for a full year and no members were recorded until 1808, when Merwin reported a society of thirteen.[45]

A year later his successor, George McCracken, tripled the membership, rented a small room for regular public worship, and made ultimately fruitless arrangements to buy a site for a chapel. James Mitchell, his replacement in 1810, also remained for only one year, and the last American missionary, Joseph Scull, departed with the outbreak of the War of 1812. Membership declined to about twenty-six under Scull's tenure, and it was a weak and disheartened congregation that turned to British Methodism for ministerial supply. Even with the commitment and financial support of businessmen such as John Shea and Peter Langlois, Methodism at Quebec remained too impoverished to pay for a minister, let alone a church building.[46]

Early Methodism in Montreal had an only slightly less disappointing history. A small group of men and women had met together for prayer and spiritual refreshment since at least the end of the American Revolution. But it was not until 1802 that Joseph Sawyer paid a short visit from his Bay of Quinte circuit to organize them into a regular Methodist class. Essentially, the same missionaries who worked in Quebec also supplied Montreal. They usually exchanged pulpits during the year because of the financial and psychological difficulties of labour at Quebec.

In 1807 Samuel Coate returned to Montreal from England with financial aid to build a chapel on St Joseph Street, which was finally opened in 1809. Coate was the presiding elder for Lower Canada and had impressive early results in gaining converts to Methodism. According to observers, "He swept like a meteor over the land, and spell-bound the astonished gaze of the wondering new settlers ... He was the Heaven-anointed and successful instrument of the conversion of hundreds."[47] Unfortunately, he later left Methodism for the Church of England and finally abandoned religion altogether. With a church building, the Montreal congregation became slightly stronger and more generous than the one in Quebec, although by 1812 it only had thirty-six members. Nevertheless, the fact that Montreal was more Protestant and more British gave hope for better days ahead. Between 1812 and 1814 Thomas Burch, an Irish-born British subject from the United States, served the congregation as the only American missionary active in Lower Canada during the war. However, during this period the society split over the issue of belonging to a foreign and enemy-controlled ecclesiastical body, and a majority of the membership petitioned the British missionary authorities to send "reliable" preachers.[48] The Methodist congregations in the town remained divided until 1820.

Within the remainder of Lower Canada, Methodism emerged only fitfully. In 1806, when the Lower Canada district had been established, it consisted of the Quebec, Montreal, Ottawa (region), Dunham, and Stanstead circuits. Both Dunham and Stanstead in the Eastern Townships overlapped the Vermont border, and the bulk of the membership was on the American side. Those residing in Lower Canada were mostly newly arrived New Englanders seeking land, who had little connection with the St Lawrence valley or the older colony. Although officially part of Lower Canadian Methodism, they were more closely allied to the contiguous American districts and usually received their missionaries directly from the United States.

Stanstead circuit was organized in 1804 and eight years later had 238 members. Dunham was set up in 1806 and shared the numerical prosperity, with 335 members by the beginning of the war. Despite the large membership, the area's Methodism was considered unorthodox and heavily influenced by the evangelical Congregational background of most of the settlers.[49] Dunham was particularly isolated, and even during the war both Canadian and American adherents persisted in worshipping amicably together for some time. Fitch Reed described an early service:

a large building was erected directly on the national line, as far as might be from the usual routes of travel ... Here they could meet and worship with their Yankee brethren, without leaving their own territory. A large company assembled in the house – the Yankees on the south side of the line, and the Canadians on the north – and yet in a compact congregation ... No one crossed the line, yet they passed very closely on both sides, and never was there a heartier hand-shaking than on that occasion – nominal beligerents, but real, heartfelt friends and brethren.[50]

Ties of kinship, friendship, and religion outweighed political divisions until near the end of the war, when the local situation changed dramatically.

The Ottawa circuit, straddling the Ottawa River northwest of Montreal, was organized in 1800 and by 1806, when it was transferred to the Lower Canadian jurisdiction, contained 105 members. William Snyder took it over in that year, and because he was French-speaking, he attempted to evangelize the considerable Roman Catholic population. However, he met with strong opposition from the local priests and gained no lasting converts.[51] Membership remained relatively stable up to the war through the ministries of Snyder, Madden, Samuel Luckey, and Robert Hibbard.

In 1809 the Methodist Episcopal Church had opened a circuit at Trois-Rivières, but it never had more than eighteen members and was left vacant from 1811 to 1815. Finally, a circuit was established overlapping the disputed boundary with Maine along the St Francis River northeast of Quebec. It too was served only intermittently and lasted until 1817.[52] Again, the majority of adherents resided in the United States and fell more properly into the American orbit. Except for the quasi-American causes and to some extent in Montreal, Methodism in the province by the War of 1812 was weak and apparently moribund.

The overwhelmingly French-speaking and Roman Catholic population generally obeyed its powerful hierarchy when faced with Protestant proselytizing. To become Protestant was to abandon both one's religious and one's cultural heritage and to accept assimilation into English-Canadian society. No Protestant denomination ever effectively overcame the hostility to such action. Methodism's relative failure was really based on its inability to convert the other Protestant inhabitants. Religious and ethnic loyalties and business and political alliances mutually reinforced each other among the Scots Presbyterians and English Anglicans. They actively opposed Methodist preaching on social and political, as well as religious, grounds. For instance, in 1794 Bishop Jacob Mountain attacked Methodist preachers as "a set of ignorant Enthusiasts whose preaching is calculated only to perplex the understanding and corrupt the morals, to relax the nerves of industry and dissolve the bonds of Society."[53] Such antagonism was evident throughout the first decades of Methodism in Lower Canada. By 1812 the movement could probably claim only about three hundred members actually residing in the province.

### UPPER CANADA

In Upper Canada, Methodism had a more propitious beginning. Other than the native population, there were only a few scattered settlements in the territory before 1783. These had their origins as fur-trading centres or as forts designed to prevent incursions from the south. Cataraqui (Kingston), Newark (Niagara), and Detroit were the only settlements of note, and even they were very small. The situation changed dramatically after the American Revolution with the settling of some 7,500 United Empire Loyalists, their so-called late-Loyalist American compatriots, disbanded British troops, and British immigrants. For the most part, the American settlers came from upstate New York, western Massachusetts, Pennsylvania, and New Jersey and represented a rich variety of ethnic and religious persuasions. Dutch-German Lutherans, Palatine Irish Protestants, New England Congregationalists, Scots and Irish Presbyterians and Roman Catholics, New Light Baptists, and English Anglicans and Methodists created a heady religious mixture. It was enlivened by Quakers, Mennonites, Tunkers, and Moravians and by those without ecclesiastical affiliation or religious beliefs at all.[54]

Outposts of Methodism quickly emerged along the St Lawrence River, on the Bay of Quinte, and at Niagara. The Hecks and Emburys and their relatives and friends recreated their class meeting in Augusta Township in 1785; Major George Neal preached throughout the Niagara region beginning in 1786 and organized a class at Stamford under Christian Warner; James Lyons at

Adolphustown and James McCarty at Ernestown lit the flame of Methodism around the Bay of Quinte in about 1788.[55] This Loyalist population had been deeply inculcated with North American religious, social, and political ideas. While wishing to create and preserve a conservative Anglo-American society, it was prepared neither to forsake its systems of beliefs and customs nor to follow blindly the British political and military élite, with its social and class pretensions, especially when religious freedom was involved. Despite the British government's decision to support a "Protestant clergy," which meant endowing the Church of England, in the newly created Province of Upper Canada in 1791, the general populace would not automatically subscribe to its Articles.[56] Methodism offered a legitimate and powerful spiritual alternative.

For Methodists, the province was a natural extension of Freeborn Garretson's upstate New York mission field and fitted easily into the regular pattern of American evangelistic expansion. William Losee, although not ordained until 1792, was the first Methodist missionary to serve in Upper Canada. He crossed the St Lawrence from his Lake Champlain circuit during the winter of 1789–90 in order to tour the settlements west of Cornwall. He returned to the United States the following summer, but at the 1790 Conference, Bishop Asbury assigned him to organize a circuit covering about a sixty-mile radius from Kingston beginning the following year. Until his premature retirement in 1793, Losee preached widely and helped establish classes and build chapels. As a preacher he was described as "more Hortatory than expository. He was impassioned, voluble, fearless, and denunciatory, cutting deep and closely, and praying God to 'smite sinners.'"[57] Although he helped to build two churches, like most of the first-generation preachers, he was more adept at awakening sinners than at constructing a permanent organization.

In 1792 Losee was joined by Darius Dunham, blunt, plain-spoken, and a strict disciplinarian. Together they alternated in the huge circuits of Kingston, which covered the area west almost to York, and Niagara, which consisted of the region around York, the Niagara Peninsula, and west to the Thames River. By 1795 Upper Canada claimed 483 members and growing societies centred on Stamford, Niagara, Augusta, Adolphustown, Ernestown, and Fredericksburgh.[58] More missionaries arrived every year from the United States, and they gradually filled in the intervening territory with preaching appointments. By 1802 there were ten itinerants ministering to over 1,500 members in the province. These numbers grew to over 2,000 members and sixteen ministers serving Upper and Lower Canada four years later.[59] At that time the Upper Canada district was divided into seven circuits.

Even though most of the settlement did not extend far back into the interior, the missionary traversed long distances on horseback or by foot to visit the dispersed homesteads and villages. Often the itinerant travelled more than three hundred miles and preached thirty-five times a month, as well as improving his education and fulfilling other pastoral responsibilities.[60] Supplies were always scarce and expensive, forcing him to beg his meals, feed for his horse, and a place to rest. Most services were held in private homes, in barns, or outdoors when the weather was favourable. The gatherings were often boisterous and undisciplined and sometimes argumentative Services were frequently broken up by shouting or criticisms or by cries of ecstasy and pleas for grace from members of the congregation. The preacher had to rely on personal fervour and a strong voice to succeed; a lively hymn was also useful in regaining order.[61]

During its early history, Methodism made little progress in the urban centres. York, the capital, received preaching only every second week beginning about 1803, and a church was not built there until 1818. Kingston, with its powerful and well-established Anglican and Presbyterian presence, was initially unfriendly to the Methodist cause. Although it was the circuit headquarters, it contributed few members and had only a small chapel until after the War of 1812. For instance, when Henry Ryan and William Case visited in 1805, they had to preach in the market square and "would tie up their horses, lock arms and go singing down the street to gather a crowd." As to their reception, "They suffered no particular opposition, excepting a little annoyance from some of the baser sort, who sometimes tried to trip them off the butcher's block which constituted their rostrum; set fire to their hair, and then blow out the candle if it were in the night session."[62]

Many of the early missionaries were as wild as their circuits. John Robinson, who itinerated from 1801 until he located in 1805, and William Snyder, who itinerated from 1806 until 1809, were both considered insane. Other preachers were noted for their ability to maintain order by physically enforcing their position. Most missionaries, however, used only an unquenchable "holy fervour" and a "burning love for the souls" of their listeners to spread the gospel. They shared a constant and sometimes oppressive concern for their own spiritual state and an all-consuming anxiety over saving souls.[63]

By far the two most dominant preachers to emerge during this pre-war period were William Case and Henry Ryan. Case had been born in Massachusetts in 1780 into a Congregationalist yeoman family. He received a good primary education and was reborn and converted to Methodism in 1803. Two years later, the connexion accepted him on probation for the itinerancy and sent him to the Bay of Quinte circuit in Upper Canada. In 1808 he was ordained elder and sent to the Ancaster circuit and to renew the mission along the lower Thames River and into Detroit. A short, handsome, amiable young man with a strong, melodious voice who captured many converts through his singing of Charles Wesley's hymns, Case was noted as a persuasive, rather than a haranguing, preacher. His talents were quickly recognized, and he was made presiding elder of the Cayuga district in New York State in 1810. He remained in the United States during the war, but returned to Upper Canada in 1815 as presiding elder to help rebuild the shattered Methodist cause. Until his death in 1855, he remained one of the most valued leaders of Canadian Methodism. Always "guileless, friendly and obliging," as well as hard working and efficient, he was warmly regarded as a tolerant Christian gentleman deeply committed to the welfare of his charges.[64]

These attributes sharply contrasted Case with his colleague Henry Ryan. Of Irish extraction, but probably born in Massachusetts in 1775, Ryan had been raised in New York. After serving as a local preacher, he was received on probation in 1800 and ordained elder four years later, and he joined Case on the

Bay of Quinte circuit in 1805. Over six feet tall, with a powerful, athletic build, Ryan physically dominated his surroundings and, when necessary, used his strength and boxing skills to prevent rowdy individuals from disrupting Methodist services. After several successful years on various circuits, he became presiding elder for Upper Canada in the newly constituted Genesee Conference in 1810. During the war he supervised both Upper and Lower Canada, stationed preachers, filled vacant pulpits, mobilized local preachers, and by the sheer force of his personality and energy, kept the church functioning. John Carroll, the noted Methodist chronicler, claimed that "he went forth as a flaming herald" and that he was a renowned preacher and gifted leader. "He had zeal, enterprise, courage, system, industry and that rough and ready kind of talent which was then more effective than any other."[65] However, Ryan's insufferable authoritarianism frequently degenerated into tyranny, causing conflict and disharmony among the preachers and laity.

Between 1790 and 1812, seventy-six different missionaries served voluntary terms in the Canadas under the auspices of the Methodist Episcopal Church; seven of these were native-born Canadians. At the beginning of the War of 1812, twenty-one missionaries were preaching to a membership of about 3,300. Excluding those who located or returned to the United States because of the hostilities, a third of the seventy-six missionaries itinerated for three or fewer years, and eleven worked for more than ten years. Although a few died on active duty, about two-thirds finished their careers in the United States, and the remainder retired in the Canadas. They often continued as local preachers and class leaders. This was a significantly better record than in other British North American mission fields. These preachers and their lay colleagues were eminently successful in attracting pioneer Upper Canadians to the Methodist fold during this period.[66]

Nevertheless, the war significantly disrupted Methodist operations in the Canadas. Upper Canada was invaded on several occasions by American forces and was constantly subject to the threat of smaller raids. Farms and homes along the frontier were looted and burned, and the population was perpetually alert to impending disaster. Genesee Conference's plan to meet at Niagara in July 1812 was thwarted by the war. When it met at Lyons, New York, the missionaries from the Canadas could not attend. As well, new recruits could not take up their circuits north of the border. The itinerants in Upper Canada met separately under Henry Ryan and attempted to supply the local work themselves, but several felt they could not conscientiously remain in the Canadas and take an oath of allegiance. Therefore some crossed over to the United States; others retired from the active ministry, although they continued to preach locally. Still others served with the Upper Canadian militia and joined with the Methodist laity in defending the province. Most Methodists, it should be noted, were sincerely loyal to the British cause.[67]

The work was extremely difficult for those itinerants who remained in the active ministry. Along with local preachers, they attempted to fill as many vacant appointments as possible. Ryan was especially skilled at choosing effective young laymen to keep up the work. Nevertheless, not only were there insufficient preachers, but the fledgling societies were themselves broken up as members joined the militia or did other war-related work. In several places, the remaining classes contained only women and children. Even where societies continued unaffected, travelling American preachers were viewed with suspicion, and the travel itself was constantly disrupted by the war conditions. Moreover, since the itinerant's salary was supplied by voluntary donations, both the absence of men and the devastation of property significantly reduced financial support. Ryan even hauled government freight to augment his income.[68]

Equally disruptive, Methodists in general and their ministers in particular were subject to the constant charge of disloyalty. The war naturally did much to crystallize anti-American sentiment and to renew the badge of distinction for the United Empire Loyalists. All things American were bitterly suspect; loyalty and conservatism became synonymous. Canadian society came to define itself as a different and superior order on the continent. The war also advanced the prestige and power of a local Anglican political élite who inextricably linked patriotism to the Church of England. By definition, Methodism, with its ties to an American ecclesiastical body and its threat to Anglican hegemony, was disloyal. Actually, many staunch Methodists shared this mistrust of American political and social predilections, had suffered from American military attacks, and questioned the acceptance of an American ministry.

To its opponents, however, the Methodist church was disloyal, not only because it was controlled by a foreign power, but much more profoundly, because it seemed to attack the intellectual, social, and political foundations that the Anglican élites were attempting to construct throughout British North America. With its democratic principles, its appeal to the emotions, and its reliance on personal experience and apparently irrational conduct, American-style Methodism appeared to threaten a conservative understanding of authority and order. Given its egalitarian leanings, it recognized no fundamental hierarchy in ecclesiastical or social matters, and it lacked the deference and trust in traditional relationships so critical for the Church of England's vision for British North America. By the end of the war, only about 1,800 members could be found in the Methodist connexion in the Canadas. Although many hundreds of others loosely allied themselves with the Methodist cause, it would take time to weld them into a disciplined spiritual institution.[69]

The war also sensitized Upper Canadian Methodism to the need to develop a native-born clergy. Several Canadian lay preachers who had been pressed into wartime service later joined the itinerant ranks, and in 1815 David Culp, David Youmans, William Brown, and Ezra Adams, all Canadians, were ordained in the province. A Canadian clergy, perhaps more than any other factor, promoted the eventual creation of an independent connexion and allowed Methodism to sustain a vital role in the country. Building on its own Loyalist heritage and its understanding of the local conditions and needs, Methodism in the region would surprisingly quickly become the most Canadian of all the Protestant churches.[70]

Within the denomination, the war also accelerated the collision between the American and British branches of Methodism in the Canadas. The American Methodist Episcopal Church had been active in the region for over two decades and could undeniably claim priority of service. It also had other advantages. It could furnish more thorough and consistent supervision, at least in peacetime; its missionaries were accustomed to pioneer North American conditions and understood the life, customs, and foibles of the inhabitants; and they could operate with little or no financial assistance from headquarters.[71]

On the other hand, British Methodism in the second decade of the nineteenth century was reorganizing its missionary operations and was flush with optimism and a heightened sense of its overseas responsibilities. It was determined to meet the requests for missionaries and to create a pure, disciplined Wesleyan church in British North America. The missionary authorities were also conscious of local denunciations of the disloyal and republican sentiments of the American preachers, their lack of respectability, and particularly their involvement, on the reform side, in colonial politics. The British Wesleyans were more willing to cooperate with the government and with the Church of England, which they still held in quasi-filial deference. They opposed any hint of radical political involvement. They were also in a much better financial position than their American co-religionists to assist the Canadian connexion and felt a particular responsibility for British subjects emigrating to North America. Finally, the British authorities, with their limited understanding of the region, could not believe that their missionaries would interfere with the few American preachers in such a vast, undeveloped territory.[72]

From the Canadian standpoint, it was natural that Quebec and Montreal should seek a supply of ministers from Britain. Quebec in particular had received only fitful service from the American church. Regular, inexpensive preaching by the Wesleyans was a highly attractive alternative when no missionary was available from the United States during the war, irrespective of any question of loyalty. In Montreal, even before the outbreak of hostilities, the society was split, and most members wanted a British preacher because they considered the incumbent, Thomas Burch, to be unsympathetic to local interests.[73]

By the end of the war, petitioners were even more adamant about being placed under British Wesleyan jurisdiction. They pointed out that as British subjects they owed it to themselves and to Britain to employ only British preachers. The political principles espoused by the American missionaries exposed the society to derision and suspicion. As a result, respectable prospective adherents were discouraged from joining, and uneasy relations were created with the general public. "It is evident to us that we have been considered a *Risk of Sedition*; this is an odium which as British subjects we cannot endure."[74] Given the increasingly chauvinistic character of American Methodism, this complaint had real substance.

On a more practical level, it would again be difficult to obtain preachers from the United States if another war occurred, and such a development seemed highly likely at the time. Leaving circuits vacant would seriously jeopardize the church's work. Even if war did not develop, since all American missionaries to the Canadas were volunteers, there was no guarantee of a steady or sufficient supply of high-quality preachers. The general unfriendly relations between the two countries might well inhibit suitable itinerants from crossing the border. The local Methodist connexion was also anxious to gain the full rights and privileges enjoyed by other recognized churches. It felt demeaned and disadvantaged at being unable to hold property on a connexional basis or to perform full ministerial offices. A committee from the Montreal circuit wrote to authorities in Britain, "We particularly wish that our preachers should have full power to perform all the duties of a ministerial character such as baptizing, burying and marrying ... This will not be granted us unless we employ British preachers."[75] Methodists were obliged to use justices of the peace or a minister from a recognized church in order to get married. And the problems of having property held by local trustees instead of by the denomination would cause division and discord for generations and seriously hamper connexional effectiveness.

The pro-British forces also expected that Canadian Methodism would benefit from having more missionaries than the American church could afford to supply, especially since they would receive a reliable income from abroad. Such a source of support would lift a heavy burden from local adherents and remove the public odium of a debt-ridden clergy. It was also maintained that British preachers were better educated, more regular in their enforcement of doctrine and discipline, and more clerical in deportment. These characteristics, it was assumed, would give them a distinct advantage in the urban centres and among the recent British immigrants.[76]

With these views in mind, the Wesleyan missionary society in June 1814 sent out John Strong to serve the Quebec circuit. He immediately began gathering the dispirited members and raised a subscription to buy a lot on St Ann Street on which to erect a church. According to Strong, a proper building was indispensable in attracting respectable citizens. The war had caused havoc in Upper Canada, but away from the fighting it had provided a great source of income to business interests, especially in Lower Canada. Without the need to provide a salary for Strong, more money was available for church construction. Strong also visited Montreal, where Henry Ryan, the presiding elder, refused him permission to preach in the Episcopal meeting-house. Despite this opposition, he joined the majority of the Montreal congregation in pressing London for more missionaries for Lower Canada.[77]

In 1815 Richard Williams answered these pleas and took over the chapel and most of the Montreal society, contrary to the wishes of Ryan and the local Episcopal Methodist minister. They were helpless to prevent this action since the building was owned by trustees loyal to Williams. The Episcopal Methodist remainder of the congregation was forced to rent rooms for its services. Williams was "a man of strong sense and equally strong will" and was inflexible in his attachment to Methodist doctrine and the Wesleyan connexion.[78] He succeeded in rebuilding the congregation and opened up new preaching appointments among the Protestants in Saint-Michel, St John's, Terrebonne, and Chambly near Montreal. Later he exchanged pulpits with Strong and pressed forward the construction of a church at Quebec.

Such British Wesleyan expansion led to increasingly acrimonious confrontations with the American Episcopal Methodists. In 1815 Ryan suggested that the issue should be resolved jointly by the British and American authorities since the local societies were incapable of reaching an accord. A year later, William Black and William Bennett, who was technically in charge of Lower Canadian Wesleyan operations and who had recently visited Montreal, were sent as representatives of the British Conference to work out the difficulties with the American General Conference meeting in Baltimore. Both Black and Bennett sympathized with the American presence in Lower Canada; Bennett had earlier attempted to convince Williams to leave Montreal rather than divide the mission. None the less, they did outline the reasons for the Wesleyan mission and the British missionary society's request that the Methodist Episcopal Church should withdraw from the province.[79]

The General Conference received these statements and also interviewed Case and Ryan, who were present in Baltimore. Ryan would accept no compromise, and his personal animosity toward the British Wesleyan intruders added fuel to the dispute and made any settlement difficult. Finally, the Conference decided to remain in Lower Canada and to seek the removal of the Wesleyans. It believed that most citizens still wanted American preachers. In order to lessen tensions, however, Ryan and Case exchanged districts, since the more amiable Case had greater respect for the British preachers. In a related move, Strong and Williams also exchanged circuits.[80]

Despite the decision of the General Conference, the Wesleyans not only refused to abandon Lower Canada, but they expanded their operations into Upper Canada. Several more British missionaries arrived in 1816, including John de Putron, a French-speaking minister from Guernsey who attempted, like others before him, to evangelize the French Canadians. However, he failed to overcome the power of the Catholic clergy or the commitment of the population to Catholicism and soon settled into regular circuit work. He claimed, "The ignorance, bigotry and prejudice of the Canadians are far too great for me to describe." But others suggested that de Putron "unquestionably lacked the persuasive element, which all will admit to be an essential one in dealing with such people."[81] Another recruit, James Booth, replaced Strong in Montreal, started a Sunday school, and opened a subscription for a larger church in the city.

Other new missionaries moved up the Ottawa River, where they took over direction of the great revival begun by George Ferguson, the Episcopal Methodist itinerant, which was sweeping the area. British itinerants also displaced the American preachers in the Eastern Townships. For instance, Richard Pope described his work along the Vermont border near where Fitch Reed had earlier reported cordial wartime relations.

St. Armand is about 50 miles from Montreal and is very contiguous to the United States of America. I preach at St. Armand one half of my time and in the Township of Dunham the other half ... Religion once flourished in the neighbourhood but the late unnatural and destructive war gave it a dreadful blow. Many pious persons, who were inimical to our government moved away to other places, whilst others were so engaged in the war as to disregard all religion ... Since the peace, the American preachers have been sent to some of the circuits as before, but in vain, the people retain their former prejudices and by far the greater part will not come to hear them.[82]

In Upper Canada, the Wesleyans organized a circuit around the village of Perth. Kingston and its surrounding region also invited and received Wesleyan clerical support. In the town, Methodism had never been able to compete with the Anglicans and Presbyterians. But in the outlying district, it was claimed a Wesleyan preacher was needed because "the people are mostly Methodists in the country or attendants on their meetings, tho' we have to lament that we see but very little real piety, but sometimes a great deal of wildfire and great irregularity in their meeting, and in their intercourse with the world."[83] The local inhabitants, who wanted a Wesleyan missionary, described the American preachers as young, inexperienced, and ignorant. Ironically, it was a young and inexperienced British probationer, Thomas Catterick, who soon answered the call.

Wesleyan missionaries also moved into Fort Wellington (Prescott) and Cornwall, where, it was claimed, two able ministers "appealed strongly to the known loyalty of the people."[84] Others began to serve the Bay of Quinte region, York, and Niagara. On the Niagara circuit in 1818, the Wesleyan preacher Henry Pope reported that he had preached to over two hundred at Stamford and had nine preaching appointments in the peninsula. He argued that if the Methodist Episcopal itinerants stayed in Upper Canada, they should serve the interior, relinquishing the more settled circuits to the Wesleyans since they "scarcely make any attempt in many of the most populous and important places on the frontier" because of the hostility engendered by the war.[85] Rather than seeking to ameliorate relations and defend the Methodist name, the British Wesleyan missionaries played on the fears heightened by the recent conflict to advance their own cause.

By 1817 there were nine Wesleyan missionaries in the Canadas, and they endeavoured to gain a degree of autonomy from the Nova Scotia district, under whose supervision they had been placed, concerning such internal matters as the stationing of preachers. The distance and expense of dealing with Nova Scotia made any relations ineffectual, particularly since important decisions were made by the missionary committee in London. It was to this committee that Henry Pope wrote in 1818 requesting at least ten more missionaries. The local Wesleyan missionaries constantly reported that American Methodists were not serving Upper Canada adequately and that there was plenty of room for both connexions. However, they were not prepared themselves to go into settlements that lacked Methodist preachers; rather, they took over existing chapels or set up societies in direct competition with their American brethren.[86]

The response of the Canadian Episcopal Methodist leaders was understandable. They tried to continue their work in Montreal and along the Ottawa River, although they were seriously disadvantaged there. In other areas, they attempted to out-preach their British competition while complaining bitterly to both their own Conference and the British Wesleyan authorities about the interference. They vehemently denied any charge of disloyalty and cited the increasing Canadian-born ministry. Statistically, they were regaining the ground lost during the war and effectively evangelizing a large proportion of the population. Ninian Holmes reported the good work taking place in the Detroit area and requested that there be no Wesleyan interference; Montreal and the Bay of Quinte circuits also complained about the divisive Wesleyan presence. At Matilda on the Cornwall circuit, little or no decline in membership was recorded, and the lack of growth was blamed on Wesleyan preachers. Despite Pope's preaching near Niagara, the members "remained firm in their allegiance to the 'American preachers,' as they are called, despite their own traditional Tory proclivities."[87] From Niagara, George Ferguson also dismissed the Wesleyan missionaries' purported advances and denounced them as agents of Satan sent to injure religion. At Kingston the Episcopal Methodists gained an ally in Edward Johnston, the newly appointed British Wesleyan minister. He informed the British connexion that it had been seriously misinformed about the religious destitution of the settlers, and he added that "the cause of religion is suffering very much by the division and contentions going on here by so much zeal for parties ... I dare not go upon the labours of other Methodist preachers until I see the reasons made clear."[88]

In all the settled areas of the province, the Wesleyans were aggressive and determined, but although they were making gains at the expense of the Episcopal Methodists, these were never as great as they wished or announced. Their impact was simply to hurt the overall work by causing disharmony and to bring Methodism into disrepute. The bitter controversy only aided the religious and political opponents of both denominations and disrupted the otherwise friendly relations between British and American Methodism. The English committee gradually came to recognize its responsibility in fostering this imbroglio and in 1819 urged its missionaries to enter unserved areas in the province, rather than compete in established localities, unless there was sufficient scope for both organizations. However, the Wesleyan itinerants maintained that doing so would mean abandoning their loyal followers, and they ignored the request.

Since it was evident that the local ministers on both sides were unwilling to cease their competition voluntarily, the issue was once again referred to the American General Conference in 1820. After hearing several memorials and considering all the arguments, the Conference reluctantly voted to leave Lower Canada to the Wesleyans but to remain in Upper Canada. It also instructed its missionaries that their loyalty was to the British crown and the Canadian political system while they were serving in the province. It went on to recommend the formation of a separate Canada Conference at some future date. It hoped these last two resolutions would answer any allegations of disloyalty and foreign domination.[89]

In turn, the British connexion accepted this compromise and agreed to withdraw from Upper Canada. The missionary authorities in Britain were quite willing to support this decision. After the first flush of enthusiastic expansion and particularly as funds decreased during the postwar depression, they were attempting to reduce their overseas expenditures. Throughout British America, British missionaries had far exceeded their budgets and had indiscriminately overdrawn on funds. In 1820 the Canada districts alone ran a £567 deficit. In the same year, the missionary committee attempted to curb this practice by establishing an annual limit of £50 per circuit. It believed that if the work was progressing as well as reported, the local societies should be able to be more self-supporting. Subsequent reports to the committee tended to stress the scarcity of local support and the consequent difficulty of sustaining the missions. These reports confirmed the suspicion that earlier statements of success had been exaggerated and also laid open to question accounts about the services provided by the American preachers in the region. The committee came to recognize the value and extent of the Episcopal Methodists' work and accepted their arguments concerning historical precedence in the country.[90]

Although the compromise of 1820 officially settled the dispute, local antagonisms remained deep. In Montreal, when the American preacher was transferred, many of the adherents moved to other Protestant denominations, and some invited an independent American Presbyterian minister to serve them.[91] In Upper Canada, the Wesleyan societies at Niagara, Fort Wellington, and Kingston petitioned the British missionary society to exempt them from the general agreement. They dismissed the Episcopal Methodists as ignorant and disloyal enthusiasts who would likely hurt the political and religious interests of the country. Only Kingston, because it was the site of a large British garrison, retained a Wesleyan missionary. Nevertheless, the case for a strong Wesleyan presence in Upper Canada continued to be made throughout the 1820s, and animosity remained just below the surface in Methodist affairs. In fact, within a decade the compromise of 1820 would be shattered and a new period of competition inaugurated.[92]

For the time being, however, Methodist energies could be directed toward building stronger, self-sufficient connexions in the separate spheres of influence in the Canadas. It was estimated that by 1820 the Wesleyans had about 750 members in Upper and Lower Canada and the Episcopal Methodists had rebuilt their societies to some 6,000 members. Priority was now given to expanding the work among the "respectable" elements in the colonies and in the growing urban centres. As if to consummate the return to normal relations both between British and American Methodism and between Canada and the United States, the Genesee Conference met at the Lundy's Lane meetinghouse near Niagara Falls, Upper Canada, in 1820. The indigenous nature of the Canadian operations was further signalled by the ordination of three native-born itinerants and the acceptance of four others on probation.[93] The period of dependence on foreign support was rapidly drawing to a close in Upper Canada, and with it the pioneer days of instability and fears of evangelical failure were passing. The connexion looked forward, confident in its ability to create a sound institutional structure that could win the hearts and minds of the whole region.

# 3 Methodism as a Personal Spiritual and Moral Movement

The Methodist movement and, indeed, the evangelical revival in general were based pre-eminently on a dynamic, personal religion. Methodism found its meaning and drew its vitality from its ability to help individuals to achieve a spiritual rebirth by opening their hearts and minds to Christ and by encouraging them to seek a living relationship to God independent of ecclesiastical intermediaries. In the early evolution of Methodism in British North America, institutional development was of secondary importance. The church did not grow from the top down through legislated fiat or even earnest injunction; rather, it expanded because it provided a satisfying home for those desperately seeking a higher spiritual and moral state. Further, its future did not lie solely in the hands of itinerant or local preachers, roving evangelists, or Sunday school teachers, but in the continued commitment of its members to the quest for conversion and sanctification, the sacredness of mutual fellowship, and the religious expression received and given at home. Methodism offered an intimate fellowship based on a set of common values and shared practices. Ultimately, private and family religious experience and worship, and the social attitudes they helped to foster, most clearly defined early Canadian Methodism.

## THE COMMUNITY OF BELIEVERS

John Wesley throughout his long life had striven to create and nurture a balanced approach to religion. According to him, religion was fundamentally grounded in the Scriptures, especially in its presentation of the person of Christ, expounded through the early church fathers and other writers who had proven their spirituality over time, experienced vitally in the heart, and sustained by the laws of logic and reason. Yet, by the time of Wesley's death, the Age of Reason, in which he had functioned most creatively, was gradually being transformed or displaced by a new Romantic age which lauded the emotional and accepted the irrational. In the face of the revolutionary changes occurring in society, the old understanding of a restrained and well-ordered universe based on natural law no longer appeared valid. Especially in North America, nature, even with humanity at its apex, proved to be wild and unmanageable, provoking distinctly irrational and emotional responses. As the appeal of Romanticism expanded, it transformed philosophy, literature, the arts, and perhaps most fundamentally, religion. The new age appeared to demand a reinstatement of God in the natural world as an active agent in the lives of all creation, and nature itself was exalted as a source of inspiration for a more intimate and personal knowledge of God.[1] As a result, evangelical religion came to rely even more on experience as the source of spiritual guidance.

Moreover, the American and particularly the French Revolution not only initiated a violent and chaotic period in history, but they also proved that reason alone was insufficient to sustain order or authority and could not be relied upon to re-create individuals as moral or spiritually alive beings. To Methodists, only a deep and personal commitment to God through the redeeming power of Jesus Christ could truly renew the individual and advance society. At the same time, emotional fervour appeared to provide a legitimate catalyst for gaining access to God's re-creative force. In early-nineteenth-century North America, tradition and reason, as sources of religious authority, were at least partially abandoned. Experience reigned instead, and the acceptable experience was often transformed into a subjective "feeling,"[2] although "enthusiasm" still had to be avoided. Church authorities continued to suspect that enthusiasts failed to live holy lives because they refused to participate actively in the appointed means of grace.[3] Of equal concern, over-emotional enthusiasm sometimes manifest itself in eccentric, unnatural behaviour and was even blamed for inciting madness in some mentally unstable individuals.

These shifts in emphasis were especially understandable in light of pioneer conditions in British America. The early settlers, whether isolated in Atlantic fishing ports, in embryonic villages, or on primitive farms carved out of the threatening forests, were ever conscious of their own insignificance. The wild face of nature was rarely absent. At times the environment might appear benevolent, but only the foolish forgot its harsh reality or believed they could truly conquer it. Defiantly hostile, nature constantly threatened the pioneer's very existence. Canadians did not march confidently across a bountiful, harmonious wilderness; they struggled to come to terms with their surroundings and gradually to transform their environment, but rarely were they at ease with it.[4]

Under these conditions, institutional religion initially tended to fall away. One must discount to a degree the vivid descriptions of immorality and irreligion portrayed by generations of pious Methodist preachers, such as Henry Pope's 1818 account: "Almost all the vices that afford gratification to the carnal mind seem pursued with unwearied avidity."[5] But it was certainly true that much of pioneer society was not restrained by the moral forces of civilization. Indifference combined with superstition and ignorance to create an unwholesome spiritual environment. As Bishop Mountain noted from his early tour of

Upper Canada, "Living without restraint, and without the eye of those whom they respect, a sense of decency and religion frequently disappears. Here the disinclination to holy things presents itself in all its deformity, a distaste for divine worship, and neglect of everything sacred, and a total estrangement from God; and although from their situation, crimes against society are few; the heart becomes entirely dead to true piety and virtue."[6]

Isolation had much to do with these conditions, but they also reflected the unsettled nature of pioneer existence. Most immigrants lived in a marginal economic state for a number of years. Poverty was endemic, except for those few with stable sources of income, and the creation of new wealth through land clearance took many years of hard labour.[7] Survival often depended on finding work off the farm and a careful husbanding of resources. Even these actions could be undone by fluctuations in the general economy, which was dependent on unstable outside forces. Often traditional kinship and community support was not available to provide temporary assistance. These conditions led to a transient lifestyle as individuals and families moved about looking for economic advancement.

Such conditions destablized family life and prevented the development of strong ecclesiastical ties. At the same time, traditional religious services were rarely available, even for those predisposed to search them out. Both ministers and places of worship were in short supply during the first decades of the nineteenth century in British North America. Therefore settlers were rarely disciplined by a strong ecclesiastical presence, by well-developed ethical standards in the community, or even by the enforcement of a mature legal code and system of justice. Not surprisingly, drunkenness, rowdyism, and even social immorality were near-normal aspects of life.

Despite the lack of institutional support, however, most Canadians resisted the degenerating tendencies of pioneer conditions. They did so by holding onto as much of their cultural and religious heritage as they could. They resisted being demoralized by their economic and social conditions and worked to re-establish as quickly as possible the style of life they had been forced to abandon. Such was especially the case for women. New settlers naturally turned to their normally more civilized former homes to satisfy their spiritual and intellectual hunger and provide a stable, disciplined social order. Over time, as well, they recognized that in the face of hostile nature and economic insecurity, they were helpless without spiritual support. It was God, after all, who had "turned a barren wilderness into a fruitful field, and made the desert rejoice and blossom like a rose."[8] It was therefore natural and vitally important for religiously trained Methodists to continue their individual quests for spiritual strength and to organize prayer meetings, class meetings, and "cottage worship" at the earliest opportunity. In addition, Methodism with its forthright and all-encompassing message, provided a congenial home for any Protestant seeking a demonstrative and vital religion.[9]

Nevertheless, it demanded significant sacrifice from its adherents. Initially, it forced would-be members to break all those ties which had sustained social relations in the "corrupt" world. "Their ties of previous kinship varied – blood, marriage, commerce, debt, class, sport, religion, [race] ... to honour the world's pattern of kinship was to reject that of Christ."[10] Methodism instituted a community of believers that defined itself against the corrupt world, embracing the "ins" and anathematizing the "outs." "We naturally imbibe the sentiments, and conform to the practices of those with whom we associate. Similarity of views, dispositions and pursuits, is necessary to friendship, and we cannot long be companions of the wicked without conforming to their habits."[11] Even when apparently harmless, such companionship had to be avoided unless the opportunity was used to evangelize. If continued, it would lead to worldliness and loss of faith.

Beyond the dangers of evil companions, simply living left one vulnerable to general social immorality. Methodists, along with other religious groups, often denounced the conduct at such social gatherings as picnics and barn-raisings, and some refused to attend.[12] In denouncing dancing, popular amusements, and drinking, they severed other important social links that helped to dispel the inherent loneliness and frustration of pioneer life. This refusal to share in the local social life appeared to attack neighbourliness, the most precious of all pioneer social graces, and weakened the fragile sense of community. Methodists were often ridiculed and denounced for being too superior to join with their fellow settlers. One of the criticisms of early Methodists was that they were too self-righteous, too sure of their own spiritual status, to fit into the general fabric of secular society. At times, this criticism in turn led to suspicion and overt opposition, especially from those in power, who believed that Methodists lacked adequate respect for authority. None the less, it should be emphasized that Methodism was not a joyless, puritanical retreat from the world. Rather, it was profoundly sociable and convivial, providing a warm, outgoing sense of fellowship which welcomed all to join.

On a broader level, the appeal of Methodism, and therefore the expansion of the Methodist community, reflected a temporary weakening of the bonds of traditional religious integration and denominational loyalty throughout the English-speaking world. The Anglican, Presbyterian, and even Baptist and Quaker churches seemed unable to satisfy the new demands of society resulting from a significant population explosion and the economic and social dislocation of the industrial revolution, coupled with the intellectual and political chaos magnified by the French Revolution and the subsequent period of warfare.[13] Authors such as Elie Halévy, E.P. Thompson, E.J. Hobsbawm, and Bernard Semmel,[14] along with their disciples, have analysed the impact of the evangelical revival in muting discord and redirecting revolutionary energy to spiritual matters, but even the existing denominations were torn by internal dissension and forced to redefine their position in society and their mission to the world. Particularly in North America during the early nineteenth century, the various forces at work helped to establish a new, undenominational model of religious affiliation which led to different patterns of religious fellowship. Community-wide preaching and interdenominational Sunday schools both reflected and promoted denominational weakness and the submersion of traditional patterns of ecclesiastical loyalty.[15] Such cooperation in pioneer areas was not only generally necessary, but it was also a part of a broader acceptance of legitimate differences among religious communions.

Elaborating new patterns of spiritual fellowship forced Methodists to break former ecclesiastical relations and sever connections with the corrupt world. These were replaced by strong personal piety and a strict spiritual and moral code. However, the quest for personal salvation could be extremely traumatic. Periods of success, with their acute ecstasy, could be quickly replaced by despondency and a sense of failure. The existing diaries, memoirs, and correspondence tend to come from those whose personal struggles were ultimately victorious; no estimate can be made of the effects on those whose failure left them psychologically scarred and permanently disheartened about their spiritual welfare and their damnation after death. These battles were difficult even when family and friends shared the Methodist heritage and offered comfort and encouragement, but they were much more difficult for those without such support.

For instance, John Carroll, who would later become one of the great Canadian Methodist propagandists, initially hid his quest for conversion and his move to Methodism from his friends and co-workers. Although members of his own family were supportive, he was afraid of ridicule and felt a strong pressure to conform to his colleagues' social practices.[16] However, his journey was not nearly as difficult as that of many others. The story of the Ryerson brothers' estrangement from their father when they left the Church of England was typical of large numbers of Methodists. The case of the prominent Bible Christian Cephas Barker illustrates even greater family and social difficulties. His father was a strict Baptist, and when the young Barker began attending Methodist meetings, "His angry father dragged him from his knees at a prayer meeting, pushed him into the street, and struck and kicked him repeatedly while on the way home. Having got there, in his rage the father … whipt him until the blood flowed freely, winding up … by rubbing handful after handful of salt into the bleeding wounds."[17] Barker senior refused to allow his son to attend any Methodist gatherings and ignored him in public. Young Cephas left home, joined the navy, and later entered the Methodist ministry, preferring to abandon his family rather than his spiritual home. Although Methodism usually opposed rebellion against parental authority, such kinship breaks were acceptable, and they became part of the "heroic" tradition of sacrifice in Methodist lore.

Once the individual had made the decision, Methodism encouraged a continual segregation from non-Methodists. Marriage outside the fellowship was strongly discouraged unless it was the providential means of bringing the spouse into the fold. The church's Discipline noted, "We are well assured that few things have been more pernicious to the work of God, than the marriage of the children of God with the children of the world."[18] Such action transgressed biblical injunction and placed the soul in jeopardy. In many ways, Methodism represented an extended family; marriage provided a critical support system which could be endangered by non-Methodist alliances. Since the family was the essential foundation for worship, the future spiritual growth and prosperity of all its members demanded marital harmony and union of belief and purpose.

For at least the first half of the nineteenth century, Canadian Methodists were also discouraged from joining secular societies that might divide loyalty and commitment to the Methodist cause. Most prominent among these were the secret societies such as the Freemasons and the Orange Order. At its first meeting in 1824, the Canada Conference of the Methodist Episcopal Church resolved "That this body consider it contrary to the spirit of the gospel and the feelings of its members for any Methodist Minister to become a member of, or frequent any Masonic Temple."[19] Although these organizations did not always have laudatory goals, they did help cement social cohesion and provided a mutual-aid network. However, Methodists believed they should give preference only to co-religionists. Also, secret oaths and secret loyalties could lead to unlawful or unchristian behaviour. James Richardson, the editor of the *Christian Guardian,* warned in 1833, "All secret associations, or those societies whose conditions of fellowship, bonds of union, rules of action, or objects of pursuit, are not known … are dangerous to any community, civil, political or religious."[20]

To replace the external community, internal bonds were forged which fostered a powerful new kinship of believers to sustain its members against outside hostility and social pressures. This relationship was based on the misleadingly simple quest to "flee from the wrath to come." Yet it was cemented by strong spiritual and emotional bonds. Individuals gave themselves wholly to Christ and to one another. A profound intimacy emerged which encompassed everyone sharing in the community. As William Jessop expressed it to Daniel Fidler, "You lay near my Heart, & nothing but Sin, shall ever part thy Soul and mine."[21] The language itself conveyed the fervour uniting Methodists. They were substantially brothers and sisters, fathers, mothers, and children, in Christ. Such relationships mitigated such temporal divisions as class, race, or nationality.

This bonding was important for all Methodists, but it was particularly vital for women, who were among the most isolated and socially dispossessed groups in the community. Although nineteenth-century Methodism opposed social equality of the sexes, it did provide a forum for shared experience that helped sustain female members against the harsh realities of the times. The only important criterion was true rebirth and conscious holy living. Since Methodism sustained the belief that all Christians, regardless of sex, were legitimate and proper ministers of Christ, it is not surprising that women often played a significant role in advancing the cause. Canadian Methodism owed a great debt to such women leaders as Barbara Heck and perhaps even more to women preachers such as Elizabeth Dart and Ann Vickery or to later women evangelists, including the Dimsdale sisters.[22]

Bound as they were in a form of spiritual kinship, Methodists were able to guard each other's spiritual and moral health; the relationship gave one the authority to interfere directly in the lives of others. In fact, mutual support, regulation, and discipline were expected within this spiritually egalitarian society. Methodists were obliged to avoid all forms of evil. Ultimate authority to discipline and expel fallen members resided with the itinerant preacher and the quarterly official board of the circuit, but most problems never reached these institutional bodies. The class leader or other members would normally exhort, instruct, or reprove the offenders. Through prayer, counsel, forbearance, and if necessary, sympathetic, but firm admonition, most disciplinary problems were resolved. Undergirded by the church's doctrines and discipline and buttressed by quasi-familial bonds, individuals could place powerful pressure on fellow members to conform, even during the long absences of the itinerant preacher.

On a different level, as in other churches sharing the evangelical revival, Methodism was strengthened by an expressive vernacular – a new, self-defined vocabulary. This idiom distinguished the evangelical denominations from other groups and promoted the mutual understanding of intimate shared experiences.[23] Even a casual reading of Methodist diaries, memoirs, or newspaper articles evinces a repetitive use of specific terms and phrases to describe the individuals' religious feelings. The use of such language among Methodists in fact started with Wesley's description of his own conversion: his heart was "strangely warmed." The search for Zion was not for a physical, but for a metaphysical place. Seekers after salvation were "trembling," "weeping," "shouting," "shrieking," and "white unto harvest." Those acknowledging God's presence were "awakened," "set at liberty," cleansed by a "shower of blessing"; they were "broken" as by a hammer, "cut down" by an axe or scythe, "struck by lightning," or most commonly "melted" by fire.[24] The great fire of revival melted away impurity in the sinner and forged members into a community of God, a community shared equally by laity and clergy.

This language became a shorthand for describing the indescribable that was clearly recognizable to fellow Methodists. Later generations (and most modern readers), who suspected that it was used only out of habit and did not spring from the innermost experience, missed the point; the idiom was intended to define who shared and who were excluded from the family. Even its highly charged imagery suited this purpose. "Excessive language fitted the occasions; how else could the drama and power of an emotional encounter between a sinner and God be described."[25] Thus nearly every aspect of doctrine, discipline, experience, and human relations were utilized to recreate a self-sustaining and holy communion of believers.

### THE INDIVIDUAL AND THE FAMILY

One of the hallmarks of the evangelical revival was its aggrandizement of the individual and the consequent strengthening of individualism. Family and friends could encourage, but spiritual growth and conversion were, under God, a personal responsibility and a personal opportunity. The significance of external restraining authorities was reduced. Priestly functions and ecclesiastical institutions served only to bolster individual religious development and to assist a personal decision for Christ. The individual became the active agent, subject to God's initiative, in the struggle for grace, rather than merely the passive recipient of undeserved favour.

This new status unleashed vast reserves of religious energy, but it also placed terrifying demands on the penitent. Humanity was naturally and totally depraved, and only through personal rebirth and holy living could the terrors of a real hell be alleviated. With this understanding came introversion, self-criticism, and oppressively morbid loneliness that could be only partially ameliorated by the support of the Methodist community. The private writings of nineteenth-century Canadian Methodists unhesitatingly expressed this anxious self-doubt. For instance, George Abbs recalled in 1892 that during his early struggle for God's grace, "I seemed to be enduring the very pangs of hell" and "losing my reason" as a result of his spiritual torments.[26] Others could neither sleep nor eat and often associated their spiritual distress with poor health or secular misfortunes. Physical isolation only exaggerated their spiritual loneliness.

These anxieties were perhaps best exemplified and elaborated by the overwhelming preoccupation with death. Death was a constant companion, tormenting pioneer Canadians no matter how old they were. It was not reserved for the aged or infirm; accidents, disease, and childbirth were too ready to carry off even the apparently strong and healthy. For the Methodist, death was God's judgment on Adam's sin and an ever-present reminder of humanity's frailty and continuing evil. Commonly, natural disasters and epidemics were perceived as special visitations of God. Like many others, George Hodgins remembered being constantly afraid of dying and going to hell. Matthew Richey warned his nine-year-old daughter that "many more die *young*, than *old*: and should this be the case with you, you can easily think how it would increase the affliction of your loss if you were not good, I mean a sincere follower of the blessed redeemer."[27]

The expectation of imminent death, either for oneself or for family or friends, was often critical in forcing individuals to contemplate their spiritual health. Of course, many turned to religion when sick, only to abandon it when recovered. However, death could strike so unexpectedly that spiritual rebirth provided the only secure haven. William Blackstock, a popular Methodist itinerant, reminded his listeners that humankind was indebted to affliction for the stimulus it provided to turn to God.[28] Death, with its incumbent rewards and punishments, necessitated constant human vigilance. Joseph Anderson warned his colleague Daniel Fidler, "O that we were always upon our guard as well becomes creatures conscious that they stand upon a narrow brink between two boundless Eternities."[29] Or as Richey morbidly pointed out, "The earth is a vast cemetery of human carcasses, and our bodies shall soon return to dust and mingle with the common mass of corruption. Oh! solemn and humiliating thought! Who can for a moment pause and indulge to such pensive meditations without perceiving and feeling that preparation for death is as our Lord emphatically calls it the 'One thing needful.' "[30]

Death, however, also afforded an opportunity for testing the quality and depth of faith. Conversion and sanctification were the only meaningful answers to the trauma of death, but these bastions of freedom and safety could be too easily breached by doubt, temptation, and sin. In facing death, the faithful Methodist exemplified all the Christian virtues and thereby gave assurance to those who would be left behind. Family, friends, and neighbours made it a point of honour to visit the dying as much for instruction as to comfort the afflicted household. The dying were constantly observed and questioned as to their spiritual condition, and by their example and often their words of warning, they encouraged religion in others.

Deathbed conversions or confessions, although encouraged and sometimes even coerced in non-believers, were not expected from sound Methodists. Rather, the last hours reflected a proper fulfilment of a holy life. John Watson died "exalting in the salvation of the gospel." Thomas Madden "endured his affliction with much patience" and was "greatly supported by the consolation of the Holy Spirit ... In some instances, he was so enraptured with divine things, that he was constrained to praise and glorify God with a loud voice." As was commonly the case, Madden used his last efforts "to deliver a solemn charge to his family." Peace of mind and contentment with one's fate were almost obligatory signs of salvation. William Slater "manifested perfect resignation at his approaching fate" despite a natural concern for his family's welfare. Benjamin Cole was in intense pain; nevertheless, "When asked if he wished to live, he said, 'I would like to labor a little longer in the vineyard but I am ready to go.'"[31]

Such deathbed scenes, especially those published in elaborate nineteenth-century obituaries, represented a major component of the life story of the deceased. Together with the conversion experience, death was perceived as perhaps the most critical element in one's existence. The accounts quickly took on a routine character, rehearsing the resolve to accept God's will and the anticipation of reaching heaven. A favourite hymn or Scripture verse was almost invariably on the lips as death carried off the tranquil victim. These scenes were faithfully recounted, and they furnished the living with consolation, warning, and a model of how a Christian was expected to face death. They proved that even death held no real terror for those who were reborn in Christ here on earth. Indeed, many Methodists could visualize death as a release from earthly pain and temptation. Moreover, the knowledge that children who had died were waiting for parents "on that celestial shore" was a "precious consolation."[32] But a triumphant afterlife could only be achieved by those who had secured a personal, heartfelt conversion.

To achieve this state of salvation, Methodists were under a strict obligation to use all the providential (God-ordained) and prudential (God-supported) means of grace available. The regular means of grace encompassed the normal elements of church life, which helped to bring the individual to that crisis of spiritual decision and which promoted the full abundance of entire sanctification. These elements were naturally numerous, diverse, and comprehensive. While institutional Methodism depended on the social means of grace, including preaching, the sacraments, class meetings, prayer meetings, love feasts, and regular church worship (which will be discussed in a subsequent chapter), behind these lay the relatively simple private means of grace. These were available to everyone, even when he or she was alone or in a family setting.

The most basic, and perhaps most essential, private means of grace was prayer. Methodists were constantly admonished: "Often pray to our heavenly Father who seeth in secret ... every morning and every evening assemble your family, and present the supplications of your household to the God of the families on the earth." Prayer was a means "without which all others will be vain and ineffectual."[33] Individuals must pray daily: when they rose in the morning, whenever they felt tempted, before making important decisions, before every meal, and as the last act before retiring at night. Everyone should maintain a private place for prayer, anywhere one could "closet" oneself away from temporal distractions and intimately seek God.

Prayer must not be used to seek material prosperity or other selfish ends. It began with an acknowledgment of one's unworthiness and guilt: "I come before thee this evening, condemning myself, and crying, Unclean, Unclean!"[34] And it continued with a confession of specific sins and weaknesses. The power and authority of God were acknowledged, and spiritual blessings, according to God's benevolent wisdom, were sought. Methodists prayed especially for the resolve to fight sin, for a visitation of the Holy Spirit, and for God's constant presence.

On special occasions or in times of extraordinary need, prayer was complemented by days of fasting. For instance, the Methodist Episcopal Conference called for fasting and prayer on the first Friday of March 1795 in order to encourage a rededication to evangelism.[35] In 1824 the inaugural Canada Conference resolved that its clergy should follow this practice on the first Friday of every month and two years later appointed "the first Friday in November be set apart for *fasting and prayer,* for the promotion of internal holiness and the spread of the work of God in general."[36] On other occasions, individual Methodists took it upon themselves to establish personal days of fasting.

Except during illness or unusual circumstances, fasting was valuable in isolating the individual from the secular world: "self-examination was instituted, humiliation and self-denial practised, and a spirit of reformation promoted. By such appointments the laws of God are venerated, and the statutes and authorities of the civil government respected."[37] The absence of food was also a clear indication of one's perpetual dependence on God. In order to prevent the sin of pride, humanity needed to be reminded that God was the source of all things and that sacrifice and hardship were part of the plan of existence. "If misfortune comes it will bring its blessings; and if prosperity mingle its more pleasing ingredients with the bitter dregs, which man is doomed to receive, it will be rendered still more welcome by the reflection that a father's hand dispenses it."[38] Thus fasting gave proof of a humble resignation to God's will and represented a renunciation of the corrupt world.

The other important private means of grace involved reading the Scriptures. Methodism was founded on a deep personal knowledge of the Bible. Its members were enjoined to read parts of the Bible daily and to ponder and discuss its important message. Scripture not only provided the one sure guide for salvation and an understanding of God's demands and expectations, but it also established rules of conduct and ethical behaviour that were essential for spiritual and moral growth. John Wesley's writings and other inspired sources were vital auxiliaries to the Bible which expanded on the biblical injunctions. Equally valuable to most Methodists were the hymns of Charles Wesley. They brought Wesleyan theology joyfully or painfully to life. Singing hymns helped instil the magnificence of God and the awful sacrifice of Christ in the heart of the singer. They reinforced Scripture and expanded the popular appeal of religion. In times of loneliness, hymns were of great consolation and in moments of joy, they encapsulated all the elements of

God. It is difficult to exaggerate their importance in the spiritual lives of Methodists.[39]

The church encouraged all who were willing to flee from the wrath to come to pray, fast, study, and sing in order to strengthen personal piety. Everyone was to follow John Wesley's example and live by a strict regime of the private means of grace. The young Egerton Ryerson was only following this general pattern of Methodist behaviour when he recorded in his diary in 1825 eight rules of conduct to promote his religious progress:

1  Endeavour to fix my first waking thought on God
2  to arise early to attend to my devotions and read Scriptures
3  Pray oftener and maintain a devotional state of mind
4  Circumspect in conduct and conversation
5  more diligently reading useful books and study
6  Self examination according to Scripture rule
7  looking to God for guidance
8  Every evening examining short-comings[40]

Such discipline was critical for the development of personal piety.

However, the individual did not struggle alone; the household and the family provided an essential supporting environment for the private means of grace. Christian churches believed the family unit had been established by God as the cornerstone of all society. Without strong families, no institution or civilization could long prosper; the family nurtured all moral impulses, sustained order and respect, and lightened the burden of isolated individualism. "Family religion underlies the commonwealth and the Church of Christ. No Christian government, no healthy conscience, no Bible philanthropics, no godly church-life can exist, unless they are rooted beneath Christian hearth-stones and family altars."[41] The *Christian Guardian* and other Methodist journals constantly repeated the same views on the importance of the family: "The first, most natural and most ardent of all the social affections, are found among those of the same blood, or between members of one family united under one common parent or head. All society, civil, political and moral, originates in, and receives its character from this."[42] When morally and spiritually enlightened, the family represented the core of the Methodist fellowship. It was especially valuable in supporting the disciplined resolve for conversion and holy living and in carrying the principles of religion to the corrupt world when the institutional church was absent or present in merely embryonic from. Only through the Christian family could one "retain the glow and simplicity of your first love, your closet communion with God."[43]

Methodists understood that the integrity of the family depended in the first instance on the sanctity of marriage, a relationship demanding a strict obedience to the obligations established between husband and wife. These included mutual support and respect, but assumed the wife's inferior social status before her husband's authority. "The good wife is one, who ever mindful of the solemn contract she hath entered into, is strictly and conscientiously virtuous, constant, and faithful to her husband ... she is humble and modest from reason and conviction, submissive from choice and obedient from inclination ... she makes it her business to serve, and her pleasure to oblige her husband ... her tenderness relieves his cares, her affection softens his distress, her good humour and complacency lessen, and subdue his afflictions."[44] She should also be a good, pious Christian, living to serve her God and her family, and she should run the household morally and economically. The wife must not dissipate her husband's property on vain indulgences, fancy attire, or other trivial things.

On the other hand, the husband also had obligations. "The good husband is one, who, wedded not by interest, but by choice is constant as well from inclination as from principle: he treats his wife with delicacy as a woman, with tenderness as a friend; he attributes her folly to her weakness, her imprudence to her inadvertency ... and pardons them with indulgence: all his care and industry are employed for her welfare; all his strength and power are exerted for her support and protection."[45] He too had to be pious and moral and must implement all the tenets of religion. The husband acted as the minister to his household, including servants, relatives, and all others residing in his home. In the absence of regular church services, he might expand his ministry to include services to the neighbourhood. The husband was also the father, and his prayers and intercessions were meant to cover the entire household; his role encompassed reading the Scriptures to his family and leading in hymn singing. He was the model for his family and governed with wisdom, charity, order, and purity.

Nevertheless, the mother was the true spiritual guide, especially for the very young. "Elevated above earthly things, she seems like one of those guiding angels ... through whose ministrations we are incited to good and restrained from evil."[46] For Methodists, Susanna Wesley became the inspiration for conscientious motherhood. And Nathanael Burwash spoke for generations of Canadians when he maintained that women "were by nature endowed with special moral virtues such as patience, fortitude and intuition, and these equipped them better than men to provide moral training to a child."[47] Most Methodist leaders paid strong tribute to their own pious mothers for their religious strength and resolve. It was vital, however, that the mother begin her training while the child was still an infant and that she taught by proper example, as well as by earnest strictures.

Children required more than simple moral guidance, however; they must be taught to look for a conversion experience in order to know their sins were forgiven and to escape the evils of the world. Childhood conversion might be spurious or its religious experiences too immature to be truly transforming, but church authorities agreed that children were the proper subjects of saving grace and their religious expressions should be carefully examined and not arbitrarily dismissed by overcautious parents.[48] Equally important, mothers could best console the young when their quest for salvation went unanswered and they were left in a state of extreme anxiety. Although conversion was the work of the Spirit on the individual, society assumed that mothers played a dominant role in moulding the conscience, thereby preparing the way for conversion.

The father and mother together established a natural harmony in the family; conventional wisdom asserted that the ideal parents divided the rule in the household. Each had a proper sphere in raising their children, yet they functioned as a single entity. Although the father's role took him beyond the confines of the home, it was generally expected that the mother would limit her work to this arena. Despite this model, however, Methodist women often went outside their recognized limits and assumed all the pastoral care of the family; they even extended their ministry to neighbours and friends through prayer, exhortation, and preaching. Although this work was often discounted or criticized by some church authorities, women none the less played a critical role in expanding religion in channels running parallel to the institutional structures.

However, women's principal influence operated through the family, and it was the family that provided the major forum for saving the young. Public worship was often considered too remote for young children, and they were felt to be too immature to undertake unsupervised "closet" worship. They required the family circle to shape their consciences until they were old enough to act responsibly. Parents were needed in order to help mitigate the sins and passions of childhood. Such assistance was essential since, at least during the first half of the nineteenth century, children, although immature, were assumed to have all the natural depravity of humanity. They were complete adults except for their simpler understanding. "In infancy and childhood, we see ... *the man in miniature*, drawn indeed, in outlines; but these exhibiting all the general traits of his intellectual and moral character."[49]

For this reason, parents were enjoined to break the inherently rebellious will and subdue the natural wildness of their children. In this battle, as in many others, the reason for controlling boys and girls was different. Both needed to have their wills broken, but in the boy it was to promote future disciplined strength and true manliness. Canadian society maintained that a man who could not rule himself could never rule others. For the girl, breaking the will was to develop meekness, submission, and good humour. "A man in a furious passion, is terrible to his enemies, but a woman in a passion is disgusting to her friends; she loses all the respect due to her sex."[50] Only through firm parental authority could vanity, pride, idleness, extravagance, and disrespect be driven from children's character.

Parental rule, however, must be governed by moderation and love. The Methodist press admonished its readers that the only way to subjugate selfishness and wilfulness was through good example, charity, and mutual respect. The child should be led, not driven, to follow proper moral and spiritual precepts. Children were an integral part of the family and if properly nurtured, could themselves serve to bring others to God. Often their pious example reproved backsliding or irreligious parents and friends. Contemporary reports were full of accounts such as this: "Two little girls, about twelve years of age ... have been the instruments in the hands of a wonder-working God, of bringing their ungodly mothers, as broken hearted penitents to the footstool of mercy."[51] Thus the whole family worked to promote spiritual Christianity.

## THE INDIVIDUAL AND SOCIETY

Nevertheless, most Canadian Methodists agreed that personal religion demanded much more than a solitary quest for conversion and moral rectitude in a strong family setting. Personal asceticism was never sufficient. Methodism reiterated the assumption that "individualism involves a suppression of half the duties and a surrender of half the blessedness of the Christian life ... Religious isolation is alien to all their healthiest instincts."[52] Methodists were not of the world, but they were in the world; Methodism was ultimately a joyful, outgoing, social religion: "Not cloistered recluses, nor the inmates of monastic cells are the true ideals of religious life but a Christian brotherhood, dwelling together in mutual helpfulness and sympathy."[53] They believed in openness and an expanding religious life, not a closed association regulated by traditional forms and procedures.

Such a Christian community, with its stress on moral reformation, naturally began among church adherents themselves. All Methodists were bound to avoid doing harm of any kind and to abstain from evils such as swearing, sabbath-breaking, drinking, quarrelling, fighting, uncharitable conduct, self-indulgence, sloth, costly apparel, or the exploitation of others. Indebtedness or immoral business practices were also condemned since they brought scandal on the church, as well as on the individual. For similar reasons, litigation between Methodists was discouraged. If a satisfactory resolution of a dispute could not be reached by the parties involved, other members were expected to arbitrate. On the positive side, Methodists were expected to employ fellow members, to buy from one another whenever possible, and to assist each other in business.[54] These requirements were in addition to the normal charitable support expected from those in a position to help their less-fortunate co-religionists. Economic and social bonds would therefore reinforce spiritual and moral links within the Methodist fellowship.

But Methodists were also expected to help improve national life as a whole. The cultural and moral requirements of Methodism demanded the reformation of individuals in the corrupt world. Only by this process could the nation and the world truly progress. On perhaps the most obvious level, Christian charity was a critical aspect of Methodism's response to society's needs. When it proceeded from a "saved heart," charity was part of the perpetual struggle for holy living. For Methodists, the support of ministers, the construction and maintenance of churches, and the establishment of missions to evangelize others remained the first priority of Christian charity. Of course, the Methodist church was not unique in this regard. All the non-established denominations were sustained by the benevolence of their members.

In addition, all denominations assisted the deserving poor, especially widows and orphans, who undoubtedly had a genuine need. In most areas, this charity was performed casually on a temporary, individual basis in times of particular distress. It was part of neighbourliness to share food, clothing, and other necessities. In some of the larger centres, however, there gradually evolved a more systematic denominational and interdenominational pattern of relief. As early as 1816, the women of Zoar Methodist church in Halifax, under the

chairmanship of William Black, organized the Halifax Wesleyan Female Benevolent Society to "relieve the wants, assuage the griefs and mitigate the suffering" of women, particularly widows with young children.[55] The combination of
the post–War of 1812 depression and an unusually severe winter provided the
impetus for this organization since individual donations could not answer the
need. In its first year, it raised over £100 and relieved more than two hundred
cases of distress, mostly among non-Methodists. However, such welfare institutions were rare. Where they did exist, they normally relied on the active involvement of women. More common, but still not widespread during the first
half of the nineteenth century, community-wide societies linked Christians
from the various denominations in the fight against local poverty. Such benevolent societies were not specifically church sponsored; they relied instead on
the organized contributions of individuals.[56] Relief programs organized by
specific congregations remained sporadic, and connexion-wide programs did
not develop until near the end of the century. It was most appropriate for
Methodists to undertake charity privately and quietly.

As well as charity, Methodism demanded the elimination of the myriad of
evils abounding in society. In particular, Methodists actively condemned any
violation of the sanctity of the sabbath. Sunday was not simply a day of rest, it
was a day of active worship. To remain late in bed, to allow children to run
wild, or to visit neighbours to carry on "worldly conversation" was a "criminal
indulgence."[57] Methodists obviously did no unnecessary work. After private
devotions for the household, the day was spent in at least two church services,
Sunday school, and sometimes class meeting, and it ended with hymn singing
and prayer. When not in religious activity, the whole family would normally be
found in quiet, reverential pursuits at home.

On all days of the week, Methodists denounced participation in any so-
called pernicious amusements. Wholesome reading was essential, but light
novels and other unedifying works were condemned. Time was too precious
to waste on reading that tended to poison faith or lead to moral ruin. At the
same time, Methodists rejected a variety of other non-religious activities. Especially by the 1830s, the *Christian Guardian* reminded its readers: "The Ball
chamber, the theatre, the gaming-house and the cricket ground, the horse-
race, the grog-shop, the house of ill-fame, and the circus, are so many ways of
leading to destruction … Whosoever would shun hell, should avoid the paths
which lead them there."[58] Nothing should be undertaken which would impair religious feelings, betray solemn modesty, or lead to vanity. Women especially were warned against fancy dress, jewellery, and particularly, frivolous
behaviour.

While sabbath-breaking and popular amusements were worldly sins, Methodists were most seriously and persistently concerned about the use of alcohol. It was considered the root of nearly all personal degeneration, vice, and
misery. Intemperance was a "gorged yet hungry monster" causing "the tears
of many scores of heart-broken females, and the soul-piercing cries of starving
orphans." It meant "destruction of the religious feeling and moral principle
of the mind" and led ultimately to torment in hell fire. It was the source of
brutality and crime, led to poverty and sickness, and undermined the sanctity

of the family. Given the vast quantity of alcohol consumed at the time, the lack of control in its manufacture, and its poorly regulated distribution, these warnings had considerable validity.[59]

However, Methodism had not always been so rigorous in its views on temperance. In fact, its attitudes gradually evolved over the first three decades of the nineteenth century. Initially at least, alcohol was divided between "ardent spirits," which included whisky, rum, gin, and brandy, and fermented drinks, such as wine, cider, and beer. Intemperance was the excessive use of either, but especially "spiritous liquor"; true temperance permitted moderate consumption of alcohol. Liquor was used to treat certain illnesses, and in some locations it was considered safer than the water. The local church's response reflected this view of moderate drinking. For example, in 1825, the London circuit attacked only the distribution of liquor at "bees, raisings and trainings," while during the same period, members were disciplined, not for the use of alcohol, but for the sale or gift of liquor, which led to disorderly conduct.[60]

By the late 1820s, however, the attack on even moderate consumption of liquor had begun in earnest. This change was reflected in the *Christian Guardian*, which in 1829 argued, "No man can say to an indulged appetite, 'thus far and no farther.' The very moment he begins with what is called 'a prudent' use of ardent spirits, he puts himself in the hands of a giant, that nine instances out of ten, will make him his prey forever."[61] The following year, a powerful total-abstinence faction convinced the Methodist Conference to declare "That this Conference believe that (what is termed) the moderate or temperate use of Ardent Spirits is the fruitful source of all the intemperance which abounds in this country, and which is the cause of so much immorality, misery and destruction."[62] The Conference then overcame the opposition which wished to permit liquor for medicinal purposes and formed itself into a total-abstinence society. Medical evidence was mustered to suggest alcohol was actually detrimental to health. During this period, the first injunctions were made forbidding Methodists from distilling or selling liquor, and the entire connexion was perceived as "a universal Temperance Society, and every class a branch thereof."[63]

These resolutions related to distilled liquor; the question of fermented beverages was originally seen in a different light. Wine was an integral part of the sacraments, and Christ's first miracle involved transforming water into wine. Even John Wesley, who was commonly cited as a staunch opponent of excessive drinking, consumed wine. It might also be added that since wine was generally unavailable to farmers and workers, it was not perceived as a source of disorder and poverty. With regard to beer and cider, these were often considered true temperance drinks, providing refreshment and nourishment and stimulating health, and were believed to be easily consumed in moderation.[64] Many temperance organizations served them as a safe substitute for liquor. Gradually, however, even these forms of alcohol were censured. Again by the early 1830s, the belief that the wine produced by Jesus' miraculous intervention was either extremely weak or totally non-alcoholic began to gain acceptance, John Wesley's drinking habits were ignored, and fermented spirits in all forms were condemned.[65] But these attitudes took longer to gain widespread popular support, even among Methodists.

While Methodists took a leadership role, much of the temperance movement was genuinely ecumenical. Methodists allied themselves with anyone who would support the cause. For instance, the *Christian Guardian* advised, "If as Methodists we are uniting our efforts to advance the interests of religion generally; as men let us unite with other men and Christians in the destruction of the enemy of our peace and our liberty."[66] The temperance crusade was aimed at instilling proper religious principles, not proselytizing for any one denomination. This cooperation took its most concrete form in the large number of temperance societies that began to appear throughout British America during the 1820s. They paralleled and expanded the work of the churches and individual temperance advocates. Through education and moral pressure, the temperance forces appeared, by the 1840s, to be remoulding social attitudes. Liquor became less acceptable at many public gatherings, and inebriated individuals were frequently censured in public. Nevertheless, the first half of the nineteenth century witnessed little long-term alteration in Canadian drinking habits.

Since reform remained personal, however, it was assumed that change could only be truly achieved through moral suasion. Government-legislated prohibitions, at least until the late 1840s, were viewed with suspicion, and throughout the century they were considered only secondary to private reformation.[67] In order to persuade the intemperate to abandon their habits, a vast campaign for individual abstinence was undertaken, and all the moral forces of society were mustered for the battle. The churches preached temperance as a scriptural obligation, and Sunday schools became critical allies, especially among young people. The religious and much of the secular press joined in attacking the evil of alcohol. The *Christian Guardian* was particularly committed to the cause. It reprinted countless sermons, tracts, reports, and letters promoting temperance. In addition, a constant stream of temperance speakers criss-crossed the country lecturing on the benefits of abstinence.[68]

Since intemperance assaulted wholesome family life, it was appropriate for women also to be strategically involved in destroying the evil. It was clearly within their sphere as moral guardians; women were considered morally superior to men, and intemperance was judged to be particularly a male vice. As well as using their moral influence, women were counselled to avoid socializing with and especially marrying any man who drank. Young women were believed to provide an exceptionally valuable example and force in the campaign. In the fight to preserve the sacred family, children were also employed as a moral influence to keep their parents on the right path.[69]

For Methodists, the temperance campaign represented a vital component in the transformation of anxiety over personal spiritual and moral health into a movement for the total reform of society. Methodists believed that it was most clearly in the realm of alcohol abuse that the obligation of self-regeneration involved securing the welfare of the entire community. Although the focus remained on the corrupt individual rather than social institutions, none the less, such broad social concern reflected an important extension of Methodism's interest in personal ethical conduct and ultimately its mission to evangelize the world. Solicitude for the welfare of the entire community was a broader manifestation of the personal necessity and power to improve.[70] Temperance and the other social reforms demanded by staunch Methodists also demonstrated the wider goal of the private means of grace, family worship, and the other non-institutional elements of religion to create a moral and spiritually alive civilization in British North America. At the same time, private Methodist religious practice, based on an emotional, experiential vision, underlay and paralleled all church work, helped to define who a Methodist was, and supplied the essential foundation for Methodist social religion in the country.

# 4 Upper Canadian Wesleyan and Episcopal Methodism, 1820–54

The compromise of 1820 between the British Wesleyans and the American Episcopal Methodists regarding the Canadas temporarily ended the period of inter-connexional rivalry. Except at Kingston and a small society at York, the Wesleyans confined their missions to Lower Canada, while the Episcopal Methodists extended their evangelization among the whites and natives in Upper Canada. Once this issue was apparently resolved, the following decade witnessed the emergence of an independent Canadian church and the formation of a splinter connexion under the leadership of Henry Ryan. However, Episcopal Methodist independence was short-lived since union with the Wesleyans appeared to be the only way of avoiding renewed competition. This union in 1833 in turn precipitated the formation of a new Methodist Episcopal church in Canada, and dissatisfaction among those who remained in the union caused a dissolution in 1840, which was not healed until seven years later. After 1847, however, a new movement to unite Methodism throughout British North America emerged, beginning with the amalgamation of Wesleyan operations in the two Canadas.

## AN INDEPENDENT CANADIAN CHURCH AND THE RYANITE DEFECTIONS

By 1820 most Canadian members of the Methodist Episcopal connexion in Upper Canada felt severely disadvantaged because of their ties to the American parent body. In fact, the Upper Canada district had first petitioned for independence as early as 1817. It hoped that local autonomy would eliminate charges of disloyalty and permit the connexion to hold property, perform marriages, and escape from other ecclesiastical disabilities. The Canadian Methodists were increasingly wary of the heightened sense of republican nationalism in the American church. The local church's increased membership, financial support, and native-born clergy gave assurance that independence was indeed practical. The American General Conference in 1820 agreed to a separate Upper Canadian Conference sometime in the future, although it firmly rejected complete connexional independence.[1]

On the basis of this promise, the Upper Canada district in 1822 formally petitioned for an autonomous conference, while still hoping that when the General Conference met at Baltimore in 1824, it would grant complete independence with only fraternal ties. Henry Ryan, the senior presiding elder, was especially adamant about gaining independence. Combining in himself a strong Canadian patriotism and a keen sense that he and his connexion had been betrayed in the dispute with the Wesleyans, he believed that the American bishops and Conference were not qualified to challenge his authority by dictating policy to Canadians. Arrogant, authoritarian, and pugnacious, he would not countenance such action from either Americans or his Canadian brethren.[2]

The 1823 district meetings appointed Wyatt Chamberlayne and Isaac B. Smith, Ryan's brother-in-law, to represent Upper Canada at the Baltimore Conference and to present the resolutions for an independent connexion. In an unusual step, both William Case and Henry Ryan, the presiding elders, were omitted from the delegation. Ryan's disruptive conduct disqualified him, and Case was passed over to avoid a charge that Ryan had been discriminated against. Ryan took his omission as a personal insult and organized a local preachers' meeting in his district, which subsequently appointed him and David Breckenridge to represent Canadian interests at the General Conference.[3] But that Conference denied their credentials, recognizing only the regularly appointed delegates.

The General Conference established Upper Canada as a distinct annual conference and acknowledged the expediency of granting independence at some future date, perhaps in 1828, but it would not countenance the change at that time. This refusal had little to do with the Canadian situation. Over the previous decades, the American Methodist church had become increasingly dominated by its episcopacy, who were supported by a coterie of leading clergy. In 1824 dissident factions were attempting to increase the relative power of the Annual and General Conferences and to introduce lay delegates in these church courts. Simultaneously, the General Conference feared that some church members would use the precedent of an independent Canadian connexion to divide the American church along geographic lines over the issue of slavery.[4] The church authorities were not prepared for an internal jurisdictional dispute precipitated by the issue of independence for Canadian Methodists. The Canadian delegates were content with the creation of an annual conference, if not totally pleased, and returned home to set up their new organization.

However, Ryan, claiming that the Baltimore Conference had insulted the Canadian delegates – meaning himself – ignored their legitimate petitions, and given no persuasive justification for denying immediate separation, called together his sympathizers at Elizabethtown (Brockville). The Elizabethtown "district conference" of some of the most prominent retired itinerants, local preachers, elders, and deacons in Upper Canada resolved to form an independent church subject to no other connexion "either in the United States or Europe."[5] Although Ryan misinformed and manipulated the meeting and many representatives later withdrew their support, the gathering did reflect deep-seated fears within the fellowship of local preachers. They believed that the church courts were attacking their legitimate status and attempting to pre-empt their influence. This dispute would create fissures in Canadian Methodism throughout the nineteenth century. During the pioneer era, there were only hazy distinctions between itinerating and local preachers. Although not "stationed," and therefore not eligible to attend Conference, many local preachers travelled nearly as much as their itinerant colleagues. During the absence of the regular ministers, who were obliged to serve immense circuits, they administered church affairs, supervised pastoral duties, and preached to congregations. Sometimes ordained, they also on occasion administered the sacraments. No functional differences divided the two categories of ministry; individuals often moved between the two offices as personal circumstances dictated.

Moreover, although some local preachers were young men preparing for future itinerant service, many others were simply located itinerants. The physical and financial hardships of full-time work frequently forced them to retire. Nevertheless, they continued to evangelize on a more circumscribed level while holding secular occupations. These pioneers of Methodism resented being ignored by the often less experienced travelling ministers. In 1824 the Genesee Annual Conference, which included the Upper Canadian districts, petitioned for lay delegates at General Conference. For a variety of sound reasons, this resolution was denied, but its defeat only aggravated the hostility among discontented local preachers.[6] It was against this background that Ryan was able to garner support for an independent church which would, according to the Elizabethtown resolutions, submit all decisions to district conferences of senior local preachers. Although he had earlier denounced the local preachers when they had questioned his authority as presiding elder, he readily acceded to this measure to insure their support. But he stopped short of accepting a democratization of the church; he refused the lay membership a place on the church courts or in its formal decision-making process.

In August 1824, shortly after the Elizabethtown meeting, the first assembly of the official Canada Conference met at Hallowell (Picton). After completing the routine organizational matters, it petitioned the American General Conference, which was to meet in 1828, for complete independence. The resolution was supported by the two bishops having immediate authority over the Canadian Episcopal Methodists, Enoch George and Elijah Hedding, who promised to use their influence to advance the cause.[7] At the same time, the Canada Conference recognized the local preachers as "brethren in Christ," at least partially deflecting their concern over diminished status. In a separate vote, the local preachers supported the resolution for independence, and even the Ryan faction agreed to postpone its secession until the matter could be dealt with by the General Conference, meeting at Pittsburgh in 1828.

The first Canada Conference was also obliged to deal with the illegal and disruptive actions of Henry Ryan. He acknowledged that the regular Canadian

*Local preachers*

delegates had been honourably treated in Baltimore, and he regretted any action that had offended his brethren. A lesser minister would simply have been dismissed, but the local church owed Ryan too much, and he had too many loyal followers for him to be unceremoniously expelled. None the less, Conference was not prepared to sanction his actions by ignoring his assault on its authority. Under the guise of easing his workload, it did not re-elected him presiding elder, but appointed him special missionary "to Chippeway and Grand River Falls, and the new and destitute settlements in those parts." He could use his extraordinary energy and talents to promote this pioneer work.[8] It was obvious to all that this decision was a severe reprimand, especially since the region was as isolated as possible from Ryan's base of support in eastern Upper Canada. The stationing of itinerants was often an effective form of discipline for a recalcitrant minister.

It did not take long for the Conference to realize that its actions would not restrain Ryan. Deeply humiliated, he used his new commission as a special missionary to travel throughout the western district holding revivals, collecting funds, and establishing new societies. He only rarely visited his own circuit and gained no new members there. The real problem, however, was that he used his meetings to foster personal support rather than to build up the connexion and that his actions conflicted with the regular itinerants. Convinced that the American church would never grant independence and that his own legitimate ambitions were being systematically thwarted by a conspiratorial alliance of his Canadian colleagues, Ryan attacked the subservient character of the Canada Conference and the conduct of its ministers.

At the 1825 Annual Conference, Ryan's character was questioned, and he was requested to explain his actions. After a series of mutual personal recriminations, he agreed to retire from the active ministry and, it was assumed, from disruptive activities. However, he almost immediately began to traverse the province denouncing the Conference, the spirituality of the itinerants, and the authority of the episcopacy. In 1827 charges were preferred against him for his improper conduct, but they could not be proved. Nevertheless, Ryan severed his relations with the connexion, although he recanted and sought readmission in 1828. But by then the connexion had lost patience with him and refused even to hear his complaints.[9]

During the remainder of 1828 and early 1829, James Jackson, Isaac B. Smith, David Breckenridge, Moses Blackstock, and several local preachers either quit or were expelled from the Methodist Episcopal Church, and together they formed the Canadian Wesleyan Methodist connexion under Ryan. They organized several meetings across the province to attract disgruntled members to their cause but met with only limited success. Most local quarterly boards and the general membership were not convinced of Ryan's sincerity and disapproved of his methods.[10] It was suggested by some of his critics that he had accepted assistance from Methodism's arch-enemy, Archdeacon John Strachan, and from the Upper Canadian government in order to split the Methodist church. Whether true or not, such accusations undermined the new Ryanite connexion. By the time of his death in 1833, the splinter group was virtually leaderless and had little financial or membership support.

In fact, much of Ryan's effective propaganda had already been lost in 1828 when the American General Conference agreed to allow the Upper Canadian Methodists to form their own church. John Ryerson, one of the Canadian delegates, reported to his brother on the affair. "About four days after the commencement of the Conference there was a committee of five persons appointed on the Canada question. The committee reported last Thursday positively against the separation declaring it in their opinion unconstitutional. Dr. Bangs brought the report before the Conference and made a long speech against the separation. William Ryerson and myself replied to him pointedly and at length and we were supported by Revs. Dr. Fisk and Luckey."[11] The discussions lasted for two days, with the Conference finally overruling its committee and voting 105 to 43 to allow independence. It also agreed to ordain a general superintendent for Canada when one was elected and wrote to the British Wesleyan Conference requesting that the compromise of 1820 remain in force. The actual wording of the General Conference resolution "allowed" the Canadians to separate; this again reflected concerns over the court's authority to grant independence and the potentially disruptive affect it might have in the United States. Hence the Canadian church declared itself independent, while retaining cordial fraternal relations and maintaining the existing doctrines, discipline, and polity.

After the mechanisms of a separate church had been established, the first task was to elect a bishop (general superintendent). His most important duties would be to chair connexional meetings, appoint district presiding elders, assist in stationing itinerants, and ordain new ministers. Anticipating the need for a bishop, Egerton, John, and William Ryerson wrote to other prominent Canadian Methodist itinerants for their suggestions even before the meeting of the General Conference. They believed that Nathan Bangs, with his international reputation, his experience in Canada, and his background in publishing, was the obvious choice. But he was an American whose election might provoke cries of foreign control. He also had a large family and was securely ensconced at the Methodist Publishing House in New York City.[12] When Bangs himself opposed independence, his proposed elevation to the Canadian episcopacy became impossible.

The Ryersons maintained that it would actually be better to elect a Canadian, and they recommended William Case, although he lacked popular support. William and John Ryerson, while acting as the Canadian delegates at the Pittsburgh General Conference in 1828, could not get a firm commitment from any senior American Methodist minister. As a result, Case was elected general superintendent *pro tempore*, and the search proceeded for a permanent replacement. Over the following years, several Americans, including Wilbur Fisk, president of Wesleyan University in Middletown, Connecticut, were offered the position, but during its short history the Methodist Episcopal Church in Canada never had its own episcopacy. Bishop Hedding continued to visit the Canadian Conferences to ordain ministers.[13]

Despite the Ryanite defections and the readjustments required by separation from the American church, Episcopal Methodist work in Upper Canada generally prospered. Between 1824 and 1828, membership grew from 6,875 to 9,678, and in 1832, after four years of independence, the total was 14,999. During those eight years, membership among the aboriginal population had risen from 120 to 1,090. As well, the number of circuits and itinerants had more than doubled. In November 1829 the connexion welcomed the weekly *Christian Guardian* as its denominational newspaper under the vigorous editorship of Egerton Ryerson. It quickly became one of the most widely circulated and influential newspapers in the province. The *Christian Guardian* complemented the Book Room, which distributed religious publications from the United States and Britain and acted as a clearing-house for important information. The connexion also established its own book and publishing house in 1829, with profits going to support the itinerants' pension fund. In its first year, together with the *Christian Guardian*, it published *The Doctrines and Discipline of the Methodist Episcopal Church in Canada* to familiarize Canadian Methodists with their own rules and regulations. The next year it issued a collection of hymns translated into Ojibwa by Peter Jones, the report of the York Bible Society, and a special report from a select committee of the Upper Canada House of Assembly. Over the following years, the Methodist Book and Publishing House grew into one of the leading publishers in the country.[14]

Equally important, the new church recognized the need for a school in the province to educate the "non-established" youth. In opposition to the Anglican Upper Canada College, the Methodists proposed a non-sectarian academy without religious tests for staff or students. Although religion and morality would be central elements in the character-building process, no theology was to be taught. They expected that the proposed Upper Canada Academy would provide an alternative to local non-Methodist schools or to going abroad for a secondary education. The connexion was particularly sensitive to the republican sentiments inculcated in the Methodist students trained in the United States.[15] Several sites were proposed for the school, but the Conference finally selected Cobourg and raised an impressive subscription to erect and endow the facilities. Disruptions within the church delayed its opening and prevented the collection of some of these subscriptions, but once the school had finally begun classes in 1836 under the young Maritime Wesleyan preacher Matthew Richey, it provided a sound secondary education and would be especially important for preparing future generations of Methodist leaders. Thus the late 1820s witnessed the beginnings of an institutional infrastructure that would prove critical for the expansion and spiritual health of the whole church.

## THE UNION OF 1833

Despite its apparently strong beginning, the Methodist Episcopal Church in Canada was confronted immediately after its creation in 1828 with a return of the old issue of British Wesleyan competition in Upper Canada. In fact, the undercurrent of ill feeling among the Wesleyans had really never disappeared. The Wesleyan William Lunn represented many in Lower and Upper Canada when he reported to his superiors in Britain that the inhabitants were not receiving the true gospel. The Episcopal Methodist preachers were considered too worldly and too political. He added that "the Government of

Upper Canada is much displeased that American missionaries are occupying their country," warning that the connexion "is the cause of much evil and I am not aware that it has done much good" and that the only remedy was to send British missionaries.[16] Joseph Stinson at Kingston also denounced the Episcopal Methodists' claim to Upper Canada, strongly opposing the suggestion from Bishop George in 1824 that the local Wesleyans should integrate into the Methodist Episcopal connexion when it gained independence. Robert Alder observed that the dissatisfaction he witnessed with the episcopal form of church government and with the office of presiding elder would lead Canadians to welcome the Wesleyan connexion.[17]

Against the claim that they were too involved in politics, the Canadian Episcopal Methodists argued that they were only reacting naturally and honestly to the discrimination they faced. When Upper Canada had been created by the Constitutional Act of 1791, provisions had been enacted giving the Church of England a preferred status in the expectation that it would promote a loyal, conservative colony. Although not fully established, it gained valuable prerogatives. These included substantial control over education, sole possession of the lucrative military chaplaincy appointments, financial support for Anglican ministers, and occasional grants for the erection of churches. Most controversial, however, the Anglican clergy alone could draw support from an endowment based on the value of one-seventh of the land granted in Upper Canada, known popularly as the "clergy reserves." Through these legislated privileges and a supportive government, the Church of England was expected to dominate the province's religious life.[18]

In 1793 the Anglican clergy had also gained the exclusive right to perform marriages. Since there were few Anglican clergy, marriage was both inconvenient and expensive. The restriction also removed one of the few sources of income available to supplement the meagre salaries of other Protestant clergy. Most critical, however, it tended to define the non-Anglican churches as second-class institutions. Opposition to this monopoly developed quite quickly among the "dissenting" churches, led by the Presbyterians. Reacting to sustained pressure, the government extended the privilege of performing marriages to churches that were established elsewhere and were therefore by definition legitimate and respectable. While this enactment assisted the Presbyterians and Lutherans in particular, the Methodist connexion, because it was neither a dissenting church nor even a distinct denomination in Britain, was conspicuously excluded. Canadian Methodists repeatedly petitioned to be allowed to perform marriages and thereby receive official sanction as a church. At least part of the desire for independence from the American Methodist connexion was in order to qualify for this status. The Methodist Episcopal church would not gain the power to perform marriages until 1831.[19]

As well as seeking legal recognition and the right to perform marriages, the connexion wanted the ability to own property corporately. Without this power, meeting places and cemeteries had to be held by local trustees, who were personally liable. In times of economic distress, the church found it difficult to convince individuals to take on this responsibility. Equally serious, if there was a dispute within a congregation or between the congregation and the connexion as a whole, the trustees could take over the property and deny access to others. This was a recurring problem and caused considerable irritation throughout British America. After years of persistent lobbying, the Upper Canadian government finally granted the Methodist Conference the right to hold property in its own name in 1828.

The use of the clergy-reserve funds, however, remained the most important and most controversial political and religious issue during the first half of the nineteenth century in Upper Canada. Again the opposition to the Anglican monopoly began with the Presbyterians, who claimed they were included in the original designation of "a Protestant clergy" since they were members of the established Church of Scotland. Although the British government eventually accepted this claim, the revenues fell under the jurisdiction of the provincial administration. Influenced by John Strachan and the Anglican oligarchy, it withheld the funds from the Presbyterians.[20]

While some Presbyterians pressed the government for a share of the money, during the 1820s a loose alliance of religious and political forces argued that government support for religious groups should be abandoned altogether. They believed that clergy-reserve revenue should be assigned to secular provincial needs such as a proper education system. These factions represented the voluntary tradition in the Methodist and Dissenter churches, and they advocated a complete separation between church and state.[21] It was this alliance which captured the provincial assembly in 1828 and challenged the authority of the lieutenant-governor, Sir John Colborne, and his executive council advisers. However, it would take another twenty-five years of deeply divisive quarrelling before the issue was settled. Eventually, part of the fund was assigned to support a limited number of Anglican clergy while the bulk of the revenue was used to assist the provincial education system and other secular purposes.

In the meantime, these issues underlay contentions between the Wesleyans and the Episcopal Methodists in Upper Canada. Much of the opposition to American Methodism legitimately centred on the question of loyalty, on different assumptions regarding the status of the Church of England, and on involvement in partisan politics. The Wesleyans doubted that when Episcopal Methodists attacked the government they were only reacting to social and religious discrimination. There were also honest disagreements concerning decorum during church worship and the role of revivals. The Wesleyans, who generally followed a more formal service modelled on Anglican worship, were distressed by the fervent and sometimes raucous Episcopal Methodist practices, which were even disrupting the connexion in Britain. Moreover, the two Methodist churches tended to disagree on the centrality of social causes such as temperance in the quest for spiritual reformation.

However, a substantial portion of the Wesleyan discontent rested on personal animosity and jealousy because of the success of Episcopal Methodism. Despite generous grants from England, the Wesleyans had never been able to sustain significant growth in the Atlantic region or Lower Canada and looked covetously on the rich potential of Upper Canada. But even in that province their enclaves were not prospering. The membership of the Kingston circuit under Stinson fluctuated wildly, but was rarely as healthy as the missionary society had a right to expect. It was too easy to blame the Episcopal Methodists for the troubles. Although the Wesleyans dismissed them as half-starved Yankee enthusiasts,[22] their church was rapidly expanding throughout the region and developing a vital institutional network.

Pressure for the Wesleyans to expand their operations mounted after the Canadian Episcopal Methodists gained independence. The local Wesleyans were supported by the British and colonial administration, by John Strachan and the Church of England, and more cautiously, by the British missionary committee, which would have to pay for expansion and was relatively less hostile to American Methodists. All these groups disapproved of the increasingly effective Episcopal Methodist criticism of the established order. They perceived it as a disloyal attack on the British constitutional system. To Lieutenant-Governor Colborne, the Episcopal Methodists were radical, disreputable, and ignorant and probably republicans in disguise who were subverting true British principles in the province. He was convinced that the only way to limit their influence was to reintroduce the more manageable British Wesleyans into Upper Canada. They recognized the Church of England as the "established" church and respected its exclusive right to the clergy reserves.[23]

The Wesleyans were also much closer to Anglicans in their attitudes and principles. Robert Alder, the leading Wesleyan missionary, with substantial experience in British North America, was especially eager, even sycophantic, in his deference both to the Church of England and to a conservative political order. Born in England in 1796, he had served as a Wesleyan missionary in the Maritimes until 1827, when he returned to Britain. From 1833 until 1851 he was one of the secretaries of the Wesleyan Missionary Society and had particular responsibility for British North America. Authoritarian and paternalistic, he detested the "democratic" tendencies which he found in Canadian Methodism. In 1853 Alder took his "measured zeal" into the Church of England, where he eventually rose to the rank of archdeacon before his death at Gibraltar in 1870. During the early nineteenth century, the conservative element among Wesleyans in England kept the connexion clearly on the side of the status quo in politics. It warned overseas missionaries in particular against "meddling with political parties or secular disputes," although it assumed they were "to enforce, by precept and example, a cheerful obedience to lawful authority."[24] The British Wesleyans in North America were often quite political, but unlike their Canadian brethren, they promoted the existing state of affairs.

By the end of the 1820s, the local authorities and the British government believed that it would be expedient to have conservative Wesleyans minister to the new British immigrants and especially to the native peoples. The British Wesleyan administration unconditionally denied that the 1820 agreement had ever extended to the aboriginal population.[25] As important military allies with a special right to British aid and protection, natives could not be handed over to hostile American Methodist influence. Under Colborne's direction, a settlement was constructed for them near Sarnia on Lake St Clair, and a reservation system was inaugurated. He had expected the Church of England to send a missionary, but when one was not forthcoming, even with government financial support, he turned to the Wesleyans. He refused to allow the Episcopal Methodists, who were already ministering to large numbers of natives, to occupy the field. He felt that they gave them "absurd advice" and could not be trusted either to provide proper religious training or to promote loyalty. The *Christian Guardian* reacted to Colborne's rebukes in a series of articles critical of the provincial administration which further antagonized relations. Although the British Colonial Office chastised Colborne for his indiscreet remarks, it was committed to the same goal. Both levels of government assured the Wesleyans of financial support for missions throughout Upper Canada commencing with the new mission at St Clair.[26]

Concurrently, the Episcopal Methodists were attempting to raise funds to expand their own extensive native missions, and they sent Peter Jones, the first aboriginal Methodist itinerant, and John Ryerson, the new presiding elder, to tour the British Isles. The British Wesleyan missionary committee had not been consulted and was furious at this invasion of its fund-raising territory. Although it provided a grant of £300, it prohibited the Canadians from securing support from Wesleyans in Britain and opposed any future unauthorized tours. Jones was allowed to fulfil his engagements but only in order to raise public awareness of Wesleyan missionary operations.[27]

However, the necessity of the tour provided sufficient evidence that Canadians did not have the resources to minister properly to the native population and the excuse the British needed in order to send missionaries. The Canada Conference apologized for not consulting the missionary committee and thanked it for the money, but opposed the formation of rival missions. As an alternative, it recommended that the Wesleyans send missionaries to the huge unserved regions north and west of the Great Lakes.[28] The committee's response was quick and comprehensive. In the presence of Ryerson and Jones, it proclaimed its right to send missionaries to both the natives and the white settlers. The 1820 agreement was now void because of the formation of the Canadian Methodist Episcopal church, and in any event, it had never included the native population. Even if the agreement were still valid, the committee announced, the vast immigration from Britain and the competition from Methodist splinter denominations had completely altered the situation and made a Wesleyan presence essential. Finally, it claimed that the political interference of the Canadian Episcopal Methodists would have justified the abrogation of the original agreement even if it were still substantially applicable. The committee had already sent Thomas Turner on a tour of the province to locate potential Wesleyan missions, and he was stationed at the St Clair mission, then under construction, to serve the natives and neighbouring white settlers. Soon after, the committee announced that at least twelve new missionaries would be sent to Upper Canada.[29]

In addition to missionary activity with the natives, the government and the Church of England encouraged the Wesleyans to minister to the white population in order to promote "sound British principles" and reduce attacks on the Anglican prerogatives. The local Wesleyans added to this chorus by claiming that new immigrants would not join the Methodist Episcopal church and were being driven to unite with other denominations. To forestall such action, more Wesleyan itinerants were essential.[30] By the end of 1828, the Wesleyans in York had bought a parcel of land and were raising subscriptions in order to erect a chapel as a focus for expanded work in the region. They argued that in spite of the apparent independence, the Episcopal Methodists were still subject to foreign control since they were expected to appoint an American bishop.[31]

Responding to this combined encouragement, the British Conference petitioned Parliament for financial aid to expand its operations in Upper Canada. It claimed that "we have every reason to believe that measures will ere long be adopted by which the numerous Methodist Societies in Upper Canada will be brought into immediate connexion with the British Conference, and placed under its influence … As the way is now open for us to extend our labours … we trust that if a new appropriation of the Clergy Reserves be made, and a portion of them be granted to the Presbyterians, a part of them will also be applied to the Methodists."[32] Any such money was to be in addition to grants from the "casual and territorial" revenues at the disposal of the lieutenant-governor in council, and both sets of grants were to be administered by the missionary committee in London.

The initial response of the Canadian Episcopal Methodists was to protest to the British missionary authorities against any interference in the province.[33] It quickly became apparent, however, that the Canadian protests would have little influence, and rather than witness a hostile rivalry, Egerton Ryerson and other Episcopal Methodist leaders suggested a union of the two connexions. However, although all the Episcopal Methodists opposed religious competition, many feared they would lose their local autonomy and be overwhelmed by what they regarded as the reactionary influence of the Wesleyans. George Ryerson, who was studying the social views of the British connexion while visiting England, was particularly critical of its policies, and he was afraid of becoming subordinate to its jurisdiction. He considered it humiliatingly servile to the Church of England and a real obstacle to religious and civil liberty in Britain. He warned his brother about the determination of the British Wesleyan authorities to dominate Upper Canadian Methodism as they were doing in the Maritimes and Lower Canada.[34]

Despite such warnings, Egerton and John Ryerson, on behalf of the Canadian Episcopal Methodists, and Robert Alder, representing the British Conference through the missionary committee, began negotiations. Both parties assumed that Wesleyan polity, doctrine, and discipline would be followed, but Alder suggested several more specific alterations to the existing Canadian procedures. He was deeply disturbed by the power of the local preachers and especially their ordination. He believed the Canadian church had abandoned one of John Wesley's fundamental principles by allowing those set apart for the ministry to hold secular occupations. There was no ordination in the British *Ordination* Wesleyan church at the time; the rights of ministry were acknowledged by an individual being "received into full connexion." In future, only full-time itinerants would be permitted to administer the sacraments, and local preachers would follow the more subordinate role common in the Wesleyan connexion.

Alder also suggested that Kingston should remain part of the Lower Canada district so as to act as a communication link between the two bodies in order to help prepare the way for a possible amalgamation in the future. He hoped that the funds from the missionary committee to the missionaries serving the natives and destitute settlers would be funnelled through this circuit in order to keep the money away from the control of Canadian officials and insure that Wesleyan priorities were implemented. He wrote to his superiors in England, "If we are to do anything with the Yankee we must be Lords of the Treasury."[35] The British connexion was also to control all appointments, the divisions of circuits, and the transferring of itinerants within British America. Such detailed administrative direction was later rejected as impractical by the British connexion itself. In matters such as the use of camp meetings, Alder suggested that further detailed discussions were required. Finally, he believed it was essential that the *Christian Guardian* desist completely from meddling in partisan politics.

Although Alder did not completely get his way, the terms accepted by the Canada Conference meeting at Hallowell in August 1832 and forwarded to the British Conference for approval were better than he had anticipated. Strachan and Colborne were also delighted. Alder promised them that if he was appointed president of the united connexion, as he fully anticipated, relations with the government and the Anglican church would be greatly improved. The new church accepted Wesleyan discipline and polity, including the replacement of the episcopacy by an annually elected president appointed from the British Conference and the presiding elders by the less-powerful district chairmen. Although the existing itinerants and local preachers would retain their functions, future candidates would follow Wesleyan regulations. This change removed sacramental functions from those pursuing secular occupations.[36]

By the terms of union, all native missions would be controlled by the Wesleyan Missionary Society in Britain, with a local committee of clerical and lay representatives handling only administrative details. The Canadian Missionary Society would become an auxiliary of the British society, forwarding all funds raised to Britain to be used at the latter's discretion. Missionaries sent to Upper Canada would become members of the Canada Conference, except that their stationing would be subject to British approval. Alder's suggestions that the Kingston circuit remain with Lower Canada and distribute mission funds were dropped by the British Conference, which instead appointed a general superintendent of missions to supervise the work among the "Indians and destitute settlers" and to direct the use of funds.[37]

After the terms were accepted by the Canada Conference in 1832, they were sent to the circuit quarterly meetings, where they were ratified by a large majority. Following established procedures, the general membership did not vote on union, and this omission was later used by opponents to denounce it. However, the terms were widely discussed, and support appeared general when Egerton Ryerson carried the resolutions to Britain for ratification. The British Conference in 1833 modified and clarified the terms and appointed George Marsden president and Joseph Stinson missionary superintendent. The amendments were accepted by the Canadian Episcopal Methodists in October

1833, and the Wesleyan Methodist Church in Canada became a reality. According to the new Conference, the union "has been accomplished upon a principle of perfect equality, without any sacrifice of principle or independence on either side."[38]

Both sides expected to gain substantially from the accord. For the Canadians it meant first and foremost the end of potentially devastating competition. The general membership probably anticipated that little else would change at the circuit level. The new church would also be able to draw on more ministers and greater and more stable financial resources, supplemented by a government grant of £900. Beyond permitting the expansion of operations to serve the whole province, these resources were vital for the health of the new Methodist school then being organized and for the institutional infrastructure of a mature religious community. Moreover, the connexion would provide a familiar home for recent British immigrants, and union would forever dispel the suspicion of disloyalty, weaken provincial hostility, and increase the respectability of the church in the eyes of the general public.[39]

Union also offered benefits for the Wesleyans. Regardless of the brave rhetoric of equality, the Upper Canadian cause had been placed firmly under the control of the British church. With only limited success in the Atlantic region and Lower Canada, the British connexion needed the existing and potential membership of Upper Canada if it was to develop a viable Wesleyan church on the continent. The fact that it required union in order to gain access to this rich potential was confirmed by the missionary authorities shortly after union was formalized:

The experiment of commencing a Mission at York has convinced the Committee of the impracticality of carrying on their Missionary operations in Upper Canada without a Union with the Canada Conference. They have not funds to enable them to execute their plans in the Upper Province, on such a scale of expenditure; and if they had the means, Christian principle forbids their making that interesting country the scene of unhallowed rivalry, and unbrotherly contention, between two bodies of Christians bearing the same name, holding the same doctrine and having one common origin.[40]

Ironically, the British authorities at last subscribed to the same assessment that the Canada Conference had reached in opposing the earlier rivalry.

The Wesleyans also expected that the union would further the cause of loyalty to Britain, extinguish republican sentiments, and eliminate partisan support of the Reformers. Important as these results might be for ending confrontations in Upper Canada, the British authorities were even more anxious to sustain good relations with the Church of England and all levels of government. Not only did such a position naturally suit the temperaments of the leading Wesleyans, but in order to advance the work throughout the British empire, it was also critical that good relations be maintained with the Colonial Office. The slavery question and powerful reform forces were already unsettling politics in Britain, and the Wesleyan leadership wished to avoid any further causes of disturbance. As later events would

Egerton Ryerson (1803–82). Pre-eminent Canadian Methodist in the fields of politics and education in old Ontario. (UCA, P5741N)

James Richardson (1791–1875). Major force in building new Methodist Episcopal Church in Canada. (UCA, P5473)

Robert Alder (1795–1870). Conservative Wesleyan leader in Britain and British North America. (UCA, Album 78.105C/OS)

Joseph Stinson (1801–62). British Wesleyan minister in the Maritimes and president of Conference in old Ontario. (UCA, Album 78.105C/OS)

prove, these hopes were never realized. Whatever the Wesleyans assumed, the Canadian leadership was far from accepting inferior roles in determining its own future.

The British were pleased to have gained total control of the native work. They would be able to eliminate all perceived American influences, but more particularly, their independent work with the natives at the St Clair mission and elsewhere had not been progressing well. Despite a heavy government subsidy to the mission, few natives were joining their cause. Through government inefficiency and delays in building, the settlement on Lake St Clair was still incomplete, and a serious cholera outbreak in 1832 worsened the situation. In spite of claims that the Canadians could not supply the religious needs of the natives, Alder gave a more valid assessment to his superiors when he told them the union would "place the whole of their flourishing Indian missions under your management, which will give you great influence at the Colonial Office, as well as in the Province."[41] In developing missions to the natives and the destitute settlements nearby, the missionary committee was most interested in the aid that the British and colonial governments could provide and in controlling these funds in Britain. Colborne assured the committee, "His Majesty's government will, I am persuaded, afford some pecuniary aid where the inhabitants are unable to build churches or provide for the residence of ministers."[42] The Wesleyan authorities, in fact, petitioned for this aid on several occasions and received support for the St Clair mission. After the union of 1833, the colonial government granted £900 from the "casual and territorial" revenues and promised an annual subsidy. With these combined benefits, the union appeared to be useful and popular to all concerned.

## A NEW METHODIST EPISCOPAL CHURCH

When the union was consummated in October 1833, everyone in authority anticipated a long era of harmonious growth and spiritual prosperity. Certainly establishing district meetings, implementing Wesleyan procedures, and modifying the local preacher's functions would have to be carried out gradually to limit confusion, but all these changes were expected to be accomplished smoothly. With over 16,000 members in more than forty circuits and 913 natives on nine missions, the Methodist church in Upper Canada had achieved an impressive base from which to extend throughout the region.[43]

However, these hopes were quickly dashed by widespread opposition. Unexpectedly, the first dissent appeared among the congregations and ministers of the former British Wesleyan connexion in Upper and Lower Canada. They had expected that the Wesleyans would displace, not amalgamate with, the Episcopal Methodists. John Barry, the new minister at York, John Hetherington at Kingston, and William Croscombe in Montreal condemned the partisan politics of the Episcopal Methodists and revived the shibboleth of disloyalty. Hetherington had arrived from England in 1831 and Barry from Jamaica in 1832, so they had little experience with the Canadian scene; Croscombe too had spent most of his career in the Maritimes, where political divisions were not so stridently sectarian.[44]

Despite the reappearance of old allegations, much of the opposition was really based on personal antagonisms and differing perceptions of the conduct of the church. The rival factions also differed on what was appropriate in worship; Wesleyans generally demanded greater decorum and criticized highly emotional conduct during worship. Stinson, for instance, was appalled by the unruly behaviour he witnessed in several congregations, and the Annual Conference denounced such activities. In 1835 it warned its members, "How irreverent, how unseemly, how indecent, to see the hat worn, to see snuffing, chewing tobacco and spitting, or to hear talking or whispering, or children running to and fro in the holy sanctuary of the Most High God!"[45] Such conduct led to the condemnation of ministers and members as ignorant, fanatical, and unrespectable. These conditions had actually been common in pioneer religious services, even in some Anglican congregations, and while not approved, they were at least tolerated by the Episcopal Methodists as long as they did not interfere with evangelical spirituality.

As significant, the two former churches also disagreed on the use of extraordinary, revivalistic means of grace. Wesleyans generally disapproved of camp meetings and other revival techniques, while to the Episcopal church they were essential, God-directed methods of expanding spiritual consciousness. For their part, the Episcopal Methodists denounced the lack of zeal among Wesleyan itinerants. They were considered too formal, too concerned with respectability and status, and therefore too remote from the lives of their adherents. They were also regarded as socially irresponsible, if not immoral, since they usually continued to oppose total abstinence. Thus lifestyle and social views divided the two Methodist communities as seriously as political and ecclesiastical considerations.

At Kingston and York, the stewards and trustees even denied Stinson, the new head of missions, the right to preach in their chapels if he persisted in preaching to former Episcopal Methodists.[46] Deeply angered by this assault on its authority and by the mistreatment of its representative, the missionary committee in London responded decisively. In December 1833, after reviewing all available information regarding the Upper Canadian work, it dismissed claims of disloyalty laid against the former Episcopal Methodists and reiterated its support for the union. The local congregations were instructed to accept Stinson as their superior and to cooperate in the union. The committee also commissioned Alder to preside over the Lower Canadian district meeting set for May 1834 in order to suppress opposition. On Stinson's advice, Egerton Ryerson and James Richardson, the leaders of the two factions in Canadian Methodism, were invited to attend. Alder and Stinson agreed that much of the hostility would disappear if their contending colleagues actually met each other. Alder was also armed with strong notes of censure for the recalcitrant missionaries. Barry was transferred to Bermuda and Hetherington to Prince Edward Island. Croscombe apologized for his conduct and agreed to promote the union among his congregations.[47]

For their part, both Richardson and Ryerson greatly impressed the district meeting. Ryerson apologized for anything he had written which had appeared partisan or caused difficulty in the connexion. Nevertheless, he explained that his church had been vigorously assaulted for decades by political and religious factions bent on destroying Methodist influence. Political action had been justified to defend Methodism and to gain legitimate ecclesiastical rights such as holding property and performing marriages. Lower Canadian Methodists had also faced these disabilities and could appreciate his arguments. Ryerson also elaborated his position on the clergy reserves and on how the union was intended to function, and dispelled suspicions about the relative powers of the presiding elders versus district chairmen. By the end of the summer of 1834, with the principal clerical opponents removed or silenced and the congregations in Kingston and York at least meeting with their former rivals, the hostility to union from this quarter was greatly muted, if not entirely forgotten.[48]

The Wesleyans were silenced relatively easily, but a more serious division was simmering among the former Episcopal Methodists. The possible abandonment of support for reform politics and the acceptance of government grants were understandable sources of irritation, but Ryerson and his friends were somewhat surprised that issues of episcopal leadership and the role of local preachers should become the focus of discontent. Disaffection among local preachers mirrored the concerns which had earlier led to the Ryanite schism. The Wesleyan polity prevented easy movement between the two ministerial categories, diminished the local preacher's authority and functions, and appeared to shift power even further to the Conference of ordained itinerants. The dissidents believed such actions would lead to ministerial despotism and ultimately to a more conservative church which would dampen the fire of pure evangelical and spiritual revival. The 1834 Conference gave a focus to this disaffection when Edmund Grindrod, the newly arrived president, refused to ordain a number of local preachers because they would continue to hold secular occupations. These men had originally entered the work on the understanding that they would be eligible for ordination. The apparent breach of faith drove several of them to abandon the connexion.[49]

In defending the abolition of the episcopacy, Egerton Ryerson denied that it was essential "to the purity or efficiency of our economy." Since no bishop had ever been elected, the move to a president involved no serious dislocation or substantial change. Moreover, the relationship with the British Wesleyans paralleled the former fraternal links to the American Methodist church. James Richardson, the editor of the *Christian Guardian*, represented a substantial faction in the Methodist connexion when he disagreed. For him, the three orders of ministry were being supplanted by a single order, and Methodism's status as a distinct church was being undermined. Unlike a bishop, who would be responsible to the Canadian Conference, the new president was the creature of a distant, separate body. As well, the Wesleyans in Britain were not truly independent of the Church of England, and their assumptions about the nature of the Methodist society threatened traditional freedom of action in Canada.[50]

Ryerson shared many of these assumptions, but he believed a president spending only part of the year in the country would never wield effective control; he anticipated that the local leadership, under his own guidance, would operate a practically autonomous church regardless of the formal terms of union. Since these views could never be articulated without jeopardizing the new relationship, many Methodists came to believe that the local leaders were destroying the integrity of the connexion. Dissension reached its peak among the old Loyalist settlements, where Methodists resented being dominated from either the United States or Britain or having newcomers dictate how Canadian Methodism should function.

The acceptance of government grants seemed to confirm this betrayal.[51] The Wesleyans had never developed a solid voluntary tradition and readily accepted the propriety of state aid. Canadians who had denounced such assistance to the Anglicans as corrupting Protestant spirituality could not tolerate this hypocrisy. Union supporters had recognized the potential divisiveness of the issue and attempted to keep it out of public discussions. Even before union, Ryerson had written to Alder that "it is indispensable to the peace of our Societies and the interests of the Preachers for me to make it appear that our preachers have no personal interest in the grant."[52] Later Stinson requested that his own salary not be paid from the grant since it would upset former Episcopal Methodists.It was vital to local harmony that the funds appear to be managed in Britain for the exclusive use of native missions and therefore beyond Canadian jurisdiction. Ryerson believed that there was a critical difference because the British would spend the money on promoting native welfare, not the general work of the connexion. To the ever-pragmatic Ryerson, however, the real issue was that the money was essential for the work. He would follow a similar rationale later regarding state aid for denominational schools.

The opponents of union also feared that Ryerson and the *Guardian* would attempt to realign the church with conservative political forces in the province. Such was certainly both the long-expressed wish of the British leadership and the assumption of local radical and reform politicians. The dissident Methodists did not want to sever ties with Britain, but neither were they prepared to accept domination from the Tory-Anglican élite or forsake their right to criticize an oppressive government. Certainly, George Ryerson, who left Methodism altogether after converting to Irvingism and joining the Catholic Apostolic Church in 1833, Franklin Metcalf and William Case, former presiding elders who were only lukewarm about union, and William and Edwy Ryerson, who supported union but opposed any reactionary shift, never accepted the restrictions on this constitutional privilege. Even Egerton Ryerson, who was never as reform-oriented as his brothers, consistently assumed he had the right to speak out on political questions affecting religion.

Although his actions upset the British Wesleyans while driving other Methodists into a new Methodist Episcopal church, Ryerson believed he was totally consistent in his political and social views. He refused to be categorized on either side of the political spectrum. His use of the *Guardian* to denounce any group that criticized Methodist loyalty and to attack the prerogatives of the Church of England naturally allied him with political reformers.[53] However, shortly after being re-elected editor by the 1833 Conference, he wrote a series of "impressions" on the Reform politicians in England. The articles were immediately recognized as a general assault on Upper Canadian reform, and since they appeared less than a month after union, it was widely suspected Ryerson had abandoned his friends in order to curry favour with the British Wesleyans. Edwy Ryerson, Egerton's youngest brother, summed up the discontent when he wrote, "The present agitated state of the societies on this circuit [Stamford], partly from the Union, and in a greater degree, from your 'impressions' which would have been a blessing to our societies, had they never been conceived ... the Guardian has turned tory is the hew and cry."[54] On the other hand, the British Wesleyans were jubilant.

In fact, however, both Reformers and Tories misunderstood Egerton Ryerson's position. He was always a moderate conservative who would not be tied to extreme political parties. In responding to criticisms of his writings, he restated his belief that Methodists "ought conscientiously and carefully to guard against indulging a political party spirit ... as detrimental to our own religious prosperity and the general tranquility and advancement of the church," but they "should, at the same time, be firm and diligent and conscientious in maintaining their constitutional and just rights and privileges." The *Guardian* must not "discuss merely political questions, nor the merits of mere political parties; but ought to support the principles of equal religious freedom and privilege, and dutiful subjection to the British Government, and be preeminently a journal of religion, science and general intelligence."[55] Critics failed to appreciate how deeply Ryerson meant these statements or that he defined "religion, science and general intelligence" very broadly. He never really changed, remaining throughout his life a loyal social and political critic attempting pragmatically to strengthen the Methodist church in a moderate and progressive Canadian society. John Ryerson, Egerton's chief counsellor, did not fully understand his brother's position, but advised him against involvement in purely partisan political issues at that time. However, he supported his brother's critique of the reform movement and hoped the *Guardian* articles would help to dissolve the ties between Canadian Methodists and the political radicals in Upper Canada.

Nevertheless, Egerton's statements did give ammunition to those who opposed the union and assisted in the creation of a viable, independent Methodist Episcopal church in 1834. On June 25 that year, shortly after the annual Wesleyan Methodist Conference, Joseph Gatchell, John Reynolds, Daniel Pickett, David Culp, John Byam, and several lay representatives met at Cummer's meeting-house north of Toronto to organize the continuing Methodist Episcopal Church in Canada. Gatchell, a semi-retired itinerant, had walked out of the 1833 union conference rather than disturb its unanimity. While still occasionally preaching for the Wesleyans, he became the focal point for the discontented.

Gatchell had been licensed as a local preacher in 1806; he entered the itinerancy in 1825 and had ceased travelling in 1831, before entering the new denomination. The other leaders had followed a similar pattern. John Reynolds had itinerated briefly before retiring in 1813 to become first a school-teacher and later a wealthy merchant and local preacher in Belleville. In 1834 he carried a large number of local supporters into the Methodist Episcopal church, and he served as its first bishop from 1835 until his death in 1857.

His liberal financial contributions were important for the institutional development of the denomination. Pickett had located in 1809 after itinerating for nine years, but remained an ordained local preacher; Culp travelled from 1813 to 1825, and Byam was "discontinued" in 1818 after two years on probation. Other local preachers, such as Silas Hopkins and John Huston, also joined the cause bringing substantial membership support with them.[56]

Perhaps the most important accessions after the formation of the new church were James Richardson and Philander Smith. Ordained in 1827, Richardson had served as editor of the *Christian Guardian* and secretary of the Conference and was one of the rising luminaries of provincial Methodism. He was the acknowledged leader of those hesitant about union with the Wesleyans. In 1836 he felt he could no longer continue in the Wesleyan fold, and after a year of service in the United States, he joined the Episcopal Methodists in Canada. He provided credibility and dynamic leadership to the church and served as bishop from 1858 to 1875. Philander Smith retired from the Wesleyan connexion in 1836 and joined the Episcopal Methodists in 1837. After serving several important circuits, he succeeded Reynolds, serving as bishop from 1857 to 1870.[57]

Initially, the Wesleyans expected that most of the dissidents would return quietly to the fold. Not only was it their legitimate spiritual home, but it also held the means to fulfil the great mission to evangelize Upper Canada. They continued to minimize the defections. Samuel Rose, for instance, wrote in December 1835, "Their cause is as 'powerless as moonlight cold, on the cold snow' in this part," and the Annual Conference announced, "Some few, influenced we believe, by misrepresentation have seceded from our communion; but the number is so small as only to justify even a reference to the circumstance ... notwithstanding the misguided zeal of certain individuals who have assiduously laboured to sow the seeds of discord throughout the fair field of our spiritual culture."[58]

From the perspective of the new Methodist Episcopal church, however, it was the majority that had seceded. The new body remained the legitimate continuation of the independent Methodist Episcopal church established in 1828. It assumed that the whole union movement had been concocted by Alder and Colborne, with the connivance of Strachan, to destroy Methodism in the province and make the church a mere pawn of the established oligarchy. The alterations in church polity and the acceptance of secular grants had been unconstitutional, especially since no vote of the church membership had been taken, and would ultimately diminish the connexion's evangelical power by making it subordinate to the secular state.[59]

The new denomination initially drew its members from dissatisfied Wesleyans. George Ferguson, a loyal Wesleyan itinerant, recorded that he and nearly all other itinerants were forced to spend most of their time defending the union and counteracting the discontent. He was on the Sydney circuit, near the heart of Episcopal Methodist support in Belleville, and after weeks of turmoil, he reported that nearly two hundred had left the Wesleyans.[60] Elsewhere ministers and members held on to the church property when they joined the Episcopal Methodist connexion. However, it did not take long for the new church to develop a sound circuit organization with an aggressive recruiting program and to initiate revival services to expand membership. By 1836 it had 2,390 members and had begun a campaign to gain recognition from the American Methodist church as the true successor of the Methodist connexion in Upper Canada and to contend in the courts for possession of several important church buildings. By 1843, after ten years in existence, it reported 8,880 members in two districts and a strong, native-born force of itinerants and local preachers.[61] It would remain the second largest Methodist church in Canada until the union of 1884 and develop a vital and impressive institutional infrastructure.

### THE DISRUPTION OF 1840 AND THE UNIONS OF 1847 AND 1854

Even with the defection of so many discontented members, the marriage of Wesleyan and Episcopal Methodists in the province was never happy. The Episcopal Methodists, especially the Ryerson faction, believed they should function autonomously. The Wesleyans were to bring financial and manpower support, along with a degree of respectability, but the president and missionary superintendent were to exert only limited influence. Union was designed to eliminate British competition, not to promote its cause in the province. Needless to say, the British Wesleyan authorities and their local congregations never subscribed to these positions and expected that the new immigrants would support their viewpoint. During the remainder of the 1830s, despite the losses to the new Methodist Episcopal church, the arrival of new Methodist splinter churches from abroad, the destructive cholera epidemics, and the turmoil of the Rebellions of 1837 and the post-rebellion conservative backlash, Wesleyan membership and vitality increased. However, serious troubles remained just below the surface, and finally in the summer of 1840 the fragile church broke apart.

Fundamentally, the dissolution of the union was caused by the refusal of the British missionary authorities to allow the local administration to run the church. The specific issues were really the same unresolved disputes that had bedevilled relations since the War of 1812. The *Christian Guardian* continued to attack the Church of England and the ruling élites. In particular, Egerton Ryerson, who was editor for all but three years during the union, used its columns to denounce any vestige of apparent discrimination against Methodism. Even when the conservative, pro-British Ephraim Evans was editor between 1835 and 1838 and the journal was more politically subdued, Ryerson and his friends battled with colonial administrators. Once re-elected editor in 1838, Ryerson re-emphasized political themes often only marginally related to religious questions.[62] Most important, however, he assaulted the exclusive claims of the so-called established churches to the proceeds from the sale of the clergy reserves. He claimed that the money should be used to support general education, not to mention his favourite project, Upper Canada Academy. In fact, Lord Sydenham, governor-general from 1839 to 1841, and members of the British government received Ryerson's arguments sympathetically by the end of the 1830s.

The Canadian Conference of 1837 had hoped to facilitate more liberal legislation on the clergy reserves by passing a series of resolutions regarding Methodist rights and religious instruction. The government proposed removing the annual grants assigned to the Wesleyan Missionary Society from the "casual and territorial" revenues and making them a permanent charge on the proceeds from the sale of the clergy reserves. Essentially, the Conference attempted to make it easier for the government by claiming no right to provincial funds, leaving it entirely "to the unbiased judgement of the authorities concerned, to decide whether any public aid can be properly and advantageously given towards the improvement of the injured aboriginal inhabitants ... and, if any, to what amount and through what agency."[63] This statement appeared to release the provincial government from its guarantee to provide grants from its discretionary funds to the British Missionary Society.

The resolutions also called for an early settlement of the clergy-reserves controversy "in accordance with the wishes and circumstances of the inhabitants," and while reiterating its desire to abstain from meddling in secular politics, Conference "expressed its decided conviction of the inexpediency of the establishment of one or more Churches in the Provinces, with exclusive rights and privileges ... and that the continued efforts of certain members of the Church of England to maintain, and the recent attempts of the Convention of Delegates of the Kirk of Scotland to secure, an ascendancy over their Christian brethren of other denominations ... will ... be in direct violation of those principles of civil and religious liberty for ... which this Conference ... contends."[64] Conference assured the government that if the reserves were properly dealt with, Canadian Methodists would only seek aid for the "religious and educational improvement of the Province." These resolutions reflected ongoing negotiations with the government independent of the British missionary authorities; they were based on the assumption that Canadians had a right to carry on such actions and that the clergy reserves was a religious, not a secular partisan question. In 1838 the move to greater autonomy was also advanced by the successful pressure to replace William Lord with the more sympathetic and manageable Joseph Stinson as president of Conference.[65]

The British missionary committee deplored these actions and particularly objected to the apparent attempt to alienate its revenues and to control the replacement grants. Visiting the Canadian Conference of 1839, Robert Alder persuaded it to rescind the objectionable resolutions, but his attempt to prevent the church from undertaking further political action and persuade it to show greater deference to the parent authorities was unsuccessful. The Canadians established a committee under Ryerson's direction to negotiate with the various levels of government on the clergy reserves and related issues.[66]

After the close of Conference, Alder reaffirmed his support for an established church with the lieutenant-governor, Sir George Arthur, and members of the oligarchy. He was even more convinced that the union was a mistake and should be nullified. Alder's actions helped raise the fear among Canadian Methodists that their interests could not be trusted to the missionary committee or its local agents. This mistrust was justified when a letter written to Lord Sydenham in January 1840 by Joseph Stinson and Matthew Richey, both members of the British Conference, was made public. Stinson was the titular head of the Canadian church and had significant experience in the Canadas. Richey was the founding principal of Upper Canada Academy. Born in 1803 into a devout Irish Presbyterian family, he had received a decent classical education before moving to Saint John in 1819. The following year, he entered the Methodist ministry and was finally ordained in 1825. His preaching balanced evangelical zeal with learning, while his courteous outward conduct camouflaged a vitriolic and suspicious nature. Politically and ecclesiastically conservative, he opposed any move which threatened Canadian ties to Britain or British Wesleyanism. In 1835 Richey was transferred to Lower Canada, and a year later accepted the position at Upper Canada Academy. Stinson and Richey wrote to Lord Sydenham that they had no objection to the Church of England being recognized as the established church with exclusive control of the clergy reserves. But if the Presbyterians were to receive a share, then support should also be given "to the Wesleyan Methodists who are now, and may be hereafter connected with the British Wesleyan Conference."[67] These funds would be distinct from the grants already given to the missionary committee. The letter gave the distinct impression that its authors anticipated a dissolution of the union and were attempting to secure control of government funding for their separate connexion.

Sydenham showed Ryerson the letter, and on January 17, 1840, Ryerson replied by rehearsing the history of government grants in a light strongly favourable to the Canadian position. In his letter, he contended that "should a dissolution of the Union take place between the bodies, as intimated to your Excellency by Messrs. Stinson & Richey, the Conference in England would claim the missions in this Province – notwithstanding their original establishment by the Canadian Conference, and the annual collections made to support them. But I apprehend no disposition on the part of the British Conference to dissolve the union, unless they can get government aid independent of the Canadian Conference to prosecute their views."[68] Ryerson concluded by requesting that any grants "intended to benefit the Wesleyan Methodist Church in Canada ought undoubtedly to be placed at the disposal of the Conference of that Church." He was confident that the British would not attempt to compete in Upper Canada, except perhaps in the native missions, without government aid, and the shift of control of funds might prevent the disruption of the union.

The members of the London missionary committee were furious. They were already planning to dissolve the union and resented Ryerson's proposed raid on their legitimate resources. They spent the remainder of 1840 attempting to persuade the British government to maintain their annual grant of £700 and prevent any money being directed to Ryerson's education projects.[69] On the same day they first laid these arguments before the colonial secretary, they drew up extensive charges against Ryerson. Ignoring established procedures, they threatened unilaterally to annul the union unless the Canadian Conference disciplined him severely and permanently broke his power.

The charges attacked his meddling in politics, his "disingenuous" conduct, his usurpation of the authority of the president to negotiate on behalf of the connexion, and his illegal and immoral attempts to procure the annual grants. The resolutions concluded by claiming all the aboriginal missions as a matter of right if union failed and requested that a Canadian delegation attend the 1840 British Conference to resolve all existing difficulties. The exact charges were of little real consequence; the issues were who would control the potential revenues from the clergy reserves, with the corollary of the suspension of grants from the "casual and territorial" funds, and whether the connexion would ultimately be directed from Britain or in Upper Canada. As for the original grants, they undoubtedly belonged to the British authorities, but altering the funding procedure might well redirect revenues to an independent Canadian connexion.[70]

At the Canadian Conference meeting in June 1840, Ryerson and his friends presented a determined front against Stinson, Richey, and Ephraim Evans, who represented the missionary society. Ryerson made especially good use of the Stinson-Richey letter to Sydenham the previous January to illustrate the unreliability of the British appointees. The final vote of 59 to 8 cleared him of all charges. The Conference went further and denied the missionary committee's right to lay charges against one of its members or to interfere in the internal affairs of the connexion. It also denied that the British-appointed president alone represented the connexion and reaffirmed Ryerson as its principal negotiator. Finally, the Conference denied that the British had any inherent right to the native missions since they had been initiated by Canadian missionaries and supported by Canadian funds.[71] As if these resolutions were not offensive enough, Egerton and William Ryerson were appointed representatives to the British Conference to discuss the existing difficulties and, equally important, to negotiate with the British government over the revisions to the clergy-reserves bill then before Parliament.[72] The British Conference was insulted by these appointees and refused them permission even to attend the sessions. It voted to dissolve the union and to create a separate Wesleyan connexion in Upper Canada.

In October 1840 the now-independent Canada Conference met in special session to reorganize its own work. Ephraim Evans, John Douse, Benjamin Slight, James Norris, Thomas Fawcett, William Scott, James Brock, John G. Manly, Charles Goodrich, Edmund Stoney, and William Case formally withdrew to form the nucleus of the British Wesleyan connexion; Joseph Stinson and Matthew Richey had always been members of the British Conference. Thomas Hurlburt and John Sunday, a native preacher, also withdrew; Hurlburt supported the Canadian position, but since he was serving in the Hudson's Bay territory with James Evans, he felt he must quit the Canadian connexion. Sunday and Case joined the British in order to continue the native work. Ironically, Peter Jones, the first ordained native itinerant, allied with the Canadians and helped retain the support of nearly eight hundred native members. He remained loyal to his friend Egerton Ryerson rather than to his former mentor, William Case, who he believed was overly paternalistic and critical of his translations of the Bible.[73]

The British Wesleyans retained the native missions at Sarnia, Alderville, Rice Lake, and Amherstburg and those to white settlers at Sarnia, Goderich, Amherstburg, Toronto, Kingston, Hamilton, Peterborough, and Guelph. In 1841 these circuits and missions scattered across the province contained only about fifteen hundred members. The work was severely hampered by lack of funds since the government suspended grants to both the Canadian and British factions and the missionary collections from Canadian circuits were cut off. At the same time, the London missionary committee was preoccupied with the new missions in the Hudson's Bay territory, and this expensive and rather unsuccessful experiment added to the drain on missionary funds. Although the British Wesleyans in Upper Canada assumed that new immigrants would flock to their flag, instead the newcomers seemed content with the Canadian ministry and the connexion grew only marginally during the 1840s. Even its journal, the *Wesleyan*, established in 1840 in Montreal and transferred to Toronto a year later to oppose the *Christian Guardian*, was forced to cease publication in 1844 because of heavy financial losses.[74]

As for the Canadian Wesleyans, after a year of separation they claimed 17,017 members, an increase of over 600 from the previous year. Although the dissolution of union had split congregations, such as those in Kingston and Toronto, membership declined only sightly in Kingston and actually grew by 50 in Toronto. The connexion experimented briefly with administrative modifications, such as stationing district chairmen and placing the native missions directly in their adjacent districts in order to increase efficiency, but few radical changes were made. It also had some success in encouraging former Ryanite and Episcopal Methodists to rejoin the connexion. However, it decided not to expand into Lower Canada since such an operation would have been too expensive and unnecessarily provocative.[75] In Cobourg, Upper Canada Academy was transformed into Victoria College in 1841 under the direction of Egerton Ryerson. Over the early 1840s, the church also shared substantially in the impressive continent-wide revival and gained significant confidence in its ability to administer its own affairs and compete with the other Methodist denominations in the region. Despite this prosperity, the disruption was difficult, especially for ordinary members, who never fully appreciated the reasons for separation.

Quite apart from internal difficulties within the Wesleyan connexion, the 1840s witnessed a radical reshaping of the religious landscape in both Britain and North America. During the 1830s, the Scottish Presbyterian minister Edward Irving, claiming that he had received direct revelations from God, had begun to prophesy "in tongues" and to preach the premillennialist doctrine of the imminent destruction of the world and the thousand-year reign of Christ. By the 1840s, his supporters, including many Methodists, had formed the Catholic Apostolic Church. The British and Canadian Wesleyans also shared the serious defection of members to the adventist crusades of the Americans William Miller, who calculated that the world would end in 1843, and Joseph Smith, who offered a new series of revelations to his Mormon followers. Such breaches in the evangelical vision of society were serious enough, but they were paralleled by extensive disruptions in the old-line churches as well. In both Scotland and North America, the Presbyterians were shattered into Free and Old Kirk factions in 1843–44 over voluntaryism and state interference, and the Church of England was divided by the Tractarian movement's struggle to revitalize Catholic elements in the church.[76] Together these movements fractured all previously understood patterns of religious affiliation and denominational relationships.

The Wesleyans in Britain were also feeling the effects of divisions in their own ranks. The Fly Sheet controversy during the 1840s led to the loss of nearly one-quarter of the membership. The Fly Sheets were a series of anonymous pamphlets, originally circulated among British Wesleyan ministers between 1844 and 1849, which attacked the controlling influence of Jabez Bunting and his conservative colleagues over Wesleyan Methodism. Although not particularly radical in themselves, they provided a focus for discontented members who wanted more power for the laity in church courts, less deference to the Church of England, and a greater use of American-style revivalism. At the same time, many Wesleyans were beginning to denounce the increase in ritual and Catholic pretensions in the Church of England and to stop according it their traditional deference. Bunting, the undisputed leader of the British Wesleyans, even acknowledged that with regard to public questions the Canadians had been right.

On the other hand, the Canadian Wesleyans were themselves badly divided over Egerton Ryerson's support for Governor-General Sir Charles Metcalfe against the Reformers in the election of 1844 and his subsequent appointment as assistant superintendent of education. Whatever the difficulties these actions caused for the Upper Canadian connexion, they did have the advantage, as far as the British were concerned, of removing Ryerson from a position of influence in Canadian Methodist affairs and especially of muting the *Christian Guardian*. Moreover, by the second half of the 1840s, the annual increases in membership had turned into losses and the Canadian connexion became less sure of its independent existence.[77]

Thus, almost from the dissolution in 1840, forces were at work to reunite the two Wesleyan branches and even to promote a broader union of all Methodists in British North America. For the first few years, antipathy toward Ryerson kept discussions from proceeding very far, and the consensus among British Wesleyans in Canada was that if union was restored, the British authorities would have to control property, appointments, publications, revenue, and legislative capacity.[78] Such a loss of autonomy was unacceptable to the Canadians and perhaps more surprisingly, to the British missionary authorities, who could not administer such an operation. In 1844 John Ryerson, the most diplomatic member of his family, presented proposals for reunion to the missionary committee, and after further discussions with Egerton Ryerson, who was once again visiting England, negotiations continued unofficially. The following year a committee of the Canada Conference was authorized to settle all outstanding issues. The British canvassed their missionaries, and after Alder and Stinson supported reunion, they established their own negotiating committee in 1846. The same year, Anson Green and John Ryerson, in England as delegates to the international convention of the Evangelical Alliance, presented proposals as a basis of reunion which, after being approved by the Canadian quarterly meetings, were accepted formally by both churches in 1847. The Canada Conference voted 82 to 8 for the measure.[79]

The terms were essentially the same as in 1833 except that the British missionaries retained their status in the British Conference and the new position of co-delegate was created. Normally a Canadian, the co-delegate would administer the church during the extended absence of the British president. In addition, the missionary society would provide an annual grant of £1,000 for native work and £600 for missions to destitute settlers. A joint application was made for the government grants, which had been held in abeyance for the previous seven years, and these funds, along with the native missions, would be controlled from Britain.[80] What had really changed was the recognition by the British Conference that Canadians should run the local connexion with a minimum of external interference. This change was made less controversial with the transfer of the clergy-reserves question to the imperial Parliament and also, ironically, because Egerton Ryerson had forever removed himself from a position of dominance in Methodist councils.

The reunion also terminated for another generation the suggested union of all the splinter Methodist denominations. The New Connexion, Bible Christian, and Primitive Methodists, newly settled in Upper Canada, were not prepared to affiliate with British Wesleyanism; they were too bound to their own evangelistic experimentations and to their quest for a significant independent mission. This quest was also strong among the Episcopal Methodists, with their substantial, well-established membership, proudly tracing their origins to the first missionaries entering Upper Canada in the eighteenth century. According to the 1851 census, the Methodist Episcopal church had over 46,000 adherents (more than 8,000 members) in two annual conferences and was expanding into Canada East.[81] Despite its optimism, however, long-term growth was still problematic since it depended on the creation of a viable institutional network and achieving a greater measure of success in the larger urban centres.

Although general Methodist union did not proceed immediately, the 1850s did witness an encouraging improvement in cooperation and unity of purpose, especially within the Evangelical Alliance. After 1847 the British missionary authorities were also increasingly determined to transfer all their North American operations to a self-sufficient Canadian church. The British and Canadian connexions agreed in principle to what the Toronto *Globe* described as "a Federal Union of the Methodists of British North America, embracing Eastern and Western Canada, the Hudson's Bay Territory, New Brunswick, Nova Scotia and Newfoundland, the whole of which to be governed by a Federal Council, after the manner of the general Council of the Methodist Episcopal Church in the adjoining republic. The movement has not originated with the church in this country, but has been suggested by the Parent Conference in England."[82]

In anticipation of this national church, the Wesleyans in the two Canadas began cooperative administration of their work in 1853 and completed their amalgamation in 1854. The 32,000 members in the west welcomed their 4,000 co-religionists from Canada East.[83] The Canadas had a natural internal integrity, and the movement of itinerants and ideas, as well as the administration of the church, ignored provincial boundaries. Regardless of its long tradition of British Wesleyanism, Canada East readily accepted integration with its larger neighbour. The expansion of Roman Catholic ultramontanism and the Frenchification of Montreal and the Eastern Townships so beleaguered Methodism in the province that, despite the existence of a few relatively strong congregations, the church came to rely on Canada West's support for its continued development. With over 125,000 adherents by 1854, the Wesleyan Methodist connexion in the Canadas was sufficiently developed to be highly and rightfully optimistic about its ability to serve creatively the expanding spiritual needs of all British North America.

This spirit was perhaps best illustrated by its agreement to assume responsibility for the missions in the northwest originally begun by the British Wesleyans in 1840. By 1854 these missions were nearly defunct, and the British missionary committee was pleased to provide an annual grant of £1,000 in order to be released from the burden. To the Canadians, the region was the legitimate homeland for future generations of settlers and the object of their nationalistic ambitions. They already claimed the heroic missionary work of James Evans and his associates, and it was in the northwest that Canadian Methodism's natural aspirations to share in the great crusade to evangelize and Protestantize the world would be fulfilled.[84] Thus, after over three decades of political and ecclesiastical struggle, a viable, prosperous, and deeply committed Canadian Wesleyan Methodism was ready to meet the new era of institutional and geographic expansion.

## 5 Divergent Visions: The Wesleyans in the Atlantic Region and the Smaller Connexions before 1855

While the complicated story of mainstream Methodism in Upper Canada spoke generally of growth and optimism, the picture of the movement in the Atlantic provinces was quite different. Most members denied any natural correlation between size and spiritual prosperity, but Methodists were never satisfied with remaining a closed, limited body of converts. Although no true measure of religious progress, "Ecclesiastics are nevertheless very sensitive to membership gains and losses, while the common man unhesitatingly judges the church in large measure by its institutional size."[1] The Wesleyans in the Atlantic region were never able to capture the evangelical revival for their denominational advantage. Despite being closely allied with evangelical Anglicans and remaining deferential to the Church of England, they still appeared too experiential and unrespectable for most Anglicans or Scottish Presbyterians. Yet the Wesleyan church was too staid and formal for those seeking an emotionally satisfying, spiritual fellowship. These people normally turned to the Free Will Baptists, who apparently offered all the benefits of Methodist evangelicalism without many of its liabilities. At the same time, unlike their counterparts in Upper Canada, Methodists in the Atlantic provinces failed to gain significant converts among the Protestant Irish immigrants entering the region after the close of the Napoleonic Wars.

In 1820 the connexion was divided into the Newfoundland, New Brunswick, and Nova Scotia missionary districts under the supervision of the Wesleyan Missionary Society in London. Newfoundland was responsible for Labrador, the New Brunswick district contained the Annapolis Valley, and the Nova Scotia district included Prince Edward Island. This arrangement was maintained until a semi-autonomous Conference of Eastern British America was established in 1855. At least until that time, the history of the connexion was characterized by a shortage of preachers, heavy debt, and the inability to sustain membership growth.

In 1827 the Newfoundland, Nova Scotia, and New Brunswick districts reported 1,100, 1,520, and about 800 members respectively.[2] With the exception of relatively strong circuits at Island Cove-Perlican, Bonavista, Saint John, and Halifax, most of the societies were small and isolated. The constraints of the region's geography and economic potential prevented the development of a large, contiguous population. Prince Edward Island reported a total of 275 members on its three circuits. The Nova Scotia district had 34 chapels, more than twice as many as either of the other two districts, but most in the region, including the large Halifax church, were unfinished and in debt. Despite a significant revival in the early 1830s, the average rate of expansion was embarrassingly slow and erratic.

During the whole period before 1855, the only marked improvement occurred during the first half of the 1840s. After three years of respectable membership increase, the region shared in the great revival sweeping North America in 1842–43. At the annual district meeting in 1843, Nova Scotia showed an increase of 747 members, with an additional 3,800 on trial. It added another 471 members the following year, reaching a total membership of 4,860. Newfoundland rose substantially to 2,333 members in 1843 and 2,530 in 1844, and New Brunswick followed a similar pattern, with a membership of 3,788 in 1843 and over 3,900 in 1844. Nearly all the circuits shared in the growth, and even the new missions on Cape Breton Island and the pioneer areas of New Brunswick seemed to prosper. It appeared that the Wesleyan cause had finally achieved the critical threshold of self-sustaining expansion.

However, these encouraging results could not be sustained. After 1844 substantial decline was followed by only a slow recovery. Membership did not again reach the 1844 peak in either Newfoundland or New Brunswick districts until 1855. In the Nova Scotia district, it took until 1852 before its 1844 membership was surpassed. In 1851, the year before the district was divided into two, it reported 4,803 members. After 1852 membership increases were most pronounced on Prince Edward Island and at Halifax. In 1855 the two Nova Scotia districts brought a total of 5,539 members to join the 3,718 from New Brunswick and the 2,633 from Newfoundland in the new Conference.[3]

The Wesleyan missionaries were quick to blame the large-scale emigration of Protestants, unfair competition from other denominations, the weak commitment of revival converts, and the hard-hearted obstinacy of the citizenry for the lack of expansion.[4] To a degree they were justified in this assessment, but the missionaries themselves must also share some of the blame. While they could with some justice complain about staff shortages, travel difficulties, and the isolation of the settlements, these conditions were common to all denominations in British North America, and the preachers themselves were generally lax about visiting the societies. They relied on a semi-settled, rather than a truly itinerant ministry.[5] Most lacked an aggressive drive to evangelize and were complacent about expanding or even properly serving their preaching appointments. For instance, in Newfoundland in 1843, the fourteen missionaries held services at thirty-two chapels and eighty-two other appointments, but by 1854 the thirteen itinerants preached at thirty-seven chapels and only forty other places.[6] Such retrenchment severely limited connexional growth and the supervision of outlying members, and illustrated the weakness of evangelical fervour.

The situation was made worse by the casual manner in which the itinerants took up their circuit responsibilities; often the stationing decisions were ignored or altered, leaving circuits with capricious clerical leadership. On average the itinerants preached only about five times per week. This translated into a very irregular ministry of two or three weekday services to the outlying appointments. The resulting gap was not properly filled by the laity because of the small number and low status accorded the local preachers. Often they had to be paid to preach.[7] Their role was even less important than in Britain since they shared no administrative responsibility beyond the circuit level. They were poorly educated and usually ignored; their vital role in expanding missionary operations was never fully exploited by the Maritime Methodist church leaders.

This attitude was further reflected in the treatment of itinerants born or raised in the region. One of the major failings of the pioneer connexion had been the absence of local men in the itinerancy. This lack was partially alleviated after 1827, when more candidates applied and were accepted on probation. The qualifications were usually similar to those of James Melvin, except he was older than most: "James Melvin, a native of Nova Scotia, 27 years of age, without a matrimonial engagement, and out of debt. He was examined as to his conversion, call to the ministry and views of our doctrines and discipline. He is totally acquainted with English Grammar, is fond of reading, enjoys tolerably good health and is willing to be sent by the Committee to any part of the world."[8] But the London committee encouraged locally born ministers at least partially because it believed they could operate less expensively than missionaries from Britain. It attempted to designate them "native missionaries," a term elsewhere reserved for aboriginal assistants, to grant them smaller subsidies, and initially to deny them access to the connexional pension plans. The local districts strongly opposed the creation of a second-class ministry, and these restrictions were removed by the 1840s.[9] Nevertheless, the inference of colonial inferiority did little to impress Maritimers with the Christian wisdom of the British Missionary Society.

Such attitudes aggravated a deeper malaise among the missionaries themselves. They only indifferently enforced the rules and regulations, let alone the doctrines of Wesleyan Methodism. The young were rarely catechized or visited in the Sunday schools; class meetings, where they were sustained, were seldom encouraged to promote their critical evangelical and economic functions; and the laity was seldom directed to strengthen the local cause.[10] Without these undergirdings, the whole Wesleyan structure remained feeble and unstable. At the top of this structure was a politically and ecclesiastically conservative itinerant missionary force who never favoured earnest revival techniques and could be induced only occasionally to use English-style protracted meetings (see chapter 6 for an explanation of this phenomenon). While appalled by the antinomianism and emotionalism of many Baptists, the Methodist missionaries failed to address the legitimate longings of the population for an emotionally fulfilling religious experience.

This problem was compounded by the fact that the missionaries were generally English, while the recent Protestant Irish immigrants, particularly in Newfoundland and New Brunswick, offered the greatest source of potential converts. Nationalistic and linguistic differences often made these two groups incompatible. Moreover, the Wesleyan missionaries were also remarkably slow to appreciate the emerging Maritime cultural and social identity. Even after decades of service, many of the leading missionaries remained Britons abroad, uninvolved and unintegrated into the national aspirations of their adopted communities. They continued to reflect the cultural and political outlook dominating Methodism in Britain and delayed the moulding of the connexion into a viable indigenous institution.

This situation was only slowly modified during the 1840s as the rising generation of itinerants gradually replaced the older missionaries. In 1842 alone, Nova Scotia district admitted five local candidates: "The acquisition of these was indicative not only of a steady growth in the number of preachers, but probably of a subtle alteration in their calibre and their outlook."[11] These advances should not be overestimated, however, since while New Brunswick's itinerant cadre advanced from thirteen to twenty-seven between 1831 and 1854, Nova Scotia and Newfoundland saw only a slight increase in missionary staff. Nevertheless, men such as Matthew Richey, Samuel Dwight Rice, Humphrey Pickard, Enoch Wood, and Ephraim Evans saw themselves as North American ministers, rather than as British missionaries. They were prepared to experiment with innovative methods and to trust in the ability of the local connexion to administer its own affairs; it was upon their shoulders that the creation of a mature religious infrastructure rested. Although they remained hesitant about severing financial ties with Britain, they were anxious to assume responsibility and were willing to risk the vicissitudes of an autonomous connexion.[12] At the same time, they were more self-reliant only to a degree, and their real influence would not be felt until the second half of the century.

No feature was more constant among the Wesleyans during the first half of the century than their annual plea for financial aid from Britain. Although local income fluctuated, it usually covered only about half of the amount spent. The missionaries were quick to recite "the distress of the times and the poverty of people" to explain the lack of support.[13] Certainly, even during good times, the economy was uneven and highly volatile, but the lack of initiative among both the clergy and the laity must also be blamed. In budgeting it was assumed, not only that the missionary committee would provide a large grant, but also that it would subsequently cover any additional deficit. Not one of the circuits ever raised a surplus to support expansion or to assist the weaker societies, and it was only after 1852 that a few circuits no longer drew support from the missionary grant.

Even Halifax, with at times over six hundred members, never became self-supporting. In 1836 its stewards requested a special interest-free loan of £1,000 for five years to help pay off the chapel debt of nearly £3,000. As a whole, the Nova Scotia district spent £1,076 more than it raised for domestic operations. Enoch Wood in 1842 also requested a £1,000 loan or a gift of £500 for Centenary Chapel in Saint John. These examples illustrate the inability of the connexion to tap into regional wealth in order to sustain its own stability or growth. In 1844, after years of impressive membership expansion and without additional labourers or substantial new territory to drain off receipts, the Nova Scotia district still complained that the reduced missionary grant of £900 was inadequate.

The British missionary committee attacked the wasteful local administration and demanded an explanation for the construction of a new chapel in Halifax when no money was available locally to pay for it. Exasperated, it also wanted to know why the long-established Wesleyan societies were still not self-sufficient while those in the Canadas and Australia, and other non-Methodist denominations in the Maritimes, were able to cover their own costs. The districts offered only trivial excuses and continued to lament the weak support from headquarters. They assumed that it was their right to rely on missionary society resources while complaining that they were overly restricted by the British administration.[14] In reality, poor management and lack of initiative kept the connexion subservient. The local church was never able to impress its membership with the necessity of strong voluntary contributions or to develop sources of consistent financial support. Without this base, the London missionary committee refused to sanction more missionaries, although they were certainly needed.

Weak financial support also inhibited the creation of an ecclesiastical infrastructure, which was essential for the development of a mature, viable connexion. As early as the 1820s, the Maritime Wesleyans had recognized the value of a newspaper in presenting a strong image to the regional community and in defending the Methodist cause against the accusations of other denominations. It would also distribute information to members at a relatively small cost, develop and satisfy a taste for reading and education, and assist in spreading Methodist doctrines, particularly to the better-established elements in society.

Partially to fulfil this want, the two mainland districts collaborated to establish the quarterly *Nova Scotia and New Brunswick Wesleyan Magazine* in 1832, with William Temple as editor.[15] Since it had not been consulted, the London missionary committee viewed this action as an unacceptable breach of its authority and as a detrimental competition for British Wesleyan journals. After its disastrous experience with the *Christian Guardian* in Upper Canada, the committee also feared the new journal would embroil the connexion in partisan politics. Essentially, however, the magazine represented another ill-conceived and poorly financed enterprise that would become a drain on society funds. The committee forced the closing of the paper in 1833. Although the Maritime districts requested a reconsideration, they confirmed the committee's fears by requesting funds for publishing since the "general poverty of our people is such as to call for special consideration in reference to a provision for their religious instruction."[16] The committee chose not to respond to the request.

In the absence of any reply, the Nova Scotia district took it upon itself to publish the *Wesleyan* in February 1838, with Alexander MacLeod as editor. Appearing fortnightly, it contained articles on divinity, literature, history, and biography as well as church and general news. When Robert Alder visited the Maritime district meeting on his way to Upper Canada in 1839, he reported the missionary committee's continued opposition, and the journal ceased publication after only a few issues. However, he did agree to use his influence to obtain the committee's sanction to start a new magazine jointly published by the two mainland districts.[17] In 1841 the monthly *British North American Wesleyan Methodist Magazine* commenced operations in Saint John under the joint editorship of Temple and Enoch Wood. Except for education, which was considered essentially a religious question, the magazine refrained from narrow sectarian or political controversy and strove to strengthen Methodism throughout all the colonies. Unfortunately, it was never popular or financially successful, and after temporarily suspending operations in 1845, it closed completely two years later.

A monthly magazine relying heavily on foreign literary and religious contributions did little to answer the real needs of Maritime Methodists. Only a weekly newspaper that focused on the local spiritual and social issues could provide a relevant and influential alternative to the secular and non-Wesleyan religious press and fulfil the nationalistic and cultural aspirations of the region. With financial support from England, the *Wesleyan*, a new, weekly newspaper, made its appearance in April 1849. Alexander MacLeod edited the journal and, as book steward, also ran the Halifax-based Book Room and publishing interests of the church. "Almost at once the morale of the Societies was strengthened by this new and effective defender of their position."[18] The *Wesleyan* quickly took the lead in promoting a regional conference and the expansion of a strong, indigenous connexion. It became especially active in seeking government assistance for denominational higher education, particularly for Methodist schools.

The idea of a Methodist school system modelled on John Wesley's Kingswood school had been proposed as early as 1828. Various plans were suggested during the 1830s, but without connexional support, a determined lay leadership, or assurances of government grants, only a few semi-official day schools, meeting irregularly, developed in Fredericton, Horton, and Halifax.[19] The whole situation was dramatically altered in 1839, when Charles Allison of Sackville, New Brunswick, offered to build a school costing about £4,000 on a seven-acre site in his home town. Allison was a native-born Maritimer of Ulster Scottish descent who had converted from the Church of England to Wesleyan Methodism in 1836. After a successful career as merchant and lumber exporter, the deeply religious Allison retired from business in 1840 to promote Methodist education full-time. He and the town of Sackville also each agreed to provide a £100 endowment annually for ten years to place the school on a sound financial base. Alder, who heard the terms during his visit in 1839, strongly supported the plan, and the offer was accepted. The Sackville Academy, later Mount Allison University, was opened in June 1843 so that "religious, moral and intellectual discipline would be fruitfully combined in a thoroughly Wesleyan atmosphere."[20]

The New Brunswick and Nova Scotia governments each agreed to contribute £200 in 1843 and 1844 to subsidize the operating expenses, and the connexion trusted that government aid would continue permanently. The districts assumed they would not have to supply additional financial aid, although they did apply for British missionary society funds for the school and encouraged private donations. When Matthew Richey was unavailable, Humphrey Pickard, his young and energetic colleague, was appointed principal. The son of a Methodist businessman of New England descent, Pickard had been born in 1813 in Fredericton, New Brunswick. Before ordination into the Methodist ministry in 1842, he had graduated from Wesleyan University in Middletown, Connecticut. He remained at the school until 1869, the last seven years as president of Mount Allison University, and his austere, but sensitive administration and his legislative skills helped build the Wesleyan educational infrastructure in the Maritimes. The school quickly became crucial for Methodist interests by providing a sound classical secondary education for the youth of the region, especially the training it gave the future Wesleyan itinerancy. First proposed in 1847, a Female Academy was opened at Sackville in 1854, allowing for Methodist-controlled female secondary education.[21]

With a denominational secondary school and a viable newspaper, the Maritime-raised leaders were finally prepared to reorganize the church into a semi-autonomous conference. However, the initiative for such a move came from the British missionary committee. Since at least the 1830s, it had believed the districts should assume a greater share of their own financial burden and had pressed for a restructuring of the local work. When Alder visited in 1839, he encouraged Nova Scotia and New Brunswick to unite their efforts. The districts feared that any alteration of the status quo might lead to a reduction in the missionary grants and opposed the suggestion.[22]

The London committee was not prepared to abandon the idea, however, and in 1843 proposed a much more elaborate plan for union. Following the disruption of the Upper Canadian Methodist connexion, the British authorities advocated the creation of one North American conference bringing together all the Wesleyans in the various colonies. Such an organization would provide a real alternative to the Canadian Methodists and would ultimately permit the districts to share resources and administer their own affairs more economically and effectively. Again, however, the Atlantic districts believed the time was not right and used the excuse of requiring more information to delay change.[23]

The British administration did not immediately pursue the proposal because it was preoccupied with the reunion of Upper Canadian Methodism. After that was accomplished in 1847, it again made overtures to unite the British North American societies into one large connexion by joining the prosperous Upper Canadian church with the weaker Lower Canadian and Atlantic-region districts. It hoped this national body would become a prosperous partner in the quest to evangelize the world. Initially, the reorganized church could take over the missions to the Hudson's Bay territories. As a first step, the Atlantic circuits would be reorganized, and in 1849 Bermuda was added to the Nova Scotia district. The declining Wesleyan cause in Newfoundland and the somewhat orphaned Canada East district were then to join the Maritime districts. The greatest opposition to this scheme remained among the older British missionaries, who feared the removal of British subsidies. Enoch Wood had described their position in 1842, and they had never really changed: "The great secret of aversion to a separate conference, still retaining connexion with 'home' is dependence upon 'home'; an unwillingness to bend to circumstances ... If you can help us you will do it, but if not, why should we not adapt ourselves as far as possible to the wants of the country?"[24]

Nevertheless, by the end of the decade, the younger leaders were preparing for local control by straightening out tangled accounts and administrative systems and by establishing educational and pension funds. The local church also hoped that its future economic position would improve since it was beginning to develop greater strength among the increasingly prosperous artisan classes, especially in urban New Brunswick. At the same time, the church leadership was becoming more active in defending Methodist rights against the prerogatives of the Church of England and in defining the connexion as a distinct community. In Newfoundland the Wesleyans particularly identified themselves with the poor and socially dispossessed, gaining a sense of cohesion by differentiating themselves from the upper-class Anglican commercial and military élites. They also gradually adopted American-style revivalistic techniques as a means of expanding their membership. Although still in their embryonic stages, these developments offered hope that the Wesleyan church could support a regional conference.

Since the region now had a newspaper to promote the idea and a leadership at least partially sympathetic, the British Conference was encouraged to present concrete proposals.[25] Preoccupied with more critical difficulties at home, it was even more desperate to unburden itself of its overly dependent missions. The Fly Sheet controversy was tearing the Wesleyan connexion apart and, among its other impacts, was drastically reducing revenues. In order to save money, the British church established conferences in Australia and France and was obliged to reduce its missionary grants and refuse to cover additional deficits. Unused to such treatment, the Maritime districts had no procedure in place to cover the shortfall except borrowing the money from the Methodist laity. By the mid-1850s, the debt had accumulated to such an embarrassing extent that the reputation of the church was in jeopardy. Although this state of affairs increased fears about independence, it also made clear the necessity of some new arrangement.[26]

The Maritime missionaries were resolved to assume greater control over their own affairs, but they were not ready to give up their operating grants or their links to the British pension plans and were not enthusiastic about joining their Canadian Wesleyan brethren or being saddled with the weak Newfoundland societies. Part of their concern was eliminated when the Canada East district joined the Canada Conference in 1854 and the idea of one national connexion was postponed indefinitely. But it was obvious that Newfoundland would have to be included in any new Maritime Conference. When John Beecham, the senior missionary secretary, arrived, only the final terms had still to be settled. The president would be appointed in Britain, the British Conference reserved a legislative veto, although most decisions remained a local responsibility, and the local missionary society auxiliaries

Enoch Wood (1804–88). Wesleyan missionary to the Maritimes and head of the combined Canadian Wesleyan mission operations after 1847. (UCA, P7178)

Matthew Richey (1803–83). British Wesleyan itinerant in the Maritimes and central Canada. (UCA, Album 78.105C/OS)

John Seybert (1791–1860). Bishop of the Evangelical Association, who expanded the German-speaking church in the United States and Canada. (UCA, P5963N)

Bible Christian Conference, 1865. The Bible Christians were attempting to build an alternative Methodist connexion. (UCA, P171GN)

would continue to contribute to the general mission fund. For its part, the missionary society agreed to continue annual grants until the Conference could become self-sufficient and to help with the accumulated debt.[27] Thus in 1855 the Wesleyan Methodist Conference of Eastern British America came into existence. The Conference was divided into the seven districts of Halifax, Saint John, Charlottetown, Fredericton, Sackville, Annapolis, and Newfoundland in order to respond more quickly and effectively to the difficulties and opportunities of the regional cause. Nevertheless, despite being better organized and led and with prospects for future prosperity, it was still a heavily dependent church that faced the challenges of the second half of the nineteenth century.

### THE SMALLER BRITISH CONNEXIONS

To return to the Canadas, clearly the Wesleyan and Methodist Episcopal churches had made impressive statistical and institutional strides during the first half of the century, particularly in Upper Canada. However, beginning in the 1820s, they had been faced by competition from splinter factions of British and American Methodists. During the first half of the century, three significant Methodist groups entered British North America from Britain – the New Connexion, Primitive Methodist, and Bible Christian churches – and two from the United States – the Methodist Protestant and the African Methodist Episcopal churches. In general, these connexions had emerged under circumstances peculiar to their country of origin, and except for first-generation immigrants, they held little appeal for Canadians. Serving settlers from a particular geographic region or with ethnic, economic, or racial similarities, overall they failed to transfer their initial rationale for existence to their adopted home. They remained isolated and, with one exception, were eventually forced to merge with the larger Methodist bodies in order to retain any vestige of their evangelical traditions. Such union was facilitated since "amid all the numerous secessions from the Wesleyan Methodist body in England, and the Episcopal Methodists of the United States, none have seceded on the ground of *doctrines* or church *ordinances*. In every instance, the seceding body has taken exception to the polity of the parent body."[28] With the gradual adoption of similar church polities in Canada, no real rationale remained to keep them apart.

Among these smaller Methodist denominations in the Canadas, the New Connexion began with the best chance of success. It was the first body to break away from British Wesleyanism. In 1796 William Thom and Alexander Kilham, two prominent Wesleyan itinerants, were expelled from the connexion for promoting discord over the status and polity of the church. The following year they established the New Connexion Methodist Church, centred in the Midlands and the industrial towns of northern England, with an initial strength of nearly 5,000 members.[29] In objecting to the continued subservience of the Wesleyans to the Church of England, it held its services at the same time as the Anglicans and permitted its ministry to administer the sacraments in its own places of worship. The New Connexion also attempted to break the so-called despotism of the clergy by instituting equal lay representation in all its courts and by permitting the local society a significant role in receiving and expelling members, electing local officers, and calling candidates for the itinerancy.[30] With only limited resources, it initially opted for intensive evangelization of the local region rather than attempting to spread across Britain, but the connexion grew only slowly on this narrow geographical base. One of the major problems was the large-scale emigration from the region during the post-Napoleonic period.

However, the church did send missionaries to Ireland beginning in 1824 and later attempted to serve its lost membership abroad. Prominent New Connexion laymen had advocated missions to the Canadas since 1820, but it was not until the fall of 1837 that John Addyman arrived in Lower Canada to scout the mission prospects.[31] Although he found only a few scattered former members, he began services in Montreal and the nearby Eastern Townships and, on the invitation of the local members of the Methodist Protestant Church, served their main Canadian circuit at Henrysburgh for the year.

The Methodist Protestant connexion was a weak offshoot of the American Methodist Protestant Church, which in 1832 had sent missionaries to serve the migration of New Englanders into the region. The parent body had split from the American Methodist Episcopal Church in 1830 after nearly fifteen years of unsuccessful lobbying to limit the power of the episcopacy and gain lay representation in the church courts. It was the controversy surrounding this movement that had helped delay the establishment of the independent Canadian Methodist Episcopal church until 1828. The Protestant Methodists replaced the episcopacy with an annually elected president and allowed equal lay and clerical representation in their Annual and General Conferences. Shortly after its creation, however, the church too was torn apart by the slavery controversy, and this issue helped drive the Canadian branch to form a partially independent conference in 1836. Consisting of six weak and disillusioned missions, it was severely limited by poor financial support and the political turmoil surrounding the Rebellions of 1837. The absence of American missionaries commended the New Connexion Addyman to the Protestant Methodist congregations. In 1838 he moved to Montreal and left his newly arrived colleague, James Hutchinson, to serve these isolated families. The following year, H.O. Crofts arrived to take over Montreal and allow Addyman to seek out better prospects in Upper Canada.[32]

He toured the upper province in 1840 and at the invitation of James Jackson, the only remaining strong leader among the Canadian Wesleyan Methodists (Ryanites), initiated union negotiations. The British New Connexion authorities were anxious to gain a foothold in the Canadas to promote their cause among immigrants from New Connexion households. They agreed to send missionaries, guarantee a minimum salary, support insolvent circuits, and open a school to train candidates for the ministry. They would also supply and pay for a general superintendent of missions who would supervise the expenditure of money and sit ex officio on the church's executive.[33]

To the Ryanites, the offer appeared providential. "Instead of falling into a state of anarchy or of becoming extinct as a church, we expect to become firmer as to our establishment and more decorous as to our economy."[34]

They desperately needed financial assistance since local contributions were insufficient to meet existing operating needs and the connexion was saddled with a considerable debt as a result of the failure of the denominational newspaper, the *Canadian Wesleyan*. Manpower support was also critical. Although the church had listed twenty-one itinerants and forty-two local preachers serving 2,481 members on thirteen circuits in 1835, there were only 1,915 members and a combined preaching staff of thirty-three by 1841. Over the intervening years, it had lost many of its most able leaders to the larger Methodist denominations. Moreover, it could ill afford to have the New Connexion as competitors in Upper Canada.

The discussions led to formal amalgamation in 1841 and the creation of the Canadian Wesleyan Methodist New Connexion Church, with Jackson as first president. He had emigrated from the United States as a young man sometime after the War of 1812 and become a probationer in the Methodist Episcopal church in 1817. Though energetic and evangelical, he lacked tact and discretion and would prove a mixed blessing for the New Connexion. There was some initial concern about the loss of autonomy and the suitableness of the British missionaries, but these fears were generally outweighed by the obvious benefits. In fact, the two churches amalgamated quickly and easily. Since the Ryanites had adopted equal lay representation in their church courts in 1829, there was no real difference in polity or doctrine or in the strong desire to maintain a liberal and popular balance of power between the ministry and the laity.[35]

In 1843 the eight weak New Connexion and Methodist Protestant circuits in Canada East also entered the new church. It was their only hope for sustaining their spiritual experiment as Protestant islands in a sea of Roman Catholicism. In reality, the union in both provinces was an absorption of the failing local operations by the British parent body. Although the president was elected in Canada, much of the dynamic leadership was provided by the missionaries from Britain and real power resided in the semi-permanent and financially independent missionary superintendent. John Addyman, as well as serving the prominent Hamilton circuit, held this post until his return to England in 1844. His fellow early missionary, H.O. Crofts, served as his successor until 1851. While both men were highly respected and personally influential, the weak financial base and the miserly contributions from Britain kept the connexion in a constant state of distress and subservience.[36]

In 1844 the New Connexion in the Canadas reported thirty-four itinerants, thirty-eight local preachers, and twenty-seven chapels on twenty-three circuits; the membership was 3,300. Part of this growth, however, was a reflection of the general revival of the early 1840s. Just as the new church was attempting to create an institutional infrastructure, much of this support evaporated. Simultaneously, the Millerite adventist movement made serious inroads into its membership. Although some growth was reported and important work commenced in the larger centres such as Toronto, its newspaper, the *Christian Messenger*, lasted less than a year and the proposed school failed to materialize.[37] Despite a deep commitment to the voluntary principle and the separation of church and state, the denomination failed to raise sufficient funds to build new chapels or even to pay minimum salaries to its itinerancy. British grants to debt-ridden circuits never made up the difference.

While the church gradually expanded into the southwestern sections of Canada West during the 1840s and 1850s, the faltering work in Canada East represented a serious liability to connexional resources. The congregation in Montreal was temporarily abandoned during the 1850s, and much of the work in the Eastern Townships was transferred to the Wesleyans. The connexion was also desperately short of suitable itinerants. Most of the native-born clergy were zealous but too poorly educated to be accepted by the more established congregations. According to the 1851 census, the New Connexion represented only .9 per cent of the 952,000 residents of Canada West and had no statistical presence elsewhere. In 1854 the church reported 4,034 members in Canada West and only 528 in Canada East. Despite its early links with indigenous Methodist groups, the New Connexion faced an uncertain future in British North America.[38]

Although the New Connexion had been the first to separate from the British Wesleyans, the Primitive Methodist connexion was the first of the splinter denominations to send missionaries to British North America. It had been formed in 1811 by the merger of supporters of Hugh Bourne and William Clowes. Both men were lay revivalists deeply affected by the camp-meeting evangelism of the American Lorenzo Dow.[39] Bourne had been converted to Methodism in 1799 and thereafter worked to convert his relatives and friends through earnest exhortation and cottage and field preaching. After witnessing Dow's success, he organized camp meetings in Staffordshire and Cheshire. In 1808 the Wesleyan Conference expelled him for disobeying its injunctions against camp meetings. To the Wesleyans, these meetings relied on excessive enthusiasm, which made them potential sources of sedition and political agitation. Their anarchistic and democratic features worried the conservative Wesleyan leadership, especially during the troubled period of the Napoleonic Wars.[40] After his expulsion, Bourne organized his followers into the Camp-Meeting Methodists and continued to arrange revivals near his home.

William Clowes had been converted from a life of self-confessed debauchery in 1805 during a revival at Tunstall, Staffordshire. Originally apprenticed as a potter, he left this trade to exhort in the Tunstall area and to organize camp meetings on the Dow and Bourne models. In 1810 he and his supporters were expelled by the Wesleyans, and the following year they merged with Bourne's supporters. Initially the new church, with a membership of about two hundred, was highly localized in north Staffordshire and the adjoining counties. At first hesitant to expand his preaching, after 1820 Clowes became a popular and influential evangelist throughout England.[41]

The use of the term "primitive" signified a return to a more basic, scriptural spirituality, which the connexion believed the Wesleyans had forsaken. Highly suspicious of the clergy, it even permitted the laity to administer the sacraments. The stress on a primitive scriptural church was carried over into a puritanical code of dress and behaviour and later to a strong advocacy of temperance.[42] The Primitive Methodist connexion was particularly popular among the industrial working class and agricultural labourers. These groups appreciated its simple, earnest, and spontaneous preaching, its colourful processions and lively services, and its open-air meetings led by working-class men and women.[43] The Primitive Methodists relied heavily on women preachers until a gradual professionalization of the clergy diminished their status and functions.

Bourne organized British-style camp meetings throughout England, but especially in Cornwall and Devon and across the Midlands. With 7,842 members in 1820, he could no longer effectively manage the cause, and a Conference was organized. Conference representation was based on two lay delegates for every ordained minister attending, although this policy was opposed by some who felt it over-represented the clergy. However, such representation did not mean that the Conference was democratic; in fact, a few prominent senior lay members shared power among themselves, with little real input from the general membership.[44]

In 1842, when both Clowes and Bourne retired, the connexion reported nearly 80,000 members, 500 travelling preachers, and 1,200 chapels. After their retirement, Conference assumed greater control from the local circuits, and a period of institutional restructuring occurred. The offices, book room, and executive of the newly created missionary committee moved from Hull to London in 1843 to improve administrative control. Overseas mission work, which had been managed by individual circuits, was transferred to the the missionary committee, and overall operations were established on more traditional connexional lines. As a predominantly working-class movement, however, the connexion was especially vulnerable to economic recession and emigration. It could ill afford weak overseas missions. "Beset by removals and rural depopulation on the one hand and the challenges of institutionalization, social reform, the rapid growth of towns and cities ... on the other, most of the Connexion's resources were devoted to domestic problems ... A movement strongly indigenous to England, it was unable to establish itself firmly outside its native soil."[45]

Despite these limitations, the connexion was anxious to promote the spiritual welfare of its emigrating members. In 1829 Hull and Tunstall circuits sent out four missionaries to New York and Pennsylvania. A mission in Upper Canada began in 1829 with the arrival at York (Toronto) of William Lawson. Originally a prominent merchant and local preacher near Brampton, England, he opened a clothing business and began preaching in the market at York in June that year. Later he rented space in a schoolhouse to hold services and meet with the embryonic society. He was soon joined in business and religious work by his former apprentice Robert Walker. Walker later became one of Toronto's wealthiest merchants and with Lawson the dominant force in Primitive Methodism in Canada. Tunstall circuit responded to their request for help by sending Nathaniel Watkins in August 1830. Energetic and enthusiastic, but nearly illiterate and a poor speaker, Watkins had formed three societies with eight local preachers and eighty-one members in the area around York by the time he left for the United States the following year.[46]

However, Lawson and Walker were disappointed with these results; they believed Upper Canada held a vast potential for Primitive Methodism. With proper preaching and financial support from England, they hoped to draw in the orphaned British Wesleyans and serve the large, unattached English and Protestant Irish immigrant population. Although the connexion was notoriously radical in England, the Primitive Methodist leadership in Upper Canada was a conservative, aspiring middle class, intensely loyal to the British crown. It opposed the politics of the Episcopal Methodists and believed the Wesleyans would be attracted by its English preachers. Former New Connexion and Bible Christians could also be won over because of the similarities in church polity. However, these hopes were never fulfilled, in part for reasons beyond the connexion's control and in part because of the slow and hesitant support from the British Primitive missionary society.[47]

With Watkins's departure, William Summersides left his station in the United States and came to York in 1831 to take over the work. Much more adept than his predecessor, he organized protracted meetings and love feasts and opened new preaching appointments in Peel and York counties. A year after his arrival, the supervision of the mission was transferred to the more powerful Hull circuit, and Bay Street chapel, seating nearly 600, was opened. With only 132 members spread across the region, the chapel and indeed the whole connexion was heavily in debt. But following the arrival of Joseph Partington and William Lyle from England in 1833, the expansion across Lake Ontario to the Niagara Peninsula, and the creation of a nearly self-supporting circuit around Brampton, it temporarily appeared as if the church would achieve its early expectations. By 1835 the denomination claimed 209 members on the Toronto circuit, including 93 in the city itself, 114 in or near Brampton, and 42 along the Niagara River, and it was expanding into Markham and Erin, northeast and northwest of Toronto.[48]

Partington and a number of local preachers soon quit the work, however, and preaching could no longer be sustained in Niagara or at many of the appointments around Toronto. As a result, there was little numerical growth during the remainder of the decade. With the 1833 union of Wesleyan and Episcopal Methodists and the arrival of African Methodist Episcopal, Bible Christian, and eventually New Connexion missionaries, the opportunities for large-scale accessions disappeared. Out of desperation, the connexion even flirted with the idea of joining the splinter Methodist Episcopal church in 1836. After Henry Jolley arrived in 1837, his evangelistic missions were initially disturbed by the turmoil surrounding the rebellions, and the following year Summersides left the country complaining of both weak local support and the open hostility of the Hull circuit in England. It was distressed at the inefficiency and laxity in the Canadian mission.[49] The 1830s were also marked by serious internal quarrels, and many demoralized members joined more stable churches.

Under pressure from England, the local connexion did tighten up its discipline, eliminate weak members and ineffective local preachers, and attempt to gain control over its expenditures. The Canadian societies constantly sought more financial support, but the British connexion urged greater efforts at self-sufficiency. As with all the Methodist missionary operations, the mother church was either unable or unwilling to provide the resources demanded by the local connexion. In 1840 the Primitive Methodists contemplated union with the newly separated Canadian Wesleyans in order to alleviate their financial problems.[50]

The 1840s, on the other hand, witnessed a modest reversal of fortunes. The decade began with a series of lively and popular protracted meetings which added over 200 members. "Profligate sinners were preached to their knees and then prayed to their feet again ... Communities were shaken as a forest in a gale; and the results of those awakenings were widespread, salutary and lasting."[51] Brampton became self-supporting, and mission operations again expanded into Niagara and the region around Toronto. With 663 members in 1842, the Canadian connexion was reorganized as a district with greater local administrative control. At its first district meeting in February 1843, a missionary committee and local executive were created, and Lawson was chosen secretary and Walker treasurer. The district had four circuits – Toronto, Brampton, Etobicoke, and Markham – five chapels, 906 members, and a substantial Sunday school population to act as a nursery for the connexion.[52]

Just as critical, the restructuring of the British Primitive Methodist church and especially the creation of a centralized missionary society presaged a period of greater support for overseas missions. Between 1843 and 1848, five new missionaries arrived to join Lyle and Jolley, and Hugh Bourne even visited the circuits over the winter of 1844–45. Jolley retired in 1845, but the connexion was by then drawing effective itinerants from its own Canadian ranks. Matthew Nicols and later James Edgar were particularly successful preachers and revivalists. Most of these ministers were too enthusiastic and unlettered to hold the better educated for the connexion. But at least with the increased numbers, the church was able to provide more regular preaching and to expand into southwestern Canada West and up to the Bruce Peninsula. In 1847 John Davison arrived as missionary superintendent; he would be the connexion's most eminent preacher until his retirement in 1866. He attempted, unsuccessfully, to publish a denominational newspaper, the *Evangelist*, in 1848 and again in 1851. He succeeded with the *Christian Journal* in 1858.[53]

Between 1853 and 1855, 12 new missionaries arrived from England, and the connexion expanded east to Kingston and consolidated its cause in the southwest. In 1854 it divided into Toronto and Hamilton districts in order to provide more immediate service, and with 35 itinerants, 151 local preachers, and 2,671 members (about 7,500 adherents) it organized a semi-autonomous Conference. The new optimism was perhaps best illustrated by the replacement in Toronto of the Bay Street chapel with a much larger structure on Alice Street.[54]

However, the connexion still had serious problems to face. Most of its new members were recent immigrants who were unable to contribute financially to the church or were revival converts who, as in other denominations, were an unreliable source of permanent support. Although it had the benefit of being narrowly confined in sections of the province, including in the relatively prosperous Toronto-centred region, the membership was widely scattered in these sections. These circumstances forced the creation of many small preaching appointments, which in turn limited effective pastoral super-vision. The conservative businessmen who financed much of the work were hesitant about subdividing these large circuits or expanding rapidly into new territories. As a result, members who moved away from Primitive Methodist strongholds were lost to the denomination. Although it was still optimistic, the connexion faced serious challenges if it was to sustain its evangelistic mis-sion in the second half of the nineteenth century.

The third of the new British Methodist groups in British North America was the Bible Christian connexion. Founded in 1815 by the lay revivalist William O'Bryan, it always considered itself a second awakening among the uncon-verted, rather than a schism within Wesleyanism. O'Bryan viewed himself as another Wesley or Whitefield arousing and revitalizing a forlorn society. The son of a prosperous Cornish farmer, he served as a Wesleyan local preacher in the Newquay region of his home county. Refusing to follow the established lo-cal preachers' plan, he ranged over the area exhorting, preaching, and form-ing new Wesleyan congregations, often where others had failed. In 1810, after being rejected as a candidate for the itinerancy because he was married, he was expelled for failing to abide by the Conference's instructions.[55]

O'Bryan was not deterred; he and his energetic and independent-minded wife, Catherine, began preaching successfully throughout Cornwall, and in 1814 he retired from his secular work to hold a series of revivals that strength-ened the local Wesleyan cause. Temporarily reinstated by the Wesleyans, he repeated his revival in the isolated and religiously neglected sections of west-ern Devon in 1815. However, he was again expelled for ignoring his regular appointments, and together with James Thorne, a recent convert from Angli-canism, he organized the Arminian Bible Christian Connexion along Meth-odist lines. On January 1, 1816, the new denomination convened its first quarterly meeting and formally commenced independent operations. After only a year, the Bible Christians reported 980 members and sixty-six local preachers in one large circuit spreading across Devon and Cornwall.[56] In 1819 the first Conference was established to advise O'Bryan, and with the as-sistance of a missionary society organized in 1821, the evangelistic crusade had spread to London and Kent by the mid-1820s.

However, a conflict between O'Bryan and the Conference weakened the internal unity of the church after 1825. He believed that, like Wesley, he was the final authority in all matters; Conference could only advise, not legislate. His views might not have posed a serious problem if he had been a better ad-ministrator. But while he could arouse and convert, he lacked the personal discipline and long-term commitment needed to provide pastoral oversight or to weld the members into an effective institution. After a prolonged series of disagreements, he finally withdrew with a small body of followers in 1829. Unable to keep even this group together, he was forced by circumstances to spend three years visiting former members in North America. In 1835 he and his remaining followers were reinstated in the Bible Christian church,[57] but he never again wielded significant power. Effective leadership remained with James Thorne, who had directed the church's development at least since O'Bryan's departure.

The Bible Christians shared a similar polity and outlook with the Primitive and New Connexion Methodists, stressing plain dress, ascetic behaviour, temperance, and a simple form of worship and, after 1829, allowing equal lay and clerical representation in all church courts. While the Primitives and New Connexion gained their converts mainly in the north and Midlands, the Bible Christians attempted to revive the south and west of England. Although apparenty complementary movements, they were in fact natural competitors for the same limited clientele and over the years, tended to restrict each other's ability to create a viable alternative to the Wesleyans.[58]

If anything, the Bible Christians were more extreme in their commitment to revivalism; they continued to rely heavily on protracted meetings and other extraordinary services long after these had declined in favour among other British Methodists. In addition to emphasizing the quest for entire sanctification, these revivals were often wildly enthusiastic, shocking even William Clowes when he attended. Dancing and shouting highlighted and disrupted the services, and O'Bryan himself often ran among the worshippers laughing, singing, and praying. Much of the conduct appeared to be closer to the old pagan Celtic festivals, a heritage shared by most Bible Christian adherents, than to appropriate Christian behaviour.[59] As a result, the Bible Christians were never really successful at expanding beyond their Devon-Cornwall constituency, with its closely knit, clannish traditions, its particular customs, and its isolating dialect.

The Bible Christians also encouraged and relied upon women to pursue active careers as itinerant preachers. Along with the Primitive Methodists, they expanded on a long tradition in Methodism of fostering female leadership. Catherine O'Bryan had been only the first of a virtual torrent of consecrated and efficacious Bible Christian women evangelists. The first Annual Conference in 1819 forcefully proclaimed the biblical and providential right of women to preach and listed fourteen, or 48 per cent, of the itinerants as women. In 1823 over one hundred women were serving in the local-preacher or itinerant ranks, and they were some of the most popular and compelling voices in the church. The careers of the dozens of able women in all the Methodist connexions were purposely masked during the nineteenth century in order to project an image of orthodoxy and respectability, and research has only recently begun to uncover their invaluable contributions to the evangelical revival. The status and numbers of itinerating and local women preachers gradually declined, but they did not totally disappear among the Bible Christians. By 1838 only 13 per cent of the itinerants were women, and lacking a vote in Conference, they fell prey to connexional discrimination. Often they ceased to travel after marriage, although they still maintained active careers in a more circumscribed field. Several of the most prominent, including Elizabeth Dart and Ann Vickery, emigrated with their missionary husbands and sustained successful evangelistic careers abroad.[60]

Closely associated with Bible Christian evangelism was the deep commitment to share in the mission to Christianize the world and especially to serve those of its own members who were emigrating to North America and later Australia. Although the connexion had only 6,650 members in 1831 and was still recovering from the O'Bryan schism two years earlier, the missionary society eagerly

responded to requests for ministers by sending Francis Metherall to Prince Edward Island and John Glass to Upper Canada. Beginning in the 1820s, a large
contingent of Bible Christian craftsmen and farmers had been working in the
lumber and shipbuilding industries and opening up farms in Prince Edward Island. Because they were relatively late arrivals with little financial backing and
preferred residing near relatives and friends from Devon and Cornwall, other
Bible Christians established a band of pocket settlements along the north shore
of Lake Ontario from Oshawa to Cobourg and into the back townships from
Lake Simcoe east through Peterborough to Madoc.[61] They too were involved in
the lumber industry while attempting to farm. Anxious to re-establish their familiar religious fellowship, they quickly organized prayer and class meetings
and appointed lay preachers. As with all the first connexional missionaries,
Glass and Metherall came to fields eager for their pastoral care.

This did not mean their task was easy; the new immigrants were still unsettled
and lacked the resources to support an itinerant clergy. The latter was also true
of the missionary society in England. Its paltry annual income of about £100
rarely covered the expenses of domestic missions, and little was available for
overseas work. Moreover, none of the Methodist parent organizations ever fully
appreciated the physical hardships or the expense involved in serving pioneer
fields. Goods cost substantially more, and the local income to pay itinerants was
limited and highly seasonal. As well, although a horse was considered a luxury
in Britain, it was an absolute necessity on the vast circuits of British America.
Most of the irritation and even hostility between Canadian and British personnel stemmed from the allocation of the inadequate financial resources.

Francis Metherall, after nine years' preaching experience in England, arrived in the isolated colony of Prince Edward Island in June 1832, ready to
serve the Bible Christian congregations. His first circuit was centred at Union
Road, about six miles from Charlottetown, but reached out nearly eighty
miles, with 46 registered in class.[62] The island presented many difficulties for
the settlers and preachers alike. Beyond its small size and limited economic
potential was the fact that the land was mostly owned by absentee landlords,
who offered only leasehold tenure to the inhabitants. According to Metherall,
although the island offered opportunities superior to England for the energetic and persevering poor, who, he might have added, were prepared to remain that way, it was unsuitable for the wealthy who wished to expand their
capital with a minimum of physical labour.[63] The poor Bible Christian immigrants, who were obliged to rent less desirable agricultural land or to work in
the unstable shipbuilding industry, were especially vulnerable to economic distress. These conditions precluded the formation of a strong, stable religious
fellowship.

In 1835 Metherall reported only 67 members, centred at Vernon River and
Wilmot Creek, but improvement was expected with the arrival of Philip James
that year. Even with the two men's energetic evangelizing, the constant reloca-
tion of converts and adherents to other parts of North America meant that
the connexion retained only about 120 members by the end of the decade.
The 1841 island census illustrates the difficulties facing the church. Of the inhabitants, 42.5 per cent were Roman Catholics, 31.5 Presbyterians, and 11.9

Anglicans. The census did not differentiate among the 7.1 per cent of the population who claimed to be Methodists, but the vast majority were British Wesleyans, who jealously guarded their own small accomplishments against this enthusiastic sect.[64]

Despite strong opposition, in the 1840s it did achieve some temporary and erratic growth. In 1842 and 1843, a significant revival beginning at Vernon River spread across the island arousing and converting several hundred. With a membership of 442 in 1845, the connexion tried to solidify its position by establishing a preaching station in Charlottetown, but the experiment failed and was abandoned. Without at least a presence in the only town of consequence and relying on unstable revival converts, the society began to decline after 1847. For instance, two years later it had only 207 members, seven missionaries, and twenty-three local preachers. The New London circuit reflected this weakness when it reported that "the past year has been one of labour and strife, accompanied with a loss of members, a falling off of our finances, chiefly by the heavy failure of our crops, and the almost total stagnation of trade."[65] When Metherall retired in 1856, there were only four itinerants and 357 members on seven weak missions. Although the new superintendent was able to build a church in Charlottetown the following year, its $5,000 cost placed the whole connexion in debt and necessitated the closing of several weak outlying appointments.[66] Some advances were made during the 1860s, but it was a gaunt and disheartened body that amalgamated with its Upper Canadian co-religionists in 1865. For the next twenty years, it would remain a serious imposition on the limited resources of the Bible Christian connexion in Canada.

The Bible Christian development in Upper Canada was only slightly more successful. John Glass had arrived in Cobourg in 1831, but after only a few months of discouraging labour, he opened a school and retired to the local-preacher ranks. Two years later, John Hicks Eynon and his new wife, the famous preacher Elizabeth Dart, commenced their extended careers in the province. Their first circuit began at Cobourg and involved a two-hundred-mile round trip through the surrounding region. They were both at work nearly constantly, exhorting, praying, and preaching to the dispersed cells of loyal Bible Christians.[67]

Elizabeth Eynon often fulfilled her popular and effective preaching excursions without her husband. One of the founders of the Bible Christian connexion in 1815, she had originally converted from the Church of England in 1811 at age nineteen, had itinerated in Britain until her marriage in 1833, and was recognized as perhaps the best Bible Christian missionary sent to Canada. There women were not listed officially as itinerants and were not allowed a salary, yet they were expected to combine their regular household and family duties with the many aspects of evangelism. Their labours are all the more impressive for these reasons. This tradition of service was shared by most of the preachers' wives. Elizabeth Eynon was later joined by her former itinerating colleague, Ann Vickery, who as Mrs Paul Robins travelled in Upper Canada from her arrival in 1846 until her untimely death in 1853. Earnest and dedicated, Ann Robins had converted to the Bible Christian church in

1819 at age nineteen and begun itinerating the following year. Even her marriage in 1831 and the subsequent birth of her two sons did not stop her from preaching.

Without the unstinting service of these women, the early Bible Christian mission could never have developed as well as it did. In 1865 the Bible Christian Conference reminded the members of their debt to this "noble band of women, whose hearts and lips God touched, before whose preaching the pride of intellect was humbled, mere status in Civil Society felt to be nothing ... and many thousands of redeemed ones brought into the fold of Christ."[68] A year later, the first Canadian Bible Christian Digest of Rules confirmed their status: "We believe that God in certain instances calls women as well as men to publish salvation to their fellow sinners; and seeing that in many cases the Almighty has sealed their ministrations by the conversion of souls ... [Conference] holds itself ready to enter into special arrangements with any sister of unquestionable piety and acceptable talents who may believe herself called of God to engage in this work."[69] None the less, regular female preaching gradually disappeared from the connexion as the desire for respectable standing in the community grew.

To return to the early years, even with the energetic preaching of the Eynons, only two chapels in the section around Cobourg were opened by 1836. John and Mary Kemeys arrived the following year to help, but only limited progress was made during the decade. The church faced stiff competition from the Wesleyans and the Episcopal Methodists and suffered as a result of the political upheaval surrounding the rebellions. Mass revival services were particularly difficult to arrange during this period, and in 1840 the church registered only 256 members. The following year an important milestone was reached when the connexion gained the right to hold property corporately, although it would not be able to solemnize marriages in the province until 1847.[70]

In 1843, after a series of protracted meetings and the arrival of more missionaries, prospects appeared to improve. The church encouraged Sunday schools at each appointment as a more reliable nursery than revivals for future members and to facilitate missionary operations. Encouraged by numerical expansion, between 1845 and 1847 it constructed twenty-four new chapels. But as was so often the case, the connexion had been overly optimistic and was left in financial trouble. It had added to its difficulties in 1846 by establishing societies in the relatively isolated Huron region north and west of London, where its missionaries had followed members from England, Prince Edward Island, and sections of old Ontario into newly opened territory.[71]

Given only 1,300 members, thirty chapels, eighty-eight local preachers, and fourteen itinerants divided among Cobourg, Bowmanville, and the new Huron district in 1849, prospects for a significant cause in the province were not promising. The Cobourg circuit alone reported that nearly thirty members had moved beyond the connexional boundaries; Peterborough circuit feared it could not sustain an appointment in town, though the rural appointments held good congregations; and Mariposa to the north announced, "In the past year we have experienced many vicissitudes which is often the case after revivals … Our money matters fell short of last year, as the times are oppressive, and the last harvest was unfavourable."[72]

However, with the return of better economic conditions, a careful husbanding of resources, and a new wave of revival converts, the connexion had become nearly self-sufficient by 1852. The Bible Christian authorities in Britain were anxious for the Canadian operation to pay for itself and to assist the weaker missions in Prince Edward Island and Wisconsin in the United States. But while providing support only grudgingly, they lectured the local connexion on the virtues of economy and self-reliance. The Canadian Bible Christians grew increasingly irritated by the detailed, though ineffectual control exercised from Britain,[73] and in 1855, with the consent of the British Conference, they organized the most nearly independent of all the British-oriented Methodist churches in the country. With twenty-one itinerants and one hundred and sixty local preachers to minister to 2,074 members, they felt sufficiently well established to administer their own affairs. The British church would still receive annual reports, would provide some funds and personnel, and could appoint a president in alternate years, although this official would normally be a minister residing in Canada.[74] Relations were to remain fraternal, rather than filial, for the following thirty years.

By mid-century, the Bible Christians were organized in two blocks in Upper Canada. The larger and more prosperous one remained the Oshawa-to-Belleville corridor with its back-country hinterland, and the newer one ran from Stratford to Goderich, especially in Perth and Huron counties. Both the strengths and limitations of the connexion were reflected in this pattern. The church could use its small resources within these restricted areas and thereby maintain an adequate presence among its members. Good relations among adherents and with the itinerants could be fostered relatively easily. The connexion remained a tightly knit community with transplanted regional and kinship ties, able to exhibit a collective vigour greater than its meagre membership suggested. These were valuable assets for a small body of enthusiastic converts in a strange and often hostile environment.[75]

But these characteristics also represented serious drawbacks for prosperity in a missionary church with regional and even continental ambitions. The same ties that bound new arrivals to a familiar and comfortable fellowship prevented a strong appeal to immigrants from other sections of Britain or especially to native-born Canadians. The connexion had great difficulty projecting a broad denominational vision to draw in a wider range of prospective members. Moreover, members who scattered beyond the connexional concentrations were lost to the church. Being so concentrated in particular regions, the connexion was also susceptible to local economic troubles, which limited its ability to provide services when they were most required. With only 5,700 adherents, representing less than .6 per cent of the Upper Canadian population in 1851, the Bible Christians, like the New Connexion and Primitive Methodists, were only weak and vulnerable religious experiments in pioneer British North America.[76]

In fact, all three splinter churches were suffering from the same problems. Highly concentrated, with only a small membership and weak financial support, they relied on new arrivals from Britain to provide their real growth. As their membership became naturalized, much of the rationale for their existence disappeared. Although their polity was more liberal than the Wesleyans in Britain and even the mainstream Methodist churches in the Canadas, a general remoulding of all the connexions by liberal political, economic, and social forces gradually blurred denominational lines. Since, at the same time, these churches were competing among themselves for the same relatively small number of potential converts, they never gained the size or stature to form an independent alternative in British North America. It was only a matter of time before they would have to merge with their Methodist co-religionists if they wished to share in the wider potentials for evangelism.

## SPLINTER CONNEXIONS FROM THE UNITED STATES

As well as the three small British denominations, there were two noteworthy English-speaking American Methodist connexions which entered British North America during the first half of the century. Strangely, these two connexions represented alien and largely unrecognized forces in Canadian church history. Despite the long and close links with the United States and with other American Methodists, Canadians only marginally noted their presence. This was at least partially due to the political and racial factors that underlay the two connexions' history.

The first of these churches was the Methodist Protestant connexion, which has already been discussed briefly. Hived off in the Eastern Townships among immigrating New Englanders, it made little impression upon native-born Canadians or immigrants from Britain. As migrations from the United States used other avenues of entry into the Canadas and as the region became increasingly French Canadian, the connexion succumbed to the disciplined Roman Catholic hostility and folded into the New Connexion or Wesleyan Methodist churches. Its separate existence had been warranted only by its indignation over American slavery and its liberal polity. Slavery never really interested Canadian Methodists, and the church's focus on American issues was anathema to nationalistic Canadians. Perhaps its only impact was to increase the awareness of these issues among the New Connexion, which remained relatively the most generous in dealing with former slaves fleeing to Canada. However, Methodist Protestants had little independent impact on the Canadian religious scene.

The second American splinter church was the British Methodist Episcopal connexion, an offshoot of the black African Methodist Episcopal Church in the United States, which continues to operate as a separate denomination in Canada to the present day. Although it answered a distinct need by serving a largely ostracized black clientele, it was substantially ignored by other Canadians. Originally, the Methodist evangelical revolution of the eighteenth century had been popular because it appeared to break the fetters of social conformity, as well as to promise universal salvation. Methodism forged a new equality in the quest for salvation, partially breaking down the old barriers of nationality, ethnicity, class, and race.[77] The evangelistic churches, especially the Baptists and Methodists, drew in the slaves and former slaves in the United States precisely because they offered freedom of worship and the potential for a transformed and emancipated community. The evangelicals held out at least liberation in the next world through personal salvation and earthly hope through self-esteem and self-help.[78]

It did not take long, however, for restrictive notions of race to divide the evangelical revolution. The southern United States gradually denied the commingling of the races in church and sometimes religion itself to slaves unless subservience was reinforced. Even the northern denominations evolved a habit of segregation while at the same time disapproving of specifically black churches. Nevertheless, beginning in the 1790s, a myriad of independent churches were created throughout the United States as much to provide a fellowship where blacks could worship freely and develop their own self-esteem as to satisfy the antipathy of whites.

One of the most important leaders in this movement to create black denominations was Richard Allen. Originally ordained into the Methodist Episcopal Church by Bishop Francis Asbury, he had travelled and preached widely to large and appreciative audiences of blacks and whites. He finally succumbed to social pressure and established the black Bethel congregation in Philadelphia. To support his ministerial duties, he also held a variety of secular occupations. In 1816 he was consecrated bishop of the newly created African Methodist Episcopal Church by a group of black ministers from several different denominations and independent congregations. Under Allen's leadership, the denomination succeeded in linking a variety of semi-independent Methodistic congregations and expanding the work among freed slaves in the northern states. It actively campaigned for social justice and the abolition of slavery. By the time of Allen's death in 1840, it had also organized missions in Haiti, the British West Indies, and the Canadas. It would later develop missions in the Maritimes and nearly take over the Methodist work among blacks in Bermuda.[79]

The entry of the denomination into British North America was an extension of its work with escaped slaves and free blacks in the northern states. Thousands had fled their former masters and were attempting to build new lives in the free states. Over the first half of the nineteenth century, as the numbers of blacks increased, many of the northern states passed restrictive "black codes" limiting their property and labour rights. For instance, in 1828 Ohio required blacks to post a bond of $500 to guarantee good behaviour. The prohibitive amount was really designed to prevent impoverished former slaves from settling and to force older black residents to emigrate. Southern legislation, supported by the federal government and a significant proportion of northern sentiment, made life precarious for runaway slaves and free blacks alike. As a result, a stream of ex-slaves crossed the border and settled in Upper Canada, especially at Niagara and east from Windsor. Others entered Nova Scotia and mingled with the existing community of native-born blacks in the province.[80] British North America had eliminated its own slavery relatively painlessly and had all but forgotten this chapter in its early history. Initially, it welcomed these refugees from American tyranny, and relief organizations developed to aid their economic, religious, and social integration.

The response of Canadian Methodists to the slavery issue was not particularly noteworthy. When the Methodist church officially noticed the question at all, it opposed slavery and in 1833 congratulated the British government for outlawing the practice in the British empire. With regard to slavery in the Unites States, Methodists generally joined their fellow citizens in arguing that despite its immorality, Canadians should not get involved in an internal American question. The only real condemnation among mainstream Methodists came from British Wesleyans, such as Ephraim Evans, who while editor, used the *Christian Guardian* to attack the institution and to call for assistance for blacks in the province. His actions reflected British, rather than Canadian concerns. After 1834 the Episcopal Methodists recorded and supported the sentiments of the Methodist Episcopal Church in the northern United States, and the New Connexion condemned the mistreatment of slaves and the evil of slavery, but these were far from central issues in their catalogue of social evils.[81]

Once blacks started arriving in Upper Canada and the stream soon grew into a flood with the ever more oppressive measures enacted in the United States, all the Methodist bodies attempted to provide religious services and to assist these poor refugees. In the Canadas, the Wesleyans were most active because of their size and resources, but the New Connexion was perhaps the most committed to the task. Usually these new members were integrated into the local circuits, where they may or may not have established distinct congregations depending on their numbers and location. For the most part the records do not distinguish between black and white membership. In 1835 the Halifax circuit did note some thirty-five black members, and in 1842 an "African chapel" was opened at Mount Pleasant near Liverpool, Nova Scotia.[82] With the financial assistance of blacks and whites in the United States, land was purchased for the new arrivals and other social and religious programs were devised. The most prominent was the internationally renowned Buxton Settlement in southwestern Canada West.

As numbers increased, so too did local hostility and racial discrimination. The blacks in Upper Canada soon after their arrival in the late 1820s requested black ministers with whom they were familiar, and the Methodist connexions were usually quite willing to leave the work to the American denominations. In 1834 a few African Methodist Episcopal ministers arrived and began organizing societies. Early statistics on the number of preachers and members are not available, but by 1838 they had become sufficiently numerous for Bishop Morris Brown to come from the United States to organize a Canada Conference. The work greatly expanded during the 1840s and particularly during the 1850s, when hostile American actions such as the passing of the Fugitive Slave Law of 1850 and the Dred Scott court decision inaugurated a vast wave of black migration. By 1860 there were an estimated 40,000 blacks in the Canadas.[83]

The Canada Conference felt disadvantaged by its ties to the American parent body, and in 1856, with that group's consent, it created the independent British Methodist Episcopal connexion at Chatham. Its adoption of the name "British" was to signify further its attempt to become a loyal, indigenous church in the

British colonies. In doctrine, discipline, and polity, it followed the American Methodist Episcopal Church. The same year William Nazrey, a former American African Methodist Episcopal bishop who had settled permanently in the province, was elected general superintendent of the new church.[84] The connexion developed a parallel role among the blacks of Nova Scotia; during the late eighteenth century, over 10 per cent of Methodists had been black. Many of these now looked to the British Methodist Episcopal connexion. For instance, the Halifax Wesleyan circuit in 1846 reported a significant decline in membership resulting "partly from the withdrawal of the great majority of our coloured members," who were being served by a black African Methodist Episcopal minister from the United States.[85] Despite the return to the United States of the vast majority of blacks during or immediately after the Civil War, the connexion has maintained a viable operation in Canada. It has remained proudly independent and resisted attempts to realign it with its American parent denomination. Its work has been supplemented on a more modest scale by the black African Methodist Episcopal Zion Church and the Wesleyan Methodist Connexion of America. As with all the splinter denominations of the first half of the nineteenth century, these churches wove their own spiritual experiments into the fabric of Canadian Methodism and into the Protestant vision for the nation.

# 6 Mass Evangelism before 1860

Revival was essential to the vital and creative existence of the Methodist church. Every service of worship, every private and social means of grace, every sermon, tract, or prayer was directed to this end. The quest for conversion and entire sanctification was unceasing and compelling; it justified all missionary activity and underlay every attempt to reform character and all ethical conduct. "Methodism was wholeheartedly a revival movement: it had been born of a revival; its churches grew through revivals; its ministers preached revival; its success was talked of in terms of revival. Sometimes, when most of those who were converted were the children of Methodist parents, the revival served to consolidate, but just as frequently it sought to break new territory and reach new pockets of population to achieve overall growth."[1]

In North America, revival was deeply rooted in the Protestant culture of the eighteenth century. In addition to the Methodist spiritual revolution, it had gained sway even in staunch New England Calvinism through the sermons and writings of Jonathan Edwards and his supporters. Their Great Awakening transformed traditional Calvinist theology and reinvigorated its Congregational, Presbyterian, and Baptist exponents. In so doing, it allied them with Methodists in the vast enterprise to evangelize the world.[2] Since the first Great Awakening and its religious aftermath deeply influenced Protestantism in the Maritime region of British North America and underlay the religious upbringing of many future Loyalist and post-Loyalist settlers, it established a critical foundation for Methodist and other evangelical missionary activities throughout the region. These people were highly susceptible to an Arminian-based preaching which offered an optimistic vision of humanity's ability to improve its own spirituality and gain immediate conversion in response to the anguish and frustration inherent in much Calvinist theology.[3] This was particularly true of new immigrants, who had already been forced to break political, religious, and cultural ties to their former homes.

Thus by the end of the eighteenth century, a fundamental transformation was occurring in Protestant religion in what is now Canada. Into a social environment defined by Anglican and orthodox Calvinist ideologies came a new trust in personal control, under God, of one's spiritual health and a deeper commitment to earnest religion. Whether individuals were members of well-established denominations or without previous religious belief, they joined with Methodists in the revival movement and either altered their religious affiliation or became active supporters of a personal, experiential spirituality within other evangelical churches. Inspired by the twin goals of converting and sanctifying the individual and spurring the community along the path of spiritual and ethical growth in order to achieve a post-millennial rule of Christ in the world, revivalism became one of the pre-eminent concerns of the nineteenth-century English-speaking world, and it redefined the very nature of religious expression.[4]

Although the search for personal growth in grace was constant, unfortunately, positive results were not always achieved. Religion, it seemed, could too easily stagnate into a dry formalism that enervated its evangelizing mission. Therefore the evangelical denominations, led by the Methodists, utilized extraordinary revival services of mass evangelism to invigorate and revitalize themselves. Confusion has sometimes developed over the term "revival" since it refers to a broad spiritual awakening in society and, as well, has come to denote the specific techniques of mass evangelism. These means of grace were required because religion did not progress uniformly. An extraordinary shock was periodically required to rekindle the spiritual intensity of the church; or as the Canadian Primitive Methodist itinerant and revivalist James Edgar claimed, "Since the dread eclipse which passed upon man in Eden brutalising his nature and devilising his soul, Revivals of Religion have been absolutely requisite ... Sinners are dead, the electric shocks and trumpet voices of Revivals burst the catacombs where they are immured under successive layers of 'trespasses and sins' and, through the agency of the Holy Spirit, impart unto them spiritual life."[5] Revivals, therefore, were essential to cleanse the church of meaningless ritual and stultifying cant, to strengthen personal regeneration, and to spread the gospel truths. During the first sixty years of the nineteenth century, these specialized elements of mass evangelism reached the peak of their influence. While still popular throughout the remainder of the century, revivals were essentially transformed or separated from the mainstream of Protestantism in Canada.

## CAMP AND PROTRACTED MEETINGS

Mass evangelism in nineteenth-century British North America normally took the form of either a "camp meeting" or a "protracted meeting." Camp meetings originated in Kentucky and Tennessee during the 1790s under the leadership of evangelical Baptist and Presbyterian clergy and were echoed by similar activities in the Delmarva peninsula (Delaware, Maryland, and Virginia) under Methodist auspices.[6] As their popularity spread north and east, their evangelistic techniques and fervour merged with the urban-centred revivalism of protracted meetings emanating from New England. The two forces combined most potently in the "burned-over" district of upstate New York.[7] During the first half of the nineteenth century, this region was scorched by wave after wave of revival fire and produced a variety of peculiar, experiential religious movements. Modified by these new surroundings, camp and protracted meetings entered the Canadas from New York while in the Maritimes protracted meetings arrived directly from New England or later in a further modified form from Britain. Although protracted meetings remained generally popular among all the evangelical denominations and they all developed versions of mass evengelism, only the Methodists continued to use camp meetings extensively in sections of British North America during the first half of the century.

Camp meetings were large, open-air gatherings lasting for several days. Under the control of leading local clergy, families and individuals travelled to a prearranged site and constructed a temporary village of tents encircling a preaching stand and a clearing containing rough benches. The Reverend Samuel Coate, himself a fervent preacher and camp-meeting promoter, attended one of the first camp meetings in New York State near Albany in June 1805. In a relatively long letter to Joseph Benson, a prominent English Wesleyan minister, he attempted to assess the phenomenon:

I attended a Camp meeting last June ... where there were visible displays of the power and presents of God ... Throughout, Bishops Asbury and Whatcoat, with the rest of the people, stayed on the ground the whole time ... constantly in the exercise of singing, praying and exhorting ... On the sabbath day the rain was measurably over, and the number that attended was computed to be about four Thousand ... a number protest to be converted, and a great many more to have the work deepened in their hearts ... A volume might be written to particularise every circumstance, however, it lasted upwards of three days, and upon the whole I believe great good was done. I impute the gracious effects of Camp Meetings partly to their novelty exciting different emotions in the mind – setting the passions afloat, and thereby rendering the heart more accessible – and partly to their nature, or continuance without intermission. The ears of the people being momently saluted with the sound of preaching, singing and prayer; at length they are under the influence of these exercises so much, that when you speak to them, they melt down like wax before the fire. It is not an uncommon thing for them to imagine they hear the same noise in the woods a week or a fortnight afterwards. We had many flaming Preachers at the Meeting, more filled with faith and the Holy Ghost.[8]

The success of this camp meeting induced the returning itinerants to organize their own meetings in Upper Canada. The first confirmed camp meeting took place at Hay Bay on the Bay of Quinte circuit in late September 1805. It was held on the property of Peter Huff, a member of one of the Palatine Loyalist families that had settled the area during the 1780s, in the true heartland of eighteenth-century Upper Canadian Methodism. Led by Nathan Bangs and supported by William Case and Henry Ryan, the two stationed itinerants on the circuit, the four-day meeting significantly revitalized the experiential faith of the estimated 2,500 who attended. The presence of the Holy Spirit, which was described as descending on the assembled worshippers like a "cloud of divine glory," was as vital as any miracles performed by Jesus in Israel. Many who attended were so spiritually aroused that they continued to seek redemption day and night without sleep. The camp meeting created a vast fellowship of earnest seekers after salvation and converted, sanctified, or strengthened many in their struggle to flee from the wrath to come. Although regular worship services, under the power of earnest preaching, had produced similar results on a small scale, nothing earlier could compare with the power of this meeting. Because of its success, such gatherings developed into regular adjuncts of Methodist services throughout the more populated sections of Upper Canada and became recognized as a providential gift sent to quicken the whole mission of the church.[9]

Over time the camp meeting assumed a regular and systematic character requiring elaborate preparations and regulations. For instance, John Carroll, a leading proponent of revivals, described the first camp meeting he attended. It was organized at Cummer's Mills just north of present-day Toronto in 1825. A week before the revival, volunteers erected a large board tent and preaching stand, slab seats were arranged across a gentle slope ringing the stand, and the whole encampment was surrounded by a high stockade. Finally, the site was cleared of brush, and arrangements were made for a supply of water and firewood. During the meetings and at night, guards would be stationed at the gates to keep out intruders.[10] This preparation was considered essential to promote an earnest, yet orderly, evangelistic gathering.

In Lower Canada, camp meetings never gained the same popularity. Initially, the local Methodist churches were probably too weak to sustain them, and the connexion had to fend off charges from Anglicans and Presbyterians of being dominated by irrational and ignorant enthusiasm. After the War of 1812, the British Wesleyans who took over the management of Methodist affairs generally opposed such uncontrolled and extravagant services. This opposition also prevailed among Wesleyans in the Atlantic provinces, where revivalistic energies were more muted and likely only to be directed into protracted meetings. Nevertheless, by the 1830s, camp meetings had taken on such a secure life of their own that they were even making their way into selective areas of Lower Canada. James Booth described the gathering at Odelltown in September 1835 in great detail since it was the first Wesleyan camp meeting ever held in the province. The site was a sugar maple bush. "Here a circle of 70 yards in circumference was formed, the under brush was cleared, and the leaves taken from the trees standing to within 12 feet from the ground, to admit of the erection of tents, and 4 fires built in fish jacks, elevated about 5 feet from the ground, and placed on the 4 corners of the range of seats in front of the stand, for the congregation, for lights during the night."[11]

The preachers' stand, built to accommodate twelve preachers and raised about five feet from the ground, was enclosed on three sides and covered by a board roof. There was also a large pew in front for a choir and a floored area for kneeling in prayer and receiving communion. The seating area contained rows of rough slab benches built along the incline of the hill to facilitate easy viewing and was divided by a central aisle to separate men and women. Several wooden tents, some 24 feet by 12 feet in size and containing a stove, were available for the campers. Others stayed in canvas tents or returned home after the evening service. A volunteer police force led by Methodist militia officers patrolled the grounds day and night and, under the jurisdiction of a local magistrate, enforced the laws of Lower Canada and the strict regulations of the camp ground. In fact, the property had been formally leased by the organizers so that they would be able to restrict trespassers if necessary.[12]

In the absence of large, permanent buildings, camp meetings were extremely valuable for assembling and evangelizing large crowds. Although most camp meetings were attended by only a few hundred, some attracted thousands. As the country became more settled and urban centres grew, larger buildings became available for year-round protracted meetings. Moreover, in the Maritimes and Lower Canada, where camp meetings were only rarely utilized during the first half of the nineteenth century, protracted meetings performed a similar and equally valuable revivalistic role in more conventional surroundings.[13]

As the name implies, protracted meetings involved an extended series of gatherings in a church or hall lasting a few days to several months. Although some continued without a break, most urban meetings gathered in the evenings to allow for the normal secular activities of those attending. These concentrated daily assemblies created a significantly pious and fervent climate. Despite the lack of isolation from outside distractions and the daily break in the program, a sense of shared experience was created. The commitment was partially sustained by visits from preachers to the penitent in their homes for individual spiritual nurturing. The protracted meeting was also more easily disciplined, and the leaders could at least partially control rowdyism, rampant enthusiasm, and extremes in theological experimentation. It therefore retained many of the best qualities of the camp meeting and had the added advantage of not being drastically affected by the weather.[14]

Because of the more respectable nature of protracted meetings, they were more widely accepted by British Wesleyans. For instance, Enoch Wood supported the protracted meeting as a providential and scriptural means of grace. While cautioning that it should be used sparingly so as not to displace regular church worship and should not be allowed to degenerate through "agitating excitements," he recognized its value in saving sinners.[15] Nevertheless, most British Wesleyans were more hesitant than Wood, who had become acclimatized to North American religious practices. In Britain the Wesleyans' experience with the splinter Methodist denominations made them wary of revivalistic innovations. Their extended services were more regular in organization, limited in scope, and restrained in nature. In addition, leadership remained more firmly in the hands of the ordained itinerants. In areas under Wesleyan jurisdiction, the British version, and not the American-style revival, was commonly used, especially up to the mid-1830s.[16]

### THE NATURE OF MASS EVANGELISM

However, all the manifestations of mass evangelism during the first half of the nineteenth century emphasized a simple, highly charged appeal to spiritual regeneration. Their goal was to awaken the dormant spirituality latent in all people. Much of the subtlety of John Wesley's theology was ignored. What remained was a highly subjective trust in experience based on a limited understanding of Scripture and a narrow definition of Methodist doctrine sustained by the strict obligations of his discipline. Revivals were occasions neither for theological debate nor for clarifying fine points of denominational orthodoxy; rather, they established absolutes to be obeyed. They were designed to force a personal rebirth and the growth to a purer religious condition. Through an individual's conviction of sin, humble repentance, and ethical reformation, the power of the corrupt world would be broken.

Camp and protracted meetings provided the occasion for the expansion of both the private and the social means of grace to serve the spiritual needs of society at large. The private means of grace, including prayer, hymn singing, and Scripture reading, were utilized on behalf of the sinner and penitent seeker after salvation. Individuals were isolated, even in this public setting, and personally assisted by the fervent prayers and exhortations of friends and neighbours. Moreover, the fellowship of public worship which bound Methodists into a tightly knit community of believers was shared through mass evangelism with the external world. The intimacy and discipline of the class meeting, the prayer meeting, and the love feast were now available to help regenerate both Methodist adherents and the wider public.[17] In fact, Methodism recognized these institutions of mass evangelism as the most appropriate means of stirring the larger society and of adapting the movement's eighteenth-century revival message to the requirements of nineteenth-century evangelism.

Without doubt, protracted and camp meetings offered opportunities to sustain traditional revivalism in a semi-official, yet distinct setting. "The camp meeting was a ritual reenactment of unities, openness, inclusiveness and flexibility that had characterized early American Methodism"[18] and helped to integrate the whole spectrum of linguistic, racial, and ethnic groups into a Protestant Canadian society. These institutions expanded the communal nature of Wesley's original revival to assist in fulfilling his mission to save the world. They became major instruments in evangelization and were especially critical in British North America, where church authority and the presence of regular church services were limited.

Mass evangelism achieved these results because it was particularly effective in creating an environment in which the individual could become sensitive to personal sinfulness and seek Christ's forgiveness. Although ultimately the battle had to be fought alone, the group could and did stimulate this decision.[19] Isolated from outside influences and temporal distractions and surrounded by friends either struggling for their own salvation or earnestly striving for mutual spiritual growth, all who attended experienced a powerful psychological pressure. Even those who had come for amusement or to disrupt the gathering were often drawn in and spiritually awakened. Through the repetition of singing, praying, preaching, and exhorting, the individual was forced consciously to accept or reject salvation. Over several days, or even weeks, the pressure became so intense that it was extremely difficult to deny God's grace in the presence of family and friends.

The psychological pressure was also heightened by the emotional release at these services. Emotionalism was a natural aspect of all evangelical religious worship, but revivals particularly emphasised deep emotional expression and earnest behaviour as the most consistent and legitimate bases for conversion. The key to the success of protracted or camp meetings was their ability to raise the audience to this emotional state; under the power of the Holy Spirit, it was difficult to avoid fervent enthusiasm. J. Wesley Johnston, an American evangelist, claimed, "He inspires, He arouses, He stimulates; He awakens the dormant energies, He stirs up the latent faculties, He creates zeal, He calls forth enthusiasm."[20] This emotional release often led to shouting and wailing, violent bodily shaking, or even fainting. However, occurrences which might appear fanatical to the sceptical observer were not to be questioned since they were the legitimate expression of the presence of the Holy Spirit. Opposition was accordingly dismissed as the imprudent criticism of the unsaved. James Watson, in his widely read book *Helps to Revivals of Religion*, answered these criticisms by maintaining "that, in the matter of spiritual manifestations, as there is a 'diversity of gifts,' we would set ourselves up as a judge of these extravagances, with very great caution."[21]

None the less, Methodist leaders were aware that extravagant, fanatical behaviour not only brought revivals into disrepute, but also undermined the credibility of the whole church. Normally, they tried to control or at least downplay such conduct. For example, Egerton Ryerson, in describing a protracted meeting at St Catharines claimed: "Disorder has been uniformly discountenanced and the extravagances of ignorant and ungoverned passion have been immediately corrected. Not a particle of enthusiasm appears to have entered into this work, nor to have received the least encouragement ... The consequence is that there has not been so much unintelligible noise ... but more deep feeling, more holy, heart-melting importunity, more ardent (not fiery) and persevering zeal, more settled and prevailing faith, more rational and sound conversions of sinners and more consistency and permanent building up of believers in the most holy faith."[22] The goal of directing enthusiasm to its proper ends and appointed times became increasingly important as Methodists centred their revivals in the larger towns and cities. But protracted and camp meetings illustrate the complex tension in Methodism between order and freedom, conformity and spontaneity.

In the search for order, revivals were carefully orchestrated and a rigid timetable was instituted, though not always followed. The spiritual quest remained spontaneous, but sermons, exhortations, hymns, and prayer followed each other in prescribed order. At camp meetings everyone rose at the same early hour, carried out private worship, and assembled punctually for the first public services of the day. Prayer and hymns were followed by powerful sermons, usually in the middle of the morning, the middle of the afternoon, and the late evening. Each sermon was followed by an earnest exhortation to seek God immediately and by long extempore prayers. Three or four ordained itinerants and a number of lay preachers, often under the direction of the presiding elder or district chairman, supervised the proceedings. Inspiring hymns, many later written specifically for such occasions, punctuated the meetings and helped the singers transcend their normally drab and lonely existence and reach out to a romantic vision of future grace. Hymns were also a useful means of refocusing the assembly and regaining order.[23] At the appropriate moment, the penitent were called forward, where they could be prayed for separately. The decision to move to the altar or the "penitents' bench" was often the most difficult one for individuals to take since it focused the attention of the whole gathering on those individuals. Once someone made this decision, however, it was hard for him or her not to continue on to a personal decision for Christ.

After this conversion experience, the "reborn" were usually interviewed by the revival leaders in order for the conversions to be authenticated and enumerated. Critics of revivals had long claimed that the conversions were transitory and the numbers wildly distorted. However, nearly every report about revivals makes it clear that the new converts were carefully examined and as much as possible, their change of heart verified. Detailed statistics were kept, and attempts were made to measure the increases in the surrounding congregations. Nevertheless, because of backsliding and the weak nature of many of the emotionally induced conversions, revival converts were not a reliable basis for long-term connexional growth. The significant declines in Methodist membership across British America after the great revivals of the early 1840s provide sufficient evidence.[24] However, often the conversions persisted long enough for new classes to be organized, new churches constructed, and more intensive ministry initiated. These in turn strengthened the institutional infrastructure and expanded the permanent base of operations in the community.

Critics also claimed that revivals were disorderly and rowdy. These characteristics were less true of protracted meetings, but camp meetings were indeed subject to lawlessness and both internal and external disruptions. Although Methodist reports normally discounted such disruptions, the general descriptions of camp meetings during the first half of the nineteenth century clearly emphasize the necessity of stockades and guards to prevent inappropriate conduct and keep out intruders. In their defence, it must be remembered that early camp and protracted meetings were not designed for the ardent churchgoer; rather, they were intended to transform the sinner. It was the drunken troublemaker or neighbourhood bully who represented the most celebrated "catch" at a revival.[25] To keep him or her out of the proceedings would remove a central purpose of the services. Revivals were not exclusive; they aimed at reshaping the entire community.

Revival services, especially camp meetings, also almost inadvertently provided other social benefits to the community. In an important sense, mass evangelism blended with the rhythm of national life and the social conventions of the times. Community projects, political questions, or aspects of moral and social reform often found their first public expression in the informal associations begun at revivals. Moreover, like barn-raisings and fall fairs, revivals permitted a social and recreational outlet, as well as a spiritual renewal. They provided an important opportunity for young people to meet in an appropriately controlled setting. Such opportunities were scarce and necessarily prized by those involved. Since entertainment was also rare, revivals

Lorenzo Dow (1777–1834). A key transitional figure in the development of professional evangelists. (Lorenzo Dow, *Complete Works*, frontispiece)

Grimsby Camp Meeting, 1859. (UCA, P2019N)

could be a source of healthy amusement, breaking the dull routine of every-day life. In general, they furnished a vital release from the isolation, frustration, and anxiety of pioneer existence.[26] In all, mass evangelism during the first sixty years of the nineteenth century answered a broad range of social and cultural, as well as religious, needs.

## THE PROFESSIONAL EVANGELIST

Camp and protracted meetings also permitted the elaboration of a new type of specialized ministry. While the great majority of revival services were led by regular itinerants, who despite a certain flair for such programs, were principally committed to the regular duties of a circuit, on occasion the church looked to professional evangelists for leadership. Whether these individuals were designated from within the connexion or were independent preachers, their gifts, skill, and training significantly improved the chances for large-scale success. Of equal importance, their example provided valuable guidance and publicity for the connexional programs. Professional revivalists redefined the functioning of mass evangelism and introduced valuable techniques for bringing the audience to a state of penitence and beyond. By their clear emphasis on a significant role for the laity, their denunciation of narrow denominationalism and Calvinistic exclusiveness, and their stress on social reform to advance Christ's dominion, they reaffirmed and extended the general attributes of revivalism in nineteenth-century society. Moreover, they infused mass evangelism with a new vitality and power. Although evangelical missionaries had brought the revival message to the unsaved population during the eighteenth century, the professional evangelist represented a substantially new model of preacher.

Most of these specialized revivalists also gave a particular voice to a new and highly controversial version of entire sanctification. "Entire sanctification," "holiness," and "Christian perfection" were synonymous terms for the central Wesleyan doctrine requiring converts to grow in grace until they achieved a complete love of God and humanity. Through private and public worship, maturing experience, right living, and good works, John Wesley believed that religious life might culminate in a second experience through which the believer achieved a state of complete earthly holiness. Although sliding back to damnation remained an ever-present possibility, this second peak of faith was a critical goal for aspiring Christians.[27] From its inception, Methodist revivalism had urged this journey on all converts, but it expected that very few would actually achieve this status and only after a long struggle. The critical element was the process, not the realization of a state of holiness. Nineteenth century revivalists significantly altered the understanding of this doctrine.

The first important evangelist for Methodism was Lorenzo Dow. He represented the transition from the old-style itinerating preacher to the nineteenth-century specialist in mass evangelism. Dow had been born in Connecticut in 1777 and at an early age had received what he believed was a vision from God instructing him to evangelize the world. Throughout his life, he relied on God's direct intervention to guide all his actions.[28] He began to exhort and preach at the age of sixteen, was ordained in the Methodist Episcopal Church in 1798, and by the end of the century had travelled throughout the United States, visited Upper Canada and the town of Quebec, and carried his evangelism to Britain. In 1802 he extended his mission from the Bay of Quinte to Cornwall in Upper Canada but had little permanent success.

Dow's real influence and lasting importance stemmed from his three tours of Britain in 1799, 1805, and 1818, when he introduced American-style camp and protracted meetings to British Protestants. He influenced the embryonic Primitive Methodist and Bible Christian connexions with his evangelistic message and techniques and thereby aggravated existing divisions within the Wesleyan societies. His anti-denominationalism, social-reform orientation, and reliance on a committed laity were generally unwelcome, but they did stimulate a minority to reassess their understanding of evangelical religion. Dow's emphasis on the need for entire sanctification among all converts and church members also reminded the British connexions of this previously somewhat neglected doctrine.[29]

He had intended to visit British North America in 1807. However, he claimed that God directed his path elsewhere, and it appears that he did not return until 1828, when he assisted at a camp meeting at Presqu'ile. By then he was nearly a spent force and he left the leadership to the regular itinerants. He died six years later. "Crazy" Dow was considered an extremely erratic, undisciplined, and eccentric character whose sickly constitution and wild appearance shocked many Methodists. Yet his preaching, writing, and especially his popularizing of the new techniques of mass evangelism stimulated future generations of evangelists in North America and Britain.[30]

Just as Lorenzo Dow represented the first generation of nineteenth-century evangelists, Charles Grandison Finney became the most influential systematizer of the phenomenon. Although born in Connecticut in 1792, he was raised in upstate New York, where he witnessed the first fires of revivalism burning across the region. He was licensed to preach in the Congregational Church in 1824, but was never satisfied with its orthodox Calvinism. During the 1820s and 1830s, he held a series of highly successful and widely publicized protracted meetings in the towns of upstate New York and in cities along the eastern seaboard. He merged the style and techniques of the camp meeting with a highly Arminianized version of Calvinism, which he presented to a diverse urban-centred audience.[31] For several years, he held pastorates in revival-oriented congregations in New York City, before accepting a professorship at Oberlin College in 1835. He became president of that institution in 1852 but continued to participate in revivals almost until his death in 1875.

Finney did not invent any specific revival methods. His importance rested rather on their systematic and comprehensive introduction through his meetings and particularly through his book *Lectures on Revivals*. First published in 1835, this source of inspiration and advice for those interested in developing a revival went through numerous editions and remained a standard evangelistic textbook until well into the twentieth century. It succinctly defined the major characteristics of revivalism and provided a ready guide for carrying out mass evangelism.[32] Finney's example also added an important measure of respectability both to the revival program and to the travelling evangelist.

Highly suspicious of the traditionally educated clergy, he used his position at Oberlin College to train generations of evangelistic ministers who were not bound by the Calvinist theories of predestination. "He helped to knock the last props from under the old Calvinist system and to establish in its place the Arminianized Calvinism called evangelicalism. In the process he firmly established a coherent rationale for the new tradition of worked-up revivals."[33] In helping to shape an evangelical consensus in American culture, he facilitated the cooperation of Calvinist and Wesleyan church members in the great mission to evangelize the corrupt world. "Denominational barriers continued to fall before a resurgent spirit of cooperation ... His encouragement of lay leadership, his openness to the ministry of women, his dissatisfaction with clerical professionalism and the state of seminary education, his disquiet with divisive sectarianism, his yearnings for holiness in his own life and in the lives of his converts, his distaste for the 'cannotism' of hyper-Calvinism, as he liked to call it, and his eager anticipation of the coming of God's millennial kingdom, all made him a rallying point around whom thousands of Christians could gather."[34]

Despite the fact that Finney was not a Methodist and never visited British North America, he had a major direct and indirect influence on early Canadian mass evangelism. This influence was particularly apparent in the new characteristics he helped to give to the doctrine of entire sanctification. His perfectionism differed from Wesley's in several important ways. To Wesley, entire sanctification meant perfect love of God and humankind; to Finney it signified a right will. According to him, sin was not caused by a depraved nature resulting from Adam's fall, but rather from a depravity of the will. Individuals had a free will, which gave them the ability to determine, under God, their own spiritual state.[35] People were depraved and therefore condemned to hell because they willed to sin, and conversely, if the will was right, then sin was not necessary. Mass evangelism helped the individual to set the will right. In consequence, the individual was not constrained by the necessity of extended right living or attendance on the social means of grace in order to achieve holiness at some future date. Complete holiness could be reached immediately after conversion through a second spiritual experience. "Since the will is free of any innate limitations on moral ability, persons can receive instantaneous power from Christ to will correctly."[36] In effect, Finney rejected both orthodox Calvinism and Wesley's teaching on the subject. This understanding of the nature of sanctification placed tremendous pressure on all revival preachers to push those attending camp and protracted meetings to this higher level of faith and experience.

In the same year that Finney published his *Lectures on Revivals*, Sarah Worrall received the blessing of complete holiness and organized a Tuesday women's meeting in New York City to promote holiness in others. Her ultimately more famous sister, Phoebe Worrall Palmer, attended these meetings and soon took over their leadership. Phoebe Palmer had been born in 1807 into a wealthy Methodist family and had married Dr Walter C. Palmer in 1827. From the time she experienced entire sanctification in 1837 until her death in 1874, she remained one of the most influential American revivalists and writers on mass evangelism and the nature of holiness.[37]

The "Tuesday meeting for the promotion of holiness" was extended to men in 1839. It quickly became "the center of Methodist perfectionism and spiritual feminism and the source of much of its social concern."[38] It was a model for similar gatherings around the world during the second half of the nineteenth century and influenced many of the Methodist ecclesiastical élite. By means of this weekly meeting, her preaching, and her writings, Palmer promoted the cause of revivalism both within and beyond the Methodist fellowship. Her talent, commitment, and money were critical elements in a renewed revivalism in the third quarter of the century, and she was particularly significant in fostering the "holiness movement" in North American Methodism.

The quest for entire sanctification was the fundamental doctrine of Palmer's evangelism. Unlike Finney, she was not inhibited by Calvinist reservations about the concept. Although she claimed that her understanding of holiness came originally from Wesley's writings and later Methodist theologians such as Adam Clarke and John Fletcher, she maintained that no evidence or authority beyond the clear biblical text was required.[39] In her seventeen books, numerous pamphlets, and most especially the pages of the magazine *Guide to Holiness*, which she published and sometimes edited, Palmer simplified and popularized the doctrine. She identified entire sanctification with a second blessing of the Holy Spirit, linked it to the achievement of personal power, and claimed it was the beginning, not the culmination, of a Christian life. She stressed the instantaneous reception of holiness, possibly immediately after conversion, rather than viewing it as a gradual process achieved near the end of one's life. Palmer reduced the gaining of holiness to a straightforward process of personal consecration to Christ, faith in God's power, and individual testimony as to the change of heart.[40] Although recognizing the importance of the striving for sanctification, most orthodox Canadian Methodists rejected her rather controversial easy road to holiness, and the doctrine would later exacerbate the split between mainstream Methodism and the holiness movement.

Nevertheless, based on the models and training provided by Dow, Finney, and Palmer, the professional evangelist became recognized as a vital auxiliary to mass evangelism. The first great revivalist to crusade extensively in British North America was James Caughey, and ironically, his first major mission was among the British Wesleyans in Lower Canada, who had been hostile to American-style revivalism. Caughey had been born in northern Ireland in 1810 but raised in New York State, where he entered the Episcopal Methodist ministry in 1834. The following year, he spent about three weeks assisting at protracted meetings in Montreal and Quebec City, and two years later he repeated his mission in those cities for about a month.[41]

However, Caughey's early fame in British North America rested on his extended mission of about ten months beginning in October 1840. After he announced that he had received a special call from God to evangelize Britain, the Methodist Episcopal Conference in June that year granted him a leave to visit Europe. He began his journey by travelling to Lower Canada and held services at La Prairie, St John's, and Montreal. Having gained only limited results, he was glad to accept an invitation from William Harvard, one of the few British Wesleyan itinerants who promoted revivals, to join him in protracted meetings in Quebec City. During his three-month stay, he finally gained the results he had anticipated.[42]

Caughey returned to Montreal at the end of January 1841. Typically, bowing to God's direction and his own commitment never to miss an opportunity to evangelize, he stopped on the way to hold services near Trois-Rivières, where "Within a few minutes of the conclusion of the discourse, an astonishing influence came down upon all present. Nothing was to be seen but weeping on every side. We fell upon our knees and poured out our souls to God ... I paced the floor on my knees, encouraging each trembling sinner to rely upon the atonement for the forgiveness of sins."[43] Completing his journey, Caughey repeated his success at St James Street Methodist church, one of the largest and most respectable Protestant churches in British North America. He hoped to carry the crusade to Kingston, but the weather was too inclement and the Montreal revival was going too well. At both Montreal and Quebec City, his largest meetings were held to assist the temperance cause. To Caughey, conversion and moral reform were inextricably intertwined.[44]

Considering that he and Harvard were ministering to British Wesleyans and that they were operating in the cautious political and religious atmosphere of Lower Canada shortly after the Rebellions of 1837, their mission was surprisingly successful. The early 1840s was a period of massive revival throughout British North America, and it is difficult to determine whether Caughey's crusade stimulated or merely shared in this wider movement. Nevertheless, he was careful to keep precise records, and these suggested that over 500 were converted and more than 120 placed on trial in Montreal congregations alone.[45] A large number also joined the other evangelical denominations. Of equal significance, the achievement was attributed to Caughey, the professional evangelist. Harvard reported in the Methodist press that "while the works of conversion and entire sanctification were both encouragingly going on among us, previously to the coming of our beloved brother; yet that the rapid and extended spread of that grace is mainly to be attributed to the blessing of God which has accompanied the impressive and evangelical ministry, and fervent and persevering toils in the prayer-meetings, of that honoured servant of God."[46]

With the conclusion of his meetings in Montreal, Caughey made a brief visit home before returning to hold services for two weeks in Quebec City. He then spent two weeks in Halifax, finally sailing to Britain in July 1841. His extensive revivals in Britain over the following few years were dramatic, yet contentious. Supporters were heavily involved in the Fly Sheet controversy, which, as previously noted, seriously divided the Wesleyan connexion and led to the expulsion of thousands of members.[47] Despite official opposition, Caughey did preach successfully, especially to Primitive Methodist congregations, and he gained a huge international following. By the time he returned to America, he was immensely popular and a major figure at subsequent camp and protracted meetings. His writings were also important in spreading the revival message throughout the English-speaking world.

Caughey visited the Canadas on several subsequent occasions. From Christmas 1852 until March 1853, he was in Kingston, where "1028 registered some special blessing."[48] From March until early July he laboured in Hamilton and was particularly influential among the Methodist clerical and lay leadership there. Under his guidance, 630 were converted from among those with no previous religious affiliation, 103 non-Methodists were also reborn, and over 400 were added to Methodist class meetings. During the same period, his revival in Toronto increased the membership to such an extent that Elm Street Methodist church had to be built to handle the crowds. John Carroll described Caughey's work: "we must also say that the original, searching and deeply spiritual preaching of our friend, clothed as it was by so rich an unction of the Spirit; and the influence of his name joined to what I may be allowed to call his admirable revival tactics, by which the official and praying members, and indeed the whole church, were enlisted, and their efforts directed in the work of saving souls, were the principal immediate means, under God, of this revival."[49] In 1853–54 Caughey again held meetings in Quebec City. In 1856 he evangelized Belleville and Brockville, where he remained "a burning and a shining light" converting hundreds and significantly increasing Methodist membership.[50]

He was also a powerful influence on the decision of young men such as William Parker, Henry Tew, and Nicholas Willoughby to enter the Methodist ministry and indirectly had a similar influence on Albert Carman, later bishop of the Methodist Episcopal church and general superintendent of the united Methodist connexion after 1884. As a young man, Nathanael Burwash, who would subsequently train generations of ministers at Victoria College, was also deeply affected by Caughey's preaching and particularly by his emphasis on entire sanctification. Burwash became a constant reader of the *Guide to Holiness*, to which his father subscribed, and "the conviction that cleansing from sin was the privilege and duty of every Christian became as deeply fixed in my soul as had been the conviction of the need for pardon in the past."[51] In fact, through Caughey's ministry, revival success was judged not only by the number of converts, but also by the extent to which entire sanctification was achieved. Indeed, even regular Methodist worship services increasingly stressed this goal.[52]

The doctrine of entire sanctification was particularly appealing to those who had grown up in a sound religious environment and were in search of a state of grace higher than that evident in the rest of the Protestant community. As well, many Methodists were suspicious of what they felt were only "half conversions" or immature religious experiences achieved by those reborn under the emotionalism and psychological tension of mass evangelism.[53] Following a revival, there was an apparently inevitable period of decline as large numbers of recent converts abandoned their elevated status and their commitment to organized religion. Revivalists believed – as it turned out, erroneously – that those experiencing the second blessing of holiness would retain their spirituality and not backslide.

After Caughey's triumphs, British North America became a fertile field for professional evangelists and a regular stage on their international tours. Walter and Phoebe Palmer especially became highly popular personalities at revivals in the territory throughout the third quarter of the nineteenth century. Although best known for their promotion of holiness, they also stressed feminism, humanitarianism, and social reform. Both supported a vital role for laymen and laywomen in preaching and ministering to the penitent. Like other evangelists, they also placed great importance on temperance and social improvement.[54]

In 1857 the Palmers carried out their most famous crusade in British North America. Travelling throughout the Maritimes and the Canadas, they were influential in converting and sanctifying thousands. Charles Ladner, a Maritime Methodist, recorded in his memoirs: "In the summer of 1857, Mr. W.C. Palmer, M.D., and his devoted wife Phoebe Palmer, of the City of New York, visited Nova Scotia, New Brunswick and P.E. Island to hold special services ... The holy spirit was pulled out. A large number of members of the Church came into the joyful experience of men and women filled with the Spirit ... [at Charlottetown] One thousand persons were reported by the Secretary as having been blessed in those services ... The city was never so moved and the Church brought up to a higher spiritual state. Out of this service, several young men went into the Ministry."[55] The Palmers also held large revivals in Hamilton, Oakville, and Toronto.

The publicity from this triumphant crusade has been credited with inspiring a massive revival in the United States and Britain the following year, although revivals had also been taking place in New England during 1857. Over a million people in the United States and a million and a half in Britain professed conversion in 1858.[56] Indeed, it was the greatest year in the nineteenth century for North American mass evangelism and the real culmination of the influence of traditional camp and protracted meetings in the Methodist connexions.

As well as the strict preaching of conversion and entire sanctification, the early effectiveness of the specialized evangelists was founded on what Carroll termed "admirable revival tactics." These men and women knew from training and experience how to draw in their audience, how to build up and sustain the emotional energy, and how to direct the penitent to that critical moment of decision. Often through their own personal prestige, they kept revivals from deteriorating into emotional chaos or being redirected by fervent members. Most evangelists had their own particular style of preaching and of focusing the spiritual proceedings. Their message was simple and straightforward, and their language generally plain, direct, and colloquial. They used any technique available to sell their message to their audience and maintain the novelty and freshness of the meeting.[57]

Revivalists were also expert at motivating and managing their lay and clerical associates. Much of their success depended on sound organization, detailed planning, and careful marshalling of resources. Despite the general autonomy of evangelists from denominational control, they were deeply indebted to the local congregations and to dedicated leadership in the community. Long before revival services began, buildings or camp grounds were secured, publicity arranged, and other preliminary arrangements made. Often beginning with special prayer meetings, the circle of people promoting the cause was systematically widened until a large proportion of the community was involved. The necessary authority and respectability was secured by the participation of the local clergy. Benjamin Slight, who studied revivalists, noted in his journal that the active cooperation of the "pious and working proportion of the church" was essential. "But where you have not co-operation by the church, one man, however earnest and desirous to save the souls of men, can do but little."[58] This cooperation was also essential for nurturing revived individuals both by visiting them during the revival and later by assisting them in regular church worship.

As the evangelists' success expanded, their message and techniques were broadcast throughout the continent and beyond. Articles, tracts, and books brought their work into thousands of households, and collections of their letters and sermons and their biographies inspired readers and spread the fame of the revivalist and the flame of revival. Of equal importance, the religious and secular press provided wide coverage of revivals. Few understood better than the independent professional evangelist how vital the popular press had become in assisting their mission. The leadership provided by evangelists and the impressions they made on the public in turn helped sustain connexional camp and protracted meetings throughout the country.

### THE IMPACT OF MASS EVANGELISM

On a wider level, mass evangelism had serious implications for Protestant Christianity. It challenged the established definition, organization, and operation of the traditional church and thereby redirected a transformed evangelicalism.[59] Central to this reordering of the church, revivals and especially professional revivalists stressed an active "clerical" role for the laity, including women, promoted anti-Calvinism and anti-denominationalism, advocated the creative reformation of society in the expectation of Christ's imminent post-millennial reign on earth, and gradually expanded the emphasis on immediate entire sanctification. Since many of these features were present in regular Methodist religious activities, mass evangelism did not represent a serious break with the past, and it fitted easily with the other social means of grace. However, camp and protracted meetings gave these features a much higher visibility and greater popularity among the general public.

In attempting to return to the essential characteristics of early Christianity, revivals reasserted the vital role of the laity in defending and expanding God's kingdom. Since the basis of ministry in the early Christian church had been God's "call," not selection by ecclesiastical authorities, any saved individual could legitimately prosecute God's work. It was not only a right but a duty to answer the summons, and no ecclesiastical body or even the individual involved could properly reject it. The real test of this call was the effectiveness of unordained preachers in bringing sinners to Christ: "How shall one person know and be able to determine and judge, whether it be the duty of another to preach or not? There are but three evidences ... 1st. Divine evidence in his own soul. 2nd. By the fruits of his labour. 3rd. The witness of his word with power."[60] These standards were not new; John Wesley had applied them to his early preachers. Moreover, some Methodists sincerely mistrusted the leadership of a trained clergy. Professional ministers could too easily be trapped in formality, irrelevant theological debates, and potentially even priestly despotism. Mass evangelism elevated earnest preaching based on a personal conversion experience and a knowledge of Scripture, and it could be carried out by a committed laity. The labour-intensive demands of these mass-evangelistic gatherings also made the laity essential for success.

Although preaching and exhorting were essential features of revivals, the actual breaking of Satan's grip was more readily accomplished on an individual basis. As the fire and enthusiasm of revival swept over the gathering, the preachers, both ordained and lay, sometimes lost control. Despite their best efforts, they could not prevent small pockets of believers separating off to pray and encourage individual penitents. Spontaneous hymns, shouts, and exaltations drowned out attempts to regain order. Under these conditions, it was the active laity, infused with the Holy Spirit, that claimed the right and obligation to carry forward the revival. Although the direction in which they took the spiritual outpouring was not necessarily that of the leader, they felt equally empowered to decide how to proceed. Sometimes these activities continued in the tents or homes of the distressed long after the regular services had ended for the day, and it was most often the converted or sanctified laity who presided on these occasions.[61]

Individual laymen and especially laywomen praying or exhorting one another in public offended some people's sense of decorum. But these activities both increased the effectiveness of revivals and expanded the sense of worth and influence of the laity in the broader work of the church. This success was particularly critical for women, who found important avenues of public service and prestige within camp and protracted meetings. They helped to break down stereotypical sex roles and linked precisely with women's expanding interest in moral and social reform.[62]

A called laity further weakened a Calvinist world-view that had already been placed on the defensive by the Great Awakening and the "new measures" advocated by nineteenth-century New England theologians and revivalists.[63] The essence of revivalism stood in stark contrast to perceptions of election and predestination and drew evangelical Protestants to an Arminian position which stressed the universality of God's saving grace. This freedom was not based on a totally free will since God initiated the process, but it did permit, if not demand, a more active participation in spiritual reformation and afforded a hope for immediate conversion and growth in grace.[64] The impact of this element in revivalism was so profound that as the nineteenth century progressed, it became increasingly difficult even for Calvinists to preach predestination, and its implications were either abandoned or ignored.

Paradoxically, mass evangelism also strengthened denominational growth and commitment while promoting a powerful sense of interdenominationalism and even anti-denominationalism. On one level, although protracted meetings were organized by various evangelical denominations, camp meetings in British North America became almost exclusively Methodist institutions. Methodism therefore received most of the credit and the numerical gains among those who supported camp meetings, but was obliged to bear the stigma of a coarse, fanatical sect from those who scoffed at the strange behaviour and questioned the validity of the salvation experience. Camp meetings were not only under general Methodist direction, but they were intimately connected with the regular work of the connexion and even semi-official branches of its denominational evangelism. They were closely associated with the church's ongoing fellowship and grew out of the regular circuit organization.[65]

As well, mass evangelistic campaigns were rarely spontaneous occurrences. God's miraculous intervention in the lives of sinners was not needed for revivals to occur. Indeed, revival was believed to be a natural event based on well-organized, cooperative action and "the result of a union of effort on the part of spiritually intensified individuals."[66] To have a triumphant revival, "the people should be publicly taught ... the congregation should be called together repeatedly and life and death set before them ... The pious portion of the congregation should engage in devout prayer ... that the spirit of awakening may run through the assembly like fire through dry stubble ... Those who are seeking the Lord sorrowing should be visited and instructed in the things of God."[67] Planning, piety, and determined action brought revival to the community.

Given the intimate connection between mass evangelism and the Methodist church during the first half of the nineteenth century, it was expected that revival converts would join the church that was instrumental in their rebirth. Studies of local congregations have shown that after a camp or protracted meeting, membership did rise dramatically, although it often subsequently declined to previous levels. However, numerical growth was not restricted to the Methodist connexions. Usually all the contiguous Protestant churches benefited numerically from the revival. This growth reflected the interdenominational appeal and character of revivals. Individual members from all the evangelical denominations and, more critically, those who disdained organized religion altogether, joined in the search for a new spiritual awareness, the conquering of animal passions, and ultimately the kingdom of God. Ministers from these different denominations often shared the preachers' stand and reaped the harvest of new members. "To place the camp meeting in the economy of Methodism is to remove it ... from its premier place in 'the great revival' ... and from its part in the production of an Evangelical ethos intended by Protestantism as a vehicle for the national establishment of Christianity."[68]

However, the interdenominationalism of mass evangelism went well beyond simply attracting new members for the participating churches. Traditional denominational loyalties were shattered and new patterns of ecclesiastical organization took their place. An anti-denominational mentality developed instead. Revival converts often refused to be bound formally to any church that they believed failed to exhibit a revival mentality. In being reborn as Christians, they were alienated from many mainstream religious ideologies. Loyalty was to an evangelical movement, not a specific communion. All Protestant churches had to come to terms with the implications of the revival message whether or not they subscribed to its principles.

Revival preachers frequently aggravated this situation by attacking institutional notions of the church and by refusing to be constrained by denominational norms. "Above all, they thought of themselves as instruments of the work of God, which was independent of all traditional forms of religious life. For that reason they insisted that the true church was invisible, except as it became visible in limited, tentative and purified form in the wake of their preaching."[69] Peter Bowslaugh, exhorting in broken English at a camp meeting in the Niagara Peninsula in 1827, claimed, "This religion is good and it is free to all ... Methodist God is the Baptist God and the Presbyterian God. Glory be his name."[70] To Bowslaugh, as to many others, denominational loyalties were secondary to experiential religion. Only the "great, central, saving truths" of Christianity were necessary and proper.

In weakening denominational loyalty, revivalism also released a myriad of countervailing forces during the nineteenth century. The Primitive Methodists and the Bible Christians were only two of a vast array of splinter churches and interest groups that emerged in Britain, all with their own particular perception of revivalism. Under the enthusiasm of revival, they could justify separation on the grounds of remaining true to vital evangelical principles. In fact, the conception of "church" was transformed from an institution based on dogmatically enforced membership to one which exalted voluntary association, although, ironically, discipline was usually made stronger than ever.

Revivalism also gave a higher visibility to what has been described as the shadow of progress.[71] A variety of apocalyptic groups emerged which condemned the entire notion of earthly progress and expected the imminent destruction of the world and the personal rule of Christ. It would be a mistake to designate groups such as the Millerites or Catholic Apostolics as churches in the traditional nineteenth-century understanding of that word, but they did build on the same theological and experiential ideologies as the evangelical revival and drew their support from the same clerical and lay clientele. They sought the conversion and sanctification of as many as possible before the end came. However, the mainstream churches, even those most influenced by mass evangelism, never subscribed to such adventist notions of the destruction of the world.[72] None the less, with the weakening of denominational loyalties and the increased association based on visionary beliefs, there was little to restrain these new movements.

These groups also diverged from the main thrust of mass evangelism in that they placed little or no value on society's ethical standards or on its moral reformation. For mainstream Methodism, camp and protracted meetings, as well as seeking to convert and possibly sanctify those in attendance, also strove to awaken a social conscience and to convince individuals to live better lives. After achieving a personal rebirth, the individual was obliged to grow in grace to a state of complete earthly holiness through the appointed means of the church, holy living, and good works. Christian charity and moral and ethical reformation were central elements in the progress to heaven. Allies from all churches, regardless of social or political differences, were welcome in the fight for a better community. This cooperative battle against evil was at least partially reflected in the creation of union Sunday schools and the broadly based temperance societies which characterized the revival-oriented, evangelical churches. Henry Pope described the results of a camp meeting: "The evidences of divine change are clear and scriptural; and their piety and zeal truly commendable. It is a most pleasing sight to see men long addicted to habits of inebriety, profane swearing, and Sabbath-breaking, now bending before the throne of sovereign grace."[73] Changed social behaviour furnished indisputable evidence of a changed heart, and moral conduct became a critical means of defining membership in the Methodist connexion.[74]

Paul Johnson in his study of the evangelical revival in Rochester, New York, summarized the socializing and reforming effects of mass evangelism: "In 1825, a northern businessman dominated his wife and children, worked irregular hours, consumed enormous amounts of alcohol, and seldom voted or went to church. Ten years later the same man went to church twice a week, treated his family with gentleness and love, drank nothing but water, worked steady hours and forced his employees to do the same ... and spent his spare time convincing others that if they organized their lives in similar ways, the world would be perfect."[75] Although this portrait is urban-centred and somewhat overdrawn, it certainly describes the social attributes sought by all forms of mass evangelism. Moreover, although campaigns for temperance and moral reform had originally been designed to control and restrain those likely to cause social and political turmoil, under the impetus of mass evangelism, reform became essential to liberate humanity from sin and to advance the postmillennial reign of Christ on earth.[76] The proponents of revivalism were highly optimistic that when individuals were changed, all social evil would be vanquished and the world would be truly transformed into Christ's earthly dominion. A favourite theme at revivals was the hope that each person would help convert one other, who would in turn do the same. Thus in only a few years the whole world would be Christ's.[77]

Methodists judged true success by the building up of church membership and the vitality of the Christian community. Connexional programs and institutions often received a vital boost from mass evangelism, and it provided a strong impetus for young men and women to dedicate their lives to Christian service. The ranks of the itinerancy and local preachers were filled with individuals who had been converted under the influence of camp and protracted meetings. In fact, all the Methodist connexions were heavily indebted to revivals for their substantial growth during the first sixty years of the nineteenth century.[78] Furthermore, revivals provided a common ground, helping to break down connexional barriers and promoting a common evangelical Protestant vision for British North America.

## 7 The Methodists and Native Peoples before 1860

By the mid-1850s Canadian Methodists optimistically proclaimed, "The two religious aspects of the nineteenth century are evangelical piety and missions."[1] With good reason, they believed the drive for emotional spirituality, social morality, and the expansion of missions around the world was well established. Although Methodism had centred its crusade on the European and American immigrants to British North America, it had also made significant gains in evangelizing the native population. The connexion was more anxious than ever to participate in bringing Christianity to the entire "heathen" world. However, while Africa and Asia beckoned, it was the native population northwest of the Great Lakes and along the Pacific coast that presented the natural field for Canadian Methodist missionary operations in the immediate future.[2] The church was confident it could meet this challenge because of the experience it had gained in Christianizing and civilizing the aborigines in the eastern half of the continent.

### THE FIRST CONTACTS

At the end of the eighteenth century, a host of widely dispersed bands of native peoples inhabited the eastern half of British North America. In Newfoundland a small number of Beothuks still isolated themselves from European contact in the interior. Some Inuit and Crees were present along the Labrador coast. In the Maritimes, three related tribes ranged across the region. The Micmacs were settled mainly along the coast from Nova Scotia to Gaspé, the Maliseets fished and hunted in the Saint John River valley, and the Abenakis lived in western New Brunswick. These peoples shared a similar Algonkian language and culture and were related to the larger Algonkian-speaking groups to the west.

Across the lower part of the Laurentian Shield, the main Algonkian peoples roamed as nomadic hunters and gatherers. The Algonquins, Ottawas, and further west, Ojibwas held loose, but unchallenged control from the mouth of the Ottawa River to west of Lake Superior. The greatest number and variety of aborigines resided south of the Shield in the fertile St Lawrence–Great Lakes lowlands. In Lower Canada, some Algonkian-speaking bands had settled in pockets among the French-Canadian settlers, but few of the original inhabitants remained.

Upper Canada was originally occupied by the Iroquoian-speaking Huron confederacy and by their allies, the Neutrals and Eries, in the southwest. More sedentary than their northern neighbours, they lived in large villages and raised crops. However, by the 1650s the Iroquois from south of the Great Lakes had nearly eradicated the Hurons and reduced their allies to submission. All the native tribes were also devastated by European diseases and commercial warfare. The Iroquois only marginally occupied the territory before Ojibwa and French forces finally drove them out by about 1700. The Ojibwas had gradually moved south following the destruction of Huronia and established themselves as masters of the region. Acquiring the local name Mississauga, they remained semi-nomadic hunters and gatherers. They scattered in small bands, especially along the shores of the lower Great Lakes, where the abundance of small rivers provided their staple diet of fish.[3]

This situation was complicated by the American Revolution and the succession of battles between American and native forces. After the defeat of the British, not only was Upper Canada invaded by thousands of American refugees and disbanded soldiers, but hundreds of loyal Iroquois moved north as well. They settled on reserves near Montreal, along the Bay of Quinte at Tyendinaga, and particularly along the Grand River north of Lake Erie. They were joined by refugee Delawares, Potawatomis, Pawnees, and other related peoples seeking to escape American expansion. The Iroquois and Mississaugas were traditional enemies, but they worked out an accommodation in the face of the common threat of European settlement and cultural hegemony and under pressure from the British government, which had promised protection from Americans and assistance to overcome the dislocation of their traditional economy.

Even after centuries of European contact with the native population, relations between the two groups were coloured by often contradictory and irrational perceptions of the aborigines.[4] For the most part, Canadians did not subscribe to extreme views; originally, the natives had been seen as valuable military allies to the French and later the British in the struggles with the region's southern neighbour and had been essential agents in economic expansion and the commercial development of the continent's fur resources. Because of the significance of these roles to both the European community in British North America and the British mercantile and defence systems, the imperial government had early recognized native ownership of the land and the desirability of providing annual gifts to maintain the friendship of the tribes. Nevertheless, British policy in this field was primarily designed to remove impediments to the white settlement of the country. This meant extinguishing native land claims as quickly and as cheaply as possible. As the value of the roles performed by the native people declined, so too did the esteem and sometimes fear in which they were held. With the diminished numbers and status, they became ready targets for exploitation and manipulation.

At the same time, even the most benevolent humanitarians were perplexed about how best to deal with the aboriginal population. If, as many so-called experts assumed, the native people were facing ultimate extinction, should white society simply insure that this road to oblivion was painless? Should natives be encouraged to adhere to their traditional way of life? Conversely, if they survived, how could their future be guaranteed and their existence improved? Should they be isolated from destructive contact with Europeans? Doing so could mean that the aborigines would continue their semi-nomadic existence in large, specially reserved territories free from exploitation and alcohol and untrammelled by alien culture; or they could be settled in independent communities under the positive and progressive influences of religion, education, and material improvement. In either case, the native population faced the prospect of dependence on public charity or government grants. The other option was for them to integrate gradually into the European society. The result might be personal independence and self-reliance, but their culture, heritage, and social cohesion would likely be destroyed and their collective rights abrogated.[5] All of these approaches were attempted by paternalistic church and state officials, generally without consulting the aborigines themselves, but all failed to resolve the problem of exploitation or the bitterness, and mistrust they felt.

Regardless of which strategy predominated, Methodist missionaries shared with nearly all members of Euro-Canadian society a powerful belief in the superiority of British culture and the Christian religion. Although sometimes critical of specific policies, "They did not challenge the concept that it was Britain's destiny to rule other lands."[6] Its political and economic system, along with its social, scientific, and technological progress, were considered immensely beneficial to native society. Methodists were also confident that Protestant Christianity would eliminate the destructive consequences of so-called pagan superstition both in this world and the next. The earthly plight of the natives was at least partially blamed on their non-Christian state, and their future happiness was considered in serious jeopardy. Missionaries implicitly accepted that Christianity was the only true religion and the only means for eternal life, and therefore specifically rejected notions that contact only debased the aboriginal society. Paganism was equated with the devil's dark realm. In converting the natives, the missionaries were assailing ignorance and false belief and truly enlarging God's earthly dominion, rather than merely proselytizing among supposed Christians of other churches. Such missionary work was the ultimate duty of Christians.[7]

Despite these beliefs, until the early nineteenth century, Methodists carried out only sporadic evangelism among the aboriginal peoples. For instance, although David Sawyer and Nathan Bangs preached to some isolated native families between 1801 and 1803, and others, including William Case, later preached to natives as circumstances arose, no concerted effort was attempted until well after the War of 1812 and these early, unsystematic approaches achieved little.[8] Most natives were still too sceptical of Christianity,

too secure in their own traditional spirituality, and too economically and socially independent to rush to a new god; their response did not justify much
optimism for Methodist success. Even those groups that appeared to be ex-
ceptions to this generalization were not unquestionably committed to Christianity. The Moravian Delawares on the Thames River at Fairfield had in fact
become increasingly hostile to religion because of their earlier mistreatment
by supposedly Christian Americans. Even the long-time Anglican Mohawks
under Joseph Brant along the Grand River received minimal pastoral care,
and the Methodists considered them only nominal Christians.[9]

In the Atlantic region, after disastrous initial contact, the Beothuks had
isolated themselves from all religious, cultural, and social intercourse with
the Europeans. Most of the Micmacs, Abenakis, and Maliseets in the Maritimes had become Roman Catholics during the French regime, but much of
the Catholic influence was removed by the British conquest. Despite concerted effort over the centuries in both Acadia and New France, the aborigines "were as yet imperfectly instructed and inclined to confuse Catholicism
with native belief and practice ... reversion to old ways seemed to be an ever-
present danger."[10] The Wesleyans in the Maritimes and Lower Canada were
too weak to undertake the evangelization of these peoples, and their chance
of success was bleak at best.

In general, little Protestant aboriginal missionary work was accomplished
before the end of the War of 1812. But the war itself did much to alter this situation. Especially in Upper Canada, it significantly accelerated the dissolution
of native society by destroying much of that society's economic base and undermining its internal cohesion and spiritual values. The contending armies
drove away the wildlife and devastated the hunting-grounds. In addition to
ravaging the native settlements, the fighting inflicted heavy casualties and
drove over two thousand destitute natives from the southwestern region of the
province to the Mississauga lands north and west of Lake Ontario. This over-
burdened territory was already unable to support adequately the local indigenous population. Devastated by disease and alcoholism and unable either to
sustain themselves through traditional economic activity or to merge into
white society, the natives were obliged to rely ever more heavily on meagre
government and charitable support.

Moreover, many of their important leaders and tribal elders had been
killed during the war. These deaths deprived the native people not only of
their natural leadership, but also of their spiritual knowledge and oral traditions. By the end of the war, traditional spiritual guides no longer seemed capable of maintaining their way of life or of firmly anchoring their society in its
natural surroundings. The local spirits had apparently fled the country in the
face of advancing white settlement, and even the Great Spirit appeared to be
inferior to the Christian God.[11] The result was a loss of pride and of the people's ability to preserve their social cohesion or their historic claims. They
were psychologically traumatized, and they seem to have lost confidence in
themselves as a people.

These problems accelerated in the aftermath of the war. The increased British immigration, with its insatiable appetite for land, hemmed in the aboriginal

people and forced the government to acquire and open up more territory for settlement. Hitherto the British Colonial Office, which had jurisdiction over the natives, had been concerned only with their pacification, maintaining their loyalty, and systematically acquiring their lands. Between 1783 and 1820 nearly all the land along the St Lawrence and the lower Great Lakes had been purchased. The corrupt, and inefficient local Indian Department was regarded as a sinecure by members of the provincial élite, and its officials did little to protect or improve native life. It merely distributed annuity payments while attempting to intimidate and stifle native initiative. Pioneer settlers rarely appreciated the native contribution to the preservation of British interests during the past conflicts with the United States and often begrudged any concessions to those they perceived as a drunken, indolent, slothful, sickly, violent, immoral, and beggarly people wandering indiscriminately over large tracts of arable land.[12]

In the Maritimes, the post–War of 1812 depression left the Methodist connexion with serious financial and organizational problems which continued to hamper any attempts to work with the native population. However, following the private philanthropic endeavours of individual Methodists, such as Walter Bromley in Halifax, to provide an education for young Micmacs, the British Wesleyan Missionary Society in 1816 urged its ministers to evangelize the natives. Despite this official interest, no specific missions were established and the work was never far-reaching or successful. As late as 1842, a government commission reported that the 1,400 natives in Nova Scotia had little or no land of their own and were being destroyed by alcohol, disease, and emigration. Although mostly Roman Catholic, they showed only a marginal understanding of Christianity and had merely a "faint hope" of becoming civilized. Almost nothing had been achieved by either church or state to ameliorate their condition. Three years later, another commission gave an equally bleak portrayal of conditions among the 600 Micmacs on Cape Breton Island. Their 12,000-acre reserve was generally infertile, yet white settlers were still encroaching upon it.[13]

Similarly, in Newfoundland, after highly publicized contact with a few Beothuks during the 1820s, the Wesleyan Missionary Society encouraged its missionaries to seek out and Christianize those remaining in the interior. Such opportunities never occurred. Because of the destructive effects of earlier meetings, the Beothuks were nearly unique in their avoidance of any contact with Europeans during the nineteenth century. They chose to isolate themselves away from the coast and gradually died out as a people. With expectations of greater success, the missionary society also instructed its Newfoundland workers to provide Christian services to the Crees and Inuit along the Labrador coast. During the summers of 1824 and 1825, first Thomas Hickson and then Richard Knight paid short visits to the seasonal fisheries and the small native population. A more permanent operation was launched in 1826 under George Ellidge, but it failed after only one season, and summer missions did not resume until 1845.[14] The Newfoundland connexion could not generate sufficient resources to maintain a viable mission in this harsh region. Besides, the ministers lacked expertise in dealing with native peoples. Without extensive language training, a sympathetic understanding of native culture, skilled native assistants, or even a deep commitment to the task, they could have little hope of converting these people to Methodism, especially since Moravian missionaries were already well established in Labrador.

Furthermore, throughout British North America there had been a substantial debate in Protestant church circles over the ability of aborigines to understand Christianity before they had acquired a mature European mindset and had reached a substantial level of civilization. In Upper Canada, William Case, the driving force behind establishing native missions, believed native survival and prosperity depended on the adoption of European habits and values. Although highly paternalistic, Case was deeply concerned for the welfare of natives and was convinced that they were capable of comprehending the complexities of Christianity even before they were transformed by secular European civilization. In fact, he argued that conversion was the critical first step to civilization.[15]

Case's view gradually became the accepted basis for Methodist evangelization. By the 1830s, James Evans, the rising luminary in native work, argued that "Christianity and civilization go hand in hand and Christianity is the elder sister ... the leaven of the gospel shall raise them out of the mire of paganism and ignorance."[16] According to the Canadian Wesleyan Conference, Christianity would "illuminate the rayless wigwam of the Indian with the Light of Life, and create around him the comforts and institutions of Christian civilization."[17] It represented the ultimate achievement. To the church, the natives' traditional existence appeared to offer nothing of lasting value either to the world at large or to natives themselves; quite properly, it was moribund and should be abandoned as quickly as possible. Comparing natives to the barbaric early Celts and Saxons, Methodist missionaries unhesitatingly assumed that progress required Christian civilization to transform aboriginal life. Once Christianized, the aboriginal peoples would become temperate, industrious, moral, educated subjects demanding the superior benefits of the British way of life.[18]

By about 1820, the Methodist establishment recognized that circumstances were finally appropriate for concerted action. Encouraged by the success of American Methodist missionaries among the Wyandots in Ohio and Upper Canada, the church began to assign a high priority to native evangelization, and the general membership was willing to supply the necessary financial support, at least in Upper Canada.[19] Initially, Case and his associates focused their hopes on converting the Iroquois bands along the Grand River. Because of their long association with British society both before and after the American Revolution, these people appeared to offer the best prospects for success. The Anglican Mohawks were the largest and most influential of the Iroquoian tribes in Canada, and Case trusted that with regular pastoral care they would enter the Methodist fold. Some Oneidas were also at least nominal Christians, and the Tuscaroras and branches of the Cayugas were becoming increasingly Europeanized. Only the Senecas, Onondagas, and some of the Cayugas appeared seriously hostile to Christian instruction. They were strongly influenced by the Longhouse religious revival originally espoused by Handsome Lake (Skanyadariyoh), the American Seneca prophet, who had attempted to reinvigorate traditional Iroquois culture and spirituality at the end of the eighteenth century.[20]

In 1822 the Genesee Conference of the Methodist Episcopal Church appointed Alvin Torry to the newly created Grand River mission with the responsibility of ministering jointly to the new settlers and the native population. As well as visiting the Mohawks and other Iroquois bands, Torry contacted the Moravian Delawares at Fairfield and other groups scattered throughout southwestern Upper Canada. However, most openly disdained his appeals; during his first season he failed to convert any to Methodism. He later recorded his initial reservations about his work: "I had received no particular instructions as to the manner of commencing or proceeding with my labor; and I doubt if there was a man in the Genesee Conference, excepting Br. Case, that believed the Indians, in their pagan state, as we now found them, could be Christianized; and I am sure my brethren in Canada did not believe I would succeed in my work. Their theory was, 'First civilize, then Christianize.' "[21]

Fortunately, by early 1823 Torry was able to make some headway. He used the home of Chief Thomas Davis (Tehowagherengaraghkwen) and Davisville, the village developing around his farm, as the centre of the mission. Davis, a cousin of Joseph Brant, had risen to the rank of war chief while fighting for the British during the American Revolution and the War of 1812. Tall, dignified, and a natural orator, he was the leader of a Mohawk band located a few miles from Brantford and was highly influential in tribal councils. In attempting to gain a more profound personal religious understanding, the Anglican Davis read the Scriptures to his neighbours and held services in his home. He became dissatisfied with the infrequent and highly structured religious worship provided by the Church of England and its relatively lax attitude regarding liquor and invited the Methodists to minister to his people. In the summer of 1823, he was spiritually reborn and joined the Methodist connexion. For the rest of his life he remained a vital link to the native bands in the region. Many who were curious about Christianity came to reside in the community. In 1824 the first native Methodist church was erected at Davisville; it served as a school during the week.[22]

During the summer of 1823, Torry had been joined by Seth Crawford, a licensed exhorter from Saratoga, New York, and Edmund Stoney, an Irish-born local preacher. Crawford was determined to assist in the conversion of the Mohawks and received Davis's permission to reside on the reserve in order to learn the language and run the day school and Methodist Sunday school for Mohawk youth. He did much to raise the band's respect for Methodism. Stoney travelled throughout the region either alone or with Torry or later with native preachers, encouraging a personal commitment to evangelical religion.[23]

Despite Davis's significance, the real blossoming of Methodist native evangelization began with the conversion of the Mississauga Kahkewaquonaby, better known as Peter Jones. Jones's mother was Tuhbenahneequay, daughter of the chief of a Mississauga band whose hunting-ground extended from the Credit River west to Burlington Bay. His father was a prosperous Welsh-born Loyalist named Augustus Jones, who worked as a government surveyor. Following native custom, Augustus was also married to Sara Tekharihogen of the

Mohawks. After Peter's birth in 1802, Augustus severed his relations with Peter's mother, although he continued to maintain an interest in the welfare of Peter and his older brother, John. The two boys were raised by their mother until 1816, when they joined their father's Mohawk household, first near Stoney Creek and later at his extensive holdings near Brantford. There they gained a decent primary education, learned farming and other artisan skills, and more important, learned to function in Canadian society. Although Peter chose never to return to his early nomadic way of life, he remained comfortable in both worlds. Devout, intelligent, and industrious, he retained the respect and even admiration of both communities.[24]

In the spring of 1823, Peter travelled to Davisville in the hope of gaining greater religious understanding. Torry and Case had organized a camp meeting in Ancaster Township near the reserve for early June and anticipated widespread native participation. Iroquois attendance was disappointing, but both Peter Jones and his half-sister Mary (Polly), the daughter of Sarah Tekharihogen, were converted. This event ushered in a new era in Methodist relations with native people. Mary provided the Methodists with additional prestige among the Mohawks and was later able to promote the status of her brother and other native Christian leaders while working herself to convert the Iroquois. More important, however, Peter was among the first and by far the most promising Mississauga to join the Methodist Episcopal church. As Case observed, "Glory to God ... now is the door opened for the work of conversion among his nation!"[25] Here was a critical first step; Jones, it was hoped, would eloquently explain one society to the other.

### CHRISTIANIZING AND CIVILIZING THE NATIVE POPULATION

Although the detailed Methodist strategy for native missions would evolve over time, the essentials had been established by 1821 when the Genesee Conference had organized a committee on Indian affairs with William Case as its leading voice.[26] Random baptizing of the wandering tribes had had its value, but to effect long-term transformation, it was vital to establish in-depth pastoral care, provide moral guidance, and break the hold of traditional native culture. Therefore the missionaries, especially after the conversion of Peter Jones and Chief Davis, introduced not only Christianity but also a completely new social system.

To these missionaries and many responsible native leaders as well, alcohol was the greatest deterrent to social and economic progress. It was the root of poverty, disease, accidental death, immorality, and outbursts of "savage passions." Many chiefs turned to Methodism because of its strong stand on abstinence. In turn, abstinence became an important component of right living and a verification of a responsible conversion experience among native people. It was partly in response to petitions from the Methodist bands that the provincial legislature in 1841 prohibited the sale or gift of liquor to natives.[27]

The Methodist missionaries also wanted the natives to give up their semi-nomadic existence and settle permanently in rural communities. They assumed that natives could never develop a viable society until they took up specific tracts of land, lived in proper houses, and created at least an embryonic village structure. Farming or working at a trade would provide substantial economic alternatives to their subsistence living, and with the accumulation of wealth, they would be less vulnerable to scarcity of game, exploitation, or malicious government policies.[28] A settled community would also be better able to police and discipline itself, keep liquor away, and prevent incursions by undesirable elements. Of equal importance, the debilitating, paganizing influence of forest life, along with the immorality associated by Methodist missionaries with the long hunting and fishing excursions, would be reduced. Also, Christian religious and educational facilities could be properly established.

As part of this civilizing process, the natives were expected to forsake their traditional communal living arrangements and reside as nuclear families in separate houses. This change was considered essential for the establishment of moral and respectable family life. The native family was to provide the same discipline, nurture, and religious training as the best British households and to become the central element in social development and spiritual progress. To achieve this, the traditional roles and relations among men, women, and children were to be transformed to imitate a balanced, patriarchal, European-style system. The father firmly ruled, yet he was expected to perform former woman's work such as chopping wood, carrying loads, and tending crops. Mothers were expected to remain at home performing household chores and caring for the young. The old practice of allowing children unbridled liberty was no longer acceptable; they must be deferential and industrious. This model of family life was considered a critical element of civilized behaviour.[29]

Converts were also expected to follow British courtship and marriage practices. Arranged marriages with gifts to the bride's family were discouraged. Mixed marriages *à la façon du pays*, or according to tribal custom without the benefit of clergy, were attacked as sinful. Christian society condemned the ease with which native marriages could end by the simple declaration of divorce by the husband and commanded Christian natives to maintain monogamous arrangements. While early Methodist ministers understood and even sympathized with the social and economic rationale for polygamy, they nevertheless insisted that all but the first wife be sent away. A man could continue to support the children from the former marriages, but any ongoing liaison with former wives was forbidden.[30] One clear indication of backsliding was renewing a relationship with a former spouse.

Native women also had a reputation for loose morals, at least partially the result of traditional marriage customs. Many were considered little better than prostitutes, and most received little courtesy or respect from white society.[31] Molestation and sexual abuse, particularly at the hands of Europeans, was a common occurrence, and while all women were poorly protected, native women were particularly vulnerable to male aggression. Christian marriage represented a shield of virtue for women and a guarantee to the community of high moral standards. Methodist missionaries made the protection of this institution a high priority.

Christianity instituted other important social and cultural changes in aboriginal society. When baptized, natives received a Christian first name and often a surname. Sometimes the last name was simply a modified version or translation of the aboriginal designation, but often it was adopted from some supportive European. Children assumed their father's surname, and descent then followed the patrilineal pattern. In some instances, this practice differed significantly from native custom and affected familial links of status and power. The adoption of anglicized names, especially when combined with European dress, became signs to the Canadian community that Christian civilization was actually taking hold.[32]

However, these changes were only preliminary to the more difficult task of inculcating industry, self-reliance, and personal pride. The missionaries strove to train their new charges to fit into the commercial and industrial nineteenth century. Agrarian society of the time was obliged to undergo similar training in order to survive in the changing economic and social conditions and, even with its cultural head start, found the transformation difficult. For North America's natives, the transition was often extremely traumatic. Not only were they required to learn basic cottage-industrial and domestic skills, but they had to adopt an entirely new mind-set. They would have to sell their goods and services for a profit and accumulate private wealth, both concepts alien to native culture.[33]

Equally important, they had to adopt modern European technology and agricultural practices in order to develop an independent farming community. More than simply learning how to plough, plant, and harvest, farming involved the acceptance of disciplined work habits and the notion of private ownership. Unlike in European society, where wealth was traditionally based on a settled and tight personal control of land, for the semi-nomadic North American native population, specific areas were generally important only because they were the particular home of a deity or were valuable sites for fishing, hunting, or trading. Since these locations represented the benevolence of the gods to the entire population, they could not be monopolized, and certainly not owned, by one individual. Similarly, while hunting-grounds were defended against intrusion by outsiders, these territories were open to all members of the local band. White society rarely appreciated the intimate links between the natural environment and native spirituality; it could see only a primitive animism which limited the ability to exploit the rich potential of the land and thereby progress economically. Natives had to abandon the old belief that land was for the use of the entire band and actually belonged to no one.[34]

However, the Methodist missionaries hoped that this economic process would not occur before their charges understood its implications. The distribution of individual freehold land presented enticing opportunities for unscrupulous land speculators to cheat the natives of their rightful property. Most missionaries and certainly the government officials in charge believed that private control of land had to be delayed until the natives were sufficiently acculturated to avoid these destructive results. Some Indian Department officials hoped this day would never come since it would eliminate their control of native resources. Nevertheless, the Methodists believed it was best to isolate native communities from negative outside influences while gradually introducing positive ones. In this way, a settled native agrarian society would have time to establish a viable strategy for advancement.[35]

Once again, the natives were never consulted about these assumptions. "Notions of freedom of conscience were not broad enough ... to allow for any serious consideration of the view that native people might be allowed to remain indefinitely outside the Christian sphere."[36] For their part, some natives mistrusted Christianity because it had failed to improve corrupt members of white society or to remedy drunkenness, disease, and immorality among so-called Christian natives. More instinctively, however, they believed that the Christian God only protected Europeans. If natives abandoned their traditional gods, they feared they would be left without supernatural assistance on earth and shut out of both heavens after death.[37] The Methodist missionaries were only partially successful in dispelling this fear, although they continued to assume that once the wisdom of Christianity was made known, old superstitions and fears would fade away.

At the same time, the natives of Upper Canada were not merely passive recipients of Christian civilization. They generally recognized both the positive and the negative implications of the social transformation presented by the missionaries. While most native leaders acknowledged that some change was inevitable and even essential, the revival of traditional forms of spirituality remained a popular alternative to Christianity during the first half of the nineteenth century. Shamans, especially in more isolated districts, were often quite successful in rebuilding native culture and resisting missionary initiatives. Sometimes these men and women integrated compatible elements from Christianity in order to expand the effective dimensions of their teachings. Even those who voluntarily accepted Christianity often followed only those practices which were compatible with their old understanding of God and nature. They were praying to their old gods in new, more effective ways.[38]

Yet there was a gradual recognition that Christianity did have value in preserving the integrity of native communities, in distancing alcohol and other immoral influences, and in enlarging spiritual prosperity. Many natives believed that social change must be undergirded by a strong religious base. Christianity also offered important temporal benefits for its native adherents. Although natives lacked real power, after two hundred years of dealing with Europeans, they were hardly the "simple children of the forest" characterized by paternalistic church and government officials. Native leaders recognized that Christians had easier access to government and private largesse and could develop more beneficial relations with the dominant society. The missionaries were also important allies, both locally and in Britain, where real decisions were made, in protecting native interests. While not necessarily comprehending why Christianity was divided into so many contending groups, the natives soon realized that they could select the branch most appealing to their social and spiritual requirements. They assessed the churches for their access to power and their commitment to aboriginal rights, as well as for their religious message. They assumed that their Christian status and religious alliances would increase their economic position. These benefits enabled Christian natives to expand their influence within their local bands. Respect and power had long resided with those best able to answer tribal needs, and by the 1820s these needs centred on the problems and opportunities created by white society.[39]

Meanwhile, in attempting to evangelize the native population, the Methodist missionaries believed that until the natives became fluent in English, it was essential to preach and to provide texts in their own languages. They therefore gave a high priority to attracting able young natives as teachers, interpreters, and preachers. These individuals might even take on the delicate task of translating the Bible. The missionaries assumed that the ultimate achievement of Christian civilization would quickly follow. Given this goal, the conversion of Peter Jones appeared providential. Recognizing Jones's leadership qualities, Case took it upon himself to make the young man a superior evangelist and translator.

Soon after his conversion, Jones was instrumental in converting several Credit Valley Mississaugas visiting Davisville, many of whom were his own relatives. He opened a small school on his father's farm, taught Sunday school, and exhorted at Davisville, where he helped to build the Methodist chapel. He also assisted Torry and Stoney with their preaching, participated in missionary tours of the province, and was responsible for spiritual improvement among the Delawares on the Thames River.[40] Soon after, he visited the Mississaugas near Burlington and at the Credit River, later reporting, "the work began in a powerful manner among the river Credit Indians who, previous to their conversion were in a most wretched and forlorn state."[41] Through Methodist ministrations, liquor was eliminated and the band members became model Christians.

In 1824 the Methodist Episcopal Church in Canada reported 56 native members, and a year later the number had risen to 104. Observers noted that they were "sober, pious persons, giving up their old habits of vice; and instead of the lazy, filthy, drunken savage, they were now clean – somewhat industrious, deeply pious and orderly."[42] Jones continued to fulfil Case's expectations by assisting in the conversion of a Mississauga band near Belleville in early 1826 and especially by convincing others, including Peter Jacobs (Pahtahsega) and John Sunday (Shawundais), to undertake careers as interpreters and preachers. Jacobs had been born in about 1807 near Rice Lake, and after his conversion, he translated and preached intermittently during the 1830s. He later served in the Hudson's Bay territories, but was finally expelled from the Methodist connexion in 1858 because of a drinking problem and failure to follow the instructions of the Missionary Society. He settled at Rama, where he taught school and acted as an interpreter until his death in 1890. Two of his sons became missionaries for the Church of England. John Sunday was about twelve years older than Jacobs and as a young man had fought for the British during the War of 1812. He took a leadership role in the development of native missions and remained firm in his faith and service until his death in 1875 at Alderville.

Almost from the beginning, long-term success in evangelization depended on the development of an effective core of native preachers and teachers. Beginning with Jones, who was finally ordained in 1829 after two years as a probationer, several young Mississaugas and Mohawks entered the Methodist ministry. By 1830 there were seventeen native teachers, interpreters, and church workers and over the following decade the number rose to nearly fifty.[43] John Sunday and Moses Walker were ordained in 1836, and later Henry Bird Steinhauer, Peter Jacobs, Allen Salt, William Herkimer, William Beaver, Abraham Sickles, and a host of other ordained and lay preachers, exhorters, teachers, and translators spread Methodism across Upper Canada, into the American west, and eventually throughout the vast northwest beyond the Great Lakes. These men were effective not only because they spoke the native languages, but also because they shared the cultural and spiritual heritage of their clientele. They were able to place Christianity in a relevant mythological context. By linking it to traditional beliefs, they made it comprehensible, gave it power, and convinced the natives that this religion was not restricted to Europeans.[44]

With the availability of dedicated, trustworthy, and moderately educated native workers, Case and the other missionary authorities could proceed more rapidly with the translation of the Scriptures, hymns, and notable Methodist writings. Case did not speak any native tongue and therefore relied on his younger colleagues to perform the task. Not only was it essential for evangelization, but Jones believed that language was an essential guard against complete assimilation. It was critical for the accurate expression of native spirituality and for the preservation of cultural identity.

Originally, selections from the New Testament had been translated and published in a crude phonetical Mohawk, but after Jones's conversion and the rapid expansion of work among the Mississaugas, translation focused on supplying accurate Ojibwa texts.[45] Methodist hymns were extraordinarily valuable in awakening Christian experience. Jones commenced this labour almost immediately after joining the Methodists and spent much of his spare time for the remainder of his life expanding the corpus of sources in the Ojibwa language. John Sunday, Peter Jacobs, and several other native workers also contributed to this program. Together these texts markedly quickened the influence of Christianity and furnished a vital resource and an enduring legacy for native people.

Native Christian workers were also essential in raising funds for the perennially overextended mission operations. Nearly every circuit was visited annually both to increase the profile of the work and to raise the money needed to sustain and extend it. Although Case and other missionary spokesmen were successful, native preachers were much more effective. Jones recorded in his journal that the audience at Ernestown was so large and exuberant he was obliged to preach outside in February, and this experience was not extraordinary. The preachers' confessions of faith and urgent pleas for their pagan brethren made a profound impression upon the local congregations and resulted in large contributions. Although women converts were not used for this purpose, they were among the most effective at organizing fund-raising activities for missions.[46]

Native preachers were especially valuable during fund-raising tours of the United States and, after 1830, Britain. Until 1828 the missions had been under the general direction of the American Methodist Episcopal Church, and Americans generously promoted the Canadian work. The American missionary society provided an annual grant and supported the special fund-raising campaigns carried out by Case and his associates. For instance, George Playter described the trip to New York City in 1828: "The Society had yearly given an allowance to the Upper Canada mission, and the benevolent of the city had contributed privately, especially last year to the Grape Island settlement ... John Sunday, from Grape Island, rose and in the Chippewa Tongue described the wonderful work of God to his people ... though the congregation understood not a word, yet his gestures, expressions of countenance, energy and appeals to heaven ... so indicated ... the sincerity of his religion ... that sighs were heard and tears seen in every part of the crowded church."[47]

With the formal independence of the Canada Conference in 1828, funds were less readily available from the United States, although native missions continued to expand at an unprecedented rate. Some funds had earlier come from Britain, and increasingly this source was looked to to rescue the mission operations. In 1831 Peter Jones and John Ryerson undertook the first of many extended tours there. The British Wesleyan Missionary Society initially opposed this intrusion and later used it as an excuse to send missionaries to Upper Canada. As noted earlier, the need for financial assistance for missions was a significant factor in the union of Wesleyan and Episcopal Methodist forces in 1833, and the disposal of missionary funds contributed to the split in the church in Upper Canada between 1840 and 1847. In any event, after the 1833 union, Canadian preachers received a cordial welcome in Britain. Jones was deeply impressed by that country, and his preaching caused a great sensation. He and Sunday were even presented at court during the 1830s, and their tours greatly increased moral and financial support for both the missionary cause and for aboriginal rights in general.[48]

As well as these church functions, native workers performed vital leadership roles within their own society. In 1825, for instance, Jones led the Christian Mississaugas at the government present-giving ceremonies at the Humber River near York. They startled the Indian agent, Colonel James Givens, and Archdeacon John Strachan by their well-ordered deportment. Strachan took the opportunity to suggest that Jones's band from Davisville should join with the other Christian Mississaugas in a permanent settlement on the banks of the Credit River.

After the War of 1812, the British Colonial Office and its Upper Canadian administration had begun to re-evaluate existing policies toward native peoples. In Britain, church and humanitarian leaders had been highly critical of the government for not promoting Christian civilization among its subject peoples. The officials in charge also recognized that much of the heavy financial burden of annuity payments and gifts could be removed if the aboriginal peoples were assimilated into the prevailing Canadian cultural and economic systems. Sir Peregrine Maitland, the lieutenant-governor of Upper Canada from 1818 to 1828, was a devout Christian, deeply concerned about the welfare of the natives. In 1820 he proposed that the government supply houses in settlements on specific reserves when the bands ended their semi-nomadic existence. When Strachan met Jones in 1825, he felt the time had finally arrived to implement Maitland's settlement policy, and he also hoped to influence Peter and John Jones to lead their band into the Church of England. Colonel Givens promised to have twenty-five acres on the river flats ploughed and to erect twenty cabins on the adjoining western embankment about three kilometres north of Lake Ontario.[49]

For his part, Peter Jones was eager for the Mississaugas to secure clear title to their hereditary Credit valley lands. He was convinced that only through permanent settlement and the acceptance of Christian civilization could the extermination of his people be avoided. The 4,000-acre site on the Credit was an excellent location for the mission reserve. The valley had long served as a convenient meeting place for the Mississaugas, and with its fertile soil, large salmon run, and excellent harbour, it would provide a good base for prosperity. The Mississaugas therefore accepted the government's offer. In April 1826 Jones and some companions laid out village lots, and the cabins were erected by the autumn. With the assistance of the young probationer Egerton Ryerson, more land was cultivated and a church and school opened. These projects were paid for from funds collected both locally and in the United States. Peter and John Jones were elected chiefs of the Credit band in recognition of their successful negotiations with the government and the leadership they had exhibited in establishing the reserve. This signal honour for such young men reflected the cultural revolution overtaking Mississauga society.[50] None the less, the Jones brothers were unable to secure clear title for the Credit lands, and this failure would ultimately lead to major problems.

While Peter Jones was usually absent encouraging the local Mississaugas to move to the mission or touring the province to gain new converts, John led the Methodist class meeting, assisted with the church services, and taught the male students at the school. In 1826 the Credit mission reported 110 members, and it reached its peak membership of 140 three years later. By that time nearly all the neighbouring Mississaugas had been baptized and now shared the benefits of the settlement.[51]

At the Credit, as at all subsequent native missions, much of the most important religious and educational work was performed by the female teachers. John Jones's first wife, a granddaughter of Joseph Brant, taught the girls until her untimely death, and his second wife carried on this work. Single women and missionary wives worked largely unheralded wherever Methodist schools operated. While the men and boys learned farming, carpentry, and other cottage-industry skills, girls and women were taught to spin, knit, sew, make baskets, manage a European-style household, and read and write. Since they served as guardians of the home, their acceptance of these aspects of Christian civilization was deemed essential for real change to occur in native culture.

The sober, devout, and prosperous Credit mission, with its neat village, cultivated fields, and healthy livestock, impressed visitors with the progress possible through Christian civilization. It remained the hub of Methodist mission operations for over a decade and furnished a vital training ground for both new Methodist missionaries and the expanding corps of native workers. In various ways, therefore, the Credit mission became a model community,

allowing the Mississaugas to remain a distinct society while gradually adopting the way of life of their neighbours.[52]

Deeply gratified by the mission's impressive results, Case worked to extend
the number of model communities. With the financial assistance of local
Methodists, he leased the eleven-acre Grape Island in Lake Ontario about
ten kilometres from Belleville to create an agricultural mission for the area's
native converts and moved to the new village in 1827. It consisted of twenty-
three cabins, a church and missionary residence, a school, a hospital, a general store, and blacksmith's and mechanic's shops. Construction costs were
paid from funds raised by Case and Jones and particularly from the private
New England Company. A stream of dedicated European and native teachers, including Case's wife, educated and trained the inhabitants. Case, Jones,
and John Sunday used Grape Island as their headquarters when they were
not at the Credit or on missionary tours.[53]

Although Case had expected that the isolated setting would permit easier
progress and avoid overly rapid or destructive contact with outside forces, in
fact, the site was recognized as a mistake almost from the beginning. Grape Island was too small for the number of inhabitants, and even when the fifty-acre
Huff's Island was used for grazing cattle, it was impossible to develop a viable
agricultural base. Methodist membership fluctuated from about 90 to 120 until 1831, but declined steadily thereafter. Grape Island was finally abandoned
in 1837, when the mission moved to Alderville in Alnwick Township on the
south side of Rice Lake.[54] Fortunately, the trust deed for the new reserve was
held by the New England Company and the residents could not be forced by
the government to move. Although the Grape Island mission ultimately failed,
while it existed, it too provided an important showcase for Methodist evangelization and native assimilation, and it trained several important church workers
and native community leaders.

The fame of the Methodist settlements spread across the province and
reached into the United States and the territory north of the Great Lakes.
Nearly everywhere that the native workers and their ordained brethren trav-
elled, the Christian message found an inquisitive audience. By 1827 the
church reported large and attentive congregations and a native membership
of 572.[55] New missions were opened for the Mohawks at Tyendinaga on the
Bay of Quinte, the Mississaugas south of Lake Simcoe, in the southwest near
Amherstburg, and at Rice Lake north of Cobourg. The region from Lake
Scugog to Rice and Mud lakes was the hunting-ground for several hundred
Mississaugas under Chief Paudash; nearly a third of the band was converted
*en masse* after visiting a camp meeting associated with the 1826 Methodist
Annual Conference held near Cobourg. Jones, Sunday, and Peter Jacobs
preached and explained the rudiments of Christianity to them in their own
language, while Case and other ministers encouraged them to make a personal religious commitment. Paudash was attracted to Methodism as a means
for the band to escape the reactionary teachings of traditional shamans while
at the same time breaking the destructive grip of the whisky traders.[56]

Beginning in 1826, Jones, Sunday, and missionaries such as Egerton Ryerson also paid several visits to the Mississaugas living south of Lake Simcoe. As

William Case (1780–1855). Presiding Elder in Upper-Canadian Methodism and founder of the mission operations among the aboriginal population.

James Evans (1801–1846). Celebrated linguist who headed the Wesleyan missions in the Hudson's Bay Territories, 1840–1845.

Peter Jones (Kahkewaquonaby) (1802–56). Mississauga chief and first native Methodist itinerant. (Victoria University Library)

Sketch of Credit Mission, Upper Canada. (UCA, P627N)

settlement moved steadily up Yonge Street, these bands gradually retreated north, settling on islands in Lake Simcoe and Lake Couchiching, at the narrows between these two lakes where Orillia now stands, and west to Coldwater and Penetang. During the late 1820s, many Ojibwa also moved into this region from north of Lake Huron, and others crossed from the Michigan territory to escape the American invasion of their homelands. By 1828 nearly four hundred, including Chief Yellowhead, had joined the Methodist Episcopal church, and Methodist schools had opened at Coldwater and on Yellowhead's island.[57]

In addition to the use of native preachers and a ministry that travelled to the natives, to a substantial degree Methodist success rested on the demand it made for a momentous, personal conversion experience and a profound commitment to Christ. The Methodist camp meetings, with their highly emotional release of spiritual energy, struck an especially receptive chord among the Ojibwa and Iroquois. The forest setting, the similarity to traditional religious festivals, the mutual prayer, the powerful, uplifting hymns, and the creation of an often overwhelming psychological pressure were reminiscent of native quests for contact with the spirit world and the formation of a new persona. At camp meetings, the essence of Christianity seemed to come alive. As well, outdoor services were less intimidating; it was easier to make Christianity appealing there than in the alien and uncomfortable church buildings. Under mass evangelism, whole bands sought forgiveness and entered the Methodist fellowship. Even the government recognized this influence by threatening to withhold the annual presents to the Mississaugas if they attended Methodist camp meetings; it wanted the natives to join the Church of England.[58]

### THE MISSIONS AND GOVERNMENT POLICY

By the late 1820s the governments in Britain and Upper Canada also began to initiate new native policies. The Colonial Office, partially in response to criticism from church and humanitarian groups, encouraged the use of every available channel to civilize and assimilate the aborigines into the British social and economic systems. The new lieutenant-governor, Sir John Colborne, who served from 1828 to 1835, was also committed to this civilizing program. Impressed by the Methodist settlement at the Credit, he believed it offered a pattern for government action and was prepared to provide financial assistance from provincial funds for similar settlements in the Georgian Bay, Lake Simcoe, and St Clair River areas. Houses and schools were constructed, teachers supplied, and the bands encouraged to settle down and engage in agriculture. Publicly Colborne also encouraged the Methodist Episcopal church to expand its native missions, although he admonished it to refrain from meddling in secular political affairs and worked privately to restrict its operations.[59]

He was dedicated to advancing the Church of England's influence and prerogatives. He recognized that prestige and broad social and political influence would accrue, both in Upper Canada and in Britain, to the church that converted and reformed the aboriginal population. He was also convinced that the Methodist Episcopal church was hostile to the best interests of the Church of England and the political and social stability of Upper Canada. Colborne feared that the Episcopal Methodists would undermine the loyalty to Britain of their native converts and add their voice to the growing chorus of opposition to his legislative policies. Hence, the evangelization of the aborigines became entangled with questions about the establishment of the Church of England and its control over the clergy reserves and the newly chartered provincial university and ultimately with the House of Assembly's challenge to the power of the governing oligarchy.[60]

As mentioned earlier, to offset the Episcopal Methodist control of native missions, Colborne and the Colonial Office negotiated with the British Wesleyans to re-enter Upper Canada. Since the Church of England lacked sufficient resources to monopolize the work, he assumed that the more docile and loyal Wesleyans, supported by a large government grant, would displace their co-religionists in the mission field. To further this plan, he instructed the Indian Department to curb the Episcopal Methodist work around Lake Simcoe and Georgian Bay. An Anglican minister was sent to the Matchedash band, and government-paid Anglican teachers dislodged the Methodists there and on Yellowhead's island.[61]

The Canadian Methodist Missionary Society in 1830 denounced such actions as inimical to the best interests of all concerned. It demanded that the bands be permitted to choose their own denominational affiliation without the threat of government reprisals and that they receive secure possession and title to their lands without fear of removal. In fact, however, without competent ministers or native workers, the initial Anglican foray at Matchedash, Coldwater, the Narrows (Orillia), and the adjoining territory failed to gain church members or children for the schools. Most of the local natives mistrusted the government officials and their Anglican allies. On the other hand, "the Methodists, while still predatory to some aspects of Indian culture, nevertheless represented to many Native people in an increasingly hostile environment an organization whose members came closest to an accurate understanding of their problems."[62] Until the mid-1830s, when new forces were enlisted, the original Episcopal Methodist Church continued to gain significant numbers of converts in this region.

The only area of Upper Canada that generally resisted early Methodist evangelization was the southwest. Except for a weak cause at Amherstburg, most of the scattered bands there remained opposed either to Christianity in general or to Methodism in particular. Along the Grand River, traditional native spirituality remained a powerful alternative, and even the more sympathetic Mohawks and Oneidas were described as "less docile, more haughty, self-willed and conceited" than the Mississaugas.[63] At Muncey on the Thames River some thirty kilometres southwest of London, Jones and Torry had converted a few Ojibwa-speaking Muncees or Delawares in 1825, and John Carey opened a school for their children, but most Delawares there remained steadfast to the religion of their ancestors. In the early 1830s, only about a quarter of the five to six hundred in the community were Christians, and some became Anglicans to escape Methodist discipline. By mid-decade, however, with the school in the care of Peter Jones's half-brother, George Henry, and with the tolerant and able Ezra Adams as minister, about one-half joined the Methodists. Eventually, in 1847 the Moravian Delawares at Fairfield also requested Methodist services, although this request was mainly due to a dispute with the Moravian missionaries over ownership of the land.[64]

On Walpole Island at the northern entrance to Lake St Clair, the natives recently arrived from the United States refused all Christian overtures until the late 1830s, when government policies and deteriorating social and economic conditions forced them to change in order to protect their community.[65] They shared the distrust of Europeans caused by past American betrayals and the aggressive expansion of settlers. They were also more isolated from the dominant British society and therefore less intimidated by social and cultural incursions. On the negative side, they were more vulnerable to liquor supplied from the United States and therefore more debauched and uncivilized.

Closer to Sarnia, the church made little headway during the 1820s and early 1830s. Again as part of its plan to settle and civilize the native bands, the colonial administration in 1830 promised to build cabins on a four-mile-square reserve. Fearful of Episcopal Methodist influence, yet unable to attract an Anglican minister, Colborne had the Wesleyans station Thomas Turner there. However, Turner had little experience in North America and none with native evangelization. Construction delays, government bungling, and a hostile clientele made his work difficult. But of greater importance, he was never able to draw on the native assistants so critical for Methodist success. In the fall of 1831, he reported that although he was treated with civility, "I now fear that they are not only indifferent, but even hostile to Christianity."[66] The local Indian agent had suggested that Turner not identify himself as a minister.

The following summer, many families abandoned their thirty-acre farms along the St Clair river because of a cholera outbreak. By 1833 only about fifteen families remained in the badly deteriorating government housing, and few cultivated even small patches of corn. Although some wished to receive a rudimentary education, they did not want religious services and no one was converted to Methodism. Easy access to American liquor exacerbated the poverty and miserable conditions. Turner failed to have any impact on native behaviour or spiritual reformation until late 1833, when he was joined by George Henry as schoolteacher and interpreter. The following year James Evans replaced Turner. He described the mission thus:

The men are all drunkards, with one exception; not drunkards in a limited sense, but the most abandoned and unblushing sots … They were *Idle* in the extreme, never attending to any business except hunting; the women being considered the proper persons to manage the agricultural department, which consisted of perhaps half an acre of maise … Nor were the women far removed from the men in vice, nay, in some respects their sex enabled them to be more audaciously obscene … In these frequent scenes of beastly intoxication they could scarcely be supposed to escape those abuses to which their sex exposed them, and, as a natural consequence, a squalid, sickly, puny race are now destined to occupy the places of this once healthy, athletic and noble race.[67]

Born in 1801, Evans had been educated in England before immigrating to Lower Canada with his family in 1822. From 1828 until he entered the Methodist ministry in 1830, he taught at the Rice Lake mission school. A year after his ordination in 1833, he began at St Clair a short, but one of the most important, missionary careers in Methodist history. Evans was a gifted linguist and quickly became expert in Ojibwa; assisted by Peter Jones and George Henry, he systematized the grammar and spelling and translated several texts. Later he would use the same formulation to develop a Cree syllabary, thereby creating a written language for most of the tribes in the northwest. His ability to write and preach in the native languages and his strong advocacy of native rights gained him widespread acceptance and respect and increased his effectiveness. In 1836 Evans recorded 101 Methodist members on or near the St Clair reserve, while three years later his successor reported 109 Methodists, with "none given to intoxication." By then, the settlement was known for its fine harvests, well-attended school, neat houses, and regular attendance on the means of grace.[68] Thus, by the end of the 1830s, the Methodists had generally evangelized the bands in southwestern Upper Canada.

During that decade they also provided religious services to the Saugeen bands scattered from Goderich to Georgian Bay. Membership at the Saugeen mission on Lake Huron doubled to about 80 over the decade. These natives roamed over the last great unceded territory in the fertile region of Upper Canada. The Methodist missionaries assisted in their attempts to gain title to the land and to prevent squatters from settling there. It was widely hoped in church circles that the government would sanction the use of this territory as a separate, permanent homeland for all the province's native peoples. The veteran itinerant Thomas Whitehead, after touring the area in 1834, expressed the views of many when he wrote, "I think the Sahgeeng [sic] will bear a comparison with any river in Upper Canada ... I indulge a cheerful hope that I shall see the most of the Christian natives settled once for all on the Sahgeeng River; it would prove to be the best of earthly blessings to the Red Men, and would concentrate the white population."[69]

However, government policy underwent a severe reversal during the administration of the new lieutenant-governor, Sir Francis Bond Head. Unlike his predecessor, Bond Head was convinced that the aborigines could never be civilized and assimilated and that they would eventually become extinct as a people. He argued that they should be isolated from European society. A valuable side-effect would be the crown's acquisition of vast new lands for settlement. Building on Colborne's earlier suggestion that the northern tribes congregate on Manitoulin Island, Bond Head reported to the colonial secretary, Lord Glenelg, in 1836, "it is evident to me that we should reap a very great Benefit, if we could persuade those Indians, who are now impeding the Progress of Civilization in Upper Canada, to resort to a place possessing the double Advantage of being admirably adapted to *them* (insomuch as it affords Fishing, Hunting, Bird-shooting, and Fruit), and yet in no way adapted to the White population."[70] Dismissing the achievements of the previous decade, Bond Head envisioned all the aborigines removed to Manitoulin Island or other northern forests.

During the same period, the situation was complicated by the arrival of hundreds of American aborigines fleeing President Andrew Jackson's genocidal policy of removing the eastern tribes to the Great Desert west of the Mississippi. Although the new arrivals introduced a virulence to native affairs, they could do nothing to prevent the partial implementation of Bond Head's removal policy. At the annual gift-giving ceremonies on Manitoulin Island in 1836, the indigenous bands agreed to give up their exclusive claims to the island in order to permit others to settle there. In a related treaty, the Saugeens surrendered one and a half million acres of land and agreed to move north either to the Bruce Peninsula or to Manitoulin. A decade later, a general council of Ojibwas petitioned to have the remaining territory north of Owen Sound established as a perpetual reserve for the provincial bands, but they likewise were forced to cede much of the Bruce Peninsula in 1854 and move to the inhospitable Cape Croker reserve. Although Bond Head reported to his superiors that the treaties were made voluntarily, in fact, the disillusioned and frustrated Saugeen bands were intimidated into submission and much of the natural tribal leadership was ignored at the signing. As well as the Saugeen lands, the native settlements at Coldwater and the Narrows were sold, with the residents moving to Manitoulin or the infertile lands at Rama. Smaller tracts of land were later ceded at Amherstburg and Fairfield.[71]

Although divided over many issues and to a degree over native requirements and the extent to which the church should oppose the government, the Canadian and British Methodist missionary leadership was committed to protecting native land claims. With the provincial House of Assembly at odds with Bond Head and his council and Upper Canadian politics generally in a state of chaos, the Methodists focused their efforts on changing policy in Britain. The Wesleyan missionary secretaries collected evidence of the successful conversion and civilization of the Mississaugas and Iroquois and between 1836 and 1838 repeatedly presented their findings to the British Parliament. Over the same period, Peter Jones, John Sunday, James Evans, and Egerton Ryerson met with parliamentary committees, the Colonial Office, and even King William IV and Queen Victoria to impress upon them the injustice of Bond Head's removal policy. They reminded the officials of past promises, pointed out the illegitimate nature of recent land transfers, and published long articles contradicting the lieutenant-governor's assessment of aboriginal conditions and attacking his treaties. Ryerson became the Canadian representative in the Society for the Protection of Aboriginal Inhabitants of the British Dominions and joined other humanitarians lobbying the government on behalf of Britain's native subjects.[72]

Bond Head was recalled because of the Rebellion of 1837, but the aboriginal lands were irretrievably lost. His successor, Sir George Arthur, recognized the evil of the removal policy and was instructed by the colonial secretary to provide some remedy. However, little was actually done, and even title to the remaining unceded lands was withheld on the assumption that the natives could not be trusted to guard their own interests. During the 1840s, the government returned to the policy of civilization, but this program included consolidating the bands on larger, and by definition more isolated, reserves. As a result, the Credit mission, including about 3,000 acres of prime farm land and town lots in Port Credit, was sold in 1847, and the Mississaugas were encouraged to resettle on Manitoulin Island or the Bruce Peninsula. Because the British and Canadian Wesleyans had been divided since 1840 and the British church was increasingly engrossed with its missions in the Hudson's Bay territory, no strong voice was raised on behalf of native rights. The Credit band itself was badly divided and felt helpless to oppose the decision. Even Jones, who considered the sale a betrayal, could do little. However, rather than move to the wilderness, he acquired about 4,000 acres on the Grand River from the Mohawks, divided the reserve into farms, and formed the New Credit settlement.[73]

Part of the rationale for consolidating the bands was to permit the establishment of better facilities, including larger and more efficient schools. The Methodist missionaries actively promoted this goal. Although both day and sabbath schools had helped to assimilate and civilize native children, most missionaries and teachers recognized that they required a great deal of improvement. Irregular attendance, lax discipline, and countervailing parental and community values obstructed real educational progress. The children were removed for the annual hunting and fishing excursions, for berry picking and making maple sugar, or when farming required their services. They were constantly subject to their family's often irresolute lifestyle. In addition to better local schools, most missionaries agreed that the best way to end these negative influences was to place the children in full-time residential schools where they could be continually supervised. Such schools would shield the youth from their own communities.[74]

The first Canadian Methodist residential schools for native children evolved out of Case's school at Alderville, which he began in 1838 principally to train girls. By the early 1840s, it had become a manual-labour school with a high-school department modelled on the American Methodist school for the Shawnees in Kansas. Manual-labour schools were also supported by the Bagot Commission of 1844 and by leading educationalists in Upper Canada. In a substantial brick building, the school at Alderville taught general education, as well as farming and artisan skills to boys and household management to girls. It was paid for from funds raised in the United States and Britain and from government annuity payments to the Mississaugas. The teachers were supplied by the Wesleyan Missionary Society. In 1847 a 200-acre farm was set aside for student training, and it also supplied part of the school's needs. As well as day students, in 1849 there were about sixty residential students from all over the province.[75]

The Canadian Methodists under the leadership of John Ryerson and Peter Jones had decided in 1842 to build a similar manual-labour school on the Muncey reserve near London. This 20,000-acre reserve was home to about 1,200 Oneidas, Ojibwas, and Muncees. They agreed to provide funds from their annuity receipts, and Jones arranged for land for the school and the adjoining 200-acre farm. After several fund-raising expeditions, the cornerstone was finally laid in July 1849 by Governor-General Lord Elgin, who took an active interest in the school. It was named Mount Elgin Wesleyan Methodist

Ojibway Industrial School in his honour and opened in early 1850. Although the Methodists were unsuccessful in securing part of the government grant previously given to the Wesleyan Missionary Society, in 1851 direct grants were made to support the schools. Alderville and Mount Elgin became the pattern for native education across the country for more than a century. Nevertheless, school attendance remained erratic, and none of the schools were ever able to displace totally the resilient native culture.[76]

Unfortunately, their advent also marked a significant shift in Methodist educational philosophy, which in turn denigrated the position of native workers in the church. The new missionary leadership believed the native population should learn English as quickly as possible. The missionaries understood the close connection between language and social traditions. In order to assimilate the children into the dominant culture, they gradually insisted that instruction take place in English. Despite the objections of senior missionaries such as Case and Jones, the church also published less material in Ojibwa and Mohawk. Tolerance and respect for the native customs and skills also declined as non-aboriginal teachers became increasingly distant from the heroic era of native culture and more intent on imposing their alien values. Missionaries such as David Wright at the New Credit wanted to "burn or destroy all Indian Books, and put an end to talking Indian in school." Within a few years, his successor noted, "The English language is used almost exclusively in the play as well as the studies of the children, which is in itself a great advantage to the Indian children, and is becoming more and more appreciated by the Indian parents."[77]

Furthermore, the church no longer considered it essential to train missionaries in Ojibwa or Mohawk. The ministers themselves were equally unsympathetic to preaching or providing pastoral oversight in the native languages, relying instead on interpreters or working in English. Such strategies undoubtedly diminished the status of native preachers; no new generation of great aboriginal leaders emerged to evangelize the Canadas. Notions of racial inferiority and the assumption that natives should not minister to their own emerged during the second half of the nineteenth century. Methodism thereby lost much of its original advantage over other churches.

Although new fields of service were opening up, native missions in Upper Canada declined in relative importance and certainly in the minds of Canadian Methodists after the mid-1850s. Methodist missions also fell prey to severe competition from other Protestant and especially Roman Catholic churches. Certainly, the Roman Catholics predominated in the north and on Manitoulin Island, but even the Anglicans were able to displace or at least confound much of the Methodist work around Lake Simcoe and in the southwest. Baptists also made significant inroads among the Six Nations on the Grand River.[78]

## THE NORTHWEST

In spite of the great challenges faced by mission operations in Upper Canada from the 1820s to the 1850s, as they were transformed, they gradually acquired a structured routine more suited to the dedicated itinerant and career teacher than to the pioneer missionary. However, while this institutionalization was taking place, the Methodist church turned to the vast regions north and west of the Great Lakes. By 1831 a preaching excursion to the mouth of the French River introduced Methodism to the Ojibwas and Algonquins of the Canadian Shield. Although few natives permanently inhabited the district, the river formed a strategic link joining Montreal to the upper Great Lakes and the territories beyond. It was therefore a valuable meeting place for natives who could carry Christianity to their distant homes. After 1835 the site became a regular part of the mission to the north shore of Georgian Bay. On Manitoulin itself, the Methodists found a huge field of labour, especially after the 1836 treaties had made it the home to numerous non-Christian bands. While attending the infamous 1836 present-giving ceremonies, as part of his broader tour of Lake Huron, James Evans described the assembly. After commenting on the Christians, he wrote that "the remainder of perhaps 2000 adults are in the gall of bitterness and in the bonds of iniquity, slaves to the most degrading vices, dupes of the most notorious villains, and like the summer hail, fast melting under the scorching flames of liquid fire ... I have ever felt, since I entered the missionary field, an ardent desire ... that the heathen might be saved, but never, never, has my soul been so truly alive to their distress and my duty."[79] Even so, the Methodists never opened a mission on the island and made few inroads in this region because of competition from the Church of England and the Roman Catholic Church.

In 1832 John Sunday had led a group of native workers in an evangelizing tour of the Sault Ste Marie area. But the region was too remote and too expensive to serve; it would be nearly two decades before a permanent mission could operate in the district. In the meantime, the Canadian church lent many of its native assistants to the American mission in the region. Henry Snake and Thomas Frasier, both trained at Grape Island, and later George Copway and William Herkimer assisted there.[80]

It was not until 1851 that the Wesleyan missionary George McDougall developed a mission at Garden River a few miles from Sault Ste Marie. With a farm and a school, as well as a church and manse, prospects appeared good; McDougall confidently expected to create a mature, Upper Canadian–style mission in the wilderness. However, the nomadic population and the poor agricultural potential of the region limited the prospects for a settled Methodist aboriginal community. The natives were also faced with the prospect of losing their lands because they lacked legal title and were being corrupted by alcohol and other European vices. These conditions were becoming more serious as the mineral and timber resources of the area began to be exploited. The developments at Bruce Mines, some thirty miles east of Garden River, foreshadowed what the future held for the indigenous population.[81]

As part of the Wesleyans' earlier advance toward the northwest, James Evans had conducted an evangelizing tour of Lake Superior in 1838–39 and pronounced as unlimited the region's potential for Christian converts. He and his associate Thomas Hurlburt held extended services at Fort William and Lake Nipigon, but at least partially because of strong Roman Catholic competition at the western end of Lake Superior, they established a permanent mission near the important fur-trading post at the mouth of the Pic River. Hurlburt was optimistic about the mission's prospects and constructed a house and church at Pic in 1840.[82] Although there was only a small population in the vicinity, the mission served those bringing in furs or travelling to or from the far west. Like all isolated missions, Pic was difficult to supply and supervise since management rested with the Wesleyan Missionary Society in London.

However, opportunities appeared to improve when the Hudson's Bay Company under George Simpson invited Wesleyan missionaries into its vast territories. It agreed to supply transportation, accommodation at its posts, interpreters, necessary provisions, and "goodwill" in the evangelizing of both its own employees and the scattered tribes. Without company favour, missionary success was all but impossible in the area between Lake Superior and the Pacific.

The Hudson's Bay Company was hardly acting out of altruistic motives. Its charter to exclusive control of the northwest had been renewed in 1837 on condition that it promote the moral and religious advancement of the aboriginal population. The missionary enterprise must succeed if the company was to answer the criticisms of reform groups in Britain. The company also expected the Wesleyans to provide Christian discipline and a bulwark against the debauching influence of the free traders. And since the Wesleyans would be located throughout the country, they would help undercut the attraction of the Red River settlement, where Anglican missionaries were drawing natives to their school and religious services. The company was anxious that no religious body gain too great a sway.[83]

After discussions with Robert Alder and James Evans, Simpson agreed to the formation of a distinct mission field directed by the British Wesleyans. They dispatched George Barnley, William Mason, and Robert Rundle from England, and James Evans was transferred from Canada to supervise the work. The native preachers Peter Jacobs and Henry Bird Steinhauer joined the group in the new district. Evans was stationed at Norway House, the clearing depot for the northern posts and the most suitable centre for missionary coordination. Barnley operated out of Moose Factory on James Bay and ministered to the Inuit and Swampy Crees in the territory surrounding Fort Albany, Rupert House, Fort George, and Abitibi. Rundle was stationed at Fort Edmonton and Rocky Mountain House, but served most of present-day northern Alberta and Saskatchewan. As well as Woodland Crees, he was commissioned to spread Christian civilization among the Assiniboines, Piegans, Sarcees, and Bloods.

Mason was initially sent to Fort Frances on Lac la Pluie (Rainy Lake), which served as a major rendezvous for company workers and various native bands. Steinhauer assisted Mason as interpreter, guide, and teacher, while Jacobs helped Evans at Norway House for a short time before assuming his appointment to the Crees at Fort Alexander near the outlet of the Winnipeg River. In 1842 Jacobs travelled to Canada to be ordained and returned to take over the mission at Rainy Lake. Steinhauer and Mason then joined Evans at the new Rossville mission near Norway House. The Lake Superior mission at Pic served by Thomas Hurlburt was also transferred to the new district in order to share in the Hudson's Bay Company assistance, but little or no supervision was exercised from the northwest.[84]

With at times generous support from the company, the mission work started out as well as could reasonably be expected. Although chaplain services were provided for the company employees, the priority remained native evangelization. Evans attempted to duplicate the mission experience in Upper Canada and sought to furnish education and agricultural training as well as spiritual guidance. Schools and model farms were tried, but they met with only very limited success. With Evans in charge, the translation and publication of texts in Cree was also a high priority. His Cree syllabics permitted the creation of a written language, and works were published at Norway House and later at Rossville.

However, the aboriginal peoples in this region were generally more independent and less susceptible to arguments about the benefits of Christian civilization than the eastern tribes. They had not yet felt the sustained destructive impact of European settlement. The Methodist missions faced a series of other problems during the 1840s which seriously limited their evangelization of the region. At the centre of much of the difficulty was Evans himself. Energetic, fervent, and practical, as well as strong-willed and independent, he soon ran foul of company officials. Most of the troubles resulted simply from contradictory expectations of the missionary's role, what was involved in Christianizing the natives, and the nature of acceptable conduct within company precincts. Evans believed the company was exploiting its employees, forcing them to break the sabbath, and encouraging a dissolute lifestyle. On the other hand, the company opposed schemes to settle the Christian natives in agrarian communities, disliked Evans's interference in fur-trade matters, and believed he was neglecting his office as chaplain. By 1845 it was glad to use his alleged sexual misconduct with a native servant to have him censured. He returned to England to defend himself, but died prematurely in 1846.[85]

Under these circumstances, Barnley and Rundle were left substantially on their own. Although both were young and inexperienced, they performed remarkably well considering the conditions they faced. Rundle was dealing with some of the most warlike tribes on the continent. Although he was encouraged to meet with the natives exclusively at the posts, he believed that the only way to have any influence was to travel extensively and to share their way of life. His doing so led to complaints from company officials that he showed "more zeal than judgement" and neglected his responsibilities to the company, but in general he worked well with the traders. More important, he deeply impressed several native leaders. Few converts were made, but he taught Evans's Cree syllabics and spread the gospel message widely. None the less, he was angered by the refusal of the missionary authorities to allow him to return to England to marry and was becoming disillusioned by growing company hostility as well as indifference from Methodist headquarters. In 1848 he left the country for medical treatment of an injured arm, and despite his expectation to return, he was not unhappy to settle quietly into the regular British itinerancy for the rest of his life.[86]

For his part, George Barnley travelled extensively across the inhospitable James Bay region. More fortunate than Rundle, he was permitted to return home in 1844 to marry and a year later brought his wife to Moose Factory. While his marriage added to his own happiness, it became a source of friction between him and Robert Miles, the chief resident trader, and led to a serious deterioration of the mission's effectiveness. Barnley's wife felt superior to the local "country wives" and especially offended Mrs Miles by not showing due respect to her as first lady of the settlement.[87]

These personality conflicts, however, only aggravated the real troubles that faced Barnley in overcoming the local indifference to Christianity and the relatively strong commitment to native spirituality. He was also confronted with a new religious movement sweeping through his district. In 1842 a self-proclaimed prophet named Abishabis convinced many natives that he was the true path to spiritual salvation. Combining traditional beliefs with a diluted Christianity gleaned from Evans's Cree translations, he deeply divided the community. Although the movement went underground because of company denunciation, even the murder of Abishabis in 1843 could not completely destroy its influence.[88] In 1847 Barnley had had enough and settled back into the regular itinerancy in England. Neither he nor Rundle had anticipated a lifelong missionary career, and both were relieved to have completed their apprenticeships in the wilds of North America.

As for the British Missionary Society, it was embarrassed by the ill will and other serious problems it had faced in the northwest. Rather than celebrate the services of Evans, Rundle, and Barnley, it was anxious to extricate itself from further turmoil and forget the entire enterprise. The Hudson's Bay Company sympathized, but wanted a new missionary at least for Moose Factory. It was worried about attacks on its management of the territory; a native delegation to England in 1847 had complained of the "legal oppression and of neglect on the part of the Company to provide for the moral advancement of the natives."[89] To combat such statements, by the 1850s the company was again prepared to encourage Methodist missions. Simpson wrote to Robert Alder assuring him that "it would have given me sincere pleasure to see the station reoccupied this season. In the absence of a Protestant missionary, the Roman Catholic priests are extending their operations in that direction, nor can the Company much longer withhold its sanction to their permanently establishing themselves at Moose."[90] Company policy preferred that the religious communities operate in distinct zones so as not to confuse the native population, but if the Methodists could not fill the need, the mission would be turned over to those who could. Ultimately, in fact, Moose Factory was lost as a Methodist mission.

However, the British Wesleyans were straining to support even Jacobs, Mason, and Steinhauer. Jacobs continued at Fort Frances until 1850, but made little progress with the transient population. The local chiefs and native conjurors were particularly hostile to his ministry. He too became disillusioned by the lack of respect shown him by both company officials and his own Wesleyan connnexion. As a native preacher, he never received the salary or status accorded the ordinary Methodist itinerant. After leaving the mission, he served for short periods at Saugeen and Rama before abandoning the church altogether in 1857. His successor at Rainy Lake, Allen Salt, believed Jacobs had been derelict in his duties, although he acknowledged the great hardships of the mission.[91]

In 1843 Steinhauer and Mason had moved to Rossville, and Mason inherited Evans's mantle of leadership two years later. Mason continued the translation and publication of texts in Cree as well as running the mission and school activities. Before travelling to Rossville, he had married Sophia Thomas, the daughter of a senior Hudson's Bay Company official and his Cree wife. Assisted by Sophia, Mason had fewer confrontations with the various segments of local society. She had received a decent education at Red River and was extremely useful in interpreting, translating, and teaching at the mission school. In 1852 Mason reported, "Never were our missions more prosperous and never were circumstances more calculated to inspire hope ... Heathenism has received its death blow and falls before the power and influence of the Gospel."[92] However, both William and Sophia Mason were becoming increasingly disillusioned by the lack of resources available. They had both been raised in the Church of England and had developed cordial relations with the Anglicans at Red River. When the Wesleyan district was transferred to the Canadian Methodist church in 1854, the Masons took the opportunity to join the Anglican Church Missionary Society and continued to translate, publish, and minister to the aboriginal population. At the same time, the Church of England proposed taking over all the Methodist missions in the northwest. This suggestion was firmly rejected by Enoch Wood, the superintendent of the Canadian Wesleyan missions.[93]

By the time the Canadian church assumed control in 1854, only Henry Steinhauer remained loyally at his post. After serving as Mason's chief translator until 1851, he had opened a new mission at Oxford House, about two hundred miles northeast of Rossville. When John Ryerson passed through on his inspection of the western missions in 1854, Steinhauer accompanied him back to Canada via Britain and spoke repeatedly at fund-raising meetings about the needs of the northwest. The following year, as part of the reorganization of the work, he was finally ordained and sent with Thomas Woolsey to the far west. They divided the territory of present-day Alberta between them. Steinhauer originally settled at Lac la Biche, but in 1858 he moved to a better site at White Fish Lake. There he built the first Protestant church in the region and served as missionary until his death in 1884.[94]

Thomas Hurlburt, Robert Brooking, Allen Salt, and a year later, Woolsey were also sent to the northwest. Hurlburt, an experienced if somewhat controversial missionary, supervised the work from Rossville recently vacated by Mason. But he remained for only two years before returning to native mission work in Canada. During his brief stay in Rupert's Land, he did little more than re-establish the Methodist presence. Brooking had been ordained as a missionary to West Africa, where he served between 1839 and 1846. After four years at Rice Lake and two more at the St Clair mission, he took over Oxford House and in 1857 replaced Hurlburt as superintendent at Rossville. Three years later he returned to mission work in Canada, serving at Rama,

Hiawatha, and Alderville. No reason was given for the expensive shifting of missionaries in and out of the northwest.[95]

Allen Salt, Jacob's replacement at Rainy Lake, also remained for only a short term. Again, his greatest opposition came from native shamans and Roman Catholic missionaries. Although relations with Hudson's Bay Company officials remained volatile and frustrating, George Simpson did offer help when it did not interfere with company priorities. The Methodist priorities remained to settle the tribes and develop an agrarian economy. However, it would take a new generation of missionaries and severe economic and social change among the natives themselves before real evangelization occurred. As in Upper Canada, only a major crisis could turn them to Christian civilization.[96]

In the meantime, the Canadian Wesleyan church was spreading its influence to the Pacific Ocean. In December 1858 Ephraim Evans, Arthur Browning, Edward White, and Ebenezer Robson set out from Canada. They arrived in British Columbia the following summer and immediately opened missions at Victoria and Nanaimo on Vancouver Island and at New Westminster and Fort Hope on the mainland. Essentially, these were not missions to the native peoples, but once established, they provided a new impetus to evangelizing the local tribes.[97] Thus by 1860 the Wesleyan Methodist Church in Canada had spread its influence from sea to sea. By stressing spiritual rebirth, moral living, education, and training in agrarian and cottage-industrial skills, it helped to prevent the extinction of the native people and, more positively, to provide them with all the benefits of Christian civilization. The church was now beginning to become a partner in the great enterprise of worldwide missionary endeavour.

# 8 The Elaboration
## of a National Methodist Church

On June 1, 1884, the Methodist Church of Canada, created in 1874 by the union of the Wesleyan and New Connexion Methodists, formally amalgamated with the Primitive Methodist, Bible Christian, and Methodist Episcopal churches to establish "The Methodist Church." The new body immediately became the largest Protestant denomination in Canada, encompassing nearly the entire family of Methodist connexions in the dominion and Newfoundland and supervising much of the work in Bermuda and a growing mission operation in Japan. Out of the turmoil of more than seventy years of competition, particularly in central Canada, one independent national body emerged to represent the denomination before the country and the world.

The union was the culmination of a drive for greater unity which had characterized Canadian Methodism for much of the century and which fitted into the general pattern of ecumenism affecting mid-Victorian Protestantism. Although the twentieth century would witness the splintering of the evangelical consensus, to a large degree by the 1880s, the mainstream churches had abandoned many of their distinguishing characteristics and become broadly Protestant Canadian institutions. They were affected by the same forces, aspired to the same goals, and were no longer estranged by conflicting theological assumptions.[1] As for the Methodists, they followed the same doctrines and theology and were becoming ever more compatible in church polity. Their original distinctions had been based mainly on British or American administrative and political questions which became irrelevant to the Canadian religious experience and mission. "Acknowledging one Lord, one faith, one baptism, one God and Father of all, we rejoice that the time has come for us to become one also as an organic whole. Preaching the same gospel of free grace, singing the same hymns of Christian faith and hope, rejoicing in the same experience of conscious salvation, it is evident that there was little to justify continued division."[2]

In fact, Methodism in British America had in large measure passed out of its "heroic age" as a missionary church serving the needs of a scattered, pioneer society as early as the 1850s.[3] Originally it owed much of its appeal to the unceasing spiritual and moral vigil it had sustained among early settlements, backwoods farmers, and isolated fishing communities. Its saddle-bag preachers had bravely served where few other clergy would venture and had brought an emotionally satisfying, fervent religion to an immigrant society deeply in need of spiritual comfort and social regeneration and to a demoralized native population on the verge of extinction. During the first half of the nineteenth century, Methodism, especially in Upper Canada, had created a vital sense of community while overcoming attacks on its loyalty to the crown and struggling against the prerogatives of the quasi-established churches and the Tory élite. It was also during this heroic period that Methodism had laid a strong foundation for the institutional infrastructure of the church.

By the 1850s Methodists were redirecting their attention to physical expansion and internal consolidation.[4] New social forces contributed to the transformation of many of the essential elements of Methodism as it attempted to serve the needs of Victorian Canada. Moreover, in the period after the union of 1884, united Methodism emphasized new mission priorities at home and abroad while sharing, and often leading, in the mounting struggle for social justice. The church's actions took both traditional and innovative forms and often relied on united Protestant solutions. These developments will be explored in subsequent chapters. Nevertheless, as the period after the 1850s unfolded, the priorities among Methodists were to expand across the continent, consolidate the home bases, and create a solid and progressive national Methodist connexion.

### EXPANSION AND CONSOLIDATION OF THE CONNEXIONS

To help explain the nature of Methodist expansion and consolidation, table 1 provides an overview of the population growth of Canada and its provinces up to 1921. In 1851 Canada West had a population of about 925,000 located in a continuous band along the north shore of the St Lawrence River and lakes Ontario and Erie and reaching back into the fertile country behind the lakes. During the 1850s, settlement moved farther up the Ottawa valley, into the Bruce Peninsula, and along the upper Great Lakes, principally to exploit the forest potential of these regions. Of greater importance, especially after the creation of a railway network, the Yonge Street corridor to Lake Simcoe and the southwestern section of the province were filling up. Pioneer conditions gradually came to an end, and the principal towns and cities expanded quickly to become centres of economic, social, and religious influence.[5]

In Canada East the 1851 population of 890,900 was concentrated along the St Lawrence lowlands for the most part.[5] Improved transportation gradually helped expand settlement in the Eastern Townships, and the forest industry and related small-scale agriculture allowed settlers to penetrate the Shield along the Ottawa, Saguenay, and other tributaries of the St Lawrence. Immigration was significantly smaller than in Canada West, and population growth relied instead on a high birth rate and a declining mortality rate. The significant shift to the larger urban centres reflected intensified population pressure and

Table 1    Canadian decennial population figures, 1851–1921

|         | 1851 | 1861 | 1871 | 1881 | 1891 | 1901 | 1911 | 1921 |
|---------|------|------|------|------|------|------|------|------|
| Canada | 2,436,297 | 3,229,633 | 3,689,300 | 4,324,800 | 4,833,200 | 5,371,300 | 7,206,600 | 8,788,500 |
| Ont. | 952,000 | 1,396,000 | 1,620,900 | 1,926,900 | 2,114,300 | 2,182,900 | 2,527,300 | 2,933,700 |
| Que. | 890,300 | 1,111,600 | 1,191,500 | 1,359,000 | 1,488,500 | 1,648,900 | 2,005,800 | 2,361,200 |
| NS | 276,900 | 330,900 | 387,800 | 440,600 | 450,400 | 459,600 | 492,300 | 523,800 |
| NB | 193,800 | 252,000 | 285,600 | 321,200 | 321,300 | 331,100 | 351,900 | 387,900 |
| PEI | 62,678 | 80,900 | 94,000 | 108,900 | 109,100 | 103,300 | 93,700 | 88,600 |
| Nfld. | 122,600 | 146,500 | | | | | | |
| Man. | – | – | 25,200 | 62,300 | 115,500 | 255,200 | 461,500 | 610,100 |
| N/W. | 5,700 | 6,700 | 48,000 | 56,400 | 99,000 | – | – | – |
| Sask. | – | – | – | – | – | 91,300 | 492,400 | 757,500 |
| Alta. | – | – | – | – | – | 73,000 | 374,300 | 588,500 |
| BC | 55,000 | 51,500 | 36,200 | 49,500 | 98,200 | 178,700 | 392,500 | 524,600 |

Notes:
Drawn from various censuses and historical statistics of Canada.
1851 and 1861: Province of the Canadas.
The northwest was divided by 1901, although the provinces of Saskatchewan and Alberta were not created until 1905.
Newfoundland did not join Canada until 1949; the figures listed here were taken from census summaries from 1857 and 1869.

declining rural wealth rather than a progressive agricultural base or prosperous urban industrialization. Inhabitants were also obliged to migrate west or emigrate to New England; between 1870 and 1900 about 400,000 left Quebec. For English-speaking Quebeckers in Montreal and the townships and along the Ottawa River, the economic problems were exacerbated by severe social, linguistic, and religious pressures.[6]

Economic instability, massive emigration, and only limited and capricious population growth marked the history of the Atlantic region during the seventy years following 1850. Prince Edward Island's population actually declined. Nevertheless, the region developed an impressive social and intellectual identity and provided educational and intellectual leadership for the entire country. St John's, Halifax, and Saint John also continued to provide regional and national leadership in commercial and financial activities. In the west, real growth began only with the opening of the Canadian Pacific Railway system after 1885, and the trickle of new settlers became a torrent during the fifteen years preceding World War 1. After 1896 massive immigration, especially from England, the United States, and eastern Europe, developed the agricultural potential of the northwest and the natural resources and transshipment opportunities of British Columbia. In 1921 the regions west of Ontario represented over 28 per cent of Canada's population.

Table 2   Relative strength of denominations in Canada, 1851–1921

| Date | Methodists | | Presbyterians | | Anglicans | | Roman Catholics | | Baptists | |
|---|---|---|---|---|---|---|---|---|---|---|
| **CANADA** | | | | | | | | | | |
| 1871 | 574,091 | 15.6 | 539,998 | 14.6 | 494,049 | 13.4 | 1,492,029 | 40.4 | 239,343 | 6.5 |
| 1881 | 742,981 | 17.2 | 676,165 | 15.6 | 574,818 | 13.5 | 1,791,982 | 41.4 | 296,525 | 6.9 |
| 1891 | 848,000 | 17.5 | 755,000 | 15.6 | 646,000 | 13.4 | 1,992,000 | 41.2 | 303,000 | 6.3 |
| 1901 | 916,886 | 17.1 | 842,442 | 15.7 | 680,620 | 12.7 | 2,229,600 | 41.5 | 318,666 | 5.9 |
| 1911 | 1,079,892 | 15.0 | 1,115,324 | 15.5 | 1,043,017 | 14.8 | 2,833,041 | 39.3 | 382,666 | 5.3 |
| 1921 | 1,159,458 | 13.2 | 1,409,407 | 16.0 | 1,407,994 | 16.0 | 3,389,636 | 38.6 | 421,731 | 4.8 |
| **ONTARIO** | | | | | | | | | | |
| 1851 | 213,365 | 22.4 | 204,148 | 21.4 | 223,190 | 23.4 | 167,695 | 17.6 | 45,353 | 4.8 |
| 1861 | 350,373 | 25.0 | 303,374 | 21.7 | 311,559 | 22.3 | 258,151 | 18.5 | 61,559 | 4.4 |
| 1871 | 462,264 | 28.5 | 356,442 | 22.0 | 330,995 | 20.4 | 274,162 | 16.9 | 86,630 | 5.3 |
| 1881 | 591,503 | 30.7 | 417,749 | 21.7 | 366,539 | 19.0 | 320,839 | 16.7 | 106,680 | 5.5 |
| 1891 | 654,033 | 30.9 | 453,147 | 21.4 | 385,999 | 18.3 | 358,300 | 16.9 | 106,000 | 5.0 |
| 1901 | 666,388 | 30.5 | 477,386 | 21.9 | 367,937 | 16.9 | 390,304 | 17.9 | 117,700 | 5.4 |
| 1911 | 671,727 | 26.6 | 524,603 | 20.8 | 489,704 | 19.4 | 484,997 | 19.2 | 132,809 | 5.3 |
| 1921 | 685,463 | 23.4 | 613,532 | 20.9 | 648,883 | 22.1 | 576,178 | 19.6 | 148,634 | 5.1 |
| **QUEBEC** | | | | | | | | | | |
| 1851 | 21,200 | 2.4 | 33,500 | 3.8 | 44,682 | 5.0 | 746,854 | 83.9 | 4,493 | 0.5 |
| 1861 | 30,844 | 2.8 | 43,735 | 3.9 | 63,487 | 5.7 | 943,253 | 84.9 | 7,751 | 0.7 |
| 1871 | 34,100 | 2.9 | 46,465 | 3.9 | 62,449 | 5.2 | 1,019,850 | 85.6 | 8,700 | 0.7 |
| 1881 | 39,221 | 2.9 | 50,287 | 3.7 | 68,797 | 5.1 | 1,170,178 | 86.1 | 8,853 | 0.7 |
| 1891 | 39,574 | 2.7 | 52,673 | 3.5 | 75,472 | 5.1 | 1,291,709 | 86.8 | 7,991 | 0.5 |
| 1901 | 42,014 | 2.5 | 58,013 | 3.5 | 81,653 | 4.9 | 1,429,260 | 86.7 | 8,960 | 0.5 |
| 1911 | 42,444 | 2.1 | 64,125 | 3.2 | 102,684 | 5.1 | 1,724,683 | 86.0 | 9,255 | 0.5 |
| 1921 | 41,884 | 1.8 | 73,748 | 3.1 | 121,967 | 5.2 | 2,023,993 | 85.7 | 9,257 | 0.4 |
| **THE MARITIMES (EXCLUDING NEWFOUNDLAND)** | | | | | | | | | | |
| 1861 | 67,669 | 10.2 | 151,249 | 22.8 | 97,305 | 14.7 | 207,371 | 31.2 | 123,220 | 18.6 |
| 1871 | 82,797 | 10.8 | 171,970 | 22.4 | 107,825 | 14.1 | 238,459 | 31.1 | 148,386 | 19.3 |
| 1881 | 98,791 | 11.3 | 189,111 | 21.7 | 114,215 | 13.1 | 273,693 | 31.4 | 171,089 | 19.6 |
| 1891 | 103,291 | 11.7 | 182,668 | 20.7 | 114,151 | 13.0 | 286,250 | 32.5 | 169,021 | 19.2 |
| 1901 | 106,865 | 12.0 | 176,627 | 19.8 | 113,846 | 12.7 | 301,072 | 33.7 | 146,000 | 16.3 |
| 1911 | 104,373 | 11.1 | 176,276 | 18.8 | 123,118 | 13.1 | 331,874 | 35.4 | 171,332 | 18.3 |
| 1921 | 105,349 | 10.5 | 177,082 | 17.7 | 137,681 | 13.8 | 370,715 | 37.1 | 178,403 | 17.8 |
| **MANITOBA, SASKATCHEWAN, ALBERTA** | | | | | | | | | | |
| 1881 | 9,941 | 8.4 | 14,831 | 12.5 | 17,463 | 14.7 | 16,689 | 14.1 | 7,796 | 6.6 |
| 1891 | 31,378 | 14.6 | 41,508 | 19.4 | 45,018 | 21.0 | 33,579 | 15.7 | 17,655 | 8.2 |
| 1901 | 76,572 | 18.2 | 96,335 | 22.9 | 76,581 | 18.2 | 75,325 | 17.9 | 15,071 | 3.6 |
| 1911 | 206,066 | 15.5 | 266,536 | 20.1 | 217,548 | 16.4 | 226,279 | 17.0 | 51,861 | 3.9 |
| 1921 | 261,774 | 13.4 | 421,357 | 21.5 | 336,013 | 17.2 | 350,168 | 17.9 | 65,177 | 3.3 |
| **BRITISH COLUMBIA** | | | | | | | | | | |
| 1881 | 3,516 | 7.1 | 4,095 | 8.3 | 7,804 | 15.8 | 10,043 | 20.3 | 434 | 0.9 |
| 1891 | 14,193 | 14.5 | 15,284 | 15.6 | 23,619 | 24.1 | 20,843 | 21.2 | 3,100 | 3.2 |
| 1901 | 25,047 | 14.0 | 34,081 | 19.1 | 40,689 | 22.8 | 33,639 | 18.8 | 6,471 | 3.6 |
| 1911 | 52,132 | 13.3 | 82,125 | 20.9 | 100,952 | 25.7 | 58,397 | 14.9 | 18,378 | 4.7 |
| 1921 | 64,810 | 12.4 | 123,022 | 23.5 | 160,978 | 30.7 | 63,980 | 12.2 | 20,158 | 3.8 |

On the whole, Methodism grew and prospered during this period, although by the twentieth century it had lost its pre-eminence among the Protestant denominations. Most church members continued to deny any natural correlation between size and religious progress or spiritual prosperity, but few Methodists were content to remain part of a limited body of enthusiastic converts. Methodists in fact laid great stress on numerical growth as a sign of the spiritual vitality of their evangelical mission. Table 2 relates Methodism's relative strength by region to the other mainstream Protestant denominations and the Roman Catholic church from 1851 to 1921.

While the 1851–52 census is notoriously inaccurate, especially in its understating of Wesleyans and its overstating of Anglicans, it does help to provide a general base for understanding how the churches developed. Clearly, Ontario evolved into the heartland of Methodism during the second half of the century; elsewhere the church was weaker numerically than the Presbyterians and Anglicans, and in the Maritimes, the Baptists were significantly stronger. Nevertheless, Methodism had more adherents than any other Protestant denomination in Canada until the twentieth century. Although these statistics provide a number of valuable insights, they submerge much of the subtlety of regional and connexional differences among Methodists, especially in old Ontario before the union of 1884.

Table 3 provides more detailed membership data for the various churches that merged in 1884 into the Methodist Church. The figures represent the number of members in good standing recognized by the church, rather than adherents claiming Methodist affiliation as in the census. Against the backdrop of these numbers, the relatively small Bible Christian, New Connexion, and Primitive Methodist churches attempted to elaborate their own religious experiments. All three shared the problem of maintaining and spreading a vital evangelical message in the face of the huge geographic demands of the country and the high mobility of their members. The three churches were concentrated in distinct sections of Ontario, while the Bible Christians also had weakly organized districts in Prince Edward Island and Ohio-Wisconsin, and the New Connexion held on to a meagre presence in Quebec. Together the three denominations faced the dilemma of having too narrow a territorial and membership base to support effective expansion, but needed physical expansion to retain the members settling beyond their reach and thereby enhance their overall mission.[7]

In 1851 the Bible Christian connexion numbered about 5,700 adherents or about 1,800 members in Canada West and some 250 in Prince Edward Island. Contributing to this overall weakness, during the 1850s the church had no effective operations in a city of any importance except for a small society in Charlottetown. As a connexion, therefore, the Bible Christians were much less visible than their Methodist co-religionists. Only with difficulty could they project a strong denominational image and thereby broaden their appeal to prospective members. Without an urban presence the church also failed to tap the local commercial élites, with their valuable administrative skills and financial resources. Even with a relatively more significant presence in some of the towns and villages, its urban limitations detrimentally affected prospects for the future.

In 1851 the New Connexion Methodist church represented just over 8,600 adherents in Canada West and another 3,400 in Canada East. These figures translated into 3,607 actual members in Canada West and 427 in Canada East. The discrepancy in the ratio between adherents and members in Canada East illustrated the connexion's inability to supply ministers and chapels for the region.[8] Moreover, the physical distances between the church's operations only

Table 3   Methodist connexional membership, 1854–83

| | Wesleyans | | New Connexion | | Bible Christians | | Epis. Meth. | Prim. Meth. |
|---|---|---|---|---|---|---|---|---|
| Date | Ont./Que. | Atl. Can. | Ont. | Que. | Ont. | PEI | Ont. | Ont. |
| 1854 | 32,364 | – | 4,138 | 373 | – | – | 10,337 | 2,671 |
| 1855 | 37,895 | 13,136 | 3,835 | 373 | – | – | 11,310 | 2,902 |
| 1856 | 39,015 | 12,855 | 4,246 | 182 | 2,384 | 357 | 12,466 | 3,039 |
| 1857 | 41,597 | 12,730 | 4,387 | 159 | 2,589 | – | 13,352 | 3,090 |
| 1858 | 48,693 | 13,511 | 4,874 | 275 | 3,106 | 403 | 15,572 | 3,399 |
| 1859 | 51,339 | 14,816 | 6,144 | 293 | 3,245 | 450 | 16,575 | 3,838 |
| 1860 | 53,238 | 15,167 | 6,690 | 294 | 3,294 | 648 | 17,727 | 4,274 |
| 1861 | 53,109 | 15,497 | 7,115 | 308 | 3,251 | 619 | 18,082 | 4,432 |
| 1862 | 53,950 | 15,389 | 7,197 | 304 | 3,459 | 581 | 19,484 | 4,842 |
| 1863 | 55,813 | 15,104 | 7,565 | 354 | 3,869 | 570 | 20,386 | 5,417 |
| 1864 | 55,073 | 15,125 | 7,688 | 340 | 3,745 | 648 | 20,086 | 5,659 |
| 1865 | 55,687 | 15,029 | 7,401 | 327 | 3,762 | 607 | 19,602 | 5,854 |
| 1866 | 56,067 | 15,275 | 7,363 | 343 | 4,005 | 527 | 18,941 | 5,891 |
| 1867 | 57,694 | 14,873 | 7,543 | 383 | 3,827 | 505 | 18,741 | 6,178 |
| 1868 | 59,626 | 15,070 | 7,632 | 394 | 3,957 | 521 | 19,468 | 6,230 |
| 1869 | 61,721 | 14,938 | 7,745 | 442 | 4,285 | 499 | 19,559 | 6,211 |
| 1870 | 63,696 | 15,021 | 7,666 | 463 | 4,342 | 517 | 20,118 | 6,432 |
| 1871 | 65,698 | 15,803 | 7,583 | 405 | 4,304 | 526 | 20,903 | 6,493 |
| 1872 | 68,274 | 15,342 | 7,610 | 381 | 4,624 | 527 | 21,103 | 6,710 |
| 1873 | 69,333 | 15,934 | 7,495 | 390 | 4,544 | 533 | 21,371 | 6,669 |
| 1874 | 72,198 | 17,580 | 7,184 | 403 | 4,826 | 627 | 22,500 | 6,781 |

| | Methodist Church of Canada | | | Bible Christians | | Epis. Meth. | Prim. Meth. |
|---|---|---|---|---|---|---|---|
| Date | Ont./Que. | Atl. Can. | Other | Ont. | PEI | Ont. | Ont. |
| 1875 | 83,364 | 18,962 | 2,410 | 4,948 | 643 | 23,012 | 7,145 |
| 1876 | 88,054 | 21,427 | 2,550 | 5,595 | 633 | – | 7,624 |
| 1877 | 92,591 | 22,083 | 2,158 | 6,268 | 639 | 26,104 | 8,008 |
| 1878 | 94,554 | 22,573 | 2,284 | 6,281 | 661 | 27,285 | 8,174 |
| 1879 | 94,722 | 23,597 | 2,449 | 5,829 | 613 | 27,798 | 8,307 |
| 1880 | 94,396 | 23,725 | 2,715 | 5,868 | 584 | 28,070 | 8,222 |
| 1881 | 95,673 | 24,211 | 2,860 | 6,300 | 638 | 27,402 | 8,218 |
| 1882 | 95,265 | 24,735 | 3,833 | 6,183 | 647 | 26,594 | 8,223 |
| 1883 | 96,786 | 25,152 | 4,286 | 6,014 | 622 | 25,671 | 8,090 |

Notes:

The Methodist Episcopal Church and the Primitive Methodist Church were only organized in Ontario. During the 1880s they both had some members in the northwest.

The Bible Christian Church also oversaw missions in Ohio and Wisconsin until the union of 1884. Over the years the American mission was slightly larger than that in PEI.

"Other" includes the missions in the northwest, British Columbia, and Japan.

All statistics are drawn from the Minutes of Annual Conference or the Journal of General Conference of the various Methodist denominations.

increased the difficulties of providing adequate services. The New Connexion was slightly better represented in the larger urban centres than the Bible Christians, but it also suffered from the lack of a strong presence.

On the other hand, the Primitive Methodists were concentrated heavily in the Toronto area, with 7,500 adherents or 2,000 members in 1851. With the highest relative urban concentration of all the Methodists, the Primitive Methodist church was not only the most visible of the small connexions, but it also had the advantage of several prominent, wealthy lay leaders. Nevertheless, even while strengthening its urban base, these advantages could not overcome the movement of members beyond the limits of effective supervision.[9]

However, the Primitive Methodist church did increase its membership annually until 1868, when it reached 6,230. The following year marked the first decline, and during the early 1870s a period of slower and more halting growth forced the church to re-evaluate the validity of its distinctive evangelical presence and seriously contemplate union with the other Methodist connexions. In 1871 the Primitive Methodists reported only 6,493 members or about 24,000 adherents in Ontario. This latter figure represented 5.2 per cent of the total Methodists and 1.5 per cent of the general population in the province. With the return of internal harmony after the disruption caused by the proposed union in 1874, the church again expanded until 1879, when it reached its peak as a distinct connexion. It hovered at about 8,220 members over the following few years, but brought only 8,090 of them into the united Methodist church. Although growth had been sustained, it was not as rapid as either Methodism in general or the provincial population. In 1881, with 25,555 adherents, the Primitive Methodist church had declined to 4.3 per cent of Ontario's Methodists and 1.3 per cent of the population.

The New Connexion Methodists suffered slow growth in Canada West during most of the 1850s. But the church apparently benefited from the great revival of 1858–59, and membership surged to 7,115 members or about 25,000 adherents in 1861. This represented an increase to 1.8 per cent of the population and 7.2 per cent of all Methodists in Canada West. However, the following years witnessed only slight membership increases and even some years of decline. The position of the New Connexion in Canada East was even more precarious. After almost completely withdrawing services during the early 1850s, the connexion grew back to only 308 members in 1861. This figure translates into only about 1,300 adherents and represents a significant decline over the decade. Many former members had either moved beyond the connexion's reach or had joined the local Wesleyans, where they could share regular religious worship. Overall, the New Connexion reached its greatest size in 1869 with 8,187 members in central Canada. In Ontario in 1871, it represented 6.7 per cent of Methodists and 1.9 per cent of the population and had 30,889 adherents. Another 1,546 adherents resided in Quebec. Three years later the church brought 7,587 members into the union with the Canadian Wesleyans.

Hopes for a viable national Bible Christian church also faltered over this period. Since it was the smallest of the three minor Methodist connexions and received minimal support from abroad, the problems that were critical for the New Connexion and Primitive Methodists were even more significant for the Bible Christians.[10] By 1861 operations in Canada West had grown to 3,251 members, or about 8,800 adherents. These figures represented 2.5 per cent of the Methodist and 0.6 per cent of the provincial population. Following a decade of growth, the church claimed 4,304 members, and the census recorded 18,225 adherents, or 1.1 per cent of the provincial population and 3.9 per cent of the Methodists. Membership generally expanded until 1878 and was aided by the addition of opponents of the 1874 union between the New Connexion and Wesleyan Methodists. After 1878, however, the Bible Christian connexion generally declined until in 1881 in Ontario it represented 1.2 per cent of the population and 4.0 per cent of the Methodists, or

6,300 members and 23,726 adherents. Finally, it entered the union of 1884 with only 6,014 members. The 762 members from the satellite missions in Ohio and Wisconsin severed their links to the Canadian church at that time.

The Bible Christians in Prince Edward Island reported 357 members in 1857 and by 1861 had grown to 619 members and some 2,061 adherents, or over 26 per cent of the island's Methodists but only 2.5 per cent of the population. In 1865 the Bible Christians united with their kindred church in Canada West and added 607 members to the combined connexion. Over the following eight years, membership on the island fluctuated between 499 and 533. In 1871, 526 members were recorded, and the census listed 2,709 adherents, representing approximately 24.5 per cent of the Methodists and 2.9 per cent of the provincial population. From 1874 to 1883 the connexion generally reported over 600 members and reached its peak in 1878. Three years later it had 638 members and 2,403 adherents, representing 17.8 per cent of the Methodists and 2.2 per cent of the population.

Numerical change was only part of the story, however. All three of these small Methodist connexions attempted to expand their operations to serve members who had moved beyond effective ministry. After 1854 the Bible Christian church gradually spread out from its concentrations in Durham and Huron-Perth counties, and in 1869 it opened missions at Owen Sound and on Lake Superior as jumping-off points for the northwest. Such centres were critical for a missionary church with national ambitions. Nevertheless, it withdrew its missionary from Lake Superior after only one year and did not commence organized work in the northwest until 1879. Five missions were briefly opened there, but the church's large operating deficit and the loss of the first two missionaries to secular occupations because of poor financial support effectively crippled the cause.[11]

The New Connexion also attempted to expand into southwestern Canada West and the base of the Bruce Peninsula, but except for rapid growth in Grey and Simcoe counties, which led to the formation of the Owen Sound district in 1853, shortage of finances and preachers forestalled any major expansion. During the same period, as well as the problems faced by the other two churches, the Primitive Methodist connexion was dominated by a few conservative lay leaders who were extremely cautious about expanding into new territories. It was only in 1859 that the Toronto and Hamilton districts were subdivided to create the Brampton district. The following year, more distant circuits were set apart to form Kingston, Guelph, and London districts, and finally in 1870 the Barrie district organized the more northerly circuits. The short-lived Primitive Methodist mission to the northwest was also doomed because of lack of resources. These three denominations continually had to walk a fine line between too rapid and too sluggish expansion, and in general their attempts to serve new regions represented ill-timed drains on their connexional resources.[12]

The Bible Christian, New Connexion, and Primitive Methodist churches gradually recognized that expansion into new territories must be limited until their home districts were in a sounder financial condition. This situation would not be reached until more local members were securely attached to their respective denominations. For instance, in 1864 the New Connexion Conference somewhat sadly reported, "Of late years we have diligently laboured to extend our borders and the cause of Christ among us ... And perhaps our zeal has been too ardent in this matter for our real and permanent good. We have almost run too fast, i.e., for our resources. The zeal will have to be more than ever directed now to the consolidation of our Connexional enterprises – to the strengthening of our stakes. Our influence will have to be brought to bear more fully in diligently cultivating the ground we do occupy, that it may indeed become a fruitful field."[13] Therefore all three connexions developed a strategy of more intensive work among the families of members and subdivided existing districts and circuits to increase the efficiency of this task. Although more labour-intensive and therefore expensive, the smaller units meant less onerous and wasteful travel for the itinerants and permitted greater energy to be spent in essential pastoral work.[14]

A major component of this emphasis on consolidation was the churches' struggle to improve their position in the urban centres. The Primitive Methodist leadership, for example, maintained, "We believe it to be a great mistake to act upon the principle that a mission should only be formed in the backwoods among a poor and scattered population. True, those should not be neglected ... But in many cases, they are not half so much neglected as hundreds and thousands in our cities and towns."[15] The Bible Christians agreed, arguing that to sustain a viable future, "we must enter the centres of population and from thence, with an increased power and efficiency only obtainable from such standpoints, prove our heaven-given mission in winning large numbers from darkness to light and from the power of Satan to God."[16] All three Methodist connexions recognized that without a significant presence in the larger centres, newly arrived members would lose their sense of denominational attachment, and the rural congregations would feel isolated. They understood that strong city circuits were better able to communicate the distinctive connexional message and to provide a dynamism to the entire church operations.

The Bible Christian connexion therefore built churches in Toronto, Hamilton, and Charlottetown and later in Belleville and St Thomas. These stations, the church claimed, gave "us as a denomination a much improved *status* in the Dominion."[17] Similarly, during the 1860s five of the six new Methodist churches in greater Toronto were built by the Primitive Methodists, and in 1876 this Toronto emphasis was capped by the erection of Carlton Street church. The Primitive Methodists also constructed large churches in Brampton and Brantford to supervise the work in the neighbouring regions. The New Connexion attempted to expand its presence in the larger centres, but except for Broadway Tabernacle, which opened in Toronto in 1870, it failed to develop a strong urban presence. It, in fact, was forced to abandon temporarily its work in Montreal for lack of resources, and although it was later able to send a minister there, the Montreal congregation was never self-supporting.

These churches also justified urban expansion on the grounds of moral need. The New Connexion claimed that cities were legitimate fields for evangelical cultivation since they were "centres of crime and moral deprivation that will smite our fair Dominion as with the breath of a pestilence."[18] The Bible Christian Missionary Society in 1867 defended its presence in cities on similar grounds:

We answer, to enter the great centres of population in this new but growing Dominion; to visit the back streets and lanes of towns and cities; to probe the festering wounds of moral corruption found there, and pour into them the blessed balm of Gilead; to enter the dark purlieus and dens of infamy, debauchery and crime, and offer mercy, pardon and peace to those who there wallow in vice; to reclaim the city arab from civilized heathendom; to collect together and educate the teeming thousands of the young and rising race, who, inhaling the pestilential vapours of the immoral atmosphere, and influenced by the corrupt example of city life, in its most debasing forms, will, if not reclaimed prove pests of society, and fill our beloved country with crime, if not with anarchy and revolution. All this, and much more in this direction, is truly and legitimately mission work.[19]

Despite such passionate declarations, however, the churches did not direct their city work at the poor and oppressed, but rather, they sought to attract the commercial and professional middle classes and the skilled artisans. They hoped that the urban congregations would provide status and increased financial support for the larger work of the denominations. Saving the wealthy was just as important as saving the poor, and it was both easier and more beneficial to the other goals of the church.[20]

However, both the Bible Christian and New Connexion churches failed to develop a viable urban base, and in the smaller towns and villages their relative position actually declined after 1861. Over the same period, although the Primitive Methodist city churches were more numerous, most were weak in membership and constrained by heavy debts. Because of lack of resources, in 1873 the connexion cut off financial assistance to all the town churches, and they could barely function, let alone provide leadership for the Primitive Methodist fellowship, under this disability. Thus, together with the New Connexion and the Bible Christians, the Primitive Methodists needed to form a united front with the other larger bodies of Methodists if their evangelical vision was to survive in Canada.[21]

Unlike the three small Methodist connexions originating in Britain, the Methodist Episcopal church had a substantial and well-established membership. By 1851 it could claim over 46,000 adherents and over 8,000 members in two conferences. Just as significant, it was led by a native-born clergy that understood the Canadian situation and was not bound to any foreign ecclesiastical body. It believed it had a destiny to mould and perpetuate a distinctive nation wide voice within the Methodist family of churches. None the less, the Episcopal Methodists shared many of the disabilities of their smaller cousin churches. They were heavily concentrated in two separate regions of Canada West and never developed an organized presence in Canada East or the

Atlantic region. The long-term pattern of growth also camouflaged the troubles the church had faced in the 1840s. Although it had claimed over 8,900 members in 1844, it did not regain that size until 1853. Therefore the Episcopal Methodists faced the future with only cautious optimism.

Of equal importance, they never established a significant presence in the larger urban centres. In Canada West, they represented only 0.4 per cent of the city population and 1.9 per cent in the smaller centres as opposed to 4.9 per cent of the total population in 1851. Such heavy underrepresentation was perhaps understandable in Toronto and the central part of the province, but even in those regions that were their strongholds, they were only marginally present in the major towns. In Kingston, a mere twenty-five individuals claimed to be Episcopal Methodists in 1851.[22] Even more than other connexions, the Methodist Episcopal church was rooted in the land, grew when agriculture prospered, and shrivelled when it suffered. Although it was of sufficient size to serve members in the remoter areas of the province and to create an institutional framework for the connexion, its failure to secure the rising urban centres limited its resource potential, institutional image, and access to the commercial leaders. It measured its success against the Wesleyans, not the small Methodist connexions, and thus, while it grew in absolute terms, it failed to achieve its goal of becoming the pre-eminent voice of Methodism in British America.

Sharing the growth spurred by the great revival of the late 1850s, the connexion by 1861 had doubled its membership to 18,082 and claimed nearly 75,000 adherents in Canada West. These figures represented 5.3 per cent of the provincial population and 21.3 per cent of Methodists. In 1871 the church had 20,903 members and 92,198 adherents in Ontario, with another 1,300 adherents in bordering regions of Quebec. However, growth had slowed and become more erratic; between 1864 and 1867 the church had experienced a net loss of members. Although the denomination grew more rapidly than the general Ontario population, it declined to 19.9 per cent of provincial Methodists in 1871. The connexion reached its highest membership in 1880, but then an absolute decline set in until the union four years later. In 1881 the church represented 17.2 per cent of Methodists and 5.3 per cent of the provincial population. The actual membership of 27,402 in 1881 fell to 24,400 by 1884. From 1854 to 1884, the Methodist Episcopal church was gradually losing ground in its competition with the other Methodist churches.

In any case, simple growth was never enough; as a missionary church with national ambitions, it needed territorial expansion as well as numerical superiority. If it did not make the extra effort to expand its borders, then it was repudiating not only God's earnest command, but also the moral justification for its own separate existence. The emphasis on expansion was especially strong during the 1850s, when it prided itself on being a rural church. "The wilderness and solitary places constitute our ground ... A wide field is open before us in the increasing extension of the back settlements of our country, and among the aborigines of the land. On you, dear brethren, depends the question – shall we go forth and cultivate it? Supply us the means and labourers will be forthcoming, and the solitary places will be glad, and the wilderness bud and blossom as the rose."[23] The 1870s witnessed the final fruition of this policy of expansion. Spurred by Canada's purchase of the Hudson's Bay territory and the perceived threat of Roman Catholic dominance of the country's future heartland, the Methodist Episcopal church joined in the struggle to Protestantize the great northwest. It sent Daniel Pomeroy to Emerson, Manitoba, and Thomas Argue to Winnipeg in 1876, and others soon followed. Bishop Albert Carman used his considerable personal and episcopal influence to support these missionary operations and attempted to generate a permanent cause in the territory.[24]

Nevertheless, the missions never achieved any true measure of independence or stability. The basic problems were familiar. Operating costs were too great for available resources, and loyal Episcopal Methodists were too scattered. For example, in 1880 A.W. Edwards reported from Rapid City: "This place is growing with wonderful rapidity ... I am negotiating for church property here. So far, except for Portage laPrairie, I have found very few of our people. There are none here but one family ... I do not think that enough of our people can be found in any one place in the country to warrant us in opening a mission but these growing centres ought to be looked after."[25] Even Robert Pope, from the stronger mission at Emerson, wrote: "Brother Edwards returned me a list of twenty-eight members, but after a diligent search, I can find seventeen. Possibly this is due to the unsettled state of the Province ... At present writing we are carrying a floating debt of nearly $600. The amount of mortgage is $3500 ... With the strong opposition we meet and the determined and persistent effort made to drive us out of this town, if not to drive us out of this Province, it will be very damaging, if not ruinous, to have it known that we are burdened financially."[26]

Later Pope reinforced this point and suggested that the Methodist Church of Canada, with its long record and more secure position in the region, represented the greatest competition. Although the Methodist Episcopal church eventually organized the missions at Winnipeg, Portage la Prairie, Emerson, Brandon, Morris, Carman, and Nelsonville into a western district under Thomas Argue, the cause never fully recovered from initial weak support and mobile membership.[27] The western missions remained a serious drain on the connexion and by 1883 supplied only 350 members.

Gradually during the 1870s, the church recognized the long-term disadvantages of over-expansion and in Ontario stressed consolidation and improving pastoral care. It reorganized circuits and appointments to permit more intensive supervision by its clergy and strove to overcome its deficiency in the larger centres. It built churches in Kingston and other regional towns and established a church extension fund in 1874 to improve the work in the towns and cities. Although the connexion was willing to make these adaptations by the 1870s, the most eligible church sites had long been occupied, and the Episcopal Methodists were ineffective at luring members from the more established local congregations. The relative position of the Methodist Episcopal church in the larger centres in Ontario actually declined between 1861 and 1871 and thereafter remained constant at about 1.4 per cent of the urban population. Significantly, no Episcopal Methodist church was ever built in Toronto or Montreal, and even in cities such as Ottawa and Kingston, which were the natural focus of large Episcopal Methodist concentrations, the congregations were heavily in debt.[28] For all its ambitions, this inability to develop a viable presence in the important regional centres demonstrated the broader failure of the church to become a significant national institution.

Among the Methodists in British America, the Wesleyans were the clear leaders. This primacy was a function of both size and distribution throughout the country. The connexion entered the 1850s highly optimistic about its future prosperity and its ability to serve the broad range of Canadian needs. Although pre-eminently a rural church, the Wesleyan Methodist connexion early appreciated the benefits of strong operations in the larger urban centres. Its ability to hold on to the urban congregations during the rift with the British Wesleyans during the 1840s was an important factor in its continued stability and growth. It also utilized the influence of the growing regional hegemony of Toronto to spread its evangelical message. Although expansion proved more difficult there, the emphasis on urban centres also grew in the Atlantic region. Not only were members of the local professional and commercial élites drawn to this branch of Methodism, but the cities themselves provided bases for a more effective use of the growing communication systems. Through the distribution of the *Christian Guardian*, the *Wesleyan*, and religious literature, Wesleyans spread their message to all parts of the country.[29]

In Ontario, except for slight decreases in 1861, 1864, 1880, and 1882, the membership of the Wesleyan Methodist church and its successor, the Methodist Church of Canada, increased every year between 1847 and 1884. In 1854, before the addition of about 4,000 members from the union with the Wesleyans in Canada East, it contained 32,364 members. In Canada West, the census recorded 218,427 Wesleyan adherents in 1861 and 286,911 in 1871. These figures represent an increase from 16.0 per cent to 17.7 per cent of the provincial population, but a rather constant 62.0 per cent of all the Methodists. Ten years later, including the additions from the New Connexion, the Methodist Church of Canada represented 436,987 adherents, or 73.9 per cent of all the Ontario Methodists and 22.7 per cent of the provincial population. After 1854, it is difficult to distinguish membership statistics accurately for Canada West since Wesleyan appointments, circuits, and districts ignored the political boundary between Canada West and Canada East.

The significant growth, however, occurred in Canada West; in Canada East, Methodism was besieged and faltering. Except for the influential congregations in Montreal and some strength in the Eastern Townships, little of substance developed in the province during this period. The missions to French Canadians and natives were constantly under attack from the Roman Catholic hierarchy, and membership showed only a slight and fluctuating growth. The Wesleyans in Canada East had about 5,000 members and 25,900 adherents in 1861. Over the following decade, support grew to only 6,200 members and 26,700 adherents. With the addition of members from the New Connexion, the united body recorded an increase to about 8,000 members and 38,000 adherents in 1881. That year there were only about 39,000 Methodists, representing 2.9 per cent of the population in Quebec. Nevertheless, despite the clear failure of the Methodist mission to Protestantize French Canada, the Wesleyans at least provided a denominational presence and an evangelical alternative for the province.

In the Atlantic region, the Wesleyans were also the only significant region-wide Methodist body and served Methodists of all stripes who could not receive pastoral care from their own communions. With the organization of a distinct Conference in 1855, the Wesleyans recorded 13,136 members, including 368 in Bermuda and 2,633 in Newfoundland. Except for rather impressive numerical growth during the late 1850s, the following fifteen years were marked by membership stagnation. Attempts to reopen missions in Labrador only weakened the financial stability of the connexion. The anticipation and final consummation of union with the Wesleyan and New Connexion Methodists from central Canada apparently provided impetus to membership growth and spiritual revival. Membership increased annually between 1874 and 1883, when the Methodist Church of Canada in the Atlantic region brought 25,152 members into the new united Methodist church. The membership of the Methodist Church continued to grow relatively rapidly in New Brunswick over the remainder of the nineteenth century, especially in the industrial urban centres. And Newfoundland provided the highest relative growth in membership for the region, remaining a Methodist stronghold until the interdenominational union of 1925.

As a missionary church with a vital Protestant, Anglo-Saxon vision, the Wesleyans were also intensely interested in the evangelical potential of the northwest and British Columbia. During the 1850s and 1860s, the native population provided the principal focus of mission operations, but gradually the emphasis shifted to the new settlers. Although the church heartily shared the heroic tradition of James Evans and his colleagues and actively promoted such men as George McDougall as they trekked across the west, hope was now placed on the developing mission to Vancouver Island in 1859 and to Red River (Winnipeg) in 1869.[30] However, the Methodists were never able to dominate these mission fields as they had older pioneer Ontario. In 1871 the Wesleyans reported 1,101 members west of Ontario, and this figure rose to 4,286 by the time of the 1884 union, including 721 overseas in the Japan mission.

Only the Wesleyans had the size and stability to develop these missions while still expanding into the newer pioneer areas in Ontario. The church hoped to maintain all of its work and in 1871 announced that "we are resolved to keep pace with the progress of population, to follow the new settler into the wilderness, to comfort him in his loneliness, and guide him in his pathway to the rest of a better home; whilst at the same time, we seek to strengthen and build up the work of God in our growing cities, towns and older settlements."[31] Nevertheless, the Wesleyan leaders mourned the removal of members beyond the church's reach, the inability to attract more converts, and the failure to bring more adherents into full and active membership.[32]

The Wesleyans therefore also recognized that to expand judiciously they must consolidate their position in the Ontario heartland. "If, on the one hand, we seek to enlarge our borders, but, at the same time, fail to preserve to Methodism her own children, the power of extension is impaired, and a collapse is imminent. If on the other hand, we care only to keep and cherish those already under our influence, we close against ourselves a field of labour which ... furnishes a sphere for the manifestation of the loftiest Christian heroism and we forfeit God's crowning benediction."[33] To improve service in Ontario, circuits and districts were reduced in size and the new districts of Whitby, Niagara, Bradford, and Sarnia were created. This administrative consolidation aided the more intensive ministry necessary to help the domestic missions become self-sufficient and the regular circuits to increase their contribution to the overall church operations. Simultaneously, most of the larger urban congregations were set apart as distinct, one-station circuits with full-time pastoral care.

Moreover, the Wesleyans increased their emphasis on developing strong urban congregations during this period. In Wingham, Ontario, for instance, Thomas Cleworth reported in 1870, "We are centralizing some of our scattered congregations with a view to render the working of the Mission more efficient." And Charles Turner wrote from Collingwood, "This is a good church in a most important place. First in relation to the North Shore, rich in lumber, minerals and agriculture to be developed; secondly to the opening up of the Great Northwest, towards which eyes are now turned, and ultimately to free through-trade with the great grain growing States of the American Union."[34] At the same time, subscriptions from across the country were helping to build a suitably impressive church in Winnipeg. It not only served the small local congregation, but more importantly, it provided services for those passing through the city on the journey farther west.[35] It was a critical reminder that Wesleyan Methodism was always near at hand.

Furthermore, the Wesleyans were the first Methodist body to undertake serious mission work in the cities. While never avowing a desire to remake social conditions and clearly not preaching an even embryonic "social gospel," with its collectivist emphasis on creating heaven on earth, the Wesleyans did transcend the rhetoric of the Bible Christians in attempting to bring religion to the urban poor. In Halifax and St John's, a long tradition of concern for the unemployed, widowed, and orphaned led to benevolent organizations and specialized preaching missions. In 1856 the Toronto West circuit hired a missionary to carry out organized city-mission work. In 1859 Hugh Carson performed similar duties in Montreal, and a mission to seamen was opened in Quebec City in 1865. These missionaries visited the poor and sick in areas not regularly served by the itinerancy and worked in the streets, hospitals, and prisons. Basically, they preached the traditional evangelical message of salvation and God's love, and cooperated with local interdenominational charity organizations to help the destitute. However, their concern was the soul, not the body; to them, true victory could only be achieved on an individual basis as the sinner received salvation through the traditional means of grace.[36]

Although not as significant in terms of numbers as the domestic missions, the Wesleyans also entered the overseas mission field. In 1873, after forceful lobbying by William Morley Punshon, the indomitable president of Conference, and with the particular financial support of the wealthy Toronto merchant John Macdonald, a mission was established in Japan.[37] Perhaps more than any other single event, this mission marked the maturity of Canadian

Methodism. Though the improved status gained by the Wesleyans remained, their aggressive missionary expansion was temporarily halted by the severe economic depression of the 1870s. Between 1874 and 1878, a mission deficit of over $70,000 forced internal reorganization and retrenchment. The church forbade the establishment of new missions, surplus missionaries were posted to secure circuits, and the missionary department was pared of all non-essential personnel. One of the two secretaries was transferred and the department's separate publications were eliminated. Furthermore, the specialized mission to Germans in Ontario, established in 1861, was turned over to the German-speaking, Methodistic Evangelical Association in 1879. It was even suggested that the Japan mission be integrated with the American Methodist mission, but the General Conference of 1878 vetoed this proposal. It was no accident that the Woman's Missionary Society was established in 1881 to tap the energy and influence of the female members of the connexion. Paralleling these developments, thirty-seven domestic missions in Ontario became self-supporting circuits between 1878 and 1882, and there was renewed consolidation of the city-mission work. Even some pioneer missions had to be abandoned.[38] By the early 1880s, therefore, the Methodist Church of Canada had joined the other Methodist connexions in recognizing that physical consolidation and the control of the important urban centres must precede expansion if growth was to be sustained.

## THE UNION OF 1884

The most sensible means of consolidating the work in British America was through a union of the mainstream Methodist denominations. Union had in fact been discussed at various times since at least the 1840s. The reunion of the Wesleyans in Canada West in 1847 presaged the essentially geographic union of the Wesleyans in the Canadas in 1854. The easy amalgamation of their operations led to discussions about the broader integration of the Canadian and Atlantic-region Wesleyan connexions. Nevertheless, the splinter denominations also recognized the benefits of union among themselves or even with the large Wesleyan church.

In some ways, it is more difficult to understand why they remained separate. Certainly, early on the parent connexions in Britain were not willing to accept the concessions required for union. The rationale for continued separation there was too strong to allow for recognition of the different circumstances and needs of the bodies in British America. Usually, the first generation of missionaries, who essentially had founded the organizations in British America, also felt too great a personal commitment to their causes to support union. After the long struggle and sacrifice, they felt it would be a betrayal of their colleagues and heritage. Each denomination claimed a distinctive, God-given mission; such beliefs were difficult to overcome. With regard to the Wesleyan and Episcopal Methodists, a full generation of legal, political, and social antagonism, often aggravated by personality conflicts at both the local and national levels, made the removal of ecclesiastical boundaries difficult.[39]

Gradually, however, as new generations of church members and leaders reached maturity, these old differences lost much of their force. Preliminary discussions for union began in the 1850s, and formal committees were established by the various connexions in the middle 1860s. Except for the Bible Christians, whose parent church could not condone union with a Wesleyan connexion, all continued to talk throughout the early 1870s. The Bible Christians expressed interest in a union of the smaller Methodist churches, but neither the New Connexion nor the Primitive Methodists believed such action would solve their problems or help fulfil their evangelical destiny. The Methodist Episcopal church supported union in principle, but it would not abandon the episcopacy or give real power to the laity in its church courts. The Wesleyans also feared greater lay power, but were willing to make some concessions. The Primitive Methodists did not feel these went far enough, and fearing union was simply a means of annexing the smaller churches, they, like the Episcopal Methodists and Bible Christians, remained separate.[40]

Nevertheless, in 1874 a basis of union was accepted by the quarterly meetings of the Wesleyans in Atlantic and central Canada and the New Connexion. The newly created Methodist Church of Canada divided itself into Toronto, London, Montreal, Nova Scotia, New Brunswick and Prince Edward Island, and Newfoundland annual conferences and established a General Conference to meet every four years. Although the churchwide boards, committees, schools, and publishing interests came under the authority of the General Conference, real power remained with the fairly independent annual conferences. The laity were allowed equal representation with the itinerants on General Conference, but not on the annual or district conferences. General Conference was led by a president who merely chaired the meetings. In recognition of his long service and the unique position he held in the history of Canadian Methodism, Egerton Ryerson was elected the first president. However, he claimed this was merely an "honourable diversion" without any real duties.[41]

Originally, the church was called "The United Wesleyan Methodist Church of Canada," but "Wesleyan" was immediately dropped in order to make wider union more palatable. The new church also ended its filial relationship with the British Wesleyan and New Connexion churches. It became a totally independent and equal partner within the international family of Methodist connexions. It also became the first truly national Protestant church, with members from Newfoundland to British Columbia and overseas in Bermuda and Japan.

Over the following decade, it became apparent that a full union of all the mainstream Methodist churches was both necessary and advantageous. When they individually looked for greater support, they found wasteful and irrational competition instead. In some small villages, three or four weak Methodist churches divided the field. It was ruefully claimed that "on a quiet Sunday evening the singing in one could be heard in the other ... in the words of the same Methodist hymn."[42] Such conditions could not be allowed to prevail if Methodism was to play a vital social and evangelical role.

Moreover, throughout at least the last quarter of the nineteenth century, powerful ecumenical forces were driving the Protestant denominations together. For instance, in 1878 Toronto hosted the First Canadian Christian

Conference. Modelled on similar British and American gatherings, the conference brought together the major Protestant denominations to discuss their evangelistic mission and to acknowledge their similar attributes and goals. These churches were also active participants in international, interdenominational missionary conferences which advocated cooperation in serving the non-Christian world. Of greater significance for Methodists, in the fall of 1881 the first Ecumenical Methodist Conference met in London to discuss common themes. It supplied an immediate and powerful impulse to Methodist union in Canada, which was consummated three years later.[43] Subsequently, talks continued in earnest with the Presbyterian, Congregational, and Anglican churches over immediate cooperation and ultimate organic union.[44]

More particularly, supporters of Methodist union claimed that opponents of the denomination used its factionalism and petty squabbling to attack its Christian character. Not only was disunity considered an insult to God's will, but it also prevented the creation of a common front against religion's many enemies. This was true whether the enemy was Roman Catholicism, heathenism and irreligion, or the scepticism, atheism, and immorality of the contemporary world. New intellectual attacks on the fundamental anchors of religion also appeared to make a united response critical for Methodist success.[45]

Further, by the 1880s all the Methodist churches were essentially broadly Protestant Canadian institutions. The social, economic, and political differences of the original connexions had all but disappeared, and the denominations were determined to build mature, independent organizations. Increasingly nationalistic, the new Canadian-born leaders were anxious to work out their own destiny and resented the ill-informed intervention of some British churchmen. Also, these new Canadian leaders had grown beyond the prejudices and animosities of many of their predecessors. Despite their heroic contributions in earlier times, the death of men such as James Richardson in 1875, Anson Green in 1879, and especially Egerton Ryerson in 1882 removed large impediments to union. Many sincere Methodists could never reside in a church which contained the Ryerson clan.[46]

Perhaps the best argument for union, however, was the lack of friction in the Methodist Church of Canada. Concerns over redundant ministers, pension plans, and possible defections were worked out fairly amicably. Some New Connexion members had joined the Primitive Methodists and Bible Christians, but charges were found for displaced itinerants, and $71,000 was collected to upgrade the New Connexion's superannuation and children's funds. As the full force of the economic depression was felt in the late 1870s, most members agreed they would have been in much worse shape without union. Its benefits clearly outweighed any pains caused by integration.[47]

Nevertheless, two substantial issues of church polity remained to be solved before broader union could be implemented. These centred on the role of the laity in the church courts and the nature of the new church's executive. The distinctive evangelical experiment of the Bible Christians, Primitive Methodists, and former New Connexion Methodists was based on the crucial role performed by the laity in church administration. The councils of the former two especially were dominated by powerful laymen who jealously guarded their

influence; the churches had been founded in revolt against the highly conservative, minister-controlled Wesleyan church in Britain. They feared that without
lay participation at all levels of administration, the institution would become
dominated by the ordained clergy. Formality and loss of dynamic fervour, if not
clerical despotism, might well result. They viewed equal or greater lay participation with the clergy as a measure of the vitality of their connexions.[48]

It should be noted that, over the third quarter of the nineteenth century,
both the Wesleyan and Episcopal Methodist churches had adopted a more extensive role for the laity. The Methodist Episcopal church recognized the role
of laymen on church boards, in unofficial organizations, or as church trustees,
stewards, and financial agents and relied heavily on them for advice on church
matters. A committee of the 1870 General Conference also studied having lay
delegates on that body. The laity was granted membership on the annual conferences in 1874 in response to the greater financial and administrative needs
of the church. In that year as well, the General Conference agreed to accept laymen in its deliberations, but when the local churches were polled, this reform
was rejected. However, over the following years, there was a change of heart,
and laymen took an equal place with the itinerants at the last independent General Conference in 1882.[49]

The Wesleyans, who had been hurt by lay schisms in both England and
Upper Canada, had joined the Episcopal Methodists in their early unwillingness to grant laymen membership on the church's higher courts. Gradually,
however, this view changed. By 1854 the laity might independently petition the
Conference for desired actions and had already gained a significant place on
committees such as the missionary board, college, chapel relief, and contingent
fund. After 1855, in recognition of the need for financial support, all church
committees dealing with money matters had equal lay and itinerant membership. Furthermore, under pressure from both lay and clerical leaders, the connexion gradually accorded a greater share of its committee responsibilities to
the laity.[50] For instance, all committees negotiating union had equal lay and
itinerant representation.

By the 1870s, the Wesleyans were prepared to cede equal lay membership on
nearly all the committees of Conference, but they stopped short of granting
membership in the actual deliberations of the annual or district conferences.
In order that union with the New Connexion in 1874 might be achieved, however, the laity was finally granted equal membership with the itinerancy in the
newly created General Conference except when it dealt with stationing, ordination, or ministerial discipline. At the second General Conference of the Methodist Church of Canada in 1878, a motion to extend lay representation to the
annual and district conferences, where real power resided, was postponed.[51]

With these compromises over lay participation already in place, many Episcopal and Wesleyan Methodists objected to a further extension of power to the laity. They feared that it might weaken the centralized control considered
essential for effective administration and discipline and the ultimate mission of
the church. The itinerants were particularly afraid of interference in areas considered purely "clerical" such as stationing, disciplining, and ordaining ministers. The clergy believed it was crucial for their independence that they be

judged and appointed by their peers.[52] Even many of the leading Wesleyan and Episcopal Methodist laity objected to the proposal; they already wielded significant power without a seat at Conference. The expansion of lay participation might well undermine their own existing status and influence. Nevertheless, in the interest of organic union, most of the original opponents were willing to accept concessions. According to the basis of union, laymen, but not laywomen, were granted equal representation on all church courts. For their part, those favouring total equality agreed that the laity should not participate on disciplining or stationing committees, although even there their influence would be felt.

But this expanded lay participation did not represent a real democratization within Methodism; rather, it reinforced the position of the traditional lay élites. Only they had the wealth and local prestige and could afford the necessary time to serve as delegates. Presence within the bar at Conference merely confirmed their existing power officially. Moreover, wealthy and influential lay Methodists, men and women, had always exercised significant power because they were too valuable to be ignored. John Williams, the president of the London Conference of the Methodist Church of Canada claimed: "They apprehended the fact that as the Church advanced in intelligence, wealth and moral influence, it required and demanded a different treatment from that which was only suited to the formative period of its history … yet the ministry felt it could hardly justify itself in assuming the entire burden and labour of carrying out and bringing to maturity the various schemes of the Church's enterprise – which its increasing culture, wealth and social position were demanding – while so much talent and energy were to be found in the laity."[53] The church required their business acumen and liberality, and the laity received a visible and responsible role in return. The move would bolster their denominational loyalty and expand their contribution to the effectiveness of the connexion's administration.

This extension of power to the laity did not mean a split in the church's government. The itinerancy and the laity fundamentally agreed on the policies the church should pursue. They shared the same aspirations to evangelize the world and to strengthen the moral base of society at home. They remained essential allies in nourishing the new church and guarding the Protestant goals of Canadian society. The status and stability of the lay leaders added to the church's respectability and permitted the clergy more freedom to deal with social and spiritual matters. Where divisions did occur, they represented factions within the two groups, not between them.[54]

The other divisive issue among the Methodist churches was the nature of the official head of the church. All institutions needed leadership, but traditional fear of ecclesiastical despotism, especially among the Bible Christian, New Connexion, and Primitive Methodists, meant that this individual's power had to be circumscribed by representative bodies. Furthermore, the conferences of all the Methodist connexions would never abandon their positions as the seats of power, while the local quarterly official boards expected to remain the arbiters of final recourse.[55]

Originally, the first Methodist church in Upper Canada had retained the American-style episcopacy as the most legitimate and scripturally sound form of leadership. However, with the union in 1833, it accepted an annually elected president of Conference. After the reunion of 1847, the British-appointed president shared authority with the Canadian co-delegate, who presided during the president's absence. In order to limit the already meagre powers of the president, the same individual could not normally hold office more than once in four years.[56] The weak Wesleyan connexions in Lower Canada and the Atlantic region were administered directly by the executive committee of the British Missionary Society until the mid-1850s and afterwards followed the Wesleyan pattern in Upper Canada. The presidents were in fact only chairmen of the Conference meetings and carried on their regular duties during the year.

Leadership never rested with the president alone. The editors of the newspapers, principals of the schools, missionary secretaries, and others holding prominent pulpits easily had as much influence. Although authority remained with the Annual Conference, personal qualities of leadership could raise an individual to significant temporary power. For instance, Egerton Ryerson never served as president or co-delegate of the Wesleyan Methodist Church, yet he retained a tremendous influence through his own personal energy and ability. Hence the Conference, although it disciplined, did not stifle able leaders.

This pattern was repeated in the smaller Methodist denominations. The presiding officer was sometimes native-born rather than from Britain, but real power remained with the Conference. Since the president merely added the duties to his pastoral and circuit responsibilities, the position tended to be an onerous, but honorary one. Again, a group of able itinerants dominated the key boards, committees, and publications where decisions were made and the ongoing administration of the connexion carried out.

In 1874, with separation from the British parent connexions, the Conference of the Methodist Church of Canada itself elected Egerton Ryerson president. On his retirement four years later, he acknowledged its honorary character but warned that the church needed stronger personal leadership. "Equally, if not more, important, will it be for you to supply some principle or authority of connexional unity, as at present our Connexion consists of a mere congeries of co-ordinate annual Conferences, and your President is the mere chairman of the General Conference, and is not even a member of any annual Conference except that from which he happens to have been elected. The oneness and unity of the body of the Church obviously requires, not merely a figure head, but a real head, like that of the head of a natural body."[57] Ryerson was then nearing the end of an illustrious career and was not prepared to press for the needed changes during his own term of office.

The General Conference of 1878 did recognize the need for continuity, but rather than increase the power of the president, it established an executive board of twelve to administer the church when Conference was not assembled. Although not a legislative body, this board could carry out recommendations and decide on measures for the general welfare of the church, as well as act as a court of appeal on questions of law arising from the annual conferences. Ultimately, this board was created to consolidate the hold of existing church leaders on denominational operations. In turn, its strength came from the powerful clerical and lay members who sat on the board. No one could easily stand up against the collective opinion of these men, who held influence throughout the connexion and in temporal society as well. However, many leading Methodists, including Alexander Sutherland, the missionary secretary, still pressed for a powerful "general superintendent" with authority to direct the church's work. "I do not hold that a General Superintendency will infallibly cure every unhealthy symptom, and usher in the millennium; nevertheless, I do believe that a Superintendency in harmony with the Connexional character of Methodism would have a powerful effect in strengthening weak points, and in promoting unity of aim, unity of effort and unity of administration."[58]

On the other hand, the Methodist Episcopal church, when it had been constituted in 1834, had been led by bishops. This fact became the principal distinguishing characteristic of the church. However, although it was a life appointment, General Conference elected and controlled the bishop. His influence rested on his status and energy rather than on strictly independent ecclesiastical power. But he was able to bring continuity and efficiency to the church's operations as its chief administrator. The first two bishops, John Reynolds and John Alley, began a tradition of conservative, responsible administration. Alley, who held office for only two years, was succeeded by Philander Smith in 1850. Smith presided with Reynolds until the latter's death in 1857 and then continued with James Richardson as co-bishop until 1870. Richardson was the first native-born Methodist bishop, and he had a profound influence on the direction taken by the church. During the union discussions of the 1860s and 1870s, he avoided taking sides and did much to maintain harmonious relations among Episcopal Methodists when organic union was subsequently rejected.[59]

The last and strongest bishop was Albert Carman. Born of United Empire Loyalist stock in 1833, he was educated at Victoria College. He then taught school and gained particular influence as principal of Albert College, the university established in Belleville by the Episcopal Methodists. Carman possessed not only a shrewd mind and a notable administrative talent, but also a strong sense of the distinct mission of the connexion. Representing the new generation rising to prominence in the church, he through his education, temperament, and detachment from the old political and ecclesiastical feuds was able to accept the new opportunities challenging the church. He believed strongly in a centralized administration and the wisdom and scriptural basis of the episcopacy, yet he was never blinded to the advantages of organic union in order to fulfil the greater destiny of service to the nation and the world beyond.[60]

As union discussions evolved during the 1870s and 1880s, the churches with a British background supported a president or perhaps a general superintendent, but they would never accept the rule of bishops. Even the title was too closely associated with dogma, ritual, and authoritarianism. However, the Methodist Episcopal church appeared equally committed to the office. It believed that its episcopacy was not open to the abuses of power which it saw in the Roman Catholic or Anglican churches. Led by Emerson Bristol, Isaac Aylesworth, and Thomas Webster, many of the older clergy refused to accept any compromise on this issue. After spending their entire lives defending the office, they felt it would be hypocritical to surrender.[61]

A compromise was worked out, however, that satisfied most members. The church's leadership would rest in two general superintendents, who would head a much more powerful General Conference. They would be elected by the General Conference for a four- or eight-year term, but would be able to succeed themselves in office. Their powers were substantially greater than former executive officers. All the uniting connexions recognized that a properly influential senior executive was needed to oversee the complex denominational operations and agreed that the general superintendency was a realistic compromise. After all, rule by committee was no less open to abuse than by an episcopacy.[62]

Although the general superintendent was not a bishop, the younger Methodist Episcopal clergy were willing to accept the compromise in the interest of union. When Bishop Carman agreed, other opposition quickly faded. With Carman as the first effective superintendent in the new church, the episcopal dimensions of the office quickly resurfaced. Even the apparent limitation on the term of office had little effect since Carman continued as head of the denomination until his retirement in 1914.[63] His colleague and successor, Samuel Dwight Chown, remained in office from 1910 until the formation of the United Church of Canada in 1925.

With the issues of the role of the laity and the nature of the church's leadership resolved, questions of the powers of the various church courts, the status of lay preachers, and the integration of the various connexions and their institutions were also quickly worked out. Only 3,403 members of the Bible Christian connexion voted on union, with 71 per cent in favour, and 78 per cent of the 3,848 members of the Primitive Methodist connexion who voted supported union. Neither the Methodist Episcopal church nor the Methodist Church of Canada held a popular vote. According to established procedure, only the quarterly meetings of circuit were asked to endorse the agreement. In the Methodist Church of Canada, 649 or 87 per cent supported union while 90 opposed and 10 tied. In the Methodist Episcopal church, the vote was 135 in favour, 35 opposed, and 7 tied. Only the parent British Bible Christian connexion opposed the union, but the local Bible Christians denied the right of that body to control the property or destiny of the Canadian church.[64]

Despite the overwhelming support for union, some members chose not to join. Some Bible Christians and Primitive Methodists who had not felt comfortable in an urban, middle-class church took this opportunity to promote an independent, conservative evangelical mission. They were no longer restrained by connexional loyalty and felt the new institution would be even less sympathetic to their interests. The Free Methodist, Baptist, or other evangelical churches provided more congenial homes. Others took the opportunity to join the quasi-Methodist Salvation Army, with its highly theatrical and emotional services and its commitment to the industrial poor. A few Episcopal Methodist preachers emigrated to the United States in order to retain the episcopacy, though this move also reflected concern over redundant itinerants in the new church, but most of the preachers who originally opposed the union finished out their careers in the Methodist Church. At the same time, since Methodism by 1884 represented a moderate, middle-of-the-road Protestantism, some members found no trouble in shifting to the Presbyterian or Anglican fellowships.

### THE NEW CHURCH

Notwithstanding the minor desertions, the union of 1884 was widely acclaimed and actively supported. It appeared to stimulate a massive revival which more than compensated for any membership losses resulting from union. It also magnified a sense of optimism and accomplishment throughout the entire denomination and reconfirmed a feeling of natural power and rectitude inherent in the members.[65] In the decades that followed, the Methodist Church was able to minister to the moral and spiritual needs of all Canadians and had the wealth and respectability to participate in a wide range of vital social experiments.

The new church was also capable of effectively dealing with many of the problems that had faced the antecedent connexions. It eliminated much of the wasteful competition in older communities by closing churches and consolidating or realigning congregations and circuits while supplying more intensive pastoral care. The newly available resources were applied to the church's expanding mission operations in western Canada and overseas. Methodism now believed it was in a position to save the northwest and British Columbia from heathenism, scepticism, and Roman Catholicism and thereby buttress the moral and spiritual fabric of the nation. It was also able to become an equal partner with other churches in the international assault on the non-Christian world. It could expand its work in Japan and open new missions in China.[66]

On another level, union permitted the church to pursue the growing demands of Canadian cities. Especially after 1896, when the country seemed inundated by non-English-speaking immigrants, Methodism was able to focus a specialized ministry on their needs. The traditional urban congregations, with their comfortable respectability and moral self-righteousness, held little appeal for most of the newcomers. Even the old-fashioned urban missions were generally irrelevant to the immigrants' experience or requirements. These immigrants represented a truly alien dimension in Canadian life. The Methodists attempted to create institutions that were both helpful and meaningful to them and that would also help assimilate them into the Protestant Canadian way of life.[67]

Industrialization also enlarged the prosperous middle class. As the cities became bigger and more functionally specialized, this stratum of society abandoned the core of the city to the factories and workers and erected luxurious houses on the outskirts of the built-up districts. The shift did not represent a flight to the suburbs in the modern sense, but rather a move uptown. Nevertheless, the large downtown churches, many of which were new and still in debt, were too distant or in too unattractive locations to retain their former supporters. Within a very few years, therefore, Methodism was obliged to build a large number of costly buildings. Without church union, it is doubtful that this need could have been met, and the denomination would have lost that group which it was most interested in retaining and serving.

As table 4 illustrates, the membership of the new church continued to expand from 1884 until it merged into the United Church of Canada in 1925. The table summarizes this growth by conference and shows the spread of the church across Canada and into Japan and China. Shifts in conference boundaries make comparisons at this level difficult, but overall the table also demonstrates the uneven nature of membership expansion, especially in Atlantic Canada. While Methodism increased dramatically in the Prairie provinces and British Columbia, it did not keep pace with actual population growth. Perhaps most interesting, the figures for members on trial fell off dramatically over the period. Except for Newfoundland, it appears that either the testing of members became less onerous or the church lost much of its evangelizing drive. In any event, from 1886 until 1925, the church increased its membership from 197,479 to 418,352.

The union of 1884 also permitted the further elaboration of a complex national organization to meet the church's expanded mission. This involved significant administrative reform, the expansion of a sophisticated institutional infrastructure, improved church facilities, and the systematizing of the means to pay for these and other developments. With regard to administration, strong centralized control, not localism or spontaneity, had always marked the Methodist revival in British America. While the church's strength rested on its well-established organization rising pyramid-like from the individual through the class meeting, appointment, circuit, and district to the Annual or General Conference, the true heart of the denomination's power was the large Conference. It enforced unity and discipline. Congregational independence never gained a foothold in Methodism.[68] At the same time, the Conference helped assure a continuing, relevant mission to Canadian society. Hence it represented a powerful focus for the church's collective aspirations and was the face of the church to the world. Since in the new church the General Conference administered the boards and institutions and brought together the leading Methodists in the country, over time, real power gravitated to this assembly.

As part of the increased institutional evolution, Methodism also developed a significant network of newspapers and magazines. They were critical in binding members to the church and transmitting its ideology and goals to the public at large. Under a succession of influential editors, the *Christian Guardian* had always represented first the Wesleyans and later the united Methodists in Canada. In 1849 the Wesleyans in the Maritimes had established the *Wesleyan* to promote their regional aims. The Episcopal Methodists started the *Canada Christian Advocate* in 1845, and the New Connexion supported the *Evangelical Witness* from 1854 until it merged with the *Christian Guardian* in 1874. The Primitive Methodists' *Christian Journal,* founded in Toronto in 1858, and the Bible Christians' *Observer,* established at Bowmanville in 1866, represented the religious and social ambitions of their respective churches.[69]

Table 4  Quadrennial Methodist membership by conference, 1886–1925

| Conference | 1886 | | | 1890 | | | 1894 | | |
|---|---|---|---|---|---|---|---|---|---|
| | Full | Trial | Total | Full | Trial | Total | Full | Trial | Total |
| Toronto | 30,497 | 2,892 | 33,389 | 35,468 | 2,260 | 37,728 | 33,697 | 1,744 | 35,441[a] |
| London | 22,233 | 2,004 | 24,237 | 25,552 | 1,687 | 27,212 | 28,047 | 2,196 | 30,243 |
| Nia./Ham. | 23,202 | 1,806 | 25,008 | 25,285 | 1,529 | 26,814 | 28,188 | 1,442 | 29,630 |
| Bay Quinte | 23,599 | 2,224 | 24,623 | 28,318 | 1,637 | 29,955 | 36,568 | 2,254 | 38,822[a] |
| Guelph | 23,506 | 2,246 | 25,552 | 26,917 | 1,311 | 28,228 | 29,386 | 1,199 | 30,585 |
| Montreal | 24,554 | 1,670 | 26,224 | 32,307 | 1,849 | 34,156 | 35,677 | 1,891 | 37,568 |
| Nova Scotia | 11,779 | 639 | 12,428 | 13,339 | 372 | 13,751 | 13,723 | 502 | 14,255 |
| NB/PEI | 9,803 | 541 | 10,334 | 10,920 | 449 | 11,369 | 11,952 | 314 | 12,266 |
| Nfld | 8,669 | 1,972 | 10,641 | 9,230 | 835 | 10,065 | 9,708 | 842 | 10,550 |
| Manitoba | 4,640 | 393 | 5,033 | 9,258 | 637 | 9,895 | 14,297 | 909 | 15,260 |
| Sask. | | | | | | | | | |
| Alberta | | | | | | | | | |
| BC | | | | 2,172 | 807 | 2,979 | 3,440 | 996 | 4,436 |
| Japan | | | | 1,716 | 0 | 1,716 | 1,876 | 105 | 1,981 |
| China | | | | | | | | | |
| Total | 181,082 | 16,387 | 197,479 | 220,495 | 13,373 | 233,868 | 246,559 | 14,394 | 260,953 |

Notes:
[a] Bowmanville and Uxbridge districts, with 5,723 members, were transferred from Toronto to Bay of Quinte Conference.
British Columbia and Japan were districts in Toronto Conference before becoming separate Conferences.

| *Conference* | *1898* | | | *1902* | | | *1906* | | | *1910* | | |
|---|---|---|---|---|---|---|---|---|---|---|---|---|
| Toronto | 41,686 | 1,632 | 43,318 | 45,004 | 1,371 | 46,375 | 51,539 | 1,562 | 53,101 | 57,418 | 1,144 | 58,562 |
| London | 46,268 | 1,515 | 47,783 | 48,142 | 1,096 | 49,238 | 49,129 | 1,284 | 50,413 | 49,962 | 661 | 50,623 |
| Hamilton | 44,740[b] | 1,338 | 46,078 | 46,595 | 1,027 | 47,622 | 49,650 | 1,069 | 50,719 | 51,868 | 620 | 52,480 |
| Bay Quinte | 38,764 | 1,866 | 40,630 | 38,562 | 942 | 39,504 | 39,249 | 1,104 | 40,353 | 39,821 | 1,055 | 40,876 |
| Montreal | 35,855 | 986 | 36,841 | 35,375 | 834 | 36,209 | 36,812 | 870 | 37,682 | 38,005 | 719 | 38,724 |
| Nova Scotia | 15,764 | 343 | 16,107 | 15,848 | 219 | 16,067 | 16,104 | 207 | 16,311 | 16,028 | 156 | 16,184 |
| NB/PEI | 13,275 | 287 | 13,562 | 13,516 | 276 | 13,792 | 13,662 | 184 | 13,846 | 14,201 | 286 | 14,487 |
| Nfld. | 10,544 | 702 | 11,246 | 10,688 | 1,163 | 11,851 | 11,668 | 964 | 12,632 | 12,146 | 1,488 | 13,634 |
| Manitoba | 16,940 | 752 | 17,692 | 21,708 | 684 | 22,392 | 15,018 | 371 | 15,389 | 16,711 | 369 | 17,080 |
| Sask. | 10,445 | 360 | 10,805 | 14,995 | 363 | 15,358 | | | | | | |
| Alberta | 5,673 | 235 | 5,908 | 10,358 | 292 | 10,650 | | | | | | |
| BC | 3,782 | 1,097 | 4,879 | 4,922 | 1,194 | 6,116 | 5,908 | 1,297 | 7,205 | 8,839 | 961 | 9,800 |
| Japan | 2,200 | 170 | 2,370 | 2,440 | 235 | 2,675 | 2,872 | 231 | 3,103 | | | |
| China | 9 | 22 | 31 | 54 | 0 | 54 | 150 | 100 | 250 | 1,625 | 0 | 1,625 |
| Total | 269,827 | 10,710 | 280,537 | 282,854 | 9,041 | 291,895 | 307,879 | 9,838 | 317,717 | 331,977 | 8,114 | 340,091 |

*Notes:*

b Guelph and Niagara Conferences were folded into Hamilton Conference. Some of the districts were transferred to London Conference.

In 1907 the Canadian and American Methodist churches in Japan united to form a quasi-independent local church. Statistics were therefore no longer available.

Manitoba includes the northwest until the Conference of 1906.

Table 4  Quadrennial Methodist membership by conference, 1886–1925 (cont'd)

| Conference | 1914 | | | 1918 | | | 1922 | | | 1925 | | |
|---|---|---|---|---|---|---|---|---|---|---|---|---|
| | Full | Trial | Total | Full | Trial | Total | Full | Trial | Total | Full | Trial | Total |
| Toronto | 61,769 | 1,348 | 63,117 | 66,614 | 924 | 67,538 | 71,435 | 916 | 72,351 | 74,916 | 729 | 75,645 |
| London | 51,037 | 914 | 51,951 | 55,350 | 461 | 55,811 | 57,829 | 567 | 58,396 | 59,538 | 243 | 59,781 |
| Hamilton | 54,668 | 710 | 55,378 | 57,720 | 523 | 58,243 | 59,387 | 466 | 59,853 | 60,097 | 334 | 60,431 |
| Bay Quinte | 40,610 | 669 | 41,279 | 41,971 | 803 | 42,774 | 44,112 | 401 | 44,513 | 43,931 | 199 | 44,130 |
| Montreal | 39,369 | 608 | 39,975 | 41,086 | 518 | 41,604 | 43,477 | 500 | 43,977 | 44,434 | 406 | 44,840 |
| Nova Scotia | 16,331 | 126 | 16,457 | 16,960 | 147 | 17,107 | 17,775 | 80 | 17,855 | 18,012 | 74 | 18,086 |
| NB/PEI | 14,381 | 242 | 14,623 | 14,961 | 208 | 15,169 | 15,694 | 146 | 15,840 | 16,189 | 107 | 16,296 |
| Nfld | 11,852 | 1,069 | 12,921 | 12,613 | 1,028 | 13,641 | 13,021 | 1,075 | 14,096 | 12,006 | 1,196 | 13,202 |
| Manitoba | 23,124 | 259 | 23,383 | 24,590 | 252 | 24,942 | 25,088 | 340 | 25,428 | 27,341 | 216 | 27,557 |
| Sask. | 17,574 | 422 | 17,996 | 18,495 | 381 | 18,876 | 20,770 | 250 | 21,020 | 21,032 | 222 | 21,254 |
| Alberta | 15,286 | 299 | 15,585 | 15,643 | 121 | 15,764 | 16,525 | 180 | 16,713 | 15,860 | 150 | 16,010 |
| BC | 13,515 | 1,210 | 14,725 | 14,107 | 871 | 14,978 | 16,216 | 675 | 16,891 | 17,164 | 639 | 17,823 |
| China | 1,462 | 140 | 1,602 | 1,863 | 0 | 1,863 | – | – | 2,694ᶜ | – | – | 3,298 |
| Total | 360,978 | 8,014 | 368,992 | 381,973 | 6,237 | 388,210 | 404,023 | 5,604 | 409,627 | 410,520 | 4,515 | 418,352 |

ᶜThis figure is from 1923; the 1922 statistics are unavailable for China.

All the central-Canadian Methodist newspapers merged into the *Christian Guardian* in 1884 while the *Wesleyan* continued to represent Methodism in Atlantic Canada.

Union also helped to enlarge the market for more specialized journals. In fact, this trend had begun in 1875 with the founding of the *Canadian Methodist Magazine* by the Methodist Church of Canada. It was devoted to "religion, literature and social progress" and was designed to advance Canadian literary, religious, and intellectual life.[70] The magazine played a subtle, yet indispensable role in introducing a wide range of controversial questions to the church membership. Edited by William Henry Withrow from its inception until it ceased publication in 1906, it absorbed *Earnest Christianity* in 1876 and the *Canadian Methodist Quarterly* in 1895. The latter journal had originally been published jointly by the faculties of theology at Montreal's Wesleyan Theological Seminary and Victoria University from 1889 until 1895 in order to promote "theology, philosophy, sociology and education."[71]

As well as regional journals such as the *Western Methodist Recorder* (1899), the *Assiniboia Church Advocate* (1904), the *Rat Portage Methodist* (1901), and the *Newfoundland Methodist Monthly Greeting* (1888), the church sponsored a wide variety of magazines on topics related to young people and missionary operations. Journals such as *Canadian Epworth Era* (1899–1916), *Missionary Outlook* (1881–1925), *Onward* (1891–1925), *Missionary Bulletin* (1903–21), and *Palm Branch* (1894–1925) were critical in the institutional evolution of the church, as well as in defining its role during the late nineteenth and early twentieth centuries.

Simultaneously, the Methodist church maintained its long tradition of operating book rooms and publishing houses across Canada. As well as acting as clearing-houses for foreign publications, they reprinted or published important religious and secular works. The Methodist publishing business became one of the largest and most important in the dominion and provided a permanent headquarters for the central bureaucracy of the entire church. The press helped expand the literary scope of church members, introduced broader religious, scientific, and intellectual questions to the public, and especially under William Briggs, provided a major forum for the growing Canadian literary community.[72]

The church also continued its emphasis on improving its facilities. This most visibly took the form of constructing large churches to serve the expanding range of social and educational, as well as religious, functions. The process had begun in the 1850s and because of its expense, was a significant factor in the unions of 1874 and 1884. Such buildings required skilled workers, detailed plans, and large amounts of money. Yet no connexion could afford to abstain from these projects. As early as 1863, the Annual Conference of the Methodist Episcopal church claimed that "it is difficult to attach too much importance to the subjects of building, improving and thus extending our chapel accommodation. We regard our Canadian chapels, not only as the glory of our country, but useful and substantial monuments of Christian liberality and enterprise ... We would urge every member of this conference, and of the church, to make church-building a personal duty, second only to

the saving of souls."[73] Church buildings were believed to be the best investment for the religious welfare of future generations of Canadians, and since
little else separated the various Methodist connexions, these structures demonstrated their continued confidence in separate connexional polities.[74] Eventually this competition led to overbuilding, but the edifices formed a network
for the spread of values and for the maintenance of stability and unity throughout the national Methodist community.

The 1860s had also witnessed the construction of a number of regional
churches which served both the local congregations and the surrounding districts. Providence church in Thunder Bay, for instance, was three hundred
miles west of the nearest Wesleyan church and five hundred miles east of
Winnipeg. The church building supplied a focus for the entire mission field
and, it was believed, "may become a centre from which shall go out an influence for good to a large section of this very extensive territory."[75] In Winnipeg, Grace church opened in 1871 to perform a similar function for the
northwest. At the summit of these regional churches were a group of well-established congregations with even more elaborate structures. These were the
"mother" churches of their communities and created and helped to support
a host of "daughter" churches in the surrounding areas. Gower Street in
St John's, Brunswick Street in Halifax, and St James Street in Montreal, for
example, all could claim this distinction.

These churches shared with other, newer buildings the status of monuments to Methodist progress. They were the pride of the denomination and of
the city in which they were located. Hamilton's Centenary Wesleyan church,
guided and sustained by Edward and Lydia Jackson, cost over $30,000 and was
designed to be the connexional landmark in the city. Built in 1866, it housed
the leading local Methodists, illustrated God's favour to the denomination,
and demonstrated that temporal prosperity need not undermine earnest piety.[76] Similarly, Dominion church in Ottawa purposely supplied a command-
ing presence and raised the status of Methodism in the nation's capital. And
Metropolitan church in Victoria opened in 1872 as "a fitting monument to
the energy and liberality, as well as evidence of the prosperity, of Victoria
Methodism."[77]

The supreme Canadian Methodist example of the monumental church,
however, was Toronto's Metropolitan Wesleyan. This "cathedral" confirmed
the Wesleyans' pre-eminence among the Methodists and demonstrated Toronto's leadership among Canadian Protestant communities. Costing over
$150,000 and housing more than 1,900 worshippers, it was formally opened
on March 12, 1872. Although many Wesleyans had misgivings about commit-
ting so much of the connexion's resources to one project, most agreed it
would be invaluable in imparting elements of Christian civilization to the
population. Edward Hartley Dewart, the editor of the *Christian Guardian,* assured his readers, "God has given us to build Christian temples more in accordance with the circumstances and tastes of the people, and the necessities of
the times. While the poor and ignorant have strong claims upon us, it would
be a great mistake to adapt our agencies to them alone and hand over the
wealthy and cultivated classes to the care and control of the other churches ...

we must not conclude that poverty and ignorance have a tendency to promote a higher type of piety than wealth and refinement."[78] Dr Tiffany, the popular American preacher who helped dedicate the building, added that "every Wesleyan Methodist in the Dominion ought to take a deep interest in seeing a central monumental structure in this city from which each would receive radiating and reflected glory."[79]

In addition to these churches, the denomination constructed specialized missions, hospitals, residential mission schools, secondary schools, and colleges to serve the maturing regional communities across the country. As part of its attempt to consolidate its operations, the church also significantly expanded its bureaucracy and systematized its internal operations. Uniform schedules, model deeds, and even a denominational insurance company had been used before union.[80] After union, a whole series of boards and standing committees evolved. Over time these became highly specialized with their own offices and personnel. By the early twentieth century, the General Conference maintained a general superintendent, General Conference secretariat, Finance Department, archivist, educational committee, and the large Department of Evangelism and Social Service. The last had field secretaries and regional offices across the country. In addition, the church supported large-scale Sunday school and young people's organizations, deaconesses, and editorial and publishing staff. It also developed the powerful Board of Missions, which had its own fund-raising and administrative network. The Woman's Missionary Society, with its nearly independent role in both domestic and foreign missions, paralleled the general mission board.[81]

In fact, the twelve boards or standing committees in place in 1884 would expand to thirty-two by 1925. This expansion mirrored the changes occurring in business and government and reflected the multiplication of special-interest organizations in society. These organizations increasingly defined their goals in terms of class, occupation, ethnicity, gender, or age and established functionally specialized operations. At least partially in response, the Methodist Church underwent significant administrative growth and sophistication and became "an increasingly larger, more complex, and more cosmopolitan structure of integrated institutions through which Methodism could interpret and influence the broader society."[82]

By the twentieth century, the denomination had a vast investment in the social, intellectual, moral, and spiritual welfare of Canadians. When these concerns were added to the requirements of the domestic and overseas missions and the social-service programs, the church needed substantially increased financial contributions from its members. Since human beings were merely earthly stewards of God's benevolence, giving was a fundamental Christian duty, and the church constantly reminded its members of this obligation. Although the unified Methodist connexion after 1884 was in a superior position to meet these needs, the church recognized that establishing order and system in its finances was a critical component of general consolidation. Traditional contributions at class meetings, even when subsidized by pews rentals or special fund-raising teas and socials, no longer satisfied the demand.[83]

Many lay and clerical leaders hoped to introduce modern business principles into the fund-raising process by establishing proper accounting and budgeting practices at both local and national levels. In order to regularize benevolence, the envelope system was introduced whereby contributors subscribed to a fixed amount at the beginning of the year and paid it in weekly instalments. Even if the subscriber was absent from worship, the amount could be paid at a subsequent service. This system permitted the church and the members to budget their resources and lessened the need for the minister to plead constantly for his salary. Many hoped the system would also encourage frugality among the poor, but it was really designed for those who could readily apportion their income in advance. In any event, it was highly effective in enlarging church income. Attempts to introduce tithing among the membership or a centralized, unified fund-raising and spending authority were less successful. The missionary societies were particularly jealous of their own prerogatives in this regard. Nevertheless, by the early twentieth century, much had been accomplished in enlarging and consolidating church finances.[84]

Together, physical, institutional, and administrative expansion and consolidation underlay the broader transformations occurring within Methodism itself. Subsequent chapters will analyse these developments within the Methodist church and among church members in greater detail. In essence, however, beginning generally in the 1850s, Methodism had emerged from its heroic period of pioneering service to become a broadly Protestant social institution ready to meet the challenges of late-Victorian society.

## 9 The Transformation of the Social Means of Grace

Although Methodism was undergoing impressive institutional restructuring, it remained deeply committed to the salvation of the individual and the moral improvement of society. It gradually emphasized different approaches and attempted to encompass new expressions of faith, but these were to elaborate, not abandon, its fundamental mission. During the late nineteenth and early twentieth centuries, all the Christian churches in Canada were buffeted by new and threatening intellectual and social forces. None the less, Methodism remained optimistic about its ability to control these forces and ultimately to Christianize Canada. Canadian Methodist leaders viewed Methodism as the truly national church encompassing the full range of Canada's cultural identity. On the one hand, this perception encouraged the church to assume a leadership role in remoulding the nation, and on the other, it forced the church to broaden its appeal by removing aspects of its system that were subject to legitimate criticism. Significantly, Canadian Methodism reappraised and reshaped many of its traditional social means of grace and even its ministry in an attempt to enhance its evangelical mission.

### MASS EVANGELISM

Typical of the transformation occurring in all the social means of grace was a shift away from dramatic revival as the basis for spiritual growth leading to conversion and entire sanctification. Revival certainly remained vital and popular, but Canadian Methodists demanded broader and more enlightened patterns of religious fellowship. The goal was to achieve righteousness and not to be limited to a particular kind of traumatic conversion experience.[1] A mature religious institution, it was felt, had to balance differing visions of the best means to achieve this private and social righteousness and not be afraid to integrate new intellectual opportunities to advance both spiritual growth and ethical humanism. Although the process was slow and uneven across the country, elements common to traditional revivalism were gradually replaced by new methods and priorities so that the church would remain relevant to the perceived needs of Canadian society.

William Arthur, a highly influential British Wesleyan preacher at mid-century, considered the Reformation, the Calvinist and Puritan purification of religion, and the Wesleyan reinvigoration of Christianity to be the pre-eminent blessings of the sixteenth, seventeenth, and eighteenth centuries respectively. He expected that the "awakening" of the nineteenth century would be equally significant. But it was crucial that the nineteenth-century revival should strengthen, not destroy, the existing Protestant churches. He hoped "that the great revival of the nineteenth century will be free from polemical strife, and will not result in raising up another distinguishing name among Christians."[2] In his view, Methodism therefore had to advance revival, but it also had to control and direct it to meet the demands of the times. Excessive claims, along with narrow perceptions, must be eliminated and revival's vitality merged with other aspects of Christian development in order to establish Christ's kingdom on earth.

To most faithful Methodists, gradual growth to a state of grace represented a more rational and appropriate basis for spiritual development than dramatic revival and appeared to be more in keeping with Wesley's original understanding of salvation.[3] Brought up in a religious family and community setting, they found that their spirituality evolved naturally until a recognizable decision for Christ was reached. Orderly, logical refinement appeared more effective, more legitimate, and more in harmony with the wider aims of the denomination and Victorian society in general. Slow, even progress better suited contemporary concepts of human development. Therefore conversion came like emergence from a long tunnel, as well as like a flash of lighting. The Reverend Stephen Rice's experience was typical of the former. "I did not experience any very terrible feelings but knew I was not living in the fear of God. I wanted to feel much more than I did and would have given a great deal to have been struck down similar to Paul so that I might have no doubt about matters. But this was not my experience. The light gradually came to me, and though I could never tell the exact moment when the change was wrought yet it did take place."[4]

Such evolutionary faith did not deny the legitimacy of dramatic conversion; it simply demonstrated an alternate method of achieving its benefits. After conversion, further spiritual growth might lead to the state of entire sanctification, which again could be accomplished gradually and undramatically. Conversion and sanctification occurred at a specific instant, but they could as equally be the culmination of a long process as a sudden acceptance of God's saving grace. To Methodists such as the calm, clear thinking Samuel Nelles, who trained generations of clerical and lay leaders at Victoria College, education and the intellectual quest for salvation were as appropriate as old-fashioned revival experiences.[5] Moreover, the results were often more permanent and valuable to the denomination. Education and methodical study, originally so important to Wesley's perception of true spiritual rebirth, were emphasized once again, and they fit more properly into the general pattern of late-nineteenth-century development. Canadian society placed a deep trust in religious-centred education as the surest foundation for economic and cultural progress. It was only a short step to the belief that education could substantially remake fallen humanity and inaugurate God's design for the nation.

Associated with the transformation of traditional revivalism was concern in some quarters over the excessive part played by emotionalism and fanatical conduct. During much of Canadian Methodism's history, extreme enthusiasm had been accepted as the surest sign of spiritual vitality. Even those who questioned violent, irrational conduct defended its validity as the workings of the Holy Spirit.[6] To a degree, this response had been necessitated by attacks on Methodism from external secular and religious groups. Although never essential to revival, irrational, emotional behaviour came to represent it in the popular mind. As a result, the motivation for revival sometimes became to stir up the emotions, rather than to evoke conversion. As Borden Parker Bowne, the prominent late-nineteenth-century Methodist liberal theologian and philosopher maintained, "There had been a tendency in the history of the church to look upon emotional ebulliencies, anarchic raptures, anomalous and spectacular experiences, as the truly classical manifestations of religion, while the interaction of religious feeling, intellect and moral will has been viewed as a falling away from the highest and only classical form."[7] Irrational behaviour did not enhance revival, and its suppression did not denote a decline in revival. But its control in mainstream Canadian Methodism symbolized the more critical changes occurring in the extraordinary means of grace.

And as the century progressed, the Methodist church increasingly censured excessive behaviour. While conversion was an emotional experience, late-Victorian Methodists shared John Wesley's early repugnance at unbounded enthusiasm and wanted instead "calm, deliberate enthusiasts."[8] For instance, Samuel Nelles argued throughout his career that true Christians should strive for tranquillity and sensible religion. "To struggle after religious fervour," he warned, "is to fall into a religious fever, a state in itself irreligious."[9] "Bonfire religion" initially created great flame and heat, but it quickly left only a heap of ashes. Methodist revival should be a furnace which purified the human metal through sustained, even heat. Such an experience never dulled or formalized true Christian earnestness, but instead strengthened moral, Christlike behaviour and encouraged dedication to total individual and social progress.

The adaptation occurring in revivalism in general was particularly visible in the special services of the camp and protracted meetings and the use of professional evangelists. After the great revivals of the late 1850s had run their course, special services fell out of fashion except for the occasional sporadic effort. It was as if Methodism required time to recuperate before recommitting its energy to these programs. However, in the early 1870s and particularly in the mid-1880s, services of mass evangelism once again swept across the country, significantly increasing both church membership and trust in these extraordinary means of grace. From Newfoundland to British Columbia, the fire of revival dominated religious activity and the columns of the Methodist press were filled with reports of triumphant camp and protracted meetings.[10]

Visiting evangelists such as Walter and Phoebe Palmer, Payson Hammond, Sam Jones, Sam Small, "California" Taylor, and William French were highly visible and eminently successful. They continued to downplay denominationalism, promote a strong role for lay women and men, attack theological exclusiveness, and preach the need for conversion and entire sanctification to herald Christ's post-millennial reign. The Methodist press normally reprinted the weekly sermons of T. DeWitt Talmage and publicized the campaigns of Dwight Moody and Ira Sankey.[11] Over the years, biographies, tracts, sermons, and newspaper reports about revivalists flooded Canada. Few individuals better understood the value of the popular press in reaching a potential audience. Whether simple propaganda or accurate representations, these accounts none the less spread the revivalists' fame and gave respectability to new generations of Canadian and foreign professional evangelists.

Nevertheless, in spite of an abiding sympathy for their services and the value of mass evangelism in the past, powerful forces in Methodism either withdrew from the special revival agencies or transformed them to suit better the goals of Victorian Canada. Such was particularly the case in the aftermath of revival campaigns, when numerical and spiritual decline led to their re-evaluation and diminished the optimism over former victories. Regardless of mass evangelism's value in enlarging church attendance, it could be a mixed blessing for Methodism. By attacking denominationalism and promoting loyalty to an evangelical movement, revival services weakened the church's control over its members and abetted schism. In the United States and Britain, camp- and protracted-meeting enthusiasts, especially those committed to immediate entire sanctification, had helped divide Methodist churches into competing factions. Late-nineteenth-century Canadian Methodism admired ecumenism and was sufficiently tolerant to encompass a wide variety of personal beliefs, but it still demanded obedience to its authority and Discipline.

Furthermore, past experience had demonstrated that revival converts were often an unreliable basis for connexional strength. Too often when the initial ardour of special services faded, the new converts slid back into sin, and some even embarrassed the church by their conduct. True spiritual awakening did not depend solely on traditional revivals, and members who lived only for revivals provided a poor foundation for institutional development.[12] However, the fault was not entirely with the converts. The highly charged spiritual environment promised by mass evangelism was not always present in regular worship services. The ordinary means of grace increasingly emphasized a moral, respectable, and some might add, complacent religious life. Regular church services and traditional revivals were diverging on fundamental issues.

None the less, the Methodist church still required all converts to utilize all the regular means of grace. Conversion and even entire sanctification did not guarantee permanent spiritual safety or even insure loyalty to Methodism. The members had to be nurtured through religious training and pastoral supervision if they were to avoid corruption and sustain their dedication and spiritual progress. Much of the post-revival decline was "due to insufficient knowledge of the cardinal doctrines of Christianity, and the duties and privileges of membership in the church of God."[13]

Thus, while recognizing the benefits of mass evangelism, the Methodist connexions re-emphasized their trust in the ordinary means of grace. In 1870 the Wesleyan Methodist Annual Conference claimed that "the progress of the gospel depends mainly upon the faithful employment of the ordinary means of grace, and the continued and general usefulness of individual Christians. Social renewal services are often found to be indispensable, and are often gloriously successful; and yet it remains generally true, that much more would be accomplished if we looked for saving fruit from every sermon and every service."[14] The Bible Christians shared this view, noting that revivalism "has led in numerous instances, we fear, to undue trust in occasional efforts and laxity in that constant attention to Christian duty so essential to a healthy state of piety."[15] Extraordinary means of grace should be used only occasionally or they would lose their beneficial results while undermining the regular work.

Mass evangelism also interfered with the daily operations of the church and placed an inordinate strain on the local itinerants and their lay colleagues. Many were forced to retire early or became ill because of overwork at revivals. During these special services, they also neglected their pastoral supervision and the business of running a circuit. The upkeep of the church, Sunday schools, youth programs, and mission activities demanded their time. As the century wore on, many conscientious lay and clerical church workers chose to fulfil these ordinary obligations rather than participate in revivals, especially since Methodism's denominational auxiliaries were crucial sources for new members. Young people in particular had to be brought fully into the connexion if the church was to prosper, and this could most effectively be accomplished through permanent organizations such as the Sunday schools and young people's societies. Although earnest, evangelical spirituality was essential, nurture in Christian values and Methodist beliefs was equally important and usually more advantageous to long-term success.[16]

Inherent in all of these concerns over mass evangelism was the old worry about over-emotional behaviour which appeared to question the maturity and respectability of institutionalized Methodism. By at least the 1860s, the church had difficulty refuting the criticism of excess that was levelled against these gatherings. Conscientious members began to describe this kind of conduct as a form of paganism and found it difficult to see God's presence in such exhibitions.[17] There was a fine line between ardent zeal and ignorant enthusiasm, and it was too easily trespassed to suit a large proportion of Methodists.

Samuel Dwight Chown recalled that while addressing revivals "there spread a contagion of hysteria manifesting itself in prostrations, shocks of glory, while some professed to be able to 'speak with tongues' … I had much to do in controlling and in some instances suppressing these hysterical outbreaks in camp meetings and elsewhere. In their inception there was probably something of a religious element but the contagion was due largely to mob psychology."[18] Bodily exercise, fainting, and shouting often appeared to be sham enthusiasm. Even when the enthusiasm was real, these activities were difficult to direct toward spiritual progress and became barely tolerable in open-air revivals, let alone in large, middle-class church buildings. With the expanding number and size of church and public buildings, the need for camp meetings to assemble large crowds diminished while the level of permissible conduct was more closely monitored. It became critically important for the Methodist church that a proper balance be maintained. Methodism had always defended earnest and emotional experiences of conversion and complete holiness, and most members were concerned about changes that might introduce formality or cause a decline in spirituality in their church. But it also opposed excessive "confusion" or conduct which brought criticism from the more respectable members of Canadian society. In general, Methodism strove to achieve the goals of revival through rational and orderly channels.[19]

Ironically, in attempting to make camp and protracted meetings more acceptable to late-Victorian Methodism, mass evangelism lost much of its value for those still bound to old-fashioned religion. These people constantly urged revival, that is, a return to the earlier style for revival institutions. Although more fervent and focused on dramatic experiential religion than other aspects of church life, these institutions too gradually abandoned many of their historic elements. The preaching that came to dominate, though still too unrefined for some, was aimed at more than arousing the emotions or even at inducing the spiritual crisis required to convince sinners of their depravity. The preachers emphasized the positive benefits of religion. Their message became more diversified in content, directed at convincing the intellect of their listeners. They also dealt with the whole range of social and moral questions in the world.[20]

The function of rousing exhortations, fervent prayers, and individual testimony also declined in the camp and protracted meetings as they became ever more systematized. Since these elements had often been the special province of local preachers and dedicated lay women and men, their decline mirrored the shifting role of the laity in the church at large. Even the counselling given to those seeking pardon and grace came more often from specially trained revival workers, not from the assembly in general.[21] These changes in turn limited mass participation, the original hallmark of revivals, and reinforced the control of those appointed to run the services. The fervent spirituality that so often hinged on group involvement tended to decline in direct proportion. Old-style mass evangelism still existed, but it was usually directed by groups such as Nelson Burns's Canadian Holiness Association or the American National Camp Meeting Association. Both of these interdenominational holiness organizations grew away from mainstream Methodism and were eventually ousted from church affiliation.

Under these cumulative pressures, Methodist camp and protracted meetings were transformed into institutions focusing on the practical needs of the individual and advancing the broad social ambitions of mainstream Methodism. An emphasis on social evangelism emerged from the transformed revivalism of the latter part of the century. Many people believed that the continued relevance of revival services depended on these new emphases. In 1885, after two years of intensive revival, the *Christian Guardian* noted that "the conditions of society, especially in the centres of population, are now so different that the most that can be said in favour of such agencies is that they are a lesser good."[22] The clearest illustration of these changes appeared in the permanent camp grounds the Methodists had established across the country. Whether in Atlantic or central Canada, they became institutionalized annual gatherings for general religious fellowship. Social refreshment, which came with a vacation from life's daily routine, kept them popular, but they bore little resemblance to the revivals of old. By the 1870s various Methodist connexions had created a group of camp grounds which stressed the healthy and moral atmosphere of a park.

At Grimsby Park on Lake Ontario near St Catharines, for instance, there were summer cottages, a hotel, boat services, and all the amenities to attract an urban, middle-class clientele. Recreation and relaxation in a moral, suburban setting became a central function. The religious services available also reflected these goals: "Due regard for the religious and intellectual wants of the people is shown in the preparation of the programme, which includes sermons, lectures, concerts and entertainments, classes in elocution and studies in literature."[23] Women's missionary societies and young people's groups often used the park for their conventions. By the 1890s the local Methodist Conference was even distressed by sabbath-breaking at the camp ground, but in 1897 was relieved to report that excursion boats were limited and the Ontario Methodist Camp Ground Company had not placed interesting programs on the sabbath which would attract large crowds.[24]

Wesley Park at Niagara Falls attracted many American visitors and a number of American-based organizations. It was described as an excellent facility for rest and relaxation for worn-out ministers. Big Bay Point on Lake Simcoe was considered suitable for Sunday schools, temperance gatherings, and other religious meetings, as well as traditional camp meetings. According to the *Christian Guardian*, the large camp ground on the St Lawrence had developed in a similar way. "There is no more healthy and pleasant summer resort than Thousand Island Park, on the St. Lawrence. The scenery is picturesque and beautiful. The water is cool and clear. The air is pure and bracing. Good order and interesting services are maintained. Fishing, boating and bathing are available to any extent. The first of the series of services of the season was begun last Friday, under the direction of Rev. Dr. Hibbard, and is now in full blast."[25] By the late 1870s the Methodist Episcopal church ran Thousand Island Park as a "coveted summer retreat from the extreme heat of city life and a favourite resort for amusement." Not only was it a "powerful impulse to all the vital interests of the church," but it also "gives definite promise of early yielding a handsome revenue to other connexional interests."[26] The religious services normally occurred in the middle of the summer for the convenience of the urban clientele and rarely featured earnest revivals.

Although these camp grounds and the types of activities they sponsored did not emphasize emotional, dramatic piety, they did address the needs of the contemporary church and of secular Canadian society in general. They remained centres of Christian communal experience and served as excellent forums for temperance and moral-reform meetings and gatherings of church auxiliaries. For instance, the Berwick Camp Ground in the Annapolis district of Nova Scotia, which served Maritime Methodism for generations after its founding in 1872 and represented to many the best elements of the Methodist tradition, provided a home for Woman's Missionary Society meetings, Sunday school and young people's gatherings, and Ministerial Association forums. A description of part of its program from 1905 illustrates the new uses of the camp ground: "The Epworth League Summer School for the study of the Bible and Christian Missions ... is an enterprise pregnant with the promises of the best results. It strikes at the root of all that makes for a stable, happy, useful, personal piety and of intelligent loyalty to the Kingdom of Jesus Christ."[27] The educative value of camp meetings expanded as sermons dealt with history, science, higher criticism, the modern Sunday school, and the practical obligations of the church and its members. Religious, social, and moral instruction and nurturing were important elements of the late-Victorian and Edwardian church. Despite the decline in the conversion function of camp meetings, they developed enterprises that helped create a stable, intelligent, and loyal attachment to Methodism and to the kingdom of God.

In general, by the late nineteenth century, camp and protracted meetings were directed at second- and third-generation Methodists who had never strayed far from Christianity and derived little sustenance from traditional revivals. As optimistic and morally progressive members of the Methodist fellowship, they sought to expand the outreach of religion and used the institutions of mass evangelism both to reinforce Christian truths and to bind the church and society together. Through a converted and sometimes sanctified membership, the gospel could be understood and implemented in all its personal and social dimensions. Hence the transformed camp and protracted meetings continued as valuable agencies for the creation of a post-millennial dominion of the Lord on earth.[28]

Even the professional evangelists faced pressure to adapt to these new requirements. Although many Methodists wished to expand the use of this specialized ministry, they also recognized its negative aspects and questioned its long-term effectiveness. The evangelists, often from the United States or Britain, were subject to no denominational disciplinary or administrative control. They disrupted regular operations and sometimes upset the harmony of the connexion or sowed dissension between congregations and their ministers.[29] Given their anti-denominational leanings and often limited formal education, un-Methodist premillennial and dispensational ideologies too often crept into their preaching. Other revivalists appeared to have no consistent theology at all and preached an assortment of strange views under the guise of biblical evangelism.

Methodist itinerants and the district and conference authorities believed that it was essential that they establish strict control over the work of transient revivalists. By the 1870s the Methodist conferences warned their membership to guard their pulpits against these preachers; "their preaching is often dangerously unscriptural ... Ministers of our Church cannot be too careful in giving countenance to men who are responsible to no Church authority, and whose chief claim to recognition seems to be their ability to disparage and slander all who will not adopt their views."[30] Eventually the Methodist Discipline was amended so that only Methodist ministers could evangelize on church property.

As well, the more conservative church members continued to assume that all Methodist itinerants should fulfil the function of evangelist. Just as every sermon and every worship service should promote true revival, every minister was called to revival work. They believed that the whole church would suffer if these abilities were lost. Charles Lench, the president of the particularly traditional Newfoundland Conference, in 1912 urged that "surely we may plead for the combination of the evangelist, the pastor and the teacher. We must hold on with a tight grip to this inseparable trio of ministerial excellencies. Every preacher his own evangelist."[31] Even when a revival service was carried on by a specialist, such individuals assumed that the Methodist itinerants were to utilize their evangelistic talents and participate.

In reality, Methodism had become too complex an institution for every itinerant to be a talented pastor, preacher, teacher, and evangelist. The numerous pastoral and administrative requirements of the church meant that many itinerants simply lacked the time for revival work. Others had lost the fervent accent to their preaching that was considered essential for successful mass evangelism. Therefore, in order to control evangelists without losing the benefits of their ministry, during the 1870s the Methodist connexions began to set apart suitably endowed lay and ordained men and women as conference evangelists.[32] This move acknowledged the specialization occurring within the ministry as a whole.

The results were generally commended by the church's membership. Among the most influential of these connexional evangelists were David Savage, the Dimsdale sisters, the team of Crossley and Hunter, and Ralph Horner. Savage was somewhat of an anomaly among conference evangelists; he had entered the work at quite an advanced age. Born in London, England, into a Congregational household in 1830, he had emigrated to Montreal with his family in 1841. After his conversion to Methodism, he entered the New Connexion ministry in 1851, had a distinguished career as editor, and was twice elected president of Conference. In 1885 he retired from regular circuit work and committed his energy to revival services across Canada until his death eight years later. Always aggressively evangelistic, he was highly successful in field preaching and other forms of mass evangelism. More particularly, he strongly supported the revival work of the Salvation Army and used it as a model to develop "missionary bands" of dedicated lay workers to help establish and operate revivals and minister to the new converts both during and after the services. These groups provided valuable assistance at both traditional and new-style revivals. "The Band work is not characterized by undue excitement," claimed the *Christian Guardian,* "but is evidently of the Holy Spirit."[33] Many young people became evangelists or regular itinerants after their experience and training in Savage's missionary bands.

This band work was particularly important in encouraging and training women to become professional evangelists. Between 1885 and 1900 at least twenty-five women led over three hundred revival services. The most popular of these were Elizabeth and Gertrude Dimsdale, Sadie Williams, and Lydia and Annie Hall. Earlier in the nineteenth century, women had been effective preachers in the Bible Christian and Primitive Methodist connexions, and in fact, Methodist doctrine and practice had been valuable in freeing women from many of the social and theological restrictions on active church leadership. The long history of women's leadership at the congregational level, the rise of women's missionary and temperance societies, and the acceptance that women had an obligation to speak out publicly on issues affecting the family all helped push them into the front lines of mass evangelism.Commended for their scriptural knowledge and their effective, orthodox preaching, women evangelists complemented and expanded the work of the regular itinerants.[34]

The women were not ordained, and they were much more vulnerable economically than male preachers; they usually worked for expenses rather than a salary. It was also expected that they would keep a low profile, and they were known for their tact as well as their ability to preach and sing. Most of these women gave up their profession when they married in order to devote themselves full time to the occupation of wife and mother. The establishment of the Deaconess Society and increased opportunities to serve as missionaries provided more stable, career-oriented occupations for dedicated single women during the early twentieth century, and female evangelists declined in significance. Although some audiences were attracted simply by the novelty and others were repelled, women preachers formed an important component of connexional mass evangelism in Canada.

Without doubt, the most popular evangelists throughout Canada after 1884 were John E. Hunter and Hugh T. Crossley. Hunter had been born in 1865 near Bowmanville, Canada West, into a Presbyterian household. He was reborn and became a Methodist at age fifteen. Four years later he entered the ministry and spent two of his probationary years at Victoria College. After ordination, he served in Ontario and Manitoba before becoming a conference evangelist and joining Hugh Crossley in 1884. Crossley had been converted at a camp meeting in 1867 at age seventeen. He taught school before entering the ministry in 1878, and after serving several Ontario circuits, he became London Conference evangelist in 1884. Hunter did most of the preaching while Crossley specialized in a "singing ministry." Together they were exceptionally successful in converting sinners and in promoting personal and social morality. Their most notable victory was Sir John A. Macdonald, the prime minister, who actively participated in the great crusade in Ottawa in 1888, but they helped an estimated 100,000 accept Christ over the twenty-five years they spent evangelizing North America. Hunter retired because of ill health in 1910 and died nine years later; Crossley continued in revival work until 1926 but remained available to assist others until his death in 1934.[35] Over their careers, they joined most other evangelists in broadening their message to promote the social reform of society.

Although the conference evangelist normally represented what the Methodist church considered to be the best qualities of the agency and followed the dictates of the church, even this office was subject to many of the abuses common among the unaffiliated revivalists. For instance, while most professional evangelists actively espoused the cause of entire sanctification, there was a significant divergence on how and when this state might be achieved. Following the ministries of Phoebe Palmer and James Caughey, most holiness preachers considered it the natural completion of the promise of conversion.

Sanctification was most profitably accomplished instantaneously right after conversion rather than as the culmination of a life of growth in grace. To many Methodists, however, this concept downgraded conversion to a preliminary experience and appeared to eliminate the need for personal morality and good works. It was too easily achieved and could lead to antinomianism. In approving the evangelistic career of David Savage, his obituary in 1893 noted that he had advanced the doctrine of holiness "as taught by the Methodist Church, without any fantastic or extravagant additions."[36]

One of Canada's leading promoters of the "easy road" to holiness was Ralph Horner. Born near Shawville, Canada East, in 1854 of Anglican parents, Horner had been converted in 1872 and at the same time claimed the blessing of entire sanctification. Montreal Conference ordained him in 1887. Problems arose immediately since he considered it a special ordination to evangelize, but the Methodist church had never accepted such a conditional ordination. Yet it did appoint him as one of the two Montreal Conference evangelists. Horner organized revivals throughout the Ottawa valley, and his powerful preaching influenced hundreds. At the same time, his services were notorious for excessively emotional conduct and what most Methodist clerical observers considered unsound doctrinal teaching.

During Horner's second year as conference evangelist, local Methodist itinerants complained that he was holding services without their permission. This was contrary to the Methodist Discipline, but he refused to be limited by the church authorities. Even when the Conference stationed him on a regular circuit in 1890, Horner hired a supply minister and continued his evangelistic services. Overlooking this defiance, the Montreal Conference again appointed him as a special evangelist in 1891 and 1892. During these years he assembled a corps of lay associates to enlarge his revival work. They were poorly prepared and not licensed by Conference. In 1893 Horner was left without an appointment, but ignoring local opposition, he bought a former Baptist church in which to continue his work. The following year he refused to accept the stationing committee's appointment and after another year of dispute was formally deposed from the Methodist ministry in 1895. He later organized the Holiness Movement Church of Canada.[37]

In conjunction with a number of traditional church leaders, General Superintendent Albert Carman had initially promoted Horner's holiness crusades, and Carman's support for revivals was crucial for their continued acceptance as vital adjuncts to Methodist evangelism. He was essentially a moderate social and theological conservative who felt that Methodism should remain broad enough to provide a congenial home for a diverse range of Protestant beliefs and approaches. He had, in fact, become a rather pragmatic bureaucrat. Carman had served as the last bishop to the Canadian Episcopal Methodists, and he continued to assert an "episcopal," if not a dictatorial, dimension to the office of general superintendent in the united Methodist cause. Combining unequalled knowledge and experience with energy, skill, and a forceful personality, he assumed a leadership role on the committees and boards which administered the church's operations and was undoubtedly the most influential voice in Methodist councils. At the same time, his dignity and authority rested

Hugh Crossley (1850–1934) and John Hunter (1865–1919). The most famous team of Canadian evangelists. (UCA, P2932)

William Morley Punshon (1824–81). President of the Wesleyan Methodist Church in Canada, 1868–72, who advanced overseas missions and improved preaching. (UCA, P5330N)

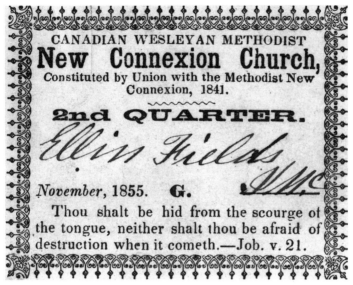

Class Ticket, 1855. Tickets were required to prove Methodist membership. (UCA, Artifact Collection)

Preachers' Plan, 1866. Ordained itinerants, lay preachers, and exhorters followed a well-defined preaching timetable. (UCA, Artifact Collection)

upon a profound sympathy for the welfare of the church's members. For Methodists he remained a respected father-figure.

Nevertheless, Carman would never accept Horner's repudiation of the church's disciplinary authority, in which he had a leading hand. Horner also antagonized the increasingly powerful, theologically liberal wing of the connexion, both clerical and lay, and even most moderates by his doctrinal and emotional excesses and his virulent criticism of institutional Methodism. For him, the construction of costly churches reflected a loss of earnest spirituality and Christian zeal, and he denounced the moral and spiritual character of any minister who criticized him or disapproved of his methods. The Methodist church would never tolerate such conduct.

During the 1890s, the Methodist church deposed other holiness preachers, including Nelson Burns and Albert Truax, for causing dissension in the denomination and refusing to accept the authority of the church. They in turn helped organize independent holiness churches and carried some disenchanted conservative Methodists with them. During the same period, the Methodist church moved to tighten its control over the training, licensing, and disciplining of the conference evangelists in order to limit their independence. Moreover, evangelists who failed to accept the broader social and moral aspects of revival that were apparent in the transformed camp and protracted meetings found themselves isolated from mainstream Methodism and normally left the connexion.

However, most conference preachers were faithful to the new priorities of Methodist mass evangelism. They accepted and indeed promoted the emphasis on gradual, evolutionary progress through education and preached against the prevalent scepticism and immorality of Canadian society, rather than limiting their message to personal conversion and sanctification. The urban poor initially seemed to provide the most appropriate audience for modern Methodist revivalism, but evangelists generally failed to attract these unchurched classes. However, by the end of the nineteenth century, much of the energy of revival was directed at remaking society in order to help establish the kingdom of God on earth, and it invigorated both the social-gospel movement and also the reform interests within the conservative, holiness movement.[38]

Although the Methodist leadership was extremely sensitive to suggestions that it was abandoning spiritual revival and becoming too formal and intellectual, especially when membership either declined or failed to increase as expected, it recognized that the manifestations of revival had to suit contemporary circumstances. The progressive editor of the *Canadian Methodist Magazine*, William Henry Withrow, maintained, "One element in the success of Methodism has been the flexibility of its mode of operation, its power of adaptation to varying circumstances. This enables it to adapt its ministrations, without losing its fervour, to the cultured and wealthy city congregation, to the frontier hamlet, to the fishing village, the mining camp, the Indian mission, or the squalid purlieus of poverty."[39] The process of adjustment was necessarily gradual and occurred at different rates according to local circumstances, but by the early twentieth century, revival was principally aimed at the "symmetrical development of Christian character," which involved personal regeneration, moral social relations, and the practical improvement of the nation.[40]

## THE REGULAR MEANS OF GRACE

Over the second half of the nineteenth century, Methodism sought and substantially accomplished a major restructuring of the extraordinary means of grace. The ability to present a meaningful church to twentieth-century Canadians was at least partially a result of these changes. They were achieved relatively easily since no major amendments to official Methodist policy or Discipline were required. The transition was handled mainly at the local and individual level at a rate appropriate for those involved.

A more significant test of Methodism's new priorities, and a greater apparent threat to traditional church operations, was the transformation of the ordinary or regular means of grace which occurred over the same period. The regular means of grace encompassed all the elements of worship and normal church life utilized to promote spiritual growth and Christian service. They were numerous, diversified, and comprehensive. They included general Protestant means such as preaching, exhorting, hymns, prayer, and the sacraments, which always were crucial elements in Methodist worship. Preaching brought God's message powerfully to the congregation, the Scriptures provided all the knowledge necessary for salvation, hymns planted doctrine and hope directly in the heart, and the sacraments were divinely instituted for remembrance and rebirth.[41]

Other regular means of grace, such as the love feast, watch-night services, and the class meeting, were more distinctively Methodist. They not only distinguished Methodists from other denominations, but they also helped enforce the separation between the saved and the corrupt world. Despite fears of a decline in personal and family worship and respect for religion, by the mid-nineteenth century, Canadians were more God-fearing and church-oriented than ever before. Religion was an integral, unavoidable part of life. Nevertheless, attendance at public worship was never as good or as consistent as the church hoped. There was a widespread fear among Methodists that any weakening of the distinctive means of grace might contaminate the evangelical purity and doom the saving mission of the connexion. Formality, indifference, and a corruption of the centrality of the conversion experience would call into question Methodism's leadership among the Protestant churches and its particular contribution to evangelical vitality.

Therefore individuals who wanted to transform the regular means of grace had to convince the church leaders and members that these changes would improve Methodism's social and spiritual mission and expand God's earthly kingdom. Reformers argued that by becoming more sensitive to society's ethical and moral goals and by removing outdated restrictions while strengthening personal piety, Methodism would better serve the entire community. Failure to adapt, they believed, would only lead to isolation and stagnation. During the second half of the nineteenth century in Canada, the emphasis and use of the social means of grace gradually shifted, but ultimately many of these changes occurred despite official policy. The individual and collective actions of the members themselves altered these institutions to fit their own expectations.

Preaching became more diversified and was directed at scepticism, secularism, and the questions posed by science and social dislocation. More elaborate, reasoned sermons replaced the fervent, but simplistic admonitions to flee from the wrath to come. Overly theatrical preaching was condemned as appealing to the baser elements of human nature. The Scriptures required critical study and explanation in order to unravel God's true meaning. It became more difficult for untutored preachers to convince others that they could present God's words accurately or place them in the context of the times. Also, the hymns had to be carefully selected to insure doctrinal soundness and to provide the proper inspiration. In many local churches, congregational singing declined or was augmented by well-trained choirs presenting the songs to the appreciative, but silent audience. Moreover, the Methodist church significantly reassessed the rights and obligations implied by baptism and the Lord's Supper, particularly their role in regenerating the individual.[42] This re-evaluation in turn held serious implications for the basis of connexional membership, the relation of children to the church, the signficance of the actual experience of conversion and entire sanctification, and the very nature of religious fellowship and church life in general.

The adaptations of traditional Christian worship services were mirrored in the particularly Methodist social means of grace. The love feast, tea meeting, prayer meeting, watch-night service, and band and class meeting, among others, all underwent significant changes. These were central elements of Methodist worship. "The peculiar institutions of Methodism are also eminently fitted to develop the elements of Christian life ... how they educate the believer to form the habit of giving expression to the conception of faith, and the rapture of love! ... How suggestive, too, of social duties are those meetings, providing as they do an opportunity for the confession of faults, the utterances of desire, and the admonitions of wisdom."[43] This description best fit the traditional love feast. However, that service gradually fell out of favour. It was opened to non-members and lost much of its spontaneity and its confessional and refreshing power. Where it survived, it became merely a moral social gathering, usually devoid of its former rich revival power. Confessions of faults or testimony of God's benevolence seemed quaint and archaic even for itinerants who had promoted the love feasts at quarterly district meetings to encourage their own spiritual progress. By the 1890s, quarterly tickets of admission were replaced by annual cards or notes, and little attempt was made to enforce disciplinary restrictions on admission. If the love feast retained a role in converting sinners, it was a markedly different one from earlier times.[44]

A similar fate befell the tea meeting. Originally useful for more informal spiritual and social refreshment and the public expression of faith, it evolved into an opportunity to raise money for local church causes. Especially under the administration of the women in the circuit, tea meetings brought together residents of the entire community to pay off debts, build parsonages, and fund church renovations, missionary needs, and other good works. If great care was not taken, the desire to entertain the audience and thereby increase revenues might mean that "in such meetings more regard is often paid to the mere tastes and desires of the ungodly than to the character of the Church and the benefits of the people."[45] In 1873 the Bible Christian Conference also warned: "It must be apparent to all that our Tea Meetings are exhibitions of finery and vanity. The recently introduced socials ... present the more odious features of being conducted generally at night, and the reading of light literature, more calculated to promote amusement and licentiousness, than piety."[46] Despite these concerns and the evident loss of spiritual power, tea meetings and socials were popular throughout the country for their recreational, as well as their financial benefits.

The decline of spiritual, experiential religion evident in the love feast and the tea meeting was further reflected in the prayer meetings, watch-night services, and "bands." Since Methodism's earliest days, the prayer meeting had been a powerful evangelical instrument used especially to promote personal commitment and revival and mission crusades. It "is an arena for the development of the spiritual life. It is a battlefield in which every member is taught to win souls, to fight for the expansion of Christ's kingdom."[47] By the 1870s, however, many Methodists felt that the prayer meeting was too emotional or too often dominated by narrow factions of the congregation and was rarely attended. In order to increase its popularity, it was altered to provide a forum for lectures, discussions, and Bible study. At other times, three or four selected leaders were called to pray for the whole assembly. Under these conditions, the spontaneity and mass participation so essential for experiential religion were eliminated. Although Methodists continually decried the poor leadership at the prayer meeting and its failing role in the church, little was done to reinstitute its former power and influence.[48]

The watch-night service had originally carried the spiritual interest of the love feast or prayer meeting into the late night, when enthusiasm faced few outside distractions and the possibility of conversion was heightened.[49] This service was most commonly held on New Year's Eve so that the believer could reflect on the past and prayerfully recovenant his or herself for the upcoming year. It substituted healthy religious activity for unbecoming, profane revelry. By the end of the century, however, the watch-night and recovenanting services either had lost their popularity or had introduced more social and recreational elements to attract members, particularly the young. As for band meetings, Wesley's small groups of most dedicated members, they were rarely organized in North America. In 1878 the General Conference of the Methodist Church of Canada removed the section on "band societies" from the Discipline since they had been "almost, if not altogether, discontinued in connection with our Church."[50]

Perhaps nowhere was the transformation of the Methodist means of grace more deeply felt than in the class meeting. In fact, this service most clearly illustrated the debate over the changes occurring in Methodism as a whole. No regular means of grace had been more crucial to the formation of a distinctive Methodist identity; consequently any challenge to its place and function was potentially extremely divisive. Ideally, the class contained about twelve members meeting once a week under the class leader. Initially, it was used to collect money for the society, but it immediately became the essential seed of Methodist expansion and spiritual discipline. The class meeting was a sincere and potent gathering, apparently blessed by God's favour, for mutual confession and experiential spiritual growth.[51]

The centrality of the class in Methodism was confirmed by the church's definition of membership. To join the connexion, one need only "desire to flee from the wrath to come" and avoid sinful behaviour; to remain a member, the church required everyone "to attend her most select and holy convocations – her class meetings."[52] Denominational strength was calculated by totalling those attending class. Unjustifiable absence, like immoral conduct, meant loss of membership rights. The ticket for admission to class was strictly guarded and presented only to those who lived according to the church's rules. Hence the class provided Methodism with its basic means of disciplining its members.

Furthermore, the class meeting fulfilled all the spiritual functions of the congregation on a more intimate and intensive level. Together the members strengthened the less experienced, prayed for the backslider, and renewed their own faith. Through testimony and encouragement, the class meeting helped overcome the loneliness, isolation, and anxiety inherent in the quest for salvation. It also entrenched religion's social principles in the membership and created a vital sense of community. In its early days, then, the class was crucial for maintaining Methodism as an earnest body of converts and for withstanding external religious and secular opposition, while providing an essential tool for expansion throughout the world.[53] Methodism preserved its integrity by dismissing anyone who would not be bound by this fellowship. When functioning properly, the class meeting epitomized the most creative features of an evangelical church.

The key to success often rested with the class leader. In early Canadian Methodism, the leaders served as sub-pastors: they recommended who should remain members, dealt with unacceptable conduct, and promoted the connexion in the community. They carried out pastoral visits to their members and helped administer the affairs of the circuit. The leaders therefore required spotless reputations, practical intelligence, and an abiding devotion to the task. They had to be respected and trusted, to guide rather than rule.[54]

None the less, over the second half of the nineteenth century, even the class meeting fell out of favour with large sections of the church and became increasingly ineffective as a vital means of grace. The majority of Methodist adherents lost confidence in it. They found the need to supply fresh evidence of spiritual failure or success week after week extremely difficult. Testimony too often digressed into a dry and repetitious sham or a rather pompous recitation of expected catch phrases. With the removal of external political, social, and economic opposition, the increased security of Methodism, and the availability of more effective means to raise money, the artificial unity of the class meeting was no longer required. Similarly, the growing economic and social stratification among Canadian Methodists removed any sense of pioneer egalitarianism and aggravated tensions in the class. People were reticent about baring their faults to their perceived social superiors and even more so, to those they considered socially inferior.[55] Finally, as the acceptability of emotional, enthusiastic behaviour diminished, the function and cohesiveness of the class meeting disintegrated. Even the disciplinary obligation to attend or lose church membership was insufficient to sustain attendance.

To retain some value and partially to justify its compulsory nature, in some places the class was transformed into a less demanding fellowship gathering. At times, seventy or eighty members might form a single class. Gone was the intimacy; gone was the demand for a personal declaration of experience and faith; gone too was the vitality that sustained the sense of distinctiveness among church members.[56] In their place, the class relied on Bible study, lectures, and general moral and religious discussions to encourage spiritual growth and a mature religious commitment. Community cultural standards and general connexional affairs also became standard concerns of the meetings. These topics were important and at times even essential as the church adjusted to contemporary conditions, but such discussions could never replace what the early meetings had accomplished. For the most part, the often-repeated attempts to rebuild the old-fashioned class meeting as an agent of personal revival failed because the membership had lost faith in its value.

The role of the class leader also changed in response to the same forces. With the decreasing size of circuits and the more consistent presence of the itinerants, the class leaders' responsibilities were heavily circumscribed. They retained only minimal disciplinary and pastoral supervision. As the century progressed, the duties of these dedicated lay leaders in the business administration of the congregation, the operation of Sunday schools and other church auxiliaries, and the promotion of missionary causes and moral reform diverted their time and energy from the already declining class meeting. They could be more usefully employed and more relevant in these other occupations. As the utility and significance of the meeting and the leader diminished, rebellion against arbitrary and authoritarian leadership further weakened their role. Such problems were exacerbated since the class leaders generally lacked the training either to give direction to the new functions assigned to the class or to re-establish its old-style vitality. The Methodist church continually attempted to upgrade the quality of class leadership, but never resuscitated the class meeting. Although the leaders received much of the blame for its moribund state, no group of individuals could restore its original vigour.[57]

Moreover, the class meeting was neither designed nor needed for the new functions it acquired. No one could object to the class as a voluntary association concerned with individual welfare and community propriety, but many doubted its continued validity as a compulsory test of membership. Some of the foremost Canadian Methodists questioned both the logic and legitimacy of retaining this requirement. The issue had first become prominent when Egerton Ryerson denounced the compulsory nature of class meetings. On January 2, 1854, he submitted his resignation as a Methodist minister in a long letter to the president of Conference.

But I resign not my connexion with, but my ministerial office in the Wesleyan Church, because I believe a condition of membership is exacted in it which has no warrant in Scripture, nor in the practice of the Primitive Church, nor in the writings of Mr. Wesley;

and, in consequence of which condition, great numbers of exemplary heads of families and young people are excluded from all recognition and rights of membership in the Church. I refer to attendance upon class-meetings; without attending which, no person is acknowledged as a member of the Wesleyan Methodist Church, however sincerely and cordially he may believe her doctrines, prefer her ministry, and support her institutions; and however exemplary he may be in life.[58]

Although he attacked the compulsory nature of the class, Ryerson did recognize that "class meetings ... are the means of immense good ... and ... should be employed and recommended as providential and useful means of religious edification to all who may be willing to avail themselves of them."[59]

However, he also recognized that as a social institution, Methodism was facing a major transition and believed that it could only retain a relevant and important role in society if it followed the direction he advocated. The utility of the entire connexion would be undermined if it failed to adjust its Doctrines and Discipline to the realities of the times. To Ryerson, Methodism was no longer a body of earnest converts. He wanted it to take its rightful place as a major cultural institution at the very heart of an educated, tolerant, progressive Protestant society. It was sheer hypocrisy to retain compulsory class meetings when few attended; they were equally pernicious when they threatened unnaturally to restrict the church fellowship. The disciplinary significance of the class had to be altered since it failed to satisfy an evangelical role, yet denied membership to moral Canadians.[60] Methodism could ill afford to lose such people. Ryerson posed a fundamental question to the church: What was the status of obviously moral Christians who would not accept the validity of the class-meeting experience? In so doing, he challenged the connexion to redefine the very nature of Canadian Methodism.

If Methodism was a broad religious fellowship rather than a body of earnest converts, the relationship of children to the church and the status of the mere adherent were significantly altered. They were both to be brought into a more intimate relationship to the denomination. Ryerson and many of his supporters assumed that membership should be based on baptism. It was the scriptural basis for sharing in the church's benefits.[61] Within Methodism, however, the conversion experience, not the sacraments, distinguished the member from the corrupt world. Conversion required a mature, conscious, and responsible decision, and infants, though they were proper subjects of baptism, lacked these requisite attributes. Was the conversion experience to be downgraded or even eliminated? How were adults to be tested concerning their willingness to flee from the wrath to come or assisted in their quest for salvation? When the ramifications of Ryerson's apparently simple alteration were clarified, they represented a radical departure from the church's accepted beliefs and presented a quagmire of divisive issues.

The more conservative elements in Methodism were quick to realize these possibilities, and they accepted the issue of Ryerson's resignation as the arena in which to meet the challenge. The question deeply divided the Wesleyan Conference in 1854, but the gathering ultimately accepted his resignation rather then amend its official policy. It did not even discuss the controversy with the church membership at large, but simply warned, "The experience of a hundred years has deeply impressed the minds of all true Wesleyans with the wisdom of the advice of our venerable founder; 'Do not mend our rules, but keep them.' "[62] Most ministers feared the internal divisions the proposed revision would cause. Although they did not wish to lose Egerton Ryerson's talents and influence, they believed it was safer to keep the rule and ignore the practice. By simply not enforcing attendance, while hoping the class would regain its former popularity and power, they expected the controversy would not unduly upset the general membership. Although they recognized the validity of Ryerson's arguments, they did not want to crack the still fragile union of Wesleyan Methodists.

Ryerson found the opposition to his logic and the hypocrisy of some of his itinerant brethren insufferable. He refused to let the matter rest, and the debate raged on, with neither side convincing the other.[63] However, his original purpose of dramatizing the question was eminently successful. All the Methodist connexions were forced to reassess their commitment to compulsory class meetings. While many opposed altering the church's regulations, they did recognize that the denomination had to be prepared to meet the changing social and religious views of Victorian Canada. With at least that accomplished, church moderates worked to bring Ryerson back into the itinerancy. He had never really wanted to resign, and few in the church desired his absence. Even if he did not recant, he was a valuable asset in connexional councils, and no other Methodist shared his stature in the nation.

Ryerson was readmitted at the Conference in 1855. He believed this action signalled his victory; the Conference thought that he would no longer press the issue. Both were wrong. Ryerson redoubled his efforts for reform and tried to stimulate public debate by forcing the church to take disciplinary action against him. However, the Wesleyan Conference refused to accept the bait; in 1856 it reaffirmed the class meeting as a vital and essential test of membership and declined further discussion.[64]

Nevertheless, the issue was far from closed. Throughout the 1860s and 1870s, all the Methodist connexions across Canada reacted to the growing opposition to compulsory class-meeting attendance. On the one hand, the Primitive Methodist Conference in 1865, while recognizing the legitimate sentiments of many of its members, still warned that it was a mistake to abandon such a valuable institution. The other Methodist connexions agreed and pleaded for the reinvigoration of class meetings and a strengthening of class leaders. They feared that if class meetings became only voluntary, there would be nothing to keep members attending. On the other hand, attendance at class continued to decline and discipline was only sporadically enforced. The attempts to improve the class meeting and to better train its leaders generally failed. According to Henry Bland, it had lost its spiritual power, it led to double standards of membership, and it fostered disrespect for the entire discipline of the church. Whether officially it was sanctioned or not, there was little anyone could do to sustain an obsolete institution. By 1873 the Bible Christians had stopped enforcing compulsory attendance, and when they amended their Discipline, they quietly omitted the controversial requirement. Compulsory attendance was also under attack in Britain and was dropped altogether by the Episcopal Methodists in the United States.[65]

The *Christian Guardian*, edited at this time by Edward Hartley Dewart, was firmly on the side of the reformers. In 1874 the paper argued that the old-fashioned church no longer existed.

But with the Methodists of the present day, the case is different. They are baptized among us, they communicate with us, they know no other membership [as did members of Wesley's societies, who, if dismissed, were still members of the Church of England]. Expulsion or dismissal is therefore something more than dismissal from a private lodge or society; and the class-meeting, in the altered state of things, is something more than a meeting for relating or hearing experience. With all our power we would sustain a vigorous and firm administration of discipline in cases where inconsistent conduct has been proved after due inquiry. But the wholesale rejection of members merely on the ground of non-attendance is a matter not to be so summarily dismissed.[66]

The controversy simmered while the union of 1874 was being consummated, but boiled up again at the meetings of the General Conference of the Methodist Church of Canada four years later. Both the Montreal and Toronto Annual Conferences recognized that a "soft theology" more appealing to the prosperous, urbane members had entered Methodism. Proposed amendments to the Discipline by some of Canada's most prominent Methodists, including Henry Bland, Alexander Sutherland, John Potts, and James Ferrier, attempted to transform the class meeting into a "recommended Christian privilege" and to base membership on a public profession of a desire to be saved and attendance at the sacraments. Once again, however, the Conference refused to sanction the change; in this instance it still believed that it was safer simply to ignore the rules.[67]

Over the following decades, the same arguments over compulsory class meetings continued to be debated while the church strove, generally without success, to improve the quality of the institution. But although the class meeting remained a test of membership until the formation of the United Church of Canada in 1925, in reality the debate had lost its relevance. Where the class meeting survived unchanged, it was exhibited as a somewhat odd example of outdated piety. Since attendance was poorly enforced, by the early twentieth century, fewer than 20 per cent of the members participated, and the limitation on attendance by non-members was removed.[68] The experiential religion fostered by the early class meeting had an essential, earnest vitality, but the modern meeting no longer retained a valid role in the transformed Methodism of the twentieth century.[69]

## THE MINISTRY

The changes occurring in the regular and extraordinary means of grace were paralleled and reinforced by a similar transformation within the Methodist ministry itself. In early British America, the classic image of the saddle-bag preachers, reading their Bible as they rode peacefully through the serene forest, was a highly romanticized creation. More often, they trudged through deep snow, hungry, frostbitten, and lost; they faced stormy seas in small, unsafe boats or, drenched by rain, forded swollen streams and flooded bogs to reach some isolated family.[70] The tales of these dauntless preachers energized their own generation and established a heritage of dedicated service that inspired Canadian Methodism throughout its history.

At their best, the pioneer itinerants were deeply pious men – and a few women – with an unquestioning loyalty to the doctrines and discipline of their church. They preached a simple, straightforward message since they had neither the inclination nor the education for detailed theological disputations. Although self-improvement was mandatory, constant travel precluded a library larger than the Bible, Wesley's *Sermons*, and a few Methodist tracts and biographies. With only a meagre and irregular salary and often no permanent home, they were limited in their accumulation of personal possessions. They relied on boundless energy, a broad range of useful information on pioneer conditions, and a sympathetic understanding of the settlers' lives. Although they were ever conscious of the depths of depravity, sin, and punishment, their religion recognized the wisdom of seeking souls through an optimistic perception of the future.[71] All these qualities made them welcome guests in the homes of people of goodwill regardless of denominational affiliation. By meeting Canadians on their own terms, the itinerants provided unmatched service and created a loyal, highly committed Methodist communion.

Unfortunately, at the other extreme, many preachers possessed less enviable attributes. Too many harboured extremely narrow and bigoted visions of their role in society. Some were blunt, unbending, and ill-humoured, preaching humanity's depravity "untrammeled with any notions of logical precision."[72] The same energy that drove them to heroic sacrifices sometimes made them stubborn and intolerant. In struggling for increased personal faith, they condemned the lack of diligence in others. The sheer, awful terror of humanity's desperate plight obliterated all else but individual salvation and other-worldly concerns. At worst, this narrow focus could lead to an over-emotional, fanatical, superstitious, and highly sectarian approach to Christianity. To such people, tolerance, culture, and breadth of vision were seeds planted by the devil to distract the individual from the primary struggle with evil. Of course, most preachers fell between these extremes of character.

As a system, the Methodist itinerancy involved both the travelling on a circuit to serve several congregations and the shifting of preachers to different circuits. A minister could generally remain on the same circuit for a maximum of three years, although shorter terms were quite common, especially for younger itinerants. This practice was considered essential for the vitality of Methodism. "By the frequent introduction of new pastors into its pulpits, it ensures the constant, varied, energetic enunciation of those great fundamental truths of our holy religion, which, applied by the Divine Spirit, become the germ and nutriment of the divine life of those who receive them. We doubt if the constant preaching of those great central saving truths is possible to a settled ministry, which is compelled to distribute general truths, and occupy itself with single points to avoid sameness and repetition."[73] The church also assumed that a settled clergy would threaten the evangelistic function of preaching by shifting the focus to more abstract issues, leading possibly to formality or even ritualistic worship. As well, the itinerancy shared both poor and exceptional preachers with the entire connexion. "Stationed ministers are like fixed stars; they always shine in the same orb and illuminate the same limited section of the firmament. By this arrangement a permanent light is, indeed, kept up; and, although it may increase in purity and intensity, the sphere of its influence is, nevertheless, measured by a contracted horizon. But the itinerants penetrate the regions beyond, and scatter light through the thick gloom that enshrouds them."[74]

The itinerant system was also a significant check on clerical independence in conduct or doctrine. Discipline, continuity, and the integrity of the denomination were more readily maintained when the Conference, through its stationing committee, could shift ministers from their bases of congregational support or, as was the case with Ralph Horner, from his independent evangelistic mission. Ministers had little time to secure a substantial personal following in the local community. The stationing committee rarely hesitated to discipline wayward ministers by transferring them to less-important circuits. During most of the nineteenth century, when the list of appointments was read out at Conference, the only acceptable response from the minister was "amen." This power at least partially explains the reluctance by the clergy to place lay members on the stationing committee. Although its conduct was sometimes questionable, as a rule the committee performed its thankless task conscientiously.[75]

Moreover, the itinerancy insured that normally all the itinerants had circuits and all the circuits had ministerial leadership. Unlike the Calvinist "call" system, where ministers frequently could not find employment or where a congregation might go for years before it could attract a minister, the itinerancy matched minister and church wherever possible. It also avoided the problem of independent ministers from non-Methodist backgrounds occupying Methodist pulpits and preaching an unwelcome theology.

Despite these benefits, however, many important aspects of ministry suffered under this system. The constant travel, especially in pioneer areas, placed a severe strain on the preacher and forced many early retirements. Perpetually out of touch with family or medical care, most suffered long bouts of ill health during their active careers. Even when preachers remained healthy, the system greatly hindered their ability to study or improve themselves. Time for study had to be seized when other duties permitted. Along with educational opportunities, itinerants also missed the myriad of social and cultural influences that were essential for forming a broad outlook. Transfers were equally difficult for the itinerants' families. They lacked long-term community contacts and were limited in the relationship they could enjoy with neighbours and friends. Children were regularly removed from school and friends and prevented from living stable lives. Absence from home also limited the ministers' ability to give proper parental leadership in their own families.[76]

Over the nineteenth century, a number of measures were introduced in order to combine the best elements of the itinerancy with the positive attributes of a more settled ministry. One critical change in fact came naturally. As the number of preachers and the membership increased, the size of circuits and the number of appointments within a circuit decreased. In most urban centres, the circuit was reduced to a single congregation. This change diminished the travel requirements and permitted greater opportunity for ministerial self-improvement and more intensive pastoral care to answer the complex needs of these congregations.

In addition, attempts were made to lengthen the maximum term on a circuit. Ministers serving on distant mission fields, teaching, editing connexional periodicals, or directing church boards had remained at the pleasure of the Conference, but all others had moved at least every three years. In 1850 in the Wesleyan church, Egerton Ryerson advocated that terms be extended to a maximum of five years. This measure was adopted experimentally in 1855 but was dropped two years later because the church believed it threatened discipline and centralized control over the ministry. However, the impulse to amend the system remained. By the 1870s pressure on the larger Methodist churches to do so was intensified by growing support for longer terms in Britain and the United States and by their adoption by the Bible Christians, Primitive, and New Connexional Methodists in Canada.[77] Led by Kennedy Creighton, a respected preacher known for his moderate views, a group of lay and clerical delegates pressed the 1882 General Conference of the Methodist Church of Canada to reintroduce the five-year term. The proposal received the support of over two-thirds of the Conference, but the president, Samuel Dwight Rice, ruled that a three-quarter majority was required. After the union of 1884, the question resurfaced at each succeeding Conference until in 1894, despite a legitimate fear of increased congregationalism, the church agreed that, with the permission of the local quarterly board and the stationing committee, an itinerant could remain for five years.[78]

At the same time, the church was gradually modifying its practice by permitting circuits to invite specific ministers and by subtly dividing the clergy into various specialized categories. Traditionally, Methodism had forbidden circuits to select their own ministers. But by the 1860s this practice was allowed on a limited basis, and it increased thereafter. Many believed that to prevent an invitation, always finally subject to the stationing committee, was an infringement of the church members' rights. They maintained that, since the local circuit was better able to recognize the best candidate for its work and was obliged to bear the financial costs, it should be able to negotiate for its pastoral services.[79]

On the other hand, numerous members of the church believed invitations limited the Conference's influence and undermined the itinerancy by turning appointments into a competitive business. The practice also made a mockery of the stationing committee and weakened the church's connexionalism. None the less, by the end of the century, the General Conference refused to limit invitations, and they became commonplace. Under such conditions, some ministers contrived to exchange pulpits or move to adjoining circuits for a term before returning to the original work. The stationing committee retained the final decision, but it tried to be as accommodating as possible. It published a preliminary list of appointments early in the Conference, and ministers could question its decisions until the amended list was read at the end of the meetings. A great deal of lobbying occurred during the interim to change the committee's decisions.[80]

These modified procedures helped to confirm a division of labour among the ordained clergy. One class of preacher tended to occupy the large rural circuits and another the compact, more cosmopolitan urban circuits. At times this trend was questioned, but the church recognized that it had been occurring for some time and had merit. Everyone acknowledged that certain itinerants were suited to pioneer work while others were required for the more sophisticated city churches. In order to attract and hold the leaders of Canadian society, the stationing committee assumed that it should place the best ministers in the larger towns and cities. In fact, some prominent itinerants moved from one distinguished congregation to another exclusively. These individuals generally assisted on the denomination's committees and boards and resided close to the seats of regional authority. Complaints from the mission fields that they suffered as a result of this concentration of talent in the larger centres were largely ignored.[81]

As the work of the church became more institutionalized and complex, even greater specialization developed among the clergy. Although the church officially maintained that every minister should fulfil the preaching, evangelizing, teaching, and pastoral functions, it recognized that each minister had specific talents that should be profitably exploited. Some ministers became missionaries in Canada, operating the native residential schools, hospitals, and missions to non-British peoples. With training in languages, sociology, and social-service skills, they presaged the era of professional social workers. Other missionaries spent their entire careers in Christian evangelization and medical and educational work in Japan or China. Still other itinerants specialized in organizing revivals, served as editors of the many journals established during the last quarter of the century, or worked in the colleges, in Christian education, or in temperance and moral-reform work. They all recognized the validity of their labour in promoting Methodism's larger mission and strove to improve their skills to match the need. The days when any itinerant was capable of any assigned task had long since passed.

With this specialization, the regular itinerants were better able to perform the increasingly complex pastoral responsibilities demanded in the Methodist church. They were expected to build up, as well as bring in, new converts. Under the heavy strain of this responsibility, ministers had to limit their activities in other areas of religious work. Visiting the poor and sick, comforting the bereaved, counselling and encouraging the spiritually and morally weak, attending business meetings, as well as performing the normal round of baptisms, marriages, and burials, left little spare time. The Sunday schools and young people's groups, missionary societies, and temperance and moral-reform campaigns competed for whatever time remained. By the twentieth century, many church buildings were open every day to serve the varied needs of the community, and ministers had to apply their "deep piety, good sense, knowledge of human nature, tender sympathy for the needy and suffering and an untiring will to work."[82] Such qualities were particularly crucial in the larger urban centres where competing denominations could supply a full-time ministry.

The transformation of the itinerancy was further mirrored in the style and content of the preaching. As early as the 1850s, some Methodist congregations had been dissatisfied with the constant repetition of the so-called simple saving truths of religion. Salvation and entire sanctification remained the central goals of preaching; the preachers' task was still "to arouse, to warm, to counsel, to exhort, to teach, to comfort, to save."[83] But much of the educated membership felt uncomfortable with frantic, confused harangues and demanded logical, well-organized, and well-delivered sermons. Especially after Canadian Methodists experienced the power and vitality of Morley Punshon's well-crafted sermons and addresses and were able to read the best works available in the English-speaking world, they refused to accept poorer preaching standards. While spiritual commitment remained essential, sermons also had to foster a deep and permanent impression on the understanding. They had to answer intelligently the serious threats posed by scepticism and biblical criticism. The late-nineteenth-century ministers accepted these challenges and adapted their preaching accordingly. Aided by the availability of university education, stronger courses of study, a myriad of published sources, and a more stable professional life, the itinerancy served the comprehensive needs of the institutionalized church and contemporary Canadian society.[84]

As the itinerancy was transformed, the other preaching agencies of exhorters and lay preachers also had to change. With the expansion of the status and function of the ordained ministry, equivalent elements in the unordained ministry either saw their work diminished or sought new areas of service. In earlier days, licensed lay workers had exhorted and preached along with the regular clergy, upheld the spiritual welfare of the circuit, assisted at revival services, and performed many of the pastoral functions in the community. They often organized and held a region for Methodism until it was sufficiently strong to support an itinerant. The lay ministry also gave practical experience to individuals who were considering entering the itinerancy, while permitting the church an opportunity to assess their "gifts and graces." Hence it provided an unequalled outlet for pious men and women to develop their own religiosity and to cultivate it in others.[85]

As most circuits became smaller and better served by the ordained ministry, the need for lay preachers seriously declined. More important, their principal talent had been in arousing emotional fervour, and this function was less appropriate in late-nineteenth-century Methodism. "The men are not changed, but the shape of the work no longer affords them the same opportunity for usefulness as preachers."[86] Some of the more sophisticated congregations also feared that the lay preachers could not compete with the professional ministry in rival denominations and would simply drive members out of the fold. As a result, their use virtually disappeared on many circuits.

Where lay preaching survived, preachers were under significant pressure to upgrade their quality. The Methodist church provided special courses of study, conferences, and educational literature in order to permit their more meaningful involvement in the life of the church. In spite of these aids, however, lay preaching never regained its former stature. Instead, deeply committed lay men and women turned their energy and talents to missionary, deaconess, Sunday school, and social-service work in the church or strengthened non-denominational organizations such as the Dominion Alliance, Woman's Christian Temperance Union, or Young Men's Christian Association. Others who wished to continue preaching turned to the new evangelical denominations emerging at the end of the century.[87]

In adapting its social means of grace and its ministry to the more complex needs of late-nineteenth-century Canadian society, Methodism had become broad enough to encompass a diversity of understandings and all but the most extreme elements of Protestantism. It combined a strong spiritual commitment with a desire to be of real earthly service and created an "evangelism in which zeal and culture, religion and theology, the heart and the intellect are yoked in one common service."[88]

# 10 Methodist Education

It is difficult to overstate the significance of education to late-nineteenth-century Canadians or the central role it played in national Methodist history as the denomination transformed its means of grace and ministry and elaborated its broader social mission. Particularly as society became increasingly propelled by urbanization, material, intellectual, and social progress depended on education. Canadians believed that it bred economic prosperity while preventing secular materialism, social dislocation, fanaticism, or anarchy from destroying the country. They considered it an important insurance against poverty, crime, and misery and that at the same time it led humanity to higher planes of wisdom. Education, therefore, both liberated the individual and conserved what the social establishment considered crucial for stability and order.

For Methodists, the desire for expanded education in the nineteenth century was influenced by the evangelical belief both in humanity's total natural depravity and, more essentially, in its ultimate perfectibility. Education could prevent wilful sinfulness rather than the sinner being reformed at some future date, and it provided the formal training for the student to benefit from life's experiences.[1] Education became an integral part of the late-nineteenth-century Methodist understanding of spiritual and moral advancement by answering fears about secular and sacred chaos and by fostering individual and social progress. It helped prepare a moral élite, as well as spreading the benefits of knowledge and wisdom broadly throughout the community. Over time, the Methodist leadership came to accept the idea that an educated membership, led by an educated ministry, would more fully appreciate evangelical religion.

However, Methodists also understood that knowledge could be either good or evil depending on how it was mastered and utilized. "Education without moral principle is a curse rather than a blessing. It is like putting a sword sharpened and furnished into the hands of a maniac."[2] Knowledge was acquired to help reveal God's purpose and works, not to undermine religion. Great care was essential in order to block perverse inquiry from weakening the foundations of Christianity and leading humanity to destruction and perdition. "Intellectual culture must be attended by spiritual culture ... for intellect without God is the true definition of Satan himself."[3]

For true progress, education must develop strong moral character, particularly among the young, who were both the most susceptible to evil influences and the most open to good. Purely intellectual attainment was secondary to establishing an intimate personal relationship with Christ. The ultimate purpose of education was to fulfil Christ's command to revere God and to love humanity. Or, according to the influential British teacher Thomas Arnold, education "must consider every part of the pupil's nature, physical, intellectual and moral; regarding the cultivation of the last, however, as paramount."[4] In this regard, the Bible was the indispensable textbook, and the moral elements in other sources also had to be emphasized. Only in this way could well-balanced men and women be created and personal piety, which Samuel Nelles described as the "harmony of all the powers in accordance with truth, purity, love and rectitude," be advanced.[5] Proper education was therefore crucial for Christian progress. "The more our minds are improved," wrote Nelles, "the more fully we can get hold of divine Truth ... Divine truth has been from the first ... the fountain of human progress."[6] Learning advanced piety and diffused virtue by extending humankind's understanding of truth. Education permitted a deeper understanding of Christian principles, helped create virtuous individuals, and ultimately promoted Christ's new world of justice, peace, and love. When properly educated, Canada would truly become the Lord's dominion from sea unto sea.[7]

At the same time, Methodists did not forget the more secular advantages of an educated population. As well as improving the chances of acquiring material wealth, education was a great ally in Methodism's struggle for equality with the other Protestant denominations and its battles to liberalize the economic and political systems. An educated population was at the heart of civil and religious freedom, good government, and social justice; neither old-fashioned aristocratic pretension nor narrow bigotry could not long survive where education ruled. Recognizing that it was both a profound Christian obligation to secure a sound education for their young and that teaching was a genuine pastoral occupation when advancing Christian nurture, Methodists conscientiously campaigned for broad educational opportunities.[8]

It was no accident that Egerton Ryerson, a Methodist minister, was instrumental in developing the public education system in Ontario. His first step was to help break the Church of England's control of state funds for education, with its emphasis upon training an aristocratic provincial élite through an Anglican university at Toronto. Drawing on his understanding of Wesley's teachings, Ryerson promoted a universal, practical, moral, and comprehensive education program. He was a determined missionary for the creation of a non-sectarian school system in which Protestant beliefs and practical knowledge intertwined naturally. In general, the Protestant churches in Ontario were exceptionally successful in forging a new, voluntary partnership between state and church through which public education inculcated broad moral precepts to reinforce the religious ambitions of the various denominations.[9]

In Atlantic Canada, it took slightly longer to clarify the pattern of public education that would prevail. Some of the governments had initially created universities to train the élites required to lead colonial society. For students, the universities relied on private schooling. The provincial elementary education programs, as in Ontario, were not designed to feed into the institutions of higher learning. Although the Presbyterian, Baptist, and Roman Catholic churches opposed exclusive Anglican control of provincial funds allocated to post-primary education, the Wesleyans were more ambiguous. Dominated by the conservative British Missionary Society and its local representatives, they were not originally prepared to deny the prerogatives of the Church of England. But as Methodists constructed their own schools, they advocated government assistance to all denominational education and the creation of a more efficient and comprehensive public system. Together the churches fostered a system that promoted their joint spiritual, moral, and social aspirations.[10]

In Newfoundland, rather than a government-run school system, the Methodists joined with the other churches in managing state-supported denominational education. During the late eighteenth century, ministers had commonly run day schools as adjuncts to their church and Sunday school operations. Lay Methodists had also operated small private schools, which were as deeply committed to religious and moral training as to literary attainments. By 1825 the Wesleyans had three fairly well established schools in the colony. In 1836 the government supplied grants to any properly functioning church school; these grants greatly facilitated the expansion of Methodist schools, especially among the scattered and often transient outport population. Government grants were augmented by student tuition and contributions from benevolent Methodists.

In 1851 the Newfoundland Wesleyan Methodist School Society helped formalize the church's educational fund-raising and organized a more consistent school program based still on voluntary student attendance. Seven years later, the government significantly expanded its funding and assigned the money in proportion to the ecclesiastical affiliation of the students. Further amendments to the education legislation in 1874 made each church responsible for training its own young people. Within two years the Wesleyan Methodist Church supervised seventy-one schools with seventy-one teachers and 8,264 students. By the end of the century, the connexion reported two hundred schools with 10,262 students, and these numbers continued to expand during the early twentieth century.[11]

Newfoundland, however, represented an anomaly in British America. Normally, denominational schools only supplemented the state-run system. With their deep commitment to serve the literary and intellectual, as well as the spiritual and moral, requirements of young Methodists, the larger connexions created an impressive group of schools across Canada. The original Methodist Episcopal Church in Upper Canada decided in 1830 to establish a permanent, coeducational institution in Cobourg. This facility would eliminate the need for young Methodists either to seek their secondary education at local non-Methodist schools or to travel abroad. The Methodists deeply resented the religious exclusiveness of the Anglican Upper Canada College, yet feared their young people might be poisoned by radical American political doctrines if they were educated in the United States. The new Canadian Methodist school was also expected to be relatively inexpensive and therefore open to a broader range of students.[12]

Upper Canada Academy, after delays caused by the church union of 1833 and the subsequent defections the following year, finally opened in 1836 under the principalship of Matthew Richey and the watchful tutelage of Egerton Ryerson. To prevent the institution from appearing sectarian, no system of theology was taught and all students were free to embrace any religious creed and attend any place of worship. As well, the faculty was never subject to religious tests, although its members were expected to be devout Protestants. Nevertheless, Upper Canada Academy provided a classical collegiate education, "where youth may be trained up in the knowledge and obedience of God, and at the same time be faithfully instructed in the various branches of human learning, which the present state of society renders essentially necessary, in order to respectability and usefulness."[13]

Again, the sources of income were tuition fees, contributions from lay and clerical supporters, and modest government grants. Ministers were encouraged to promote the school among their constituents since its prosperity "involves the character of our Church, is closely allied with our permanent advancement, and is essential to our exerting that influence over the public mind which interest and duty alike impel us to obtain and to cherish."[14] After the Upper Canadian legislature refused, the colonial executive provided an initial grant of £4,100, and the school subsequently received annual government grants. Despite this support, however, it was always in financial difficulty.

Under similar circumstances and with essentially the same goals in mind, the Maritime Wesleyans opened Mount Allison Academy for young men in Sackville, New Brunswick, in 1843 to provide elementary and later higher education. Charles Allison, a prosperous Sackville merchant, donated property and money to start the school and remained a constant benefactor and counsellor until his death in 1858. He hoped the academy would provide a sound education for prospective Methodist ministers, as well as serve the general educational needs of young men in Atlantic Canada. Mount Allison Academy was located in Sackville, rather than in one of the larger centres, partially because Allison's home was there, but more importantly because of the town's central location in the region. It proved a healthy, moral, semi-rural setting close to the traditional Methodist heartland in the Maritimes. Moreover, the location attracted students from all segments of the population, especially those of modest means from rural backgrounds. Allison had insisted that, like Upper Canada Academy, there be no required denominational tests, but the teachers impressed "constantly upon the youth committed to their charge, the superior claims which Religion ought always to have upon their attention."[15]

Although both Mount Allison and Upper Canada academies drew students from various Protestant denominations, the former was more successful in presenting itself as a non-sectarian institution. This success was partially due to the more tolerant religious atmosphere in the Maritimes. Egerton Ryerson's close association with Upper Canada Academy meant that his religious and political opponents assumed their children would not be well served there. Both academies educated students from a variety of age groups and with different scholarly attainments. Although primary training was provided, they saw their principal function as supplying collegiate education to prepare young people for business, for the professions, including the ministry, and for university study. Female students were being trained to take leadership roles in their own perceived spheres of interest, including the home and the church.

Throughout the nineteenth century and up to church union in 1925, Methodists established a host of schools across the country based on the models provided by Mount Allison and Upper Canada academies. Most often coeducational or for females only, these institutions either were controlled directly by the connexion or were proprietary schools administered by boards dominated by Methodists. After female education ceased with the reorganization of Upper Canada Academy into Victoria College in 1841, Professor Daniel Van Norman and his wife opened the Cobourg Seminary the following year to fill the gap. They severed their ties with Victoria College and Cobourg in 1847 and opened the Burlington Ladies Academy in Hamilton. After four years, they transferred their work to New York City. Also in 1842, Mrs Maria Hurlburt, formerly Maria Boulter, who had been the last lady preceptress at Upper Canada Academy, and her husband, Professor Jesse Hurlburt, established the Cobourg Ladies Academy. They too left Cobourg, moving to the Adelaide Ladies Academy in Toronto.[16]

The Reverend Samuel Rose opened the Dundas Ladies Academy in 1857 but soon moved it to Hamilton, where it merged into the large Hamilton Wesleyan Female College. Chartered in 1859, the new school opened two years later and remained an impressive city landmark until 1897. It offered a more substantial collegiate education for girls than the smaller schools had been able to provide. Graduates received either the mistress of English literature (MEL) or mistress of liberal arts (MLA) diploma. Although these diplomas fitted the students to enter teaching or other professions, for the most part, marriage and the home represented the ultimate career.[17]

As early as the 1840s, the new Methodist Episcopal church had recognized the need for a connexional school to train its own young people apart from the Wesleyan-controlled academies. But it could not muster sufficient resources until 1857, when Belleville Seminary opened under the principalship of J.H. Johnston. The church leaders acknowledged, "The influence of our connexion at large, and the efficiency of our ministry in future, as well as the attainments of the youth of our people, are to a great extent bound up with the success of the Belleville Seminary."[18] After only one year, the college board forced Johnston to resign because of suspected financial mismanagement, and Albert Carman served as principal until 1875. Over the years he and his colleagues spent much of their time convincing the church members that they should support the school financially while, at the same time, defending the acceptance of limited government grants. The Episcopal Methodists were the most "voluntary" of all the Methodist connexions and generally opposed any breach in the separation of church and state. However, Belleville Seminary could not afford to abstain from state aid while it was available. In 1862 the school affiliated with the University of Toronto in order to teach university subjects, and four years later, as Albert College, it became an independent university with the power to grant degrees in arts subjects.[19]

At that time, the female department was transferred to the newly created Alexandra College. This institution provided a broad academic training to the equivalent of first-year university. A decade later, the Episcopal Methodists created a comparable academy in St Thomas, Ontario, to serve the western section of the province. Originally chartered in 1877 as Alma College, it formally opened three years later as an affiliate of Albert and Alexandra colleges. As well as preparing women for responsible positions in society, these two female institutions became important sources of students when women were finally permitted to attend university.[20]

Earlier, in 1874, the Wesleyans in central Canada had commenced the short-lived Dundas Institute for boys under Edward B. Ryckman, the Ontario Ladies College in Whitby, and the coeducational Wesleyan College in Stanstead, Quebec. At Whitby a Methodist joint-stock company refurbished Sheriff Reynolds's Trafalgar Castle, where it ran the college. A group of dedicated Quebec Protestants established their own school as a "people's college" in Stanstead to provide quality education at a reasonable cost. They hoped to attract French-speaking Protestants and to train new lay and clerical leaders for that community. Stanstead was selected because of its proximity to the historic centres of Protestantism in the Eastern Townships and Montreal, its easy rail access to New England, and its healthy, moral rural setting. In 1881, after several years of financial difficulty, the Methodist Church of Canada assumed direct control from the original interdenominational board of managers.[21] Both Stanstead College and Ontario Ladies College continue to carry out effective educational work in their respective provinces.

In Atlantic Canada, the Methodists developed a similar pattern of private schools. Mount Allison added a long-anticipated female academy in 1854. It quickly became an integral part of education in the Maritimes. In recognition of Mount Allison's broad regional appeal, the governments of both Nova Scotia and New Brunswick provided financial assistance for a number of years. The only real Methodist competition came from the short-lived Wesleyan Methodist Academy, which operated from 1871 until 1876 in Charlottetown. However, Prince Edward Island's small population could not sustain its own private high school.[22]

In Newfoundland, the Methodists opened Wesleyan Methodist College in St John's to provide collegiate facilities for their elementary education system. Later it was supplemented by the Carbonear Grammar School. After some years of only sporadic service to female students, both became coeducational, with a curriculum similar to the Mount Allison academies, and educated young men and women to the equivalent of first-year university. The Methodists later joined with the other Protestant denominations in an unsuccessful attempt to establish an interdenominational, state-supported system of education to eliminate wasteful competition.[23]

In western Canada, the Methodists opened schools as local conditions warranted. Columbian College in New Westminster, British Columbia, was founded in 1892 and incorporated a year later. It initially offered collegiate and some university courses, including theology, and was affiliated with the University of Toronto through Victoria University until 1914, when it transferred its university program to the University of British Columbia. In 1923, when Ryerson College finally opened, it assumed responsibility for theological training.[24] Throughout the period, Columbian College gradually expanded its work as a coeducational, residential school serving the west-coast Protestant community.

Alberta College North opened in Edmonton in 1903, blending the traditional Methodist high-school education with training to meet the particular needs of the Prairie region. It offered extensive correspondence courses for the scattered farm communities and was proud of its role in assimilating the nearly forty distinct nationalities attending its classes. Its partner academy, Alberta College South, located across the Saskatchewan River, operated for only a few years before transferring its high-school program to Alberta College North and concentrating on training Methodist ministers for Alberta and Saskatchewan. In 1910 Methodists established Mount Royal College in Calgary as a junior college of the University of Alberta; it later served as a community college teaching applied arts and technology. In the same year, they opened Regina College as a high school with some university-level courses to serve southern Saskatchewan. It became a junior college associated with the University of Saskatchewan in 1925, but was closed during the economic depression of the 1930s.[25]

The almost continuous struggle to sustain all these schools in the face of inconsistent and insufficient financial support testifies to the deep commitment of Canadian Methodists to a high-quality moral and literary training. The schools drew students from all segments of society and from all Christian groups. While preparation for university became an increasingly important function, developing respectable Christian citizens who could succeed spiritually and socially in whatever occupation or situation they found themselves was more crucial.

The pedagogy changed over time to suit contemporary educational philosophies and the perceived needs of the students and Canadian society in general. The curriculum generally began with elementary courses, but these were abandoned as the public school system supplied the work. Thus the connexional schools could concentrate on secondary instruction. During the nineteenth century, a relatively small proportion of students followed a comprehensive program or even intended to matriculate. Normally students selected individual courses over several years to prepare themselves for what was essentially apprentice training in business, in the professions, on the farm, or in the home.

The courses at all the Methodist institutions tended to fall into three basic categories, although students were not constrained by these boundaries. At the most select academic level, Greek, Latin, and occasionally Hebrew were augmented by natural history, natural science, natural and mental philosophy, and Christian evidences to prepare students for university or the ministry.

These subjects were usually supplemented by logic, rhetoric, geography, modern languages, and English grammar to develop confident and articulate men and women. A second group of subjects was designed for those interested in commercial or other practical occupations. These included mathematics, chemistry, botany, astronomy, surveying, navigation, bookkeeping, and telegraphy. Finally, there were the "ornamental" or "accomplishments" subjects including vocal and instrumental music, drawing and painting, and in some instances, calisthenics and riding. When combined with English grammar and modern languages, they furnished what many considered the proper education for Canadian women.[26]

As the proportion of schools indicates, the Methodist authorities gave a high priority to female secondary education. This support was clearly an aspect of the greater freedom and authority accorded women in the Wesleyan evangelical tradition. "Woman should be educated, because she is an intelligent and accountable being, endowed with reason and judgement, and sustains the same relationship to her Creator, to time and eternity, as man."[27] Nevertheless, Methodism still assumed that the purpose of education was to expand the effectiveness of women in their special spheres of home and church by supplying a variant of a liberal education which would make them "useful, moral, cultivated and polished." Or, as Alma College announced, to supply "proper training and culture of the future 'Queens of the Home Circle.' "[28]

Female students were encouraged to take the ornamental subjects, and indeed these remained the most popular courses throughout the period. However, they were usually optional extras requiring additional fees, and they attracted some male students as well. Methodist educators did not want to create a class of idle, snobbish women and refused to permit their institutions to devolve into "finishing" schools for the élite. Rather, they hoped to supply "a good substantial education in which the moral powers have been cultivated in harmony with the intellect ... Woman was destined by the Creator to be the companion of man; but how can she fulfill this, her high destiny, in this day of increasing light and knowledge, if not permitted to drink with him from the golden font."[29]

Mary Electa Adams, perhaps the most influential female educator in Protestant Canada during the second half of the nineteenth century, was particularly adamant that women teachers and administrators should not automatically be subservient to male authority or to narrow perceptions of the appropriate education for women. For nearly forty years, she held leadership positions in several Canadian Methodist academies and prevented the ornamental subjects from dominating female education. Always a determined advocate of academic studies, she strove to obtain access to Canadian universities for her graduates.[30]

Even as early as the 1830s at Upper Canada Academy, female students took natural history, natural philosophy, botany, chemistry, algebra, geometry, astronomy, physiology, natural theology, Christian evidences, rhetoric, and composition, with senior students reading at the university level. Although, as in all coeducational institutions of the time, young men and women were taught separately, these women were recognized for their strong scholarship. In 1840 the school had ninety-six male and seventy-six female students.[31]

The other academies followed equally rigorous programs. In 1858, for instance, Albert Carman prepared a study program for his sister which included arithmetic, algebra, French, philosophy, rhetoric, and, "for a diversion," music. At Mount Allison, female education did not generally concentrate on classical subjects and omitted those pertaining to social roles considered inappropriate for women,[32] but it was not limited in scope or intellectual demand. At Alexandra College, the mistress of liberal arts diploma involved university-level work, with courses and examinations similar to those taken by men. Women at Alma and Stanstead sometimes took the more career-oriented technical subjects and were especially involved in teachers' training. With their later start, the Methodist schools in Western Canada provided even more significant academic opportunities for young women.

Although Canadian Methodists were actively involved in collegiate education, they believed secondary and elementary schooling were primarily the responsibility of the state. Only the government, working through local boards, could create and sustain a comprehensive, universal, and responsible system. The church's role was to insure that the programs were fair, moral, and Christian in their principles and curriculum. It claimed the right to keep the Bible as a fundamental part of all courses and Bible study and prayer as essential components of each day's operations. Parents, teachers, and clergy united to prevent secularism or infidelity from entering the classroom. They attempted to re-create a religious family setting in the school as the surest guarantee that the acquired knowledge would strengthen the students' character.[33]

## UNIVERSITIES

At the same time, many Methodist leaders assumed they had a sacred right and duty to build schools of higher learning. Universities were essential capstones to the provincial educational structures and were particularly valuable in creating a moral élite that would help to guarantee that Canadian society developed on Christian principles. The idea of a secular university was completely alien to the mind-set of all the churches in Canada. The discipline of the intellect and the advancement of moral and ethical character, which were the supreme goals of higher education, could only be achieved in a religious setting.

Therefore it was natural for the Canadian Wesleyans to expand Upper Canada Academy into Victoria College in 1841. In his important *Inaugural Address on the Nature and Advantages of an English and Liberal Education,* Egerton Ryerson, the first principal and president, enunciated the guiding principles for Victoria College. Relying heavily on contemporary British educational philosophies, he called for a balanced liberal arts program with a substantial role for the sciences which still maintained the best elements of the classics. English language and literature also held prominent positions. However, moral science and Christian beliefs were the true heart of the curriculum. Ryerson was a staunch supporter of denominational universities. Methodist theology was excluded since it was considered appropriate only for those entering the ministry and because Ryerson feared such instruction might appear overly sectarian

Upper Canada Academy, later Victoria College, served from 1836 until the school moved from Cobourg to Toronto in 1891. (UCA, P351N)

Alma College, St Thomas, Ontario. Opened in 1881 by the Methodist Episcopal Church to serve female students. (UCA, P1569)

Mary Electa Adams (1823–98). Promoted higher education for women. (UCA, P8N)

Margaret Addison (1868–1940). Dean of women at Victoria University, 1903–30. (UCA, P15)

and therefore jeopardize government grants, but the college's charter anticipated its inclusion at some later date. The ideas Ryerson proposed for Victoria
in fact underlay all future Methodist colleges and strongly influenced the development of other Canadian universities.[34]

Along with its new provincial charter, Victoria College received an annual
government grant of about $2,000, but even when this amount was added to
the other sources of income, the school continually ran a substantial deficit.
Throughout the 1840s, the college had great difficulty attracting and holding
suitable faculty and students or improving its facilities. Although Victoria
graduated Oliver Springer as the first bachelor of arts in the province in
1845, most matriculating students went elsewhere to complete their studies.
The formation of the college was really little more than an extension of its senior high school since the majority of the scholars remained in the collegiate
division. During the first decade the difficulties were aggravated by a lack of
effective leadership. In sum, the college was a serious drain on the Wesleyans'
resources and in danger of closing.[35]

The situation was made even more precarious by the government's repeated
attempts to redefine the position of the universities in Canada West. These actions culminated in Robert Baldwin's University Act of 1849. The central purpose of this legislation was to remove church control of higher education by
centralizing government support in a newly reorganized, secular University of
Toronto with University College as its teaching arm. Although subsequent
amendments allowed limited public aid to denominational colleges, the resulting dislocation forced Victoria to reassess its operations. It seriously considered
moving to Toronto or dropping its arts program and becoming a theological
college on the model of the Presbyterians' Knox College. There were even ru-
mours that the institution would close altogether. The summer session of 1850
was cancelled, and in the fall only four college students appeared for the opening of classes.[36]

Under these bleak conditions, in October 1850, the twenty-six-year-old Samuel Sobieski Nelles took over as acting principal. Of German extraction, the
Nelles family had originally moved from the Mohawk Valley in upstate New
York to a farm at Mount Pleasant, near Brantford, Upper Canada, shortly after
the War of 1812. Samuel was born in 1823, the eldest of nine children. Never
liking farming, he attended Victoria College from 1842 to 1844, but graduated
from Wesleyan University in Middletown, Connecticut, in 1846. He entered
the Wesleyan ministry the following year and shortly after his ordination in
1850, reluctantly accepted what he assumed would be the only temporary principalship of Victoria out of a sense of duty to Egerton Ryerson. Over the following thirty seven years, as principal, president, and ultimately as chancellor of
Victoria University, Nelles moulded the school into one of the premier centres
of learning in the country. Faculties of Law (1854), Medicine (1862), and Theology (1873) helped to build Victoria into a full-fledged university by the time
of Nelles's unexpected death in 1887. As part of this process, the high-school
department was transferred to Cobourg Collegiate and only fully matriculated
students were accepted after 1862. Victoria opened Faraday Hall in 1878 to
provide facilities for the concentrated study of the sciences.[37]

Throughout his career, Nelles was heavily involved in putting Victoria on a sound financial standing. Known as an astute and effective debater, but an only adequate preacher, he none the less preached constantly to church members on the value of higher education and the need for voluntary support. Just as constantly, he worked to gain access to government endowments. Both these processes became even more essential when the Ontario government cancelled annual denominational grants in 1868. The most promising long-term solution appeared to be the creation of one provincial university with federated church colleges either in their present locations or grouped together in Toronto. Queen's and Regiopolis in Kingston, Trinity and St Michael's in Toronto, after 1878 the University of Western Ontario in London, and Victoria in Cobourg would then share an increased endowment heretofore the exclusive preserve of University College in Toronto. This scheme went through several permutations over the decades and in the end all the church colleges except Victoria initially chose to stay independent. After assessing the alternatives, including the formation of one national Methodist university with federated colleges across the country, the Methodist General Conference of 1886 voted to federate Victoria with the University of Toronto if sufficient funds could be raised to build new facilities at Queen's Park. A provincial enabling act was passed in 1887 and finally proclaimed in 1890.[38]

During the middle of the nineteenth century, the Episcopal Methodists had also felt the need for their own university and reorganized Belleville Seminary into Albert College in 1866. The denomination required a separate university to supply its future leaders if it was to become a respectable national church. Nevertheless, both Albert Carman, the first principal, and his successor, Jabez Robert Jaques, modelled Albert College on Victoria College while paying special attention to the natural sciences and civil engineering. However, by the 1880s it was apparent that the Methodists could not afford two universities in Ontario. With the Methodist union in 1884, Albert and Victoria colleges merged into a new Victoria University, and Albert reverted to a high-quality, private collegiate.[39]

Like their co-religionists in Canada West, the Methodists of the Atlantic region believed an institution of higher learning was vital for their future development. They particularly required a locally educated clergy to strengthen the regional church and to compete with the other Protestant denominations. From its inception, the promoters of Mount Allison Academy had envisioned the creation of a university as the cornerstone of their educational work. However, their superiors in Britain were ever conscious of the local connexion's weak economic base and the serious financial implications of a university. Moreover, they generally did not share the North American Methodists' emphasis on denominationally controlled higher education or the need for a university-trained clergy. Furthermore, they were concerned that such a move would be seen as an affront to the Church of England and, at least until the 1850s, were anxious not to arouse antagonism. As a result, real progress toward establishing a college could only begin after the semi-independent Eastern British America Conference was organized in 1855. Mount Allison College was chartered three years later, but its opening was delayed until 1862 by financial problems and uncertainty over the status of the University of New Brunswick. Mount Allison granted its first degree a year later. From the college's inception, theology was expected to be an integral part of the curriculum, but in general Mount Allison was designed to provide a relatively inexpensive liberal arts education, regardless of church affiliation, for the young men of the Atlantic region.[40]

In this task, it faced strong competition from the other church colleges in the Maritimes, and despite state assistance from both New Brunswick and Nova Scotia, it suffered during most of its early history from a poor endowment, an underpaid and undersized faculty, and generally inadequate library and classroom facilities. The Methodist church attempted to establish scholarships to assist the more impoverished students, but again there was never enough money. The situation deteriorated even further when, in 1871, New Brunswick eliminated grants to all colleges except the University of New Brunswick in Fredericton. As a result, Mount Allison believed that its goal of supplying a first-class education could best be achieved by joining in one strong Maritime university modelled on the University of London. The denominational colleges would remain, but degrees would be granted after examination by a central board. Government funding would be based on student enrolment in each of the colleges. There was some hope that this scheme might be realized when the Nova Scotia government created the University of Halifax in 1876. Loosely affiliating Mount Allison, King's, Dalhousie, St Mary's, Acadia, and St Francis Xavier, the University of Halifax promised to become a major institution. However, most of the colleges feared losing their independence and were unsympathetic to the arrangements. A new and hostile provincial government allowed the plan to die in 1881 while also cancelling grants to the denominational colleges.[41]

In response, Mount Allison turned even more to its Methodist clientele. Fortunately, the reception was more positive than in the past. After twenty years of work, President Humphrey Pickard and the other college authorities had overcome much of the apathy toward higher education in the region. The community had come to recognize the value of a trained lay leadership to promote the social, moral, and economic prosperity of the country, and much of the earlier fear that an educated clergy might lose its experiential religion had faded. Others who had opposed government aid as an infringement of the "dignity and independence" of Mount Allison were able to contribute in good conscience. Furthermore, the college gained substantially, if only temporarily, from the new commercial and industrial prosperity of the region during the 1880s.[42]

In the northwest, the authorities in both the Methodist Episcopal church and the Methodist Church of Canada recognized the usefulness of an institution of higher learning during the 1870s. The Methodist Church of Canada received a charter for Wesley College in Winnipeg in 1877 as part of a federated University of Manitoba, but nothing could be done until the Methodist union of 1884 freed more resources for work in the region. Through support from the national church, the generosity of the congregation of Grace

Methodist church in Winnipeg, and other local Methodists, Wesley College was rechartered in 1886, and a year later the Wesleyan Theological Institute was organized. Classes in both arts and theology commenced in 1888.

Wesley College constructed more permanent, stone buildings in 1895 on a large site near the Presbyterian Manitoba College, which had been founded in 1871. Eventually the two institutions shared lectures and worked in concert to educate the youth of Manitoba and the northwest. This arrangement was formalized in 1913 with the creation of joint courses and a common registration. However, after only one year, Manitoba College dropped its arts program to concentrate on training Presbyterian clergy. In response, Wesley reverted to its independent teaching in arts and theology until after the formation of the United Church of Canada, when the two colleges merged.[43]

Heavily influenced by Ontario's educational and cultural traditions, Wesley played an important role in transmitting these values to the newly settled west. None the less, the college also adapted these value systems to serve its particular regional interests. The faculty and students saw themselves as the legitimate voice of the northwest. Wesley College reinforced this view by giving priority to training men and women who could fulfil the essentially missionary nature of much of the church's work in the region and assumed a leading role in dealing with the challenges created by the arrival of vast numbers of non-English-speaking immigrants. It helped assimilate these new Canadians into the dominant Protestant culture of the nation.[44]

From its inception, Wesley College admitted women on the same basis as men. Some Methodist churchmen had argued that since women had a different destiny, they should be educated separately. Only in this way could "the true ideal of womanhood" be developed. While acknowledging the need for women's higher education, they viewed the social inequality of the sexes as perpetual and feared that anarchy would result from attempts to alter their status. However, more enlightened educators argued that woman was intellectually man's equal, if not superior, and should be socially equal as well. Coeducation at all levels would promote this broader equality. Women required a sound university education to prepare themselves as wives and mothers, to participate in community service, and to enter business.[45]

In fact, the Methodist colleges across Canada took a leading role in promoting higher education for women. Mount Allison never legally barred women, but none attended until the college board formally accepted them in 1872, partially to replace revenue lost when New Brunswick cancelled government grants. Three years later, Grace Lockhart, with a bachelor of science and English literature, became the first woman to receive a Canadian university degree. Mount Allison also gave the first Canadian bachelor of arts degree granted to a woman, to Harriet Starr Stewart, in 1882. Victoria College first accepted women in 1880 and granted the first degree in Ontario to Nellie Greenwood three years later. Although they were initially segregated from the male students, in general, the Methodist colleges adjusted to the presence of women students more readily than other Canadian universities.[46] Nevertheless, women would have to wait until World War I before their relative proportion to male students rose significantly.

## EDUCATION FOR THE MINISTRY

While the Methodist universities were genuinely committed to the education of men, and later women, for positions of moral and social leadership, the church itself was more concerned about training its own ministers. Despite Methodism's birth in the rich literary environment of Oxford, the early Methodists had had little interest in superior educational attainment. Throughout their history, the debate over a "called," experience-based clergy versus an educated, professionalized ministry continually unsettled Methodist councils. If God had truly selected a person to preach and that person illustrated this selection by personal "gifts and graces," was it within the mandate of the church to delay or even deny this work on the basis of artificial scholarly tests? The essential criteria of a converting ministry were a sound conversion experience and the ability to bring others to Christ. Some Methodists feared that too great an education might lessen the spontaneity of preaching and spoil the preacher's ability to convey Christianity's simple message by introducing complex vocabulary and seemingly trivial theological niceties that would confuse the general membership and create unnatural boundaries between the congregation and the preacher. It could also undermine the emphasis on practical training in the field. Charles Stewart, who would later teach theology at Mount Allison, was also concerned that training the intellect often involved introducing the students to secular rationalism, which led to the perversion or destruction of their moral capacities.[47]

No Methodist ever denied the necessity of a conversion experience or a true calling to the ministry. But the church constantly affirmed not only its authority but also its duty to establish adequate educational standards for its clergy. At least as early as 1825, the Canada Conference of the Methodist Episcopal Church had viewed "with concern the want of intellectual improvement among our young preachers ... in order to meet the wants of society now improving in literary acquirements."[48] By mid-century, most agreed that the ministry must be well educated to meet the spirit of the times. In fact, if it was to lead the nation, it should be better educated and more cultured than society in general. Even the older ministers acknowledged they would have been more successful if they had had greater educational opportunities.

Narrow, overenthusiastic ministers were increasingly perceived as unsuitable and even dangerous to the long-term health of the denomination. As the revival mentality was replaced by a trust in evolutionary progress, an educated clergy was considered critical for proper connexional development. Ministers had to be teachers and pastors, rather than bombastic preachers; they had to convince the intellect, as well as sway the emotions. Samuel Nelles spoke for most Methodist leaders when he claimed: "We live in an intellectual age and men who are behind the age in cultivation are not the men to lead the age in religion ... It is therefore always binding on the Christian ministry to be ready to preach in the Portico as well as in the Market place, to meet the polished skepticism of the learned as well as the coarser iniquity of the ignorant."[49] In reality, the danger was not that an educated itinerancy might outdistance the congregation, but rather that the old-fashioned, untutored minister was becoming

increasingly irrelevant both for the educated members and for the rising industrial working classes with non-traditional religious needs. A good minister,
therefore, "combines depth with brilliancy, accuracy with ardor, sound judgement with fervid enthusiasm, a capacity of logic that will baffle the sceptic, with
a skill in rhetoric that will attract the crowd."[50]

Although the stress on a good general education expanded over the nineteenth century, for most of the period a very small proportion of ministerial
candidates acquired advanced formal education. Originally, those seeking admission to probationary status required only a good elementary knowledge of
grammar, arithmetic, and geography and a rudimentary understanding of
biblical and ancient history. Gradually these qualifications improved to a general secondary-school training, and by 1884 candidates required matricula-
tion in subjects equivalent to the admission standards at Mount Allison or
Victoria College. By this time, they generally had at least two years at university
before they applied to the church. Preliminary study also included familiarity
with Wesley's *Sermons* and *Notes on the New Testament* and perhaps Pinnock's
*Analysis*. It was assumed the candidate was familiar with connexional polity
through attendance at Methodist services, but if this was not the case, he informed himself by studying the particular Doctrines and Discipline of his
church.[51]

In order to become a probationer, he presented himself to his circuit quarterly board, which satisfied itself as to his "gifts and graces," that is, his conversion experience, his call to the ministry, and his ability to perform ministerial
duties. The district meeting then examined his moral character and general
efficiency, and the Annual Conference tested his educational qualifications.
The rigour of these tests increased over time, but by all accounts they were
never severe. The Annual Conference also insured that the candidate was in
good health and free from debt. Normally he had to be single in order to
make him easier to place and to save money on his salary.

Once accepted as a probationer, the young man was stationed on a regular
circuit to assist and learn from a seasoned itinerant. In his spare time he was
obliged to improve his literary and theological knowledge. Again, the time
and energy expended in these pursuits often depended on the conditions on
the circuit, the demands placed on the young man, and the attitude of the
church leaders at the time. In 1816 the original Methodist Episcopal Church
in Upper Canada formalized its apprentice-style training by assigning senior
itinerants to supervise and examine the recruits. This pattern became fairly
common across the country and in all the connexions. However, under pioneer conditions and with the overtaxing demands of circuit or mission work,
little time and few resources were available for intensive study.[52] In fact, it was
surprising how well the probationers did under the circumstances. Of course,
as conditions improved, so too did the ability of the recruit to study.

The scholarly Nelles, who served on relatively small circuits, recorded his
schedule for 1848. It included one hour of biblical study before breakfast,
four hours of thinking about and writing sermons before lunch, reading in
Proverbs, systematic theology, and church history in the afternoon, and doing
practical religious studies in the evening. He also assigned time to the much-

honoured practice of recording his spiritual state in a diary.[53] However, this regime was constantly interrupted by pastoral and other duties. Although Nelles must be considered exceptional among probationers both in his academic leaning and in his circuit responsibilities, all probationers were expected to regulate their time and energy in order to fulfil their educational requirements. For instance, John Maclean reported to then-president Nelles in 1882 from Fort Macleod in the Northwest Territories, "Examination papers on Cicero and Romans sent this mail … It is sometimes difficult to study Latin and Greek by the camp fire or when the thermometer is down to 40 degrees below zero, yet I always continue to carry with me my Greek Testament and some sound work on Geology, Philosophy or English Literature."[54]

Except under rare circumstances, the probationary period lasted four years, and the recruit was obliged to pass a prepared course of study each year in order to advance. Conference committees examined the candidates, but standards varied widely. Charles Eby, an advocate of a university degree as a prerequisite for theological study, considered the examinations a farce.[55] A passing grade was normally 40 per cent on each written paper, but the probationer could repeat failed subjects. Although the testing of theological knowledge was suspect, the curriculum was probably as rigorous as similar university courses and for ministers in other denominations at the time.

In the first year, as a prerequisite to a deeper analysis of the Bible and Methodist doctrine, students improved their standing in English, rhetoric, geography, and arithmetic. They also familiarized themselves with the Bible and Wesley's understanding of atonement, justification, regeneration, and sanctification. With only slight variations, all the Methodist connexions assigned essentially the same sources for study. These included Wesley's *Notes on the New Testament* and his first *Sermons*. Parts of Pinnock's *Analysis*, Horne's *Introduction*, Watson's *Apology*, Benson's *Commentary*, Paley's *Evidences*, and Angus's *Handbook* were also read to gain a broader understanding of the Bible and theology. Wayland or Peck's translation of Ganot introduced moral and natural philosophy. Core theology came from Wesley and part of Watson's *Institutes*. To improve preaching, the student minister studied Kidder's *Homiletics* and the sermons of Watson, Benson, and Adam Clarke. Each connexion studied its own Doctrine and Discipline and perhaps Fletcher's *Appeal* or Hare on justification. For history, Smith, Kurtz, and Mosheim provided information on the early church, while denominational histories gave insight on specific developments. Probationers were also encouraged to read biographies of Wesley and other notable Methodists.[56]

In subsequent years, the probationer did more intensive work in all these areas. The later sermons of Wesley, his *Notes on the Old Testament*, and the latter parts of the sources listed above expanded and deepened the understanding. As well, Fletcher's *Checks to Antinomianism*, Paley's or Comstock's *Moral Philosophy*, and more church history strengthened the doctrinal and biblical basis of the training. The probationer was also examined annually on an essay or sermon and before ordination, preached to the assembled Annual Conference. This last requirement was intended to demonstrate the crucial ability to transmit knowledge effectively to the people and was never taken lightly. Over time, especially as the preliminary education of probationary candidates improved, the church expanded the courses of study and raised the requisite standards. The creation of the Methodist universities and their theological institutes was at least partially designed to facilitate these developments.

However, clerical training involved much more than theological subjects; the hope was to create broadly educated individuals who could function in all circles of society. Latin and Greek were considered essential to a liberal education, and English literature, French, and German opened new vistas of intellectual interest. Samuel Nelles was particularly concerned about the narrow range of knowledge he found among his colleagues and students. Writing to his friend George Hodgins, he explained, "Thus I have chosen for a young sprig of Methodist divinity the plays of Shakespeare as a suitable antidote to the biases of sectarian crotchets ... Alas, how much reason have I seen for giving this advice to those around me, especially Methodist preachers."[57] Probationers were encouraged to seek knowledge and wisdom from a broad range of suitable sources and, if possible, to spend time at a university.

Once Victoria College was established, ministers were permitted to spend one of their probationary years there. However, between 1842 and 1855, only fourteen men took advantage of this opportunity. In 1854 the Wesleyan Methodist Conference created an education fund to assist ministers attending Victoria, and in 1870 the Maritime Conference began a similar fund for those wishing to attend Mount Allison. These funds supported increased enrolment and assisted the colleges with their financial problems. At Victoria the student could study moral philosophy, Old Testament history, ethics, and evidences of religion, as well as the classics, Greek, and literary subjects, as part of the regular arts program. Such training was considered the best method of supplying the church with efficient and devoted workers.[58]

As well as improving general education, by the 1850s all the Methodist connexions were striving to upgrade the specialized training of their itinerants. Only the Bible Christians failed to commit themselves to institutional theological education, and even they granted university graduates the equivalent of two years' standing in the probationary ranks. Among the Episcopal Methodists, Albert College always offered theological training as part of its arts program, graduated its first bachelor of divinity in 1873, and maintained a Faculty of Theology from 1876 until it united with Victoria College in 1884. The New Connexion Methodists appointed William McClure as a theological tutor in 1856 to run what amounted to a correspondence course for probationers. After his death in 1871, no replacement was made, but McClure's work had improved the theological knowledge of the new preachers. From 1867 to 1870, the Primitive Methodists ran a Theological Institute in Toronto, with Thomas Crompton providing training in theology and pastoral duties. However, the institute was financially destitute and never well patronized since the church could not afford to allow its ministers to absent themselves from circuit work. Like the New Connexion, the Primitive Methodists returned to local itinerant supervision of probationer training.[59]

Before the Methodist union of 1884, only the Wesleyans had the strength to maintain specialized divinity schools. Much of the original rationale for opening Mount Allison College had been recognition of the urgent need for an institution to train ministerial candidates. In 1860 the Conference stationed Charles DeWolfe at Sackville so that he could serve part-time as professor of theology at the college. DeWolfe had been born in Wolfville, Nova Scotia, in 1815, but studied and was ordained in England before being sent back to the Maritimes as a missionary in 1838. Respected for his learning and broad culture, he taught theology, homiletics, church history, Hebrew, and the Bible from 1861 until 1868 to a few probationers and to arts students intending to enter the itinerancy. On DeWolfe's death, it was left to the forty-eight-year-old, Scottish-born and educated Charles Stewart to organize a Faculty of Theology in 1875, with himself, David Allison, David Kennedy, John Burwash, and Alfred Smith teaching apologetics, moral science, Old and New Testament, systematic theology, homiletics, church history, Greek, church doctrine, and Methodist polity. These professors also continued to teach in the arts faculty. The theological program was originally three years long or, if combined with undergraduate arts, five years in total. Tuition was paid by the Conference from its education fund. In 1878 a Theological Society provided more specialized lectures and readings to promote advanced education for ministers in the region, and in 1883 the first bachelor of divinity graduated. Although faced with stiff competition from other Methodist theological schools, the faculty did a creditable job in meeting the changing challenges of ministerial training.[60]

In central Canada, the Wesleyans had begun promoting university-based theological education in the 1850s. However, it was not until 1866, in anticipation of creating a theological professorship, that Victoria College appointed Nathanael Burwash to teach science. The fear of jeopardizing government grants by appearing sectarian was removed when Ontario cancelled all support for denominational colleges in 1868. This loss, however, also precluded the immediate establishment of new programs. Many of the church leaders, including Egerton Ryerson, Morley Punshon, and George Douglas were promoting the idea of independent theological institutes in Toronto and Montreal. Ryerson, in particular had little respect for the young Burwash and wanted Punshon to teach theology. If created, the institutes would require all the available church funds.[61]

Although Nelles and his supporters were able to kill the idea of an institute in Toronto, strong lay and clerical forces pushed the scheme forward in Montreal. They considered it a vital anchor for the church in Canada's largest city and crucial for promoting Methodism in Quebec, particularly among French Canadians. In 1868 David Torrance, a wealthy Montreal businessman, promised to endow a chair of theology, but the scheme was shelved until about $50,000 was raised from James Ferrier and other members of the local business community. The Wesleyan Theological Institute, later Wesleyan Theological College, was established in 1872; George Douglas served as principal and professor of theology until his death in 1894. The school formally opened in September 1873, with six students taking classes in Dorchester Street Methodist church. A new building was finally erected next to McGill University in 1883, and the institute received the right to grant divinity degrees in 1887. Two years later, of its forty students, eight were in the bachelor of divinity, fifteen in the licentiate, and ten in the arts program, while the remainder were taking the prescribed Conference course of study. In 1898 the college finally gained access to the church's education funds, originally available only to Victoria University, and with a bequest from the estate of Hart Massey, was able to begin postgraduate work in theology in 1900. One of the prominent features of theological education in Montreal was the high degree of interdenominational cooperation. The Congregational, Presbyterian, Methodist, and Anglican theological colleges affiliated with McGill University in 1865, 1873, 1878, and 1880 respectively. After years of intermittent mutual assistance, the Methodist and Congregational schools amalgamated certain classes in 1899. This development in turn led to more interaction with the other schools, and in 1913 a joint board oversaw a common basic theological education among the four groups.[62]

Despite the work done in Montreal, the major Methodist focus for theological training remained Victoria College. The original obstacles were finally overcome through the bequest of $30,000 by Edward and Lydia Jackson of Hamilton and the support of the Methodist education fund. In 1871 Nathanael Burwash and John Wilson taught several classes specifically for theological students, and the following year Burwash headed a new Department of Theology. He himself taught biblical history, theology, and Hebrew. Wilson lectured on biblical antiquity and New Testament exegesis, while Alfred Reynar added rhetoric and church history and President Nelles supplied ethics, evidences of religion, and homiletics. Finally, Victoria created a Faculty of Theology under Burwash's deanship in 1873. The faculty added classics and elocution and taught religious studies, as well as the normal body of subjects, in the Faculty of Arts. A Theological Union, founded in 1877, arranged special lectures to promote greater interest in theology among the clergy and to expand the college's library. It also sponsored a fellowship for probationers based on an original written thesis. In general, it acted as the precursor of formal graduate work in divinity.[63] Victoria faced the inevitable problems with the new intellectual challenges of the late nineteenth and early twentieth centuries, but it emerged relatively unscathed and developed into one of the largest and most progressive theological schools in the country.

In the west, the Methodists repeated the pattern of small theological schools to serve their regional needs. The first meeting of Manitoba Conference proposed a theological school to serve that province and the northwest beyond. In 1887 a Theological Institute was organized, and it was transformed into a full Faculty of Theology at Wesley College in 1894. In the same year, it graduated its first bachelor of divinity. However, since a preliminary degree was expected before divinity courses at the college were pursued, most probationers opted for the Conference course of study. Later, St Stephen's College in Edmonton, formerly Alberta College South, and Ryerson College in Vancouver were also established to train ministers for the Methodist church. Although incorporated in 1912, Ryerson did not begin teaching classes until 1923 and merged into Union Theological College at the University of British Columbia four years later. During its brief history, it cooperated with the Pres-

Humphrey Pickard (1813–90). Head of educational work in Sackville, New Brunswick, 1843–69. (UCAMa)

Nathanael Burwash (1839–1918). Dean of theology, 1873–1900, and president of Victoria University, 1887–1913. (UCA, P791*)

Charles DeWolfe (1815–75). First theology professor at
Mount Allison University, Sackville, New Brunswick.
(UCA, Album 78.105C/OS)

Albert Carman (1833–1917). Last bishop of the Methodist
Episcopal Church, general superintendent of the Methodist
Church, 1884–1914, the pre-eminent conservative voice in
Canadian Methodism. (UCA, p901)

byterians and Anglicans in teaching divinity students. All three western Methodist colleges provided innovative ministerial training to candidates drawn mostly from their own sections of the country, training which was designed for the particular needs of their regions.[64]

## NEW INTELLECTUAL CHALLENGES

The need for higher education and sound theological training for the increasingly professionalized clergy was particularly evident as Protestantism faced the unparalleled social and intellectual challenges of the late nineteenth century. Against a background of increasing urban and industrial dislocation and the fear of anarchistic, socialist, and secular ideologies, the Darwinian scientific revolution had significantly unsettled the Canadian churches. Experiential religion appeared to be jeopardized by a rationalism unbounded by belief in God, and orthodox notions of biblical and natural theology seemed incapable of withstanding the assaults of the new scientific and philosophical theories. The mission of the clergy changed somewhat from converting the sinful or introducing religion to those hitherto unreached by evangelical ministry to preventing scepticism and agnosticism from undermining the faith of the community.

The great expansion in scientific knowledge during the nineteenth century was not, in itself, a problem as long as science remained the study of God's mysterious works in the realm of nature. Theology was the supreme science because it performed the same task in the more crucial spiritual realm. While biblical theology sought to understand God through the Scriptures, natural theology recognized that God's revelations could also be gleaned from his works in the world. Through God's handiwork in nature, humankind could readily see the divine design and creative power. Moral science, the core of traditional higher education, linked science and theology by demonstrating the dutiful relationship between humanity and God and among all people, and it kept the intellect under judicious control. To most Methodists, all knowledge was ultimately part of one great whole leading to an illumination of God, or as Samuel Nelles argued, "the laws of nature are the laws of God and should be made to lead the mind upward to such divine contemplation."[65]

Moreover, scientific inquiry had historically been carried out by talented amateurs, particularly by loyal churchmen who made little attempt to question traditional understandings of nature. The fields of botany and geology, which became the most contentious scientific pursuits, were especially advanced by a myriad of individuals studying their own local regions and contributing to the growing catalogue of knowledge by identifying and recording what they found. This work fitted well with the basic scientific method of the period, originally advanced by Francis Bacon, which called for the systematic collection, arrangement, and classification of data, without preconceptions and along inductive lines. Induction simply involved careful, unbiased observation of the phenomena. The cumulative effect of this Baconian scientific method was expected to be the establishment of fixed laws and true axioms, or rather, the revelation of those laws which God had previously established. However, induction could not be assumed as certain until all the evidence had been examined. Such an approach also blended well with the concept of Scottish common sense philosophy that humans had an intuitive capacity to understand both the natural world and the fundamental principles of morality. Methodists particularly appreciated the essential role of personal experience in the process of systematically expanding knowledge, wisdom, and truth.[66]

However, by at least the early nineteenth century, new generations of scholars were advancing revolutionary scientific theories of nature. These were concerned with the real age of the earth, the concept of evolution, and how nature functioned. Nevertheless, the natural theology proposed by men such as Richard Owen, the prominent British anatomist, conformed with the pronouncements of internationally famous geologists, including Hugh Miller and Louis Agassiz. God had created the world, but the days listed in Genesis were of immense duration. Science and theology could still march together to reveal God. Where this harmony appeared impossible, it was simply that humankind had not yet unravelled God's meaning. As the preliminary discussions over the relationship between the creation described in Genesis and the findings of geology emerged, the evidence provided by the latter was too incomplete to pose a serious threat to the biblical account. The Methodist church readily condemned arguments for a pre-Adamite creation as pure whimsy. Indeed, scientists could not agree among themselves, as theory denounced theory. With science itself in such a state of flux, the church leaders wisely counselled their members to avoid being diverted by the discussion.[67]

Into this already unsettled state of affairs came Charles Darwin's *On the Origin of Species by Means of Natural Selection* in 1859. It provided, through the theory of natural selection, a logical and easily comprehended means of understanding how evolution worked. Darwin's theory denied that all species had been created at one time. Rather, the almost infinite variations had appeared by adapting to the contingencies of their environment over immense periods of time. The concept replaced the notion of a benevolent God working to a great design with the assumption of a random, hostile nature that rewarded any mutation which increased a species' ability to compete for food and to reproduce. Darwin went even further in 1871 in *The Descent of Man* to include humanity in the animal world and therefore in the pattern of evolution. Humankind was no longer a unique creation. At the same time, many of Darwin's disciples analysed human development more specifically within this evolutionary process. They sought to anchor social ethics in their new understanding of the natural order and to shift the basis of moral action from God to society. The works of Darwin and his followers refocused the debate concerning evolution, the age of the earth, and the laws governing nature and humanity.[68]

If Darwin was correct, human beings were deposed from a supreme position in the world. How could humanity claim to be created in the image of God? Moreover, if it had simply evolved from some lower species, how could it have fallen into sin, and without a fall, how could Christ atone for humankind's original sins? Equally unsettling, what was God's role in creation and nature? Was God limited by the natural forces of evolution? Although Darwin never denied God as the ultimate creator and functioned within an orthodox framework of natural theology, his God seemed almost irrelevant to the process and an afterthought in his theory. The new scholarship provided a fundamentally new way of looking at the world and threatened both the harmony between science and religion and the legitimacy of faith. Darwin came, somewhat unfairly, to symbolize a sceptical and even perverse scientific community bent on destroying the foundations of Christianity.[69]

The initial reaction of Canadian Methodist educators was to reaffirm the traditional Protestant values. Samuel Nelles, for instance, claimed that most of the scientific work that attacked religion assumed evolution was a fact, not a theory, and simply searched for information to confirm this belief. Darwin had clearly followed a deductive method, arguing that if evolution occurred, the results noted in nature would likely have happened. No Darwinian was able to show one species transmuting into another. To Nelles and other Methodist teachers, this method was unscientific because it did not follow well-established Baconian scientific procedures; since Nelles could not accept the legitimacy of the approach, he could not accept the results. Others simply maintained that there was insufficient evidence to support such speculative conclusions.[70]

At the same time, a new liberal theology emerged which attempted to provide a more relevant underpinning for Protestantism. Liberal theology both resulted from the altered social and intellectual conditions and supplied a comforting explanation of these developments. Proponents of liberal theology were particularly influenced by the debate over Darwin's theory of evolution, but they also found Darwinism useful in answering their own pre-existing troubles with orthodox theology and with the traditional priorities of evangelical spirituality. The influence of liberal theology was felt by Canadian Methodism in areas such as the growing trust in education as a means of grace, the transformation of revival, and the emphasis on the ethical dimensions of religion.

Liberal theology developed gradually in Europe and North America over the second half of the nineteenth century and came to dominate Protestant theological understanding during the first three decades of the twentieth century. It represented a complex reformulation of the manner in which God functioned, the essential qualities of Christ, the nature of sin, and the basis of salvation. It owed much of its initial popularity, however, to its ability to harmonize Darwinian scientific theories of evolution with Protestant religious belief. Its success was perhaps best demonstrated by the fact that conservative and fundamentalist forces were for the most part obliged to abandon the mainstream denominations and form their own associations.

It was liberal since it attempted to make religion more human-centred, was more confident and optimistic about the human condition, and therefore advanced the status of the individual. Orthodox theology claimed that humanity had inherited a corrupt nature from Adam because of his fall from grace. Liberals assumed that human beings had a dual nature: on the one hand, corrupt, finite, and subject to death because of sin and, on the other, the children and image of God with a moral personality, capacities of reason and freedom, and the ability to gain dominion over sin and death. Some theologians claimed that sin was personal and could not be inherited from Adam; as a corollary, infants were therefore sinless at birth. Since the world and humankind in it had been created to institute a community of perfect love, a kingdom of God on earth, individuals must have the innate capacity to fulfil this goal. Under these conditions, democracy came to imply giving all individuals the maximum freedom for self-development. In general, such beliefs fitted with Wesley's concept of prevenient grace, but furthered the decline in traditional Calvinist notions of predestination and election.[71]

Liberal theology was based on the belief in an immanent, rather than a transcendent, God. In the view of those who believed God was transcendent, or stood outside the natural world, God had benevolently designed and created the world once and for all time, placed humans at the summit of creation as the only spiritual beings, and then withdrew to allow the world to operate according to normally immutable laws. The knowledge given to humanity was "the unveiling or disclosing of God's purpose in Jesus Christ to restore man to fellowship with Himself," and this unfolding of truth could be manifest "not in and through nature, but above and beyond nature, by special intervention of God."[72] As a supernatural being, God could still work miraculously to supersede his own laws of nature to help humankind understand the world. Any denial of such power undermined the biblical miracles and the Bible's entire credibility.

An immanent God, however, was constantly at work in the world. "God," according to the American liberal theologian Borden Parker Bowne, "is the omnipresent ground of all finite existence and activity."[73] Nature, instead of being self-sufficient and mechanical, depended on an active divine presence. Such beliefs gave a powerful sense of immediacy to spiritual religion and prevented natural theology from falling into a crude pantheism. Although still working through divine laws, God was part of the processes of history and did not require miraculous manifestations to demonstrate supremacy over nature. God, not nature, was the subject of wonder and worship. With God intimately involved in the universe's ongoing functions, there could be no proper division of the world into sacred and secular spheres; everything belonged to God's kingdom. Religion provided divine principles both for achieving heaven and for all aspects of earthly conduct. As well, while a transcendent God might be seen to require earthly regents, such as kings and popes, to rule over minor matters, an immanent God needed no intermediaries; this view strengthened the individualistic and democratic nature of religion and society in general.

Liberal theology emphasized the human aspect of Christ and placed him within the normal processes of human history. Accordingly, Christ was God's agent in leading humanity to understand God's will. Because Christ was human, he provided a suitable model for human behaviour; humanity could become Christlike and thus appreciate the divine aspect of God. Christ's authority rested on his unlimited moral and spiritual excellence, not on his ability to step outside the normal laws of nature and perform miracles. He was attempting to institute universal love in personal and social life and thus initiate a divine social order on earth. When accomplished, the earthly reign of God would be part of human history and not mark its end. In this view, Christ became first and foremost a social revolutionary who attempted to transform, not simply modify, society.[74]

With such a Christ as guide, liberal theology stressed the moral and ethical aspects of religion. Individuals must confront and transform, not accommodate themselves to, an evil and unjust secular society. Ultimately, secular society would cease to exist. Salvation occurred both as a victory over nature and as the acceptance of the earthly ideals of Christ. Since humankind had moral capacities, it must seek a moral transformation or sanctification. Because liberal theologians also assumed an organic relationship between the individual and society in general, both sin and salvation had social dimensions. Religion stressed the Golden Rule and the Sermon on the Mount as the clearest expressions of proper social relations. Thus cooperation and fellowship became integral parts of the quest for salvation. Liberal theologians, therefore, supplied much of the power and influence of the social-gospel movement, which will be discussed in subsequent chapters.[75]

Liberal theology was also characterized by a mistrust of historic creeds and confessions and was particularly averse to biblical inerrancy and literalism. Liberal theologians believed that although many creeds had supplied valuable expressions of belief, they were too culturally conditioned by the age which had fostered them and they required continual re-evaluation to remain relevant to contemporary needs and understanding. Both spiritual and intellectual progress relied on undertaking new fields of inquiry, not on mastering existing knowledge. The adoption of liberal theology, therefore, exalted the intellect and replaced certainty and conformity with a healthy prescription of doubt and questioning. The desire for progress supplied the unifying purpose to the late-Victorian generation of Protestants. As a corollary, liberal theology was strongly anti-sectarian and ecumenical, looking forward to ecclesiastical cooperation and even the reunification of Christianity. Traditional revivalistic religion sometimes shared these views, but liberals further believed that narrow denominational boundaries, by unnaturally dividing Christianity, limited inquiry and slowed progress. They prevented a true understanding of Christ's earthly role and interfered with the proper processes of history and the unfolding of divine revelation. Liberal theologians, therefore, supported faithful inquiry as essential to reveal the mysteries of God's truth.[76]

The key to liberal theology's popularity, however, was that it suggested a means to re-establish stability in the Canadian religious and intellectual community by reconciling Darwinism and Christianity. Liberal theologians modified Darwinism by eliminating much of the process of natural selection and changing survival of the fittest into survival of the best. With these modifications, evolution need not necessarily depose God from a position as the ultimate creator. An immanent God used the natural, ongoing processes of evolutionary creation to fulfil his purpose for the world. To Nathanael Burwash's son Edward, who was an active scientist with a strong interest in theology, "the supernatural may be regarded as but the presence of a personal God in His universe, to whose active will all the forces of natural law must be traced back as their first cause."[77] To many liberal Methodists, God was the beginning and remained the root of all development; the role of science was to "bring the progress of the world into an intelligible and natural order."[78]

The understanding of evolution was transformed from a pessimistic acceptance of a mindless nature into an optimistic trust in providential progess. God was perceived as directing humankind's development along altruistic channels. Works such as Henry Drummond's *The Ascent of Man* were popular sources for sermon material among Methodist preachers at the end of the nineteenth century since they retained God in the evolutionary system and emphasized human advancement. In fact, since evolution confirmed God's continual presence in the world and creation was an ongoing process, existence achieved a new sense of continuity and the future appeared to have unlimited possibilities.

Although many Methodists worried that social morality would be weakened if evil, like all other human impulses, was assumed only to be part of humanity's animal nature, in fact, evolution suggested that moral advancement would parallel physical and mental progress and animal behaviour would be left behind. For most Methodists, nothing could displace God as the source of moral action. At the same time, if species changed by adapting to the environment, it was a short step to the belief that by improving the social environment, humanity's evolution would be quickened. Moreover, this view reinforced the evolutionary role of education in gradually and progressively expanding Canadians' knowledge, understanding, and character. Evolutionary, not cataclysmic, conversion experiences also fitted more clearly into the accepted pattern of transformation. Together, these beliefs appeared to give scientific support to moral reform and to the ultimate possibility of creating heaven on earth while retaining Christian faith as the true guide to enlightened human intellectual, spiritual, and moral conduct. In adopting what appeared valuable from the new theological notions, Methodism had abandoned nothing which it considered essential for a meaningful evangelical religion.[79]

Interacting with liberal theology and with science in general was an increasing application of the new scientific methods to the Bible. Traditional Methodists feared that this represented an assault upon the basis of faith. Although Methodism relied heavily upon reason and personal experience for spiritual growth, it nevertheless was founded on the Bible as the inspired word of God, as the source of God's revelation, and as the sacred history of antiquity. The Scriptures demonstrated God's benevolent design in creating the world and particularly in placing humankind at the summit of creation. Thus the Bible was the one sure foundation for doctrine and morality, supplying everything necessary for redemption and eternal life. The Old and New Testaments were linked by the central figure of Christ; the former prophesied and prepared the way for his coming, while the latter unfolded his atoning covenant for humanity. Any apparently learned defamation of the Bible seemed to promote scepticism, agnosticism, and a perilous decline in the practice of evangelical religion.

The new "critical" scientific and historical approach to the Bible was principally undertaken by German theologians and philosophers and their British and North American students. It was intended to provide both a better understanding of the Scriptures and a new sense of human history. The biblical criticism took both "lower" and "higher" forms. Lower, or textual, criticism involved detailed study of the biblical texts themselves to ascertain their correct meaning. Generations of scholars had accepted the legitimacy of such work. For instance, Thomas Horne's *An Introduction to the Critical Study and Knowledge of the Holy Scriptures* had been a standard textbook in Methodist theological education almost from its publication in 1818. Although comprehensive and analytical, it did not attack the inspiration or unity of the Bible. Most Methodists agreed that language could only imperfectly present the mind of God, and therefore careful reflection and correction were appropriate in the appreciation of God's inspired words. This type of analysis was valid as long as the proper tenets of research and faithful inquiry were maintained. Indeed, many Canadian Methodist scholars, including the conservative Albert Carman and Charles Stewart, supported the validity of this work, and some supplied important corrections to the biblical texts.[80]

But higher criticism assumed that the Bible could be examined in the same way as any other literary or historical work and called for a reappraisal of the authors, nature, and authority of the Scriptures without reference to Christian doctrine or without being subject to the final arbitration of faith. In so doing, it attacked the authenticity, unity, and uniqueness of the Scriptures. In the past, critics had attempted to answer biblical anomalies, and even John Wesley had called for reasonable reappraisals of obvious inaccuracies. For instance, he dismissed Moses' authorship of the first five books of the Bible since they described Moses' own death. Higher criticism, properly conducted, was not a threat; what mattered was the spirit of truth that underlay the investigation. Wesley and most of his orthodox nineteenth-century followers assumed that the Bible was the directly inspired word of God, not merely the writings of certain individuals who had been endowed with special insight in order to record and explain God's purpose, and humankind must approach it with humble and abiding faith.[81]

However, higher critics appeared to threaten the very anchors of Christian faith and the historic harmony between reason and religion. To most Methodist leaders, Darwinian and social Darwinian scholarship gave a new integrity and licence to the social sciences and to higher criticism. Higher critics, in turn, by assuming an unqualified right to question everything, gave scepticism and agnosticism an unwarranted power and respectability. By suggesting that the Bible was full of allegory and legend, that it was designed to suit a primitive Hebrew society, or that the chronology and information in its books were faulty, higher and historical criticism appeared to many to illustrate a heretical breakdown of faith and a contempt for organized religion.

Such human analysis appeared to transgress the proper limits of inquiry. For those theologians who discounted humanity's positive spiritual qualities, original sin and natural depravity had made the intellect faulty and therefore placed limits on human reason independent of God's aid. Reason was limited because humanity was limited. Some things had to be accepted on faith; it represented a higher truth even than reason. In essential doctrinal areas, Albert Carman spoke for the conservative members of his generation when he succinctly claimed, "You cannot tell the why: you can only believe."[82] Religious truth should never be questioned; the facts of the Bible were above philosophy or science. Reason should be limited to authenticating the revelations of God. If the two were incompatible, then reason was faulty. John Burwash and his colleagues at Mount Allison were able to mute the discord between science and religion for a time by stressing the limits to understanding human origins, destiny, morality, and spiritual development.[83]

Some liberal theologians, however, turned this argument on its head by suggesting that orthodox views of the Bible were only partial because human knowledge was incomplete. Only by searching diligently for the truth using all the tools of analysis provided by God could the understanding of God's revelation be gained. Attempts to limit the search for the truth not only alienated scholars from the Christian church, but also weakened the structure of Christian doctrine. These thinkers maintained that without proper scholarship, theology would lose its relevance and be cut off from the advances in learning; this was an unpardonable disservice to the Christian faith. As knowledge grew, so would faith.[84]

Arguments on the limits of inquiry were used to buttress the old theological order. But many progressive Methodists, most of whom were by no means theological liberals, while agreeing that there were limits to human understanding, dismissed suggestions that free inquiry should be curbed. Throughout his long career, Samuel Nelles never retracted his deep commitment to the quest for the truth. Although he maintained that learning needed to be sanctified since, without religion, it "is apt to degenerate into vain jangling and idle speculation, it is apt to grow proud, shallow and unprofitable," nevertheless he also attacked stale dogmatism and the "dirt and grime" of centuries of accumulated church authoritarianism. "Religion," he wrote, "when dissevered from learning is apt to degenerate into superstition and fanaticism, and some form of idolatry." And he later proclaimed, "Let the theologian especially rejoice in the labours of men of science in giving at times a freer action and wider scope to religious thought."[85] He insisted on the right of all students of theology to seek the truth and argued that since past writers had no monopoly on wisdom, their views should never become so crystallized that new insights were automatically rejected.

Nathanael Burwash and, to a degree, even conservatives such as Albert Carman and Edward Hartley Dewart, the editor of the *Christian Guardian*, agreed on the principle of free inquiry. Burwash assumed that "spiritual truths must be judged by spiritual tests and by spiritual men" with a clear religious faith in order to sustain the balance between reason and conscience, but he supported free inquiry even when he could not conscientiously accept the results.[86] Using the Baconian approach, especially in his *Manual of Christian Theology on the Inductive Method*, he attempted to instil in his students a trust in disciplined inquiry as the best means of harmonizing theology and science and undergirding Christian faith. Although by the twentieth century this book appeared dated, it reflected Burwash's half-century of grappling with the serious intellectual problems of his age. For Dewart and Carman, the real concern was the presumption of the new biblical analysis in attacking the Bible through what they considered improper means.

In Canadian Methodism, the clash of ideologies occurred principally over the work of two Victoria University professors, George Workman and George Jackson. Workman, a student and protégé of Nelles and Burwash, had graduated in 1875 and was appointed to teach metaphysics seven years later. From 1884 until 1889, he immersed himself in the rigours of higher criticism in Leipzig before returning to introduce his research to the Canadian Methodist community. His early work on Jeremiah was well received, but in 1890 he delivered a lecture to the Victoria Theological Union entitled "Messianic Prophecy." Well documented and not particularly radical by the standards of biblical criticism, it suggested that the Old Testament prophets were concerned about the evils of their own society and, except in a few instances, did not predict the coming of Christ. Rather than the prophets pointing directly to Christ, "it is the moral truths and spiritual principles in them that bear direct witness to him and find divine fulfillment in him."[87] In making this claim, Workman appeared to be removing Christ from the Old Testament and thereby assailing the inspiration and integrity of the Scriptures. Later he claimed that he was merely part of a long tradition that had revised the texts to meet the general level of public understanding. No one claimed the Bible was undermined when scientists proved that the earth was round or that the sun was the centre of the solar system and hence did not rise as the Scriptures said.[88]

None the less, in addition to his actual conclusions, the traditionalists in the church, and Dewart and Carman in particular, were angered by Workman's assumption that he could determine the meaning of God's inspired text. They quickly mounted a campaign to censure him and refute his conclusions. R. Payne Smith's *Prophecy, a Preparation for Christ* and Edward Riehm's *Messianic Prophecy* were placed on the course of study for divinity students. Burwash published his own findings on Isaiah and argued that Christ was the central fact of both the New and Old Testaments. While opposing Workman's results, Burwash continued to support his colleague's right to pursue his research. However, although no formal charges were laid, the outcry was such that Workman was removed from the Faculty of Theology and allowed to teach only in the arts program. Appointments in theology were controlled by the church, not the university.[89] As a result, he resigned. Although the conservative forces won this battle, during the 1890s it was much more common for the extreme holiness and fundamentalist preachers to find themselves forced out of mainstream Methodism. In 1894 the General Conference replaced Dewart as editor of the *Christian Guardian* by the more liberal Andrew C. Courtice, who was a leader among the younger, progressive ministers.

Some twenty years later, George Jackson faced a similar attack on his work. He had originally been invited to join the Victoria faculty in 1905 to teach homiletics. Although he turned down the offer, he did request information from Burwash about the degree of academic freedom enjoyed by the professors in the pursuit of higher criticism. Burwash replied, "As to intellectual freedom, some of us have fought that battle here, and I think now the course is perfectly clear. There are still a number of older men who are very much afraid of the new exegesis, but our motto in our College has been 'candid, honest pursuit of truth associated with the culture of the most earnest spiritual life.' "[90]

In 1909, after serving at Sherbourne Street Methodist church in Toronto for three years, Jackson accepted the professorship of English Bible. He was well known for his research into the Old Testament and his belief that historical study of the Scriptures would lead to a stronger Christian faith by making it more logical and rational. Critical investigation would not alter the fundamental importance of the sacred texts as the record of Christ's redeeming love. At the same time, however, he claimed, "Whether the early chapters of Genesis are, in the strict sense of the word, historical, whether David actually wrote any of the Psalms, whether the book of Jonah is history or allegory – these and other questions must be determined."[91]

In an address to the local YMCA, one of the most significant religious organizations for Victoria University students, in 1909, Jackson questioned the creation story presented in Genesis. He was immediately attacked in the press by Albert Carman, the chairman of the Board of Regents at Victoria University, and his allies, many of whom were from non-Methodist evangelical denominations. However, Jackson received strong support from Burwash and other Victoria faculty members, who added a concern over academic freedom to one of religious liberalism. He was also supported by the wealthy laity at Sherbourne Street church, who had originally invited him to their congregation. They were some of the most powerful individuals in Methodism and in Canada. As well as being heavily influenced by liberal theology, they were struggling to modernize the denomination's work in home and overseas missions and in its internal practices; they were not prepared to allow Methodism's educational institutions and especially its theological schools to become a restraint on the church's progress.[92]

The times had indeed changed. Jackson's position was vindicated, and Carman was forced to retreat. However, it was as much Carman's authoritarian style and his unwillingness to share power as his conservative beliefs that fostered opposition. He was not an extremist; it was actually his attempt to keep the church on its traditional middle course that caused most of his problems. By the 1890s, he was caught between contending and apparently incompatible social and theological visions for Methodism. Although theologically orthodox and conservative by the standards of the contemporary church, he remained faithful to his mid-Victorian religious views.

To Carman, both liberal and ultra-conservative theology were unnaturally dividing Methodism and crippling its mission in the world. He could accept neither the apparent attempt by liberal theology to make humanity, not God, the focus of religion nor the work of higher critics which, he believed, claimed that humankind could select the aspects of biblical teaching most compatible with its own limited understanding. For Carman, such attitudes tended to define spiritual responsibilities in easy and simplistic terms and seriously undermined the traditional Methodist appreciation of the need for a continuous, disciplined battle against personal sin. Conversion and holy living placed onerous responsibilities on the Christian, and they could be ignored only at great peril to the eternal soul. As well, he feared that irreverent and so-called scientific meddling with the Scriptures would seriously weaken religion. When religion was based on some vague and illusive public good, the door was opened to a weak and insipid Christianity, and pragmatism replaced eternal principles. In turn, society's defences against evil were breached and left vulnerable to attack by scepticism and materialism. In the long run, the liberal church would be ill prepared to provide meaningful answers to the deep spiritual needs of Canadians and would be cast adrift without anchors in the tumultuous seas of secularism. At the same time, while Carman believed that the Bible was the literal word of God, he was never prepared to entertain the dogmatic position of the extreme fundamentalists, especially in the United States and in the new splinter churches which were influenced by a more rigid Calvinism. They were dividing Protestantism to promote their own narrow agenda. He also assumed that some knowledge remained beyond human comprehension, yet he accepted the value of education and the necessity of free inquiry.

On another level, Carman strongly advocated social reform and the transformation of Canada into Christ's earthly dominion through the tenets of a socially relevant Bible, but he mistrusted radical changes that sought to overturn the social order and also undermined personal salvation. He looked for middle-class leadership in the creation of a cooperative, "brotherly" society, but he denounced the pretensions of the wealthy laity and attacked their attempts to control the church's administration and mission through their financial contributions. Finally, Carman actively promoted a broad Protestant outlook for Canada and applauded the growing strength of this vision, but he remained wary of attempts to integrate the Protestant bodies into a single, uniform church. In all these beliefs, he retained the support of a surprisingly large proportion of the church membership. When the General Conference of 1910 elected the liberal social reformer Samuel Dwight Chown as co-general superintendent, ostensibly to assist the aging Carman, the choice reflected the successful alliance of wealthy lay élites with the theologically liberal forces in the church and especially the victory of the opponents of Carman's dictatorial administration and increasingly abrasive personality.

Although important for defining in Canadian Methodist terms the fight over higher criticism, the Workman and Jackson cases were really anomalies. The faith of the average Canadian Methodist was not unduly shaken as he or she gradually adopted the reasonable results of scientific inquiry into the Bible. Most recognized both the need and the benefits of reverent criticism to unfold the mysteries of God. Truth thus revealed to a few would soon become the common inheritance of all. The leading church educators sought to reconcile traditional religious spirituality with the advances in biblical scholarship. They argued that the Bible had never been intended to provide scientific information that was beyond the capacity of the early church to understand. Mature biblical criticism removed the need to apologize for parts of the Bible that were designed for the primitive church or to attempt to harmonize every part of God's testaments. The authority and majesty of the Bible rested on its obvious truths. These truths proved that it was inspired; it was not God's inspiration that proved the revelations were true. Empirical testing helped reveal the truth. Church educators believed that, as scientific inquiry advanced, God's revelation would become clearer and the practice of religion on earth would increase.[93]

Through the pages of the *Canadian Methodist Magazine,* founded in 1875 under the progressive William Henry Withrow, and beginning in 1889, the *Canadian Methodist Quarterly,* the Methodist church attempted to disseminate the new scholarship to its more educated members. The magazines were designed to supply antidotes to "the free thought, the infidelity and other evils of our times" and "to produce and circulate a literature that will resist the insidious and subtle influences of every form of scepticism and the various aspects of erroneous theological teaching."[94] They strove to harmonize religion and science and prevent disruptions to the practical experience of spiritual religion by presenting articles that demonstrated the competent research of some higher and lower critics and by condemning the unsound pronouncements of others. The magazines helped advance logical discussions on a number of intellectual subjects and in so doing promoted the cause of free inquiry while sparing the church the brunt of public controversy.

The Methodist church urged its membership not to fear modern thought since it did not threaten the essential elements of spiritual religion. Christian revelation and a supernatural God remained firmly entrenched, and a personal experience of the grace of God was still the critical fact of religion. Although the new scholarship appeared to question the existence of God, the person and work of Christ, and the unity and authority of the Scriptures, when the studies were complete, they would show that these threats to traditional understanding were groundless. God was progressively unfolding former mysteries through the advancement of science as humanity was able to appreciate them. Indeed, religion was strengthened when biblical criticism corrected past misapprehensions and supplied new proofs of the majesty of God and the grandeur of the Bible. Many progressive Methodists also recognized that biblical criticism helped to establish a new sense of order to human understanding.[95]

In addition, the work of Methodist biblical critics such as George Workman, in distinguishing between the historical legends and the essential moral lessons in the Scriptures, reinforced a vital social mission for the church. The Old Testament prophets may or may not have foretold the coming of Christ, but they were recognized as powerful social critics of the dissolute Hebrew society of their own times who spoke directly against immorality and for the poor and dispossessed throughout history. In the New Testament, Christ, the social critic who preached the Sermon on the Mount and attacked the materialism and perversion of religion in the Temple, emerged in full force. This portrayal of Christ helped to justify Methodism's role in disciplining and guiding human conduct. To the generation of preachers coming of age in the 1880s and 1890s, biblical criticism helped confirm their increasing emphasis on social and ethical considerations over the need for individual conversion. The Bible embodied a social gospel demanding humane treatment for all members of society on earth as much as it provided a means for preparing individuals for heaven.[96]

The gradual acceptance of higher criticism at the Canadian Methodist divinity schools was also assisted by the generally circumspect and non-confrontational manner in which critics did their work. Ralph Brecken, who taught with the conservative Charles Stewart at Mount Allison University until 1901, saw no real conflict between higher or historical criticism and evangelical religion. Stewart's successor, William G. Watson, was a moderate biblical critic who quietly replaced Butler and Paley with more modern authors and added a broad spectrum of readings to the students' program. At Victoria University, the devout Francis H. Wallace gradually introduced biblical criticism, and John McLaughlin superseded the controversial George Workman. McLaughlin in particular combined a strong support for higher criticism with popular devotional services and Bible classes. These made him appear safe in the eyes of Victoria's alumni and the general public. More concerned with practical religious expression than theoretical discussions, both McLaughlin and Wallace also gradually reformed the curriculum and reading lists for their divinity students.[97]

By the twentieth century, therefore, Methodist professors had slowly reduced their emphasis on systematic theology. Assuming that values derived their meaning from their relationship to society at large, they increasingly relied on philosophy and the new social sciences to prepare their candidates for the real world. Infused with "idealism" and assured by the preliminary results of psychological and sociological investigation, Methodist educators and their divinity students believed they could safely relegate the study of theology to the background. Sociology, in particular, was considered valuable because it used modern scientific principles of inquiry to deal with essentially spiritual and moral questions. Its straightforward answers were easily understood, were eminently practical, and appeared to provide intellectual stability and order where traditional theology seemed to offer only esoteric abstractions and insoluble questions founded on an essentially naïve faith. At the same time, these educators claimed that the social sciences provided legitimate substitutes since they helped to make intelligible, and thereby improve, human beings' place in society and ultimately supplied a more relevant appreciation of God's role in the world. In so doing, they helped to prevent materialism and secularism from dominating society.

Although the Victorian age was marked by doubt and questioning, it was also a period of great optimism. Science and technology were improving the daily lives of Canadians and permitting humans to govern, if not master, nature. Most Canadian Methodists hoped that science would also help unravel God's mysterious revelations and supply a clearer understanding of God's purpose for humanity. Over time, as the insights of higher criticism and scientific inquiry were absorbed by the general public, the new knowledge lost much of its apparent destructiveness. The church gradually recognized that the Darwinian revolution did not lead to spiritual, moral, or intellectual anarchy and did not undermine the faith of most Canadians. By dismissing or transforming the unpalatable elements of Darwin, his social Darwinian colleagues, and the biblical critics, the church authorities were able to select what they wanted in order to maintain the balance between faith and reason in a revitalized Christianity. Natural and biblical theology were thus infused with new light without the comforting instinctive flame of faith being extinguished. Despite the need to reconcile scientific inquiry with traditional beliefs, Canadian Methodist theologians and educators could still affirm the essential unity of knowledge, with God standing supreme in the universe.[98]

Late-nineteenth-century Methodism remained aggressive and expansive, and it was flexible enough to sustain a creative dialogue with the new advances in knowledge. But despite the powerful interaction between science and theology, neither could they be harmoniously reintegrated nor was a return to traditional, settled religious understanding possible. The Protestant churches were faced with the difficult task of supplying a meaningful religion while reorienting their work in order to retain a mission relevant to the transformed society they now faced. By the twentieth century, Methodism had seemingly infused a new vitality into its traditional commitment to personal and social salvation. However, by basing its clerical training on the new social sciences, the church increasingly created a pragmatic, problem-solving ministry which not only lacked a clear sense of history, but also came to mistrust historical precedents and intellectual traditions. These developments, in turn, added to the church's confused and rather hazy theological beliefs.[99] As theology ceased to be the queen of sciences and became only one of several means of understanding the world, the distinctive mission of the church was left open to assault from those who did not share its priorities. But the struggle for personal regeneration remained central to the dynamic tension in Canadian Methodism; the victory of liberal theology was never as complete as its proponents hoped or as its orthodox critics feared. While Methodists were perhaps not logical, they were able to accept aspects of liberal theology's emphasis on the need for Christianity to serve the present age on earth, at the same time as they defended orthodox theology's commitment to the absolute necessity of individual conversion in preparation for a future heaven. The creation of the Lord's dominion demanded that the church promote both. Nevertheless, with the support of liberal theology and the general acceptance of a progressive, evolutionary approach to society, the church increasingly emphasized social action and Christian ethics.

Methodist church authorities never lost faith in education to expand the knowledge and wisdom of Canadians. As the twentieth century unfolded, they trusted that the new insights would assist in reshaping society according to Christian principles and thereby enlarging the kingdom of God on earth. They recognized that ultimately there was no inherent difference between the so-called secular and sacred spheres of human conduct. Since all the world belonged to God, the church's duty was to make it worthy of God. Institutional Methodism did not seek to accommodate itself to the corrupt world, but it reaffirmed its commitment to remain active in the world. The clergy undertook their social mission recognizing that they must both prepare their members for heaven and make society a proper place for Christ's post-millennial reign. If they denied this latter role, they would be turning a blind eye to the severe problems facing Canadian society and would be announcing that they were no longer able to contend with the evil and immorality they witnessed. They had no option but to attempt to ameliorate society according to religious principles if they did not wish to abandon Canada to the forces of secularism. They could not legitimately relinquish their rightful role to secular critics, many of whom had less than laudable motives or methods, without betraying Methodism's long history of service. Certainly, in the ongoing conflict between the sacred and the profane, Methodist leaders during this period assumed the final victory of the sacred. They were confident that Canada could be transformed into Christ's dominion within the foreseeable future.

# 11  Methodist Missions in Canada, 1854–1925

All the Methodist connexions had been committed to the crusade to evangelize British North America and eventually the world beyond. By the mid-1850s, they were prepared to expand their fields geographically while consolidating their original bases of operations. Methodism demanded a constant readiness to serve wherever needed, especially on the fringes of new settlement, and to provide religion to the spiritually unenlightened and those who had moved beyond regular church worship.

As the northwest and British Columbia were opened up to settlement, Methodism claimed the right to infuse these regions with the benefits of evangelical, Protestant religion, believing that only in this way would the country be strengthened and the debilitating influences of Catholicism, scepticism, and irreligion be overcome. Eventually this missionary enthusiasm called Canadian Methodists to Japan and China, but North America remained the principal field for missionary endeavours. It was the natural first step in Protestantizing the world and was essential both to make Methodism Canada's national church and ultimately to transform the country into God's kingdom on earth. The church strove to mould Canadians into a holy people in a moral, spiritual, and progressive nation serving God in all things.[1]

## MISSION ORGANIZATION AND LAY SUPPORT

All the Methodist connexions had started missionary societies as soon as was practical after organizing their own local circuits. Except for the continuing Methodist Episcopal church after 1834, all these operations were administered by missionary superintendents, normally appointed by the parent connexion in Britain. The missions therefore represented semi-autonomous organizations within the churches. Local auxiliaries raised money for the requirements of missions wherever the parent church decided these should be located. However, as the Canadian churches gained greater autonomy, they came to control the expenditure of missionary funds directly.

By far the largest and best organized missionary society belonged to the Wesleyan Methodist church. In 1847, with the reunion of British and Canadian Wesleyanism in Canada West, Enoch Wood was appointed missionary superintendent by the British authorities. He had been born in Britain in 1801 and raised as an Anglican. After his conversion to Methodism, he was sent by the Wesleyan Missionary Society to the West Indies, where he served between 1826 and 1829. He was transferred to Saint John, New Brunswick, and ordained the following year. After more than a decade of effective service in the Maritimes, he moved to the Canadas, where he helped reunite the British and Canadian branches of Methodism. In 1851 he assumed direction of the missions in the Hudson's Bay territory. These missions were finally transferred to the Canadian church in 1854. The mission work was reorganized in 1869 with Wood as secretary of the Board of Missions. The Canadian Methodist Episcopal church administered its missions through its annual conferences until 1874, when a general Missionary Society took over the missions in Manitoba. In reality, however, Bishop Albert Carman became the guiding force in promoting missionary expansion for the denomination.[2]

By 1878 the Methodist Church of Canada had 44 native missions with 30 white and 10 native missionaries and 3,013 members, 5 missions to German Canadians with 3 missionaries and 284 members, and 9 missions to the French Canadians in Quebec with 274 members. Beyond this specialized work, the church had 24 frontier missions spread across northern Ontario, the northwest, and British Columbia. The bulk of its missions, however, involved circuits which relied on assistance from headquarters. Any circuit that needed financial support came under the jurisdiction of the Missionary Society. These 323 domestic missions contained about 35,000 members. In total, the 405 missions in Canada, with 39,165 members and 422 missionaries, interpreters, and teachers, accounted for nearly a third of the membership and ordained workers in the connexion. Moreover, these figures reflect an increase of 178 missions and 163 missionaries from the 1874 totals. Because of harsh economic times, the society ran a deficit in 1878 of nearly $9,500, and among other restraints gradually integrated the German missions in southwestern Ontario and the Ottawa valley into neighbouring English-speaking circuits or, as noted earlier, transferred them to the German-speaking Evangelical Association in 1879.[3]

The other Methodist connexions had only domestic missions; they never developed specialized ethnic or native work. Although the New Connexion acknowledged its obligation to send missionaries to the northwest and British Columbia, it could never afford to do so. Even with an annual grant from its parent missionary society and the $7,700 it raised locally for missionary purposes in 1874, the denomination remained heavily in debt. Similarly, during the 1870s, about 60 per cent of the Bible Christian circuits were domestic missions, and they contained about a third of the total membership. Although the church opened a mission in Manitoba, it could not sustain a viable expansion program in the region and had to abandon members who moved beyond its Ontario base. By 1882 it had accumulated a debt of nearly $20,000 and was in danger of failing financially even in its traditional centres. The Primitive Methodist church in 1860 had 10 regular circuits but 19 domestic missions in Canada West, and by 1874 it had expanded to 45 missions but only 16 self-supporting circuits. Despite the annual grant of $3,000 from Britain, it too continued to run a large deficit. During the early 1880s, nearly two-thirds of its members resided in the 42 missions, while the remaining third were contained within the 27 regular circuits. The mission in the northwest to the church's temperance colony at Saskatoon was a particularly serious drain on funds.[4]

Even the relatively large Methodist Episcopal church found it difficult to develop viable missions in the newly settled regions of the country. During the late 1870s and early 1880s, it made a concerted effort to establish itself in Manitoba. Its strategy was to buy property in centres of growth in the hope of gaining a head start on its major competition. By 1882 it had missions in Winnipeg, Emerson, Morris, Carman, Nelsonville, Portage la Prairie, and Moosomin. However, prices were often highly inflated, especially during the pre-railway-building boom, and Episcopal Methodist support in the towns was transient and meagre. In fact, the church had heavily miscalculated potential growth. In addition, most of the itinerants sent west failed to attract new members, complained bitterly about conditions, and soon returned to Ontario, went to the United States, or left the ministry to take up secular occupations.[5]

Much of Bishop Carman's efforts involved trying to solve the difficulties posed by these missions. With a debt of nearly $13,000 in 1883 and no apparent means of improving the financial outlook, the church had no option but to close down its less-prosperous missions, sell property, often at a loss, and withdraw from direct competition with the Methodist Church of Canada. In admitting that it was not making real progress and in seeking Methodist cooperation in the region, the Methodist Episcopal church finally recognized that its dream of becoming the pre-eminent Methodist connexion in Canada had failed. Union was the only viable means of preserving its tradition in the nation. In fact, only through union could any of the various Methodist connexions share in the evangelization of the transcontinental nation.[6]

With the unions of 1874 and 1884, the smaller denominations' work merged into the original Wesleyan programs and the Canadian church gained complete independence in its missionary operations. Alexander Sutherland was appointed Enoch Wood's assistant in 1874 and replaced him four years later. Born in 1833 near Guelph, Upper Canada, Sutherland had spent a short time at Victoria College before being called into circuit work. He early displayed a sound administrative ability and continued as the missionary secretary until 1906. At that time, the board was divided into home and foreign departments, and Sutherland served as head of foreign missions until his death in 1910. He was succeeded by his assistant, Egerton Shore, until 1913 and then by James Endicott. The home department was administered first by James Allen until his death in 1918 and subsequently by Charles Manning. The secretaries had deputies in Toronto and regional superintendents across the country. In fact, the Methodist church developed a large and highly centralized mission bureaucracy with an impressive fund-raising and publishing program.[7]

Table 5    Methodist missions in Canada, 1885–1925

| Year | Domestic | French | Native | Chinese | Japanese | Total |
|------|----------|--------|--------|---------|----------|-------|
| 1885 | 418 | 12 | 47 | 0 | 0 | 477 |
| 1890 | 408 | 9 | 47 | 4 | 0 | 468 |
| 1895 | 425 | 7 | 60 | 4 | 0 | 496 |
| 1900 | 446 | 7 | 61 | 5 | 3 | 522 |
| 1905 | 430 | 5 | 66 | 5 | 1 | 507 |
| 1910 | 561 | 0 | 60 | 7 | 4 | 632 |
| 1915 | 613 | 0 | 62 | 7 | 5 | 687 |
| 1919* | 455 | 0 | 59 | 14 | 5 | 533 |
| 1925 | 423 | 0 | 57 | 12 | 6 | 498 |

* The 1920 results are not available because of a printers' strike.

The home department oversaw the domestic missions and the French, city, immigration, and part of the ethnic mission work. As well as the overseas enterprises, the foreign department ran the Oriental missions in Canada and until 1920 the native missions since they both required specially trained missionaries. There was also a fear that native missions would be overlooked if they were tied to domestic operations. Table 5 indicates the basic composition of the Methodist missions in Canada from 1885 to 1925.[8] The expansion in native missions by 1895 reflected growth in British Columbia. Beginning in 1905, domestic missions were declining in eastern Canada, but the northwest was growing rapidly. This pattern continued until after World War I, when many of the missions in the west became self-sufficient, merged into union congregations, or became cooperative missions with the Presbyterians. Furthermore, many of the domestic missions were actually city or ethnic missions serving particular clienteles in the expanding urban centres.

The Methodist mission organization was also significantly supplemented by the parallel Woman's Missionary Society. It mirrored the Episcopal Methodist Woman's Foreign Missionary Society in the United States founded in 1869 and those of the Canadian Baptist and Presbyterian churches begun in the 1870s. The Methodist Episcopal Church in Canada established a national women's missionary society in 1876 under the close direction of its general Missionary Society. Two years later, the General Conference of the Methodist Church of Canada authorized the creation of a similar organization. There was a particularly strong interest in Montreal for a woman's missionary society to evangelize the French Canadians. Alexander Sutherland actively promoted the cause in order to strengthen the overall mission operation.[9]

Many in the church initially felt any division of effort would hurt mission contributions and ultimately the missions themselves. Since its inception, the missionary board had relied heavily on women as fund-raisers and supporters and did not want to lose this auxiliary network. There was also an underlying apprehension about women administering their own organization and getting involved at this level in activities outside of the home. Nevertheless, circumstances soon proved that when an active Woman's Missionary Society was functioning, the whole mission movement benefited. Women also proved to be first-rate administrators and productive missionaries when given a chance.

The first local branch of the WMS of the Methodist Church of Canada was organized in Hamilton in 1880, and within a year an embryonic national organization was in place. It helped establish local auxiliaries and subordinate circles and bands for younger women. These were bound together at the Annual Conference level and came under the ultimate direction of a national executive. This extremely influential group of prominent Methodist women set general policy, examined missionary candidates, and directed the expenditure of funds. It both ran its own missions and supplied personnel and funds for joint evangelistic, educational, and medical work with the Board of Missions. The WMS tenaciously guarded its administrative and financial independence at headquarters and constantly sought greater respect and independence in the field.[10]

In its first year, it raised $200 for the Indian Girls' Home in Port Simpson, British Columbia, and soon became a critical element throughout all levels of home and foreign mission work. By 1890 it reported a membership of 8,534, and this figure rose to 43,590 by 1915 and 62,212 by 1925. This latter membership number represented 1,621 auxiliaries, 614 circles, and 956 bands. The Methodist WMS became the largest and most active women's organization in Canada. Many other women, although not members, were supporters and deeply sympathized with its goals. Over its history, the WMS raised nearly $6,000,000 for missions, $500,000 in 1924–25 alone. Of this, about 75 per cent was spent in Canada and 25 per cent abroad. It also supplied over three hundred missionaries, teachers, and doctors to the Methodist mission force.[11]

The WMS played a vital role in the lives of both the professional women missionaries and those who only supported the work. The local auxiliary often attracted women who were not involved in other church organizations and provided a valuable forum for developing speaking, organizational, and administrative skills, as well as a respectable outlet for social action. It broadened horizons and fields of service from the rather mundane congregational level to encompass the whole world. For the missionaries, the WMS allowed a concrete dedication to God's service. Mission work gradually became accepted as a natural outreach of family and therefore the legitimate occupation and concern of women. As Mrs Albert Carman stated in 1886, "I believe missionary work to be preeminently suited to woman; she was last at the cross, first at the sepulchre, honoured to be the bearer of 'good tidings' from a risen Saviour to his sorrowing disciples; think you this was all chance?"[12] Mission work was also in keeping with the evangelical revival's mandate for women and was true to late-Victorian British Protestant values. Women should lead in the creation of a holy world.

The women were recruited from across Canada, but not surprisingly about 60 per cent came from Ontario. In general, the missionaries were well educated, often with university, teacher, or medical training, and were strictly screened by the society before admission. The WMS provided prestigious occupations for young, middle-class women who would otherwise be restricted to teaching, volunteer, or family work. Women doctors were especially valued in mission work, but often ostracized in Canadian medical and public circles. Mission service also provided a legitimate and fulfilling alternative to marriage. Women missionaries had to remain single; if they married, they were normally removed from the ranks. However, many who did marry continued to serve as wives of male missionaries. But, perhaps the most underrated advantage of all, becoming a missionary offered adventure and a romantic escape from boring and unsophisticated farm and small-town life. Although actual service soon dispelled such notions, none the less the lure of exotic people and places was a real attraction.[13]

As well as supporting the WMS, women contributed significantly to the church's missionary work by joining the Methodist Deaconess Society. This organization was modelled on the American Methodist deaconess movement and similar organizations in other denominations, and the deaconesses were trained to serve in any capacity the church required. Originally, it was concerned that such an organization might appear to be a religious order on the Catholic model or that it might acquire clerical functions and become a back door to the quasi-ordination of women. However, the deaconess took no vows and was not required to stay permanently in the society. She did not compete with the clergy, but rather worked voluntarily at the mission and local church level. Deaconesses received no salary; the employer supplied only room, board, and a small allowance.[14]

Under pressure from the wealthy Massey family of Toronto, the General Conference in 1890 voted to permit the annual conferences to set up a deaconess order. Quickly, church leaders recognized the vast energy and power women possessed and wanted their "feminine aptitudes" applied to the broad social and evangelistic needs of the Canadian community. Religious and reform work were desperately in need of an infusion of trained and experienced church and social workers. The deaconesses themselves generally reflected a conservative feminist interest in applying maternal virtues to social ills. By the turn of the century, there was a growing belief that every church should employ a deaconess.[15]

The duties of the deaconesses were "to minister to the poor, visit the sick, pray for the dying, care for the orphan, seek the wandering, comfort the sorrowing, save the sinning," and in fact to devote themselves wholly to Christian service. They were to save the body as well as the soul, and by supplying nurses, caseworkers, teachers, home-mission evangelists, and helpers, they became the "foot soldiers of Methodist applied Christianity."[16] They visited homes, ran fresh-air camps for girls, held sewing and cooking classes, and taught in Sunday schools. They also assisted travellers, the unemployed, and new immigrants and distributed relief supplies and religious and moral tracts. They were devoted servants of the church willing to work wherever needed.

The establishment of residential and training facilities was crucial to their success. The first Canadian deaconess training school and home was opened in Toronto in 1894 with six students; it was generally underwritten by the Masseys and the Flavelles. The purpose of the school was "not primarily literary ... but rather preparation for Christian service."[17] Lasting two years, the courses included Bible study, Christian doctrine and evidences, the history and methods of Christian work, sociology, and applied Christianity. Practical training covered household science, hygiene, sewing, basket-making, and gardening. Specialized courses for native, ethnic, and immigration work were added later. There were three divisions based primarily on the level of pre-enrolment education. The training was carried out by dedicated ministers and church workers, and the students received some lectures from faculty members of Victoria University. Similar facilities were opened in Hamilton in 1903, Montreal and Winnipeg in 1906, and Vancouver in 1910, and together they formed an important network of residences, as well as training centres.[18]

By 1905 there were 33 deaconesses at work, of whom 18 were employed in Toronto. As regional centres developed and the deaconess work gained recognition, however, the order achieved a truly national scope. In 1910 there were 80 deaconesses working across the country and in Newfoundland. The order reached its peak of service in 1912, but generally declined thereafter. Between 1894 and 1925 the church trained over 900 women, many of whom became WMS missionaries and 235 became deaconesses.[19] None the less, the deaconesses never achieved the status of the WMS missionaries; they routinely came to be viewed quite literally as servants to be exploited but otherwise ignored.

After World War I, the Methodist church did attempt to strengthen the position of women in its operations and to reinvigorate the deaconesses' work. They had proven that their careers did not interfere with their femininity or make them "unwomanly in their misdirected ecclesiastical zeal."[20] Improvements in working conditions made life more tolerable for them, and the fact that they could accept a salary from their employing agency and, starting in 1920, could receive a pension after twenty years of service placed the order on a more professional basis. In 1923, in reaction to a continuing serious decline in the order, a special commission found its effectiveness hindered by low educational standards, poor training, and lack of appreciation by local church officials. As well, alternate employment opportunities, coupled with competition from untrained church workers, seriously hampered the work. The commission recommended more efficient and higher-quality training in order to return the society to its former effectiveness. Despite its problems, however, the Deaconess Society played a valuable role in spreading Methodist moral and spiritual values throughout the home mission field.[21]

In addition to the WMS and the Deaconess Society, a variety of lay support groups developed to promote missions at home and abroad. The most prominent of these was the Young People's Forward Movement for Missions. With the increasing success of the Canadian branches of the Epworth League and the Student Volunteer Movement in encouraging young people to volunteer for mission work, there was an embarrassing lack of funds to send them to the mission fields. Although the Board of Missions found it difficult to resist the appeals for immediate extension of its work, it did not have the resources even to keep existing missions functioning properly.[22]

One of the aspiring young missionaries was Frederick Clark Stephenson. Dr Stephenson had been born in Aurora, Canada West, in 1864 and worked as a clerk before entering Albert College and later Trinity Medical School. Disappointed at not being sent to China as a medical missionary, in 1895 he established the Young People's Forward Movement for Missions in order to mobilize the vast reservoir of young people's energy and money for the cause. Not a society but "an inspiration," this movement worked through the inter-denominational Student Volunteer Movement and other existing young people's organizations to raise the consciousness of missions among Canadian Methodists. Having as its motto "Pray, Study, Give," it rapidly extended its influence throughout the Canadian church and inspired similar movements in the United States and Britain.[23]

With the able assistance of his wife, Annie, Stephenson published vast quantities of mission literature, organized local study groups, lectures, and summer mission schools, led fund-raising campaigns, and generally kept mission needs before Canadian Methodists. The movement was able to support its first missionary to China in 1896 and two years later had raised nearly $60,000. In 1902 the YPFM was adopted as a department of the Board of Missions with Stephenson as its secretary, and he continued to direct this work in the United Church of Canada until 1936. The annual contributions constantly increased during the first quarter of the twentieth century, except for a slight decline during World War I. In the 1918–22 quadrennium, the YPFM raised $777,766, an increase of nearly $300,000 over the previous four-year period. In 1922 it was supporting ninety-three missionaries in Japan and China and another fourteen in Canada. By 1925 it had raised more than $3,000,000 for missions. Equally important, it had encouraged hundreds of young people to make mission work their life vocation.[24]

Another important support group was the interdenominational and international Laymen's Missionary Movement, which was founded in the United States in 1906 to encourage men to participate more actively in mission work. Many Protestant leaders were concerned that the church in general and missions in particular were becoming women's business. Prominent Toronto lawyer Newton Wesley Rowell was present at the inaugural meeting, and the following year he organized a Canadian council to supervise its work throughout the dominion. In 1911 the organization was formally adopted by the Board of Missions under the direction of J.H. Arnup. Heavily ecumenical, it sought to promote cooperation among the Protestant denominations in mission work and strongly supported church union. As a movement rather than an organization, it did not administer programs or have a permanent bureaucracy; but where it functioned properly, it was able to increase mission contributions dramatically.[25]

However, its underlying interest was to expand the influence of the laity in the church councils. Many leading lay Methodists believed the denomination was not always spending their contributions wisely, and they were also anxious that the burden of mission support be spread more evenly among church members; the church should rely less on the benevolence of a few wealthy contributors. As well, the Laymen's Missionary Movement hoped to introduce greater system and better business practices, thereby reducing waste and duplication while increasing givings. Although the organization reflected a rather conservative view of the church, it did much to interest laymen in mission work. When its activities were combined with those of the other missionary organizations, every available Methodist constituency was tapped for the crusade to evangelize the nation and the world.[26]

### DOMESTIC MISSIONS

With regard to the actual mission endeavour in Canada, domestic missions comprised by far the greatest, if least glamorous, part of the labour. Throughout the church's history, these missions continued to dominate on the pioneer fringes and in the poorer regions of the country. For instance, even though Newfoundland and Labrador had been settled for generations, isolation and physical hardship remained the hallmark of church operations in the region's outports. The Reverend Thomas Allen at Stoyles Harbour, Labrador, recorded in his diary in 1867, "I held a prayer meeting after tea. Did not enjoy myself over much. A pig kept running in and out during the morning service. Afternoon was a dull, sleepy affair & at the prayer meeting a child was crying ... Squalling children, smoky houses and this kind of life are not favourable mentally or morally to me."[27] Allen blamed his own weak spirituality and lack of commitment to spreading the gospel when in fact the problem was common to many in similar circumstances. Disheartened and emotionally drained, missionaries found it difficult to keep up enthusiasm. Other missions reflected even more deeply the poverty of the people. At Blackhead in 1885, even though the church added 289 new members to its existing total of 561 as part of the great revival sweeping North America, the area remained a mission for several more years. Similarly, Freshwater mission, with 602 members, did not feel competent to give up its mission grant.[28]

Domestic missions were more to be expected in pioneer northern Ontario and the northwest. New settlers from eastern Canada, the United States, Britain, and increasingly after 1896, continental Europe swelled the population but provided only weak and transient support for the church. The lumber and mining camps of northern Ontario and the construction camps for the transcontinental railways offered difficult, but necessary fields of labour. Here many new immigrants, especially young men from southern and eastern Europe, received their first contact with Canadian life. If they had family members in the country, these were left on a farm or in a larger centre while the men were occupied in seasonal labour. Religious services were required to offset the lack of moral family life. In 1901, for instance, the *Rat Portage Methodist* noted that in the Lake of the Woods area, "One cannot travel much on the lake without realizing what godlessness, and vice are rampant. The gambling, swearing, drinking and lawlessness are simply astonishing."[29] Nevertheless,

Methodism was committed to Canadianize and Christianize these settlers while providing familiar church worship for those from Methodist backgrounds. The mission outposts had to add this new clientele to their traditional ministry.

Even more momentous, the settlement of Manitoba and what in 1905 became Saskatchewan and Alberta placed huge demands on the Methodist domestic mission operations. Here the church hoped to fulfil the dream of making the twentieth century Canada's. But it believed that this would only occur if paganism, scepticism, and Catholicism could be met and overcome. As well, in providing familiar worship services, the church offered vital relief from the isolation and loneliness of prairie life. However, the new settlers would not be able to pay for regular church services for some time. Until they could, the more-established eastern congregations would have to support church expansion.

At the same time, domestic missions in the northwest had trouble retaining suitable missionaries. Although many ministers went west, most considered it only a temporary move until they could find a more advantageous position. Because of the poor pay and demanding lifestyle, the ministers were generally young, single men with limited preaching or pastoral experience. Furthermore, these missionaries gained little recognition from the church or society in general for their sacrifice. As the *Christian Guardian* noted in 1901, "We are ready to vote that man or woman a hero who goes to China or India to preach Christ, but there may be more glory as God sees it in going into the next township."[30]

The Methodist church adopted a variety of strategies to supply the huge demands while faced with little money and an inadequate number of workers. At one level, James Woodsworth, the superintendent of western missions from 1886 until 1915, recruited young missionaries from Britain. But for the most part these men were not suitable for pioneer western work. They were unprepared for the climate, the arduous conditions of labour, or the congregations themselves. Complaints from both the missionaries and the membership were common.[31] At another level, the Methodist church promoted cooperation with the other Protestant churches in the region. It not only divided the work with the Presbyterians, with whom it was negotiating union, but it also worked with the Baptists and the Anglicans, who were having similar difficulties in supplying the field. A minister from any one of these Protestant denominations might serve a congregation that included members of all these churches. Ultimately, however, the Methodist church expected to bind the regional membership to its own denomination as more ordained manpower became available from eastern Canada and from the northwest itself.

A generation earlier, the church had faced similar problems on a smaller scale in British Columbia. With the development of fishing, lumbering, and mining and especially after the discovery of gold in the 1850s, the colonies of Vancouver Island and mainland British Columbia had been inundated with new settlers. For the Canadian Methodist church, the region offered an immense opportunity for evangelizing both the native and immigrant population, and it was also the natural jumping-off point for future mission work in

Asia. In 1858 the Canadian Wesleyans, with the assistance of a £500 grant from the British Wesleyan Missionary Society, sent out a party of four missionaries under the superintendent, Ephraim Evans.[32] The younger brother of the celebrated James Evans, the inventor of the Cree syllabics and first Wesleyan missionary to Norway House, Ephraim had already had an impressive career in Upper Canada and the Maritimes. He was joined by Ebenezer Robson, a probationer fresh out of Victoria College, and Edward White and Arthur Browning, young ministers with less than a decade of service in Canada.

Arriving in early 1859, Evans took up his post in the town of Victoria and the following May, opened a church on land donated by the Hudson's Bay Company. Robson initially went up the Fraser River to Fort Hope and Yale to evangelize the gold miners, but in 1860 exchanged missions with Browning, who had been sent to the coal-mining settlement at Nanaimo on Vancouver Island. Nanaimo had originally received preaching from Cornelius Bryant, a British Wesleyan schoolteacher and lay preacher. The fourth missionary, Edward White, was stationed at New Westminster, the capital of the mainland colony until it united with Vancouver Island in 1866, where in April 1860 he dedicated the first Methodist church in the province. Thus began what Methodists expected would be "the foundations of civil and religious society in British Columbia."[33]

However, over the following few years, the church made little real progress in the region; no new ministers arrived and the membership increased only haltingly to 155 in 1864 before falling off to 131 four years later. The missionaries exchanged stations on a regular basis, but with the amalgamation of New Westminster and Fort Hope in 1865 and Robson's temporary return to Canada, the district reported only three missions. Browning and Evans did make brief excursions into the interior to preach to the gold miners in the Cariboo and even opened a small chapel which was made available to all Protestant denominations in the absence of a Methodist preacher. But it was not until 1868 that a missionary, Thomas Derrick, was stationed at Barkerville. Although he built a new church to replace the original chapel, which had burned in 1868, with the decline of gold mining and the scattering of the population, the mission was finally closed in 1887.[34]

However, the provincial situation had begun to improve in 1868. That year, as well as the mission to the Cariboo, Amos Russ took over the missions at Victoria from Evans, who returned to Ontario. By this time the congregation was large enough to clear the church debt and remove it from the mission ranks. Metropolitan Methodist church in Victoria became the driving force behind much of the denomination's expansion in the city and surrounding districts. Over the following six years, some progress was recorded and work with native peoples was expanded. Although normally distinct from domestic missions, in British Columbia the native work was initially integrated into the domestic mission functions. Even with the posting of Thomas Crosby to native work in 1868, many natives remained with the domestic missions.[35]

Following the union of 1874, more money and missionaries were sent to the province. The regional church also attracted able local men into the ministry to bolster the missionary forces. For example, Cornelius Bryant, who had begun to serve in 1871, and Charles M. Tate, who was ordained in 1879, brought local expertise and commitment to the mission operations. Both men began as teachers and lay evangelists to native communities. After 1884, with the larger Methodist union and especially with the expansion resulting from railway construction which bound British Columbia to the rest of Canada, the Methodists enlarged their operations around the new port of Vancouver and expanded into the Kootenays and later into other interior mining and lumbering centres. The Methodist presence in the province gradually assumed the same pattern as in the rest of the country. In fact, British Columbia had matured to such an extent that in 1887 it became a distinct Conference with a membership of nearly 2,500.[36]

Domestic missions, however, were not limited to the pioneer areas of Canada. Even though the missionaries themselves believed that it was "a reproach and a shame that circuits in older settled parts of the country ... should be pensioners upon the charity of the Church for a missionary grant," these circuits remained an important part of Methodist work in Ontario.[37] Usually, however, there were particular reasons for the continuance of their mission status. Most were like Strathroy in 1885, which was only a mission because of the large debt it had incurred in building a new church. Others were like Dawn Mills: it had been independent, but was forced back on the mission rolls because of disruptions caused by the reorganizations over union. When a circuit was prospering, the rural hinterland was sometimes separated from the town headquarters and forced to rebuild its membership in order to regain its former status. Still others were like Napier, which in 1885 included four churches in a four-mile radius. After consolidating into two viable churches, it joined the regular circuits. As well, many circuits were forced into temporary dependence because of a local economic recession, crop failure, or natural disaster.

Methodism faced a more serious long-term problem in the abandonment of many rural parts of eastern Canada for resettlement in the west, the United States, and the larger urban centres. By the twentieth century, the church felt particularly obligated to respond to the migration from a rural to an urban setting. Not only did rural churches lose significant membership and financial resources, but the shift also threatened the denomination's vision of the future kingdom of God in Canada. Many Methodists saw country and small-town society as the true heart of the nation and essential to its moral and spiritual progress. Virtue rested its hand on the plough. On the other hand, the city was considered inherently immoral, foreign, and corrupting. It not only offered sinful temptations, but its very atmosphere seemed tainted with unchristian licentiousness. However, rural society failed to supply the freedom and opportunities available in the city, especially for young men and women.

The Board of Home Missions hoped to improve rural life and thereby keep the young in the countryside. It encouraged its local missions to provide greater recreational, social, and intellectual opportunities. It promoted libraries, better schooling, medical facilities, and a myriad of secular and religious activities that would provide a real alternative to city life. On a more practical level, it assisted in farm training programs in the hope that farming would be more profitable and lobbied the various levels of government for rural electrification and better roads and services. In general, it sought to create an attractive rural environment, to gain greater respect for farming as an occupation, and to instil a sense of pride in the rural inhabitants.[38]

None the less, most rural domestic missions tended to receive only sporadic ministerial services. They were often served only during the summer by probationers or students from the Methodist colleges. Although the congregations in the pioneer areas complained about lack of support, the transfer of able young ministers to western Canada or to specialized mission work often left rural Ontario and the Maritimes desperately short. Where ministers were available, they normally received only a minimum wage, poor housing, and little social, recreational, or intellectual opportunity. Like other rural young people, young ministers often wished to move to larger centres.[39]

In spite of the needs of rural society, the Methodist church could not abandon its traditional obligations to the middle class in the larger urban centres. In Ontario and Quebec, much of the uptown urban expansion after the 1870s, and particularly at the beginning of the new century, required an extensive commitment from mission authorities. In Montreal, for example, Douglas church sponsored a number of outreach missions which quickly developed into regular congregations serving the Protestant population moving away from the core of the city. Even these new churches were themselves often forced to relocate after only a short period of time, or at least to expand or rebuild. Every large Canadian city needed outreach assistance. While it was critical for Methodism's overall success, it drew extensive funds both from the local membership and from the central missionary society.[40]

The domestic missions also encompassed more-established congregations that had fallen on hard times. For instance, Grace Methodist church in Winnipeg was one of the largest churches in the west and had a prestigious congregation and broad outreach operation. However, after World War I, it was unable to pay even the interest on its accumulated debt of over $300,000 and became a mission of the central board. In 1921, fearing embarrassment to the entire denomination if Grace church went bankrupt, the mission authorities permitted the congregation to organize a nationwide fund-raising campaign. Ultimately, even this campaign could not save the church. Nevertheless, the mission authorities did all that could reasonably be expected considering the extraordinary demands on their limited funds.[41] At other times, similar conditions had prevailed temporarily at St James Street Methodist church in Montreal and other prominent churches across the country.

### NATIVE MISSIONS

Although domestic missions consumed the bulk of the church's resources, within the national mission field the specialized missions to native peoples, to the urban poor, and to new immigrants received the greatest publicity and stirred the imagination of Canadians. Throughout most of the nineteenth century, the Methodist church believed its most vital responsibility was to evangelize and anglicize the native peoples, and even by mundane statistical measurement, the scope of its involvement was impressive. With the assumption of

John C. McDougall (1842–1917) and Henry Bird Steinhauer (c.1818–84) flanking native converts from their missions in the northwest. (UCA, P3980N)

Ebenezer Robson (1835–1911). Served missions in British Columbia, 1859–65, 1880–1900. (UCA, Album 78.105C/OS)

control over the 4 remaining British Wesleyan missions in the northwest, the Canadian Wesleyan Methodist church in 1855 had 20 native missions, including the Mount Elgin and Alderville residential industrial schools. The 24 missionaries, 20 teachers, and 10 interpreters served 1,289 native members and about four times as many adherents.

Methodist native missions expanded significantly over the following seventy years. By the mid-1870s, there were 22 native missions in Ontario, 1 at Lake of Two Mountains in Quebec established in 1868, 4 in Manitoba, and 5 in the remaining northwest territories, and in 1875, 5 native missions were set apart in British Columbia as well. A decade later, the church reported 20 native missions in central Canada, 14 in Manitoba and the northwest, and 13 in British Columbia. This growth particulary reflected expansion into southern Alberta and British Columbia.

Finally, by 1925, although native missions had declined as a priority, the church still maintained 57 across the country. Of these, 22 were in central Canada, including the mission at Lake of Two Mountains in Quebec, 17 in the three Prairie provinces, and 18 in British Columbia. These missions were served by 40 missionaries, 32 teachers, 20 nurses, and 7 interpreters and had a combined membership of 4,641. The Methodist schools on the reserves had 1,896 students, of whom 784 were in the 6 residential schools, and 1,112 attended the 57 day schools. The Board of Home Missions also ran 5 hospitals for native Canadians in British Columbia. In addition, the Woman's Missionary Society ran girls' homes at Port Simpson and Kitimat, assisted with the Coqualeetza Institute in Chilliwack and the hospitals at Bella Bella, Port Simpson, and Hazelton, all in British Columbia, and supplied a nurse at Nelson House in Manitoba.[42]

Despite this commitment to native missions, the church showed little willingness to change its traditional attitudes or programs over the period. They had been fixed by the late 1840s and continued to reflect a conservative mandate to Christianize and civilize. Especially after the deaths of William Case in 1855 and Peter Jones a year later, most of whatever sympathy had existed for native culture had disappeared. Native spirituality, language, and family heritage were considered serious hindrances to the natives' beneficial transformation into proper Canadians. Whether hunters on the Great Plains, semi-sedentary fishermen on the Pacific Coast, or residents in agricultural settlements in central Canada, they were all forced to conform to Protestant, Victorian notions of progress and civilization. These priorities were implemented through traditional evangelization, through schools for young people, and later by providing medical assistance for the isolated communities.

Although generally insensitive to native values, the Methodist church did work tirelessly to protect native civil rights and temporal interests, especially those involving land claims and government assistance. In Ontario and Quebec, for years it had complained to the government over the poor and unhealthy lands at Rama and on the New Credit reserve. The Mississaugas and Iroquois had been forced to abandon their prosperous farms to move to these sites, and the church believed they deserved better compensation. After the creation of the Dominion of Canada in 1867, the federal government assumed control of the native peoples, but it showed even less interest in their welfare than had the previous authorities. During the economic recession of the 1870s, the government reduced its grants to the tribes while encouraging them to move to the less desirable lands in the north. The Methodists helped them to resist this policy. At the same time, they opposed cuts to the subsidies for students attending residential schools. The church had turned Alderville Industrial School into a day school in 1861, but Mount Elgin continued to operate as a manual-training residential school. In 1870 it had twenty-seven boys and nineteen girls in residence, but the government provided grants for only thirty students. The contentious relations between the church and the government over native peoples did not improve until the late 1880s.[43]

Perhaps Methodism's most serious concern in the region, however, was over the treatment of its native clientele on the Oka reserve at Lake of Two Mountains in Quebec. The seigneury was owned by the Sulpicians and had served as a mission and seminary to the local Iroquois and Algonquins since at least 1717. The Iroquois had long disputed the ownership by the Sulpicians, and in 1867 most of the band under Chief Joseph Onesakenrat separated from the Church of Rome and invited the Methodists to open a mission. The Algonquins remained loyal Catholics. The Montreal Conference sent Xavier Rivet in 1868, and he, his successors, and Onesakenrat, who entered the Methodist ministry in 1876 and served the mission until his death in 1881, worked to convert the remainder of the band.[44]

By 1869 the mission could report 110 members. In the early 1870s, ignoring the opposition of the Sulpicians and the Catholic church, the Methodists erected a small church. This was forcibly dismantled in 1875. Claiming that the mission "has been subjected to a tireless, heartless, and most provoking persecution," the Methodists assisted the Iroquois band in a long and costly legal battle to gain title to the land and to permit them equal rights with the Roman Catholics on the reserve. However, both the Quebec courts and finally the Supreme Court of Canada ruled that the land belonged to the Catholic church. Nevertheless, this land-claims dispute continues to bedevil native-white relations. The bitterness of the issue was reflected in a long series of articles in the *Christian Guardian* during the late 1870s and 1880s. It seriously aggravated Protestant-Catholic tensions and intensified the already prevalent anti-Catholic and anti-French-Canadian sentiment in the Methodist church.[45]

While the legal proceedings were moving slowly through the courts, the Methodists encouraged their native members to move to the reserves at St Regis, Caughnawaga, and Cornwall Island. By 1881 the church had also convinced the federal government to establish the Gibson reserve in Muskoka, Ontario. The popularity of this reserve among Methodist leaders reflected the continuing belief that the native peoples would benefit from being isolated from improper European contact. The Gibson reserve initially attracted about thirty-three families from Oka. The others were not enthusiastic about abandoning what they considered their hereditary lands or moving into the wilderness and again relying on hunting, fishing, and government charity. In 1884 the Methodists had 157 members at Oka, 30 at Cornwall Island, and 36 at Gibson. This membership remained essentially static over the following half-century; in 1925 the missions in Quebec reported 151 members.[46]

In Manitoba and the northwest, the operation of native missions reflected the pattern already established in Ontario. Conversion to Christianity, temperance and moral reform, education, and the general assimilation into Protestant, Victorian society remained the missions' functions. After their near collapse by the early 1850s, the Wesleyans had spent the following thirty years rebuilding the churches, schools, and farms associated with the Norway House, Oxford House, Edmonton and Rocky Mountains, and White Fish Lake missions. This task was made particularly difficult by the transfer of the northwest from the Hudson's Bay Company to the Dominion of Canada in 1869. In the ensuing power vacuum, Louis Riel and his Métis associates were able to lead a successful revolt and in 1870 bring the settlement around Red River into Canada as the province of Manitoba. From 1869 until the mid-1870s, communications were erratic and supplies for the missions, which the Hudson's Bay Company had previously guaranteed, were expensive and difficult to obtain. Riel's execution of Thomas Scott for opposing his revolutionary council's authority also embittered the church.

It was also during the period after 1870 that the tribes throughout the western plains truly lost control of their destiny. Westward migration in the United States, especially after the construction of the railroads, nearly eradicated the migrating buffalo and other game, and the accompanying genocidal wars accelerated the destruction of native society. Although war with the tribes was not part of the Canadian government's settlement policy, events in the United States foreshadowed the similarly destructive advance across the northwest by eastern Canadians. As well as causing starvation, the loss of traditional game also undermined the mystic and spiritual elements of native culture. The buffalo had provided a particularly vital link with the cosmic rhythms and harmony of nature and was central to the time-honoured customs and ceremonies that marked native life. The western tribes were rapidly losing their traditional spiritual anchors and were deeply traumatized by events over which they had no control and for which their deities offered no solutions. It was within this framework that the Protestant and Roman Catholic missionaries were attempting to inculcate Christianity and European-style civilization.

In ministering to the native tribes, the Methodist missionaries showed great skill and dedication. The native preacher Henry B. Steinhauer, who served the White Fish Lake mission area from 1855 to 1884 and opened the first school there in 1863, was particularly noteworthy. He was joined in the region by Thomas Woolsey from 1855 to 1864. Woolsey travelled to the nomadic bands rather than waiting for them to come to the mission. As well, Egerton Ryerson Young, despite his troubles with the Hudson's Bay Company, ministered successfully to the Crees in northern Manitoba between 1868 and 1876. Later, John Maclean served in what is now southern Alberta among the Blood bands from 1880 to 1889. These missionaries and their missions, with schools and small farms, finally established a credible presence for the church.[47] In addition to their evangelistic and educational work, several missionaries wrote extensively on the northwest and thereby expanded the knowledge of the region among Canadians and helped popularize the church's mission labours.

However, the central characters in the Methodists' western missions were George and John McDougall. George McDougall and his eighteen-year-old son arrived in the west in 1860. Together they strengthened the church's presence while gaining the respect and confidence of the various tribes. Although George McDougall's accidental death in 1876 initially stalled much of the work, it did provide Methodism with a legitimate martyr. John McDougall, who was ordained in 1866, succeeded his father and carried out his plans for an orphanage at Morley, Alberta, and for a more sympathetic treatment of the local population. He was assisted by his wife, the daughter of Henry Steinhauer, who, like most of the missionary wives, served quietly to expand the work of the church.[48] The McDougalls, father and son, left an indelible impression on both the native peoples and the church's operations.

The official missionaries and their wives were sent out by the Board of Missions. As well, the WMS and, by the twentieth century, the Deaconess Society dispatched assistants to the region. Furthermore, the church relied heavily on the large number of male and female teachers who laboured to educate the various tribes. In addition to the fifteen day schools opened in the northwest by the Methodists during the nineteenth century, they established residential industrial schools at Brandon, Norway House, and Red Deer. This last operated from 1883 to 1919, when the work was transferred to a similar institution in Edmonton. These schools were enlarged several times to meet the increased needs.

During the 1870s, in an attempt to stabilize conditions, the Methodist missionaries had also assisted in the federal government's program of signing treaties with the roaming tribes and settling them on reserves. George McDougall served as an official translator. The Methodists believed that this process was an essential prerequisite for Christianizing and educating the inhabitants and for their transition from hunting to an agricultural economy. The church assumed that these changes were the only guarantee for survival and progress. The missionaries also petitioned the government to provide greater assistance in order to prevent disease and starvation from destroying the tribes. By the early 1880s, these problems had grown to catastrophic levels and were aggravated by the incursions of white settlers on native hunting grounds. John A. Macdonald's government in Ottawa, preoccupied with the transcontinental railway, turned a deaf ear to all pleas for help and also ignored the claims from the Métis, mixed-bloods, and even new settlers along the North Saskatchewan River. These conditions led in 1885 to the Northwest Rebellion under the leadership of Louis Riel.[49]

The Methodist church was appalled by the rebellion. Officially, it condemned the machinations of the Roman Catholics, in both the northwest and Quebec, but centred its denunciation on Riel himself. Although demanding unconditional loyalty, it sought to quell much of the misdirected uproar in English Canada. For instance, the *Christian Guardian* in April 1885 maintained, "Though this outbreak is a great and inexcusable crime, we must not forget that most of those drawn into it are half-starved, ignorant fellow-countrymen,

who are easily misled by unscrupulous people."[50] Throughout the disturbances, the church was concerned for the welfare of the native peoples and
denounced their mistreatment by the government; it called for generous redress of their grievances. In the west, John McDougall acted as guide and interpreter for the British and Canadian forces sent to subdue the disturbances,
and all the missionaries sought to keep their native flocks out of the combat.
The western missionaries confirmed that few if any Methodist converts had
joined the insurgents. For Methodists, the revolt reinforced the need to civilize the native population and restrain Roman Catholic influence, and it also
gave credibility to their claim that they were doing vital national service in the
northwest. But by the 1890s, native mission work had passed beyond its heroic, pioneer stage in the region and was declining in relative importance as
new immigration dramatically altered the region's population and redefined
the nature of Christian nation-building.

In fact, the centre of Methodist work among native people had shifted to
British Columbia. In that region before European intrusion, the numerous
semi-sedentary native tribes had created a prosperous and sophisticated society based on powerful clan and family ties and a rich and deeply rooted spiritual heritage. However, European settlement, with its destructive diseases and
alcohol, was steadily eroding native culture and destroying the tribes' economic and social viability. The most valuable lands and natural resources were
confiscated for the benefit of the white settlers. The Methodist church officials believed that the best long-term hope for British Columbia's native population rested on its adoption of Christian civilization and its assimilation into
the prevailing Canadian Protestant community.

Although the first wholly native Methodist mission was established in British
Columbia only in 1868 and the work was not set apart until 1875, Christianizing the coastal tribes had been a major component of Methodist work from its
inception in the colony. Ebenezer Robson had preached and opened a school
to the local bands first at Hope and then at Nanaimo in 1860. He erected the
first native chapel there in 1861. Ephraim Evans preached to the natives in
and around Victoria, many of whom were visiting from more northerly villages, and the other missionaries evangelized the native families as opportunities presented themselves. By 1875 the Methodists had native missions at
Victoria, Nanaimo, Sumas and Chilliwack, Port Simpson, and Burrard Inlet.
Gradually the Methodist missions also expanded into the interior of British
Columbia and in 1883 to the Haidas at Skidegate on the Queen Charlotte Islands. The church also employed several native assistants to serve the more
isolated settlements and to preach in the local languages.[51]

The work at Port Simpson perhaps best illustrates the extensive Methodist
commitment to the native tribes. This community of Tsimshians about six
hundred miles north of Victoria had grown as a result of the Hudson's Bay
Company's decision to open a trading post there in 1834. The coastal Tsimshians quickly entered the commercial trading network and enhanced their
wealth and status by acting as middlemen for the interior bands. William Duncan, a somewhat erratic Anglican missionary, began his crusade to Christianize
the local natives in 1857 and after some success moved his converts up the

coast to Metlakatla. In 1873, while visiting Victoria, Chief Alfred Dudoward and his wife converted to Methodism and invited a missionary to their village. The following year, Thomas Crosby and his wife moved to Port Simpson, and they made it their headquarters until 1897. From there, Crosby and his associates evangelized the Nass River valley, the coastal villages south to Kitimat, and the fishing settlements as far north as Alaska.[52]

After some initial success in converting the band to Christianity, the Crosbys began to establish an institutional complex to serve the region. Mrs Emma Crosby, the daughter of the Methodist minister John Douse, opened an informal orphanage in her home in 1879. This project began receiving WMS financial support in 1881, and the following year a paid matron, Miss Hendrie, arrived from Brantford to supervise the project. A separate home was opened in 1883, and in 1890 the WMS took over direct control of the orphanage and its associated school and moral-redemption programs. However, as long as she was alive, Mrs Crosby remained the dominant force in the mission operations. The facilities were enlarged and rebuilt several times and began receiving government grants in 1903. Although the British Columbia Conference voted in 1889 to establish a similar boy's institute at Port Simpson, the missionary board refused to fund it or to expand the number of workers there. However, a boy's home was eventually opened with support from British Columbian Methodists, the local band, and the provincial government. In 1889 Dr Bolton also opened a small hospital at Port Simpson, and the WMS supplied a nurse.[53]

As well, Thomas Crosby travelled extensively by canoe along the coast visiting the isolated native and European communities. The first steamer, the *Glad Tidings*, was purchased in 1884 in order to systematize this marine mission. In 1913 the first of many mission boats was named the *Thomas Crosby* in honour of his pioneering work. In addition to missionaries, Captain William Oliver and his successors delivered supplies, medical assistance, and mail to the canneries, mills, and fishing and lumber camps, as well as to the native population. By 1925 the Methodists had four steamers in operation along the coast and on the Fraser River, and provided services that would have been impossible through ordinary missionary means.[54]

Beyond the normal mission activities, day schools, and agricultural training, the Methodist church established the Coqualeetza Institute, mentioned earlier, at Chilliwack in the Fraser River valley as a residential training school for native boys and girls. Opened in the missionary's home in 1887 with 5 children, three years later it had its own comfortable building and a staff of three. By the mid-1890s it had 97 residents and a large contingent of day students, and by the late 1920s had grown to 230 students. As with all the Methodist schools, it worked to diminish native language and culture and to create "progressive" Canadian citizens. Nevertheless, this institute became one of the most important early educational centres in the province and trained generations of native leaders.[55]

However, perhaps the most innovative work centred on the development of medical facilities for the native bands. In British Columbia, the Missionary Society eventually supported five hospitals at Port Simpson, Bella Bella (R.W. Large Memorial), River's Inlet, Port Essington, and Hazelton (H.C. Wrinch).

Although the hospitals were usually owned by the doctors, they did receive personnel and financial aid from the church. The WMS paid the salaries of eleven nurses at these hospitals and at dispensing stations such as Kitimat. The medical facilities which developed at Bella Bella were typical. In 1897 Dr J.A. Jackson opened a clinic there in association with his evangelistic work. The following year, he was replaced by Dr R.W. Large, who constructed a twelve-bed hospital in 1902. The hospital was the special project of the Toronto Epworth Leagues through the Young People's Forward Movement for Missions. As well as providing for normal medical needs, it helped during the periodic epidemics that were particularly hazardous to native peoples and trained native nurses. By 1925, like all the hospitals, it was nearly self-sufficient in its daily operations and was preparing to open a new nurses' home. Beyond its obvious health benefits, the Methodist church had discovered that medical assistance was the best way of gaining the respect of the natives and of undermining the authority of the traditional medicine men and thus transforming native culture.[56]

By the time the Methodists became active in British Columbia, the local tribes had already developed significant links with European society. They were deeply involved in the fishing, lumbering, canning, and trading operations, and several bands were attempting to operate their own commercial ventures. Although the Methodists usually considered them simple and barbarous children who needed to be transformed, the natives themselves often saw Christianity as a means of acquiring greater access to European goods and the benefits of citizenship and protecting land and legal rights. In Port Simpson, for instance, although many natives became sincere and devout Christians, Crosby was successful as long as it appeared that he represented the secular interests of the Tsimshians and had influence with the provincial and federal governments. By the mid-1890s, when it became clear these conditions were not being met and the tribe could not get a satisfactory land-claims settlement, many Tsimshians asked the Methodist church to remove him, invited the Salvation Army to the community, or stopped practising Christianity altogether.[57]

The Methodist church did try to protect the rights of the natives and actively protested against many government policies, but ultimately it had little real influence. It believed that the best way for the natives to protect themselves was to acquire all the cultural and spiritual trappings of white society. The church attacked the gambling, drinking, feasting, and immoral behaviour of the natives and attempted to destroy what it considered the superstition and witchcraft of the medicine men and other spiritual leaders. The Methodists also worked to have marriage, family life, and housing conform to Protestant, Victorian ideals, to destroy the totem poles with their symbolic mysteries, and to replace the culturally important burial ceremonies with Christian practices.[58]

The church consistently assaulted the potlatch as the institution most closely associated with the old barbarism. The potlatch was an elaborate feast given by a prominent individual intent on demonstrating and enhancing his social status which ended with the distribution of valuable gifts to the guests. This traditional practice had been made more excessive by the increased wealth created by European trade. The church believed the potlatch was immoral and led to impoverishment and economic distress; its disappearance was a clear sign of progress and Christian civilization. The government agreed and outlawed the practice. In general, although the natives' traditional culture was clearly faltering, many practices were only temporarily halted or were continued secretly. At the same time, other natives did enjoy a genuine personal religion and believed Methodism had had a constructive influence on their destiny.[59]

## CITY MISSIONS AND WORK WITH IMMIGRANTS

None the less, native work was only one aspect of the Methodist church's missionary commitment, and in fact, by the late nineteenth century, other priorities had gradually taken over. Specialized city missions increasingly preoccupied the urban congregations and eventually came under the sway of the Board of Missions. Beginning in the 1860s, cities such as Montreal, Quebec, Halifax, and Toronto developed ministries to the unchurched poor. The missionaries generally followed traditional evangelistic practices and sought to encourage attendance at one of the Methodist congregations in their cities. Like most others, the Halifax Wesleyan City Mission, established in 1872, was designed "to spread religious and moral truth among the poor and neglected portions of the population."[60] Charity and social service were originally performed informally as required and usually involved men and women from various congregations working outside official church connections.

However, by the 1880s the urban centres were becoming significantly larger, more industrialized, socially stratified, and spatially segregated. Middle-class residential neighbourhoods were separated from the growing commercial, financial, and particularly industrial sections of the city. In order to take advantage of temporary employment opportunities in labour-intensive industries, large numbers of unskilled workers moved into the core of the city, where they usually lived in unhealthy and overcrowded conditions. To middle-class observers, "The results are seen in children that are feeble physically and mentally, and delinquent morally; in faithless fathers and deserting mothers; in all manner of social, physical and moral ills."[61] Although bewildered and even frightened by what they considered to be unnatural blights on the Canadian landscape, city taxpayers were rarely prepared to pay for necessary improvements, and municipal officials were normally even less likely to promote proper housing or sanitation for these districts. They were overwhelmed by the magnitude of the problems facing them and lacked the knowledge, will, or resources to respond.

In the face of these deteriorating conditions, many Methodist lay and clerical leaders gradually awoke to the fact that the church must concern itself with the social and economic, as well as the moral and spiritual, needs of the urban poor. While these requirements were expanding, most of the older city churches were losing their congregations in the flight from downtown. To answer these churches' desperate financial situation and to provide them with a meaningful religious function, the Methodist church's mission arm transformed their basic services. For instance, Central Methodist church in

Vancouver was taken over by the city's mission board and in 1915 became the Turner Institute. It administered a broad range of social and relief programs for the unemployed and some forty different immigrant nationalities. Under the Toronto Methodist Union, Elm Street and Agnes Street churches were transformed along similar lines to serve "the Ward," a densely populated immigrant section of the city.[62]

As well as remaking traditional congregations, the church also established specialized new missions. The YMCA's Jost Mission in Halifax was taken over by the Methodist church in 1878 and intermittently served working-class women in the city for generations. In Montreal the Old Brewery Mission, originally set up in 1889 as a soup kitchen by the women of Douglas Methodist church, was adopted by the Montreal Mission Society, and new quarters were opened on Craig Street to serve a wide range of needs for the indigent population. Similarly, in 1912 a Seaman's Institute was opened in St John's, Newfoundland, to provide accommodation and moral recreation for sailors and fishermen visiting the city.[63]

The model for most Methodist city missions was the Fred Victor Mission in Toronto. In 1883 a Mrs Sheffield had begun services for street children, and three years later she rented a room to hold her large Sunday afternoon meetings. As the work expanded, the mission moved several times until in 1894 a large building was opened at Jarvis and Queen streets. Originally the work had been assisted by gifts from members of Metropolitan church, but gradually the Massey family, in conjunction with the downtown churches, supplied most of the support. The administration of the Fred Victor Mission, named after Fred Victor Massey, was assumed by the Toronto City Mission Society in 1894. It was made up of representatives from the Methodist churches in the area and members of the Massey family. In 1910 it amalgamated with the Toronto Social Union, also a creation of the Masseys, to coordinate city missions and church extension and to systematize funding for urban work.

Although the programs at Fred Victor were better funded and more elaborate, they exemplified the approaches that developed in all the specialized city missions. As well as providing some worship services and a Sunday school, it held temperance, children's, and mothers' meetings, ran evening classes and young people's organizations, and taught people how to grow vegetables and run a household. For the poor, it set up an employment agency, a savings bank, a free drug dispensary, and an inexpensive restaurant and boarding-house, and distributed money, food, and clothing to the deserving. Picnics, special suppers, and a gymnasium allowed for recreation and social interaction. The staff, which included several deaconesses, visited homes in the neighbourhood and prisoners in the jails and attended the juvenile courts to help the young offenders. The mission also established a rescue home for girls which eventually developed into the semi-independent Victor Home. Although philosophically conservative, the Fred Victor Mission adopted the most up-to-date sociological methodology and attempted to deal humanely with the indigent urban population. It hoped to create moral, upright, and progressive Canadian citizens.[64]

To the Methodist church, as to many Canadians, the greatest threat to Canada's wholesome development appeared to be the vast immigrant population entering the country. In 1901 Canada had a population of only 5,371,300. That year nearly 50,000 people legally immigrated to the dominion. In 1910–11 the number of new arrivals had jumped to 311,084. In fact, in the period between 1900 and early 1912, 2,118,712 immigrants settled in Canada. Of these, 89,474 located in the Maritimes, 309,422 in Quebec, 504,126 in Ontario, 353,100 in Manitoba, 608,965 in Saskatchewan and Alberta, and 240,414 in British Columbia. This immigration was seriously altering Canada's make-up and placing huge demands on its institutions. However, 823,188 of these immigrants came from Britain, 601,963 from England alone, and 752,120 arrived from the United States. Many had been Methodists in their homeland. The Canadian church believed it was essential to supply a friendly hand to these co-religionists and encourage them to join a Methodist congregation. Therefore the church assigned chaplains to the major ports and dispersal centres to provide information and advice. These chaplains were assisted by deaconesses working in Traveller's Aid centres in many of the large cities.

The Methodist church also collaborated with organizations in Britain, such as the Methodist Emigration League and the Brotherhood movement. These groups advised Methodists interested in settling in Canada about local economic conditions and Methodist facilities before their departure and provided lists of emigrants to Canadian church officials. Unfortunately, this chaplain work met with only limited success. There were never sufficient chaplains, and procedures to follow immigrants to their final destination were rarely implemented. The Methodists were not as active as the Anglicans, Presbyterians, or Salvation Army in this work. Moreover, World War I interrupted the immigrant flow, and when the program was reinstituted after the war, there were misgivings in Britain about recommending the Methodist Church since it was about to disappear into the United Church of Canada.[65]

At the same time, some Methodists complained that Britain was dumping its criminal and beggarly surplus on Canada and claimed these new arrivals were too weak and unadaptable for Canadian life. Furthermore, they seemed to be constantly complaining or telling Canadians how superior Britons were; Canadians disliked being dismissed as mere colonials by people who appeared not to appreciate their adopted land. Many Methodist businessmen also denounced the radical political and labour positions assumed by British immigrants, while Canadian workers feared their competition for jobs. Often poorly educated and unemployed, the immigrants were a serious drain on the largesse of the Methodist city missions. For instance, most of those using Fred Victor Mission were British immigrants.[66]

However, Canadian concern over British immigration was mild in comparison with its attitudes toward non-British immigrants. In the period between 1900 and early 1912, 543,404 immigrants arrived from countries outside of Britain and the United States. Of these, 142,652 were listed as Austro-Hungarians, 71,407 as Italians, 53,997 as Hebrews, 48,755 as Russians, 45,148 as Scandinavians, 25,809 as Germans, 15,144 as Finns, and 14,451 as Polish. At the same time, 17,571 Chinese, 13,893 Japanese, and 5,203 Hindus were reported as immigrants. Although northern European immigration was usually regarded favourably, eastern Europeans were considered a possible menace to democratic government, Italians were deemed violent and often criminal, Finns were viewed as socialists, and Asians were believed to be impossible to assimilate and a threat to the nation's moral standards.

Although the institutional Methodist church was far more tolerant than the general population and called for humane and generous treatment, it did advocate limiting foreign immigration to levels that the country could effectively assimilate. The desire to assimilate the stranger reflected deep-seated nativist sentiments among Canadians and a profound desire to maintain the purity, virility, and power of the British nations. It was believed that this could only be achieved by restraining the passions of non-Anglo-Saxons and disciplining them in the political, social, and religious tenets of traditional Protestant Canadians. Assimilation was considered a duty not only to Canada but also to God since it was part of God's plan that the dominion should help house, civilize, and Christianize the world. According to the church authorities, the main beneficiaries would be the new citizens themselves since they would learn how to use democratic institutions and gain the benefits of Anglo-Saxon civilization. This was why they had come to Canada.[67]

The Methodist church modelled its specialized work with non-English-speaking groups on its missions to native peoples and to French Canadians. Although they lacked the Presbyterian commitment to converting the Catholics in Quebec, the Methodists had begun French missions in 1855 in Quebec City and gradually opened others across the province. In 1878 the Ladies French Missionary Society, a forerunner of the WMS, was founded to assist with the education and evangelization of French Canadians. In the same year, the first French Methodist church opened in Montreal. Although the French missions were never successful in converting large numbers and remained a low priority among missionary officials, the work did have a substantial influence through its French-language schools. By the end of the nineteenth century, the Methodists and Presbyterians were cooperating in this work in order to avoid duplication while providing an antidote to what they perceived as aggressive and unholy Roman Catholic influences.[68] However, Methodist French missions were discontinued in the early twentieth century as the congregations became part of the regular circuit operations in the province.

In the 1880s, again in cooperation with the Presbyterians, the Methodist church began foreign-language work with the Chinese and Japanese settlers on the west coast. The Chinese had first come to British Columbia from California during the periodic gold rushes that marked the province's history after 1858. The Canadian Pacific Railway and local mining companies had brought in others as inexpensive contract labourers. When these jobs finished, the Chinese continued to operate small mining claims or scattered to find work in the lumber mills and fish canneries. By the late nineteenth century, they represented a significant proportion of British Columbia's population. Many Canadians considered the Chinese as a particularly immoral threat to white, Anglo-Saxon civilization and believed that it was neither possible nor desirable to assimilate them. In response to anti-Oriental sentiment, particularly in British Columbia, the federal government imposed a head tax on non-contract immigrants in

1885 and discouraged further immigration. Except for merchants, it had always been illegal for the Chinese to bring wives or families into the country, and the workers were expected to emigrate when no longer needed.[69]

The first Chinese mission in Canada grew out of these restrictions. Some Chinese merchants in Victoria began importing young girls, under the guise of relatives, and forcing them to work as prostitutes. A Chinese-speaking Presbyterian layman, John Gardner, opened a rescue home for these girls in 1886, and a year later the Methodist WMS adopted the home and sent Annie Leake as matron. The home protected, converted, and educated these victims until they could be married or returned to China. As conditions gradually changed, the home added an orphanage and school and became a safe haven for Chinese and, after 1895, Japanese women and children until it closed in 1942.[70]

From this beginning, the WMS cooperated with the Board of Missions to improve the condition of the Chinese in Victoria, Vancouver, New Westminster, and the smaller coastal fishing villages. Female and male Chinese assistants worked with the Canadian missionaries, many of whom had gained experience in China, in this evangelistic and educational work. The missionaries also attempted to allay the fears of the Canadian public and constantly attacked the irrational bigotry they met. The Chinese population had reached about 15,000 by 1910, and it remained fairly constant for the next several years. Although most Chinese remained on the west coast, there was a significant migration to the urban centres on the prairies and in Ontario, where the Methodists continued to serve them. In 1925 the church operated twelve Chinese missions and thirty-one preaching appointments and claimed 635 members.[71]

The Japanese had also been brought to British Columbia under contract to work in the mines and had later entered the fishing and canning operations. However, because they were considered more civilized and were allies of Britain, family immigration was permitted and they were able to establish a more stable social life. None the less, Japanese children were not permitted to attend Canadian schools until 1906. From about 4,700 Japanese in Canada in 1901, almost exclusively in British Columbia, the population rose to over 19,000 by 1908. But after the anti-Asiatic riots the previous year and an ensuing Gentlemen's Agreement between Britain and Japan, immigration fell off dramatically and many left the country. During the year 1907–08, 7,601 Japanese entered Canada, but the following year, only 495 arrived. By 1910 there were only about 8,000 Japanese in the dominion.

The history of the Japanese missions differed from the Chinese; the first missions and schools were begun by Japanese Christians themselves. In 1892 the Reverend Mr Kanabe arrived in British Columbia from San Francisco and organized revival services at Vancouver, Victoria, and Cumberland. This tour was followed up by visiting lay preachers, including Mr Okamoto, who before his return to Japan in 1896 helped found a hospital and mission at Steveston on the Fraser River, and Kazuo Tajima, who ran various missions until his death from tuberculosis in 1900.[72] Even after the Canadian Methodist church assumed control of the Japanese missions, it relied heavily on Japanese assistants and worked with the Methodist church in Japan to supply church workers and information.

By 1906 the church had five missions, including the hospital at Steveston, a self-supporting Japanese church, and a weekly newspaper in Japanese, and it also ran evangelistic services wherever Japanese congregated. The WMS held meetings with Japanese women in Victoria, Vancouver, New Westminster, Port Moody, Barnet, and Steveston and carried out home visitation, domestic training, and other regular social-service activities. A Japanese WMS auxiliary formed at False Creek in 1910 demonstrates the Japanese women's commitment to expanding Methodism. By 1925 the Methodists claimed 567 members in six missions and twenty-two preaching appointments. Typically, the principal work revolved around evangelization and, more importantly, education. Although only a limited number showed an interest in becoming devout Christians, many wanted to learn English in order to expand their economic and social opportunities. Nevertheless, the Canadian church did ordain several Japanese to serve in both Canada and Japan.[73]

Beginning at the turn of the century, the Methodist church also became deeply involved in medical, educational, and evangelistic missions to the immigrants from eastern Europe and Italy. The former were generally called Ruthenians or Galicians although they came from Russia, Poland, the German and Austro-Hungarian empires, and especially from Ukraine. While the Poles, Germans, and Austro-Hungarians were usually Roman Catholics, the Ukrainians and Russians were more commonly Eastern or Greek Orthodox. The eastern Europeans concentrated in the rising towns or in blocks of rural townships in a band along the route of what would become the Canadian National Railways from Winnipeg to Edmonton.

The Methodist church began ministering to these immigrants near Edmonton in 1898 as part of its regular domestic mission work, and it noted that there were already about 6,000 eastern Europeans in the area without regular worship services. They could not obtain their own priests, and the Methodists hoped to anticipate the Catholic and Orthodox churches by providing Sunday services. By 1902 the Methodists had established six special preaching appointments and claimed thirty-four members. The first Galician mission was located at the former native mission at Pakan, northeast of Edmonton, where Dr Charles Lawford opened a hospital in 1906. Over the following decade, missions were opened in Edmonton and at Wahstao, Lamont, Bellis, and Smoky Lake employing eleven WMS workers and nine missionaries appointed by the missionary board. The Norwood Methodist church in Edmonton was also transformed into a city mission to help with this ethnic outreach.[74]

The work slowly grew under the extended leadership of W.H. Pike, Taranty Hannochko, and a number of the other Ukrainian-speaking ministers. Again, the most successful elements involved hospitals and schools to take care of the pressing temporal needs of the new settlers. Subsidized by the Alberta government, the hospitals were valuable for training Ukrainian nurses as well as dispensing medical aid. The WMS operated the Edmonton Ruthenian Home for girls and major training and residential facilities at Wahstao and later at Pakan. These facilities reflected the strong priority Methodists gave to converting and training children as the best way to transform immigrant society. By

1925 the church operated nine missions to new Canadians in Alberta, four in Saskatchewan, and six in Manitoba.[75]

The Methodists also established a Ruthenian Press in Winnipeg, which produced valuable religious and secular works including a hymn-book and several tracts on Canadian citizenship. More important, however, the Methodists published a Ukrainian-language newspaper called the *Canadian* in Edmonton. Although its circulation was never large, it did assist new Canadians to understand their adopted country. The church also helped promising young immigrants attend secondary schools and encouraged them to go to university. It hoped that some of these men and women would return to minister to their own people. In addition, it began to train some probationers in foreign languages so that they could more effectively minister to this population and ease its transition into Canadian citizenship. Missionaries working in the field even suggested that Russian, German, or Ukrainian be substituted for Greek or Latin in clerical training.[76]

The Methodist church also specialized in evangelizing the Italian community. Normally unskilled farmers and labourers from the poorer regions of southern Italy, these individuals settled for the most part in the industrial or mining towns, where they could find employment in construction, transportation, or heavy industry. Large numbers settled in Sydney, Montreal, Toronto, Hamilton, Sudbury, Sault Ste Marie, and Thunder Bay, along the Welland canal, and in the coal-mining centres of Alberta and British Columbia. Like other immigrants, the Italians were fiercely clannish, and many considered themselves only temporary sojourners in the country. A high proportion were single young men who expected to return to Italy after they had made their fortunes and were therefore not interested in understanding or integrating into Canadian society. Mistrustful of police, government officials, and others in authority, these young men often found themselves in trouble. They lacked the intricate network of family and village discipline and restraint, and encountered an apparently hostile environment in which they performed physically demanding, yet essentially menial tasks, but were forbidden their traditional drinking and social customs. It was therefore easy for Canadians to stereotype Italians as immoral, dishonest, violent, and untrustworthy. Moreover, the Irish- and French- dominated Roman Catholic church was slow to minister to the Italian settlers and particularly to employ Italian-speaking priests.[77] For these reasons, the Methodist church believed special treatment was required.

The first Methodist Italian mission opened in Toronto in 1905 adjacent to the immigrant ghetto known as "the Ward." Although it is impossible to ascertain how many Italians resided in this small area, its total population grew from about 4,000 in 1902 to over 14,000 in 1912. Like all immigrant districts in the larger cities, the Ward combined elements drawn from the host society and the various immigrant groups which occupied the area. Supplying cheap accommodation, easy access to temporary employment, and goods and services familiar to the immigrants in their native languages, the area helped to ease the transition into Canadian life for new arrivals while creating a rich and vital social environment.

However, it was also characterized by a severe deterioration in its inadequate housing and sanitation facilities. Backyards and lanes were choked with peddlers' carts, stocks of goods, and discarded rubbish; single-family dwellings became overcrowded rooming-houses with limited water and toilet facilities or were replaced by equally miserable tenements. The city rarely supplied garbage collection, road cleaning, or other essential services. Since most immigrants were intent on saving as much as possible in order to support relatives who had remained at home, to be able to return home in triumph, or to buy land in Canada, they were usually willing to put up with the conditions or at least were not prepared to complain openly. Under these circumstances, the district "was a visible alien presence in a highly homogeneous society" and its inhabitants appeared dirty, sickly, and backward. At the same time, most Canadians were already highly prejudiced against foreigners and particularly despised their apparent lack of discipline and restraint or appreciation for Canada's social and political institutions and its British heritage.[78]

Under the direction of the Methodist Social Union and the Fred Victor Mission, Giuseppe Merlino, Frank Catapano, and their successors fought to overcome the effects of the squalor they witnessed in the neighbourhood and to help the Italian population fit into Canadian society. Typically, they emphasized education and training, especially for the young, and opened schools and developed social-welfare programs, as well as providing ordinary religious services at the Elm Street mission. As the city's Italian population gradually shifted north and west, the Methodist church opened two new missions and several preaching stations. However, although many Italians received a basic education and some economic support, few chose to become Methodists. Especially after the Roman Catholic church in Toronto began to concentrate on the Italian immigrants, attendance at Methodist worship declined sharply. After 1913 the Methodist missions also suffered when severe unemployment forced many Italians to leave the city to find work. During World War I, a large number, including lay and ordained church workers, returned to Italy for military service, and under the pressing wartime needs, the church reduced its commitment to all ethnic missions. After the war, despite again actively pursing the immigrant communities, it did not fare substantially better.[79]

As well as Toronto, the Methodist church was active in Montreal and the other centres with a high Italian population. A Miss Tognotti opened a Bible class for Italians at the Old Brewery Mission in Montreal in 1907, and a year later the Montreal Ministerial Association hired Laborio Lattoni, a former missionary of the American Methodist Episcopal Church, to supervise the operations. Lattoni developed a substantial congregation and French language program. He also preached throughout the province and visited the Italian population in Ottawa. Of all the Italian mission work in Canada, Montreal's was the most successful. The Methodist church also developed a mission to the thousands of Italians working in Sydney, Nova Scotia, where it opposed unfair hiring practices and job discrimination. Although it was forced to cut back on its work in Ottawa, Niagara Falls, Welland, and Copper Cliff and eliminate grants to Italian students after 1912, it maintained substantial missions at Hamilton, North Bay, Bellevue, and Crow's Nest Pass in Alberta.[80]

Where concentrations of non-British immigrants were high, but no one nationality dominated, the Methodists established "all people's missions." While these were present across the country, they were best represented by the work done in Winnipeg. That city was the great dispersal centre for western Canada, and thousands of immigrants passed through its railway station or remained until they could get established elsewhere. Many never left, and they gave the city, especially the north end, a strong European flavour. The Methodist mission began in 1899 and provided services in both English and German, initially under Alexander Thompson and later under Hamilton Wigle. Its best known director, however, was James S. Woodsworth, the son of the superintendent of western missions. His well-known career as social reformer and politician began with his work among the poor immigrants at the All People's Mission.

It established a centre on Stella Street to assist the main mission near the Canadian Pacific Railway station and eventually provided services in Ukrainian, Polish, and Russian, as well as English and German. With the aid of Methodist deaconesses and a large number of foreign-born assistants, the mission offered a wide range of services and programs, including evangelization, education for all family members, social relief and unemployment assistance, training in household sciences and domestic skills, and opportunities for recreation and social integration.[81] Like all the Methodist missions, its essential purpose was to Christianize and civilize, to assimilate the immigrants into English-Canadian society, and ultimately to make them devout Protestants who could help expand the moral and progressive dimensions of the Canadian nation.

Unfortunately, the church as a whole was rarely tolerant of the non-English-speaking immigrants. It advocated restrictions on immigration in order to give the country time to absorb the new settlers and wanted block settlements in the west broken up to encourage assimilation. Even reasonably enlightened missionaries such as James S. Woodsworth considered the foreigners to be crude peasants and believed restrictions on voting rights should be instituted until they had learned to appreciate the Canadian political and social systems. Such concerns were particularly strident during World War I, when nearly 8,000 Europeans immigrants were interned as enemy aliens. Many of these were arrested simply because they were unemployed. At the same time, there was a massive campaign to eliminate foreign-language publications in the country and to suppress ethnic activities. Although attitudes improved after the war, the economic recession and labour problems meant that anti-foreign sentiments were never far below the surface.[82]

Nevertheless, while the Methodist church strongly supported assimilation, some of its better-informed members recognized that this policy had to be promoted carefully. They realized that immigrant communities were not automatically going to accept notions of Anglo-Saxon superiority, and Canadians themselves must reassess such ideas if the country was to function properly. Most of the European immigrants had come from regions where for generations they had fought to retain any vestige of their national identity, and they were not prepared to discard it simply at the behest of Canadian government or church officials. They also resented being treated as criminals or inferiors. Most experienced Methodist missionaries were sensitive to these concerns and sought to guide, rather than to force change.[83]

# 12 Methodist Overseas Missions, 1873–1925

The Methodists developed an elaborate mission system in Canada, Newfoundland, and Bermuda, but they were also proud to share in the evangelization of the entire "heathen" world. In fact, they assumed that their absolute right and duty to transform every aspect of life was greatest in the non-Christian lands; at home "heathenism" was a personal fault since Christianity was everywhere available, but abroad much of the population had never heard the saving truths of Protestantism. Moreover, the nineteenth-century spiritual revival had enhanced the sense of guilt in failing to live up to Christian principles and created a profound anxiety over the fate of the unbeliever. This response, in turn, invigorated the desire to proclaim universally the benefits of personal salvation and Christian morality. The saved could best prove their love for God by showing their love for all humanity. Failure to participate in mission work was a confession of spiritual poverty.[1]

Foreign missions attracted support across the whole spectrum of Methodist theological belief. Although the reasons and expected results often differed, mission work united liberals, conservatives, and proto-fundamentalists as few contemporary issues could. For instance, premillennialists struggled to save as many as possible before the coming destruction of the world and humankind's final judgment. The call of the Student Volunteer Movement for "the evangelization of the world in this generation" was therefore a critical necessity. Other theological conservatives believed that only Christians could enter the "Christian heaven." Conversion was essential since all the unredeemed, even those who had never been introduced to Christianity, would ultimately be damned.

By the end of the nineteenth century, although this belief was still current, the emphasis on damnation had declined among mainstream Methodists, and the suspicion grew that a just God would not condemn to hell those who were unaware of the benefits of Christianity. Theological liberals, who essentially accepted a post-millennial resolution of human affairs, stressed the innate goodness of humanity through the indwelling Christ. Personal conversion remained essential for the creation of heaven on earth and to insure Christ's reign; but equally critical, the present human condition needed improvement. Thus while religious conservatives stressed personal conversion in foreign mission work, liberals tended to emphasize the spread of social justice and ethical humanitarianism as appropriate goals in themselves. They wished to extend social welfare, morality, and democratic institutions to the world.[2]

Beyond pure evangelism, the liberals promoted temperance, education, and other progressive attributes of Western civilization while attacking corruption and immorality. As well, they attempted to institute what they considered to be the best elements of the Protestant Victorian family in the mission field. They encouraged the local authorities to outlaw prostitution and polygamy, to raise the education level and status of women, and to protect children from exploitation. Eliminating the binding of women's feet and the sale of children might not lead to conversion, but they were manifestations of the higher social and ethical standards of Western, Christian society. Such actions would lead to the general improvement of the "heathen" lands and thus to the advancement of the whole world. Similarly, while medical and educational facilities provided opportunities to contact and convert, they also relieved human suffering and provided enlightenment. From the beginning of their overseas work therefore, Canadian Methodist missionaries combined ethical and social-service reforms with traditional evangelistic campaigns to fulfil the ultimate goal of Christanizing and civilizing the world.[3]

At the same time, foreign mission activities could never be isolated from larger economic, political, and ideological goals. The non-Western countries offered immense opportunities for profit, power, and prestige. Missionaries usually accepted and even promoted the manifest destiny of the Western nations to command and shared in the secular support for expansion. As the *Christian Guardian* noted in 1875, missions "plant the outposts of civilization … and commerce and the arts follow in the track they have cleared."[4] In turn, government and business supported missions as a corollary to their self-interested involvement in these countries. In return for such aid and protection, the churches sanctioned economic and political imperialism and made it more palatable by their altruistic mission goals. The most obvious example during the 1880s was the great imperial struggle in the Sudan. It was characterized as an attempt by the Christian General Gordon to enlighten cruel, Islamic barbarism.

Yet missionaries, diplomats, and traders were just as likely to oppose each other in the field. Missionaries were often denounced for interfering in secular affairs, while they themselves considered crass commercialism, military intimidation, and the sordid immorality of many Europeans as an important reason for the lack of progress among the local population. How could they speak of the higher morality of Christianity while individuals exemplified all the worst that the West had to offer? When preaching Western superiority, the missionaries were forced to distinguish between the ideal and the all too apparent reality. Thus critics of expansionism claimed that although the West was neither pure nor indispensable to progress, still, God had chosen it as the instrument to advance the principles of Christianity. And Christianity was sanctioned as the only universal religion that transcended narrow tribalism and withstood the tests of science and reason. It offered a unique avenue for true moral and spiritual progress. Moreover, while notions of racial superiority were never far below the surface, they were often qualified by Methodism's traditional interest in breaking down the barriers of race and class in the creation of a broad fellowship of believers.[5]

Of course, beyond the deeply felt hope to Christianize and civilize the world, missionaries saw overseas work as a means of advancing their own spiritual and social self-awareness. With improved transportation and communication facilities, travel was relatively safe and comfortable, and middle-class Victorian men and women took the opportunity to visit exotic cultures. Missionaries shared this interest in exploration and the uncovering of natural and human wonders. It did not represent a shallow escapist sense of adventure, but rather, at its best, a desire to understand God's whole creation. For the more enlightened, this broadening of intellectual horizons led to a greater appreciation of different civilizations. Their great age, sophistication, and variety suggested that they had much to teach the West or, at the very least, would be extremely difficult to transform.[6]

The church's selection of foreign missionaries was normally based on a variety of practical considerations. Beyond having a demonstrable piety, they had to be in sound physical and mental health and be self-motivated and able to work well with others. Missionaries had to combine intellectual ability with sound professional skills in order to communicate ideas and project a positive image of Christianity to the indigenous population. Adaptability to strange situations and proficiency in languages were also assets. The church was of two minds with regard to the most appropriate age for missionaries. It wanted mature, married men who brought stability and proven talents to the work and who would not be seduced by the host society, but it also believed young men would be able to master languages more easily and have longer careers. Over time, the mission board sent both types; it relied heavily on personal recommendations and recognized individual talents in selecting men who would make mission work their permanent careers.[7]

As for women, they were considered an indispensable adjunct to the missionary movement. They could serve where men were forbidden by cultural taboos or social customs and were less likely to be suspected of having ulterior motives. Moreover, it was claimed, "They have more tenderness, more patience, and can endure more hardships and privations, with less complaint, than men."[8] It was also easier for women to extol the benefits of Christianity without giving offence since they were perceived as the natural guardians of spirituality and morality and were particularly suited to promoting household progress and family life in general. One of the key elements of mission work was to elevate women in foreign cultures. The church was convinced that "lift women and you lift the race";[9] they were the primary builders of a moral and progressive society. Without female missionaries, there was little hope of success in addressing the needs of women.

To fulfil these roles effectively, the Methodist church felt that the female missionary should have piety, common sense, cheerfulness, womanly independence, tact, refinement, courage, self-control, dedication, and discipline. Neither modesty, propriety, nor decorum would be abused in mission work and should not be seen as obstacles to such a career. The female missionary also needed to be healthy and hard working and have a thorough education. Perhaps most important, she needed a deep and abiding sympathy for her task and for those under her care. In fact, she needed all the attributes expected of the best Victorian, middle-class woman.[10]

## JAPAN

Although the Canadian Wesleyan church believed in the crusade to evangelize the world, it did not feel strong enough to take on the added responsibility alone. During the third quarter of the nineteenth century, it was heavily involved in rebuilding the missions in the northwest and opening up British Columbia. However, William Morley Punshon, the ever-optimistic president of Conference, pushed the connexion to accept an overseas role. With the expected increase in revenues from the forthcoming union of Canadian Wesleyans and with a special grant from the wealthy Toronto business leader Senator John Macdonald, by 1872 the church had agreed to open a mission abroad. The West Indies, Africa, and China were considered, but British Wesleyan missionaries were serving in all these regions. In order to fill an obvious gap, the Canadian Methodists decided to send a small contingent to Japan in 1873.[11]

Japan had been opened on a limited scale to Westerners by Commodore Perry's gunboat diplomacy in 1853, and over the next seventy-five years, Japanese attitudes toward foreigners fluctuated according to local, national, and international conditions. They were restricted to working and owning property in selected treaty ports and trading centres until 1899, and the ease with which they could acquire property or even travel depended on local acceptance as much as government regulation. In addition, the Buddhist and Shinto priests periodically roused their followers to make life difficult for Christians or to compel the government to enforce restrictions. As a result, Canadian Methodist missionaries were instructed to "carefully abstain from interference in any questions pertaining to the politics or commerce of the country."[12]

Such advice was of little assistance during and immediately after the Satsuma Rebellion in 1877, when nationalism and anti-foreign sentiment made conditions even more difficult. Patriotism and wartime bigotry again caused problems for foreigners during the Sino-Japanese War in 1894–95 and the Russo-Japanese War a decade later. Had the Japanese not been victorious on both occasions, the reaction might have been more severe. However, national pride was also quickly aroused by apparent slights to Japanese honour, including continuing European involvement in what Japan viewed as its spheres of interest in China and Korea, the Gentlemen's Agreement of 1907–08 whereby Japan restricted its emigration, and the United States' Oriental-exclusion legislation.[13]

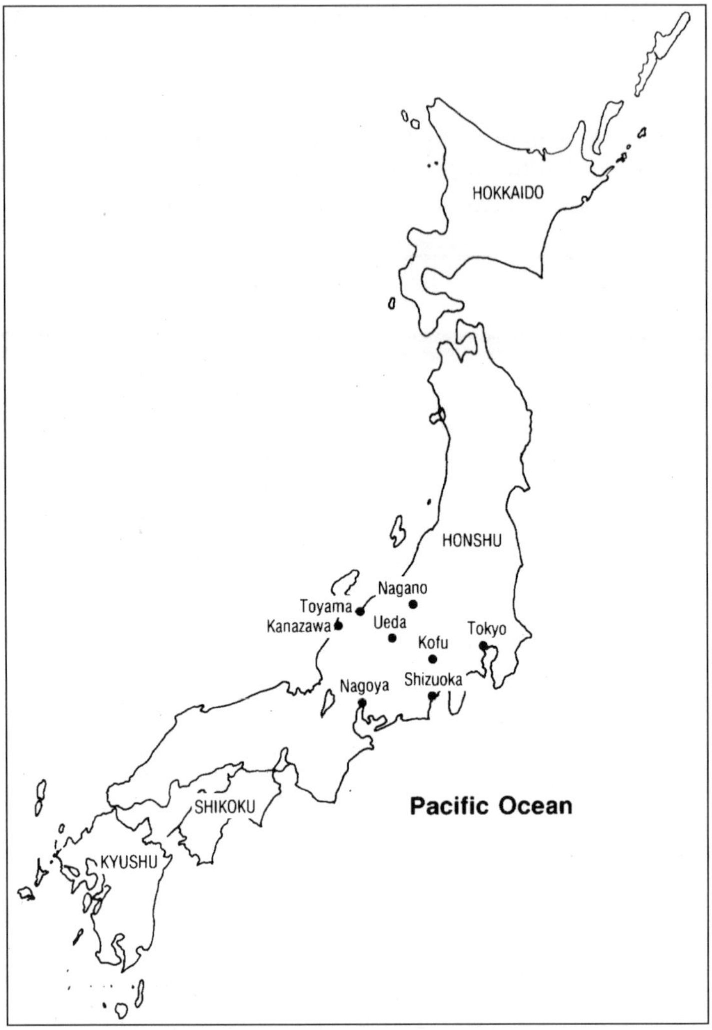

Map 1   Canadian Methodist missions in Japan

Despite such ongoing hostility, American Presbyterian and Episcopalian missionaries had arrived in 1859 and were joined by Congregational missionaries in 1869. Both the American Methodist Episcopal Church and the Canadian Wesleyan Methodist church sent missionaries in 1873, and in 1885 the American Methodist Episcopal Church, South arrived. Japan also received missionaries from several smaller Methodist connexions and other Protestant churches and had a large Roman Catholic contingent. In general, the Protestant churches worked harmoniously together, and ecumenical cooperation grew over the following decades. Although there was some overlap, the Methodists divided the field rather than compete in specific centres. The Canadian mission zone was located in the middle of Honshū island, eventually running in a semi-circle from Tokyo to Nagoya in the south and Nagano in the north.[14]

For many Japanese, the arrival of the Christian missionaries provided a valuable opportunity to enlist European civilization and technology in the promotion of national progress. They viewed Christianity as the key to understanding Western culture. Missionaries also offered facilities for learning English and other European languages. If Japan was to compete with the West, it must open its doors to new ideas while protecting the essentials of its own heritage. Japanese scholars were also intrigued by the ethical and moral aspects of Christianity and viewed it not so much as a spiritual movement, but as an important philosophical system. This was particulary true among the well-educated samurai class, which was losing its power and status in peacetime Japan. In fact, many recognized an advantage in adopting Christianity since it was generally not a bar to economic advancement or government service and was useful in international relations.[15]

On June 30, 1873, Dr Davidson Macdonald and the Reverend George Cochran arrived at Yokohama. Macdonald was a thirty-six-year-old ordained minister who had just graduated from Victoria College's medical school while serving as the minister on the Davenport and Seaton circuit in Toronto. Cochran was his senior by three years and had most recently been the minister at Metropolitan Wesleyan church in Toronto. Because of the legal restrictions on foreigners owning property or residing outside the treaty ports unless they were sponsored and employed by a Japanese citizen, most of the Christian missionaries were huddled in Yokohama or the other foreign zones. Macdonald became the first Protestant missionary to break this pattern when in April 1874 he accepted a position to teach English in a Japanese school and moved with his family to Shizuoka, south of Tokyo.

In addition to carrying out his modest teaching duties, he preached and ran a medical dispensary. By 1878, when he visited North America for a year to take specialized medical training, the local church had 118 members, most of whom were associated with his teaching. For the following eight years, Japanese lay and, later, ordained pastors expanded the Christian community at Shizuoka. After Macdonald's return, he settled in Tokyo, where, despite primarily practising medicine for the Western community, he continued to play a leadership role in mission affairs. He resigned in 1898 but maintained his private practice until 1904, when he returned to Canada. He was the only Canadian Methodist missionary to undertake medical work in Japan.[16]

George Cochran soon followed Macdonald's example and accepted a teaching position in Tokyo, where he also combined evangelizing with educational work. In 1878 and 1879 he opened the first two Canadian Methodist churches in the city. Cochran returned to Canada in the latter year, and after he went back to Japan in 1884, he served as principal and professor of systematic theology at the Anglo-Oriental College (Aoyama Gakuin) in Tokyo until 1893. He then retired to Los Angeles, California, where he died in 1901. Known particularly for his sound theology and his preaching ability, Cochran converted and trained many Japanese to carry forward the Christian cause.[17]

Although Canadian Methodism was seriously in debt and trying to restrict its overall mission operations, it did send George Meacham and Charles Eby in 1876 in order to establish a real presence in Japan. With these additions, the work was reorganized from a mission of Toronto district to a marginally more autonomous missionary district of Toronto Conference. Meacham was forty-three when he arrived to teach at Mr Ebara's academy in Numadzu; after a few years there, he moved to Tokyo to teach systematic theology. Like all the other missionaries, he spent much of his time evangelizing the local population and helping to train native workers. He retired and returned to Canada in 1903, but continued to promote overseas mission work through lectures and writings until his death in 1919.[18]

Born in 1845 and ordained in 1871, Charles Eby had worked for five years in German missions in Ontario before volunteering to go to Japan. He served there from 1876 until 1885 and again from 1887 until 1895 and was a dynamic, if somewhat troublesome, addition to the mission. He was always promoting grand schemes which often disrupted normal mission operations. During his first tour of duty, as well as teaching and preaching at Kofu and Tokyo, he published the *Chrysanthemum* from 1881 until 1883. He hoped that this magazine would promote his long-standing goal of converting the Japanese intelligentsia, but it had only a small readership, normally limited to the mission community. In 1883 Eby also published *Christianity and Humanity*, an important series of lectures on the benefits of Christianity to the Japanese. Furthermore, before the Methodists established a theological school, he worked with George Cochran to train Japanese ministers through a specialized course of study. Along with the majority of missionaries, Eby believed, "The patriotism of the Japanese, their politeness, their self-reliance, their high and splendid courage, their versatility and love of knowledge are acknowledged by all ... we might expect for them a brilliant future, and a leading place among the nations of the East."[19]

Eby returned to Canada in 1885, and during the two-year hiatus in his missionary career, he lectured and wrote extensively, including *Methodism and the Missionary Problem* in 1886. He also took the opportunity to enlist a volunteer band of missionaries to return with him to Japan in 1887. They were paid for teaching in Japanese schools and therefore did not require support from the mission board. In their spare time, they evangelized in the outlying regions and settled their converts in Methodist churches run by either Canadian missionaries or the growing corps of Japanese pastors. In all, fifteen men and one woman served through this "self-supporting band," and several of them were integrated into the regular Canadian Methodist mission in 1891 when the band was dissolved. Despite its success, it was never popular with the Canadian mission authorities since they had no administrative or disciplinary control over its work.[20]

Eby was also the driving force and first director of the Central Tabernacle, which opened in Tokyo in 1890. Modelled on Hugh Price Hughes's London mission, it combined traditional church worship with social-service activities. As well as a church, the tabernacle had a large residence and was particularly designed to attract Tokyo's intellectuals and students from the nearby Imperial University. Often new missionaries stayed there while learning the Japanese language before they settled in other missions, and it became an unofficial local headquarters for the Canadian mission operations. In 1923, along with ten other Methodist churches in Tokyo, it was destroyed by a devastating earthquake and fire. A special fund of $125,000 was raised in Toronto to repair the damage, but Central Tabernacle was not rebuilt until the end of the decade.

Although the tabernacle remained the principal Canadian mission in Japan, many missionaries and local Japanese ministers believed it was a mistake. It alone swallowed up one-eighth of the annual mission grant but gained few converts and attracted few university students. Even the institution's supporters, who maintained that it had been undermined by Alexander Sutherland in Canada and by Macdonald in Tokyo, felt unless it was run according to Eby's original plan, it should be closed. It also became a source of sometimes bitter contention between the Canadians and their Japanese colleagues. Central Tabernacle had two divisions: the Canadians ran the residence and evangelistic work while the Japanese operated the regular church. There was a growing consensus that either the Canadians or the Japanese should supervise a more intergrated operation.[21]

By the mid-1880s, the Japan district was ready to become a full conference. In anticipation of greater local autonomy and because the Japanese already represented a majority in the district court, many Canadian missionaries were apprehensive at the prospect of being subject to their Japanese colleagues. In response, the Methodist General Conference in Canada in 1886 permitted the creation of mission councils to handle local matters in foreign fields. Given this authority, the missionaries organized the Japan Mission Council, with Macdonald as secretary-treasurer, to serve as a buffer between the church courts in Japan and the missionaries. It stationed missionaries, administered funds, and reported to the Canadian headquarters. The council continued to function until the mission was closed in 1941 because of World War II.[22]

Over its history, Canadian Methodism supplied forty-seven missionaries to Japan, several of whom remained after the formation of the United Church of Canada. The Methodist mission combined traditional evangelizing with moral reform, social service, and humanitarian activities. For instance, the Reverend and Mrs Daniel MacKenzie opened an orphanage for boys in 1905 in the important garrison town of Kanazawa. This institution complemented the Woman's Missionary Society orphanage established there in 1893 and the missionary board's other orphanage at Shizuoka. The missionaries were also increasingly active in urban reform, temperance work, and settlement houses.[23]

However, above all the Methodists emphasized secondary and university education and theological training for the Japanese. These priorities again reflected their interest in converting the middle and upper classes and fostering a sound native leadership. In 1883 the mission board began to raise money to purchase property in Tokyo for a boy's school and university. It opened Toyo Eiwa Gakko Kwaisha in the Azabu district in 1884. Within a year it had 150 students and would grow to an enrolment of over 500 by 1902, when it was obliged to close. In 1898 the Japanese government, in yet another anti-foreign move, forbade the holding of Christian services or the teaching of Christianity, except as an ethical system, in accredited schools. Rather than abandon their principles, the Methodists closed the middle school at Azabu. In addition to supporting their own schools, the missionaries also helped to pay for the land and salaries for English-language schools such as the one established in 1889 at Kanazawa. However, success fluctuated with the ability of the students to secure academic standing in government schools and universities.[24]

By the early 1880s, the Canadian church also recognized the need for a Methodist theological seminary. In the near future, the Japanese must be prepared to run their own independent church; most missionaries did not anticipate a permanent role in Japan. The original approach to training, which had relied on a course of study and practical experience in the field, was not satisfactory for modern Methodism. Rather than establishing a joint school with the American Episcopal Methodists, the Canadians opened their own theological facility with eighteen students in December 1884 in conjunction with their educational work at Azabu. Canadian missionaries, such as Arthur Borden, also continued to share in the theological teaching at Aoyama Gakuin. As well, although the Methodist church was hesitant about training Japanese ministers in Canada, a few did receive scholarships to attend Victoria University in Toronto.[25]

By the twentieth century, there was a growing debate in Canadian Methodist circles over whether to locate their educational work in Tokyo or move to a smaller centre. In 1889 the American Methodist Episcopal Church, South had established Kwansei Gakuin in Kōbe, and in 1910 the Canadian Methodists became equal partners in the large, multifaceted institution. By 1922 it had grown to 850 students in the middle school, 750 in the college department, and 30 in the theological seminary. Ten years later Kwansei Gakuin became a fully accredited university. The Canadian missionary educator Cornelius Bates was dean of the college department from its opening in 1912 until 1920, when he began his distinguished twenty-year term as president.[26]

This brief survey hardly does justice to the missionaries' dedicated service. At the same time, their story is reminiscent of the original missionaries to British America, who, while working in a sometimes fractious relationship with the local church, believed their parent authorities never understood local conditions. The Japan mission always suffered from a lack of financial support considering the high cost of living, the need for a respectable presence in order to make a good impression for Christianity, and especially the immensity of the task. In particular, wages for the Japanese pastors were embarrassingly low, and many Canadian missionaries were hired by Japanese schools because they would work more cheaply than Japanese teachers.

However, the missionaries rarely appreciated the financial woes facing Methodism at home. As early as 1876, the costs of the Japan mission had quadrupled, while two years later the mission board had an accumulated debt of nearly $120,000. To save money, the board suggested that the mission join the American Methodist operations, but this idea was defeated by General Conference. The board was also obliged to oppose cooperation in theological education with the Episcopal Methodists in 1882 because it could not afford to commit future resources which might not be available. Such action could lead to embarrassment. Although financial conditions did improve, there was never sufficient money to meet the expectations of the overseas missionaries.[27]

Money was only one of the sources of friction between the missionaries in the field and the executive in Toronto. The Mission Council and Sutherland soon began contending for control of the Japan mission. Sutherland jealously guarded his authority and especially the executive's control of mission finances. Most missionaries believed that Davidson Macdonald was simply Sutherland's local agent and that the two were working to subvert the Central Tabernacle and the influence of the council in directing mission affairs. They also maintained that Macdonald was pushing missionaries into the field before they were properly trained in the Japanese language and that he sided with the WMS missionaries against the best interests of the Mission Council. In 1894 the council elected Eber Crummy, rather than Macdonald, as its secretary-treasurer, but Macdonald refused to turn over the books. This development led to a public airing of the troubles and widespread, acrimonious recriminations.[28]

Sutherland therefore recalled Charles Eby, the leader of the anti-Macdonald forces, and refused to send Francis Cassidy back to Japan after his furlough (he would later serve in Japan with the American Methodists). In 1895 the mission board in Toronto investigated and cleared Macdonald, but not before it had seriously questioned Sutherland's handling of the dispute, especially his recalling of missionaries without specific charges and his attack on Eby's character. Nevertheless, D.R. MacKenzie, Eber Crummy, Harper Coates, J.G. Dunlop, William Elliott, and John MacArthur resigned claiming they no longer had the confidence of the mission authorities. All were Eby supporters and most had come out as part of his self-supporting band. The board accepted Crummy's resignation, but the others later recanted and promised not to disturb internal mission harmony. Although the affair hurt relations with the native Japanese church, by the end of the century, internal calm had returned.[29]

Despite the role played by the Canadian missionaries, they were not the principal promoters of Christianity in Japan. The missionaries themselves acknowledged, "It was the work and devotion of the Japanese pastors and laity that was the real spearhead of the work of the Canadian mission."[30] This was inevitable considering the small number of missionaries, the shortage of resources, the difficulties with language, and the restrictions on foreigners regarding travel, residency, and ownership of property. Also, because the Japanese owned the property and ran the schools and other institutions, they were obliged to handle much of the administration and to deal with the local and central government authorities. Very early, therefore, the Canadians were forced to rely heavily on the local workers and assign a great deal of independence to their evangelizing.

Soon after the mission opened, Japanese preachers, who were trained in the same way as native preachers in Canada, began evangelizing the neighbouring areas and developing class meetings and circuit structures. In 1881 Davidson Macdonald ordained the first four Japanese itinerants, and within two years, eight Japanese were serving on the mission circuits. As the number

of Japanese ministers increased, they went from assisting Canadian missionaries to running their own local churches and evangelistic campaigns. Moreover, as more Japanese were converted, a dedicated laity emerged that was
anxious to administer its own affairs. Ever sensitive to slights upon their nationalism or to suggestions of their inferiority, the Japanese did not accept advice easily. Although not financially self-supporting, the Japanese mission was
raising an increasing proportion of it own costs and looked for every opportunity to advance its independence.[31]

In 1889 the Methodist church finally established the Japan Conference, with
three districts and a measure of local autonomy. However, while the missionaries remained members of this Conference, they retained a substantial degree of
independence from it. Their salaries and pensions were supplied from Canada
and they were subject to discipline only from their home conferences. Furthermore, the Mission Council continued to administer the mission grants. Such a
division of power would remain a constant and considerable irritant in church
relations and aggravated the problems the Mission Council was having with its
own executive in Canada. Macdonald was elected president of Conference annually from 1889 until 1898. Although the Japanese wished to lead their Conference, they had great personal respect for him and were divided internally
over a Japanese candidate. Gradually, however, the Japanese ministers and lay
leaders assumed greater control over church affairs. In 1901 Yoshiyasu Hiraiwa
was selected as the first Japanese president. He had been born in Tokyo in 1855
into the samurai class and was converted at age twenty while studying science at
the Imperial University. After training under George Cochran, he became pastor of the Tokyo Methodist congregations and evangelized in some of the outlying districts before his ordination in 1881. He spent a year preaching and
lecturing in Canada in 1887. A true pioneer in the Japanese church, Hiraiwa
remained a devout and respected Christian leader until his death in 1933.[32]

It was only a matter of time before a national Japanese Methodist church
was established, especially since the other foreign Protestant denominations
had moved in that direction. Any such organization, however, only made
sense if it included the various foreign Methodist missions in Japan. Discussions on creating a unified, independent church had begun in the early
1880s, and the Canadian Methodist General Conference accepted the proposal in 1886 and again in 1890. But the independence movement was delayed by the unwillingness of the American Methodists to accept the idea.
They were particularly concerned about the development of an episcopacy in
the new church, and their position reflected divisive issues at home as much
as in Japan. In addition, while the North American general conferences and
the missionaries in the field always assumed that an independent church was
advantageous and inevitable, many Americans and Canadians felt the Japanese were not ready to lead their own church. Indeed, some were never convinced that the time would ever be right. In part, this attitude was based on
racial stereotypes and assumptions of Oriental inferiority and immorality.
Although Japan was often complimented on being a progressive, Western nation, far in advance of China, India, or Korea, deep-seated misunderstanding,
ignorance, and intolerance still coloured relations.[33]

There was also worry that the Japanese ministers were not soundly trained in Methodist doctrine, could not be trusted to present an accurate Christian theology, and had little sense of financial restraint, trusteeship, or steward-ship. Alexander Sutherland was hesitant at least partially because he wished to direct mission operations personally and did not believe either the Cana-dian missionaries or the Japanese should challenge his authority; he wanted to abolish both the Japan Conference and the Mission Council. At the same time, many missionaries worried about their role in a national church. In 1898 George Meacham argued, "They will take from them [Canadians] the superintendency, make them mere assistants to the Japanese pastors who ... are very much their inferiors in piety, learning and experience."[34] Again, these attitudes were reminiscent of the hostile relations between early British and Canadian Methodist church authorities.

However, as the Japanese proved themselves effective evangelists, especially during the revivals that swept across the country during the early twentieth century, and the size and complexity of the Conference increased, the Cana-dian and American Methodist churches recognized that changes must be made. In 1901 the six Methodist connexions with missionaries in Japan met to discuss the formation of a united, independent Japanese church. But negotia-tions were again delayed by the withdrawal from discussions of the three smaller American groups. Nevertheless, tensions continued to hurt the effec-tiveness of the mission work. For instance, in 1902 the Canadian missionary W.W. Prudham was formally charged with sexual misconduct, although few be-lieved he was guilty. His trial took place in Hamilton Conference, not in Japan. Such an insult to the fairness and authority of the Japan Conference reflected badly on Methodism among converts and non-Christians alike. Canadian Methodism would never have accepted such a procedure from foreign mis-sionaries serving within its jurisdiction.[35]

These developments were also set against the Canadian Methodists' grow-ing appreciation of the international status that Japan had achieved. The missionaries clearly favoured Japan in its wars with China and Russia and recognized that it was the key to opening Asia to Christianity and Western civilization. During the Sino-Japanese conflict, the *Christian Guardian* had re-ported, "The war goes well and there is hope that Corea [*sic*] will soon be liberated and opened to the gospel." A month later, it commented, "The Christian who has learned to look for the hand of God in national affairs, must see in the victories of Japan the breaking down of a Chinese wall for the progress of Christ's kingdom."[36] The *Missionary Outlook* added, "China has an object lesson which will teach her, as nothing else can, the superiority of Western ideas and civilization."[37]

The decisive victory over Russia in 1905 also demonstrated how far Japan had advanced. Although Russia was a Western, Christian nation, Canadian missionaries considered it corrupt and intolerant and therefore identified God's presence with Japan. This support was made tangible by the extensive relief measures the missionaries undertook during the two wars. The opening of the orphanage at Kanazawa in 1905 especially for the families of the mili-tary was appreciated by the government. Earlier, the Canadian Methodists had been quicker than the Buddhists or Shintoists in establishing relief programs for the victims of the extensive earthquakes in 1891 and for the needy during the Sino-Japanese War. Such actions had done much to moderate anti-Canadian sentiments.[38]

Finally, in 1906 the mainstream Canadian and American Methodist churches agreed to create a Japanese church. The Nippon Methodist Kyokai was formally established at impressive services in Japan in 1907. It united ten ordained missionaries from Canada and forty from the United States with ninety-five Japanese ministers and included fifty-eight unordained men and eighty-three Bible women. A total of sixty-nine Canadian and American WMS missionaries were also operating within the church's jurisdiction. The Canadian component totalled 3,318 members, twenty-three ministers, and twenty-nine missionaries, while the church as a whole reported 9,403 members, 254 Sunday schools with some 18,000 students, and a significant institutional infrastructure, including church buildings, schools, orphanages, and a publishing house. Bishop Yoitsu Honda of the American Methodist Episcopal Church was selected as the first general superintendent.

Born into an important samurai family from northern Japan in 1848, Honda had been sent to Yokohama to learn Western languages and culture. While there he became a Christian and organized a small, independent congregation of recent converts. Four years later, in 1876, he brought his followers into the American Methodist Episcopal mission and continued as their pastor. He became principal in 1887 of Aoyama Gakuin University and later served as president until 1907. He had studied in the United States for two years before his ordination in 1890 and had also been elected a member of the provincial government. Considered the foremost personality in the founding of Methodism in Japan and exercising a formative influence on Japanese moral and spiritual life, Honda was largely responsible for forcing the North American missions to create the independent Japanese Methodist church in 1907, and he led its councils until his death in 1912. Yoshiyasu Hiraiwa was also soon raised to the episcopal ranks and made president of Kwansei Gakuin College. Foreign missionaries retained their semi-autonomous relationship with the new church, but better cooperation and more sympathetic understanding quickly developed on both sides.[39]

The Japan mission, however, was not a male preserve. In many ways, the activities of the Methodist Woman's Missionary Society were even more remarkable than those of male colleagues from Canada. Beginning with Martha Cartmell, a thirty-six-year-old teacher from Hamilton, Ontario, who served for two terms from 1882 to 1887 and 1892 to 1898, seventy-four Canadian WMS missionaries laboured in Japan. After language training, Cartmell organized and started teaching in what became the Toyo Eiwa Girl's School at Azabu in Tokyo in 1884. Both the mission board and the Woman's Missionary Society recognized the real need to educate and train girls and young women. It was the surest method of creating a body of Japanese women who could transform the households and therefore shape the future of Japan. By 1887, under the direction of Eliza Spencer, the female residential school at Azabu had 127 boarders, 65 of whom had become Christians.[40]

Following this success, and at the request of local Japanese, the WMS opened a residential school at Shizuoka in 1887 to complement the men's mission established since 1874. Two years later the society also opened a school at Kofu under Agnes Wintemute and in 1898 established a fourth residential school in Nagano as part of the general expansion of Methodist operations in central Honshū. The schools were actually owned and operated by the Japanese and had both local instructors and Canadians, who were assigned and paid by the WMS. Since there was a tuition fee, the schools were nearly self-supporting, but enrolment was generally limited to the daughters of the more prosperous classes. In 1918 these schools were fully accredited by the Japanese government. As well as the residential schools, the WMS operated several day schools and eleven kindergartens in the missionary districts of Tokyo, Shizuoka, Kofu, Kanazawa, Nagano, and finally Nagoya, which the Canadian Methodists assumed from the American Methodists after 1920.[41]

The Canadian WMS also participated in the Woman's Christian College, the Yokohama Training School for Christian Workers, and the Kindergarten Training School at Ueda. The Woman's Christian College was founded cooperatively in 1918 by the Protestant churches in Japan and offered courses in English and Japanese. Female higher education had never been a priority with the Japanese government, and foreign missionaries were allowed to pursue this activity with greater freedom. The WMS under Martha Cartmell had also set up a training program for local Bible women in the hope that they would be able to bring Christianity more easily and directly into the lives of their fellow citizens. After a three-year course of study, Bible women assisted in evangelizing, visited homes, and worked in the Sunday schools and other Methodist institutions under the supervision of WMS or male missionaries. The society paid them a modest salary. By the twentieth century, the Protestant churches who used this native female ministry had established the Yokohama Training School for Christian Workers and the Kindergarten Training School to enlarge and systematize the training program.[42]

While education remained of paramount importance, the WMS was also involved in a broad range of evangelistic and social-service activities. In fact, it was generally more successful than the male missionaries in these programs. Daniel Norman claimed in 1911 that while the men were hesitant to develop programs or were waiting for Japanese leadership, the WMS operated female orphanages in Kanazawa and Tokyo, ran classes in cooking, nutrition, and household sciences, visited hospitals, and promoted female temperance. After World War I, it gave priority to evangelizing in the factories and slums, relief work, running nursing and public-health clinics, providing hostels for working women, and ending crime, prostitution, and urban poverty.[43]

Although the WMS worked closely with the other missionaries and the indigenous Japanese church, it ran an entirely independent organization. Its missionaries were never asked to participate in the Mission Council and had no status in the Japan Conference or its successor, the Japan Methodist church. Because the society raised its own money and had a highly efficient budgeting and administrative system, it never required financial assistance from either body. Despite the formation of a WMS Council in Japan in 1888, the executive in Canada maintained rigid control over mission operations. As a result, the implementation of programs was sometimes slower, but they were more likely to be sustained. The executive also jealously guarded its own autonomy and strove to insure that its missionaries in the field operated with a similar freedom. Doing so was not always easy; friction arose on several missions between the WMS and male missionaries. The men assumed that the WMS was there to assist them and was subservient to their authority. But the women refused to be at the beck and call of their male colleagues or to relinquish independence in the field. A meeting of the WMS Japan Council in July 1892 failed to resolve the difficulties, and relations continued to deteriorate. Over the following years, the internal problems of the men's Mission Council and its relationship to the central board in Toronto and to the local Japan Conference also involved attempts to pre-empt the WMS.[44]

Much of the criticism of the WMS centred on Mrs Eliza (Spencer) Large who chaired the women's council and was particularly outspoken in her attacks on the actions of the men. She had originally come to Japan in 1885, and her work as principal of the Azabu girl's school had been considered so exceptional that she was allowed to remain even after her marriage to the Reverend Thomas Alfred Large in 1887. Three years later her husband was murdered and she was badly injured by burglars, but after a furlough to recuperate, she returned to Tokyo and continued to play a major role in local church affairs. Although the female missionaries saw her as an heroic defender of their rights, many of her male colleagues considered her the source of ongoing friction. When the mission board met in 1895 to resolve its various problems in Japan, it asked the WMS to recall Mrs Large. The society's executive agreed, despite protests from Japan, in order to calm the waters. But it refused to allow its missionaries to assume merely an auxiliary role, despite the wishes of Sutherland and several male missionaries.[45]

Although relations generally improved after 1895, the presence of strong personalities and the close working conditions inevitably meant that tensions would never disappear. The male missionaries never abandoned their desire to have the WMS work under the Japan Mission Council, and by the twentieth century this question was entwined with a movement to increase the status and official role for missionary wives. They had been the first women to labour in Japan and had continued to serve in evangelistic and educational work without pay or recognition. As well, many were at least as well educated and competent as the WMS missionaries, and several had been missionaries before their marriages. However, pleas to the mission board for official recognition and financial assistance so that they could hire domestic help to free themselves for service went unanswered. Since these women were not responsible to the WMS, and it feared they would side with their husbands and draw the female missionaries into the Mission Council orbit, the society was not prepared to grant them official status either.[46]

Despite such turmoil, the WMS continued to carry out dynamic and effective work in Japan. Because it was independent and did not seek to dominate the native Japanese work or compete in church affairs, the society had more harmonious relations with the Japan Conference and its successor, the Japan

Methodist church. Moreover, unlike the male missionaries, the Japanese did not attempt to dictate to the WMS or view it as subsidiary to their work. Instead, both laboured as natural allies in their somewhat distinct specialities. The WMS was also successful because it committed more time to language training than the men did. As a result, its women developed greater fluency and comprehension. Furthermore, as a group of females, the WMS was more often ignored or exempted from restrictions placed by the Japanese government on foreign groups.[47]

The first decade of the twentieth century was a time of readjustment for the increasingly independent Japanese church and the Canadian missionaries. To many Japanese, these Canadians tended to be overly narrow and inward-looking. They remained foreigners in an exotic land, continuing to eat Canadian food, live in Canadian-style housing, play Canadian games, and associate most freely with non-Japanese. They took their holidays together in "a little Canada" away from Japanese life. Such actions created suspicion and limited the ability of the Canadians to function in Japanese society. In 1913 the missionaries established the Canada Academy in Kōbe. Originally a high school for missionary children, it later offered a full education from kindergarten to grade thirteen, based on the Ontario education system, and drew children from the local multiracial diplomatic and business community.[48]

Over the same period, the Japanese church saw the actions of the Canadians as a potential threat to their autonomy or to their national pride. In 1908, remarking on the desire of the Japanese church to proceed without Canadian assistance, Robert Armstrong wrote, "Our pastor is a very typical Japanese. He says 'I am not anti-foreign, but I think the very presence of the foreigner in the work of evangelization in Japan compromises us native workers.'"[49] The Japanese Methodists were particularly sensitive about their missions to Korea and their training of visiting Chinese and Koreans in Japan. These parts of Asia were increasingly coming under Japanese influence and in some cases were part of the Japanese empire. The Japanese Methodist church therefore believed it should control their evangelization.

However, after a relatively short period of adjustment surrounding the creation of the independent Japanese Methodist church, relations among the WMS, the indigenous church, and the male missionaries gradually improved. This change reflected in part the greater acceptance of foreigners and a desire to modernize and enter the world community of nations by the Japanese government and in part a new confidence and trust in cooperation by both the Japanese and Canadian Methodists themselves. With independence, the Japanese church gained a new self-assurance and was less fearful of accepting advice. And with its more aggressive evangelizing, it recognized that it still needed personnel and financial assistance and that it had much to learn from the missionaries.[50]

After some hesitation, the Canadian Methodist church again committed itself fully to the work in Japan. In this, it was assisted by the increased personnel and financial resources supplied by Methodists in Canada. While trying not to offend, the mission board and the WMS accelerated their placement of missionaries, especially in positions auxiliary to the Japanese church. The

Canadian missionary contingent rose from nine in 1910 to twenty-one in 1914. The confidence was at least partially justified by the increased status that Christianity had achieved in Japan during this period. This new respectability was perhaps best symbolized by the government-sponsored Three Religions Conference of 1913. In arranging formal discussions among Shintoists, Buddhists, and Christians, the authorities appeared to be placing Christianity on an equal footing with the dominant religions in the country. The Methodists assumed that the Japanese leaders were also searching for a more profound moral and ethical base for their culture.[51]

Over the same period, more missionaries came to appreciate the depth and richness of Japanese culture. For instance, Harper Coates became an expert on the Buddhist reformer Honen, while Cornelius Bates studied Japanese philosophy and Robert Armstrong helped explain Confucianism, Buddhism, and Shintoism to previously sceptical North Americans. Although such interest demonstrated a natural maturation of missionary experience, it also reflected a certain disillusionment with Western society. In the aftermath of World War I, it was more difficult to espouse notions of Western moral or racial superiority. Missionaries were less sure of their civilizing role. None the less, by the 1920s the Canadian Methodists still believed that they had provided critical service in the great mission to evangelize the world.[52]

### CHINA

During the 1880s, the Methodist church had contemplated opening a mission in France since it already had experience in French evangelism in Canada; later India, Formosa, and the West Indies were considered but quickly rejected. China was the magnet. Japan had provided a window on the needs and opportunities for Asian missions, but for Canadians the great, lost land was China. "A World open to the Gospel of Christ, but with two-thirds of its population yet unreached by the missionary ... give rise to questions touching Christian fidelity, zeal and methods ... A timid, worldly-wise policy must give place to a fearless faith that undertakes great things of God."[53] China represented half the world's unevangelized population. Until it was saved, there would be no hope of fully establishing Christ's kingdom on earth.

The great Methodist union of 1884 and the subsequent religious revival that swept across Canada helped infuse the church with a renewed sense of optimism and enthusiasm to save the world. In particular, the desire for more overseas missions was also focused on China by the earnest and intrepid Hudson Taylor, who was on a recruiting tour for his independent, non-denominational China Inland Mission. In 1888 he left Toronto with thirteen Canadian men and women and two Americans committed to enlarge his evangelistic crusade. In addition to the 1888 contingent and the six Canadians who had earlier joined his international mission, the Canadian Presbyterians had opened a mission in Formosa in 1870 and north Honan in 1888, and they would enter Korea in 1893 and south China nine years later.[54]

A few Canadian Methodists had also served with distinction in China for many years under the American Methodist Episcopal Church. For example,

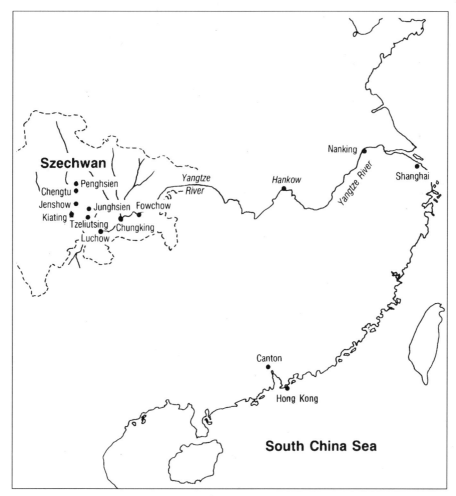

Map 2    Canadian Methodist missions in China

Adelaide Gilliland of Athens, Ontario, travelled with her American husband, Virgil Hart, to China in 1865, and the two served in central China and Szechwan (Sichuan) until ill health forced Virgil's retirement in 1888. After graduating in medicine from the University of Michigan in 1876, Dr Leonora Howard, also of Athens, Ontario, joined the Episcopal Methodist mission in 1877 and opened a hospital at Tientsin in northern China. In 1884 she married the Reverend Alexander King of the London Missionary Society. Howard was the second woman doctor sent out to China by any denomination, and she pioneered the field of medical treatment for women. She also made important contacts among China's aristocratic élites.[55]

Finally, in 1890 the Canadian Methodist General Conference authorized the formation of a mission in China. The following summer, Virgil and Adelaide Hart and their grown daughter, Estelle, the Reverend and Mrs George Hartwell, Dr and Mrs Omar Kilborn, Dr David Stevenson, and Miss Amelia

Mrs Eliza Spencer Large (d. 1933) and Japanese Christian women. (UCA, P3533)

Central Tabernacle, Tokyo. The centre of Canadian Methodist Mission operations in Japan. (UCA, uncat.)

First Canadian Methodist missionaries to Szechwan, 1891. (UCA, uncat.)

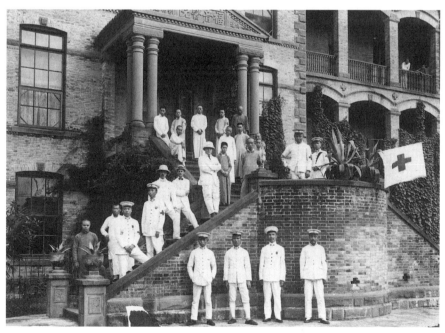

Men's Hospital, Chengtu, Szechwan, 1918. (UCA, uncat.)

Brown journeyed to Shanghai in anticipation of their final settlement at Chengtu, the capital of Szechwan. Amelia Brown had been sent by the WMS as a nurse, but she retired from the society when, after a year in China, she married David Stevenson. At the instigation of Mrs Hart, who had convinced her husband to come out of retirement to lead the new mission, the church decided to focus on the fertile province of Szechwan, which had a population of some sixty million densely packed into an area smaller than Ontario. It was bounded by Tibet on the west, and it contained the eastern terminus of the fabled silk road to Asia Minor; only the Yangtze River cut through the mountain ranges to break Szechwan's isolation from the rest of China.[56]

The two-thousand-mile trip up river from Shanghai to Chengtu took almost three months. The only real break was at Chungking, where the London Missionary Society and the Episcopal Methodist missions offered some Western comforts. However, the Canadians were delayed in Shanghai by anti-foreign riots in the interior and did not reach Chengtu until May 1892. At that time, the city had Roman Catholic, Episcopal Methodist, Quaker, and Baptist missionaries, as well as representatives from the China Inland Mission, but the Canadian Methodist force quickly came to represent the greatest commitment to the region. Upon arriving, it leased property and began construction of a mission house, chapel, schoolroom, and medical dispensary, although the dispensary work had to be curtailed since it left no time for language study.[57]

In 1893 James Endicott and Dr Mather Hare from the missionary society and Dr Alfretta Gifford and Sara Brackbill from the WMS joined the force in Chengtu. With these reinforcements, the mission expanded to the city of Kiating one hundred miles south of Chengtu in 1894. As well, since the contingent was now large enough, it organized a West China Mission Council to administer local affairs. Such a council was even more critical for China than for Japan because of the isolation, the time required to communicate home, and the hostile surroundings. The WMS was not involved in the Mission Council, but formed its own council in 1900.

Nevertheless, the two mission groups cooperated much more readily than their counterparts in Japan. By the end of 1894, in fact, the WMS executive in Canada was somewhat dismayed by the fate of its missionaries, reporting, "Our efforts to begin work in a second field, China, seem thus far to have consisted chiefly in providing helpmeets for lonely members of the General Mission."[58] Of the first three women sent out, Brown had married Stevenson, and Gifford had married Kilborn, whose first wife had died shortly after arriving in China. Dr Gifford-Kilborn did remain with the WMS on half pay for her first five-year term in China since she operated a hospital for women and children. As well, Dr Hare married Estelle Hart. Thus, from its inception, the China mission was bound together by formidable ties of marriage and kinship.

In addition to the isolation, mission work in China was extremely dangerous. As well as facing normal medical problems, the missionaries suffered from extremes in climate and unsanitary conditions, which led to dysentery, pneumonia, and severe fevers. Cholera and smallpox carried off several of the missionaries and forced others to recuperate for extended periods. Psychological distress and nervous breakdowns sometimes accentuated the physical difficulties. For some protection, as well as a break from the tension and the heat of Chinese summers, the Canadian missionaries retreated to Mount Omei, one of the four sacred mountains of China, where they established friendly relations with the Buddhist priests and developed a vacation compound. At other times, the missionaries visited Japan and spent furloughs in Canada after every term of service.[59]

Lawlessness, rioting, and revolution, however, posed much more significant threats to mission operations. Just as work was beginning in Chengtu and Kiating, the missionaries were forced to flee back to Shanghai for protection from anti-foreign rioting spurred by the Sino-Japanese War. The uprising arrived in Chengtu in late May 1895, and the missionaries did not reach safety until July 4. Upon their return in early 1896, they discovered that their mission buildings had been destroyed. They immediately began to rebuild, with compensation for their losses from the Chinese government and new recruits from Canada. The architecture maintained the Chinese style in order not to antagonize the local inhabitants.[60]

However, the Canadian Methodist missionaries were never secure from harassment, banditry, or personal attacks. Periodically, these were overtaken by nationwide anti-foreign campaigns, civil wars, or revolutions. In protest against European control of natural resources and the railways and fanned by discontent over the high cost of rice, a powerful popular uprising against foreigners in general and Christians in particular spread out from north China in 1898. The movement was sanctioned by the Empress Dowager and led by bands of "righteous and harmonious fists" (*I-ho ch'uan*), or to Europeans, the Boxers. Over the following two years, the Boxer Rebellion destroyed much of the church property in China, and the Boxers murdered nearly 250 missionaries and over 30,000 Chinese Christians. Isolated from the initial troubles, the Canadians in Szechwan remained at their posts until they were ordered to Shanghai in 1900. When they returned the following year, they found their property intact, but local bands of Boxers continued to attack Christians. Only by using drastic methods did the Chinese army bring order to the region by 1903.[61]

After nearly a decade of relative calm, the Revolution of 1911 posed another serious threat to mission work. No longer willing to tolerate the decadent and ineffectual Manchu regime, Dr Sun Yat-sen in the south and General Yüan Shih-k'ai in the north overthrew the new emperor and attempted to establish a republic. This time the outbreak began in Szechwan in the neighbourhood of the Canadian missions. Although the rebels were anxious to protect foreigners and the native Christian church, the missionaries feared a return to the excesses of the Boxers and for the third time in their short history fled to Shanghai. During the trip down river, Richard Orlando Jolliffe's five-year-old son, John, was killed by a stray shot from the shore.

While some missionaries at first were optimistic that the Revolution would improve Chinese life and that the new Kuomintang government would perhaps even "usher in a modern Commonwealth," others recognized that "the Drama is only just commencing ... It is easy enough to pull down the Manchu Dynasty but quite another thing to establish a Republic ... Quarrellings amongst the respective 'Presidents' ... may be the order of the day soon, &

then looting, firing property, & thieving, & plunder follow."[62] The Revolution led to years of civil war and lawlessness as local warlords carved out their own fiefdoms. With only limited centralized control, the country was again rocked by strong anti-foreign sentiment in 1919 as a result of the perceived mistreatment of China in the Treaty of Versailles and again from 1922 until after 1925, when Christian schools and hospitals were attacked and the missionaries were obliged to leave.[63]

Despite these troubles, the Methodists never gave up hope. After returning to the mission in 1896, the Harts, Endicotts, and Hares had gone to Kiating, while the Hartwells, Kilborns, and the newly arrived Dr and Mrs W.E. Smith were joined by Sara Brackbill, Jennie Ford, and the following year, Dr Maud Killam and Mary Foster at Chengtu. Despite Ford's death in 1897 after only two years' service, there was a large Canadian force optimistically engaged in mission work. By the time of the Boxer uprisings, the missionary society had seven missionaries and their wives and was beginning work in Omei, about twenty-three miles from Kiating. This work, however, was later turned over to the China Inland Mission. The WMS was building a school, orphanage, chapel, hospital, and home in its three-and-a-half-acre compound in Chengtu and was expanding its operation at Kiating.[64]

In 1905 the Methodists began missions in Junghsien, Jenshow, and Penghsien, although the last was undeveloped until 1907. The missionary society had eleven missionaries on duty and one on furlough, and the WMS had an additional ten missionaries. The work before 1907, however, was meagre in comparison to what followed. With the great success of the Young People's Forward Movement and especially the Laymen's Missionary Movement, hitherto undreamed-of resources became available for overseas work. Furthermore, Methodist businessmen in Canada such as Newton Wesley Rowell, Alfred E. Ames, Henry Fudger, and Joseph Flavelle were taking over the direction of the mission board, reducing Alexander Sutherland's conservative influence, and leading the way into a new era of expansion.[65]

By the end of 1907, the missionary society had twenty-two missionaries with eighteen wives and the WMS had eleven labourers. In that year, Penghsien was fully occupied and work at Tzeliutsing begun. In 1908 the west China mission field was divided among the Protestant churches in order to eliminate competition. The Canadian territory, centred on Chengtu, contained about 14,000,000 Chinese. In the same year, the missionaries commenced work in Luchow and two years later assumed the London Missionary Society's missions in or near Chungking. By 1910 there were fifty-three missionaries from the general society and twenty-five from the WMS operating, with a combined budget of about $90,000. Except during World War I, the following years witnessed significant growth and the elaboration of a sound institutional structure. In 1925 combined expenditures reached nearly $400,000, and there were thirty-one WMS missionaries on duty and another seven on furlough, while the missionary society had eighty more, most with wives. In addition to over sixty outstations, the church had extensive operations at Chengtu, Kiating, Junghsien, Jenshow, Penghsien, Tzeliutsing, Luchow, Chungking, Chunghow, and Fowchow.[66]

Statistics, however, tell only part of the story. The Methodist church was deeply committed to a "preaching, teaching and healing" mission, and these elements would be quickly augmented by a massive printing and publishing business. While all aspects of mission work were interrelated and all at least initially aimed at Christianizing and civilizing the Chinese, from early in the twentieth century, direct evangelism was the specific priority of nearly one-half of the ordained and WMS missionaries. Churches were constructed in the missionary compounds, but although many flocked there, especially in the aftermath of anti-foreign riots, they appeared to have only a limited influence in developing firm members. Even the WMS, which believed real progress could not be achieved unless women were converted, had little real impact with its programs of catechism and Sunday school classes for women after church services.

The evangelists relied more on going out to the people. They preached and distributed Christian literature to curious Chinese from street chapels, rented rooms, and storefronts. Market days were especially important for attracting and evangelizing large crowds. However, even these activities were never very successful. Traditional emotional appeals were generally misunderstood, and the Chinese ridiculed and often harassed these men and women. Evangelism could only succeed if it was practical as well as spiritual. Those who did join the church were generally from the lower classes and rarely comprehended the intricacies of Christian theology or polity. Moreover, the missionaries were always suspicious of "rice" Christians who only joined for immediate economic advantage. It was also apparent that if individuals became Christians, they were usually ostracized from their community and even their families. As a result, the evangelists encouraged whole families to join the church together. During the second decade of the twentieth century, membership remained about 1,700, and during the 1920s it fluctuated at just over 3,000, although a significantly larger number took advantage of Methodist facilities.[67]

The second component of Methodist mission work also began as soon as the missionaries reached Chengtu. On the basis of the experience among native Canadians and in Japan, the mission fostered education as a critical prerequisite to intelligent conversion. R.B. McAmmond noted that "when the light has entered his intellect as to what this Gospel means and what it brings, then I can lead that man to his knees."[68] Education was also essential to the practical social-service work that became a priority among twentieth-century liberal missionaries. The first day schools were disrupted by riots, but they still carried on under Chinese teachers during the absence of Canadians. The WMS and the missionary society generally coordinated their educational programs to reach as many young people as possible.

The real breakthrough came in 1905 when the Manchu government abolished the traditional élitist Confucian examinations necessary for government employment and encouraged the creation of a Western-style education system. In response, the various missionary authorities in west China united to create the West China Educational Union in 1906. With significant leadership from Edward Wilson Wallace, who served as principal of a boys' school as well as an active representative on the Educational Union committee, the new system established graded schools, uniform texts, standard examinations, and teacher certification. Its purpose was "to search out the best in Western education practice, to retain what is of true educational value in the time-honoured method of the Chinese, [and] ... mark the whole with the impress of Christianity."[69] It was assumed that this approach would help to modernize China by creating a new democratic élite that would eventually guide the nation out of its backward condition. By 1925 the Educational Union supervised some 32,000 students in west China.

The Canadian Methodist mission had by far the largest number of students enrolled of all the Protestant churches in the region. Beginning with Hartwell's small school in Chengtu, started in 1893 with twenty-nine pupils, and Brackbill's WMS girls' school, opened in 1896, the educational work had expanded rapidly. With the assistance of local Chinese Christian teachers, boardingschools developed in every main station, and over 125 day schools eventually carried the work to the small centres. Secondary schools were also opened in cooperation with the Episcopal Methodists and Quakers in several locations, and in 1909 a school for missionary children was started in Chengtu. Most surprising to the Chinese, the missionaries operated both primary and secondary schools for girls. Female students eventually received training as teachers and attended university. The schools taught a full range of arts and science courses as well as traditional Chinese subjects. To make the system work, the Canadian Methodists, under the authority of the West China Educational Union, ran a Normal School to train teachers.[70]

The Protestant missions also united to create a Western-style university. Acknowledging the need for a university as early as 1905, the Canadian Methodists prodded the Quakers, Baptists, and Episcopal Methodists into establishing West China Union University in Chengtu in 1908. It was inaugurated two years later, but because of Sun Yat-sen's revolution, did not offer classes in arts and science until 1913. The original sixty-acre site just outside the city eventually grew to over one hundred and fifty acres. The university was initially made up of four colleges representing the founding denominations, but it had expanded to more than twenty teaching buildings by the 1920s. A Faculty of Medicine was added in 1914, Religious Studies in 1915, and Education in 1918. A Faculty of Dentistry was created in 1920, and the formerly independent Pharmacy College begun by Edwin Meuser in 1918 joined as the Faculty of Pharmacy. In the same year, the Canadian Methodists' Virgil C. Hart Memorial College opened its permanent building. The university was incorporated in New York State in 1922, but gradually Chinese officials assumed supervision of its internal affairs.[71]

As well as preparing teachers and civil servants, higher education was essential for training a native clergy and a medical corps, and even for offering opportunities to women. Hundreds of students studied theology in the various separate programs run by the Protestant churches. In 1924 there were also seventy-five students preparing to become doctors, and they were soon serving in hospitals throughout China. After the WMS had lobbied the university officials in America and China for years, a woman's college was finally established in 1922. The WMS accepted the supervision and additional costs of the female students, and the first class of eight women began attending in 1924.

With its broad range of programs, West China Union University became a model for higher education throughout the country.[72]

The Methodist church also established a joint Publishing House and Book Room as a key partner in its educational and evangelistic mission. Originally begun by Virgil Hart when he brought presses back from Canada after his furlough in 1897, it was taken over in 1900 by James Endicott, who rapidly expanded its output. In 1904 he moved it from Kiating to spacious quarters in Chengtu. With Canadian pressmen and locally trained assistants to run the technical operations, the presses were soon supplying millions of pages annually in English, Miao, the language of the original indigenous west China population, Tibetan, and Chinese for Protestant missions all across China. Through its facilities, Bibles, tracts, magazines, and general Christian literature were made available at a relatively low cost.[73]

Of all the mission activities, however, the elaboration of Western medical facilities had the most immediate and dramatic impact on Chinese life. Originally, they were developed primarily as a means of attracting and converting the Chinese. Evangelizing was easiest among those who were facing possible death or who presented a captive audience while receiving treatment. According to Virgil Hart, medicine was "one of the best chisels ever devised to cleave the flinty mountain of heathenism."[74] However, the younger generation of medical missionaries were generally more concerned with the progress of society on earth than with purely spiritual matters. They were convinced that Western medicine answered a real human need and would help move China from the ranks of the backward nations of the world.

Both the WMS and the general missionary board developed hospitals at their main stations and an elaborate network of dispensaries and nursing stations throughout the region. Although most of these were quite small, Chengtu and Kiating eventually housed large and impressive facilities with a well-trained Canadian and Chinese staff. By 1925 there were thirty-two hospitals and dispensaries at Canadian missions, with over thirty male and female doctors. Thousands were treated annually and the medical work was especially critical during the many civil disturbances. The Canadians also supplied rare dental treatment and a skilled pharmacist who not only dispensed, but also prepared, pharmaceutical products. As well, the medical personnel promoted improved sanitary conditions and led public-health campaigns.[75]

Equally critical, the Methodists also instituted training programs for nurses, dentists, pharmacists, and doctors to prepare a future generation of skilled medical personnel who would spread the benefits of Western medicine to the entire population. Most medical education, even in North America, was still based on an apprenticeship system of hospital work, and this approach was instituted as soon as language problems were overcome. Although it continued to be the basis of training for nurses and other hospital workers, the Methodists soon after their arrival envisioned a large and modern medical college in Chengtu. While waiting for the resources to build this school, the Canadians cooperated with the other Protestant medical missionaries to produce a body of skilled local doctors, and when the Medical College opened in 1914, most of the doctors divided their time between teaching there and practising in the hospitals. Nevertheless, it was their hope that the Chinese would be able to assume both the medical work in the field and the basic training of new personnel.

At the same time, it was impossible to separate the Methodists' practical medical and educational programs from their attempts to institute social and moral reform. As well as traditional concerns such as intemperance, slothfulness, and dishonesty, the Methodists fought the evils of opium as both a medical and a social problem. A great deal of the medical treatment in fact dealt with drug overdoses and related suicide attempts. Therefore the church was eager to assist the government in implementing anti-opium legislation. In addition, all the Methodist missionaries were actively committed to improving family life, particularly the condition of women and children. As well as operating an orphanage in Chengtu, they condemned polygamy, abandoning female babies, and selling girls into prostitution. When the government outlawed the traditional practice of binding girls' feet, the missionaries helped to enforce the new law because of the greater freedom it gave to women. They also attempted to institute proper hygiene, Western household practices, and dietary reforms as a part of a comprehensive program for social reconstruction.[76]

In all the Methodist operations in China, the missionary society and the WMS functioned with little of the friction so apparent in Japan. Although they carefully maintained separate local administrative councils, their annual joint meetings helped prevent any overlap in activities and encouraged an integrated approach to problems and opportunities. The two groups also provided a united front in dealing with the Chinese and the other foreign mission organizations. This cooperation was made easier by the status given to wives of missionaries by the West China Mission Council. After 1900 they were invited to attend the meetings, and their advice regarding work with women and children was often adopted. Although they still had no official voting rights, their considerable contributions to mission operations could not be ignored, and in some instances they even received financial support for their labours.[77]

Most Canadian Methodist missionaries also recognized the critical need to develop an indigenous church. Not only would it relieve Canadians of much of the administrative and financial burden, but it would also answer anti-foreign criticism and promote legitimate nationalistic sentiments. The Methodists realized that real membership growth would not occur until the church was led by a native clergy. Unordained Chinese men had originally served as interpreters, but they gradually began to preach under missionary guidance and were particularly valuable in carrying Christianity to the outstations beyond the larger centres. After a decade of unfortunate, but unavoidable delay, the Methodists established their first systematic course of study for Chinese evangelists in 1904. Three years later, 34 licensed Chinese preachers were working under the auspices of the West China Mission Council, and this number rose to 45 by 1910 and to over 130 by 1925. As well, the WMS trained Bible women to assist in the Sunday schools and during visits to Chinese homes. In 1925, twenty-six Bible women were operating within the mission's jurisdiction. The West China Mission Council stationed the more exceptional male evangelists at the principal missions and also provided them with formal theological training, first at a theological institute founded in Chengtu and eventually at West China Union University. Finally, in 1918 the church ordained its first six Chinese ministers and stationed them throughout west China.[78]

The West China Mission Council had in 1908 begun organizing the general membership, setting up local church boards, and creating provisional district meetings. Over the years, it also held open conventions of native Christian leaders to encourage greater participation in the decision-making process. Although hesitant to proceed too rapidly, the missionaries did finally establish a quasi-independent Annual Conference for the Chinese church, or Mei Dao Hwei, during the 1920s and gradually assigned greater responsibility to native clergy and laity.[79] Of course, some missionaries were never convinced that the Chinese could manage their own affairs, but in retrospect, the Chinese Christian church proved to be extremely vital, adaptable, and resilient.

In both China and Japan, the general Methodist missionary society and the Woman's Missionary Society fulfilled a crucial role in laying the foundations for modern, national Christian churches. Their dynamic, socially progressive missions helped modernize these countries and led them, not always willingly, into the twentieth-century community of nations. The original goal of civilizing the world had been significantly modified, but the new churches were able to survive intense hostility, social turmoil, and oppressive regimes to provide meaningful spiritual and social benefits. Moreover, Canadian Methodists also benefited from the increased opportunity overseas missions provided for focusing and intensifying Christian service. Together these developments at home and abroad represent profound testimonies to the advantages of the great evangelistic and social-reform crusades undertaken by Canadian Methodism overseas.

# 13 Methodism and
## the Creation of a Moral Order

By the late nineteenth century, Canadian Methodists perceived themselves as members of the truly national church situated at the very heart of Canadian life, and they felt a deep responsibility not only to nurture and protect their own members, but also to transform the entire nation into a highly moral social order. All aspects of life were part of God's sacred domain and therefore legitimate subjects for Christian action. Moreover, the Methodist church optimistically believed that with dedicated and strenuous labour it could transform the corrupt dominion into a true kingdom of God. By using the most progressive means available, it therefore expanded the limits of its pastoral oversight to cover the complete range of personal and community activities and to meet the moral, social, and economic challenges of the times.

Despite its desire to attract everyone into its fellowship, the Methodist church increasingly defined its goals and social values according to the attitudes of an upwardly mobile middle class and in particular by a small group of wealthy commercial and industrial leaders who hoped to create a nation in their own image and who were willing to spend their resources to see it achieved. This group changed over time to reflect the shifting basis of wealth and opportunity in Canada itself. In the early nineteenth century, prominent local business leaders such as Billa Flint in Belleville, John Torrance and James Ferrier in Montreal, and James Rogers Armstrong in Toronto or the jurist and politician Lemuel Wilmot in New Brunswick had dominated local Methodist affairs. In fact, nearly every community across the country had lay leaders, usually merchants or substantial farmers and their wives, who provided much of the impetus for building and administering churches and therefore for establishing the moral and social norms for the community.

However, it was not until the latter part of the century, when the laity gained substantial power in administering the national Methodist church and the clergy itself conceded leadership in its councils, that the rising commercial élite truly wielded power.[1] Blending sound business practices and devout personal habits, men such as John Macdonald, the "merchant prince" of Toronto, impressed upon all who would listen the need for discipline, hard work, integrity, frugality, benevolence, and patriotism. Canada needed individuals who showed patience, self-denial, self-control, good sense, and honesty. Respect for order and authority were also considered essential for progress to the kingdom of God on earth.[2]

Macdonald directed his credo predominantly at young, white-collar workers and the children of Ontario's farmers. To promote their business, as well as their moral advancement, he integrated his commercial precepts with this moral code. He stressed the need for complete honesty in business as in all other aspects of life. Shrewdness was commendable, but one should never take advantage of others. Never lend or borrow excessively, always meet financial obligations, and maintain a fair price for services or products. Fair wages were essential, but excessive payments might promote laziness or immorality in workers. Macdonald was hardly unique in these views. The new, large-scale Methodist retailers such as Timothy Eaton and Robert Simpson in Toronto, as well as the host of merchants across the country, readily subscribed to the same blend of morality and business practices.[3]

Gradually, many of Canada's leading manufacturers, particularly in Ontario, added their own priorities to the definition of a moral Canadian society. Massey's farm implements, Gurney's stoves, Mason's pianos, Flavelle's meat processing, Birge's steel, Sanford's clothing, Gooderham's railways and milling, and Gibson's lumber were only some of the most prominent of the rising industrial operations led by Methodists. By the late nineteenth and especially in the early twentieth century, they were joined by land and railway promoters and by the directors of banks, insurance companies, and other financial institutions. Men such as George Cox, Henry Fudger, James Austin, Clifford Sifton, James Ashdown, Richard B. Bennett, and James Lougheed shared the power and influence that accrues to individuals with unprecedented wealth.

They also shared certain characteristics and beliefs. In their personal and business activities, they were aggressive, energetic, and hard-working as well as autocratic and paternalistic. While anxious to retain spotless reputations, they nevertheless chose to live quite ostentatiously for Methodists. Generally self-satisfied and optimistic about the progress of the world, they were at the same time deeply troubled by the social and economic conditions they witnessed. Socially and politically moderate, they trusted responsible individualism and opposed class-based responses to national problems. Society was divided between the saved and the fallen, not among social or economic classes. Industrial and social harmony depended on benevolence, tolerance, and the amelioration of class differences.[4]

These men's vision was broadened and elaborated by an expanding class of skilled professionals who helped run the commercial and industrial operations. Lawyers, accountants, and business administrators such as Newton Wesley Rowell, W.P. Gundy, A.E. Ames, Bartle Bull, George Kerr, and a host of others in the larger Canadian cities saw themselves as civil servants in the true sense of the word. While still stressing social and class cooperation, they could afford to be more tolerant of working-class arguments for a greater share in the wealth of the nation since they did not feel personally threatened by these demands. They also could look more favourably on an active role for the government in ending social ills. Deeply committed to the welfare of their church, they believed it should lead in preparing a safe, religious, and ordered social environment.[5]

Although strong critics of these values abounded within Methodism, the middle-class attitudes and social understanding were generally accepted by Victorian and Edwardian Canada. They were the common intellectual currency of secular, as well as sacred, forces and were widely shared by farmers and labourers as well as merchants and industrialists. But they were reinforced and given added sanction by the influence of the church. Methodism inculcated sober respectability and moral absolutes as indispensable components of its social cohesion and religious fellowship, and its influence naturally transcended its denominational borders.

Perhaps the most visible demonstration of the shift to a middle-class church was the network of impressive, even monumental, regional churches that came to dominate the urban landscape during the last quarter of the nineteenth century. An earlier generation of Methodists, especially the non-Wesleyan connexions, had considered elegant churches to be detrimental to profound spiritual worship. Such buildings seemed contaminated with the decadence and worldliness of Roman Catholicism. For instance, Albert Carman believed, "The simplicity of the gospel in its militant and aggressive state ill comports with expensive buildings, sumptuous appointments, and large emoluments."[6] Other conservative, evangelical Christians continued to promote this view into the twentieth century.

With the rise of middle-class respectability, however, fine church buildings were seen to demonstrate the authority and influence of the Methodist denomination, as well as the wealth and status of its membership. The "old, irregular and suffocating" churches had generally been devoid of style and harked back to a primitive, earnest spirituality and even to uncouth religious practices that no longer satisfied late Victorian Methodism. Most church leaders came to assume that the bounty of nature and industry should be used for God's glorification. A fine building "evinces an increasing spirit among the brethren and friends of the church, of liberality and regard for the interests for Zion."[7] Such buildings were also useful, if not essential, in attracting and holding new members and expanding even further the Christian community.

In the construction of its larger churches, Methodism considered various traditional architectural styles. Classical architecture, which drew on the inspiration of Greece and Rome, suggested stability, reason, and individualism and was particularly popular in buildings housing public and financial institutions. However, it failed to answer many of the nineteenth-century Romantic understandings of spirituality. As an imitation of pagan temples, the style also seemed an inappropriate way to express Christian faith and communion. It was part of the profane assault by the world on the sacredness of society. Late in the century, a number of government buildings, schools, and important churches were built in the Romanesque-revival style. With its massive, rough-hewn stone exteriors, asymetical composition, and dark, cavernous interiors, it hinted at a return to random natural forms. Nevertheless, the overwhelming choice was a revised Gothic style. Gothic architecture immediately identified the building's religious purpose. To even the most casual observer, it also marked both the spiritual and temporal prosperity of the church and the community. To all who entered the church, the Gothic style asserted well-understood divisions of space and form. With its large stained-glass windows to let in the light, it raised the vision heavenward and inspired awe, piety, and an intense sense of sacred order.[8]

The new church construction also reflected the hierarchy developing in institutional Methodism, with its accompanying centralization of power. While Metropolitan in Toronto and, to a lesser extent, St James in Montreal represented the cathedrals of Methodism, a new generation of uptown churches were important regional centres of Methodist strength and missionary outreach. Sherbourne Street Methodist in Toronto was known as the "millionaires' church" and was described as having an "opera house feeling," with a soft and rich architecture, irreproachable in taste.[9] It was not unique, however; churches such as Dominion in Ottawa, Centenary in Hamilton, Grace in Winnipeg, Central Methodist in Calgary, and Wesley in Vancouver served the same social groups and needs. They joined the older generation of local "mother" churches, such as Gower Street in St John's, Brunswick Street in Halifax, Centenary in Saint John, Sydenham Street in Kingston, First Methodist in London, and Metropolitan in Victoria. In fact, every major centre built large and refined architectural monuments to Methodist spirituality.

Similarly, many smaller centres and prosperous rural districts built more limited versions of the same churches. The new buildings often followed the amalgamation of local congregations after the church unions of 1874 and 1884 or a shift into town from a rural crossroads setting. Whether they were in Owen Sound or Moncton, Thunder Bay or Saskatoon, both the connexion and the community looked upon these impressive churches as important indications of urban maturity, prosperity, and vitality. Their foundations were securely rooted in the rich Canadian landscape, and they were the outward sign of living and growing institutions. They told the world that the community was solidly Christian. Not only had it reached a high level of economic, social, and religious civilization, but the future promised even greater progress. As well as being sources of community pride, the buildings illustrated Methodism's important status in mainstream Protestantism.

In these structures, fashion and conduct accompanied design; they became cultural, as well as spiritual, centres. Every church worthy of its name required a large organ. "That grand and solemn instrument has banished therefrom the reedy squeaking pipes and string-breaking fiddles, which too often broke the harmony of religious worship." Surpliced choirs and a church service that, while strongly spiritual, was "carefully refined, that it should not jar upon cultivated people" became normal. These churches often reintroduced a more structured liturgy based on John Wesley's *Sunday Service* which included many aspects of Anglican worship. Unnecessary ritual was staunchly opposed, "but this does not preclude a recognition of what is reverent, graceful, and in harmony with good taste ... there should be a discerning recognition of the natural social tastes and human instincts of hearers and worshippers, and a wise adaptation of our services to the wants of the people."[10] Bach recitals or other concerts became part of a community's cultural life which were as appropriately located in a church as evangelistic meetings or temperance lectures. Under these conditions, refined behaviour and dress were expected and became the outward means of identifying the members of the religious fellowship.

Whether large or small, the new churches differed significantly from their predecessors in other ways. The plans, often supplied by leading Canadian architects and reprinted in Methodist publications, not only spread style, but they also marked the elaboration of functions in the modern church. The buildings were adapted to the broader social concerns which were becoming fundamental aspects of church life. Space was set aside for an office for the minister and for meetings of the trustees and official board, as well as for auxiliary organizations such as Sunday schools, the Woman's Missionary Society, and the Ladies' Aid and the proliferation of other groups associated with the congregation. Often the congregation built an adjoining hall for home-mission work and for recreational, social, and intellectual gatherings.[11]

Even though Methodism became dominated by middle-class values, this shift did not preclude a highly divisive debate on the direction it was taking and the implications of these developments for its future. Originally, this debate centred on the notion of wealth and the wealthy, but by the twentieth century it also involved Methodism's social contract with those it served. On the personal level, many Methodists believed that too much material prosperity could seriously weaken piety: "the love of gain shuts-up the conscience, glazes over the moral question."[12] Riches could lead to idleness, arrogance, and oppression and were too often the source of the vicious condition of society. The children of the wealthy were especially to be pitied since they were subject to a worldly home environment and encouraged to be haughty or to disdain work. There was no more beneficial inheritance than "the hard but kind bosom of poverty."[13] Indigence was a blessing as long as it was not the result of personal failure or immorality; hard work made better individuals. Certainly, Methodists knew they should never pray for wealth or seek to acquire it by immoral means.

The Methodist church also recognized the danger to its integrity of relying too heavily on its wealthy members. Although the middle class sustained the church's operations, its mission to the corrupt world could be seriously weakened by "depending and looking solely to those who can pay pew rents, who have good dresses for the Sabbath, who can visit with the minister and the minister's family, and maintain among themselves a genteel society."[14] Also, by relying on such fund-raising methods as tea meetings, social entertainments, and especially the pew-rent system, the piety and sacredness of the church was threatened. Many Methodists realized that renting pews to the highest bidder instituted a reprehensible distinction between the rich and poor in the house of God. It also fostered social pride, unnatural competition, and strife in the congregation. Moreover, the élites who controlled the pews often sought to dominate church affairs and the selection and the message of the minister. There was a considerable apprehension that too many Methodist churches had become expensive luxuries beyond the reach of the working classes where only the comfortable and contented could be found. And these groups were not always the most pious or spiritually energetic. Methodism was potentially in danger of becoming socially lethargic and of abandoning the poor and thereby losing the community's respect and, more important, Christ's favour. For the church to succeed in creating a moral order, it must welcome back the dispossessed and not hive them off in mission chapels or drive them to the Salvation Army or other evangelical denominations. Renting pews was therefore generally abolished by the late nineteenth century.[15]

But the Methodist church nevertheless remained pre-eminently a middle-class institution and assumed it could best serve all segments of society by remaking the world in its own image. For it to be relevant to the status of its leading members, a different style of spiritual message seemed necessary and appropriate. Traditional appeals stressing the terrors of hell fire and the unbounded depravity of humanity seemed less credible. In their stead, a more optimistic message played down humankind's natural sinfulness and emphasized God's love, the advantages of salvation, and the benefits of right living. Sermons sometimes became simply practical addresses on moral and religious obligations. Many critics argued this emasculated theology and transformed Christianity into a benign humanism, but more liberal lay and clerical members felt it was the only way to stimulate and consolidate Methodism's appeal.[16]

Again, these attitudes were exemplified by the treatment of wealth and the wealthy. How could the Methodist church deny the religious worth of members who had gained earthly prosperity? Their faith and spiritual health was witnessed in the elegant and inspiring churches, their missionary contributions, and their morality and influence for good. Thus, while acknowledging the potential perils of wealth, the church could not justify an attack upon wealth itself. No one could buy salvation, but acquiring wealth merely reflected the use of God-given talents. "It is not a sin to be rich. Some men ought to be rich as other men are learned or talented. They have the gifts to secure it."[17] The biblical injunction that it was easier for a camel to pass through the eye of a needle than for a rich man to go to heaven was ignored. The sin was not wealth itself, but wealth immorally acquired or not directed to God's service. Not only was there no harm in being rich, but it was considered a blessing promised to the righteous.

Neither spiritual health nor the quest for salvation necessarily diminished with wealth and respectability, and they could be, in themselves, positive aspects of social and moral progress. They were important means, among others, of strengthening the family, providing social order, and promoting public morality. The growing temporal success of church members might be a legitimate sign of spiritual progress since it reflected at least a partial victory over untamed nature. Making and saving money also encouraged diligence, hard work, and discipline and stimulated frugality and benevolence. Many Methodists argued that wealth could not and should not be evenly distributed; the rich must receive due credit for improving the nation and providing work for others. The Scriptures assumed the existence of the rich as well as the poor.[18]

Such beliefs reflected a deep-seated emphasis on the work ethic. Idleness was a sin; work was essential to true happiness; diligence and hard work were Christian duties. Industry, then, helped awaken the higher nature of human-kind and led to a fuller religious experience. Since most leading Methodists believed that the natural world contained sufficient means for all humanity's needs, it was only immorality, indolence, and sloth that restrained human be-ings from achieving earthly prosperity. Following this logic, many Methodists came to view the poor as inherently sinful or at least poor stewards of God's benevolence. Drunkenness and improper behaviour were extensions of this spiritual depravity. Nothing could fully substitute for personal spiritual reli-gion, but hard work, moral behaviour, and Christian liberality illustrated vir-tue and spiritual health.[19]

Accordingly, a rift not unnaturally developed between organized religion and the poor. An urban, industrial society naturally produced an underem-ployed, socially static class that not only was uncomfortable amid the Sunday finery in the elegant churches listening to sermons on the sin of poverty, but also could find little spiritual warmth in the church's optimistic message of a post-millennial reign of Christ on earth. The poor were becoming ever more isolated, not from God, but from institutional religion, because they could not share equally in the emerging social fellowship that was displacing the evangelical pietism of earlier Methodism.

However, Methodism did not abandon the poor. It continually stressed the obligation of the more fortunate to assist their poorer neighbours and worked for moral and social reform. The industrialist Hart Massey summed up the hopes of his class: "As rich men see their wealth in the light of eternity, catch-ing glimpses of the divine order, surely they, too, will consecrate the usufruct of their lives for the good of others, then the Kingdom of Heaven will take tan-gible shape, chaos, unrest and social disorder will disappear, and this round earth will become the Kingdom of the Lord."[20] Human beings were only stew-ards of God's wealth and were obliged to spend it in God's service. Sumptuous living and unnecessary possessions were sinful wastes. Since the Bible taught that the rich must help the poor, spending money properly was a religious test and an act of worship. In fact, some Methodists advocated raising charitable giving to the dignity of a means of grace. The first obligation of this benevo-lence was to expand the work of the church since it promoted true spiritual health and led humanity to a higher life. The second obligation of charity was the amelioration of the often-desperate conditions found in society. Ulti-mately, however, Christian stewardship rewarded the giver more than the re-ceiver. It increased temporal prosperity and spiritual progress and assisted in the conversion of the world and the creation of Christ's earthly dominion.[21]

### THE ROLE OF THE FAMILY

In attempting to create a new moral order, the Methodist church, and indeed Victorian society in general, placed its primary hope on the family. Despite a growing appreciation for democratic individualism, the family was assumed to be the core of social organization, the cornerstone of civilization, and the foundation of national life. Methodists had traditionally utilized it as the basic institution for separating themselves from the corrupt world and for establishing a moral, spiritually vital fellowship. Indeed, like all Protestants, they recognized, "The family is the ordinance of God. Conceived in divine love, founded by divine wisdom, organized in a life of purity, surrounded by solemn sanctions of reward and retribution, it is the corner-stone of human life ... The home is the inner sanctuary for purity and power in the work of God in the earth. It gives firmness and fortitude in grappling with the deadly principles and powers of evil."[22]

In keeping with general middle-class assumptions and prejudices, the broken or malfunctioning family was considered particularly a problem with the poor and the new immigrants. These groups failed to appreciate the crucial value of the family, or at least did not share the prevailing view about the proper nature and function of family life. For instance, the new immigrants and urban poor too often appeared to betray the image of the ideal family by having their women and children work outside the house. Many Methodist leaders viewed such employment as pure exploitation and highly destructive to the home. They did not recognize its economic necessity. In addition, immorality and crime were generally viewed as pre-eminently the problems of the poor. "Poverty is the mother of dirt, vice and crime." "Vice naturally delights to haunt the most filthy lanes of cities and most neglected homes in the country."[23] Conversely, clean, middle-class homes were inherently more moral. The public was always shocked to learn of middle-class immorality.

During the late Victorian era, the middle-class family was beginning to be transformed and to acquire new social functions. The nuclear or conjugal family was gradually replacing the extended family as the norm. Especially in urban centres, other relatives were no longer as necessary for domestic duties. Non-related members of the household, such as boarders or servants, also decreased in status within the home circle. They participated less frequently in home worship or social activities and often rejected the family's discipline and control. These trends permitted the greater degree of privacy and introspection which marked late-Victorian family life.[24]

The era also witnessed a declining birth rate and increased health and life expectancy among the middle classes. At the same time, low wages for servants and new labour-saving inventions helped to free women from many domestic duties. These factors permitted greater leisure; more time could be spent with family members or in other social pursuits. Women especially found it easier to participate in activities outside the home. While still limited, their legitimate pursuits grew to include church, charitable work, social-reform movements, moral recreation, and even some forms of paid employment. Moreover, the family was less important for teaching the young traditional craft skills. Regular education provided much of the preparation, and the specific needs of industrial society could only be demonstrated in the work place. The home remained central for training girls to manage a household, but many of the domestic skills required by earlier generations were no longer needed.

Under these changed circumstances, the family became more than an essential economic unit or an agency for religious training and moral protection. It provided the base for an aggressive strategy of total social regeneration. With adolescent children remaining at school longer and therefore in a dependent state in the home, the family had both greater opportunities and more responsibilities for training. The demands of urban industrial society forced parents to prepare their young for the disciplined, ordered life considered essential for economic advancement. Children had to be "socialized" to the new circumstances. It was also critical that they be prepared to face the challenges posed by the more prevalent immoralities threatening society at a time when the family could rely less on relatives or community vigilance for assistance. In a rural setting, neighbours and friends formed an informal network to enforce moral standards. But as the industrial, urbanizing society became more anonymous, the nuclear family and the state were expected to assume these duties. Because the functions and values inherent in the family formed the foundations of society, state agencies could legitimately interfere in what had once been considered strictly private affairs.[25]

The family was so central that Victorian society assumed marriage was the only natural state for men and women. Social progress was impossible if they functioned simply as individuals. Commentators normally agreed, "The complete man is husband and father, and the complete woman is wife and mother"; also, "motherhood is the divinely-ordained and most sacred crown of womanhood."[26] Furthermore, because Methodists believed that marriage predated Adam's original sin and was "the only relic of a paradise that is left us ... to be a symbol forever of the primal love," it was vital that marriage remain a Christian ordinance.[27] It should never be reduced to a crass social or economic contract, and it should occur in a religious setting under the supervision of a Christian minister. Both partners should be mature, moral, spiritually alive Christians. Accordingly, Methodist authorities opposed mixed marriages between Protestants and Catholics unless the Catholic spouse converted; it was better to remain single than to abandon Protestant principles.

Moreover, the church denounced divorce as a cancer on society which deeply scarred and stigmatized both parents and children. "The maintenance of individual marital bonds thus symbolized the preservation of virtue and rectitude in all Canadians and upheld the model for intersexual relations, a beacon in a world all too darkened by sin and selfishness."[28] However, divorce rarely occurred. More often men and women simply separated or abandoned their spouses and sometimes adopted bigamous relationships or "lewd cohabitation." These were denounced as assaults upon the family and upon decent notions of sexual conduct. But even within the confines of marriage, sexual misconduct was all too prevalent. The Methodist church argued that the government should take greater action to insure that proper family responsibilities were fulfilled. Adultery and incest broke the fundamental laws of God as well as of the nation. Prostitution was not simply a harmless yielding to human weakness; it undermined the family and caused the seduction, debasement, and mistreatment of women. Methodism advocated better protection for women, particularly in the cities, where they were most vulnerable to sexual assault or to falling into a life of sin, and it was particularly concerned that native women be protected. Many Canadians had long assumed that native women were inherently immoral, and they generally received little sympathy from the legal system.[29] Methodists also urged the government to deal with illegitimate children and the other social consequences of extramarital sexual liaisons, not only to assist those involved, but also to insure the future welfare of the entire nation.[30]

It was within the context of keeping the family whole and functioning properly in an urban, industrial society that much of the debate during the late nineteenth century concerning suitable roles for women occurred. Three views prevailed during this period. One group would confine women strictly to domestic and related duties and shut them out of all other work. It assumed, "The division of labour between the sexes is primordal – older and deeper than all social development, and a fundamental condition to it"; marriage was a union of interests "which made their respective spheres of occupation supplementary to each other."[31] A women was considered at her best as a blessed minister to her family in the home. Both sexes had their proper sphere of duty and opportunity, and a husband's dominion over his wife was inherently right, but the Methodist church maintained that women's sphere should not be undervalued. Women were by no means inferior; they should never become men's servants. There was no more dignified occupation than wife and mother. As a corollary, in fact, this maternal power and authority made women superior to men. However, the argument continued that women would lose this status if they abandoned their territory or became competitors in occupations assigned to men, and "nature would revolt at this violence to physical and intellectual energy."[32] Women in particular would suffer from the ensuing social havoc. These ideas remained strong throughout the history of Canadian Methodism.

A second view assumed that "great battles are yet to be fought and won, by which women will be more fully emancipated from past usages and placed side by side with men in all the activities of life."[33] Such a radical perception was not popular among either women or men at the time. Between the two extremes, a third approach believed that God had created men and women with different constitutions which led them to occupy distinct spheres of activity. However, although some functions were particularly suited to one or other of the sexes, where they were equally suited, women should have equal access. By thus expanding the opportunities, women would improve the home and further Christian civilization. Despite disagreement over the extent of functions equally suited to men and women and the remaining limitations on women outside the home, this approach was probably the most popular with Canadians. By the late nineteenth century, it was acknowledged, "Women have taken a place among the intellectual, industrial and social forces of society greatly in advance of the position they formerly occupied."[34] And women's proper sphere was expected to continue to grow.

Beyond the traditional nurturing activities in the home and the church, women's organizations helped to expand the horizons of appropriate behaviour. From at least the 1830s, the Ladies' Aid societies had supplied important forums for community enterprise. They were crucial for the ongoing operations of local congregations. The proceeds from socials, bazaars, sewing, and a myriad of other enterprises helped maintain the church buildings, pay the minister's salary, reduce the debt, and fund other projects. By the late nineteenth century, the Ladies' Aid societies were also assisting the poor and the sick in the community and promoting mission work, particularly among females. Furthermore, these groups often financed and directed the deaconesses working in the congregation and supplied the moral suasion needed to develop social-improvement campaigns. For the women involved, these activities expanded social and intellectual horizons, provided a sense of community, and eliminated much of the loneliness and monotony of their lives. Many women also used the experience to move into national and international organizations with even more progressive programs.[35]

Both single and married women also actively participated in the Woman's Missionary Society at the local and national level. They played exceptional roles in both domestic and foreign mission work as supporters or as missionaries. Women also functioned at least as well as men in a broad range of charitable and reform programs. With their increased practical training and higher education, they gave dynamic leadership to these movements. They were also accepted and, indeed, expected to excel in such occupations as deaconesses, nurses, and teachers. By the twentieth century, a growing number of Methodists strongly opposed the social injustice of limiting women in the workforce and argued that "neither law nor social prejudice should shut them out from any employment which they may deem it proper to enter."[36]

Nevertheless, women's new freedom to participate professionally in secular affairs should not be exaggerated. For most Canadians, home and family remained women's proper sphere; after marriage, middle-class women were expected to give up paid employment and not allow other activities to interfere with their primary duties. In response to calls for equality, there was a fear that feminist leanings would lead to selfish individualism and eventually to the ruin of the family. Even among reform-minded men and women, many believed that any opportunities for developing a freer and more cultured womanhood would be best utilized in improving family life. In broader terms, Methodism assumed that women's influence rested on their personality and moral righteousness, not on any economic or political power they wielded. Romantic notions of womanhood continued to prevent real changes in social attitudes, and women's authority remained based on an acceptance of their maternal instincts.[37]

Discussions of the family most often centred on women's roles, but the church maintained that men too had functions that needed recognition and strengthening. They supplied the economic resources, protected the family, led home worship, and directed other social activities. It was the father's duty to discipline and morally train the young; it required a father's firm disposition to root out evil passions and direct latent energies. Men were especially expected to keep boys and youth from falling into the traps of the world and help to develop a "robust, physical, social, ethical and spiritual manliness."[38] Through example and counsel, they prepared children and adolescents to become responsible adults.

At the same time, Methodism expected men to continue to dominate the central activities of the church. There was a rising apprehension among its leadership that men were reducing their commitment to Christian work as they participated more fully in the economic, political, and social life of the community and the country. The possibility of a moral national order and even the authority and power of evangelical Christianity itself appeared threatened if the church became too feminized. Although never functioning as well as women's groups, laymen's organizations did seek to engage men more fully in the day-to-day life of the church and the community. But these institutions tended to concentrate on church adminstration, ministerial relations, or the promulgation of relatively conservative, middle-class priorities in the church.[39] In truth, however, men at the local or even the national church level had never required special organizations to promote their interests. They already held real power individually as ministers, editors, trustees, delegates, administrators, financial contributors, and political and social arbiters.

## THE SOCIAL-GOSPEL MOVEMENT

By the late nineteenth century, Methodism had become secure in its middle-class value system and was confident about its right and ability to lead Canadian society in making Victorian family values the basis of social progress. However, at the same time, new forces were transforming Protestantism throughout the English-speaking world. The broad consensus on the nature and function of religion that Protestantism had achieved over the previous century was seriously assailed from both the left and the right, and this assault caused serious trouble for institutional Methodism. This complex process occurred over a period of thirty or forty years and reflected attempts to answer the challenges posed by the new scientific and intellectual forces that were attacking the anchors of Christian belief, as well as to respond to the social and economic turmoil that was undermining social stability.

One response came from the liberal theologians with their strong activist and anti-metaphysical bias, who at least partially rejected the doctrinal content of traditional Protestantism in favour of ethical and moral values. To them, sin was no longer a violation of God's laws; it was conduct which injured others. Justice called for the reform of society, not punishment for defiance of God. The liberal theological belief in the innate goodness of humanity diminished the need for a dramatic conversion if humanity could be prevented from personally sinning. Such beliefs advanced the role of science by freeing society from outworn dogma and liberating it from physical and intellectual restraints. Darwinism and the accompanying social sciences provided evidence which helped legitimize cooperation among individuals to advance moral as well as physical progress. Under these terms, religion became essentially social and human-centred. It shifted from personal introspection and nurture to outward action. Liberal theology justified such action as necessary to improve temporal conditions in order to expand spiritual horizons.[40]

The trust in scientific inquiry was mirrored in the work of higher critics, who sought to glean the true meaning of the Bible by subjecting it to rigorous

Hart Massey (1823–96). Major Methodist industrialist and philanthropist. (UCA, P3938N)

Newton Wesley Rowell (1867–1941). Lawyer, businessman, and politician who helped to modernize Methodist administration and promoted church union. (UCA, P5686)

Metropolitan Methodist Church, Toronto. Opened in 1872 as the "cathedral" of Canadian Methodism. (UCA, P813N)

St James Methodist Church, Montreal. Rebuilt in 1887 as the monument of middle-class Methodism in Quebec. (UCA, Album 78.105C/OS)

analysis. They questioned traditional evangelical assumptions and substituted doubt for certainty by demanding historical relativism. Meanwhile, archaeologists and clergy were scouring the Middle East for evidence to support or refute the biblical texts. Their work helped alter the nature of the debate over the Scriptures. Even fundamentalists gleefully reported minute findings which seemed to support biblical descriptions of events such as Creation or the Flood. They too dissected the book for proof texts to advance their theological positions, even while they denied the legitimacy of interpreting the Bible in this way. Some leading Methodists sought to go beyond what they considered a narrow biblical base to find the answer to their spiritual questions. For instance, to Samuel Dwight Chown, religious truths rested not only on Scripture, but also "They rest upon nature ... They rest upon our moral constitution, upon conscience, upon history, upon the corporate religious consciousness of the Church and upon the experience of each individual Christian."[41]

The new-found understanding of religious truth reinforced Methodism's attempts to create a moral nation as a basis for God's kingdom on earth. What was perhaps most controversial was the assumption that humanity could actually effect such change. Methodism had never been significantly distracted by premillennialism, and by the late nineteenth century it was explicitly committed to a post-millennial vision for Canada and the world.[42] In fact, this vision offered a vital counterbalance to the sense of foreboding occasioned by urban and industrial expansion. The quest gave Methodism a dynamic and exciting mission. Meanwhile, this commission to establish a holy dominion appeared to sanction the heightened nationalism emerging in late-Victorian Canada. One of Protestantism's functions was to strengthen the nation, and it, in turn, would become a vehicle for a moral imperialism that would spread Christian civilization around the world. Assuming that the nation could become a sacred community, religious interests became intimately entwined with national ones.

Unfortunately, in its attempt to protect the nation's cultural heritage, this apparently righteous nationalism also intensified a bigoted nativism. Most Protestants defined the basic character of Canada needed to underpin God's earthly kingdom as a white, Anglo-Saxon, Protestant country. To develop such a nation, Methodism appeared to justify strong anti-foreign and anti-Catholic sentiments. It sought to assimilate all new immigrants, to convert non-Christians to the "true" faith, and to bestow on native Canadians the benefits of Protestant civilization. Moreover, it attempted to curb, in the national interest, the power of Roman Catholics and therefore French Canadians. To Methodists, Canada could not fulfil its true mission in the world until these goals had first been achieved; when they were accomplished, Canada would be well advanced as a proper home for the post-millennial reign of Christ.[43]

Although most Methodists strongly supported this mission, there was serious disagreement over how it could be achieved. Some responded to the changing intellectual and social milieu by emphasizing the need for personal conversion and holiness; these they saw as the only means for religion to be advanced and for believers to survive society's temporary aberrations. They advocated the old-fashioned revivalist approach, which at its narrowest viewed religion as the means to bring individuals to heaven. True reform was individual and other-worldly. Sin was not a matter of hurting others or even of evil social conditions, and therefore salvation could never be achieved through social reforms. It required a living relationship with God.[44]

Even though they continued to maintain that a good society required saved individuals and that improving social conditions was not the central goal of revived religion, most of this conservative group still sought a moral nation and advocated good works and social improvement. Social and personal holiness were both Christian duties; true revival exalted spiritual life while deepening ethical purpose. Service to others was an outward sign of a transformed spiritual nature, and better social conditions often illustrated the difference between the saved and the fallen world.[45] Furthermore, these individuals expected that the combined emphasis on personal salvation and social holiness would help restore the spiritual cohesiveness and sense of community they believed characterized an earlier time.

But the Methodist church was becoming increasingly polarized. Some of its most conservative members, including fundamentalists, holiness proponents, and opponents of higher criticism and Darwinian science, found themselves isolated in Methodist councils. Eventually, because they could not satisfy their aims within institutional Methodism and could neither conscientiously accept contrary opinions nor the church's disciplinary restrictions, they sought independence. Significant factions led by Nelson Burns, Ralph Horner, and others either left on their own or were expelled as much for their disobedience to the will of General Conference as for their specific evangelical priorities. Since they were part of large international and interdenominational movements, they had divided loyalties and refused to submit to the restrictions of Methodist polity.[46] After leaving the mainstream Methodist church, they found the Salvation Army, the Free Methodists, the Holiness Movement Church of Canada, the Gospel Workers church, the Church of the Nazarene, the adventist churches, and various splinter pentecostal groups more suitable. Even within these bodies, however, they continued to maintain their independence and rarely permitted denominational loyalty to overshadow their theological views. Despite these defections, the vast majority of conservative Methodists continued in or eventually returned to the Methodist church. But, as the language of revival was assumed by non-Methodists, and often by narrow sectarian movements, conservatives were less able to find a sympathetic hearing within the Methodist communion.

Despite the continuance of traditional evangelical attitudes, as early as the 1880s an influential band of young itinerants and social critics began to espouse a new "social gospel" for Methodism. They were spurred on by the support given by liberal theology and higher criticism, and they expected to create a new nation which could resolve the contemporary social and economic problems.[47] For the most part, they were frustrated by the apparent failure of traditional Methodism to respond to what they considered the real needs of humanity and by the irrelevance of middle-class, institutional religion to the most distressed elements of society. Just as the evangelical awakening and the rise of mass evangelism had marked and transformed Protestantism during the eighteenth and nineteenth centuries, the social-gospel movement was expected to be influential in the modern world. Indeed, the movement captured and reinvigorated the determination and crusading enthusiasm which had earlier characterized mass evangelistic campaigns. It appeared to supply a rationale for a direct mission that would infuse the entire nation with superior Christian principles without relying on future punishment or reward. As with most of the other intellectual and social influences on the church, the social-gospel movement was neither exclusively Canadian nor Methodist in its origins, development, or effects. Moreover, not even its most avid supporters clearly defined the social gospel; a variety of progressive individuals and groups laboured under its theological and intellectual umbrella.

The movement was greatly influenced by the mission work of Hugh Price Hughes in London during the 1880s and by the writings of the American Walter Rauschenbusch during the early twentieth century. In Canada, the social gospel's most eloquent spokesman was Salem Bland, who taught at Wesley College in Winnipeg from 1904 to 1918. Although as a young man he had contemplated joining the Salvation Army and was impressed by the holiness revival, he came to accept the social-gospel movement as the best means of reforming Methodist spirituality. To Bland and his more committed supporters, the kingdom of God on earth was impossible without comprehensive, radical social reform. In 1920 he summed up his attitudes in his controversial book *The New Christianity*. In this partisan review of the history of Christianity, Bland argued that medieval feudal society had relied on the Roman Catholic church to preserve Christianity from pagan barbarism, and as a result the church had naturally adopted aristocratic and authoritarian principles and practices. The Protestant Reformation represented the ecclesiastical expression of a revolt by the rising commercial middle classes against Roman Catholic despotism. According to Bland, under the new Christianity of the social gospel, the churches would celebrate the victory of the common man and the progressive principles of justice and democracy. The most noted practitioner of a more radical social gospel was James S. Woodsworth, the director of All People's Mission in Winnipeg from 1907 until 1913. After resigning from the ministry during World War I because of his pacifist sentiments, he became a labour organizer and helped to found and led the socialistic Co-operative Commonwealth Federation party in Parliament until the beginning of World War II in 1939.[48]

Believing that preparation for heaven was only a secondary aspect of the church's work and that sin was pre-eminently action which hurt humankind, the social gospellers attempted to improve human relations and the human condition on earth. To achieve this goal, they maintained, "We must refuse to accept the alternative of a social or a personal gospel. The gospel of Jesus as he first announced it was wholly a social gospel with a personal appeal ... Forgiveness of sins and the blessed hope of the future came quite incidentally."[49] True progress could only be measured by the advancement of the social good. They argued that an ultra-individualistic theology might in fact prevent personal salvation by encouraging selfishness and even pride, and they assumed that the individual must subordinate private interests to the welfare of society.

Social salvation must precede, not follow, individual salvation. By their reading of Scripture, Christ and the prophets were pre-eminently social critics who had attacked the immorality and irreligion they found in ancient Israel. John the Baptist had been beheaded for denouncing Herod's court, not for announcing the coming of the Messiah. And the Jesus they worshipped had overturned the money-changers' tables and preached the Sermon on the Mount. Humanity had to imitate Christ and reinstate the Golden Rule and the Sermon on the Mount in its daily life before the kingdom of God could be established on earth. The application of Christianity was the true substance of religion. A starving, exploited family living in a slum was not in a position to contemplate heavenly salvation; only a truly just society could produce good individuals.[50]

Canadian social gospellers also stressed the role of education and Christian nurture in advancing the movement's goals and assumed that substantial improvement required a collectivist approach through institutions transformed to implement progressive strategies. These assumptions coincided with general social attitudes of the time and particularly with the collectivization taking place in society to meet the seemingly overwhelming demands of urbanization and industrialization. Many individuals felt isolated and impotent in the presence of these challenges. Whether in the form of business associations, labour unions, farm cooperatives, women's groups, or reform societies, organized action seemed necessary to regain control of one's destiny, as well as to create a new society. This approach was widely supported by the new social sciences, such as sociology and political economy, which had at least partially replaced traditional theology as the principal guide to understanding social relations and supplying practical solutions for national problems. The social gospellers increasingly trusted experts to implement reforms.[51]

They also adopted an environmental approach to reform, derived at least partially from the assumptions of Darwinian science. Darwin had demonstrated scientifically the significance of specific environments in the evolution of species' characteristics. If the environment had this influence and if it could be manipulated for the better, then the physical and even moral progress of humanity would be quickened. The new insights of science appeared to offer the means to achieve this goal. Christian environmentalism also assumed that an immanent God was actively involved in transforming humanity, both individually and at the social level. Under these conditions, Christianity had a critical duty to assist in the evolution of society to a higher stage of development by promoting reforms.[52]

By the turn of the century, these views helped legitimize a wider spectrum of attitudes toward wealth and the wealthy among Methodists. Although some continued to laud the unbridled accumulation of riches, many liberal and conservative church leaders could no longer subscribe to this approach; extreme economic individualism could have detrimental consequences for society and could circumscribe the church's heroic redemptive and reformist elements. Critics as diverse as the conservative Albert Carman and the social-gospel leader Ernest Thomas also believed that the dominance of the wealthy in church affairs could distort Methodism's social mission. Carman warned of "the peril arising from the sinister and controlling power of an influential moneyed group within our Church," while Thomas maintained, "Ten thousand dollars for philanthropic work and starvation wages for his workmen ... is not the sign of Christianity for which the heart of the world is hungering today."[53] Leading social gospellers also warned that too many Methodist organizations appeared more interested in preserving traditional middle-class values than in redeeming society. They believed that under such leadership, the connexion shuffled the social critic out of sight while promoting the ideologically safe minister who raised the most money or built the largest church.

Methodist critics particularly questioned the morality of accumulating huge fortunes. Were they truly a sign of God's reward for Christian service or simply a measure of humanity's selfishness? Even when the money was not made illegally or did not come from evil businesses such as brewing or distilling, it too often represented the exploitation of workers or consumers. Progressives argued, "The Church must uncompromisingly proclaim the deadly perils of riches. She must substitute co-operation for the absolutely and incurably unChristian principles of competition."[54] There was no sanction in natural law either for competition or for pre-existing property rights. To be true to Christ, the Methodist church must denounce as a social crime any distribution of wealth which made a few enormously wealthy and a multitude desperately poor.

In this regard, business monopolies appeared particularly sinister in their manipulation of individuals and their control of governments for selfish financial gain. Beginning in 1904, the revelations concerning John D. Rockefeller and his Standard Oil Company's nefarious activities in the United States seemed to illustrate the dangers of big business for Canadians. Western Canadians especially mistrusted the railway, steel, meat-packing, and wheat-marketing conglomerates that dominated business. In addition, the manipulation of the stock market appeared to be no more than sophisticated gambling, while the rise of large-scale banking and insurance companies exemplified businesses that did not appear to operate in the national interest. Many Methodists complained that the acquisition of wealth and its conspicuous display had become iniquitous passions which subordinated higher goals by establishing false standards of success.[55] The assumption of social superiority and the ostentatious flaunting of prosperity betrayed true Christian stewardship. While wealth used in God's service retained a moral quality, for the social reformers all wealth must be used for the benefit of society; businessmen must be ruled by the Christian principles of comradeship and justice.

The most doctrinaire social gospellers demanded a complete overhaul of the existing social order. It was not enough to eliminate a specific evil. To them, real progress would only occur when democracy ruled and the traditionally powerless working classes had a dominant role in economic, political, and social affairs. However, although active and vocal, the membership of the extreme social-gospel wing of the Methodist church was never numerous. Like the extreme conservatives, it drew much of its influence from its membership in large international and interdenominational movements. It reacted against legislated doctrine and attempted to tackle the problems of the period pragmatically. When mainstream Methodism failed to follow its lead, some members found more receptive homes, at least temporarily, in the short-lived Labour churches or moved out of institutional religion altogether. They found they could spread their message more clearly from the union hall or the political platform.[56]

However, for the most part, the social gospel did not represent a significant break with the goals that had dominated Methodism for generations. Even the wealthy, middle-class lay leadership was not frightened by the social gospel and continued to promote significant reform. Leading businessmen such as Henry Fudger and Joseph Flavelle subscribed to liberal theology and appreciated the social gospellers' attempts at social redemption and kinship through the inculcation of justice and cooperation in all facets of life. But they instinctively opposed what they assumed were the unscriptural goals of class warfare and the overthrow of the existing social order espoused by some under the guise of the social gospel. In fact, most Methodists viewed the movement simply as faith and works articulated in concrete terms for the modern generation in order to make evangelism more aggressive and relevant. Few had difficulty combining the holiness stress on personal regeneration with the social-gospel emphasis on reshaping society. Mainstream Methodism had always acknowledged that one of the purposes of Christianity was to create a harmonious, moral society, and supporters of the social gospel never rejected traditional spiritual religion. In fact, they hoped to recapture the energy and commitment that had characterized evangelical revivalism and to link them to a more modern religious experience and social evangelism. The more adept revivalists provided a ready-made pattern for action when directed at social, rather than individual, salvation.[57]

Moderate social gospellers also readily proclaimed the necessity of personal salvation as a corollary to social reformation. Samuel Dwight Chown, for instance, preached, "Regeneration consciously experienced and testified to by the spirit of God was the outstanding doctrine of Methodism, and it is still our paramount mission to proclaim it."[58] The blending of personal and social regeneration became a fundamental canon of Methodist belief and practice during the twentieth century and was institutionalized in the Department of Evangelism and Social Service. It advocated preventive, redemptive, legislative, and punitive means to end evil. Even the classic statement of the social-gospel program enunciated in the department's report to the Methodist General Conference in 1918 claimed that many of the reforms would have been unnecessary if "the Methodist doctrine of holiness or perfect love had been followed in all its social and economic implications."[59] The Methodist church's purpose in reforming social conditions was to improve spiritual life and make Canadian society sacred.

Even the extreme social gospellers were not radical by contemporary, international standards. For instance, Ernest Thomas, who, along with Salem Bland, was condemned as the most radical and controversial Methodist official, remained inherently moderate in his approach to social questions. Coming from Britain at age twenty-four in 1890 in response to Canadian appeals for men for home-mission work, Thomas had studied theology and philosophy at Wesleyan Theological College in Montreal and Queen's University in

Kingston in preparation for his ordination in 1894. He served churches in Montreal, Saskatchewan, and British Columbia conferences until his appointment as field secretary to the Army and Navy Board and the Department of Evangelism and Social Service in 1918. Widely read and with a keen analytical mind, he hated anything that tended to degrade the individual or limit social justice. He worked throughout his long career to promote harmony between capital and labour. Although he was progressive for his times and supported the idealistic goals of organized labour and labour politicians, he often criticized their tactics and firmly allied social reform with personal evangelism.

Some social gospellers did experiment with socialism, but they generally desired a moderate Christian socialism. Communism and other forms of European socialism were too closely associated with class warfare, revolution, and anarchy. But Christian socialism was defined as the religion of Christ and resulted from the application of biblical principles to the problems of the times. It stressed class cooperation and called for social harmony and mutual respect. Methodism as a whole strongly opposed the division of its religious fellowship into social classes. It too affirmed that once the reign of "cooperative brotherhood" had been achieved, Canada would become a truly Christian cooperative commonwealth and would progress to a higher humanity. However, while most Methodists would accept the rhetoric, they would not readily subscribe to the tenets of even Christian socialism if pushed too far. Although all wealth was a social product and the state had a right to some of it for social purposes, the individual also had a right to retain the free use of honest gain. These Methodists maintained that inequalities were both inevitable and natural and that no philosophy advocating an artificial equality could be practically applied.[60]

The Methodist church continued to encourage its members to donate their surplus wealth to the connexion on a voluntary basis. Despite wishes to the contrary by some members, it relied heavily on the wealthy for the support of its operations. The church constantly reminded its members that "Christianity does not teach either public or private ownership of wealth, but it insists upon Christian stewardship."[61] Nevertheless, by the early twentieth century, the original emphasis on stewardship and Christian benevolence as essentially acts of personal faith and the means of personal growth in grace had become, under the influence of the social gospel, social duties. In addition to acknowledging God's right to the wealth, the Christian must also consecrate his or her worldly vocation and resources to uplift the entire community. The purpose of work was to acquire goods so that they could be spent in the world's service. The assumption that money could help initiate God's earthly dominion was novel, but the example of individuals such as Hart Massey gave promise that perhaps "the first interest of businessmen will be the Business of the King."[62]

Although traditional charity remained the basis of most Methodist giving, it was often highly paternalistic and reflected middle-class biases or was coupled with racial and ethnic prejudice. Charity failed to appreciate the views of the wage-earner or the poor and called for sympathy rather than social justice. "In some cases we find a patronizing paternalism which seeks to do for the needy what a juster social order would enable them to do for themselves.

Paternalism may do for the weak, but it will not develop the strong."[63] In order to advance social justice, the true philanthropist should attempt to elevate society and thereby eliminate the need for charity.

To accomplish this goal while providing meaningful social services, most social gospellers advocated a new and stronger partnership with the state. The church claimed, "True democracy makes the state the organized will of men to do the will of God."[64] The historic concern over the separation of church and state had never been meant to imply a divorce of religious principles from politics or the actions of government. The state represented the common elements of belief and practice for its subjects and must therefore be infused with sound principles. Christ came to establish his dominion, not to build a church. Only the state had the authority and power to implement and enforce substantive changes in the country. Improvement in working and living conditions, the elimination or at least control of crime and immorality, and the implementation of social justice all relied on the combined strength of a progressive church and an active state.

## THE CHURCH AND SOCIETY

In this partnership, Methodist leaders intended to utilize their power and status to infuse society with the church's standards of moral conduct. They claimed the right to set standards for their own members and to have these enforced throughout the country. Methodism had always attacked unhealthy or frivolous social amusements. The church assumed that activities such as dancing, card-playing, attending the music hall or light theatre, horse-racing, and reading novels were broad and slippery paths leading to perdition. They were normally associated with immodest or fashionable dress, gambling, smoking, unsupervised late night activities, or evil companions and were unhealthy as well as immoral in themselves. They also wasted time and money better spent in personal spiritual growth and advancing God's work. To Methodists, not only did such activities weaken the mental, moral, and physical character of the participants, but they also led to the degeneration of the entire community. They were no longer simply personal sins; they were sins against society and a disgrace to the entire nation.

These irreligious amusements had been detrimental enough in rural Canada, but they were even more perilous in crowded towns and cities where strict supervision was impossible. Where once Methodism had assumed it could provide sufficient bulwarks against evil on its own, by the end of the century it was forced to seek alliances with other Protestant churches and secular organizations and to use the authority of government to protect and promote its value system. As well as denouncing inappropriate reading, it influenced the government to ban the publication or importation of such literature and to censor books and plays. Pool halls, carnivals, racetracks, and other public amusements were to be restricted through licences and closely monitored for indecent conduct. The church also claimed that the government should ban dancing in schools and place a curfew on young people. While recognizing the advantages of healthy recreation and sports, church officials urged the government to eliminate professionalism and any associated gambling from tainting the activity. When any such laws were passed, the Methodist clergy often became an unofficial policing agency informing the authorities about infractions.

Beyond these traditional concerns, the church, again informed by the crusading vigour of the social gospel, attempted to eliminate activities that were even more clearly threats to the family and the community at large. On one level it campaigned for sexual restraint and social purity. The arrival of large numbers of non-English-speaking immigrants added a sense of urgency since they were considered a serious threat to the development of Canada as a pure and virile nation. The Methodist church claimed that the hospitals and insane asylums were full of individuals who lacked sufficient personal restraint to overcome perverse sexual drives and who were so physically and mentally weakened that they could not function properly in society. It believed that the use of prostitutes was a particularly evil example of such conduct since it also exploited women and helped spread venereal diseases. Church officials demanded long jail terms for pimps and madams and Christian rescue homes for the fallen women. As well, particularly under the enlightened leadership of Beatrice Brigden after World War I, the Department of Evangelism and Social Service provided sex education programs to local groups and distributed vast quantities of literature on the dangers of illicit sex.[65]

Red-light districts had developed in most large cities where prostitutes could operate with relative impunity. The police and local officials generally turned a blind eye to the business unless there were public complaints. The districts were usually set up in cheap hotels and boarding-houses near the railway station or harbour, out of sight of middle-class residential areas but adjacent to immigrant housing. The church was deeply disturbed by the evil example they gave to new Canadians, as well as the lure they provided for young men away from home. However, attempts to get these districts closed down permanently were generally unsuccessful.[66]

Methodist officials also laboured to reform the criminal and prison systems in Canada. Believing in the role of the environment in shaping individuals and in the potential divinity of all humanity, they supported prevention and rehabilitation rather than simple punishment. While advocating better law enforcement and even the introduction of women police officers, they placed greater trust in the new expertise of criminologists and penologists to root out crime.[67] The church boards advocated better classification of prisoners in order to separate juvenile and first-time offenders from hardened criminals and more probation or reformatories where appropriate since prisons only further contaminated their inmates. More counselling, training, and support were also necessary in the jails and after release. The boards maintained that juvenile delinquents should be placed in good Christian homes, where they could receive the discipline, guidance, and love they had obviously been denied in their own homes. At the same time, the church was distressed by the jailing of the poor and the mentally ill simply because there were no other facilities available. In all these matters, it and the various levels of government could work in a harmonious and productive partnership.[68]

In addition to their involvement in these issues, Methodist reformers sought to transform the social environment. Overcrowding and slums had become common in the growing industrial centres, and most of the newcomers, either from rural Canada or abroad, were too poor or inexperienced to avoid or improve these conditions. Municipal governments lacked the resources, expertise, and often the will to deal effectively with the issues of inadequate water supply, sewage disposal, electricity, transportation, and social services. Recognizing these problems, the Methodist church led in the struggles for public health, sanitation, and housing reform. It also campaigned for honest and efficient government in order to get these reforms implemented.[69] Furthermore, it encouraged middle-class attempts to reform the city as a whole through urban planning. Modern planning helped eliminate the worst social conditions and, perhaps of equal importance to the reformers, protected the middle-class residential districts from urban decay and undesirable development. These measures were implemented by professional city planners and managers who, it was hoped, would make the urban centres function better while removing their administration from the whims of local politicians and special interests. The best example of this type of planning was the City Beautiful movement, which encouraged the introduction of parks, boulevards, and monumental public architecture into the cities. These amenities did little to help the poor directly, but they added to the respectability and beauty of the city and improved land values.[70]

However, most church leaders also recognized that real progress in Canadian society required an end to the exploitation of workers. Once they were paid a fair wage, protected from the vicissitudes of the economic system, and treated humanely in the work place, much of the endemic misery, crime, and vice would cease, and individuals would be able to improve their own social environment. Therefore, the church called for factory safety, higher wages, the eight-hour workday, a minimum wage, the prevention of child labour, pensions, unemployment insurance, and compensation for job-related injuries. Believing that immigration, especially from non-English-speaking countries, provided cheap competition for Canadian workers, the church also advocated a restrictive immigration policy and programs to transform new arrivals into responsible citizens.[71]

In order to improve labour conditions and enhance moral rectitude, Methodism also strove to protect Sunday from desecration. Throughout the nineteenth century, the church maintained that personal piety, home worship, and religious fellowship demanded obedience to the Fourth Commandment. As one of the providential institutions given to humanity, the sabbath was a weekly reminder of God's love. Methodists objected to using the day for travel, picnics, social visits, or other secular pursuits. More than a day of rest, it was crucial for active personal and social religion; home worship and attendance at church and Sunday school helped spiritual, moral, and intellectual growth. Methodists held it as an article of faith that the sabbath also renewed the vigour, enlivened the spirits, promoted healthy family life, and protected the peace and good order of society. If the sabbath was destroyed, it would "shake the moral foundations of our national power and prosperity."[72]

However, commercial and industrial developments, especially in the transportation field, complicated attitudes toward the sabbath. People were forced to service the ships, stagecoaches, and trains operating on Sunday, and their availability encouraged secular activities by the passengers. Sunday streetcars were especially visible and popular, but they were seen as contributing to irreligious behaviour. In addition, the government was becoming a major offender by permitting public works and postal delivery to be carried out on Sunday. To facilitate these activities, shops, restaurants, and other services opened, and the multiplication of such operations further weakened the special status of the day.

The movement to preserve the sabbath united middle-class and radical reformers, business associations, and labour unions. While sabbatarianism reflected an attempt at middle-class control and the desire to assist business interests, it also sought to create a harmonious moral order and to protect the inherent rights of workers. The need for mental and physical rejuvenation was particularly strong for the working class. Without laws to protect all classes of labour, the church believed humanity would become machine-like, ignorant, and brutish. While laws could not make people religious, the church argued that they could protect employees from "the tyranny of capital" and "the imperious will of a grasping capital."[73] Furthermore, small businesses needed legislative protection from unfair competition since informal closing agreements had not been effective.

Although it had originally relied most heavily on moral suasion, over time the Methodist church cooperated with business and labour groups, other Protestant churches, and interdenominational organizations such as the Lord's Day Alliance and the Social Service Council of Canada to advance government legislation. In fact, sabbatarianism in Canada was led by the Presbyterian church, especially under the leadership of John Shearer. Because the municipal, provincial, and federal governments all had jurisdiction over aspects of Sunday activity, these groups directed their efforts at all three levels of government. Gradually legislation protecting the sabbath was passed, culminating in the national Lord's Day Act of 1907.[74] The Methodists in Newfoundland continued to press for comparable legislation, while in Canada the churches were vigilant to ensure the legislation was enforced.

Clearly, however, the issue dearest to Methodists was the abolition of intoxicants in Canada. They considered it to be the linchpin of all social reform. No real progress could be achieved while drinking remained; its prohibition would immediately advance all other reforms. In many cases, the emphasis on prohibition blinded church leaders to other social questions or at least allowed them to deal less rigorously with more fundamental social and economic issues. Many middle-class businessmen could condemn liquor yet abstain from implementing social justice in their own work places. For instance, when a drunken fourteen-year-old boy was killed by falling into a machine in a factory, the condemnation was chiefly over his drinking, not that he was perhaps too young to be so employed, that his family was too poor to allow him to attend school, or that the factory should have been safer. Most Methodists also failed to recognize that drinking was often the result, not the cause, of social and economic distress or that it sometimes simply reflected different cultural traditions. Nevertheless, alcohol was a legitimate problem. Under prevailing conditions, there was little control of the drinking age, hours of sale, or quality of the product sold. Indeed, few would disagree that the fourteen-year-old should not have been able to buy and consume liquor.

Fundamentally, the church believed drinking was evil. It was contrary to the Bible, hindered spiritual growth, and was a barrier to religious progress. How could an apparently civilized country such as Canada expect to evangelize the non-Christian world if it tolerated such behaviour at home? Liquor businesses were described as agents of the devil abusing God's bounty; no Christian could use intoxicants.[75] However, the litany of evils promoted by intemperance went far beyond its harm to religion. Drinking caused children to lose respect for parents, prevented the family from serving its moral and disciplinary roles, and weakened the whole fabric of the home and ultimately of the nation. Not only was intemperance considered evil in itself, but it was also the root of other social immorality and of debased society. It led to participation in unhealthy and immoral amusements, caused much of the desecration of the sabbath, was often accompanied by gambling, and diminished personal moral restraints. According to the Methodist church, most prostitutes had fallen while under liquor's spell, and men were generally drawn to them while intoxicated. Methodists maintained, "Abolish the liquor traffic and not one brothel out of twenty would survive."[76]

For Methodists, the list of problems caused by alcohol was nearly endless. It was denounced as an addictive poison which attacked the body and the mind, dethroning reason and causing insanity and death. It prevented the body from fighting off disease and was a significant cause of accidents. Intemperance weakened the work ethic, destroyed valuable talents and resources, and led to financial ruin. The inebriate businessman lost the confidence and respect of the community. In addition, many Methodists believed that wages were generally sufficient for basic needs if workers did not squander them on drink. Therefore drinking forced them to live in unsanitary slums without proper food or clothing and caused pauperism. Alcohol also undermined respect for authority and was blamed for much of the labour unrest and the violence that sometimes accompanied strikes. In fact, most of the crime in society at large was attributed to alcohol.[77]

By the late nineteenth century, the church attacked even moderate drinking and denied that the decision to abstain was personal and should remain voluntary. It argued that moderate drinking of even wine or beer led to heavy drinking. Alcohol was a poison; no one could advocate the moderate use of poison. Since alcohol abuse hurt the entire country, society had a right to impose restrictions on the individual. Furthermore, despite the use of educational programs, a flood of temperance literature, sermons, abstinence pledges, and other traditional means, Methodists came to recognize that moral suasion and voluntary abstinence would never reform the hardened drinker or end the social misery caused by alcohol. The church therefore advocated complete, legislated prohibition.

Although total prohibition was the ultimate goal, the Methodists cooperated with the other Christian churches, with a host of temperance organizations including the Templars of Temperance, the Woman's Christian Temperance Union, and especially the Dominion Alliance, and increasingly during the twentieth century, with business and labour groups in a number of more limited campaigns to weaken alcohol's influence. For its own part, the Methodist church replaced communion wine with grape juice except in Newfoundland. On a broader level, because of the split jurisdiction over various aspects of the production, transportation, and sale of intoxicants, the campaigns for specific changes were directed at all three levels of government. The temperance forces worked successfully to limit the sale of alcohol by the glass, reduced the number and hours of operation of saloons in St John's, prevented social clubs in Winnipeg from being licensed, kept alcohol out of the northern mining and lumber camps, abolished its sale in grocery stores in British Columbia, and had the drinking age raised in various jurisdictions. They also worked to limit the "treating habit," by which they felt inexperienced drinkers were lured into debauchery, and demanded that alcohol in dry areas be dispensed only by legitimate druggists for medicinal purposes. As well, they attempted to have bars banned altogether since these produced the "frowsy, blear-eyed, sodden derelict, destitute of self-respect, whose horizon is bounded by the liquor bottle."[78] Failing such a ban, the temperance agents at least wanted bars removed from rural or residential areas, where they threatened respectable society.

As more temperance measures were introduced, much time and energy was spent insuring that they were properly implemented. The licensing and operation of drinking establishments were closely monitored. Methodist ministers were especially vigilant and developed an elaborate network to report any infractions. In western Canada, for instance, the North-West Mounted Police were continually prodded to enforce anti prostitution and temperance laws. As in many other jurisdictions, the police were usually reluctant to enforce regulations against what they considered harmless personal vices. Methodists were also committed to assisting problem drinkers. They called for special hospitals for the inebriates, encouraged social workers to help the families, and assisted Prisoners' Aid societies to deal with ex-convicts. Because much of the alcohol reaching the consumer was actually poisonous, the church also supported legislation to monitor the quality of its production.[79]

These activities, however, were subsidiary to more systematic campaigns to have the various levels of government institute complete prohibition within their jurisdictions. Methodists believed that the influence of liquor would only be overcome through compulsory action. The state had a duty to protect its citizens from injury; this was not an infringement of inherent personal or property rights since no one had a right to impair others. Good citizenship and public interest demanded prohibition. The principal temperance legislation was the Canada Temperance, or Scott, Act of 1878, which permitted municipalities or rural townships to stop the sale of intoxicants if three-fifths of the voters agreed. Here then was an opportunity for local citizens to establish community standards. Over the next thirty-five years, under the leadership of the Methodist church and the various temperance organizations, most of the country took advantage of this local option and went dry. However, this was a slow process which covered only part of the problem; liquor was still widely available and could be consumed at home.

The temperance forces constantly petitioned the governments to hold plebiscites to determine if the provinces and the federal government could pass stronger measures. In some parts of the country there were even attempts to introduce "direct legislation" whereby citizens could bypass the perceived liquor-controlled politicians and introduce legislation directly into Parliament. Although legislation alone would never make society moral, the Methodist church believed that without such laws society would never improve. The church recommended that since this issue was so important, its members should only nominate and vote for candidates committed to prohibition. Politics needed these good men. Finally, in 1898 a national plebiscite favoured prohibition, but since the vast majority of voters in Roman Catholic Quebec opposed the measure, Sir Wilfrid Laurier's Liberal government refused to introduce legislation. At the same time, the Supreme Court ruled that the Manitoba and Prince Edward Island temperance acts of 1898 were unconstitutional since they infringed upon federal jurisdiction.[80] None the less, although faced with constant frustrations, by the early twentieth century, the temperance forces were becoming confident that in time liquor would be abolished and the Lord's dominion would be advanced in Canada.

Despite their optimism, it took the impetus of World War I to bring in total national prohibition. For most Canadians, the war was a great patriotic and moral crusade; it was unconscionable not to sacrifice at home while so many were sacrificing their lives on the battlefields. It seemed particularly unpatriotic, if not criminal, to waste badly need resources producing alcohol, which weakened both the soldier abroad and the worker at home. Nearly every country involved in the struggle introduced some form of prohibition, and by the middle of the war, every Canadian province had either prohibition or strict government control of the sale of liquor, beer, and wine. Finally, Sir Robert Borden's Union government, under the powers of the War Measures Act, passed an order-in-council establishing national prohibition. It came into effect in April 1918 except in Quebec, where it was to take effect a year later, and ran until the end of the war. Under pressure from Methodists, and particularly from Newton Wesley Rowell, then president of council in the Borden government, the measure was extended for a year after the war as a means of protecting returning soldiers.[81]

However, after the war, as the federal restrictions eased and the Scott Act again took effect, there was a gradual decline in temperance sentiment across the country. The general populace and especially the returning soldiers, tired of sacrificing and disillusioned by the failure of moral crusades, saw prohibition as a narrow restriction of their liberty. So many Canadians were disobeying the laws that bootlegging, political corruption, and other criminal activities threatened to bring the whole legal system into disrepute. Local communities increasingly voted to allow licensed establishments, and although seven provinces retained prohibition for several more years, British Columbia's and Quebec's policies of government control of the sale of intoxicants gradually became the norm. While never satisfactory to the Methodist church, government licensing and control did answer some of the worst abuses of alcohol.

The temperance movement fought a rearguard action to restrict the expansion of drinking, but as with most other issues of moral restraint, looser standards gradually came to prevail in Canada.[82] Despite a growing pessimism after the war concerning the post-millennial reign of Christ, the Methodist church remained a powerful force for social amelioration and uplift throughout its remaining history and passed on this spirit and determination to the United Church of Canada in 1925. While retaining a strong, yet moderate, middle-class value system, it continued to blend the influence of the social gospel with a renewed interest in personal piety in order to strengthen the family and improve the nation. The Methodist church remained convinced of its right and obligation to create a profoundly moral order in Canada, and in reality, it had been highly successful in establishing the framework of acceptable personal and social conduct.

# 14 Young People and the Methodist Moral Order

The Methodist church was thoroughly committed to the moral transformation of Canada by the latter part of the nineteenth century and acknowledged its obligation to bind everyone in spiritual and moral fellowship. This sense of obligation was particularly strong with regard to children. Religion was the greatest gift that society could offer its young, and religion, in turn, would sustain both their own spiritual and moral health and the prosperity of the church and the nation. The Methodist church also gradually realized that its future strength and therefore its influence for good rested on integrating its own children into the connexion rather than on converting outsiders. Since children were so vital for the future, they had to be retained in an intimate relationship to the denomination under a strict spiritual and moral discipline, and their special status had to be protected.

Part of this belief evolved out of an appreciation of childhood as a distinct phase of life. Such appreciation developed in response to a complex web of social, demographic, economic, and intellectual forces beginning in the late eighteenth and running throughout the nineteenth century.[1] Over this period the child became the primary focus within the family and a vital concern of society in general. Simultaneously, the developing industrial system required children to be trained and disciplined without providing unfair competition to adult labour. Both circumstances demanded the prolongation and protection of childhood. Thus social and economic conditions came together as never before to accord children a pre-eminent status.[2]

Although the family remained central to any concerted effort at improvement, it was not always capable or willing to advance the children's best interests. Too often they were sacrificed to more immediate and overriding financial requirements. The respectable, middle-class Methodist leaders were concerned about this aspect of life among the poorer and immigrant families, but they also recognized the need to shape their own children into moral individuals. This could best be accomplished by increasing the church's care for the young and by promoting other moral, child-centred institutions. Using the insights provided by the new scientific, philosophical, and psychological disciplines, a variety of secular institutions focused on the child as most vulnerable to mistreatment and exploitation, but also as most appropriate for reformation. To these groups, education offered the best hope for reform since it was widely assumed that crime, vice, and misery could not survive among a truly educated people. Through gradual evolution advanced by education, the very instincts for anti-social behaviour would be eliminated. This belief corresponded with an increasing trust among Methodists that spiritual progress depended on gradual growth to grace. Christian nurture therefore became an essential feature of Methodist operations.

Much of the Methodist church's response to the young was guided by a re-evaluation of the theological assumptions concerning their original spiritual condition. Belief in children's total depravity changed first to an acceptance of their innocence and their ability to be shaped into adult Christians and, ultimately, to the belief that at birth, children were in a preferred condition of spiritual safety. Under such assurance, the church could logically protect and support childhood. This new understanding was reinforced by an altered appreciation of the implications of baptism for church membership and bolstered by a more substantial alliance with religious auxiliaries such as Sunday schools and young people's societies.

However, Canadian society was by no means unanimous in its acceptance of the special condition of children; old fears continued to exert considerable influence on their treatment. In fact, an individual could retain a confusing array of contradictory beliefs in this regard, depending on the circumstances or the issues at stake.[3] Although the nineteenth century "discovered" childhood, it would have to run its full course before a preferred status was assured. Nevertheless, by the end of the century, parental and institutional discipline and affection had commingled with the new economic and social conditions in an optimistic view of childhood and in the attempt to create a harmonious, ordered, and progressive community.

## CHANGING PERCEPTIONS OF CHILDHOOD

Traditional Wesleyan doctrine declared that all humankind was heir to sin and death through Adam's fall. Christ's atonement did not dissolve this punishment, but rather permitted his advocacy for spiritual life on behalf of those who truly confessed their faults. The new covenant of God, through Jesus Christ, promised a dispensation from damnation to those who consciously, responsibly, and decisively rejected Satan and actively sought redemption.[4] By definition, the very young lacked the maturity, and its accompanying responsibility, to make a conscious decision for Christ. Little attempt was made to place an age limit on this irresponsible state, but it was generally assumed to end at age four or five when a child recognized the difference between right and wrong. Children were therefore in a state of irresponsibility and shared humanity's damnation until they were reborn later. Late-nineteenth-century Canadian Methodist theologians such as John Marshall and Nathanael Burwash continued to argue that all humankind was unconditionally depraved and to repeat that Christ's atonement simply made humanity's regeneration possible. However, they added that since young children were irresponsible, they did not commit sin, which was a conscious and wilful renunciation of God, but they possessed a proneness to evil which would lead them to sin when they matured. Children were innocent of sin, not depravity.[5]

However, by the 1870s, many Canadian Methodists, along with Protestant churchmen throughout the world, were searching for a more positive appraisal of childhood. Led in Canada by Henry Bland, Alexander Sutherland, and Egerton Ryerson, they argued that children were not subjects of humanity's original fall. Quoting Romans 5:18, they maintained that if infancy was dead because of Adam, then it received the gift of grace through Christ. Christ's atonement was superior to Adam's sin. To them it appeared unnatural and illogical that Adam's sin condemned humankind, and especially innocent children, to total destruction while Christ's glory only gave promise of salvation. No valid understanding of the Bible or the nature and wisdom of God could be founded on such principles.[6] Apart from scriptural arguments, there was growing support for the view that guilt had to be personally acquired through actual, not inherited, sin.

In practical terms, both Burwash and Marshall found it extremely difficult to suggest that a benevolent and merciful God condemned innocent children who died in infancy to eternity in hell simply because they had not consciously rejected sin. Burwash had no particular answer to such concerns, but he maintained that God would intervene to look after the dead infant. Marshall went slightly further and suggested these children were actually regenerated through a special intercession of the Holy Spirit.[7] Thus the ardent supporters of infant depravity felt obliged to soften the harshness and undermine the consistency of traditional theology. Even those who could not support the view that children were saved when born did agree with Wesley about the existence of a prevenient grace, of a germ of salvation given to humanity at Creation and magnified by Christ's atonement.

But by the second half of the nineteenth century, the infant was too deeply ensconced at the heart of the family for such haziness to suffice. Romantic sentimentalism favoured a more triumphant status for the dead infant. A minister preaching at a child's funeral found it impossible on a practical level to imply natural depravity. Such theological precepts were too harsh for a church attempting to fulfil a positive social and moral mandate in the Victorian community. Moreover, if God, with an unbounded capacity for mercy, redeemed the dying infant, why not the child that survived? For those who believed that children were already in a state of grace, no special intercession was necessary; infants legitimately proceeded to heaven upon death. This latter belief appeared more rational to a generation of Methodists who had never strayed far from spiritual religion and who were raising their own children in a moral environment.[8]

As the optimistic perception of the status of the child became more popular, many Methodist leaders attempted to gain full membership rights for children. This attempt opened a debate over both the ability of the young to have a mature conversion experience and the relationship between the sacrament of baptism and church membership. During the second half of the nineteenth century, Methodism sought to define the benefits actually received through baptism. Historically, baptism had been the "new circumcision," the New Testament method of initiating all members, but especially children, into Christ's covenant. It was an outward and visible sign of this inward promise. Nevertheless, the nature of baptism did have to be clarified in order to illuminate the proper relation of children to the Methodist church. Officially, the Methodist Doctrines and Discipline declared, "We regard all children who have been baptized, as placed in a visible covenant relation to God, and under the special care and supervision of the Church."[9] In 1853 the Wesleyan Methodist Conference had added that baptized persons "are made members of the visible Church of Christ; their gracious relation to Him as the Second Adam, and as Mediator of the New Covenant is solemnly ratified by divine appointment; and they are thereby recognized as having a claim to all those spiritual blessings of which they are the proper subjects."[10]

To determine what these statements actually meant, Methodists re-entered the debate on the spiritual condition of childhood. Few Canadians returned to Wesley for guidance. In fact, he had been part of the Anglican tradition and, while never clearly defining a distinctly Methodist position, had at least initially supported baptismal regeneration. However, in Canada most Methodists agreed that baptism was only an initiation and a symbol with no regenerative power. Baptism did not cause regeneration; rather, salvation was promised to those who sustained the early vows made on their behalf.[11] Traditional spokesmen argued that no one could be regenerated without consciously repenting his or her faults; repentance and regeneration were inseparable. Baptism did not regenerate because it was not necessarily accompanied by a mature and responsible decision. Since it did not grant membership in the invisible or spiritual church, it should not initiate children into the visible church on earth. For those people who assumed that children were totally depraved, no sacrament performed by human beings on their behalf could undo the initial condemnation of God. In consequence, the Methodist church should not grant membership based on baptism, and children must continue in a subordinate relationship in the church.[12]

This position was attacked by those who believed children were already saved. While denying baptismal regeneration, they held that regeneration was not necessary; baptism merely confirmed an existing condition. It was "a beautiful and expressive symbol of the Holy Spirit's work, and the seal which outwardly attests the child's covenant relation with God."[13] They also disagreed that repentance and regeneration were inseparable. The symbolic rejection of sin was possible even when regeneration was not necessary. Furthermore, it would be unconscionable for the church to administer baptism to children if they were totally depraved. Unlike the Baptists, who felt children should therefore be barred from baptism, they maintained there was an initial justification in children which not only entitled them to the sacrament as a symbol of the promise to continue in that state, but also equally entitled them to the benefits of full membership in the visible church on earth. "The rite of baptism admits to membership with the visible church one whom Christ has already adopted and received."[14]

In 1866 the American Methodist Episcopal Church appeared to grant membership for baptized children after six months' probation in class meetings. There were many Canadian Methodists who wished to follow this model. Nevertheless, although during the last quarter of the century, the church was moving to accept the more optimistic view of the moral status of children and the implications this held for baptism, the acceptance of children into full membership had serious obstacles to overcome. Reformers such as Egerton Ryerson and Henry Bland believed that all connexional tests which interfered with the rights of children should be removed. Ryerson's resignation from the ministry in 1854 over the status of the class meeting as a test of membership had actually been an attempt to gain recognition for baptized children. He maintained "that each child baptized by the Church is thereby enfranchised with the rights and privileges of citizenship in it until he forfeits them by personal misconduct."[15] Despite the failure to remove the compulsory status of class meetings, the wider aim of improving the position of children was at least partially satisfied. During the 1880s, other administrative changes removed liabilities on children, such as the tax on members to support the ministry. Children increasingly shared in the adult means of grace and the fellowship of the church.

## SUNDAY SCHOOLS

Paralleling these developments, the Methodist church went outside its own structures and even beyond the family to train children in spiritual and moral principles and to bind them to institutional religion. Many Methodist leaders believed that, rather than waiting to redeem adults, the church would lose an invaluable opportunity to minister to those most receptive to good if it failed to evangelize the young.[16] To assist in this task and to help create a moral order appropriate for respectable Victorian society, Methodists turned naturally to the Sunday school to supply Christian nurture. It combined all the best elements of organized religion with the seminal features of the public school system. The Sunday school offered the principal source of new church members and the best hope for the creation of a moral, spiritually alive Canadian society. Sunday schools were later supplemented by more specialized young people's organizations to meet the broader demands and different understandings of youth; together they formed an unparalleled network to evangelize children and marshall their strength for Christian service.

From the late eighteenth through the nineteenth centuries, Sunday schools normally developed from non-sectarian community organizations run by dedicated lay men and women interested in basic moral and educational training, to semi-independent church auxiliaries nurturing the young at arm's length, and finally to departments of the local churches with highly organized clerical and denominational control working to bring young people into a direct relationship with the church. In the early twentieth century, the denominational organizations functioned cooperatively to expand the work among the differentiated groups of children, adolescents, and young adults and to use these groups to promote missionary, moral-reform, and evangelizing goals. Religious education experimented with liberal theological approaches and progressive pedagogy to make itself relevant to the goals of contemporary society.[17]

Originally developed in Britain by Robert Raikes and other reformers to meet the challenges posed by dispossessed children in the burgeoning industrial centres, Sunday schools were designed to train and discipline the young and integrate them into the new economic, social, and political order. Fear of crime and anarchy had as much to do with their initial popularity as a desire to provide the poor with a means to acquire basic literary skills. The "ragged schools," as they were sometimes called, provided literary and moral training on the only day free from labour so that the working classes could read the Bible and function in their limited spheres. In Britain the Sunday schools remained for a considerable period the particular institution of the poor, who had little other opportunity to learn to read and write.[18]

Sunday schools complemented the work of both the churches and the day schools, but initially had little connection with either. However, the leaders of the evangelical revival, including John Wesley, quickly utilized them as voluntary, lay organizations dedicated to converting the young to Christ. Women were particularly suitable for the work since it was essentially an extension of the best elements of family worship and training. In Protestant Canada the secular educational role was relatively quickly displaced by the evangelizing function. Reading and writing were retained only for the very young and usually only in areas where common schools were not operating or among new immigrant children, who often missed the opportunity to attend day schools. Although many Sunday school promoters continued to assert that, in reducing ignorance, basic education in itself encouraged morality, others saw this as a secular function and potentially as "a desecration of the day, and a frustration of the holy purpose our Church contemplates in extending Sabbath School exertions."[19] Nevertheless, Sunday schools often did precede regular schools and supplied a significant educational function, especially in isolated pioneer areas such as outport Newfoundland.

Perhaps their greatest educational role, however, was in supplying reading material for the local communities. Before the establishment of the public library system or the availability of inexpensive publications for the general public, adults as well as children drew heavily on the Sunday school libraries for edifying literature. These supplied Bible tracts, hymnals, temperance material, magazines, religious biographies, and general stories and were a moral alternative to trashy novels and the secular press. The Methodist church led the way in this movement and by the end of the nineteenth century had nearly 400,000 books and pamphlets in its Sunday-school-library system.[20]

At the same time, limiting Sunday schools to the poor was less common in North America. Although the schools were sometimes used as agencies to help the disadvantaged in the local community, these individuals were not considered the lower-class outcasts of industrialization, but simply those who had not yet improved their economic condition in pioneer British America.

For the most part, the schools catered to the rising middle class or at least those with middle-class aspirations. These individuals were both accessible and most ready to take advantage of the opportunities that the Sunday schools afforded.[21] As a result, the social control the schools exhibited was based on the desire to transform all young people into respectable Christians, rather than on a perceived need to suppress the lower classes.

The first Sunday, or Sabbath, schools had appeared during the late eighteenth century in British America, but the institution did not take hold until the nineteenth century. Usually Sunday schools developed in the larger communities first and then expanded into the surrounding rural districts. Generally non-sectarian, community organizations, they united the efforts of a dedicated laity independent of the churches, although they often also served as the foundation for future congregations. These "union" schools stressed biblical teachings while playing down doctrinal issues; they "inculcate moral and religious instruction ... no sectarian sentiments shall be taught."[22] The schools accepted students and teachers from all Christian backgrounds and particularly sought children without any religious associations. The union schools were designed to lead the young to God and to be nurseries of piety and morality. To facilitate this work, they affiliated in organizations such as the Canada Sunday School Union, established in Montreal in 1836. Jealous of their independence from clerical and denominational control, the union schools operated parallel to the specifically denominational schools that began to emerge in the late 1820s. Many respected Methodists recognized the value of this ecumenical autonomy and continued to work for their success. In fact, union schools remained relatively influential in pioneer areas and were particularly popular in western Canada well into the twentieth century.[23]

But as the Methodist connexions came to acknowledge the improved status of children and sought to bring them up "in the nurture and admonition of the Lord" and as they accumulated the resources to commit to this work, they began either to take over the independent schools or to create their own denominational institutions. The churches recognized that, in conjunction with parental instruction, the Sunday schools were valuable auxiliaries for initiating young people into the Christian fellowship. In addition, since religious instruction was central to the creation of a Christian society and church doctrine was vital for religious instruction but was unavailable in union schools, many Methodists feared that traditional spiritual and social values would not be protected by non-sectarian bodies. As a result by mid-century, the Methodist churches attacked union schools for failing to foster an intimate relationship with institutional religion. For instance, although the Methodist Episcopal church believed that union schools were useful if no other agency was present, it feared it was losing its own children and jeopardizing its future membership by not developing denominational Sunday schools. The Wesleyans were even more adamant: "The evil influence of Union Schools on those connected with our Church, is almost everywhere felt and complained of."[24] The subsequent relative decline in union schools was applauded, but the Methodist churches continued to warn that such institutions were antagonistic to Methodism's best interests.

All the Protestant denominations came to view Sunday schools, not only as nurseries of piety, but also as the essential source for new members. "They are the nurseries of the Church, and fertilizing streams to the moral soil of the country"; "Sabbath school instruction stands directly connected with the future prosperity and stability of our beloved Church, and indirectly with the salvation of thousands of the youth of our land."[25] With the debate over the status of baptized children and the proper function of the class meeting dividing Methodism, the emphasis on binding Sunday school converts to the connexion was a source of deep comfort and consensus. Methodists could all agree that their youth should join Methodist churches. The Methodist Episcopal church asserted that Sunday schools were the only reliable source of members to replace those who died, and it was noted that the scholars who enter the church were "more likely to prove valiant and faithful soldiers of Christ than those who are rescued from the service of Satan after years of rebellion against God."[26]

Nevertheless, initial attempts to develop a Methodist Sunday school system were rather haphazard and remained for a considerable period under the control of the laity, with only minimal interest shown by the itinerants. For instance, in 1829 the original Methodist Episcopal Conference had established a Sunday school union, but it did little more than recognize the need for more sensible work among the young. Gradually over the following few decades, Methodist church authorities encouraged their ministers to get more deeply involved in the Sunday schools and attempted to ensure that young people adopted Methodism as their religious home. By the 1850s most communities across British America had developed connexional schools, which the church attempted to bring under direct clerical control. In 1853 the Wesleyan Conference in Canada West established a Sunday school union based on the church's districts and under the supervision of the editor of the *Sunday School Guardian*. A year later a similar union was organized for the Montreal region, and in 1857 the Wesleyans in eastern British America created a committee to coordinate the work in the Maritimes. These organizations promoted the use of Wesleyan catechisms, doctrines, and publications. By the 1860s the church directed that the circuits' quarterly boards should approve all teachers and superintendents, although this policy was never totally enforced.[27] The smaller Methodist churches quickly implemented similar regulations. Such attempts to control the Sunday school movement, however, represented only a subtle evolution of the traditional relationships.

In 1869 the Canadian Wesleyans appointed John Carroll secretary of the Sunday school union to promote the schools through lectures, writing, editing, and the distribution of connexional Sunday school literature. His expenses were expected to be paid by the affiliated schools, but this attempt at coordination was a distinct failure. It was not until the 1870s that Methodism made a concerted effort to dominate the Sunday school by making it a department of the church's operations. The Methodist church established a joint lay and clerical committee to administer the denominational system and to create and assist local schools supervised by the itinerant. The Sunday school superintendent automatically became a member of the local quarterly board to ensure the close integration of Christian nurture into the church's regular proceedings and to guarantee that proper doctrine was taught.[28] Through these means, the Sunday school evolved from a loose auxiliary into the church's right hand, serving to nurture children, convert them to Christ, and evangelize non-Methodist young people in the community.

The growth of Methodist Sunday schools after mid-century was truly remarkable. In Atlantic Canada, the Wesleyans reported 11,331 students and 205 teachers in 205 schools in 1860. These figures had increased to 25,518 students, 3,383 teachers, and 457 schools by the time of union in 1884. The most significant feature was the expanding number of teachers per school. In central Canada in 1855, the Wesleyans listed 20,708 students, 3,166 teachers, and 345 schools. These grew to 33,232 students, 5,242 teachers, and 771 schools in 1860 and to 175,052 students, 22,134 teachers, and 2,707 schools in 1883. In the Methodist Episcopal church, the student enrolment increased from 5,787 to 23,733 between 1860 and 1883, while during the same period the number of teachers increased from 851 in 106 schools to 3,285 in 430 schools.

The New Connexion Methodist church, which merged into the Methodist Church of Canada in 1874, listed 2,178 students, 363 teachers, and 86 schools in 1855 and 9,000 students, 1,089 teachers, and 154 schools in its final year of existence. The Primitive Methodist church expanded its schools from 69 to 152 between 1860 and 1883, while its enrolment rose from 3,450 to 9,065 students and from 540 to 1,172 teachers. To complete the survey of mainstream Methodist churches, the Bible Christian Sunday schools grew from about 50 with 500 teachers and 2,500 students in 1860 to about 150 with 8,000 students and 1,000 teachers in 1883.

In 1886, the first year that the united Methodist church recorded Sunday school statistics, 191,185 scholars and 24,246 teachers met in 2,675 connexion schools. These numbers increased until 1915, when 420,210 children and young adults, with 41,929 teachers and officers, attended 3,824 Methodist schools. Another 10,128 Methodists met in union schools. During World War I, the Sunday school operations grew at a much slower pace. In 1922 the church had 431,498 students, 42,861 teachers, and 3,525 schools, and on the eve of union with the Presbyterians and Congregationalists, it reported 471,104 students.[29]

With the union of 1884, the church further integrated Sunday schools into its institutional framework. A General Conference committee supervised the publication of Sunday school magazines and literature, assisted poor schools, organized conventions and teacher training institutes, and generally directed the curriculum and structure of the schools. Student contributions financed the committee's work. During the 1890s Methodism also developed significant denominational young people's organizations outside the Sunday school. A permanent bureaucracy, including at its peak seven secretaries, closely monitored all these operations. As well, the church encouraged the schools to contribute to its expanding missions and evangelistic operations and to promote temperance and reform causes.[30]

In order to increase the efficiency of this work, it began to cooperate with the other evangelical denominations. The interaction, however, was based, not on non-sectarian principles as in the union schools, but rather on strong denominational structures. In 1914 this cooperation was formalized in the International Sunday School Council, which worked to elevate standards and took over the preparation of the uniform lessons. Four years later, the Religious Educational Council of Canada was created to coordinate Protestant Sunday school operations. It brought together all the provincial organizations to establish national policies and administered, through its Work Advisory councils, the Canadian Girls in Training and the Canadian Standard Efficiency Training programs. The internal organization of the Methodist committees dealing with the young reflected these broader developments. However, despite the fact that there was increased cooperation, especially with the Presbyterians as union approached, the Methodist church was always jealous of interference in its own young people's organizations and tried to dominate the Religious Educational Council. With the assistance of the Presbyterians, the Methodists in fact used the council to promote their own social and religious agenda and as a result, raised objections from the other churches.[31]

The rationale for the integration of Sunday schools into the church's structures was the encouragement it offered students to seek conversion and to become full members of the Methodist church. Such an outcome was considered crucial both for the future strength of the church and for the spiritual safety and happiness of the young people themselves. The church constantly enjoined its Sunday school teachers to "direct all your efforts to awaken the conscience, to interest the feelings, and to engage the whole soul in the pursuit of salvation."[32] Part of this emphasis rested on the assumption that children and youth not only could be saved, but actually represented the most appropriate candidates for conversion. Those who failed to recognize these facts were condemned for weakening Methodism and hurting all young people.

In 1863 the Canadian Wesleyans had estimated that about 4 per cent of students were converted, while in 1878 the Methodist Church of Canada was disappointed by a 13 per cent converstion rate. Over the previous quadrennium, it noted that 20,986 students had been converted. In the peak year of 1915, over 25 per cent of the Sunday school students were church members, and 14,590 joined the church that year. In total, between 1900 and 1925 an estimated 225,000 students became members of the Methodist church.[33] Sunday schools had become the principal source of new members as Methodism increasingly drew its numerical strength from within its own religious community rather than attracting converts from other denominations or from the corrupt world at large. Furthermore, the reliance on religious education to bring the young to Christ reinforced the church's emphasis on a gradually evolving experience as the basis of true spirituality.[34]

RELIGIOUS EDUCATION FOR THE YOUNG

In order to remain relevant to the changing needs of the church and the Sunday schools, the curriculum, indeed the entire pedagogy of the institutions, was dramatically transformed during this period. Originally, beyond the occasional spelling book or grammar, the study sources were the Bible and lessons prepared by the teachers themselves. Methodist hymns were also a fundamental and widely appreciated method of implanting doctrine in young minds. However, there were few common standards, and the curriculum was extremely limited. Sharing these scarce resources and lessening the cost and difficulty of producing material was the basic rationale for cooperation among the local schools.

The most important denominational doctrines were taught through the connexional catechisms. Whether separate or part of the regular school program, Bible and catechumen classes were deemed to be essential elements of instruction, particularly for those more dedicated students preparing to become members. *The Catechism of the Wesleyan Methodists* was first published in 1838 and revised in 1868 to make it easier for children. After the union of 1884, the 1838 version was reprinted and used, with some modifications, until 1898, when it was replaced by a substantially amended volume. However, its declarations were often beyond children's comprehension and lent themselves more to simple memorization. Perhaps for this reason, although catechumen study remained a high priority with the supervising committees, only a small percentage of students actually participated.[35]

In the adoption of pedagogical principles or the establishment of curriculum, there was often a vast difference between what was recommended and what was actually practised in the local schools. Moreover, authorities often disagreed on which practices should prevail. For instance, from the beginning of organized work, some Sunday school authorities opposed the simple memorization of Bible verses. As early as 1829, the Canadian Sunday School Union directed, "Labour to cultivate the understanding, more than to load the memory." Forty years later the Toronto Sabbath School Association declared that "in going over the lesson, it should not be for the mere statistical store of those verses, but to gather the leading ideas which are communicated to our hearts and minds by them."[36] Children, it was argued, should not be crammed with information and should be taught how to acquire truth, not just lectured on what they should believe. They should be prepared to ask and answer incisive questions.

However, other leaders strongly recommended the memorization of hymns and Bible texts. "So far as he is capable, even the youngest child should commit Scripture to memory as an exercise of intelligence."[37] The standard view of education focused on discipline through the acquisition of useful, factual information. The child would thus have a body of habits, knowledge, and rules of conduct that were required in the adult world. Following the inductive method of inquiry, this "encyclopedic" approach to education would provide an essential basis for future decision-making. In fact, during the nineteenth century, the success of students and schools was invariably measured by the number of Bible verses memorized. Often students achieved little more than reciting verses, and rewards of books or library privileges, although sometimes questioned, were given to those most accomplished in this activity.

To improve the analytical study of the Bible, various Sunday school teachers developed lessons based on specific texts. By the 1860s, the Sunday school associations had also developed a variety of lesson systems with helps for the teachers, but the majority of schools continued to muddle on with their own resources. Perhaps the most profound innovation in the nineteenth century to systematize the work was the introduction of the International Uniform Lesson Series. Recognizing the confusion caused by a diversity of approaches, the American Sunday School Association, which included Canadian representation, developed a seven-year cycle of uniform lessons in 1872. These lessons were written principally by a Baptist, Benjamin Jacobs, and a Methodist, John Heyl Vincent, and they were designed to allow students in all schools to study the same Bible verses at the same time. The first cycle of lessons ran from 1873 to 1879, and after 1893 the cycle had a six-year span. Originally, the lessons covered forty-eight weeks, with one week per quarter allowed for review and the study of mission or temperance issues. Later this coverage was shortened to forty-four weeks to permit more time for denominational interests. Over the six or seven years, the lessons encompassed between four and five thousand Bible verses. Most Canadian denominations quickly adopted the lessons, and as a measure of their considerable popularity during the late nineteenth and early twentieth centuries, they were widely printed in both the Protestant and secular press.[38]

There were several advantages to this new system. At the most basic level, it greatly increased the efficiency of the Sunday schools and the teachers, and motivated Sunday schools to operate throughout the year, rather than only on a seasonal basis. It was also easier for children who moved to fit into their new schools. The increase in circulation of the Sunday school magazines was a partially unexpected bonus. The lessons also provided an important weapon in the ongoing struggle against scepticism and unbelief in Canadian society. William Henry Withrow, who edited the Methodist Sunday school magazines, claimed, "This is the best antidote to the sceptical tendencies and abounding iniquity of the times ... One of the principal advantages of the international uniform lesson system is that it brings to bear on the selected portions of the Scripture the best critical scholarship of the age, and makes it accessible to millions."[39] The gospel message was thus spread to countless individuals who would not otherwise receive it. Moreover, the lessons helped give evangelical Protestantism a common language when dealing with the young and were particularly appropriate in counteracting sectarian bigotry. The Sunday School Banner reported in 1873, "There is something very beautiful in this united and simultaneous study of the entire Evangelical Christian world on specific themes of God's word."[40] Hence the uniform lesson series both reflected and assisted the growing spirit of ecumenism within Canadian Protestantism. Not only did this outcome help interdenominational cooperation, but it anticipated the future union of many of the churches in Canada.

However, not everyone was pleased with this aspect of the uniform lesson series. Although the new lessons reflected strong clerical and denominational input and control, there were still Methodists who wished to expand their connexional component of Sunday school training. The shortening of the series to forty-four weeks reflected this feeling, and Methodist literature, catechisms, and doctrine also continued to augment the lessons. As well, almost from their inception, some Methodists attempted to amend the lesson guides and even the lessons themselves to reflect connexional priorities.[41]

By the late nineteenth century, there were also those who argued that different lessons should be provided for the various age groups in the Sunday schools. Supporters of the uniform lessons maintained that these differences should be brought out in the teaching. In fact, the uniform lessons, while dealing with the same biblical text, did provide three levels of analysis and questions based on the different levels of the students' knowledge. Junior, intermediate, and senior students were each presented with their own material. Nevertheless, during the 1890s, attempts were made when creating new lesson series to take these differences more into consideration.[42]

The whole issue of appropriate religious education was complicated by the new understandings that science, psychology, and sociology were bringing to human development. Children were no longer considered miniature or weak adults who warranted only discipline and restraint until they were mature enough for a responsible conversion experience. The increased status accorded childhood added new dimensions to society's responsibility to nurture and sustain. It became clear that there were several stages of human evolution from infancy to old age, which required different treatment.[43] Infancy and childhood, for instance, were seen as periods of intense selfishness when the world was only an extension of the child's immediate needs. However, this selfishness was merely nature's protection to ensure survival, and it lacked any power to harm society. Childhood was also a period of powerful, though short-lived, enthusiasms as great plans quickly succeeded one another. New sensations constantly redirected youthful ambitions. Most clearly, however, an aura of innocence, or even sinlessness, appeared to surround childhood. This ambience combined religious safety with the special protection that humanity had created as it evolved its moral sense. Because of such innate innocence, society limited its punishment of children's mischievous activities and enlarged its affectionate sympathy for the young.[44]

Although some children were considered capable of meaningful thought, care was required to ensure this did not turn into arrogance or precocity. The young needed time to evolve gradually into mature individuals who were capable of a reasonable and responsible commitment to spiritual religion and moral habits. This need to conserve childhood as a special period was reinforced by the social and economic transformation occurring in urban Canadian society. Under the new conditions, children were being forced out of the work place. From a variety of perspectives, then, Canadian society believed this formative period of development had to be prolonged in order for the natural processes of growth to operate.[45]

Just as in the late nineteenth century childhood was seen as the most important period of life, adolescence replaced it in the twentieth century. Childhood should be prolonged because of the terrible frustrations and temptations awaiting adolescents as they discovered the physical changes of puberty. Canadians were greatly worried by the awakening of sexual capacity and appetites without the self-restraints of adulthood; sex was the serpent in the Garden of Eden. Furthermore, the highly complex industrial developments in urban

Canada added an economic component to these concerns about the physical development of young women and especially young men. Society forced the young to remain dependent on their parents in order that they acquire a suitable education or training; such dependence often increased young people's sense of frustration.[46]

The adolescent was also undergoing a traumatic emotional and psychological transformation. "The period of youth is well known ... one of companionships and strange questionings, when the fountains of thought are stirred, and black doubt casts its shadow over early instruction – when passion pleads for indulgence, and the restraints of home are felt to be irksome, and the boast and bravado of impudence or irreverence is apt to be mistaken for manliness."[47] Under such conditions, the juvenile was exposed to potentially dangerous moral and intellectual assaults. While society expressed concern over the threats that adolescence offered to females, it assumed that their superior moral sense and their limited involvement outside the home would provide a measure of protection. Certainly, this need for protection was a major factor in limiting the occupations and social activities of young women. However, young males were potentially more dangerous to society and to themselves and therefore required more direct and concrete action.[48]

Nevertheless, while adolescence potentially involved great dangers, many reformers chose to emphasize the young person's capacity for good. They associated the metamorphosis of adolescence with meaningful spiritual growth and religious awakening. The critical period of spiritual danger and opportunity shifted from birth, since infants were not necessarily damned, or adulthood, by which time a conscious personal affirmation should already have occurred, to the point where childhood was lost and adulthood not yet achieved. Conversion was perceived as particularly the experience of reaching adolescence since in psychological terms it represented a new birth or at least a new consciousness. Adolescence also released vast stores of energy which, if properly directed, could serve to improve humanity. It was pre-eminently the heroic stage in life when fame and glory, sacrifice and honour, were uppermost in the mind. Adolescence was the age when selfishness was sublimated into service for others. Thus the young felt real satisfaction as they conquered obstacles and adjusted to adult life.[49]

These ideas underlay much of the child-centred reform of the late nineteenth and early twentieth centuries, including labour legislation, social and moral protection, and education. Paradoxically, Canadians demanded reform which confirmed established values and conserved the fundamental anchors of Protestant Victorian society. The unsettled intellectual atmosphere intensified by the new scientific knowledge and the Darwinian revolution reflected a sincere optimism chained to a fundamental fear of contemporary developments. The order, peace, and harmony of the nation and the stability of its institutions appeared under attack. Reform therefore attempted to improve the capacity of society to withstand these assaults.[50]

Within this intellectual and social framework, many educational innovators elaborated a new, so-called progressive education constructed on the belief that the child should be the focus of the entire system. Education should develop the child's natural qualities rather than simply supply regulations and information appropriate for adult life.[51] The freedom to experience problems and sensations and to accomplish meaningful tasks would develop character. Rather than education being aimed at the encyclopedic accumulation of facts, they maintained that the best way to prepare the young and thereby promote progress was to encourage adaptability to the evolving world. Since no particular body of information was essential for this preparation, schools should shift from a book-centred to a child-centred curriculum.

This new education assumed an optimistic belief in the "goodness" of the young. For many somewhat romantic and sentimental progressive-education promoters, "the child was a bundle of happy divinity whose trailing clouds of glory only inept adults marred."[52] Children learned by doing, and this made school more interesting and, in the long run, more successful in forming lasting habits. Moreover, as children matured, they quite naturally rebelled against parental control. They needed to develop self-control rather than rely on external restraints; they had to be trusted and influenced, not commanded. These reformers assumed that giving free rein to the students' enthusiasm developed initiative and responsibility and expanded the heroic drive for service to the community.

However, most educators would never permit liberty to sink into licence or allow freedom of experience to devolve into selfishness. The young student still required a strong dose of discipline. The problem remained, who was to decide when the child was ready for freedom and how far this freedom should go. In reality, the weight of both the religious and secular educational community remained on the side of authority, conformity, and the moulding of students into proper adults. Liberty in education had to remain within well-established bounds. Since child-centred education still required a firm moral base, conformity to community standards of conduct had to precede any removal of social restraints. Thus any sense of real youthful liberty was actually illusory since it was severely circumscribed by the intellectual and social predilections of those in authority.[53]

Nevertheless, despite these limitations on the practice of progressive education, many elements of child-centred training intertwined with the new emphasis on the stages of human development and transformed the traditional Victorian Sunday school. Sunday schools promoted individual growth in harmony with social efficiency, trusted the advice of modern experts, and integrated scientific methodology and the belief in evolutionary progress into their programs. At the same time, mental discipline, the formation of moral character, respect for authority, loyalty to Canada, and a broadly Protestant vision for the nation remained at the heart of all pedagogical developments. In addition, Sunday school work utilized many of the practices common in secular education. In regular education, "Bigger schools, graded classes, teacher training, better advice to, and more supervision of the children, teacher, parents and local educational authorities connected with the schools were all considered essential aspects of the campaign for educational improvement."[54] All these elements were mirrored in the Sunday school as it sought to embody the most intelligent and progressive components of education. Spiritual and intellectual development were inseparable.

By the 1890s, the original Sunday school divisions into junior, intermediate, and senior classes were gradually replaced by a graded system in order to involve everyone from birth to the late twenties and to target specific groups with the appropriate material and educational approaches. The Sunday schools enrolled infants on the "cradle roll" shortly after birth and placed them under watchful care. Representatives visited the parents, supplied moral literature, and encouraged them to bring their children to school when they were old enough. This first contact was considered valuable in fostering later commitment to the Methodist Sunday schools, and it also drew parents to church. In 1914 some 40,000 infants' names appeared on the cradle roll.[55] As well, by the early twentieth century, the Sunday schools were divided into elementary, secondary, and adult departments in order to segregate students by age. Beyond those on the cradle roll, the elementary department contained beginners from age four to five, primary students from six to eight, and juniors from nine to twelve. The secondary department included intermediates, aged thirteen to sixteen, and seniors, from seventeen to twenty. The adult division supervised those over twenty, as well as the home department, Bible classes, and teacher training.

Beyond the ordinary school operations, the adult classes formed an intermediary between the school and the congregation and also served as an outreach into the general community. Through its home department, volunteers distributed systematic study courses and general literature to those who were unable to attend Sunday school in person. The department also stimulated these people to take weekday Bible courses and, if possible, get involved in regular church activities. Thus it was an important evangelizing agency which attracted many who would otherwise have been overlooked. Thousands of people took advantage of this Sunday school extension program.[56]

In many ways, the keys to Sunday school success were the dedicated voluntary teachers. They were required to be earnest and active Christians with an extensive and accurate knowledge of the Bible. They had to be able to impart religious knowledge, form moral habits, train the young for Christian service, and stimulate conversion and holiness among their charges. The best teachers were at once grave and dignified, punctual and conscientious, yet affectionate, conciliatory, patient, and adaptable. "Religion itself becomes offensive, especially to young minds, when it does not beam with cheerful kindness, but is coupled with forbidding manners, with moroseness, with rigorous severity and intolerable exactions."[57] Teachers must communicate their wisdom in appropriate terms and deal equitably with their students. Equally, they had to show that moral delinquency was a sin against God, not just contrary to the rules of the school.

Originally, Methodist lay leaders had been reluctant to become Sunday school teachers, and often only casual churchgoers had undertaken the work. Over time, however, as the Sunday school became more deeply integrated into the church's regular activities, it drew heavily on the local church's lay leadership, particularly among the women. They came to recognize that the Sunday school was critical for promoting a middle-class, industrious, moral social order. This shift in interest also reflected the parallel declining influence of other traditional lay functions, such as local preacher and class leader. Men and women, including many nationally prominent Methodist leaders, found important and respected roles as Sunday school teachers and superintendents.[58]

The churches and Sunday school associations constantly strove to improve the quality of the teaching. The first Sunday school periodicals were generally for teachers rather than students and introduced new pedagogical trends. Books, lesson helps, and other literature, as well as stressing the vital role teachers were performing and their duty to improve, also provided invaluable guides to better teaching. Sunday school conventions and assemblies, often taking place in the restyled camp grounds, also became popular by the 1870s as means of conveying new Sunday school techniques and information. In addition, courses were offered at local or district teachers' institutes or at weeknight sessions run by the teachers themselves. More comprehensive programs were also offered by such bodies as the American Chautauqua Institute, which was established in 1874 by John Heyl Vincent to promote international and interdenominational Sunday school work. It offered summer schools, lectures, and assemblies at Lake Chautauqua in upstate New York and supplied extensive correspondence courses for Sunday school leaders. Vincent did not want Chautauqua to be confused with traditional revivals, but he did hope their energy and enthusiasm would be transferred to teacher improvement.[59] In addition, Nathanael Burwash at Victoria University offered courses on the inductive method to help teachers improve biblical instruction. By the end of the century therefore, teacher training courses were widely available, and many had competitive examinations and diplomas after graduation.

By the beginning of the twentieth century, the Methodist church hoped its teachers would be intellectual as well as earnest Christians. The Discipline was amended to improve the status of instructional classes for teachers. As well, in 1906 the theological colleges began short courses for their divinity students and others interested in teacher education, and four years later the Board of Sunday Schools established a teacher training department to supervise this work. By 1914, 2,858 teachers were enrolled in training programs sponsored by the church. Four years later the Methodists adopted the Canadian Standard Teacher Training Course, with certificates and diplomas for successful graduates. As well, during the first two decades of the century, the training became more specialized in order to suit the needs of particular groups, especially older children and adults, and reflected the new studies of childhood and adolescence.[60]

The Methodist connexions distributed and published vast quantities of Sunday school literature and, more important, supplied a variety of periodicals to assist both teachers and students. Almost from their inception, the *Christian Guardian*, the *Canada Christian Advocate*, the *Wesleyan*, and the other smaller denominational newspapers published Sunday school lessons and information for their respective clienteles. The Wesleyan Methodists also distributed the British *Wesleyan Sabbath School Magazine* from its creation in 1857 and joined the Episcopal Methodists in importing American publications.

In 1845 the *Christian Guardian* advertised a new Canadian Wesleyan Sunday school magazine, and within two years the *Sunday School Guardian* was selling over 800 copies. It was joined in 1868 by the *Sunday School Banner* for teachers and in the 1870s by the *Sunday School Advocate* for young people. During the following decade, there was a marked proliferation of periodicals designed for specific age groups. In 1880 *Sunbeam* was begun for young children, and the *Sunday School Guardian* was transformed into the bi-monthly *Pleasant Hours* for the intermediate classes; it was joined three years later by *Home and School* on alternate weeks. This last magazine emphasized temperance and missionary activities and was specifically designed to replace British and American magazines. William Henry Withrow, the editor of the Sunday school periodicals, believed that it was vital to support Canadian magazines since they were "loyal to the institutions of our own country, and to the doctrines of Methodism, while the foreign papers patronized by some of our Schools are often hostile to both."[61] Increasingly, the Canadian Methodist church recognized the value of Sunday schools in shaping young people's attitudes toward Canada's identity and wanted to insure that the literature promoted their proper development.

By 1884 the *Christian Guardian* had a circulation of 13,517 and the *Canadian Methodist Magazine* was selling 2,787 copies, but the Sunday school magazines were much more popular. The circulation of the *Sunday School Banner* was 8,460, *Sunbeam* 20,723, *Pleasant Hours* 37,149, and *Home and School* 23,795. In addition, 30,200 copies of *Scholar's Quarterly* and 39,303 copies of *Berean Leaf* were distributed. These two magazines contained the uniform lessons and teacher's aids. The Sunday school journals were successful because they were "adapted to the comprehension of the humblest" and provided "a noble vantage ground for moulding in large degree the future of the Church and nation, in influencing toward piety and godliness in the most susceptible and formative period of the minds of the young people of Methodism."[62] As well, they introduced scriptural knowledge to many who would not otherwise receive it.

To meet the growing demands of adolescents in both the Sunday schools and the other young people's societies, in 1890 *Onward* began its long career. The *Canadian Epworth Era*, started in 1898, focused more precisely on the work of the Epworth leagues and Endeavor societies. A year earlier, the church began publishing *Dew Drops*, which joined *Sunbeam* in addressing the needs of the primary classes; these two magazines merged in 1907. In the same year, the church created *Playmate* for the junior classes. Finally, in 1909 it launched the *Adult Class* to serve Sunday school students in their twenties, the adult Bible classes, and teachers in training. Except for the *Canadian Epworth Era*, which maintained a rather steady, but unsatisfactory, circulation of slightly over 5,000, the other magazines expanded their sales to reflect the growth in the Sunday school population in general. During World War I, the Board of Publications also established a slide and film department to complement the periodicals.[63]

Although the language and style of the magazines differed according to the age group addressed, they presented a fairly consistent focus and message. They all promoted loyalty to the nation, the monarchy, and, particularly before and during World War I, to the empire. Mostly they expressed a deep concern for Canada, however, and were not overly anglophile. The Sunday school periodicals and Sunday schools in general also strongly emphasized a deep loyalty to evangelical Christianity and especially to Methodism. The use of publications from the United States was sometimes discouraged because they reflected republican or nationalistic American values, but British and American journals were equally suspect if they appeared to challenge Methodist doctrine or discipline.[64]

Beyond these recognizable nationalistic assumptions, Methodist Sunday school literature also featured the work of the church's domestic and overseas missions. As well as providing information on the heroic service by missionaries, the magazines encouraged students to contribute time and money to develop missionary enterprises. Juvenile missionary societies became a common feature in the Sunday schools. The missions to Canada's native peoples attracted a great deal of attention in the literature, but nothing compared to the excitement and spirit of adventure created by tales of Christian missions in Africa, the South Seas, and Asia. After 1872, when Canadian Methodists had their own missions in Japan and later in China, there were Canadian heroes for Sunday school students. In addition, older students sometimes helped in the local city or ethnic missions that were a regular feature of Methodist operations in the early twentieth century. As important as the youthful service and support were, however, the church believed that the real benefit would be realized when the students became adults.[65]

While Sunday schools had a clear mandate to develop missions, Methodist authorities assumed that their more crucial function was to help create moral, self-disciplined, and spiritually alive individuals at home. Through every conceivable literary means, Sunday school periodicals sought to mould the child's character. Every issue of every paper had some advice for young people which mirrored the concern Methodism had about proper behaviour for all members of society. The Sunday school was considered one of the best institutions for advancing a moral order in Canada. The will of children had to be subdued and even broken so that they developed a proper obedience and deference to parents and others in authority. Children must learn patience, submissiveness, acceptance of their proper place, and a resignation to God's will. At the same time, they must be honest and polite, avoid profane conduct, and seek to become pious, earnest Christians and punctual, industrious citizens. Children were also enjoined to spread these values to their associates and to reprove evildoers wherever they met them. The Christian child served as a valuable example to change the conduct of misguided adults.[66]

Methodists shared with other Protestant denominations the assumption that young people needed to develop certain characteristics. Girls and young women were taught to be practical, economical, and neat and tidy, especially in running a household. Their delicacy was rarely questioned, but idle or frivolous behaviour was strongly denounced. They had to accept and master the difficult tasks nature had assigned. Certainly, they should never be wild or even appear promiscuous. Boys and young men, on the other hand, must particularly tame their sexual passions, learn respect for women, and strive always to become brave, self-reliant, and honourable. During the early twentieth century,

Christian manliness merged into "muscular Christianity," with its assumptions that the true Christian was not weak or insipid, but rather bold, virile, physically fit, and assertive.[67]

In order to develop their proper character, children were constantly warned about the evils of dancing, the theatre, smoking, gambling, bad books, evil companions, or anything that tended toward a dissolute life. No decent person wasted a moment on idle amusements. Sunday school literature was full of examples of the disastrous effects such activities had on both the young and society in general. However, many Sunday school workers recognized that they had to do more than simply denounce. In place of such negative admonitions, the schools attempted to offer healthy recreation and beneficial social relations. Picnics, excursions, and concerts became common features, and sports programs, summer camps, and other moral amusements played a significant role in attracting the young to Sunday school while serving a sound educational function as well.

The Sunday school also provided an excellent forum for kindling an interest in social reforms. Although Sunday schools promoted every positive reform, the principal concerns were sabbatarianism and temperance. Not only did the schools keep children off the streets on Sunday, but they also actively encouraged children to keep the sabbath holy by opposing any activity that did not lead directly to religious ends. Sunday was more than a day of rest; it was a day to witness before God. Everyone benefited from the spiritual and physical refreshment.[68] However, the most critical issue for Sunday schools was temperance. The best hope for a pure and prosperous society in the future was the avoidance of drink in youth. Alcohol was denounced as a cancer gnawing at the very heart of Canadian society. It was viewed as the cause of poverty and crime, and it led to evils such as prostitution and the destruction of the family. Alcohol also weakened the industrial development of the country by causing accidents and absenteeism, particularly among the immigrants pouring into the country by the late 1890s. As important, since the adolescent was considered particularly susceptible to its evil temptations, drinking posed a serious threat to the discipline and work habits of the young. The Methodist Sunday schools instructed their students on the evils of drink, established temperance societies, and urged all young people to sign temperance pledges. They therefore held vast reservoirs of volunteers to assist in the numerous temperance and prohibition campaigns undertaken during the late nineteenth and early twentieth centuries throughout Canada.[69]

## OTHER YOUNG PEOPLE'S ORGANIZATIONS

Despite the valuable roles the Sunday schools performed, they could not supply all the needs of the young, especially during the rest of the week, when there were few alternatives to immoral amusements. As a result, parallel organizations developed both inside and outside the church structures. Late-Victorian society placed great trust in clubs to help release young people's natural energy and enthusiasm, and this belief blended nicely with progres-

"How to Bridge the Gulf." Symbolized the Young People's Forward Movement for Missions founded by Dr Frederick Clark Stephenson. (MC, *Missionary Society Reports*, 1907–08, 83)

Berwick Campgrounds, Summer School, 1907. A favourite site for young people's gatherings in the Maritimes. (UCA, P932)

sive education's assumptions about the group nature of proper training. Such organizations "vent the anarchistic instincts in ways least injurious to the community and make docility and subordination more easy and natural in their turn."[70] They also permitted the first, often symbolic, abandonment of self to the interests of the larger community or to some heroic purpose. Here the emerging capacities of adolescents and young adults could be channelled into fulfilling God's purpose, and youth could be assimilated into respectable Protestant society.

For instance, the Young Men's and Young Women's Christian associations and the Mechanics' Institutes had spread from Britain to Canada during the middle of the nineteenth century and were originally designed to provide educational opportunities for young working adults. The YMCA and the YWCA gradually sought out younger members and added recreational, social, and moral training to their operations. The YWCA in particular provided a valuable training ground for women to administer their own programs. It also helped women who were entering the urban labour market by supplying respectable boarding-houses, lasting friendships, and safe intellectual and social contacts, and it worked closely with the WCTU to promote temperance and reform causes.[71]

During the first decade of the twentieth century, a variety of other young men's improvement societies, including the British-based scouting movement, also became extremely popular with Canadian youth. Lord Baden-Powell, the founder of the Boy Scouts, believed urban, industrial society was weakening the physical and mental capacities of the young and that this would have disastrous effects on the future of the British empire. He therefore established physically demanding programs in which the young learned how to survive in the wild away from the debilitating and immoral urban influences. The scouts thereby developed self-reliance within a cooperative group setting. Scouting put a premium on duty, honour, and loyalty and had the added advantage of supplying an antidote to evil companions and immoral behaviour.

Methodism, while supporting the general goals of these groups, feared that they would lead youth away from church associations and from active participation in purely denominational enterprises. It always held somewhat ambiguous views on organizations that were not directly related to a church. The most common response was to adopt the popular programs and adapt them to Methodist organizations. For instance, the camping movement, popularized by the scouts and other contemporary groups, was integrated into Sunday school and young people's programs. Likewise, mid-week social, recreational, and sports activities were used to bind the young to Methodist groups.

Often the Methodist leadership was similarly suspicious of interdenominational church organizations. In Portland, Maine, in 1881, a new young people's organization commenced operations in the Congregational church, and it quickly spread across North America. Known as the Christian Endeavor Society, it involved its members in missionary work, moral reform, and evangelization. It strove to expand inner spiritual growth as the basis for social action. In many ways, Christian Endeavor drew individuals from a Calvinist background to a more Arminian theological position by its emphasis on the universal ability to be saved. By 1901 Christian Endeavor reported 3,600,000 members through-out the world, but it gradually declined as its novelty wore off and other organi-zations attracted its members.[72] Although Canadian Methodists were actively involved in Christian Endeavor, the church tried to bring that society into the orbit of its own young people's work. Despite encouraging cooperation with other Protestant groups, the church assumed its young people should remain under its doctrinal control.

The Methodist answer to Christian Endeavor was the Epworth League. Grow-ing out of John H. Vincent's Oxford League, originally set up in the Methodist Episcopal Church in the United States in 1884, the Epworth League was founded five years later to provide tighter control of young people's associa-tions and to put the knowledge acquired in Sunday schools into active service. It hoped to develop "a hitherto latent strength and talent in behalf of civic righ-teousness and social and moral reform that will be of untold value in the future of our country."[73] An extension of Sunday school work, the Epworth League began in Canada in 1889, and the following year, the two elements of Method-ist training were placed under the Board of Sunday Schools and Epworth Leagues. This reorganization permitted more comprehensive and effective pro-vision for the spiritual and moral needs of children and young people. The Ep-worth League was designed to be an umbrella organization uniting all the groups except the Sunday school in order "to avoid confusion, distraction, mis-direction of energy and even contention; and to secure harmony and unity of action, wise and effective employment of resources, safe instruction and doc-trine, and loyalty to the church."[74] The Canadian Methodist church urged all the Endeavor societies to affiliate as Epworth Leagues of Christian Endeavor, but many remained loyal to their interdenominational organization.

The Epworth League attempted to develop a commitment among the young to spiritual growth, education, and mission work and provided a vari-ety of moral social activities. Throughout most of its history, the league had about twice as many female as male members. Local leagues were divided into five departments each headed by its own vice-president. The key depart-ment was known as Christian endeavour, borrowing the name of its fellow or-ganization. It ran prayer meetings and weekly devotional services, organized evangelistic work, and kindled spiritual rebirth among young people.[75] Main-taining that only a converted citizenry could bring about meaningful reform, the department fostered a reconsecration of Canadian youth for "Christ and his kingdom."

A second department administered the missionary interests of the league. Arguing that the time had come to establish the Lord's dominion on earth and optimistically looking forward to Christ's post-millennial reign, its mem-bers raised money, visited homes, distributed tracts, worked in the city mis-sions, and generally advanced the cause of worldwide Christian ministry. When Dr Frederick Clark Stephenson founded the Young People's Forward Movement for Missions in 1895, it initially became affiliated with the Epworth League, but quickly absorbed those interested in mission work from all the young people's societies. Under Annie Watson Stephenson's leadership, the women members of the Forward Movement were also linked to the training of deaconesses for Christian service at home and abroad.[76]

The league's department of citizenship dealt with social and political questions and stressed patriotism and moral reform as the best means of creating a strong and virtuous nation. The department offered courses, supplied reading material, and encouraged the study of Canada's history and politics. At the local level, young people participated in sabbatarian and temperance campaigns, pressed for honest, progressive government, and attempted to institute social and urban reform. At the national level, the department promoted the Methodist church's policies on immigration and the development of the northwest. It also oversaw the athletic activities of the league. This was no accident since the league believed that physical fitness was directly related to mental fitness and both were necessary if Canada was to progress according to God's plan.[77]

The literary and social department organized debating societies, lectures, essay contests, reading courses, prayer meetings, and Bible study sessions, as well as the musicals and social gatherings of the league. The league recognized that if it did not provide a suitable social life for its members, they might well be drawn to immoral amusements or at least into other, non-Methodist organizations. Equally important, the department sent volunteers into the community to gather and encourage new members and supplied badges and all the other paraphernalia and ritual so critical for a club. In this sense, it was both an evangelizing agent and the face of the organization for most of the general public. The department also ran an employment bureau to assist members looking for work.[78]

Finally, the Junior League was a nearly independent organization. It duplicated most of the activities of the Epworth League for children under fourteen years of age. For this reason, it was more directly controlled by the local itinerant, who appointed the vice-president and had immediate influence in its deliberations. Although young, Junior League members were expected to take a temperance pledge and support the general society's goals. The League specialized in catechumen and Bible classes, often on Saturday, by which the young were drawn into a more intimate relationship with the connexion. The Methodist church was anxious that the Junior League expand from its essentially Ontario base to the rest of Canada and that members be trained to take an active role in the senior league when they were older.

From its inception, the Epworth League followed the pattern established by the Sunday schools and other young people's groups. It was directly integrated into the local church's operations, with the president normally being a member of the circuit's quarterly board. Although one of the keys to its success was the fact that it offered its programs during the week, it also held meetings immediately before or after church services and therefore provided an incentive for attendance at Sunday worship. The league also held annual conventions at the local, district, and Conference level, and every four years, representatives met from across the entire national church. In 1893 Canadian Methodists participated in the first international convention of Epworth leagues, and four years later the third convention met in Toronto. The Methodist church also began publishing the *Canadian Epworth Era* in 1898 to advance the league's values among the younger generation of Canadians.[79]

The Epworth League, and indeed all the young people's societies of the period, initially made impressive gains, but they eventually declined as new organizations and new interests took their place. In fact, in the pre-war period they reached their peak in 1896, with over 82,000 members in 1,947 clubs. From there, they declined until in 1905 the church recorded only 1,776 local societies, including 106 not affiliated with the Epworth leagues, and a total membership of 70,338. After several years of uneven development, by 1914 the Epworth League reported 55,549 members in 1,332 branches, while other Methodist young people's organizations had 17,560 members in 462 groups. In that year, the church officially altered the name of its supervising committee to the General Board of Sunday Schools and Young People's Societies to reflect the trend away from the Epworth League. A year later the *Canadian Epworth Era* changed its name to *Youth and Service* to reflect the broader needs of the societies and to encourage greater support.[80]

The league also declined during World War I as young people took up new interests, became disillusioned with progressive institutions, or simply were absent on war duty. In 1922 further administrative changes altered the Epworth League into the Young People's League in order, once again, to clarify the administrative control of the diverse organizations that had developed in the church and to integrate them more effectively into the goals of the committee on religious education. By that time, other associations for young people were challenging the ability of the church to control this important aspect of its work. Simultaneously, the junior societies reduced the maximum age of membership from fourteen to eleven, and many of the societies were uniting with Presbyterian groups in anticipation of church union. Still, in 1922 the church reported 124,632 members in young people's groups.[81]

Despite these numbers, after World War I, the Methodist church was faced with declining interest in its young people's societies, especially among older boys. Many in the church worried that this decline would have a serious, negative impact on Methodism's numerical growth and institutional health. It was therefore forced to develop a new partnership with non-Methodist organizations in order to retain some control over the social and spiritual life of the young. By far the most significant of these new organizations was the Student Christian Movement, which had grown out of the YMCA. The SCM demanded that its members pledge their lives to Christian principles and especially to missionary endeavours, and it worked to raise the social conscience of its members and to encourage active participation in programs to ameliorate social ills. The SCM was particularly important for the young men and women attending university; no other organization touched so critically the lives of this body of Protestant youth during the 1920s. Many future ministers, missionaries, and lay leaders decided on their careers after participating in the SCM.[82] In fact, all the young people's societies provided important training ground for the future leaders of Canadian Methodism. Along with the Sunday schools, they also helped create a unity of vision, a discipline, and a commitment to evangelical religion and ethical principles. They were essential to the growth and stability of the denomination. In addition, they answered those critics who feared for the future of the nation by demonstrating the great potential of youth, and they worked in concert with the church's regular operations to help create a respectable moral order throughout Canadian society.

# 15 Methodism in the Early Twentieth Century

## MEETING THE CHALLENGE OF THE NEW CENTURY

The twentieth century appeared to offer immense opportunities both for Canadian society in general and for the Methodist church in particular. If, as Prime Minister Sir Wilfrid Laurier maintained, the twentieth century belonged to Canada, then Methodism assumed that no other denomination had a better claim to leadership in moulding and directing the nation in its spiritual, moral, and social progress in this era. The church was apparently unified, well administered, and materially prosperous. Its religious and intellectual institutions were among the best in the country, and its auxiliary organizations were involving huge numbers of members in religious activity and helping to evangelize and nurture all levels of society. Although resources were never sufficient, the prospects for expansion at home and overseas had never been better. Methodism's great crusades to evangelize and to establish Christ's earthly dominion appeared to be succeeding rapidly.

In 1898 the last General Conference of the old century acknowledged this material and spiritual prosperity. Although the previous quadrennium had witnessed a slower level of membership growth, this could reasonably be blamed on the removal of members to the United States, particularly from the Methodist heartland of rural Ontario, because of a severe economic depression and also on a more thorough revision of the circuit rolls. Membership still stood at over 280,000, with 2,091 ministers and nearly 1,000,000 adherents. More importantly, the church looked forward to new solutions to the remaining hindrances to ecclesiastical success, "such as secularism, materialism, false liberalism, reckless criticism, old methods of thought, or old methods of work."[1] Rather than drawing solely on its "heroic" heritage to supply as a model a mythological golden age of spirituality, the church was more inclined to modernize its methods and modes of thinking and adapt its institutions to the special needs of this progressive age.

As a final tribute to the success Methodism had achieved during the nineteenth century, as a demonstration of its continuing piety, and in order to bolster its future mission, the General Conference of 1898 authorized the collection of a special Twentieth Century Thanksgiving Fund. The money would subsidize the Methodist educational institutions, the ministers' retirement fund, and domestic and overseas missions and help pay off the debt of the local congregations. Contributors could designate which of these beneficiaries would receive their support. The Conference established a fifty-member board representing all the geographic regions of the church, with the Reverend John Potts as chairman and Senator George Cox as treasurer, to supervise the local collections and to keep a "historic roll" of supporters. Potts and Cox were the obvious choices to head the financial drive. John Potts in 1898 was sixty years old and had lived in Canada since 1855, yet he still retained an Irish lilt to his booming voice and had an equally impressive physical appearance. He had functioned for years as a one-man bureaucracy effectively raising money for Methodist educational and missionary causes. George Cox had been a loyal contributor to Methodist institutions, and as a major shareholder, president, or director of the Canadian Bank of Commerce, the National Trust, the Central Canada Loan and Savings, and numerous other companies, he was considered a financial wizard. Equally important, he was an intimate business associate of A.E. Ames and Joseph Flavelle and had important connections with wealthy Methodists throughout Canada. With a goal of $1,000,000, the committee inaugurated the Twentieth Century Fund at special services across the country on October 8, 1899. The campaign paralleled, but generally did not interfere with, the church's ordinary fund-raising and ended in April 1901. Even though many Methodist leaders feared that the target would not be achieved because Canada was just emerging from the worst depression in its history, nevertheless, $1,234,657 was finally pledged and over $750,000 was actually collected and distributed by the deadline, while most of the remainder arrived at headquarters in due course.[2]

The significance of the Twentieth Century Fund transcended the actual money raised or the improvement it guaranteed to the church's institutional infrastructure. The campaign demonstrated Methodism's strong connexional unity and deep commitment to advancing the educational and missionary goals of contemporary Christianity at a time when fundamentalist and anti-modernist forces were denying the vitality of the mainstream churches. The Methodist church was clearly a wealthy and powerful institution that retained its spiritual and moral vitality and deserved its leadership role in Canadian society. In addition, the success of this financial campaign illustrated the respectability and status the church had gained and reinforced the sense of optimism among its middle-class lay leadership as few other achievements could. Most already assumed that only money and commitment were required to inaugurate the kingdom of God on earth.[3]

The revenues from the Twentieth Century Fund, as well as the increased receipts from normal contributions to the church's work, were needed to sustain and expand its membership and mission. This need became particularly apparent early in the new century as the Methodist church assessed the results of the

1901 census. Although it constantly disclaimed any significant correlation be-tween the number of adherents and the health of the denomination, in fact, the church analysed the figures closely for signs of progress or decline. Out of a total Canadian population of 5,371,315, the census reported 916,886 Method-ists. Although the church remained the largest Protestant denomination, this figure represented an increase of only 69,121, or just over 8 per cent, during the previous decade against a general population increase of about 11 per cent.

The Methodist church was not overly concerned by the results since the ar-rival of immigrants who were either non-Christian or who would require ex-tensive evangelizing to bring them into the Methodist fellowship partially excused the relative decline in Methodist affiliation. Furthermore, the census enumerated approximately 18,000 in Methodist offshoots such as the Salva-tion Army and Hornerite and United Brethren churches. In comparison, the Anglican population had risen by about 5.5 per cent to 681,494. Even the Presbyterian church's growth to 842,442, an increase of 11.5 per cent, could be given a positive interpretation because the Presbyterians were natural Prot-estant allies. Much less satisfactory, and potentially dangerous to the Method-ist vision for Canada, the Roman Catholic church had expanded by 11.4 per cent to 2,229,600 during the previous decade. Although the Methodist lead-ership argued that one census did not necessarily represent a trend and that membership growth, which was the only true test of denominational strength, continued at a good pace, Methodists still believed that they must redouble their efforts.[4] The church was not expanding nearly rapidly enough in west-ern Canada, and conservative theological groups were increasingly gaining supporters at its expense.

In order to recapture its former rate of growth and insure its pre-eminence, the Methodist church did not attempt to retreat to a sentimental reconstruc-tion of its revivalistic past. Traditional evangelical rhetoric and programs ap-peared inappropriate for the conditions of the new century; Methodism had not been a small body of earnest converts for many decades. It recognized that such a position would only isolate it from contemporary Canadian society, weaken its ability to deal meaningfully with the problems facing the nation, and drive its progressive membership into other denominations. The church never denied the legitimacy or importance of personal regeneration. S.D. Chown and T. Albert Moore, perhaps the church leaders most consciously dedicated to a strong social mission, could still argue, "With the broadening of the social outlook of the people has come not a lessened, but a deeper and more compelling, conviction of the need of individual regeneration."[5] But the separation from the corrupt world so long espoused by Methodism now meant moral, as much as spiritual, distinctiveness and superiority. The secret of mod-ern evangelism was to remain as aggressively personal and spiritual as ever but to blend evangelism with a passion for social reform. Spiritual rebirth was only the first step and must be integrated into a "full-orbed" evangelism that re-made the whole individual for this world as well as the next. True holiness was necessarily social and reshaped both the inner and the outer life.[6]

Furthermore, this attitude reflected an appreciation of what was practical in church life in the twentieth century. Although there remained those who wished to see the traditional social means of grace reinvigorated, in reality the class meeting, love feast, and lay preaching could never recover their former power. Individuals who were both moral and spiritually alive but who refused to follow these old-fashioned Methodist agencies had achieved influential and valuable roles in the denomination at both local and national levels, and the church was not prepared to abandon them or lose their talents. In the more mission-oriented northwest, the social means of grace retained only a minor evangelizing or disciplinary role, and in the more settled regions, they were only rarely popular or effective. Where they still operated, they were more likely to assist in creating a moral social fellowship and in instilling a strong social conscience rather than promoting a personal conversion experience in their members.[7]

Similarly, Methodist leaders continued to argue that most professional revivalists were out of harmony with modern, progressive society, were often ill informed, and had little lasting influence on expanding church membership. Equally problematic, twentieth-century revivalists too often were driven by fundamentalist, adventist, premillennialist, and other non-Methodist theological assumptions. Church leaders such as the rarely controversial William Black Creighton, editor of the *Christian Guardian,* maintained that the old-fashioned revival approach hurt, rather than advanced, the church's goals. Believing that the kingdom of God on earth was at hand, probably within a generation, and that humanity now had the power to transform the world, they maintained that their duty was to build this kingdom and not just enlarge their own narrow denomination. Such a goal could best be achieved by gradual growth through Christian nurture until the entire world was bound into a religious fellowship. Even when temporarily successful, revivalists only retained a positive influence when they preached moral reform, social justice, or causes such as church union.[8]

By the early twentieth century, Methodist lay and clerical circles were well informed by liberal theology, and they were unwilling to relinquish their perception of the proper function of religion or their vision of the future of Canadian Christianity to the forces of reaction that were emerging to destroy the hard-won consensus in mainstream Protestantism. The proliferation of fundamentalist, adventist, premillennialist, dispensationalist, pentecostal, and even spiritualist groups was causing a serious upheaval throughout the Protestant community. These groups adopted the rhetoric of the historic spiritual revival and were attempting to assume the mantle of nineteenth-century evangelicalism. In fact, significant numbers of conservative Methodists who denounced higher criticism as irreligious and who mistrusted the implications of liberal theology and the emphasis on a social gospel were attracted by these new religious bodies. But while not willing to surrender their heroic traditions to what they considered upstart sects, most Methodists refused to reshape their theology in unnatural ways in order to fight the issue.

Although the holiness churches, which were often allied with the fundamentalist and other conservative groups, had grown out of the Wesleyan tradition, Canadian Methodism had never been seriously influenced by the theology that guided the new reactionary bodies. Since the days of John Wesley, Methodism had followed the Arminian theological belief in the possibility of universal salvation. It would never accept the notion of salvation being limited to a few prechosen by God or to those under a special dispensation. Furthermore, to key Methodists, theological authority rested upon the four pillars of Scripture, tradition, reason, and experience. Although the Bible was the inspired word of God and the final arbiter of religion, it was only one of several sources of spiritual truth and guides to behaviour. The Canadian Methodist church was rarely distracted by fundamentalists' concern over the literal truth of the entire book. In addition, Methodism had never given much credence either to premillennialism or to adventist notions of the impending end of the world.[9]

While the church was eager to welcome the return of individuals who it felt had been misled into quitting its communion and believed it was able to accommodate a broad range of theological beliefs, it would not deny its progressive mission in the world. With the adoption of the basic tenets of liberal theology, the church's leadership was clearly on the side of the modernist forces, and it sought out alliances with the Presbyterian, Congregationalist, Anglican, Baptist, and other mainstream Protestant churches. The clearest manifestation of these goals will be discussed in the next chapter as institutional Methodism looked for ecumenical cooperation and eventually union with like-minded Protestant denominations.[10]

If Methodism was to take its rightful position in building the twentieth-century Canadian nation, it was essential that the church modernize its institutional infrastructure. Fundamental to this process was the enlargement and strengthening of its educational facilities. Proper education would train a lay and clerical leadership for Canadian society, promote the proper avenues to spiritual growth, and advance the implementation of progressive social reform. Despite marked improvement in the public education system, the church believed its own secondary schools were better able to provide moral and spiritual guidance to young people in their critical adolescent stage. This was the strategic period for winning converts to Christ and for shaping Christian citizens. Over the first twenty-five years of the new century, the church enlarged the endowment, erected new buildings, increased enrolment, and improved the quality of teaching at its schools throughout the country. In turn, these institutions served as important sources of candidates for Methodist universities and for its ministry.[11]

While retaining a strong interest in the welfare of its secondary schools, the church recognized that in order to meet the challenges of the twentieth century, more Canadians must acquire a university education and this education must be open to all classes of society. It continued to believe that as long as universities were guided by Christian principles, they would "make all learning subservient to the highest ends, to the culture of the soul," and would advance a mature and responsible faith.[12] At the same time, modern liberal education appeared less concerned with establishing an intimate relationship with Christ and more with developing a proper place in society for the student. The social sciences were promoted as the most appropriate subjects for gaining an understanding of human and social development. Nevertheless, the church assumed that advanced study would help determine the essentials of religion and supply the best means to fulfil its goals. Ultimately, a grander intellectual and spiritual social order would result. Modern higher education would also train the experts needed to solve the complex problems facing the Canadian nation. In so doing, these experts would eventually assist the church in inaugurating the kingdom of God on earth. In order to facilitate this process, Methodists gave a high priority to expanding and updating their universities.

At Mount Allison University, these goals were partially met by the opening of the McClelan School of Applied Sciences in 1903 and, through the generosity of Lillian Massey Treble, a Faculty of Household Sciences the next year. Since Victoria University was part of the University of Toronto, it helped to promote the church's goals through the evolution of the modern University of Toronto during the first decade of the twentieth century. In 1900 engineering and medicine became formally associated with the University of Toronto, and later, again through Lillian Massey Treble's support, a School of Household Sciences opened adjacent to Victoria University. History, sociology, psychology, political science, and economics were also gradually added to the arts programs of the various universities. By the beginning of World War I, Victoria had built new women's and men's residences and a large library. A similarly dramatic expansion of facilities and modernization of curriculum occurred at Wesley College in Winnipeg.[13]

New or expanded facilities were also constructed at the theological colleges. For instance, Ryerson College erected a new building in downtown Vancouver, although it hoped to relocate near the University of British Columbia. Over the same period, the theological faculties were expanded and diversified to provide better training for ministers. They were able to supply more specialized courses and to introduce subjects such as sociology and psychology along with programs designed to help the itinerants, missionaries, and deaconesses better understand human development and deal with the practical requirements of their chosen occupations. Significant transitions were marked during the first thirteen years of the twentieth century as most of the Methodist educational institutions witnessed the retirement or death of academics and administrators such as William Shaw, Nathanael Burwash, David Allison, and Joseph Sparling, who had run their respective schools since the late nineteenth century.[14] Their replacements were generally more willing to refashion and modernize the courses of study.

Perhaps the most significant change, however, was the beginning of cooperation in theological education across denominational lines. In Montreal, in association with McGill University, ministerial candidates could take certain courses from any of the Methodist, Presbyterian, Anglican, or Congregational colleges by 1914. The Presbyterians and Methodists also experimented with joint programs in Winnipeg in 1913, and after World War I, Knox and Victoria colleges followed similar practices in Toronto. As well, beginning in 1923, Ryerson College cooperated with the Anglican and Presbyterian theological schools in Vancouver. Such action both anticipated and promoted church union among the Presbyterian, Congregational, and Methodist churches and furthered discussions for a broader union with the Anglicans.[15]

All these changes were expensive, especially since new facilities and faculty represented an ongoing drain on the colleges' financial resources. They were managed only because of the generosity of wealthy Methodists who donated millions of dollars to advance the educational cause. As well as a large share of the Twentieth Century Fund, Mount Allison and Montreal's Wesleyan Theological College received $50,000 each from Hart Massey's estate after his death in 1896, while Wesley College in Winnipeg received $100,000 and Victoria University gained $200,000 from the same source. The other Methodist schools received smaller amounts. Hart Massey's children, especially Lillian Massey Treble and Chester Massey, also eventually contributed over $2,000,000 to Methodist education before 1925. However, the Masseys were by no means alone in their generosity. Several more millions were donated by Methodist businessmen across the country. For instance, Victoria University had been built in Toronto in 1891 principally through a bequest of more than $200,000 from the estate of William Gooderham, and the $90,000 donation by wealthy members of Sherbourne Street Methodist church to the Twentieth Century Fund was designated for Victoria. In addition, several members of Victoria's Board of Regents, including A.E. Ames, George Cox, Joseph Flavelle, and A.E. Kemp, personally covered the school's annual operating deficit and donated money for student scholarships.[16]

All the schools also held periodic fund-raising campaigns to help sustain their programs, facilities, or endowments. For example, in 1912 Wesley College raised over $250,000, and Mount Allison collected a similar amount in 1914. In the latter year, friends of Victoria contributed $500,000. Ten Methodist "gentlemen" donated $390,000, and after a week of further canvassing in Toronto, another $80,000 was raised. On a national level, in fact, the Methodist church's already substantial educational assets more than doubled between 1910 and 1914. However, the decline in the Maritime and western Canadian regional economies, aggravated by the dislocation of World War I, left the colleges in a precarious position. Grants of $750,000 from the $4,800,000 donated to the Methodist National Campaign by 1922 helped alleviate some of these problems.[17]

In addition to improving its educational facilities, the Methodist church also utilized its publishing operations to help create a moral, cosmopolitan Canadian culture and thereby advance its nation-building goals. The *Christian Guardian*, *Wesleyan*, and *Western Methodist Recorder* had developed a long tradition of supplying religious and secular news and guidance in political, social, and religious matters. From 1875 until 1906, the *Canadian Methodist Magazine* was one of the most popular and valuable journals in the country dealing with current religious, scientific, and literary topics. It joined the various Sunday school and young people's magazines in supplying literature that was moral and uplifting, as well as articulate and joyful. In so doing, these periodicals provided some of the few outlets for Canadian writers and allowed them to improve their skills and earn an income while preparing their larger literary works. In fact, many of Canada's leading writers published in these magazines, which were particularly important for developing women writers.

The Methodist publishing house, especially under William Briggs and Lorne Pierce, also gave a high priority to promoting Canadian writers and did much to create a national literary tradition. After initially training for business in his native Britain, Briggs had emigrated to Canada in 1856 at age twenty and was ordained into the Wesleyan ministry seven years later. More of a businessman than a preacher, he served as book steward from 1879 until 1919. He was succeeded by the thirty-year-old Lorne Pierce, who added a keen perception of potential talent to the necessary business acumen. In 1913, after more than a decade of record profits, the Methodist church bought a block of land at Queen and John streets in Toronto to erect a five-storey publishing house. The new Wesley Buildings, which was occupied in early 1915, also held the growing church bureaucracy. The facilities cost nearly $1,000,000, but were paid for out of the profits from publishing and at the same time, according to the publishing house's ongoing mandate, significant contributions were also made to the church's superannuation funds. The new building allowed the press to publish huge quantities of Canadian history, poetry, short stories, and novels and to continue to supply school texts written by Canadians. These works demonstrated the breadth and vitality of the country's writers. Furthermore, since its publications were extremely popular with Canadian readers and it made substantial profits, other publishers across the country followed its example of encouraging Canadian authors. In fact, the English-Canadian publishing industry became dominated by Methodists who followed substantially similar publishing priorities.[18]

### WORLD WAR I

Unfortunately, although they were not immediately aware of it, Canadian Methodists' relatively comfortable and optimistic world came to a dramatic end in August 1914. The quest for personal regeneration, social justice, a moral social order, and ultimately, the kingdom of God on earth had a new and terrible hurdle to overcome. In fact, all of Methodism's cherished values would be tested over the following four and half years of world war. As a result, many Canadian Methodists came to fear that the seemingly perpetual march of progress was slowing, if not stopping altogether, and even questioned whether their own ecclesiastical success and significant contribution to the great worldwide evangelical revival was finally over. No other event in history had anything like the impact of World War I in disrupting and transforming Canadian society.

Even though the church was hesitant to support war as a means of changing the world or altering human nature, at least initially it still saw in this horrendous struggle some hope for progress. Certainly, if real progress did not emerge from the carnage, then Satan was indeed in control and humanity was doomed. Methodist leaders, especially those most involved in the church's war work, tended to see the war as a new washing away of the world's sins in blood. Thus it was a just and a holy war. Despite the fact that most Methodists believed war was inherently evil and hoped that international cooperation would prevent its occurrence, when it began, they, like all the mainstream churches in Canada, immediately offered their full support. Ordinarily, war was evil, but this was a great moral and spiritual crusade and the allied soldiers were "missionaries of the cross."[19] The Methodist church assumed that the British empire, with Canada as a vital component, was particularly God's moral instrument in the battle with evil. The imagery of a holy crusade seemed especially appropriate when the Holy Lands were finally wrested from the Ottoman empire late in the war.

At the same time, the war was sometimes considered a punishment from God for humankind's sinfulness. While some believed that the empire was God's avenging agent and some theological conservatives even suggested that Germany deserved destruction because of its leadership in the introduction of higher biblical criticism, others claimed that that country was in fact God's instrument to punish Canada and the allied nations. All the combatants equally deserved God's wrath. But as the war dragged on, casualties mounted, and the senselessness of the conflict became more evident, those who had actually participated were more inclined to recognize it as evidence of humanity's evil folly, rather than the will of God.[20]

However, Methodists could also believe that if God had a purpose in allowing the war to devastate the Western world, that purpose was, ironically, to end forever the menace of militarism. The horrors of modern warfare clearly indicated that war should never again be considered a sane or legitimate component of national policy. This was a war to end war. As such, it must be fought totally, "until the menace of militarism is broken." "There must be no partial victory, there must be no residual of militarism left."[21] Canadian propaganda was extremely effective in assigning all the blame for the conflict to Germany and its militaristic leadership. The allies were portrayed as merely defending the innocent victims of aggression and the principles of civilization. The General Conference of 1914 maintained, "When the barbarism of militarism has been recognized and destroyed, human interests the world over will be safer. To this cause, we dedicate our men and our millions, and pray that through the Empire's sacrifice, war may sooner cease in all the world."[22] Therefore Germany must be utterly defeated before the foundations of permanent peace could be laid.

Since militarism was only an extremely virulent strain of materialism, selfishness, and inhumanity, the war effort became a continuation of Methodism's long-standing battle to help regenerate the world. To the church, therefore, the struggle became a means of grace, a method by which the individual and the world would be imbued with Christian principles. Militarism would only end when individuals were spiritually reborn and humanity lived by the Golden Rule. The church believed that the war had value in calling Canadians back to the virtues of courage, loyalty, discipline, and sacrifice. The conflict forced them to think about God in concrete terms, ended their narrow complacency and selfish preoccupation with worldly pleasures, and would therefore ultimately institute real social and individual progress. The soldiers did not fight for personal glory, territorial gain, or love of battle; they were fighting for the rule of God's laws and the advance of spiritual and moral principles.[23]

Therefore patriotism transcended any petty jingoistic nationalism and represented a commitment to the principles of democracy, liberty, and justice. It preserved and advanced all the best elements of civilization. Patriotism became cloaked in religious garb and was a spiritual condition that eclipsed simple battlefield heroism. Not only did it demand sacrifice for brothers-in-arms and for country, even at the cost of one's life, but it demanded an equal commitment to the war's higher goals. The whole nation was called to patriotic service and sacrifice. Patriotism, therefore, would end corruption, eliminate immorality and injustice in human relations, and lead to a better social order after the war. The killing and destruction could be only partially justified if Christian principles were eventually victorious.[24]

The Methodist leaders believed it was their profoundly patriotic responsibility to advance the national interests during this crisis. As members of Canada's national church, they could follow no other course. In this task, "No churchmen in Canada worked harder at hammering their ploughshares into swords."[25] Every department of church work and every congregation was forced to gird on these swords until the war was won. More particularly, in November 1915 the Methodist church established the Army and Navy Board to supervise military chaplains and coordinate domestic war-related activities. Associated with the Department of Evangelism and Social Service, it became an activist propaganda agency sanitizing the war for home consumption while advancing the government's restrictive domestic policies and enlistment for overseas service. It also worked to protect Methodism's reputation and interests from domestic and foreign critics.

The Methodist war effort was led by Samuel Dwight Chown, the general superintendent, and T. Albert Moore, the secretary of General Conference and head of the Department of Evangelism and Social Service. Chown had been born in 1853 in Kingston, Canada West, and after graduating from the Kingston Military School and serving a short stint in the Prince of Wales Own Rifles, he had joined his father's successful hardward and sheet metal business. In 1874 he entered the Wesleyan itinerancy and was ordained five years later. His subsequent ministry demonstrated a deep commitment to temperance and social reform combined with a sincere sympathy for the traditional elements in the church. From 1902 until his appointment as general superintendent in 1910, he organized and led the new Department of Evangelism and Social Service. By the beginning of the war, he had firmly established himself as the leading voice in the Methodist church and one of the most influential churchmen in Canada. His critics, both inside and outside the church, noting his power and ambition, called him the Methodist archbishop. Chown was ably assisted by his chief lieutenant, Albert Moore. Moore was a native of Acton, Ontario, where he ran a newspaper before entering the Methodist ministry. After studying at McGill University, he was ordained in 1884 at age twenty-four. A tireless worker who had an intimate grasp of details, he succeeded Chown as secretary of the Department of Evangelism and Social Service and made himself the most influential bureaucrat in the Methodist church. Chown and Moore fired a nearly constant barrage of articles, sermons, and letters calling Canadians to enlist and encouraging the Methodist ministry to promote local recruiting and the total war effort. For instance, Chown argued, "At this supreme crisis every Canadian of military age, and in mental and physical health, if he has not already enlisted, must give an account to himself, to society and to God, as to why he wears civilian clothes."[26] Methodists proudly proclaimed that "our pulpits have become our best recruiting stations."[27] Even with declining enlistment by 1916, the church leaders continued to reassure the government that they would do all they could to influence Methodists to join up.

Despite the church's work, the initial enlistment statistics caused it considerable embarrassment. The Department of Militia reported that by September 1916, only 18,418 Methodists had enlisted, as opposed to 124,688 Anglicans, 63,146 Presbyterians, and 32,836 Roman Catholics. Later government statistics appeared to reconfirm the weak Methodist commitment and left the church open to public criticism. In reaction, it condemned the registration forms for calling Methodists "Wesleyans," to which many would not subscribe, and for not recording those Methodists from union congregations. It also attacked the overall accuracy of the statistics and undertook to collect its own. The Army and Navy Board defended Methodist participation and claimed that about 85,000 of its adherents were in the active forces by 1918. Even this somewhat inflated estimate, however, was well below the involvement of the Church of England and disproportionately low among the Protestant denominations.[28]

Although church leaders continued to believe that Methodist enlistment was much higher than the statistics suggested, they also justified lower involvement since Methodists were more likely to be native born and therefore married with families. New immigrants from Europe, who were still bound to their country of birth and often did not have family responsibilities, were much more likely to enlist. Indeed, a high proportion of enlistment in 1914 and 1915 represented new arrivals from Britain; less than 30 per cent of the first Canadian contingent was born in Canada. In addition, Methodists were proportionately more rural than other Protestants and could not easily abandon their farms to take up arms. While jobs in factories would wait for the returning veteran, crops would not, and the farm would quickly deteriorate. At the same time, farming was considered a moral occupation and an essential war industry. In spite of the validity of these arguments, when they were also proposed to explain weak enlistment among French-Canadian Catholics, the Methodist church dismissed them as hollow excuses. In fact, regardless of the enthusiasm for the war among most of the Methodist leaders, they were seriously out of touch with their membership. Although there was never a widespread vocal opposition among Methodists, most quietly abstained from joining the military.[29]

As for the Methodist ministry, more than 425 clergy and probationers served overseas as chaplains, YMCA workers, members of the medical corps, or combatants. In total, about 90 per cent of the ministers involved bore arms. The reasons for enlisting were as individual as the clergy themselves, but most found that it was extremely difficult to preach the need to participate while remaining safely at home. Theology students in particular were under enormous moral and social pressure to join. Many had family members or friends who had been killed, and some had been publicly humiliated for shirking their duty. Others believed the war was a great battle with the forces of the anti-Christ and agreed with Irwin Beatty, who wrote to the Army and Navy Board, "I wish to volunteer because I believe it my duty to take part in now bearing a share of our national sins. It is the voice of Christ, not the voice of my Country, that I hear."[30] Wartime service was not considered a denial of God's call to ministry; it was another, more active field of opportunity. A minister was called to serve, not merely to preach. Still other volunteers felt that it was imperative to participate actively if they hoped to understand and lead the veterans after the war.

However, after the initial surge of clerical enlistment, even the Army and Navy Board was more cautious about encouraging ministers to leave for war service. Many enthusiastic volunteers were unfit for battlefield action, and the chaplain authorities were becoming more selective. Also, while the board acknowledged that enlistment was "Truly a call of God and an insistent call," there was a tremendous shortage of ministers at home, and it maintained, "It is essential to preserve, exhort and enthrone the soul of our people here, and fit them to stand the strain of this terrific war."[31] The conflict greatly increased the pastoral duties of the ministry in areas such as counselling and assisting families in the absence of husbands and older sons, as well as filling in for absent colleagues. The ministers were told to get permission to enlist from their pastoral charge and their annual conference or mission authorities, and such permission became increasingly difficult to obtain.

The chaplains who did go overseas provided a remarkable service to the armed forces. Cooperating with the clergy from all the Christian churches, as well as with the Red Cross and YMCA, they suffered many of the same hardships and privations as the regular troops. They led church services, supervised church parades, prayed before battle, distributed tracts and religious literature, comforted the wounded and dying, and encouraged the disillusioned. They also helped distribute packages from Canada and encouraged moral behaviour among the troops. However, the clergy quickly discovered that they were most successful when they emphasized a traditional personal religion, rather than the social-gospel ideals of corporate, community regeneration. Respite from the horrors of war, it appeared, could only be secured by a spiritual recommitment to God. While these clerical functions were expected, the chaplains gained even more respect for their determination and courage under fire. They often carried litters, retrieved casualties from the battlefields, and gave practical assistance to the soldiers in the trenches.[32]

Despite the commendable performance by the Methodist clergy, the authorities who oversaw the church's war work were dismayed by the decline in voluntary enlistment during 1916. They concluded that the only solution to the growing shortage was to conscript able-bodied men for overseas service. If Canada failed to fulfil its obligations to help win the war, they believed the nation was betraying both those who had already died and the noble goals of the war itself. Even before the federal government agreed to conscription in 1917, the Methodist church was actively preaching the value of calling up all available resources for the war effort. Samuel Dwight Chown claimed that the opponent to conscription "degrades the term Canadian from a synonym of glory to a badge of dishonour."[33] Conscription was particularly necessary since the best allied military estimates assumed the war would continue for at least four more years. As a preliminary step, the registration of available human and economic resources would provide a basis for their just allocation. Many men who were working as farmers or in essential war industries were under unfair attack for not enlisting; conscription would show that they were not avoiding their patriotic responsibilities by granting them exemption from military service.

Moreover, wealth would also be conscripted through responsible taxation. Most members of the Methodist church supported legitimate profits, but given the soaring prices and evidence of profiteering, the church demanded government intervention. Opposition to excessive profits was especially prevalent among the farmers of western Canada, who blamed the nation's businessmen for most of its problems. Through conscription of wealth, the ill-gotten gains would be returned to the government to fight the war. At the same time, general Methodist opinion favoured the formation of a national union government to prosecute the war and eliminate shallow partisan politics. While cautious about any drastic interference with natural rights and liberties, the church also supported the War Measures Act and later the Wartime Election Act, which disenfranchised enemy aliens resident in Canada and gave the vote to female relatives of soldiers overseas. These and other equally drastic measures appeared necessary in order to facilitate conscription, unite the nation, and ensure victory over Germany.[34]

But to many, the real purpose of conscription was to force shirkers into the armed forces. Pre-eminently, this meant French-Canadian Roman Catholics. Colonel Charles Williams, Canada's chief recruiting officer, believed the Roman Catholics were not doing their duty and that the Catholic church was traitorously anti-British. He feared that the church's position might lead to an anti-French backlash after the war. Albert Moore was hesitant to be as outspoken, but he did report confidentially to Williams, "There is a festering sore in Canada, and every day I pray that it may not develop into bloodshed and Civil War."[35] Although some ministers believed French Canada was hoping to see the breakup of the empire, others were even more blatantly anti-French and anti-Catholic. In September 1916, for instance, James Putnam complained that "we have done our duty in this great war but the papists have not and for my part I would hail conscription in order to make those French cowards do their duty."[36] He went on to suggest that the pope was waiting until the Protestant youth were killed to make it easier for the Catholic church to take over Canada. With proper exemptions, the true purpose of conscription could be achieved and French Canada forced into active participation.

Beyond its concerns over military service, the Methodist church also worked tirelessly for the moral uplift of the troops. It believed they should be as pure as the motives for which they fought. While battlefield conditions made supervision impossible, the church sought to protect the innocent and reform the wayward among the troops in Canada, in Britain, or behind the lines in France. It strove to maintain the sanctity of the sabbath and discouraged gambling, smoking, card-playing, and the reading of offensive books and magazines. In their place, the Methodists provided moral and uplifting reading material and innocent amusements for the military both in Canada and abroad. Where possible, they attempted to re-create a friendly family environment for the young men, who were often away from home for the first time. They also supplied quiet retreats segregated from irreligious associations and worked in conjunction with the British Methodist connexions to encourage spiritual and moral growth.[37]

Most prominently, however, Canadian Methodism focused on eliminating the twin poisons of alcohol and sexual promiscuity. Many ministers and parents even opposed their young people joining the armed forces because of the evil influences facing them and viewed alcohol and sexual misconduct as greater threats than battle. Military canteens in Canada often did not sell liquor, and the church encouraged similarly dry canteens in Britain. Church authorities also petitioned the British government and the army high command to eliminate the rum ration and to prevent the sale of alcohol near military bases. The campaign against alcohol by some individual Methodists reached ludicrous proportions which would never have been sanctioned in peacetime. Although the church was encouraged by support for temperance from the British royal family, in general, the military was not sympathetic, and drink was readily available throughout the war.

The Methodist church also associated the disruption of wholesome family life during the war with the apparent rise in prostitution. Young women were entering the industrial workforce away from parental supervision, and young men, either while travelling or in military training, were often on their own for the first time. Prostitutes were readily available in the larger cities and near the military camps in Canada and especially in Britain and France. Young soldiers were also under a certain amount of peer pressure to take advantage of these opportunities to "sow their wild oats," and the military authorities attempted only weakly to suppress the business. As a result, as well as moral values being dissolved, venereal disease reached epidemic proportions, and returning troops spread the infection throughout Canada. However, although many of Methodism's programs were legitimate and its fears warranted, in its condemnation of the troops' non-military conduct, the church showed a rather naïve lack of appreciation of war conditions and sometimes left itself and its enlisted membership open to ridicule.[38]

In addition to its own work with the troops, the Methodist church cooperated with a variety of government and private agencies, usually organized at the community level, to marshall the civilian population for the war effort. Many regular church groups, such as the Ladies' Aid and the Woman's Missionary Society, reoriented their work to concentrate on providing comfort for soldiers or their families. Local churches organized teas, socials, and recreational gatherings for soldiers stationed in Canada to protect vital public works and later provided returning veterans with material aid and help in finding jobs and resettling into civilian life. As well, the individual congregations provided healthy, moral, and familiar surroundings for the thousands of agricultural and industrial workers who were far from home in war-related occupations.

Generally working through community organizations or international agencies such as the Red Cross, Methodists also forwarded shiploads of hospital supplies, blankets, socks, gloves, scarves, food packages, and reading material to Britain. Like all Canadians, they contributed heavily to the national fund-raising campaigns, such as the Belgian Relief Fund and the various Victory Bond issues. While the church officially promoted these causes and gathered statistics to demonstrate the extent of Methodist support, individual ministers and members often refused to view war work in narrow connexional terms and tended to operate in non-denominational, community-wide organizations. As the war dragged on, Canadians increasingly learned to accept government intervention in nearly all aspects of life and to practice economy and self-denial. As well as accepting income tax and rationing, individuals forsook unnecessary expenditures and adopted measures to help relieve the shortage of foodstuffs, such as planting vegetable gardens. Thousands of women and young people also travelled to rural Canada to bring in the harvests. The institutional church did what it could to facilitate all these operations.[39]

It also advanced its social and moral concerns on the home front. Canada had to be pure to live up to the obligations of the war. In concert with the other Canadian churches, secular agencies, and the government, the Methodist church fought to achieve a national moral social order. In this regard, the war served as a great catalyst to reform activity by providing a new urgency to the traditional Methodist campaigns. Prohibition now became a patriotic duty; alcohol wasted precious food and productive capacity while poisoning the troops and workers and making them less morally and physically fit to win the war. Drunkenness was unacceptable behaviour; abstinence was a legitimate wartime demand. Under this emergency, the federal government proclaimed national prohibition to reinforce local-option and provincial prohibition legislation.[40]

Wartime conditions also caused a significant disruption in traditional Canadian life. From nearly nothing, Canada developed one of the world's largest munitions industries, and this meant huge increases in mining, steel making, and subsidiary manufacturing. Of immediate concern to the church, the rise of war-related industries and the accompanying shift from the countryside to large urban centres often accelerated the destruction of the informal sources of community stability and discipline. These were impossible to replicate in the anonymous city precincts. At the same time, the associated breakdown of parental authority was exaggerated by the absence of fathers overseas and mothers working outside the home. These features, along with greater financial independence for young people, helped to increase juvenile delinquency and petty crime. For older young people, the possibility of imminent death in the armed forces combined with a growing disillusionment with society to produce rebellion against social and religious restraint and an increase in immorality.

In reaction, Methodism redoubled its efforts to achieve social progress and purity. It campaigned against prostitution and sexual promiscuity on both moral and medical grounds and began to initiate sex education programs. In 1914 alone, over 1,000,000 leaflets concerned with protecting the young from social vice were distributed, and W.L. Clark and Beatrice Brigden lectured on social morality and sex education across the country. Taking advantage of the need and increasing willingness among Canadians to sacrifice for the national good, the church attacked gambling and tobacco and promoted sabbatarianism and healthy amusements. Both in recognition of their wartime service and to introduce socially and morally advanced programs, the Methodist church pressed the government to expand women's franchise. It also helped rouse Canadians against inefficient and corrupt government policies. The war demonstrated that the state had a responsibility to interfere dramatically in the daily lives of Canadians and reduced much of the opposition to such interference.[41]

However, despite the best efforts and noble rhetoric of the church's leaders, the war in fact fractured and polarized Canadian Methodism. The senior lay and clerical leadership's monopoly of the means of communications and main institutional agencies exaggerated the appearance of unanimity about the war. Most of those who questioned the church's official position feared being branded as unpatriotic. But there was always a strong undercurrent of opposition among the Methodist ministry and laity. Certainly, the optimistic belief in the war as a holy crusade that would lead to a more Christian society was quickly shattered by experience in the trenches. War itself broke Christian principles and was the antithesis of morality and ethical conduct. Moreover, actual battle conditions made it difficult to trust that humanity had ever progressed beyond its depraved animal state or even to believe in God.[42]

Some Methodists denounced the church for acting as an agent of the government in pursuing its militaristic goals. They argued that if Methodism could not officially oppose the war, it should at least remain neutral. It should certainly not encourage young men to betray their Christian principles by forcing them to enlist. A number of Methodist ministers quietly refused to act as recruiting agents, but asked the church officials not to publicize their personal opposition. There was even greater opposition to conscription as a betrayal of the rights of the individual. Conscription would seriously divide the country along ethnic, racial, class, and geographic lines and shatter any hope that the nation could face the challenges of the postwar world united. Similarly, censorship and anti-democratic government measures such as the Wartime Election Act, the War Measures Act, and the numerous orders-in-council were considered threats to the very principles the war was being fought to preserve. Finally, some prominent Methodist ministers led in the pacifist campaigns that directly opposed Canadian participation in the war. To them, war could never be justified on any grounds. They argued that conscientious objection was legitimate and should be encouraged, not denounced, by the Methodist church. James S. Woodsworth, for example, was ostracized and effectively forced out of the church for his pacifist beliefs.[43]

POSTWAR SOCIETY

The end of the war on November 11, 1918, came as a surprise to military, government, and church officials; no one had really foreseen the sudden collapse of imperial Germany. The Canadian government was faced with the

Samuel Dwight Chown (1853–1933). First secretary of the
Department of Evangelism and Social Service and general superintendent of the Methodist Church, 1910–25. (UCA, P1005N)

Rev. Maj. George Williams (1866–1945). Military chaplain reviewing troops in Queen's Park, Toronto, 1916. (UCA, P7195)

Salem G. Bland (1859–1950). A major advocate of
the social gospel in Canada. (UCA, P484N)

James S. Woodsworth (1874–1942). Left the Methodist ministry and led the socialist Co-operative Commonwealth Federation party in national politics.
(UCA, P149)

difficult task of demobilizing and reintegrating a huge military force into civilian life, while the private sector had to shift from a wartime to a peacetime economy. The federal and provincial governments were highly conservative and lacked both the skill and the determination to participate actively in solving the postwar problems. Their major priorities were to balance their budgets and return to traditional preoccupations. Simultaneously, with the removal of the need for patriotism, sacrifice, and unity, the deep cracks in Canadian society which the war had both aggravated and papered over re-emerged to confound hopes for national harmony and progress. The nation was fractured by geographic, ethnic, and class tensions that cried out for social, economic, and political redress.

On the economic level, although the war had temporarily relieved the high unemployment, wartime prices had far outstripped wages or returns from agricultural production and caused a decrease in the standard of living for working Canadians. After the war, this impact was coupled with a return to severe unemployment and a deep recession as consumer spending failed to replace the demand for war supplies. Farmers throughout the country believed they had been exploited and that their value to the war effort and to the economic health of Canada was underestimated. Western Canada felt especially aggrieved, believing that the population growth of that region had not been reflected in an appropriate shift in political power. Politicians from Ontario and Quebec seemed to make decisions which ignored the interests of Canada's other regions. As well, industrial workers felt that they had been forced to bear the brunt of the war at home while manufacturers enjoyed excessive profits. Like the farmers, labourers wanted better social and economic security, an end to corrupt and exploitive policies, and a greater share in power. For their part, French Canadians felt isolated and politically powerless, particularly because of the imposition of conscription. In addition, the thousands of returning veterans assumed they had a legitimate claim for jobs and generous treatment, but they quickly became disillusioned by the situation they found in Canada. They complained that the best jobs were held by those who had not served their country or, worse, by alien immigrants.

In reaction, veterans used the comradeship forged in France to mobilize a powerful political lobby for special treatment and actively participated in other protest organizations. French Canadians instinctively turned inward to nationalist institutions to protect their interests. Workers and farmers developed unions, cooperatives, and other organizations which called for apparently radical economic and political action to advance their rights. They believed that they could only be successful against the might of modern capital and industry by adopting a confrontational, collectivist strategy and soon added class- or occupation-based political action. In any event, they felt that they had little to lose by trying. Moreover, international communism and other extreme social and political movements provided a highly visible backdrop to events in Canada. The combination of these elements made the situation extremely volatile.[44]

The ruptures in Canadian society also exaggerated the polarization within institutional Methodism. To some disillusioned Methodists, the social, economic, and political upheavals added to the unsettled theological and ecclesiastical conditions to produce a deep anxiety over the future of Methodism in the country. Secular and modernist concepts, promulgated by a growing force of articulate individuals, appeared to threaten the Methodist vision of itself and of its role both in Canada and around the world. After the brutality and devastation of the war and the serious problems facing postwar society, it was particularly difficult to preach the superiority of Western civilization or to assume that the world was actually advancing. This uncertainty led some Methodists to advocate radical new directions for the church while it convinced others of the need to return to the religion of an earlier, seemingly less controversial era.

A radical group of Methodist social gospellers believed the mainstream churches were controlled by the wealthy business class, which would never accept the drastic measures required to forge a just society. The war had destroyed their faith in individualistic, voluntary measures and they turned to socialism. While individuals such as the socialist J.S. Woodsworth and the communist Albert E. Smith would abandon institutional religion for the union hall and political platform, others such as William Ivens and Salem Bland continued to work within an ecclesiastical framework. Ivens joined the Christian Socialist Labour church in Winnipeg, and Bland attempted to transform the Methodist church into a working-class institution. Bland argued that the postwar world was the dawn of a new social order and called for a new Christianity to guide it. For him, old-style religion suppressed the practical spirit of Christianity in stale forms and outworn dogmas and worked to justify the dominance of the upper classes. The new Christianity demanded social justice for all. The twentieth century belonged to the working class, and pure religion must be based on a socially active Christ preaching the Sermon on the Mount.[45]

The other end of the Methodist theological spectrum claimed that the answer to injustice, as well as to the postwar divisions in Canadian society and the apparent decline in moral principles, was a renewal of traditional evangelism. Canada's social problems were viewed as merely the external manifestations of a much more profound spiritual malaise. Faithfully preaching Christ crucified did not deny a sympathy for the economically, socially, and politically dispossessed, but social welfare programs without Christ as the foundation could never bring about permanent progress. Those who held these views called for aggressive evangelistic campaigns, perhaps run by professional revivalists, to answer humanity's real needs through personal regeneration, to draw more Canadians into active church membership, and to revitalize the core spirituality of the nation. A central element of the 1918 Methodist National Campaign was to increase the spiritual commitment of Canadians and to add 100,000 new members to the church and another 100,000 to the Methodist Sunday schools.[46]

This re-emphasis on a personal religious experience often represented a reaction to the complexities of contemporary society and even to the optimistic assumption that a post-millennial world was imminent. In light of the increasing doubt about the future, many Methodists simply wished to regain some control over their own lives and perhaps to recapture part of their nineteenth-century evangelical heritage. Spiritual religion provided a sense of purpose and a release from the pressures of war and the agitations of postwar reconstruction. It held a particular appeal for many returning soldiers and for former Methodists who had moved to more evangelical denominations. However, most conservative Methodists did not wish to reopen the fundamentalist-modernist debate and felt no comfort in adventist or pentecostal answers.[47]

The vast majority of Methodists continued to call for a sensible blending of evangelistic and social-service work. The church did organize several evangelistic campaigns which emphasized personal spiritual conversion, but it also maintained that "the real spirit and purpose of evangelism ... must in our day manifest themselves not less in a deep inward experience of God in the individual soul of man, but more in the courageous and consistent, and sacrificial expression of this inward experience in all the social, industrial and political relations in life."[48] Religion must operate to assist the individual, the family, and the community; personal and social religion were inseparable. In addition, although the war created more doubt, the Methodist church's leadership was not prepared to abandon its dream of transforming Canada into Christ's dominion.

The war had deeply divided Methodism, but it had given a tremendous impetus to the implementation of specific reforms and called Canadians to "press forward fearlessly and confidently toward the ideals of the Kingdom of Christ."[49] Most Methodists agreed that Canada owed its citizens a just nation and a civilization based on "brotherhood" and liberty. They argued that the principles of sacrifice that ennobled the war effort had to be embodied in the postwar reconstruction. The church and the nation must mobilize the same conviction and energy that had gone into winning the war and apply them to eliminating injustice, poverty, and vice. Methodism must become even more aggressive in the new world order since only Christianity supplied sound ideological underpinnings for evolutionary progress and guaranteed an essential respectability to reform. Indeed, only the churches could provide an acceptable moral and spiritual leadership in moving the nation from the old order to the new.

Methodists also continued to believe that with the advances in technology, there was no need for poverty; society now produced enough to meet the normal requirements of all Canadians. Christians were merely stewards of God's special benevolence to Canada, and proper trusteeship demanded the just distribution of wealth. Methodists asserted that the community had a natural right to share in the nation's wealth and that the public good took precedence over the narrow claims of all economic interest groups. When these rights were protected, cooperation rather than competition would guide all human relations.[50] However, this goal would never be achieved without a real partnership between church and state. Just as the church had to lead in the fight for justice and morality, the state must implement the required political, social, and economic reforms by enshrining democratic and Christian principles in the laws of the land. Only the state had the power and authority to guarantee the rights of the individual and the prerogatives of the community. It was the church's duty to strengthen the government's resolve, keep politicians from succumbing to dishonest or short-sighted policies, and ultimately to transform the political system into an agency of moral, economic, and social righteousness.[51]

Along with the other mainstream Protestant denominations, the Methodist church recognized that simple appeals for the implementation of Christian principles were no longer sufficient. Canadians had lost their naïve faith in the eventual victory of justice without specific, concrete action. The general conferences of the Methodist church during the twentieth century had endorsed a wide-ranging program for social improvement and increasingly emphasized the need to protect workers, the poor, and the old. Building on the pre-war social programs and the official policies of the church, the report of the Department of Evangelism and Social Service to the General Conference of 1918 represented the culmination of this process and provided a substantially radical blueprint for postwar social reconstruction. It denounced special privilege and called upon the government to establish old age pensions, mother's allowances, and other progressive social welfare measures to protect the most vulnerable members of the community and especially to assist women and children. Such programs were the only real guarantee against poverty. Further, they did not bear the stigma of old-fashioned charity; they were part of the natural expectations of a just society. When these goals were accomplished, Canada would be well on its way to establishing the kingdom of God on earth.[52]

More immediately, however, postwar society was in desperate need of a modern, large-scale public-health system. Hundreds of thousands of Canadians had been wounded, maimed, or poisoned with gas during the war, and many required long-term treatment. In fact, nearly all members of the armed services had been weakened and made more susceptible to disease or physical breakdown. This fact represented a significant, ongoing element of Canada's medical requirements. However, the postwar influenza epidemic was an even greater threat to the nation's health. In fact, more Canadians died from the flu than had been killed during the war, and Canada's inadequate medical facilities were overwhelmed by the sick. These factors, however, only complicated the medical problems caused by such things as urban slums and inadequate regulation of food and drugs. The Methodist church urged the various levels of government to implement public-health measures and programs to assist Canadians in paying for medical services. It also supported urban reforms to clear slums, provide decent, affordable, and sanitary housing, and supply healthy parks and wholesome recreation. In addition, it influenced the government to regulate and supervise the food and drug industries to insure quality and purity.[53]

The Methodist church maintained that society had an equally immediate obligation to help reintegrate the returned soldiers into civilian life. Nearly 625,000 men had served in the armed forces, and the government should move quickly to establish agencies to assist these men. Many casualties would spend the rest of their lives in hospitals or were too badly hurt to take up full-time jobs. These men deserved generous pensions and other forms of economic assistance. Others were psychologically traumatized or brutalized by the war. After years of camp life, they could not readily settle down in now-unfamiliar surroundings among relatives and former friends with whom they had little in common. They were too restless or disillusioned to resume civilian occupations or to rejoin traditional institutions.

The Methodist church assumed that it had a special responsibility to restore former combatants to spiritual health and to win them for God's service. It believed this was a critical aspect of their reintegration into normal family, community, and national life. The church worked for a great spiritual revival after the war at least partially to satisfy these goals. It also advocated proper assistance, even for those who returned generally unscathed by their war experience. They should receive good jobs and generous treatment from both the government and the private sector. The church believed that support should be given to those who wished to improve their education or take other forms of training. Although somewhat sceptical about the programs, it also supported the various plans for resettling disbanded troops in the north and west. In general, the church believed that if Canada failed its veterans, it would be betraying all the ideals and sacrifice of the war. Such a betrayal might drive veterans to support communistic or anarchistic forces in the country and contribute to the nation's social unrest.[54]

Immediately after the war and increasingly during the 1920s, the Methodist church reconfirmed its belief that the key to long-term social regeneration was the elimination of war as an instrument of national policy. Although some church leaders recognized war's necessity if civilization was threatened, even they believed that it reflected humanity's barbaric nature and was the antithesis of Christian living. Peace and goodwill were the true bases of Christianity. Other Methodists were embarrassed by their church's former jingoistic spirit, especially as information about the causes of the war and the way it had been conducted became available. They maintained that war was based on commercial and industrial competition and that militarism was reinforced by class and racial prejudice. War wasted resources, destroyed property, and more importantly, maimed and killed innocent people. It was an instrument of tyranny that attacked fundamental social morality. Even Chown and Moore assumed a leadership role demanding that physical force be replaced by intellectual and moral force in international relations. The church strongly supported the League of Nations, international courts of justice, and the growing disarmament movement as the best hope for a peaceful, Christian world order.[55]

The Methodist church also promoted the claims of rural society as an important element in social reconstruction. It continued to assume that agrarian society preserved core national values against the destructive influences of urban life. Rural and small-town Canada was also the heart of Methodism and the major source of new members. But the wartime industrialization of the country had accelerated rural depopulation, especially in Ontario, and deepened the church's fears for its own, and therefore the nation's, future. Methodism sought to reverse this trend by eliminating rural isolation and improving recreational, intellectual, and social opportunities in the countryside. It promoted community centres for reading, discussions, and appropriate amusement and trained a more effective rural ministry. It also petitioned the government for rural electrification and improved facilities and services.[56]

However, depopulation of the countryside was essentially a response to lack of economic opportunities. The church therefore supported better agricultural training for farmers and promoted the operations of institutions such as Guelph's agricultural college and government experimental farms. At the same time, most farmers were economically disadvantaged because they had to sell their produce in open competition yet buy machinery and equipment made overly expensive by protective tariffs. The church advocated lower tariffs on manufactured goods, an easy-money policy to assist the rural debtor society, the regulation of commodity prices through agencies such as marketing boards, and cooperatives to help farmers buy and sell more competitively. The Methodist church also sought a land speculation tax to limit developers holding large tracts of land for future use. Such a policy would make more land available for agriculture at cheaper prices. In addition, it called for a limit to combines and monopolies, which were able to charge unreasonably high prices, and the nationalization of natural resources, railroads, and utilities so that they would serve the national good rather than private avarice.

Many rural ministers and several national church leaders also assumed prominent positions in the embryonic farmers' organizations and in the growing agrarian political revolt. These organizations utilized the ideology of the social gospel and the rhetoric of democracy and morality to advance their economic and social goals. New farmer-based movements evolved a group identity strongly opposing what they considered corrupt, business-dominated national parties. Although they also reflected a growing regional dissatisfaction in western Canada, they gained significant support in rural sections of Ontario and the Maritimes. With the formation of provincial farmers' parties and the national Progressive Party, these movements effectively shattered the existing political structures during the 1920s and helped to implement significant social and political change.[57]

The progressive, liberal church that Methodism had become was not, however, interested in the plight of only one economic group. It considered itself the national church and was particularly committed to aiding all disadvantaged elements in society. In fact, the church leadership became even more deeply concerned with the plight of industrial workers. The pre-war growth of industrial unions had been partially stifled by restrictions on strikes and limits to wage increases during the war. But increased business profits and a high cost of living, coupled with severe unemployment and falling wages after the war, led to a growing radicalism in the union movement. It was also partially influenced by the class-based ideologies current in Britain, Europe, and the United States. Increasingly conscious of the need to take direct, collective action to end social injustice and further its economic demands, the labour movement was prepared – and more importantly, appeared to have the power – to bring Canada's industrial system to a halt to further its aims.

To those who argued that the labour movement was dominated by bolsheviks and anarchists who were attempting to overturn the natural order of society, the Methodist church asserted that labour unrest was merely a sign of workers' intelligent ambition. The disturbances were the birth pangs of a new, more Christian order as society asserted itself against oppression and injustice.

Even many Methodist business leaders maintained that workers had a right to share more equitably in the fruits of their labour and to enjoy a more significant place in society. According to the church, if this movement was guided by Christian principles, it would not lead to anarchy or class oppression by labour, but to true brotherhood and the reign of Christ's Golden Rule and his Sermon on the Mount.[58]

To accomplish these ends, the Methodist church led the fight to protect the rights of labour and to prevent its alienation from the community at large. It trained a specialized, committed ministry to work with the poor and working classes. The church courts actively supported the natural right of labour to decent living and working conditions, as well as leisure for the enjoyment of life. Workers, no less than the middle class, deserved time for rest, recreation, education, and enjoyment of the arts. Therefore the church officially supported labour's claims for a minimum wage, an eight-hour day, and a forty-four-hour, later a forty-hour, week. It also maintained that workers should receive a decent and secure wage. Company-owned towns should be eliminated and factories, mines, and mills made safe and healthy. Protection must particularly be guaranteed for children and women in the workforce, and women's economic, as well as social and political, equality must be assured.[59]

Against the immense power of capital, the church recognized that labour needed the right to bargain collectively and to strike. However, it hoped that arbitration on fair principles and cooperation in the management of industry would prevent economic and social disruption. The state had a responsibility to insure the protection and progress of labour's rights and to foster, as far as possible, full employment. Employment was essential in order to prevent the breakdown of the family and the loss of self-esteem and respect among the workers. To meet the immediate problem of high unemployment, the church asked the government to assist those who wished to return to farming and to develop a national unemployment insurance program in place of the embarrassing charity of temporary municipal relief.[60]

Despite its support for the rights of labour, the Methodist church was not and did not intend to become a working-class institution. Its primary goal was to advance social justice and harmony and to hasten the creation of Christ's kingdom on earth. In the year following the end of World War I, strikes and labour unrest appeared to threaten Canada's political and social stability. These disruptions culminated in the Winnipeg General Strike of 1919. The original goals of gaining the right to collective bargaining and an eight-hour day in the metal trades were soon overshadowed by organized labour's attempt to break the fundamental power of the owners of the businesses. When bargaining broke down, sympathy strikes crippled all the services in the city and spread to other communities across the country. Observers quickly recognized that the Winnipeg strike was a watershed in the history of Canadian labour.

Like much of Canadian society, Methodists were deeply divided by the dispute. Many of the strikers and strike supporters were themselves active Methodists. Beatrice Brigden, who was visiting Winnipeg as an agent of the church's Department of Evangelism and Social Service, claimed that the strike illustrated the idealism and generosity of workers and should therefore be officially sanctioned by the church. Ernest Thomas, another official in the Department of Evangelism and Social Service, sympathized with the goals, if not always the tactics, of the strikers. As well, the former Methodist itinerant and professor William Ivens provided advice and assistance to the strikers from his Winnipeg Labour church, and James S. Woodsworth, who had by then left the Methodist ministry, would later assume moral leadership of the movement. Both men were arrested for seditious conspiracy when the government forcibly ended the strike. Although in a minority, these individuals articulated sentiments shared by many working-class Methodists. However, other Methodists saw the strike as the beginning of class warfare, with the leaders of organized labour attempting to establish a tyrannical proletarian dictatorship as had recently occurred in Russia. Most businessmen denounced it as an attempt to establish the radical "one big union" and through it to usurp political power from the democratically elected officials. If it was successful, they feared that it would initiate a communist revolution, replace law and order by mob rule, and destroy Canadian society. The only suitable response was the immediate and determined use of force to end the strike and break the illegitimate power of organized labour.[61]

For most moderate Methodists, a general strike went too far in undermining the rule of law and interfering with the rights of the people. As a member of the federal government, the prominent Methodist Newton Wesley Rowell had supported the rights of labour, but he feared the Winnipeg general strike had been taken over by a small coterie of disloyal Marxists who threatened national security and social stability. Most prominent lay and clerical Methodists believed that the community, as distinct from labour and capital, had rights that must prevail. The church officials called for fairness, tolerance, patience, and calm, but they maintained that justice could only be achieved through cooperative brotherhood, not class warfare. Society must evolve through a democratic use of the ballot and the strengthening of Christian principles.[62] While this position helped to drive some socialist-leaning Methodists out of the congregations, it remained the basis of mainstream Methodism's labour policy throughout the 1920s, especially as conditions returned to a more normal state.

With regard to its own internal labour relations, the Methodist church remained highly paternalistic. Its ordained ministers, as well as its missionaries, deaconesses, and other church workers, generally received poor salaries or other social benefits. But this was considered a natural consequence of serving God in a called profession. The church also believed that its ordinary employees, particularly at headquarters and in its publishing operations, should be satisfied with lower wages since they worked for a religious institution. In 1921, when the Toronto Typographic Union went on strike, the Board of Publications argued that it could not afford to increase wages while implementing a shorter work week. The church courts supported this position. Although its publishing work was highly profitable, the church considered itself a distinct case since the profits subsidized the itinerants' pension funds. Organized labour, as well as more radical Methodist ministers such as Ernest Thomas, severely criticized the church, claiming it was hypocritical in preaching the rights of labour but itself following selfish business principles.[63]

The Methodist church demonstrated a similar ambivalence with regard to the rights of women. It certainly supported expanding opportunities in higher education. During the war, the proportion of female students at Methodist universities had risen dramatically. For instance, in 1914 Victoria University had 147 women among its 622 students while four years later 191 of the 331 students were women. Even with the return of men in greater numbers after the war, women continued to supply a high proportion of students, and female faculty members began to make an appearance. The Methodist church supported this development although some leading Methodist educators, including Margaret Addison, the dean of women at Victoria University, advocated independent women's colleges. Nevertheless, the Methodist universities continued to provide generations of Canadian women with a first-class education.[64]

The church also supported economic and social equality for women. Although significant advances would have to wait for another half-century, there were nevertheless relatively more occupations open to women in business and the professions. The church encouraged this process and sought to end prejudice and eliminate regulations in the private sector which disabled middle-class women. Most working women, however, had low paying jobs in factories, offices, or stores. The church strove to improve their working conditions by advocating safety, sanitation, and health legislation, by encouraging improved holiday and recreational benefits, and by supporting higher wages. At the same time, the church still maintained that the proper condition for women was marriage and that married women should remain at home to raise their families.

In the realm of politics, the Methodist church had long advocated women's suffrage and viewed its achievement nationally in 1918 as a major indication of Canada's progress. It also encouraged women to participate actively in reforming the political system and supported their claims to full rights in Parliament. However, the church was much more hesitant about sharing power with women in its own highest courts. The issue of allowing women to become members of the Methodist General Conference was first officially raised in 1902, but it was not until 1918 that the General Conference voted to accept them. And the ordination of women, the final demonstration of full and equal rights in the church, was never achieved during the life of the Methodist church. It was not until 1936 that women were ordained in the United Church of Canada.[65]

Nevertheless, despite hesitation in some fields, the Methodist church provided a significant leadership during the first quarter of the twentieth century in attempting to make Canada a just, moral, and progressive nation according to its own understanding of these terms. In 1924 the church marked the centenary of the formation of its first Annual Conference in Canada. With church union imminent, the celebrations provided an appropriate opportunity to review Methodism's many accomplishments. Methodists could look back with legitimate pride at their heroic enterprise, their missionary contribution to spreading evangelical religion across the nation and around the world, their progressive social and educational institutions dedicated to advancing Canadian culture and morality, and ultimately to their labours on behalf of a worthy dominion for Christ. But the anniversary provided an even more opportune occasion for looking forward to ecumenical cooperation and union with the other Canadian Protestant denominations. Methodists believed that they should build on the past to create an institution that was even more dedicated to Christian service.

# 16 Methodism and the Formation of The United Church of Canada

The central feature of Methodism's crusade for spiritual and moral progress during the twentieth century was ecumenical cooperation and the union of Protestant forces into one dynamic national church. It did not advocate its own demise, but rather believed that its great commission to spread Christianity throughout the world could best be fulfilled within a broadly Protestant institutional framework. The Canadian Methodist church concluded that there remained little or no justification for a divided Canadian Protestantism while a world of opportunity awaited united action. It seemed improbable that Christ's earthly rule could arrive as long as Christians continued in their narrow, competing denominations. All Christians throughout the world belonged to the same family, shared the same values, and worked for a common end. Under God's benevolent direction, this family must eventually harness its efforts into one collective whole in order to meet the challenges of evil. It was a significant aspect of twentieth-century Canada's national destiny to lead this ecumenical effort.

Canadian Methodists recognized that the most important development for mainstream Methodism during its entire history was its amalgamation with the Presbyterian Church in Canada, the Congregational Union of Canada, the General Council of Local Union Churches, and various independent congregations to form The United Church of Canada. On June 10, 1925, the first General Council of the United Church, along with over 8,000 visitors, met at the Mutual Street Arena in Toronto to inaugurate this new church and to oversee the end of a separate presence for mainstream Canadian Methodism. This gathering was the consummation of decades of spirited and sometimes rancorous debate, endless meetings, and tireless effort. Over the following days at Metropolitan church in Toronto, the General Council cautiously set the new church on its course as Canada's premier "national" religious body.[1]

## THE BASIS OF UNION

Although the union was primarily a twentieth-century experiment in church relations, it was deeply rooted in the ethos and experience of late-Victorian Canadian Protestantism. Paradoxically, in spite of the strengthening of denominational pride and loyalty, throughout the last half of the nineteenth century, Bible societies, YMCAs, ministerial associations, Sunday school and young people's organizations, and temperance and reform groups had brought together individual men and women from all the Protestant churches throughout the country. Meetings such as the Ecumenical Methodist Conferences, the Canadian Christian Conference, and the Evangelical Alliance provided forums for the expression of common Protestant values and were designed "to manifest and strengthen Christian unity" and to illustrate "the spiritual unity of God's people."[2]

During the same period, representatives from the various mainstream denominations also reflected the growing Protestant consensus by advocating closer cooperation leading ultimately to organic Christian union. For instance, in 1871 the Episcopal Methodists' *Canada Christian Advocate* had looked forward "to our blending at some future day with the Presbyterians, Congregationalists and ... Baptists."[3] The idea of Christian union had also formed the basis of Enoch Barker's address to the Congregational Union of Ontario and Quebec in 1873, and this theme remained popular in Congregational church councils. Moreover, in 1875 John Cook, the first moderator of the new Presbyterian Church in Canada, saw its creation as only preliminary to broad Protestant union. Twenty years later, Charles Eby, after considerable experience in mission work in Japan, called for common action among the churches that would "make us ashamed of the narrowness of these infant days."[4]

On an institutional level, the success of the Presbyterian union of 1875 and the Methodist unions of 1874 and 1884, which created nationwide churches, not only appeared to make interdenominational union practical but also provided an obvious direction for the future. Even the gradual integration within the loose Congregational Unions added momemtum to this movement. As well as forming institutions that reflected the political and social reality of Canada, the unions helped to elaborate a vital national vision within the denominations. These developments were expanded in 1887 when the Presbyterian General Assembly accepted in principle the idea of cooperation with the Methodists in evangelizing thinly settled sections of the country. The Methodist General Conference agreed three years later, and the missionary societies of the two churches began to take each others' operations into consideration when planning for the future. A tolerant spirit of international and interdenominational cooperation had also been the hallmark of overseas mission operations for the two churches.[5]

Also, throughout the last half of the nineteenth century, Canadian Protestantism had been deeply troubled by the rapid expansion of what it considered aggressive and intolerant Roman Catholicism. The revival of ultramontanism, which emphasized a hierarchical and centralized structure for the Catholic church with the papacy supreme in defining belief and practice, culminated in

Inaugural Service, the United Church of Canada, June 10, 1925, in Mutual Street Arena, Toronto. (UCA, P343N)

the promulgation of the doctrine of papal infallibility in 1870. Ultramontanism helped strengthen Catholic piety and cohesion, and it gave renewed energy to Catholic aggrandizement and, as a corollary, to French-Canadian nationalism. For many Protestants, such activities appeared to threaten their grand vision for Canada by promoting mixed loyalties, anti-democratic institutions, and unbiblical theological beliefs, as well as by making it more difficult to proselytize among the Caltholic and native populations.[6]

The Riel Rebellion in the northwest in 1885 was blamed on Roman Catholic conspirators attempting to destroy the British empire and establish a popish state in the west. The 1888 Jesuits' Estates Act in Quebec, which invited the pope to settle an internal provincial dispute over the distribution of compensation for the previously expropriated Jesuit lands to both Catholic and Protestant religious organizations, seemed to confirm the corruption of Roman Catholic politics and the attempt by the church hierarchy to dominate national life. Even the Catholic influence in education in Ontario and the northwest provided evidence of the need for united Protestant action to restrain this powerful force. Virulent anti-Catholic sentiment reached a peak during the 1890s, especially in Ontario, in quasi-political organizations such as the Protestant Protective Association and the Equal Rights Association, but the sentiments would remain close to the surface in Protestant thinking at least for the first half of the twentieth century. From the Protestant churches' point of view, wasteful competition not only limited individual denominational progress, but it also helped Roman Catholicism and thereby threatened the common set of spiritual and moral values which they hoped would govern and bind Canadians together.[7]

The first concrete move toward church union had actually been organized by the Church of England. In 1881, while addressing an informal synodal gathering in Toronto, Canon James Carmichael had suggested a conference on Christian unity. Five years later, the Anglican church appointed a committee to explore whether there was general Protestant interest in union. In 1886 and 1887 the Methodists, Presbyterians, and Congregationalists set up similar committees. The next year the Lambeth Conference of worldwide Anglicans, again at Carmichael's urging, enunciated a four-point program that strongly appealed for Christian reunion. This in turn led to the popular Conference on Christian Unity in 1889 in Toronto, which discussed existing areas of mutual assistance and assessed the various churches' theological positions on the Scriptures, the creeds, and the episcopacy. Members of this conference formed the Toronto-based Canadian Society of Christian Unity.[8]

Union discussions between the Anglicans and the other Protestant denominations continued throughout the 1890s, but even with the formation of the Canadian Society of Christian Unity and later the Montreal laymen's Church Union Society, serious difficulties remained. While the first three points of the Lambeth program were generally acceptable, or at least provided a basis for negotiations, the fourth point, which called for the retention of the "historic episcopate," was more controversial. The Presbyterian General Assembly in 1890 recognized the validity of an episcopacy but assumed that the historic presbyter more clearly represented this office in the early church. The Methodists and Presbyterians refused to base union discussions on the assumption that bishops would exist in the new church, and the Anglicans would not begin negotiations based on the precondition that the episcopacy would be abandoned. In reality, the Anglicans wanted to reunite what they considered to be splinter groups into the Church of England, not to create a new, inclusive church.[9]

The difficulty with the Baptists was that no one body represented the entire denomination, and the various independent regional bodies held such divergent views that they could not unite among themselves, let alone present a single delegation to Protestant union talks. At the same time, their distinctive views on baptism remained a stumbling block to organic union. Among the smaller Methodist connexions, the Free Methodist Church was not interested in uniting with other denominations at least partially because of its emphasis on entire sanctification. The black British Methodist Episcopal Church received assistance from the Methodist church, but because of racial differences, there was little sympathy for closer union on either side. In 1890 the Methodist church did undertake formal union consultations with the Evangelical Association in western Canada, but these were adjourned in 1894 with little progress made. Four years later, Hamilton Conference received permission to commence similar negotiations with the Evangelical Association in Ontario, and these continued intermittently for decades.[10]

The 1890 Methodist General Conference also proposed continuing informal union discussions with the Congregationalists, the Presbyterians, and where possible, the Anglicans and Baptists. As a preliminary step, it believed all the larger Protestant denominations should recognize the validity of each other's ordination and ministry, welcome each other's members at the sacrament of the Lord's Supper, and encourage the exchange of pulpits. In addition, congregations should cooperate in special services and community-wide evangelistic crusades. If organic union proved impossible in the near future, the Methodist church also suggested creating a joint federal court essentially to help coordinate Protestant mission work and especially to supervise a joint French Protestant church in Quebec. Such measures encouraged greater harmony among the denominations and gradually popularized the idea of organic union.[11]

These talks took on new seriousness after the 1901 Canadian census showed large Roman Catholic advances, especially in eastern and northern Ontario, and the much smaller growth of Methodism. Although the Presbyterians had expanded substantially, the Congregationalist cause continued its long stagnation. In addition, the census demonstrated that new, non-Anglo-Saxon immigration was altering Canada's ethnic and religious composition. The Methodist leadership recognized that union would help alleviate the expanding requirements of both its home and foreign missions and the church at large. In his address to the 1902 General Conference, General Superintendent Albert Carman, who remained cautious about the benefits of the movement, still reiterated his call for the serious consideration of church union, and this appeal received support in a memorial from Samuel Dwight Chown as the president of the Canadian Society of Christian Unity.

Therefore it came as no surprise that when the General Conference received fraternal greetings from William Patrick of Manitoba College on behalf of the Presbyterian General Assembly, it responded favourably to the informal overtures for cooperation and possible union. The Methodists established a committee to study union and to meet with similar committees from the Presbyterians and Congregationalists. The Anglicans and Baptists were also invited, but declined to participate. Although the Methodist church hoped to include all the evangelical denominations, it believed that it was beneficial to start with the Congregationalists and Presbyterians and to further educate its own members about the benefits of union. These churches inaugurated formal cooperation in the home mission field. Concurrent local experiments in joint action, such as the Montreal Church Union Society and the Ottawa Federal Council of Protestant Churches, supplied momentum to full union negotiations.[12]

The committees began to meet together in April 1904 and quickly agreed that union was both practical and desirable. A joint union committee was established which created five working subcommittees to study the issues of doctrine, polity, ministry, administration, and law. By early 1906, preliminary reports from the subcommittees were available for discussion, and a proposed basis of union was presented to the Methodist General Conference in September 1906. Although initially cautious, the Methodists confidently accepted union as the best option for future development. The Conference called for the circulation of details of the proposed basis of union in its newspapers and from its pulpits, and it announced a day of prayer to help guide its negotiators. It also invited the Evangelical Association to participate and accepted the Presbyterian union committee's initiative, which again requested the Baptists and Anglicans join the union proceedings.[13]

The joint union committee, which was significantly enlarged to permit a broad representation from across the country, met in December 1906 and published the proposed Basis of Union in early 1907 in order to allow informed discussion among members of the various denominations. Although the joint committee never divided on issues based on denominational affiliation, the Congregational members were most adamant about the relationship of ministers to the doctrines of the church. They objected to the proposed article which forced ministers to pledge adherence to the united church's creed and argued that the new church should be free to revise its standards internally as circumstances demanded. Many Methodists and even some Presbyterians also assumed that formal creeds too often ossified and became unadaptable to new conditions. The offending article was quietly dropped. At its fifth annual meeting in 1908, the joint union committee adopted the slightly amended Basis of Union and forwarded it to the negotiating churches for further action.[14]

For the most part, the doctrines of the new church represented a rather straightforward consensus of central Protestant beliefs expressed originally in nineteen and finally in twenty brief articles. In attempting to reconcile Arminian and Calvinist principles, the committee opted to include as much as possible from each tradition and to avoid compromising fundamentals, but at the same time to eliminate any specific doctrines that tended to divide the churches. All three negotiating churches agreed that principles must be preserved, but prejudices abandoned. Moreover, the advanced age and experience of the committee members made them generally unwilling to experiment, and they particularly had no desire to open the wounds of the modernist-fundamentalist debate then confounding Protestant harmony. Samuel Dwight Chown would later add that theology should stimulate a higher life and enlarge vital spiritual experience, not establish formal creeds, and that with its trust in universal salvation and broad Protestant doctrines, Methodism looked eagerly to organic union. Most of the church leaders were also at least initially guided by liberal theology, which downplayed the centrality of creeds and emphasized the practical application of religion in everyday life. They agreed that the function of the United Church was to be a holy instrument for the construction of the kingdom of God on earth. Because of the essential unanimity in theological matters, there were no substantial debates over these issues in the union committees.[15]

In establishing a polity for the United Church of Canada, the Basis of Union suggested that the corresponding levels of courts in the three churches, despite differences in names, carried on essentially the same functions and that where they differed, they could still contribute to the overall welfare of the denomination. The local congregations could therefore retain familiar structures if they wished, and the United Church would amalgamate names, practices, and structures. The basic unit of organization would be the pastoral charge, which could involve several congregations. In ascending order, the pastoral charges would be organized in presbyteries, which approximated the Methodist districts, annual conferences, and a biennial General Council. Instead of a powerful general superintendent, the General Council would be led by a moderator who only chaired the various sessions and represented the church on ceremonial occasions.

With regard to ministry, the Basis again attempted to integrate the different practices of the Presbyterian system, which involved a called, settled clergy, and the Methodist stationed, itinerant system. Under normal circumstances, all pastoral charges were guaranteed a minister and all effective ministers a pastoral charge. If a minister was not called or if a pastoral charge could not obtain a minister, a settlement committee would arrange matters. As well, there were no restrictions on the length of a minister's term. It was hoped that this combined approach would eliminate the worst features of both the call and itinerant systems and create a flexible and practical system able to meet the diverse needs of the new church.

The administration of the United Church would essentially adopt the powerful Methodist bureaucracy and integrate the missions, publishing operations, school systems, and benevolent funds of the three churches. These would be rationalized later by the United Church. Organizations such as the women's missionary societies were expected to unite on their own and affiliate with the United Church in much the same relationship as they had with their founding churches. The provisions of the law subcommittee dealt with protecting the rights of the United Church and ensuring proper legal standing within the various jurisdictions in Canada, Newfoundland, and Bermuda. Their implementation would take place as the final step in the consummation of union when the United Church sought incorporation through legislation.[16]

In general, the Basis of Union was neither innovative or particularly detailed nor apparently controversial. It permitted the retention of familiar practices, especially at the local level, and assumed that the United Church would work out the necessary details as its wisdom and as circumstances demanded. It allowed for diversity and attempted to permit substantial congregational freedom within a strongly connexional structure. The tension created by this apparent contradiction would provide a key element of the United Church's administration in the future. The most important criterion seemed to be that the new church would be a true union and not the absorption of one denomination by another. The United Church would thus be able to combine the talents and resources of its members to help create a moral, spiritually alive nation for God.[17]

### DIFFERING VIEWS ON UNION

The main arguments supporting and opposing union had been discussed since the late nineteenth century, but they took on new urgency as the actual terms were presented for consideration by the membership of the three churches. Fundamentally, union supporters agreed with Egerton Shore, the secretary of the Board of Foreign Missions, when he wrote: "I am heart and soul and life in favour of Church union in this country ... We absolutely believe that in the providence of God, and under the leadership of the Spirit, this movement cannot fail ... it is inevitable ... the movement is of God."[18] It would demonstrate a "oneness in Christ," or as William Caven, the principal of the Presbyterian Knox College in Toronto, had declared, "real organic union ... would represent in a far truer and more perfect way the body of Christ."[19] Continuing denominational rivalry might glorify Methodism or Presbyterianism, but it did not glorify God; disunity therefore was considered an act of impiety. Organic union would answer Christ's own prayer "that they all may be one." All other considerations were secondary.

Since union was of God, it would surely intensify the spiritual commitment of Christians and both enlarge mainstream Protestant membership and strengthen Christian practice. As a corollary, continued Christian disunity would limit personal spiritual progress. While this optimistic motivation was perhaps strongest in Atlantic Canada, even in the west the church hoped that, with joint action "devoted to Christian evangelism and high forms of service, we will see at least the dawn of a new day of spiritual progress."[20] Many Methodists fondly remembered the revival that had coincided with their 1884 union and expected an even greater spiritual outpouring in the wake of a broad Protestant amalgamation. In this belief, they were joined by traditionalists from all three negotiating churches and by sympathetic supporters throughout Protestantism.

While traditionalists and even theological conservatives hoped spiritual renewal would be the primary benefit of union, for the majority of Methodists, evangelism and social service were inseparable. They maintained that union would promote the spread of Christian justice and the creation of God's kingdom on earth. On one level, it would force the government to recognize the status of Protestantism and strengthen its political voice. The provincial and federal governments in Canada could ignore the individual churches more easily and were wary of the zealous denominationalism they had often witnessed in the past. A United Church would have both the influence and the moral authority to demand honest and active governments and could rightfully demand measures such as the oversight of religious instruction in the schools. On another level, it would be better able to produce moral human beings and implement social reforms, such as prohibition and sabbatarianism, as stepping stones along the path to the realization of Christ's earthly dominion.[21]

For liberals who were increasingly defining Methodist theological understanding, historic creeds and traditional theology held little meaning. At the same time, the opportunities associated with union suggested a way of effectively integrating the current intellectual ferment with the dramatic social changes in contemporary society without abandoning religious influence to secularism. The rise of the social-gospel movement in fact reflected the displacement of traditional doctrine and metaphysical biases by an activist, humanistic Christianity, which in turn demanded union or at least hearty cooperation to enlarge the practical work of the churches. Some believed that to remain relevant, the churches must replace their traditional denominational structures and rivalries with a broad Protestant ecumenism. The social-gospel movement crossed denominational loyalties and could not be confined within narrow institutional boundaries. It therefore supplied a powerful motivation for union since united action was considered the best means of realizing its goals of creating a new, progressive social system.[22]

Promoters also argued that union would advance the broad Protestant consensus that had emerged during the late nineteenth century. The elements which had historically divided mainstream Canadian Protestants appeared to have lost their relevance. The Methodist General Conference in 1902 had suggested that church relations "are already marked by a great degree of spiritual unity, and they have become closely assimilated in standards and ideals of Church life, forms of worship and ecclesiastical polity."[23] Although Christian fundamentals were still firmly held, distinctive denominational doctrines were rarely preached, and it was believed that they would never regain their former standing except among dogmatists. Over time, as theological and doctrinal differences had declined in importance, the Presbyterians, Congregationalists, and Methodists had come to share a common ethos, with similar views on the sacraments, the nature and function of ministry, and common approaches to secularism and modernism. As well, they were the most self-consciously Canadian of the churches and shared a common desire to assimilate native peoples and new immigrants and a similar dynamic national vision. At once liberal, evangelistic, and moralistic, they were particularly pragmatic in ecclesiastical affairs. In addition, pro-union Methodists maintained that John Wesley would have supported merger since it actually represented a return "to the broad catholicity of spirit that marked our founder."[24]

It was also hoped that union would effectively answer the various threats to the progressive Protestant vision for Canada. Foremost among these perceived threats was the Roman Catholic church. With its apparently monolithic and undemocratic structure, it maintained a distinct advantage over a divided Protestantism, and Catholicism's historic power and influence were considered potentially much greater because of its appeal to the vast array of non-Protestant immigrants flooding into the country. If these new arrivals were not met by an equally united and committed Protestantism, they might well be lost for all time. Such a loss would be detrimental both to the immigrants themselves and to the nation at large. Unionists could readily claim, therefore, that along with immoral materialism, the chief beneficiary of the failure of union would be "the organized, aggressive, centralized system of the Roman Church."[25]

Nevertheless, the Protestant consensus was also threatened by the emergence of evangelical splinter denominations. In trying to include all theological perspectives, the mainstream churches had alienated individuals who felt that they could not remain loyal to these ecclesiastical bodies without abandoning essential elements of faith. Holiness, pentecostal, adventist, dispensationalist, and fundamentalist churches were especially angered by the ready acceptance among the larger Protestant churches of higher criticism, non-literal interpretations of the Bible, and the reduction of emphasis on personal conversion. Many of these new denominations claimed to be the true inheritors of Wesleyanism or the defenders of traditional evangelicalism. While their rapid growth during the early twentieth century threatened the expansion of membership in the mainstream churches, it also removed many members who opposed the new Protestant priorities and who might have opposed union.[26]

Canadian unionists were also influenced by the broad ecumenical spirit manifesting itself throughout the English-speaking world and more particularly by the various church union movements then underway. In the United States by the early years of the twentieth century, the Congregationalists and the United Brethren in Christ were negotiating organic union, and they were later joined by the Methodist Protestants. In Britain, union among the New Connexion Methodists, Bible Christians, and Methodist Free churches was consummated in 1907. The Presbyterians and Methodists in New Zealand were also discussing union, as were the Presbyterians, Congregationalists, and Methodists in Australia. Over the same period, various missionary operations were uniting to form national churches such as the Nippon Methodist Kyokai in Japan in 1907. In turn, the Canadian union discussions and the Basis of Union were themselves studied as a possible model for these various uniting denominations. Samuel Dwight Chown maintained, "The movement toward the union of the Churches of Christendom, in order that they may speak with moral authority to divided and sometimes hostile nations, is part of the divine plan for the unification of the world in righteousness."[27]

As with all the denominational unions, one of the primary motivations for organic union was that it made economic sense. In the older settled parts of the country, small communities could no longer maintain viable congregations that were able to provide the expected functions of the modern church. With union, the Presbyterians, Congregationalists, and Methodists in a community would supply enough members to sustain a debt-free operation while improving the work of the Sunday schools, missionary societies, and other church auxiliaries. As well, union would allow the amalgamation and rationalization of the churches' institutional infrastructures. Newspapers, magazines, and publishing operations could draw on a wider audience and improve both their quality and their efficiency. The same could be said for the church schools, colleges, and theological programs. They could expect larger regional support and provide better teachers and educational facilities. Union supporters also suggested that the resources freed by amalgamation would permit better salaries for the ministry. This was a considerable incentive for the increasingly educated and professionalized clergy, who believed they were falling behind the new professions in status and remuneration. It would also be a consideration in attracting young men into the ministry.[28]

The waste of resources on unnecessary competition was especially damaging to the various churches' missions in western Canada. With the rapid settlement of the region and especially with the arrival of non-British immigrants, all the Protestant denominations were finding it impossible to provide the required ministers and religious services. And again, the churches' work went well beyond strictly spiritual concerns. They were involved in supplying practical assistance, helping to Canadianize new arrivals, and meeting the challenges of modern, industrial society. At the same time, the social and spatial mobility so common in the west were helping to weaken the traditional denominational loyalties that had so often relied on kinship and community relations for sustenance. Under these circumstances, there was a much readier acceptance of any legitimate minister and of community-wide worship. Cooperation in the home mission field had been forced on the churches by the needs of the west, and the west, in turn, provided the most enthusiastic supporters for union. The very success of cooperation in meeting the needs of the region provided one of the strongest arguments for broader organic union.[29]

In addition, the needs overseas were daunting. Millions in Africa and Asia remained to be evangelized, and there were never sufficient resources to meet the challenge. To make effective use of the available resources, the missionary authorities had already learned to cooperate and even to unite their operations across national and denominational lines. This was certainly the experience of the Methodists and Presbyterians in Japan and China and the Congregationalists in Angola. They had also been forced by local circumstances to present a united front to the unbelieving populations and not to confuse them with what appeared to be irrelevant theological niceties. Moreover, the new ecumenical Christian mission churches were not prepared to perpetuate denominational differences that seemed to reflect western European social and political history. Based on their experiences abroad, the missionaries usually advocated organic union in Canada.[30]

Beyond the needs of home and foreign missions, union made economic sense for the whole range of day-to-day church activities since it clearly reflected current business practices. During the first decade of the twentieth century, mergers among industrial and commercial enterprises were transforming economic activity in North America. The larger units were able to compete more effectively and were supposedly able to supply goods and services at reduced costs. Lay promoters of church union such as Joseph Flavelle and Newton Wesley Rowell were heavily involved in this business practice and clearly recognized its importance for the church at large. The growth of huge industry-wide unions and the cooperative movement in the agricultural sector reflected a similar impulse. Most leaders in the mainstream Protestant churches viewed these developments as progressive, economically sound, and morally correct. For the church, however, union was not simply a means of saving money; the United Church was expected to raise more money than the partner churches combined had collected. Rather, it was considered indispensable for the proper Christian stewardship of God's benevolence to Canadians.[31]

Competition was not only an economic, but also a spiritual and social evil. Proclaiming cooperation in economic activities as the will of God, could the Protestant churches settle for less in ecclesiastical affairs? And the creation of a United Church was much more than an economic enterprise. The new institution would be greater than the sum of its original parts; it would be a unique and significant experiment in church relations. The Basis of Union declared prominently, "It shall be the policy of The United Church to foster the spirit of unity in the hope that this sentiment of unity may in due time, so far as Canada is concerned, take shape in a church which may fittingly be described as national."[32] As a uniting as well as a united church, the amalgamation of Methodists, Presbyterians, and Congregationalists was the next logical preliminary step in creating a genuinely national church without the disabling limitations of the old-fashioned denominations. Being a national church was in fact already a central element in Methodism's self-image; it had always been inclusive and indeed universal in its theology and mission and had increasingly felt constrained by its denominational boundaries.

The support for church union was heavily bound up with the optimistic vision for Canada itself. With the settlement of the west and the growing population and prosperity, it finally appeared that the original promise of Confederation was about to be achieved. This belief heightened loyalty, nationalism, and the sense of a great destiny. It would be the duty of the newly created United Church to help mould Canada as a nation. If Canada's destiny was to have a spiritual and moral base, a patriotic national church must instil a common set of Christian principles, help preserve national and social stability, guide the country's conscience, and make Canada a legitimate model for the entire world. In helping to define and elaborate a mature national identity, the United Church must strive to eliminate political, geographic, and ethnic differences, and ameliorate racial and class tensions. It must also assist the state to rise above purely temporal matters by providing it with a coherent and legitimate social and moral role. Church union, therefore, was perceived as vital for the creation of a complete, modern nation. The church was then both a reflection of the Canadian experience and an important instrument in refining and perpetuating that experience.[33]

Regardless of the grand objectives and promising opportunities, there were still Methodists who opposed union in general and the terms of the Basis of Union in particular. Traditional Methodists believed that union forced the connexion to abandon its historic social means of grace, Wesley's disciplinary rules, and the spiritual commitment leading to entire sanctification. Attendance at class meetings would no longer be required for church membership, and prayer meetings, love feasts, and lay preaching would be negligible in the new church. Such a rejection of Methodism's evangelical heritage would mean the end of its revival spirit. The result, they argued, would be an institution devoid of God-given power. In fact, the United Church seemed to be merely an artificial creation to institutionalize the social gospel in Canada. It would be far too involved in politics and secular affairs. Thus it represented an immoral lust for ecclesiastical empire that would undermine the commitment to save sinners. Those who held these views called for a reinvigoration of Methodism, rather than union, as the basis of a continuing dynamic mission in Canada.[34]

This criticism was closely associated with opposition to the apparent destruction of the itinerant system. The stationing of ministers for a limited term on one circuit and their transfer to where they were best suited and most needed had been the core of Methodist evangelical expansion. It had also helped bind the Methodist church together into one strong, disciplined, and dynamic community. Opponents maintained that the Basis of Union established a called ministry, which had demonstrated in the past its inabilty to promote a dynamic, spiritual religion. It was considered "a recipe for disaster"[35] in the United Church. It would also further aggravate the serious assault on the connexional nature of the church. Critics asserted that the Basis of Union already threatened the principle of connexionalism by permitting extensive congregational independence in worship, administration, polity, and the control of property.[36]

In response to these criticisms, church leaders such as Albert Carman argued that nothing had been abandoned that was fundamental to Methodism. The class meeting had long since ceased to be a vital institution and was not a current test of Methodist membership. Similarly, the prayer meeting, love feast, and lay preaching had lost their popularity and were only incidental to Methodist worship or evangelism. The spiritual fervour which had perhaps been Methodism's hallmark during its pioneer development was both impossible to retrieve and inappropriate for the modern church or the needs of Canadian society. Those who blamed the decline of spiritual zeal and the Methodist social means of grace or the growing sophistication of church operations on union seriously misread the changes that had occurred in Methodism over the previous half-century. They were not caused by the move toward union and would not be reversed by denominational independence.[37]

Similarly, union supporters maintained that many of the historic features of the itinerancy had already disappeared. Most ministers were invited by the local circuit, with the stationing committee usually only confirming prearranged agreements. Ministers serving on missions, at Methodist schools, in the publishing operations, or in other special circumstances were already exempt from term limitations, and the stationing system had shown itself open to abuse in the past. A more settled ministry was also advantageous for the clergy and their families and, more importantly, was better able to supply the required pastoral care and to serve the diverse functions required by the modern church. Moreover, the Basis of Union called for an amalgamation of the best features of the Methodist stationing and Presbyterian call systems. Actually, most itinerants recognized the difficulties with their form of ministry and were quite pleased to gain the benefits of the Presbyterian-style pastorate as long as there would be some degree of security in obtaining a church.[38]

Some Methodist critics also believed that the theology of the United Church was overly conservative and fundamentally obsolete. It would limit the church's ability to meet the contemporary and future needs of Canadian society. On the other hand, some maintained that Calvinism dominated the doctrinal statement of the Basis of Union. For instance, J.A. McCamus, in a series of articles in the *Christian Guardian*, argued that Article III appeared to make God the author of sin and promoted predestination by removing humankind's ability to choose between right and wrong. Similarly, Article VI appeared to support special election in the statement "God ... gave to His Son a people, an innumerable multitude, chosen in Christ unto holiness, service and salvation." An "innumerable multitude" could be interpreted as a finite number bound for heaven. Defenders of the Basis of Union replied that McCamus and similar critics did not understand Article III and that "an innumerable multitude" in Article VI might include everyone. They used the phrase to argue that Methodists and Presbyterians were preaching a similar Arminian doctrine of universal salvation.[39]

However, the often-repeated pro-union argument that little of substance divided Canadian Protestantism also met with disapproval. If it was true, opponents claimed, then the ministers had been unfaithful to their ordination vows and were not presenting their denominations' true beliefs. In fact, union critics maintained that a truly uniform amalgamation of beliefs was both impossible and undesirable. Past attempts to create uniform national churches had led to oppression and eventually to schism. The established churches in Europe and indeed Roman Catholicism provided ample proof of the danger involved. At the same time, the assumption that the nineteenth-century denominational unions demonstrated the feasibility of organic union was also discounted. These churches, despite sharing a common history, theology, doctrine, and polity had not always amalgamated harmoniously. Certainly, at the local level, congregations had often been unwilling to combine even with other Methodists or Presbyterians. Critics also warned that attempts at union would probably lead to the creation of new Methodist, Presbyterian, and Congregational churches. Even some union supporters feared that the British and American Methodist churches would, in answer to local encouragement, establish branch operations in Canada. In addition, groups such as the Free Methodists certainly anticipated an increase in their membership from anti-unionists.[40]

Union critics were also unconvinced that organic union was necessarily God's will. Such a claim by union forces represented only a narrow interpretation of

Scripture and certainly was extremely presumptuous. The unity Christ prayed for could as likely mean oneness in "nature, affection and service," and, critics suggested, "Union of spirit, purpose and action in separate ranks is better than organic union with internal divisions and strife."[41] Many Methodists who supported cooperation believed that the negotiating churches were not yet ready for organic union, in part because the issues involved had not been thoroughly publicized or analysed, and they advocated church federation instead. Federation would allow cooperation while leaving the more difficult questions of doctrine and polity to be dealt with when the churches had become more familiar with each other. They suggested that "Dominion Unity and Denominational Liberty"[42] would better answer the needs of contemporary society. However, unionists for the most part dismissed federation as simply a plan to block union without providing a legitimate alternative; to them, it represented a substitution of fear for faith in the future of Canadian churches. Since everyone agreed union was the ideal, it was the duty of Christians to see it accomplished.

Nevertheless, some Methodists were unhappy about an organization that based much of its rationale on economic advantage and appeared to abandon its normative statements of faith for a new creed of business efficiency. They feared that the result would be "a great, dead, compromised, creedless church."[43] And it was questionable whether business, and especially the development of monopolistic combines, provided a suitable model for a spiritual and moral institution. Even if they did, the unionists could supply no proof that the United Church would be able to raise more money than the individual churches combined had done. In fact, critics of union suggested contributions would fall since union would allow more adherents to reduce their commitment. Even the incentive of better salaries was questioned; higher pay did not guarantee a more dedicated clergy.[44]

At the same time, many Methodists were concerned about the financial arrangements associated with amalgamating the three churches. The Methodist union of 1884 had placed a significant burden on the Wesleyan pension plan and other benevolent funds, and there was every likelihood that similar problems would arise with the formation of the United Church. The Basis of Union provided no protection for Methodist assets, and there was concern that it would initiate a raid on the Methodist superannuation and mission funds by the financially weaker Presbyterian and Congregational churches. Moreover, although most Methodist property was owned by the connexion, much of the Congregational and Presbyterian property belonged to the local congregations. It was not clear how the United Church's collective property rights would be assured, especially if individual congregations chose to reject union. These fears were intensified by worry over the loss of historic church buildings and by local antipathy and personality conflicts often based on perceived class, status, or ethnic differences.[45]

Finally, Methodist opposition had a regional dimension, which was most clearly expressed in Newfoundland. Although closely linked with the Dominion of Canada, it was a separate colony of Britain, and despite its long association with Canadian Methodism, the church there remained significantly closer to British Wesleyanism than any other part of the Canadian church. It still received a disproportionately high number of British ministers. At the same time, it had evolved differently from the rest of the Canadian Methodist connexion. Traditional revivalism and the Methodist social means of grace continued popular there long after they had been transformed or abandoned on the mainland. Perhaps more important, however, the insignificant Presbyterian and Congregational presence meant that the Methodist heritage in Newfoundland would be abandoned without gaining measurable spiritual, numerical, or financial benefits.[46]

### THE CHOICE FOR THE UNITED CHURCH OF CANADA

Despite the years of discussion, the Basis of Union was only slightly modified to clarify its meaning, and it was officially sent to the negotiating churches in 1909. The Congregational Union of Canada, which two years earlier had amalgamated the former Congregational Union of Ontario and Quebec with the Congregational Union of Nova Scotia and New Brunswick, forwarded the document to its member churches for a tentative vote to aid discussions. The twenty-four former United Brethren congregations that had joined the Congregational Union in 1906 were also included in the procedure. With only about 11,000 members, the Congregational Union spoke from a position of considerable weakness. Nevertheless, regardless of its tradition of congregational independence, it had long recognized the advantages of organic union. Only 813 voted against the Basis of Union and about 82 per cent of the 3,749 who chose to vote supported the measure. The church therefore decided no further official action was necessary and waited patiently for the other churches to proceed to union.[47]

When the Methodist General Conference met in 1910, it assumed that the Basis of Union did not require an alteration in the church's doctrine and that the General Conference therefore had substantial authority to decide on union. Nevertheless, after overwhelmingly supporting union, it decided to send the plan to the 1911 annual conferences and, if they approved, to hold a national plebiscite in early 1912. Voters were asked the single question: "Are you in favor of Organic Union between the Methodist, Presbyterian and Congregational Churches upon the proposed *Basis of Union*?" Separate votes were recorded for members of the official boards, members over eighteen years of age, members under eighteen, and adherents. Results were reported by district and annual conference. Table 6 provides a detailed breakdown by conference.[48]

Of those voting, about 88 per cent supported union and only Newfoundland Conference voted about 70 to 30 per cent against union. With these results, the church in 1912 officially agreed to proceed with union when the Presbyterians and Congregationalists were ready. No further vote was taken. Although some opposition remained, there was a general belief that Methodists should follow the will of the majority and obey the dictates of the church courts. This had always been an important component of Methodist discipline and was fundamental to the idea of connexionalism. Moreover, the union

Table 6   Methodist church-union vote, 1912

| Conference | Official Board | | Members 18+ | | Members 18- | | Adherents | |
|---|---|---|---|---|---|---|---|---|
| | Yes | No | Yes | No | Yes | No | Yes | No |
| Nfld | 369 | 622 | 1,731 | 4,045 | 98 | 198 | 1,194 | 2,787 |
| NS | 990 | 215 | 6,345 | 1,650 | 422 | 92 | 2,341 | 434 |
| NB/PEI | 1,107 | 192 | 7,003 | 1,160 | 498 | 81 | 2,879 | 427 |
| Mont. | 2,552 | 593 | 17,312 | 3,744 | 1,854 | 415 | 5,655 | 877 |
| Quinte | 2,586 | 340 | 19,416 | 2,252 | 2,167 | 241 | 4,308 | 532 |
| Tor. | 3,364 | 453 | 25,690 | 2,743 | 3,537 | 285 | 5,172 | 385 |
| Ham. | 3,122 | 576 | 21,325 | 3,498 | 3,010 | 691 | 3,823 | 576 |
| Lon. | 3,644 | 446 | 22,923 | 3,326 | 2,977 | 371 | 4,753 | 610 |
| Man. | 1,857 | 170 | 10,732 | 782 | 1,295 | 89 | 4,151 | 261 |
| Sask. | 1,739 | 96 | 7,754 | 474 | 840 | 39 | 4,103 | 180 |
| Alta | 1,294 | 53 | 5,985 | 290 | 703 | 39 | 2,721 | 95 |
| BC | 951 | 113 | 4,725 | 393 | 517 | 24 | 1,015 | 70 |
| Total | 23,475 | 3,869 | 150,941 | 24,357 | 17,818 | 2,465 | 42,115 | 7,233 |

forces controlled the major church journals, which effectively cut off debate, and anti-unionists would have little claim to any denominational property if they withdrew from the United Church. Even the members of Newfoundland Conference were not prepared to stand against the overwhelming will of their co-religionists without some viable alternative to union.[49]

The Presbyterian story was considerably more complicated. In 1909 the General Assembly had received the Basis of Union and voted 160 to 42 to accept the plan and to send it to the presbyteries for their information. They were to vote on it after the Methodist General Conference of 1910 had dealt with the plan. That year the General Assembly, by a vote of 184 to 73, instructed the presbyteries to vote on union. With a majority of presbyteries in favour, the General Assembly sent the issue to the general membership in early 1912. Separate votes were recorded for elders, communicants, and adherents, and the ballot asked three questions: "Are you in favour of organic union with the Methodist and Congregational Churches? Do you approve of the proposed *Basis of Union?* Have you any suggestions or alternatives?"[50]

On these questions, 90 per cent of the elders but only 54 per cent of the members voted. The results with regard to the organic union question were 6,245 elders, 106,755 members, and 37,175 adherents in favour and 2,475 elders, 48,278 members, and 14,174 adherents opposed. In total, 150,175, or nearly 70 per cent, supported union and 64,925, or about 30 per cent opposed. By congregation, 1,391 had a majority supporting union and 339 had a majority opposed. On the specific plan of union, 110,853 were in favour and 49,705 were opposed. Hundreds of suggestions were made to amend the

Basis of Union. Several called for the insertion of an article on prayer in the section on doctrine, and this was later done. Most of the other suggestions were designed to strengthen the Presbyterian nature of the union by providing more power to the presbyteries, re-establishing the call system, and having ministerial candidates declare their adherence to the doctrines of the church. These changes were not acceptable to the Methodist or Congregational union committees. The most popular suggested alternative to union was church federation.[51]

After reviewing the results, the General Assembly in 1912 decided to increase its cooperation with the Methodists and Congregationalists, especially in the home mission and theological education fields, and to bring the plebiscite recommendations to the joint church-union committee. In light of the significant minority, however, it decided to proceed cautiously and use the time to convince the minority to change its mind. Hoping to gain a greater consensus, the Assembly also appointed several well-known opponents of union to its negotiating committee. But in general these members used their position to further delay and disrupt proceedings and normally presented a minority report to subsequent general assemblies. Over the following years, the Presbyterian unionists continued to reiterate the well-known reasons for union and maintained, "We are as a Church on trial before the whole of Canada and the Christian world ... our divided Protestantism must draw closer together for the sake of the advancement of God's Kingdom in our beloved land."[52] They also argued that the minority should not dictate to the majority, that opposition would hurt the international church-union movements, that a rump Presbyterian denomination would lose its standing as a vital, national institution, and that with 70 per cent support, the church was honour bound to proceed to union.

Nevertheless, Presbyterian opposition grew and became more intransigent over the following years. In 1914 the anti-unionists formed an organization to preserve the Presbyterian church even if union went forward. For Presbyterians such as Ephraim Scott, the editor of the Montreal-based *Presbyterian Record* from 1892 until 1925, the union appeared to abandon the Westminister Confession and the creedal norms of Presbyterianism. They denounced the doctrinal articles as being too Arminian, and the rebuttal that the plan of union contained many central Presbyterian doctrines meant little since there was no insistence upon a rigid subscription to formal creeds and doctrines by the members or ministry. These anti-unionists further believed that union was proceeding in a radical, unsubstantiated, if not unbiblical, theological direction, and they were joined by theological conservatives who opposed the social-gospel nature of the proposed new church. These groups also mistrusted the higher church courts and their officials and denied that the General Assembly had the authority to pursue union. A similar constitutional position had been successfully argued by the Scottish "Wee Frees," who opposed the creation of the United Free Church of Scotland in 1900, to claim all church property.[53]

Although Presbyterian anti-unionists were scattered throughout the country, the main opposition resided in the Toronto-centred region, Montreal, and pockets in the Maritimes. The wealthy and well-organized congregations in Toronto and Montreal believed they could sustain a continuing national Presbyterian church, especially if the weak and expensive home and foreign missions were transferred to the United Church. They also appeared to resent the diminution of their status and influence in the proposed church. Conversely, the Presbyterians in Pictou County in Nova Scotia and in Prince Edward Island shared a strong local identity, which they feared would be undermined by union with the other Protestant churches. In Prince Edward Island, their dissent was "reinforced by a largely rural, close-knit, stable, traditional and community-centred Island social context"[54] that inhibited the formation of a broad national sentiment, accentuated regional grievances, and was led by popular and articulate dissident ministers. Similar arguments could be made for other parts of the Maritimes.

Opposition was as diverse as the individuals involved. Across Canada, members feared they would lose their church buildings, their power on local church boards, or their historic style of worship. Rigid Scottish ethnic and national pride, particularly among recent immigrants, linked denominational loyalty with patriotism. Perceptions of different class or social status, local animosities, or personality conflicts also played important roles in keeping individuals from accepting union. Others simply disliked change or felt union would betray their historic commitment to the international Presbyterian cause. In addition, there were still inherently schismatic members and clergy who had never been comfortable with the Presbyterian union of 1875 and saw the debate on a larger union as an opportunity to undo that amalgamation; they opposed other Presbyterians, not Congregationalists or Methodists. Moreover, a respected antiunionist, or indeed a pro-unionist, minister could sometimes convince his congregation to follow his lead or suffer the loss of his services. Emboldened by the size of the oppostion, union critics could argue for the complete abandonment of the project or, as a compromise, the federation of the Protestant churches. For instance, John MacKay, the principal of Westminister Hall in Vancouver from 1908 to 1919, led the early fight for federation; however, when this ceased to be an acceptable alternative, he subsequently entered the United Church and served as head of Manitoba College from 1919 to 1938.[55]

The Methodists and Congregationalists were somewhat dismayed by the failure of the Presbyterians to proceed. They believed that with 70 per cent of the vote the union cause had received overwhelming Presbyterian support and the church should follow the will of the majority; if it did, many early critics of union, such as John MacKay, would probably enter the United Church. The Methodist church was also worried that delay would allow the consolidation of anti-union sentiment among Methodists or permit the further disintegration of its societies in western Canada. S.D. Chown devoted much of his energy and his considerable personal influence keeping the union forces intact. Furthermore, the Methodist church could not understand how the opponents of union within the three churches could fail to recognize that the United Church blended the distinct traditions of the three denominations while permitting the greatest possible latitude for individual religious expression.[56]

It and, to a lesser degree, the Congregational Union were also apprehensive about the returns from the 1911 Canadian census. Even with the addition of many of the United Brethren members, the Congregationalists reported an increase over the previous decade of only 5,761, for a total of 34,054 adherents in Canada. Ten years later, the 1921 census listed a decline to 30,730 Congregationalists in the country. The somewhat offhand remark that union would provide a funeral for Congregationalism appeared to be coming true. In 1911 the census also reported 1,079,892 Methodists. This was an increase of 163,006, or over 17 per cent, but the Presbyterian church was now larger and the Anglican church was only marginally smaller. According to the census, the Presbyterians had 1,115,324 adherents and the Anglicans 1,043,017. Clearly, the Methodists were not keeping pace with the major Protestant denominations or with the expansion of the nation as a whole. The Church of England in particular had grown as a consequence of the large English component of early twentieth-century immigration, while the Methodist church was losing members through the depopulation of rural Ontario and its inability to evangelize as effectively as its competitors in western Canada.[57]

The Methodists therefore re-emphasized their commitment to union and to winning support among the Presbyterians. But without a substantial, pro-union church bureaucracy, control of publications, or an indigenous connexional identity, Presbyterian unionist forces had a difficult battle against the entrenched, articulate, wealthy, and well-organized anti-union minority. In 1914 and again in 1915, the General Assembly supported union and prepared the church for another vote on the issue. In order to prevent many of the earlier difficulties, this time the only question was, "Are you in favour of Union with the Methodist and Congregational Churches of Canada on the *Basis of Union* approved by the General Assembly of 1915?" No suggestions were requested, and the membership was informed that the decision would be based on the results of the vote. There was no promise that a consensus need be reached.[58]

When the vote was taken, the returns demonstrated that little progress had been made in convincing the opponents of union. In spite of the minor amendments to the Basis of Union, the Presbyterian returns in fact demonstrated increased hostility. A majority in 1,331 pastoral charges supported union and 494 opposed. Among communicants and adherents, a total of 143,458 supported union, while 89,917 opposed it. Nevertheless, the General Assembly of 1916, although frustrated by the continuing opposition, moved to support definite organic union at some time after the war by a vote of 406 to 90. Recognizing the size of the minority, however, it also guaranteed to protect the rights of the dissenting Presbyterians. Between 1917 and 1921, principally because of the demands of World War I, negotiations were adjourned.[59]

Meanwhile, paralleling the internal developments within the three negotiating churches, union was complicated by the emergence of cooperative, union, and affiliated congregations. Cooperation in home mission work had been accepted in principle late in the nineteenth century, and by 1903 the Presbyterian and Methodist mission authorities had begun to adjust their work to eliminate overlap. In 1911 the two churches formally agreed not to compete in new territory or to build within six miles of each other. Thus local Methodists or Presbyterians received permission to attend each other's services if they did not have a congregation of their own. By 1923 the denominations reported 1,014 cooperative pastoral charges, with 132 in British Columbia, 692 in the Prairie provinces, and 190 east of Manitoba. This cooperation also extended to overseas missions, social, service work, religious education, and theological training at the church colleges. As well, between 1911 and 1915, the churches cooperated in taking social surveys in order to gather information to improve urban and rural mission work.[60]

After the tentative Basis of Union had been formulated in 1908, a number of new congregations, especially in western Canada, had organized themselves according to its principles. With characteristics similar to the old-style community churches, these union churches also included members and ministers from the Anglican and Baptist communions and quickly became independent of any denominational control. Impatient with Presbyterian delays, in 1912 they organized themselves into a semi-independent general council. Four years later the Council of Local Union Churches had three presbyteries, and this number quickly expanded to six after World War I. For the pro-union forces, the union churches provided concrete proof that Protestants could work together to forge a powerful Christian presence. However, they also hurt the work of the mainstream denominations by not contributing to the financial needs of their parent churches or accepting their discipline and eventually by threatening to form a new Protestant church. While the expansion of these union churches gave the Methodists and Presbyterians a strong argument for union, it also provided the impetus for immediate action if they were not to lose their connexional presence across the west. In 1921 the General Council of Local Union Churches was given formal status as a separate body on the joint union committee. Two years later there were three union churches in British Columbia, forty-eight across the Prairies, and four east of Manitoba. Their presence quickened the consummation of union, and they entered the United Church as a distinct institution in 1925.[61]

In order to forestall the growth of union churches, the Methodists, Congregationalists, and Presbyterians also permitted the formation of "affiliated" pastoral changes. Members cooperated in a single congregation, but remained directly associated with their own denomination. The congregation was affiliated with one or more of the churches depending on its make-up. Thus single, double, and triple affiliated charges developed. This meant that the parent denominations retained control of property and financial contributions and authority over the ministry and doctrine, as well as continuing to direct general operations. These affiliated congregations were also able to pre-empt Baptist, Anglican, and other evangelical influences. In 1923 there were 176 affiliated pastoral charges, with 4 in British Columbia, 136 in the Prairies, 30 in Ontario and Quebec, and 6 across the Maritimes. Combined, the cooperative, local union, and affiliated pastoral charges represented over 3,000 preaching appointments and thus a sizable proportion of those finally entering the United Church.[62]

While the period witnessed the rapid expansion of interdenominational pastoral charges, the mainstream churches were preoccupied with meeting the needs of the World War I and assisting in Canada's postwar reconstruction. The cooperation required to solve these problems and to advance Christ's dominion in Canada helped to reinforce the desire for organic union. By 1921 the joint committee on church union decided that it had postponed its work long enough and authorized its subcommittee on law to prepare federal and provincial enabling legislation. The three churches had already become so entwined in their local and mission work that it would be virtually impossible to sort out their distinctive operations if union was not finalized. In the same year, the Presbyterian General Assembly voted overwhelmingly to proceed to union. The following year, the Methodist General Conference approved the proposed legislation, and in 1923 both the Presbyterian General Assembly and the Congregational Union decided to proceed immediately and authorized their committees to finalize the technical details of the legislation to incorporate the United Church.[63]

By 1923 the joint union committee had also created the Bureau of Literature and Information to run a massive pro-union propaganda campaign. Under the management of the Presbyterian minister R.J. Wilson, but heavily funded by the Methodist business community, the bureau defended union and attempted to discount opposition attacks on Methodists and pro-union Presbyterians. It reprinted speeches, published articles and information on the union legislation, organized hundreds of meetings, placed advertisements, and did all it could to muster the support of the secular press. Among the leading newspapers, the Toronto *Globe*, the Ottawa *Free Press*, the Hamilton *Spectator*, and the Halifax *Morning Chronicle* opposed union, while the Toronto *Star*, the Montreal *Star*, the Winnipeg *Free Press*, the Vancouver *Sun*, and the Halifax *Herald* actively promoted the cause. After union was consummated, the bureau continued to defend the United Church and to encourage support for its claims before the various property commissions.[64]

Meanwhile, the Presbyterian minority carried on its agitation against union and again declared that if union proceeded, it would withdraw and form a separate church. The anti-union Presbyterian Church Association also argued that the General Assembly had promised union would not proceed without nearly unanimous support of the membership. Since this was impossible, union negotiations should cease immediately. As well, the anti-unionists insisted that the 1919 Forward Movement fund-raising campaign had claimed the contributions would be for the benefit of the Presbyterian church. Many had contributed on the understanding that union was no longer a viable option. Finally, they reiterated their assumption that the General Assembly did not have the authority to disband the Presbyterian church. In response, the Assembly maintained that union would not destroy the church, but would carry "the same church into a higher unity and a larger service."[65] To the increasingly rancorous debate, George Pidgeon, one of the most prominent pro-union Presbyterians, added, "If the use of the name Presbyterian must go, it is only the bursting of the acorn shell in order to let the oak develop."[66] This position was supported by the civil courts and by the recognition of the international Presbyterian community. In 1924 the Alliance of Reformed Churches holding the Presbyterian System ruled that the United Church was sufficiently Presbyterian to remain a member of that organization. The General Assembly in 1924 voted 426 to 96 to confirm its support for union.

Manitoba became the first province to pass church-union legislation in March 1924. Most of the other provinces quickly followed, although in Prince Edward Island the anti-union lieutenant-governor refused to sign the legislation and the bill had to be reintroduced in early 1925. The major opposition developed in Ontario, where the private bills committee added an unacceptable amendment that forced the withdrawal of the legislation. A new bill that strengthened the position of the non-concurring Presbyterians by, among other things, forcing all non-concurring congregations to become members of the continuing Presbyterian church was finally passed on April 9, 1925. Quebec followed Ontario's lead in adding amendments to strengthen the position of the anti-unionists and on March 24, 1926, became the last province to enact the legislation. On May 20, 1926, after complaining about being ignored by the Canadian authorities, Newfoundland also incorporated the new church. Finally, in 1930 the Wesleyans in Bermuda overcame certain legal problems and, although still locally independent, affiliated loosely as a presbytery in the United Church.[67]

The federal Parliament had passed the legislation as a private member's bill on July 19, 1924. Although the bill was introduced by the Presbyterian Robert Forke, the leader of the Progressive Party, and was strongly supported by the Presbyterian Arthur Meighen, the leader of the National Conservative Party, Prime Minister Mackenzie King's hesitancy allowed the anti-union forces to muster significant opposition and gain important concessions. Among these were the protection of minority rights and the holding of another nationwide vote. The Congregationalists and Methodists declined to participate, but the Presbyterian church proceeded to canvass its membership. Across Canada, 108,840 out of 374,951 voted themselves out of union. The main opposition was in Ontario, where 78,584 of the 203,707 members voted non-concurrence. There were 368 non-concurring Presbyterian ministers, and of the 3,904 preaching places that had the right to vote, 667 opposed union. As well, 325 of the 1,128 self-sustaining charges voted non-concurrence. However, only 31 of the 321 missionaries abroad voted to stay Presbyterian. Thus about one-third of the Presbyterian Church in Canada opposed union. Although it was heavily concentrated in Ontario, there were also pockets of anti-union strength in Montreal, Pictou County in Nova Scotia, Prince Edward Island, and even Alberta.[68]

Those voting to remain out of union were later granted the right to retain the title of the Presbyterian Church in Canada, which had significant financial implications regarding wills and trusts, and they received a proportionate share of church property through a national and several provincial property commissions. With great difficulty, all the assets of the Presbyterian operations were totalled and then divided. In a few instances, former Methodist property was handed over to the continuing Presbyterians. However, the most significant loss for the United Church was Knox College in Toronto, which had recently constructed new quarters. In 1927 the two churches agreed that the continuing Presbyterian church should receive 20 per cent of the foreign mission budget and retain North Formosa, British Guiana, and part of the India missions. Although the foreign missionaries had overwhelmingly supported union, some agreed to remain under the Presbyterian church until it was able to supply its own workers. The final property settlement took over fourteen years and caused significant hard feelings between the continuing Presbyterians and the United Church.[69]

None the less, on June 10, 1925, "The United Church of Canada" formally came into existence. In a final gesture of conciliation and generosity, the normally ambitious general superintendent of the Methodist church, Samuel Dwight Chown, refused to stand for election and instead nominated the Presbyterian George Pidgeon as the first moderator of the new church. It combined all but 7 of the 174 Canadian Congregational churches and 3,835 Presbyterian and 4,797 Methodist preaching places. It contained 85 Congregational, 2,065 Methodist, and 1,669 Presbyterian ministers and another 648 missionaries and had a total membership of nearly 700,000. However, the formation of the United Church of Canada was the beginning, not the end, of the process. The new institution was a uniting, as well as a united church. It welcomed discussions with other independent Protestant churches that would lead to a still wider union. It believed that the Baptists and Anglicans in Canada, as well as many small denominations, were natural allies and that they could retain the best elements of their theology and tradition while entering into a grand Church of Christ in Canada. The United Church maintained, "Our intention in uniting is to come together in an enriched embodiment of the one Church of God, not to create a new church or to bring into being a merger of existing ecclesiastical bodies."[70] The United Church was not designed to be simply another competing denomination or in fact a church like any other; it was to fulfil Methodism's dream of becoming the church for the nation.

# Epilogue:
# Methodism – the Continuing Legacy

## METHODISM'S CONTRIBUTION TO CANADA

What then was Methodism's legacy? Certainly, it introduced and was the major exponent of the evangelical revival in British North America. Through the promulgation of John Wesley's particular conjunction of Catholic and Protestant theological understanding and practice regarding universal salvation, conversion, and entire sanctification, Methodism offered an optimistic, forward-looking spirituality for all who wished to partake of its benefits. It adapted the first Great Awakening to the particular spiritual needs of the settlers in the new land. In so doing, it helped to fulfil the fundamental Christian mission to spread scriptural holiness throughout the world and make disciples of all nations. The Methodist church continuously struggled to provide an experiential religion suitable for all Canadians. During the early nineteenth century, Canadian Methodism also became the major national voice for the revival of religion then transforming Protestantism throughout the English-speaking world, and it oversaw the widespread transformation of theology from a Calvinist to an Arminian perspective. It supplied an inclusive and profoundly spiritual and moral religious experience to pioneer society.

As the needs and expectations of society changed, Methodism transformed its means of grace and its overall strategies without abandoning its central beliefs. The church also created a significant range of dynamic literary and educational institutions to expand its mission. Through its schools and universities, it improved the general level of education throughout the country and trained generations of Canadians to take advantage of the opportunities in agriculture, commerce, and industry. These institutions were perhaps even more valuable in building a moral, socially responsible élite of men and women to confront the contemporary challenges to the country's intellectual and spiritual harmony. Methodist education was designed essentially to form and strengthen Christian character, especially among those individuals who would ultimately define Canadian culture, rather than to impart a particular body of information or to prepare the student for a specific career. Although it was circumscribed by social restraint and regimented by narrow, sometimes inhibiting or apparently sanctimonious, notions of proper personal conduct, it nevertheless supplied a valuable purpose and continuity to life. Even as it prepared its own ecclesiastical community for a meaningful place in Canada's future, it rooted this future securely in an ethical, Christian past. At the same time, the Methodist churches' newspapers and publishing operations helped to inform Canadians about the important political, social, and intellectual issues both in their midst and around the world. They became major assets in the formulation and expansion of Canadian culture. They also helped the Methodist church relate a relevant message to its members even as it changed from a small body of earnest converts to a large, broadly based social institution.

Furthermore, Methodism greatly improved the condition of individual Canadians. It preached a mission of hope, love, and joy. It never isolated itself from the community in which it functioned and constantly sought to demonstrate God's benevolence to humanity. Truly a social religion, it inculcated humane values and democratic principles in Canadian society and harnessed the vast Canadian reserves of energy for crusades to evangelize and transform individuals, institutions, and society in general. Many of the Methodist church's campaigns to improve the individual and the broader society centred on avoiding or ending unhealthy or immoral amusements, strengthening rather than desecrating the sabbath, and especially defeating the evil influence of liquor. When taken to the extreme, the reforms demanded by the church quickly deteriorated into attempts by middle-class Anglo-Protestants to define and limit the social norms and to impose these on all Canadians. In turn, despite the fact that many of the changes were positive and addressed serious problems, such measures have often led to a dismissal of the Methodist church and the moral reforms it advocated as naïve and priggish, if not intolerant and racist.

Yet Wesley had demanded a totally transformed human being. This transformation required both a new spiritual life and disciplined, holy living. Religion could not be contemplated merely at church; it must be manifest in every activity. Canadian Methodism could never accept the idea that sinfulness was purely relative or that it should be defined by current attitudes and conduct in the corrupt world at large. And Methodists shared with other Protestants the belief that a pattern of proper restraint was essential for decent religious and community life. While at times too uncritical of its own motives and too insensitive to legitimate criticism, none the less, the Methodist church anchored its evangelism in the needs of society both to achieve heavenly safety and to live an exemplary life on earth. For over one hundred and sixty years, it strove to erect a moral and just nation, usually through moderate and well-conceived means. By its determined example, Canadians and Canadian governments came to accept their legitimate responsibility to assist the disadvantaged and to strive for a humane and broadly moral social order.

The Canadian Methodist church rarely let a subscription to narrow creeds limit its expansive enterprise. With its broad theological understanding and catholicity of spirit, it recognized that religious progress often demanded new doctrinal precedents rather than merely a rehearsal of those fixed by earlier authorities. Methodism never feared experimentation as long as it was well grounded in biblical sanction, Christian tradition, and Wesleyan "experience." Although it was bound by its contemporary culture and social conventions, it provided a progressive forum for the advancement of the rights of the individual and especially for those of women. Ironically, it was within the context of the church's highly centralized, ministerial-controlled government that a powerful laity representing Canada's various regions emerged to carry out the church's mission to transform Canadian life. For women, the Methodist church supplied a training ground and a vehicle for positive change, as well as a natural ally in their struggle for equality and social justice.

The church was also successful at least partially because of its rich legacy of music. The hymns used by Methodists, especially those of Charles Wesley, made religion accessible and popular by spreading doctrines to a wider variety of adherents than preaching or writing ever could. In the words of a modern writer,

Poetry is perhaps the most appropriate form for a theology of the heart; the words often communicate to the soul even before they are understood by the mind. The power of Wesley's poetry is its evocative nature – the words call forth images that are immediately sensible and personally relevant. Wesley's poetry is conceived within a vibrant sense of the divine-human relationship, and from the experience of this reality emerge words that convey the depth and breadth of Christian experience. Charles has mastered the art of poetic expression by marshalling verbal symbols that give perceptive form to the palpitations of his heart.[1]

Hymns encapsulated and magnified God's glory, Christ's sacrifice, and humankind's duty. They brought theology joyfully or painfully to life, consoled the lonely or distressed, and helped communicate Christian principles and practices. They provided an immediate and vital sense of community in local worship, while linking worshippers throughout the Christian world.

The Methodist church also strove to make Canada the natural home for the kingdom of God on earth. It therefore sought to Christianize and civilize all its subjects, including new immigrants and the native population, and thereby make the nation a proper dominion for the Lord. It profoundly believed that Christianity was the only true religion and that God demanded its adoption throughout the world. Inspired and challenged by these assumptions and reinforced by a moral altruism, the Methodist church promoted a Canadian manifest destiny to bring Protestant Christianity to the entire world through its missionary campaigns. Unfortunately, it was initially also motivated by a keen sense of its own racial and cultural superiority and by a predisposition to denigrate all non-British societies. Accordingly, it attempted to destroy what it understood to be merely primitive magical and animistic beliefs and to assist in the evolution of what it assumed were less-progressive religions. Over time, however, it gradually came to appreciate and respect the diverse cultures around the world, while working to ameliorate the universal problems of disease, poverty, and social injustice. Throughout its history, the

Methodist church never abandoned its belief in the need for a spirit of sacrifice at home or abroad. In fulfilling its mission, Methodism significantly influenced Canada's attitudes to the world community of nations and helped to shape the country's foreign policies. At least partially through Methodism's example, Canada was imbued with a deep sense of duty to provide moral leadership in the world.

In fact, surprisingly quickly, Methodism had evolved into the most Canadian of all the churches. Especially as the various Methodist bodies united into one nationwide church with a strong sense of connexionalism and a clear set of aspirations, it assumed the prerogatives of a popular, national institution and, indeed, believed it was the national ecclesiastical body. As a matter of course, the Methodist church promoted loyalty to Canada and remained throughout its history a major force for a united and progressive nation. With its broad appeal to the diverse components of Canadian society, it strove to break down the ethnic, geographic, political, economic, and social divisions apparently confounding national unity. Unfortunately, it believed that the anti-Catholic, nativist, and racist assumptions which underlay its assimilative policies were positive attributes. Harbouring no ill will to any particular individuals, the Methodist church nevertheless wanted Canada to become as homogeneous as possible in order to promote an evangelical Protestant national destiny. As its understanding grew, however, the church strove to improve ethnic relations and to dissipate racial tensions through tolerance and mutual respect. Although it never became as universal as it wished, it was remarkably successful in defining the religious, political, and social agenda for at least the Protestant component of the Canadian nation.

Several modern Canadian historians have seen in the intellectual debates and the rise of a socially active Christianity during the late nineteenth and early twentieth centuries the roots of modern secularism. However, it is rarely clear what they mean by secularization. Does the term imply the removal of God from the central place in the cosmos, the loss of belief in the power of the supernatural, the rise of materialism, the decline of institutional religion, the interjection of the state in previously ecclesiastical functions, or all of these? If secularization, however understood, is such a potent force, did it arise in the late nineteenth century or was it in fact more visible when rational deism dominated intellectual understanding in the eighteenth century? Some critics believe that it was dominant when Protestantism undermined the universal Roman Catholic expression of European Christianity. The use of secularization as an organizing principle is usually relative and is based on hindsight since it assumes that a previous age was sacred, or at least more sacred, than the present and that a clear linear path can be traced illustrating the rise of the profane. Such assumptions are not born out by closer examination.

In Canada the changes wrought in the Methodist understanding of Christianity more likely delayed the onset of a social order founded on a narrow vision of science or a selfish materialism by, among other things, encouraging the civil government to adopt and advance moral and religious goals. The factors which helped to create the belief that the social order could be self-sufficient and human-centred, without the need for ecclesiastical or supernatural guidance, arose independently of the churches. Although Protestant theological vagueness perhaps inadvertently weakened the church's ability to meet these challenges, they had more to do with the apparent ability of technology and industrialization to mitigate nature's caprices. As well, it is perhaps too early to declare final victory for the profane. History has shown that secularization and revivals of religion rise in waves to displace each other over time and that the resilience of spiritual beliefs should never be underestimated. The decade of the 1950s was perhaps the most religious in Canadian history, as measured both by membership growth and new church construction and also by the influence of religious ideas on Canadian culture. In actual fact, over its history Canadian Methodism manifested a rich and heroic faith and a powerful legacy of service to humanity and to God.[2]

## THE CONTINUING METHODIST CHURCHES

The church union consummated on June 10, 1925, did not mean that all Methodist churches in Canada ceased to exist, and certainly the influence of John Wesley and Methodism continued within evangelical churches and especially in the United Church of Canada. Arminian theology was deeply entrenched in the ideology of the United Church and had become a significant factor even in many of the Calvinistic denominations. They also shared common spiritual, intellectual, and social assumptions that had long been the hallmark of the Methodist church. A host of independent churches remained in Canada that claimed direct descent from John and Charles Wesley although they generally served an ethnic or racial minority or emphasized particular doctrines that separated them from contemporary mainstream Methodism.

The oldest of these continuing Methodist churches were the Evangelical Association (Evangelical Church after 1923) and the United Brethren in Christ. They had begun organized work in Canada during the 1830s among the German-speaking population in what is now southwestern Ontario and the Ottawa valley and had expanded to the western prairies as that region opened up before World War I. They maintained close fraternal relations with mainstream Methodism, with which they shared similar doctrines, polity, and commitment to evangelism and social service. Twenty-four of the United Brethren congregations entered the United Church in 1925 as part of the Congregational Union. Following the example of their American parent connexions, the remainder of the United Brethren and the Evangelical Association united in 1946 to form the Evangelical United Brethren Church. With the gradual decline in the use of German, the Ontario and Quebec section of the Evangelical United Brethren saw little justification for remaining independent. Immediately after its own amalgamation, this section of the church opened union negotiations that were finalized in 1968 when it joined the United Church of Canada. However the more conservative Northwest Conference opposed many of the liberal policies of the United Church and declined to participate.[3]

The British (African) Methodist Episcopal Church also continued outside of the union of 1925, although it has subsequently cooperated with the United Church. In fact, the black Episcopal Methodist church had never been invited to unite with its fellow Methodists, and preliminary discussions regarding union with the United Church fell through in the 1940s. It had led in the anti-slavery campaigns before and during the American Civil War and had provided a safe haven for thousands of fugitive slaves and a warm, congenial fellowship for free blacks. Despite emerging from the American social and political experience, the church quickly developed, and has since guarded, a strong loyalty to Canada and to independence from foreign control. Along with a trust in dynamic evangelism and a strong sense of mission, it maintains a proud heritage of reform and service, especially in the areas of civil and human rights, and continues to provide a vital Wesleyan community for blacks across Canada.

By 1925 the country was also home to numerous independent holiness churches that to a greater or lesser degree reflected Wesleyan doctrines and practices. Synthesizing Wesley's doctrine of Christian perfection with the revivalism of Charles G. Finney and Phoebe Palmer, these groups gained substantial support among disenchanted Methodists, Mennonites, Quakers, Baptists, and Presbyterians, who often so caricatured Wesley's influence as to make it unrecognizable. In the disputes over biblical literalism, the holiness churches usually sided with conservative evangelicals, pentecostals, and more recently, charismatics, but they still retained Wesley's commitment to experiential religion combined with a powerful ethical and moral concern. "The Holiness movement differs from fundamentalism and evangelicalism in that it is more oriented to ethics and spiritual life than to a defense of doctrinal orthodoxy."[4] As the debate over higher criticism and the literal veracity of the Bible has changed during the twentieth century, many holiness churches have sought to underline their distinctiveness and particularly their differences from other conservative denominations by re-emphasizing their Wesleyan heritage. In so doing, some have also played down the somewhat simplistic "easy road" to entire sanctification, which has always found a more receptive audience in the United States than in Canada.

The Free Methodist Church was the first of the holiness-movement institutions to enter Canada and initially ministered to some of the Methodists who felt uncomfortable in the mainstream Methodist church. With the formation of the United Church of Canada, the Free Methodists expected to attract a large number of opponents to union, but this did not occur. Contrary to the views of modern apologists, the church was heavily bound to its American parent until after World War II and was never able to convince Canadians that it was the true inheritor of the mantle of Canadian Methodism. Since at least the 1970s, in defence against attempts by its conservative wing to move the connexion into alliances with fundamentalists and pentecostals, the Free Methodist leadership has also chosen to highlight its links with traditional Canadian Methodism.[5]

As well, the twentieth century witnessed the transformation and growth of other holiness churches. Ralph Horner, originally a Methodist evangelist, moved from his Holiness Movement Church of Canada into the Standard Church of America in 1916 and dabbled with pentecostal blessings of heaven-sent wind and fire to empower preaching and healing. The Church of the Nazarene, which combined holiness and fundamentalist ideas, entered Canada in 1902 from its California base. While claiming John Wesley as a parent, it has generally misunderstood or ignored his legacy. In 1958 it absorbed the remnants of the Gospel Workers Church of Canada. The Gospel Workers began in revivals in 1898 and grew principally among Methodists in the Collingwood area of Ontario under the leadership of Frank Goff. A former Hornerite, Goff formed a separate church in 1902, which was infused with a belief in a third work of grace, or baptism of the Holy Ghost. The Wesleyan Methodist Church of America, which began operations in Canada in 1897, was even less recognizably inspired by Wesley. It combined holiness revivalism with the Quakerism of the Pilgrim Holiness Church and elements of the Reformed Baptists from Atlantic Canada. Attempts to unite with the Free Methodists during the 1960s caused considerable dissension in both camps.[6]

The Salvation Army is the most influential of the holiness churches in Canada. It has blended social action with Christian perfectionist evangelism and attracted many disaffected Methodists who maintained that society could be truly reformed only by converting the individual. Most late-nineteenth-century Methodists were suspicious of its agitating style, but welcomed its service to the underprivileged in the community. It directed its message of personal conversion and sanctification primarily at the poor and labouring classes. This interest was shared by the radical Labour churches that entered Canada from Britain at the end of the nineteenth century. Directly influenced by Primitive Methodism's concern for the rights of workers and its commitment to trade unionism, the Labour churches also emphasized Fabian socialist ideas and programs in their religious meetings. Without a clear spiritual dimension, however, these churches could not sustain a long-term, distinct existence.[7]

### THE METHODIST HERITAGE IN THE UNITED CHURCH

While many denominations have been directly informed by Wesleyan teachings, Methodist influences have become so deeply entrenched in Protestant Canada that their parentage has often gone unrecognized. Nevertheless, the United Church of Canada remains the major inheritor of Methodism in the country. But again, since by the early twentieth century the Methodist, Presbyterian, and Congregational churches had grown so similar, particular influences in the United Church are difficult to identify. The new church enunciated a consensus of general Protestant beliefs and was at least partially convinced that a reliance on particular doctrinal and theological statements would only divide its members. The first generations of church leaders also assumed that actions should not be justified by reference to any specific historical confession, and in the interest of internal harmony, they disregarded the individual contributions of the founding denominations. As a result, the United Church quickly lost a clear sense of the value of its own history in supplying perspective to its policies and practices. It assumed that problems should be solved pragmatically as they arose.

At the time of union, in the attempt to clarify the central characteristics of the partner churches, Presbyterians were generally identified with education, sacred learning, and church order, Congregationalists with spiritual freedom and the enforcement of civic justice, the Local Union churches with community life and unity, and finally, the Methodists with audacity of enterprise and with "evangelical zeal for human redemption, the testimony of spiritual experience, and the ministry of sacred song."[8] Obviously, none of the denominations held a monopoly of the virtues attributed to them, but most Methodists were pleased with the idea that they infused the United Church with experiential religion.

The crucified, atoning Christ is the central fact of United Church life, and the church continues to try to balance experience and reason in light of tradition and Scripture. While rejecting overt emotionalism, it has also maintained the Methodist battle against spiritually deadening formalism and the spread of secularism. An emphasis on personal revival underlay all the church's programs during the late 1920s and the 1930s and was manifest most prominently immediately after World War II. The church's postwar Crusade for Christ and His Kingdom helped initiate perhaps the greatest religious revival ever witnessed in Canada. In attempting to reintegrate the returning veterans and providing stability to families disrupted by the war, the crusade converted thousands. It was followed closely by the church's National Evangelistic Mission, which helped raise church membership to its highest level and inaugurated the largest church-building program in Canadian history. Although a typical post-revival decline was aggravated by changing demographic patterns and modern modes of behaviour, spiritual experience remains central to church life.[9]

However, in the United Church, as in its Methodist antecedents, this spirituality is not designed to isolate the individual or to promote a rejection of the world. Rather, it accentuates the commitment of the membership to social action and social progress. The church blends evangelism with social service to advance both the sacred and the temporal communities. In staying relevant to the social, intellectual, and cultural currents of twentieth-century Canada, it has expanded its religiosity by carrying its spiritual and moral message to the heart of society. In fact, the United Church assumes that one of its pre-eminent functions is to transform the secular community into a sacred society. It has helped to convince Canadians that they share the fundamental obligation to advance social justice, human rights, and moral progress. The success of the church can perhaps be best measured by the degree to which the state has accepted this prescribed role and implemented many of the social-welfare programs originally advocated by the Methodist and United churches.[10]

On another level, the systematic theology that survived in the United Church generally ignored John and Charles Wesley. For the most part, the Wesleys were dismissed as lacking a coherent theology and being interested only in promoting emotional spiritual experience. Few United Church clergy have read Wesley's published sermons or other Methodist standards, and contrary to the practice of the Uniting Church in Australia, they were never an authorized basis of church doctrine. Through ignorance or indifference, John Wesley has usually been trivialized and has received little appreciation as a major theologian, evangelist, and church builder. Furthermore, Charles Wesley's hymns were rarely recognized for their contribution to Christian theology, Protestant doctrine, or the exploration of the human condition. Indeed, the teaching function of these hymns has never been fully understood in the United Church. Given the church's "tempered enthusiasm" and emphasis on educational progress, which marked its shift away from a theology of the heart, Wesley's hymns no longer appeared to speak to the core of modern religious experience. At the same time, the church's emphasis on ecumenism and pluralism, along with its need to balance a host of ecclesiastical traditions, has meant that most of these hymns have been omitted from United Church hymnals.[11]

None the less, Methodism's ecclesiastical traditions and theological and practical elements were never far beneath the surface and have re-emerged as they were needed. Certainly the social gospel and its related liberal theology, although not uniquely Methodist, were major components of the intellectual and social contribution of Methodism to the United Church. However, by the late 1930s, there was a growing reaction against liberal theology. Support for beliefs that asserted the nobility of humanity, the benevolence of an immanent God, distrust of ancient creeds, and reliance on historical processes to advance human progress until it ultimately achieved the kingdom of God on earth seemed misplaced. Although many of the church's leaders attempted to solve the human problems associated with the Great Depression by implementing radial social policies, the suggested remedies provided little comfort for the average church member and appeared to accelerate a declining interest in religion. While these members acknowledged that the social gospel, properly understood, still demanded personal regeneration, the emphasis on social action alone seemed too shallow to solve humanity's needs. In many ways, the reliance on pragmatic problem solving had developed in the Methodist and Presbyterian churches as a means of avoiding the disruptive influences of the nineteenth-century debates over the implications of Darwinian science and biblical criticism. In retrospect, although these churches emerged relatively unscathed by those debates, it sometimes appears that as a result they bequeathed a lack of theological consistency to the United Church.[12]

If the United Church's mission was not to be betrayed, many felt the need to re-establish a balance between social service and individual experience. However, the elaborate nineteenth-century debates over biblical literalism were no longer appropriate, and these disaffected members of the United Church refused to subscribe to the narrow vision and outdated formulas of fundamentalism. Instead, they searched for a new orthodoxy based on personal faith that placed God at the centre of religious experience without denying a socially relevant mission to Canadians. Even many leading social gospellers underwent a traumatic crisis of faith and sought a spiritual revival for themselves and for the entire church. They did not always recognize their debt, but they turned instinctively to Wesleyanism as the most appropriate model of a spiritually awakened institution.[13]

In 1943 the United Church reopened formal union discussions with the Anglican Church of Canada and later entered into negotiations with the Evangelical United Brethren Church and the Christian Church (Disciples of Christ). As a uniting as well as united church, it found significant value in the breadth of Wesleyan precepts. Not least of these was the belief in organic union itself. "The Wesley heritage is evident rather in the Catholic spirit which has promoted Methodists to attempt to move again and again throughout this century into a larger organic Christian unity."[14] Methodism was content to see itself as an interim institution, not a necessary end in itself; the world did not require a Methodist church to fulfil Wesley's mission.

Moreover, in order to provide a credible beginning, the negotiating churches felt it was desirable to define their fundamental denominational principles. When this was accomplished, it would presumably be easier to formulate common standards for the new church. Ironically, this was the first time that the United Church had analysed many of its own doctrines. In this process during the 1950s and 1960s, it rediscovered Wesley as an important father of the denomination and found that many central Methodist doctrines supplied useful links among the various communions. United Church officials were somewhat surprised to discover Wesley's complexity and his substantial contribution to Christian understanding. During the same period, the new openness and ecumenical spirit surrounding the Roman Catholic discussions at Vatican II increased the interest in John Wesley as a valuable bridge between Protestants and Roman Catholics.[15]

More recently, the United Church has adopted popular currents from the third world's liberation theology. Rejecting both a Catholicism that too often translated into unquestioning obedience to those in secular power and a distorted version of Calvinism that suggested God had preordained one's status and therefore supported the oppression of one race or class by another, liberation theology identified the church's obligations to society's victims. The United Church has applied the tenets of liberation theology to the rights of minorities, women, and aboriginal peoples both in Canada and abroad. Liberation theology has a ready-made authority in John Wesley. He opposed any form of oppression and through his stress on universal salvation showed the way for personal growth and progress. He also put the Bible into the hands of the people and thereby provided direct access to divine authority. At the same time, his support for universal education helped to advance political, economic, and social freedom. In addition, institutional Methodism offered valuable opportunities for training and practice in secular leadership.[16]

Beyond theological considerations, the United Church of Canada has also inherited much of the Methodist mind-set. Until the late 1970s, which saw the failure of union with the Anglicans and disillusionment with the whole union process, the United Church did not consider itself a denomination like the others. As the embodiment of Protestant values, it viewed itself as a precursor to a totally integrated organic Christianity. Like original Methodism, it was established to create a new, all-inclusive fellowship designed to participate in the world. Everyone was welcome regardless of race, class, ethnicity, or nationality. As long as fundamental Christian beliefs were intact, the United Church accepted a wide divergence of ecclesiastical, theological, and doctrinal beliefs; it never demanded uniformity in Christian understanding. The United Church believed that it was the national church. As such, it also assumed that it had the right and the duty to reshape Canadian society in Christ's image and that its status empowered it to provide a tolerant and unbiased forum for diverse interests from both the religious and secular communities.

Thanks to its Methodist roots, the United Church also retained a strong sense of connexionalism. Although this connexionalism has been challenged recently by the introduction of divisive regional and congregational semi-autonomy, for the most part the church has recognized the benefits of maintaining an integrated institution. Connexionalism was strengthened by the adoption of the Methodist bureaucratic structure of boards, departments, and committees. This structure, although sometimes undemocratic, supplied efficient direction to the church. Connexionalism was also enhanced by centrally directed and unified Christian education programs, missionary operations, and church newspapers and publications. The ability to mobilize a united, national church was vital in times of crisis such as the Great Depression or World War II. In both instances, the United Church became a model for action by the government and other institutions.[17]

As well, the United Church has inherited the traditional Methodist concern for missions. This has taken two principal forms. First, the church has maintained an active partnership with indigenous churches throughout the world and supplied financial assistance, expertise, and guidance. There is no longer a question of imperialistic intervention, but rather fraternal cooperation. Help has been provided to develop essential infrastructure and to train teachers, doctors, and other secular and spiritual leaders. Second, the United Church has functioned within the international ecclesiastical community, such as the World Council of Churches, and has taken an active role in inter-church and interfaith dialogues in order to promote social justice and economic progress. The modern trust in unity, if no longer organic union, has also reinforced Christian solidarity with suffering and oppressed peoples in order to further their human and social rights.[18]

Moreover, the United Church has maintained the Methodist leadership in developing a creative role for its own laity. Lay men and women have established a significant partnership with the clergy in all aspects of church life. In fact, the definition of ministry includes the whole people of God. Wesley certainly supported the idea of encouraging all church members to become active Christian workers. At the same time, the United Church has advanced the status and role of women both as members of the laity and, beginning with the ordination of Lydia Gruchy in 1936, as part of the order of professional ministry. The hesitancy of many congregations to accept female clergy, the difficulty of placing married women whose husbands also work, and the competing claims on women to remain at home to preserve stable family life all slowed the numerical growth of women clergy, but the United Church continues to work to overcome these obstacles. The church has also reflected its Methodist heritage in pursuing equality for women throughout society.[19]

Finally, the United Church is not a static or monolithic institution, and although it is seriously challenged by internal and external forces, it still seeks the best means of advancing the spiritual and moral welfare of Canadians. Over the last thirty years, the importance of Canada's Methodist heritage has been increasingly demonstrated to the church. As the generations of members who considered themselves Congregationalists, Presbyterians, or Methodists are replaced by those who have known only the United Church, it may well be even more willing to look to its own rich heritage for guidance and to accept the impressive legacy that Methodism has to offer in making the Dominion of Canada into the dominion of the Lord.

# Notes

The vast majority of records cited in this study are located at the United Church Archives at Victoria University in Toronto. In many instances, records located in Britain, the United States, and other centres in Canada have been copied by the church and are held in Toronto.

INTRODUCTION

1 Ps. 72:8; Zech. 9.10. See also William Westfall, *Two Worlds: The Protestant Culture of Nineteenth-Century Ontario* (Kingston: McGill-Queen's Univ. Press, 1989), 3–4.

CHAPTER ONE

1 John Wesley, *Journal*, 1, May 24, 1738. This reference is routinely repeated in studies of the life of John Wesley. However, it should be added that while the date has come to represent the founding of Methodism, since it reflected the climax in the evolution of Wesley's spirituality, he himself in later years downplayed its significance. He had earlier and later spiritual crises, and after his split with the Moravians, he was hesitant to make too much of an occasion dominated by their leadership. See Albert Outler (ed.), *John Wesley* (New York: Oxford Univ. Press, 1964), 51–52.

2 The dating and consequences of the first three "beginnings" of Methodism – 1729, 1736, and 1738 – have been long established since Wesley repeatedly described the events. However, recent research has shown that in all three instances, he telescoped events which actually took place over several months, exaggerated the numbers and commitment of those involved, and tended to give himself a more central role than was warranted. See Richard Heitzenrater, "John Wesley as Historian of Early Methodism," CMHS, *Papers* 7 (1989): 37–54.

3 Frank Baker, "Susanna Wesley: Puritan, Parent, Pastor, Protagonist, Pattern," in James Udy and Eric Clancy (eds.), *Dig or Die* (Sydney, Australia: World Methodist Historical Society, 1981), 86; Sidney Dimond, *The Psychology of the Methodist Revival: An Empirical and Descriptive Study* (Oxford: Oxford Univ. Press, 1926), 50–56.

4 "John Wesley" and "Charles Wesley," *Encyclopedia of World Methodism*, 2:2491, 2495.

5 Maldwin Edwards, "John Wesley," in Rupert Davies et al. (eds.), *A History of the Methodist Church in Great Britain* (London: Epworth Press, 1965–88), 1:44, 46–47; "Charles Wesley," *Encyclopedia of World Methodism*, 2:2491; Outler, 11.

6 "John Wesley," *Encyclopedia of World Methodism*, 2:2496; Outler, 13–14; "Bands and Classes," in *A History of the Methodist Church in Great Britain*, 4:25.

7 Frank Baker, "John Wesley at Leisure," CMHS, *Papers* 7 (1989): 23–35; Kenneth Rowe, "The Search for the Historical Wesley," in Kenneth Rowe (ed.), *The Place of Wesley in the Christian Tradition* (Metuchen: Scarecrow Press, 1976); Dimond, 42, 46–49; Owen Chadwick, "John Wesley and the Origins of Methodism," in Charles Scobie and John W. Grant (eds.), *The Contribution of Methodism to Atlantic Canada* (Montreal: McGill-Queen's Univ. Press, 1992), 11–31; Horton Davies, *Worship and Theology in England*, vol. 3, *From Watts to Wesley to Maurice, 1690–1850* (Princeton: Princeton Univ. Press, 1961), 144.

8 John Tyson, "Charles Wesley, Evangelist: The Unpublished Newcastle Journal," *Methodist History* 25 (1986): 41–43; A. Harold Wood, "Our Heritage in Charles Wesley's Hymns," in *Dig or Die*, 49; Horton Davies, 3:201.

9 Frank Baker, *From Wesley to Asbury: Studies in Early American Methodism* (Durham, NC: Duke Univ. Press, 1976), 24; Heitzenrater, 46.

10 "George Whitefield," *Encyclopedia of World Methodism*, 2:2553; Horton Davies, 3:144–9; Harry S. Stout, *The Divine Dramatist: George Whitefield and the Rise of Modern Evangelicalism* (Grand Rapids: Wm. Eerdmans, 1991), 2–3, 66–70.

11 Frank Baker, "The Trans-Atlantic Triangle: Relations Between British, Canadian and American Methodism in the Eighteenth Century," UCA, *Bulletin* 28 (1979): 6; Baker, *From Wesley to Asbury*, 25; Stout, 155, 276–287.

12 "George Whitefield," *Encyclopedia of World Methodism*, 2:2553, Stout, 5–6, 16; Albert Outler, "The Place of Wesley in the Christian Tradition," in *The Place of Wesley in the Christian Tradition*, 26; Horton Davies, 3:145, 155–158. Wesley adopted the term Arminian, but he was also influenced by a variety of other theologians. After Whitefield's death in 1770, the question of predestination would again undermine Methodist fraternity.

13 Bernard Semmel, *The Methodist Revolution* (New York: Basic Books, 1973), 7; Outler, "The Place of Wesley in the Christian Tradition," 16; Charles S. Eby, *Methodism and the Missionary Problem* (Toronto: Wm. Briggs, 1886), 14–15; Horton Davies, 3:143–144.

14 Albert Outler, "John Wesley's Interests in the Early Fathers of the Church," UCA, *Bulletin*, 29 (1983): 6–7; James Thomas, "How Theology Emerges from Polity," Bicentennial Consultation on Wesleyan Theology, Emory University, 1983, 3, 13; Abel Stevens, *History of the Methodist Episcopal Church in the United States of America* (New York: Carlton & Porter, 1866–67), 1:29.

15 "Doctrinal Standards," *Encyclopedia of World Methodism*, 1:698–703; Samuel Warren, *Chronicles of Wesleyan Methodism* (London: John Stephens, 1827), 1–30; Rupert Davies, "Justification, Sanctification and the Liberation of the Person," in Theodore Runyon (ed.), *Sanctification and Liberation* (Nashville: Abingdon Press, 1981), 67–68; Ole Borgen, "Baptism, Confirmation and Church Membership," *Methodist History* 27 (1989): 91–92; John Fletcher, "First Checks to Antinomianism, 1771," in *A History of the Methodist Church in Great Britain*, 4:166–167; Thomas Langford, "John Wesley's Doctrine of Justification by Faith," UCA, *Bulletin* 29 (1983): 47–62.

16 "Justification," *Encyclopedia of World Methodism*, 1:1303–1304; Horton Davies, 3:151; John Wesley, "Salvation by Faith, Sermon #1," in *A History of the Methodist Church in Great Britain*, 4:20–23; Robert J. Hillman, "Grace in the Preaching of Calvin and Wesley," in *Dig or Die*, 282; Methodist Episcopal Church, *A Collection of Interesting Tracts, Explaining Several Important Points of Scriptural Doctrine* (New York: J. Soules, 1817), 359; William Cannon, "Salvation in the Theology of John Wesley," UCA, *Bulletin* 27 (1978): 44–46.

17 Hillman, 284; "The Conference of 1745," in *A History of the Methodist Church in Great Britain*, 4:76–7. In answer to a question on the early history of Methodism, Wesley responded in part, "When Satan could no longer prevent this, he threw Calvinism in our way" (*Minutes of Annual Conference*, 1765, 50). See also the articles by Victor Shepherd and Thomas Langford comparing the teachings of Wesley and Calvin in UCA, *Bulletin* 29 (1983).

18 Horton Davies, 3:154; "Christian Perfection," *Encyclopedia of World Methodism*, 1:489; Thomas Langford, "John Wesley's Doctrine of Sanctification," UCA, *Bulletin*

29 (1983): 63–73; Cannon, 50–51; A Harold Wood, "Charles Wesley's Hymns on Holiness," in *Dig or Die*, 67–76.

19 Outler (ed.), *John Wesley*, 9–10; Stanley Hauerwas, "Characterizing Perfection: Second Thoughts on Character and Sanctification," Bicentennial Consultation on Wesleyan Theology, Emory University, 1983, 2; Rupert Davies, "Justification, Sanctification and Liberation," 69; John Wesley, "Plain Account of Christian Perfection," in *A History of the Methodist Church in Great Britain*, 4:137.

20 Antinomianism was a heresy within Christian thought which theorized that once justified, the believer could no longer sin and was set free from all obligations to carry out the commands of God. To Wesley, this concept meant the antinomian was not obliged to live a holy life or observe the appointed means of grace or church sacraments (Tyson, 46, note 30; "Checks to Antinomianism," in *A History of the Methodist Church in Great Britain*, 4:167).

21 John Wesley, "The Character of a Methodist (1742)," in *A History of the Methodist Church in Great Britain*, 4:52; Theodore Runyon, "Wesley and 'Right Experience,'" CMHS, *Papers* 7 (1989): 55–56.

22 Goldwin S. French, *Parsons and Politics* (Toronto: Ryerson Press, 1962), 15; John Wesley, "Scriptural Christianity," in H. Sugden (ed.), *John Wesley's Fifty-Three Sermons* (Nashville: Abingdon Press, [1921] 1983); Wesley, "The Character of a Methodist," 4:51; Leon Hyson, "Christian Love: The Key to Wesley's Ethics," *Methodist History* 14 (1975): 44–55.

23 William J. Abraham, "The Wesleyan Quadrilateral," Bicentennial Consultation on Wesleyan Theology, Emory University, 1983; Lovett Weems, *The Gospel According to Wesley* (Nashville: Discipleship Resources, 1982), 5; Allan Coppedge, "John Wesley and the Issue of Authority in Theological Pluralism," in Michael Peterson (ed.), *Spectrum of Thought* (Wilmore, Ky: Francis Asbury Publishing Co., 1982); Paul M. Bassett, "North American Methodist Biblical Scholarship and the Authority of Scripture," Bicentennial Consultation on Wesleyan Theology, Emory University, 1983; Rupert Davies, "Justification, Sanctification and Liberation," 70; Peder Borgen, "Biblical Authority and the Authenticity of the Church in Relationship to Auxiliary Keys such as Reason, Experience and Social Contexts," *Epworth Review* 8 (1981): 72–81; Paul Ballard, "Evangelical Experience: Notes on the History of a Tradition," *Journal of Ecumenical Studies* 13 (1976); Runyon, 62; Outler, "John Wesley's Interests in the Early Fathers of the Church," 7; Ted Campbell, "The 'Wesleyan Quadrilateral': The Story of a Modern Methodist Myth," *Methodist History* 29 (1991): 87–95.

24 Outler (ed.), *John Wesley*, 9–10; Outler, "John Wesley's Interests in the Early Fathers of the Church," 10–17; William Cannon, "John Wesley and the Catholic Tradition," CMHS, *Papers* 2 (1980); John C. English, "John Wesley and Francis Rous," *Methodist History* 6 (1968). 28–35, Robin Scroggs, "John Wesley as a Biblical Scholar," *Journal of Bible and Religion* 28 (1960); John Wesley, *The Sunday Service for the People Called Methodists*, preface.

25 Rex Matthews, "'With the Eyes of Faith': Scriptural Experience and the Knowledge of God in the Theology of John Wesley," Bicentennial Consultation on Wesleyan Theology, Emory University, 1983; Stuart Andrews, "John Wesley and the Age of Reason," *History Today* 19 (1969): 25–32; Fred Dreyer, "Faith and Experience in the Thought of John Wesley," CMHS, *Papers* 3 (1982); Colin Williams, *John Wesley's*

*Theology Today* (London: Epworth Press, 1960), 30; John Wesley, *Earnest Appeals to Men of Reason and Religion* (1743), in Gerald Cragg (ed.), *The Appeals to Men of Reason and Religion, The Works of John Wesley*, vol. 11 (Oxford: Clarendon Press, 1975); Ralph Gabriel, "Evangelical Religion and Popular Romanticism in Early Nineteenth-Century America," *Church History* 19 (1950): 34–35; Runyon, 58.

26 Runyon, 60–61; Cragg, intro., 24–27.

27 Runyon, 62.

28 Standish Meacham, "The Evangelical Inheritance," *Journal of British Studies* 3 (1963): 91; Runyon, 63; John Wesley, *The Works of John Wesley* (bicentennial ed., Nashville, 1984), 4:174.

29 Semmel, 14; Mary Ryder, "Avoiding the 'Many-Headed Monster': Wesley and Johnston on Enthusiasm," *Methodist History* 23 (1985): 214–222; John Wesley, *The Nature of Enthusiasm: A Sermon on Acts 26:24* (London: 1755); Cragg, intro., 24–25. Wesley believed that clear emotions, sound reason, and a healthy body were inseparable. His concern with medicine derived from his interest in the whole nature of humanity. See Phillip Ott, "John Wesley on Mind and Body: An Understanding of Health and Wholeness," *Methodist History* 27 (1989): 61–72.

30 Horton Davies, 3:184, 190–195, 205–209; "John Wesley to George Boyce (1750)," in *A History of the Methodist Church in Great Britain*, 4:107; Ole Borgen, 89–91.

31 Alan Gilbert, "Patterns of Religious Practice, 1740–1914," in Robert Currie et al. (eds.), *Churches and Churchgoers: Patterns of Church Growth in the British Isles since 1700* (London: Clarendon Press, 1977); *Minutes of the Annual Conferences, from the First, Held in London* (London: Conference Office, 1812), 1:99, 151, 244. Early membership statistics were not recorded in the *Minutes*. The British Conference also reported 64,146 members in America in 1791, of which 150 were in Newfoundland and 780 were in Nova Scotia.

32 Baker, *From Wesley to Asbury*, 16; "Rules of the Band Societies (1738)," in *A History of the Methodist Church in Great Britain*, 4:23–5.

33 Michael Hennell, "Evangelicalism and Worldliness, 1770–1870," in G.J. Cumming and Derek Baker (eds.), *Popular Belief and Practice* (Cambridge: Univ. Press, 1972); John Wesley, *Rules of the Society of the People Called Methodists* (Toronto: Wm. Briggs, n.d.); "The Nature, Design and General Rules of the United Societies (1743)," in *A History of the Methodist Church in Great Britain*, 4:59–61.

34 N.P. Goldhawk, "The Methodist People in the Early Victorian Age: Spirituality and Worship," in *A History of the Methodist Church in Great Britain*, 2:140; "Class Meeting," *Encyclopedia of World Methodism*, 1:519; "A Plain Account of the People Called Methodists (1748)," in *A History of the Methodist Church in Great Britain*, 4:95; David L. Watson, "The Origin and Significance of the Early Methodist Class Meeting" (PhD, Duke Univ., 1978).

35 Russell Richey, "Conference as a Means of Grace," Wesleyan/Holiness Conference, Asbury Theological Seminary, 1989, 11.

36 Horton Davies, 3:191; Russell Richey, "Community, Fraternity and Order in Methodism," CMHS, *Papers* 4 (1984): 3; Goldhawk, 141. The expression "feast of love" appears in Freeborn Garrettson's diary, August 17, 1781.

37 Goldhawk, 127.

38 Langford, 38; see also James Garlow, "John Wesley's Understanding of the Laity as Demonstrated by His Use of Lay Preachers" (PhD, Drew Univ., 1979); Paul

Chilcote, *John Wesley and the Women Preachers of Early Methodism* (Metuchen: Scarecrow Press, 1991), 49–75.

39 Nancy Hardesty, "The Wesleyan Movement and Women's Liberation," in *Sanctification and Liberation*, 168–73; Chilcote, 4–17, 92–113.

40 "John Wesley to 'an Evangelical Layman' (1751)," in *A History of the Methodist Church in Great Britain*, 4:109–110.

41 Horton Davies, 3:189; Outler (ed.), *John Wesley*, 384; Frank Baker, *John Wesley and the Church of England* (London: Epworth Press, 1970), 4–6.

42 "Conference of 1747," in *A History of the Methodist Church in Great Britain*, 4:86–87.

43 *Reasons Against a Separation from the Church of England*, in *A History of the Methodist Church in Great Britain*, 4:128–134; UCAMa, William Black Papers, Thomas Coke to William Black, September 7, 1791.

44 Wesley believed that American Methodism was already distinct from the Church of England in the 1770s and should not be forced to rejoin (John Wesley, *Works*, Telford ed., 7:239; A Raymond George, "Ordination," in *A History of the Methodist Church in Great Britain*, 2:143–59). In 1786 Wesley recorded in the *Minutes of Annual Conferences*, 191: "After Dr. Coke's return from America, many of our friends begged I would consider the case of Scotland ... I at length consented to take the same step with regard to Scotland, which I had done with regard to America. But this is not separation from the Church at all ... Whatever then is done either in America or Scotland, is no separation from the Church of England" (Baker, *From Wesley to Asbury*, 17).

45 Eby, 10–11; Baker, "The Trans-Atlantic Triangle," 17; N. Allen Birtwhistle, "Methodist Missions," in *A History of the Methodist Church in Great Britain*, 3:1, 4–5.

46 Joseph Belcher, *George Whitefield: a biography* (New York: American Tract Society, 1857), 65, 154. Whitefield visited New England beginning in 1740, when he built on the work begun by Jonathan Edwards in 1734. See also Stout.

47 Baker, "The Trans-Atlantic Triangle," 6–7; Hans Rollmann, "Laurence Coughlan and the Origins of Methodism in Newfoundland," in *The Contribution of Methodism to Atlantic Canada*, 53–54; James Lewis, *Francis Asbury, Bishop of the Methodist Episcopal Church* (London: Epworth Press, 1927), 25–30.

48 Baker, *From Wesley to Asbury*, 59, 85–98; Birtwhistle, 3; Lewis, 15–19, 32, 110, 162; Charles Ludwig, *Francis Asbury: God's Circuit Rider* (Milford, Michigan: Mott Media, 1984), i, 1–10.

49 Albea Godbold, "Francis Asbury and His Difficulties with John Wesley and Thomas Rankin," *Methodist History* 3 (1965): 3–19; Albea Godbold, "Methodist Episcopacy," *Methodist History* 11 (1972): 15–29; Baker, *From Wesley to Asbury*, 98–103; Frederick Norwood, "A Crisis of Leadership: The General Conference of 1792," *Methodist History* 28 (1990): 195–201.

50 Baker, "The Trans-Atlantic Triangle," 9; Baker, *From Wesley to Asbury*, 99.

51 K. James Stein, "Baltimore 1784 – Historical-Theological-Ecclesiastical," *Methodist History* 23 (1984): 25.

52 Baker, *From Wesley to Asbury*, 102–103.

53 "Thomas Coke," *Encyclopedia of World Methodism*, 1:528–531; John Vickers, *Thomas Coke, Apostle of Methodism* (Nashville: Abingdon Press, 1969), 31–32, 142–144; Baker, *From Wesley to Asbury*, 99, 157; Cyril Davey, *Mad about Mission: The Story of Thomas Coke* (North Marston, England: Marshall Publishing, 1985), 1–15.

54 Stein, 25.

55 Thomas, "How Theology Emerges from Polity"; Stein, 38–39; Russell Richey, "The Social Sources of Denominationalism: Methodism," *Methodist History* 15 (1977): 168–169; William Nash Wade, "A History of Public Worship in the Methodist Episcopal Church and the Methodist Episcopal Church, South, from 1784 to 1905" (PhD, Univ. of Notre Dame, 1981), i–iv.

56 Stein, 29; Baker, *From Wesley to Asbury,* 163–182; Frank Baker, "The Americanization of Methodism," *Methodist History* 13 (1975): 5–20; Richey, "Community, Fraternity and Order," 10.

57 Baker, *From Wesley to Asbury,* 140; Eby, 20.

58 Russell Richey, "The Four Languages of Early American Methodism," CMHS, *Papers* 7 (1989): 155; Thomas, 7; Theodore S. Linn, "Religion and Nationalism: American Methodism and the New Nation in the Early National Period, 1776–1844" (PhD, Drew Univ., 1971); Stout, 205; Nathan Hatch, *The Democratization of American Christianity* (New Haven: Yale Univ. Press, 1989), 3–16, 81–93.

CHAPTER TWO

1 N.P. Goldhawk, "The Methodist People in the Early Victorian Age: Spirituality and Worship," in Rupert Davies et al. (eds.), *A History of the Methodist Church in Great Britain* (London: Epworth Press, 1965–88), 2:114; John Kent, "The Methodists to 1849," ibid., 2:228; N. Allen Birtwhistle, "Methodist Missions," ibid., 3:1; E.A. Payne, "The Evangelical Revival and the Beginnings of the Modern Missionary Movement," *Congregational Quarterly* 21 (1943): 223; W. Reginald Ward, "The Religion of the People and the Problem of Control, 1790–1830," in G.J. Cumming and Derek Baker (eds.), *Popular Belief and Practice* (Cambridge: Univ. Press, 1972), 237–238; George Rawlyk, *The Canada Fire: Radical Evangelicalism in British North America, 1775–1812* (Kingston: McGill-Queen's Univ. Press, 1994), xiii–xix, 3–4.

2 T.Watson Smith, *History of the Methodist Church within the Territories embraced in the Late Conference of Eastern British America* (Halifax: Methodist Book Room, 1877–90), 1:45; Hans Rollmann, "Laurence Coughlan and the Origins of Methodism in Newfoundland," in Charles Scobie and John W. Grant (eds.), *The Contribution of Methodism to Atlantic Canada* (Montreal: McGill-Queen's Univ. Press, 1992), 53–58.

3 Smith, 46. See also David W. Johnson, *History of Methodism in Eastern British America* (Sackville: Tribune Printing, 1925), 242.

4 Laurence Coughlan, *An Account of the Work of God in Newfoundland* (London: W. Gilbert, 1776), 9.

5 Arthur Kewley, "The First Fifty Years of Methodism in Newfoundland," UCA, *Bulletin* 26 (1977): 16; Johnson, 242; Rollmann, 67–68.

6 Kewley, 17; Rollmann, 62–63.

7 UCA, WMSC, Richard Taylor to Missionary Committee, February 1, 1813.

8 Johnson, 243; Smith, 60; Naboth Winsor, *Hearts Strangely Warmed: A History of Methodism in Newfoundland, 1765–1925* (Gander: B.S.C. Printing, 1982), 29; Kewley, 16.

9 Winsor, 29.

10 Johnson, 244–245; John W. Grant, "Methodist Origins in Atlantic Canada," in *The Contribution of Methodism to Atlantic Canada,* 33–36.

11 WMSC, Richard Knight to Missionary Secretaries, June 2, 1812.

12 Kewley, 10, 21; Winsor, 34.

13 Kewley, 21, 23; David Pitt and Marion Pitt, *Goodly Heritage: A Centennial History of the Congregation of Wesley United* (St John's: Jesperson Press, 1984), 1; WMSC, John Walsh to Missionary Secretaries, October 26, 1821; Wesleyan Missionary Auxiliary Society, Nova Scotia District, Annual Report, 1818. A £50 limit per circuit was established in 1821.

14 Kewley, 24. See also Grant, 37.

15 George Rawlyk, *Wrapped up in God* (Burlington, Ont.: Welch, 1988), 2–3; Norman McNairn, "The American Contribution to Early Methodism in Canada, 1790–1840" (ThD, Iliff School of Theology, 1969), 14. Originally, Nova Scotia included the whole Maritime region. New Brunswick was established as a separate colony in 1784. St. John's Island was renamed Prince Edward Island in 1799 after becoming a separate colony in 1769. Cape Breton Island was set off from Nova Scotia in 1784, but the two were reunited in 1820.

16 John S. Moir, "American Influence on Canadian Protestant Churches Before Confederation," *Church History* 36 (1967): 441–442; Rawlyk, *Wrapped up in God*, 1–54; Rawlyk, *The Canada Fire*, 5–18. Jonathan Edwards (1703–58) was one of the great theological and revival figures produced in America. Born and raised in Connecticut as a member of a prominent religious and intellectual family, he through his preaching and writing helped reawaken the spiritually dormant New Englanders and brought about a great evangelical resurgence throughout the English-speaking world.

17 "William Black," *DCB*, 6:62–67; Rawlyk, *The Canada Fire*, 20–24.

18 R. Scott Robertson, "William Black and the Making of Maritime Methodism" (BA, Mount Allison Univ., 1977), 90–92; Johnson, 16–17; R.M. Hattie, *Old Halifax Churches* (n.p.), 56–58; Robert Wilson, *Methodism in the Maritime Provinces* (Halifax: S.F. Huestis, 1893), 6. Many of the Maritime churches date their origins to Black's preaching.

19 UCAMa, William Black Papers, William Black to John Wesley, 1788; ibid., John Wesley to William Black, July 13, 1783; ibid., John Wesley to William Black, May 11, 1784; Rawlyk, *The Canada Fire*, 26–32.

20 Thomas W. Acheson, "Denominationalism in a Loyalist County: The Social History of Charlotte, 1783–1940" (MA, Univ. of New Brunswick, 1964), 1. See also Goldwin S. French, *Parsons and Politics: The Role of the Wesleyan Methodists in Upper Canada and the Maritimes from 1780 to 1855* (Toronto: Ryerson Press, 1962), 29–31.

21 Quoted in Acheson, "Denominationalism," 6. See also Thomas W. Acheson, "Methodism and the Problem of Identity in Nineteenth-Century New Brunswick," in *The Contribution of Methodism to Atlantic Canada*, 108–109.

22 Rawlyk, *Wrapped up in God*, 56–58, Robert D. Simpson (ed.), *American Methodist Pioneer: The Life and Journals of the Rev. Freeborn Garrettson, 1752–1827* (Madison: Drew Univ. Press, 1984), intro.

23 E. Arthur Betts, *Bishop Black and His Preachers, The Story of Maritime Methodism to 1825* (Halifax, 1974), 73. The appendix gives biographical information about all the Wesleyan missionaries. Hattie, 57; Johnson, 17; Rawlyk, *Wrapped up in God*, 57; Simpson, 125–131; Rawlyk, *The Canada Fire*, 44–47.

24 Rawlyk, *Wrapped up in God*, 55.

25 Ibid., 55–56.

26 WMSC, Robert Alder to Missionary Secretary, December 4, 1822; ibid., William Black to Missionary Secretary, October 10, 1804; Joshua Newton to Daniel Fidler, August 25, 1796, in Goldwin French (ed.), "Daniel Fidler Papers," UCA, *Bulletin* 13 (1960): 30; James Mann to Daniel Fidler, October 15, 1796, ibid., 33.

27 Robert Alder, *Zeal in the Cause of Missions, Sermon* (Saint John: 1822), 6; Robert Cooney, *The Autobiography of a Wesleyan Methodist Missionary* (Montreal: Pickup, 1856), 150–151; Acheson, "Methodism and the Problem of Identity," 114–115.

28 Rawlyk, *Wrapped up in God*, 64; Winsor, 29; Robertson, 90–91; Joseph Angwin, *Methodism in Cape Breton, 1789–1914* (Sydney Mines, 1914), 9.

29 Cooney, 161, 166. See also WMSC, Robert Alder to Joseph Taylor, June 1824.

30 William Jessop to Daniel Fidler, January 1793, in Goldwin French (ed.), "Daniel Fidler Papers," UCA, *Bulletin* 12 (1959): 5; James Boyd to Daniel Fidler, April 11, 1793, ibid., 7; Thomas Martin to Daniel Fidler, August 8, 1797, ibid., 13 (1960): 38.

31 WMSC, William Black to Missionary Society, October 10, 1804. See also ibid., William Black to Missionary Society, September 17, 1804; ibid., Minutes of Halifax Conference of Ministers, July 6, 1804.

32 WMSC, William Black to Thomas Coke, November 21, 1808. See also ibid., William Black to Thomas Coke, July 1, 1813.

33 WMSC, James Priestly to Missionary Society, January 27, 1813. See also ibid., William Black to Robert Smith, July 11, 1814, with excerpt from Duncan McColl to William Black, May 28, 1814.

34 Betts, 71–79; Acheson, "Methodism and the Problem of Identity," 111.

35 WMSC, William Black to Missionary Society, October 10, 1804; Betts, 71–79.

36 Smith, 369.

37 WMSC, James Knowlan to Missionary Secretaries, June 15, 1820; ibid., Robert Alder to Joseph Taylor, April 1, 1819; ibid., William Black to Missionary Society, October 10, 1804. A close reading of the Daniel Fidler correspondence in UCA, *Bulletin*, 1959 and 1960, will also give clear evidence of this problem.

38 French, *Parsons and Politics*, 36; Smith, 370; WMSC, Robert Alder to Missionary Secretaries, February 15, 1820.

39 WMSC, James Knowlan to Missionary Secretaries, June 15, 1820; ibid., Duncan McColl to Missionary Committee, August 6, 1804.

40 See, for example, WMSC, Robert Alder to Missionary Secretaries, January 23, 1823; ibid., Robert Alder to Missionary Secretaries, June 4, 1823.

41 Betts, 71–79; WMSC, Robert Alder to Joseph Taylor, June 1824.

42 Rawlyk, *Wrapped up in God*, 74; Wesleyan Missionary Auxiliary Society, Nova Scotia District, Annual Report, 1818, "Address to the Public," n.p.; WMSC, Robert Alder to Missionary Secretaries, December 4, 1822.

43 John Carroll, *Case and His Cotemporaries* (Toronto: Samuel Rose, 1867–77), 1:6 Katherine M. Crawford, "The Beginnings of Methodism in Quebec City," CMHS, *Papers* 8 (1988): 1; Robert Stewart, *St. Andrew's Church, Quebec: An Historical Sketch of the Church and its Ministers* (Quebec, 1928), 8.

44 Abel Stevens, *Life and Times of Nathan Bangs* (New York: Carlton & Porter, 1863), 160.

45 George Cornish, *Cyclopaedia of Methodism in Canada*, (Toronto: Methodist Book Room, 1881, 1905), 1:287.

46 Carroll, *Case*, 1:121, 137–138; Cornish, 1:287; Crawford, 2–4; Scull's replacement, Robert Hibbard, drowned on his way to the city.

47 Carroll, *Case*, 1:20–21, 139, 177. See John Carroll, *Past and Present* (Toronto: Alfred Dredge, 1860), 16; Cornish, 1:252, 287; William R. Phinney, "The New York Conference and Canadian Methodism," UCA, *Bulletin* 26 (1977): 38; Abel Stevens, *History of the Methodist Episcopal Church,* (New York: Carlton & Porter, 1867), 3:197–8.

48 WMSC, James Hallowell to Missionary Committee, May 26, 1812, with addendum, March 26, 1813.

49 Cornish, 1:202, 302; Cooney, 116; Carroll, *Case*, 1:119, 139–140, 277.

50 Carroll, *Case*, 1:279.

51 Ibid., 1:134–135.

52 Cornish, 1:307, 313.

53 John S. Moir, *The Church in the British Era* (Toronto: McGraw-Hill Ryerson, 1972), 65–66, and Curtis Fahey, *In His Name: The Anglican Experience in Upper Canada, 1791–1854* (Ottawa: Carleton Univ. Press, 1991), 10–11, citing John Strachan's 1826 sermon on the death of Bishop Mountain.

54 John Webster Grant, *A Profusion of Spires: Religion in Nineteenth-Century Ontario* (Toronto: Univ. of Toronto Press, 1988), 22–32; George Playter, *The History of Methodism in Canada* (Toronto: Anson Green, 1862), 40–41; Carroll, *Case*, 1:4. See also Bruce Wilson, *As She Began: An Illustrated Introduction to Loyalist Ontario* (Toronto: Dundurn Press, 1981), and Gerald Craig, *Upper Canada: The Formative Years, 1784–1841* (Toronto: McClelland & Stewart, 1963). Curtis Fahey cites the SPG "Journals," XXVIII, November 8, 1803, regarding the religious affiliations of Ernestown in 1803: 160 Anglicans, 398 Methodists, 250 Lutherans, 498 Presbyterians, 11 Quakers, 63 Universalists, 16 Roman Catholics, 33 Deists, 10 Baptists, and 688 who professed no religion.

55 "Charles Justin (James) McCarty," *DCB*, 4:494–495; UCA George Neal biographical file; Carroll, *Case*, 1:6–7; Norman McNairn, "Mission to Canada," *Methodist History* 13 (1975): 50–51; Arthur Kewley, "Some Early Sites of Methodist Camp Meetings on the Niagara Peninsula," *Proceedings of the Niagara Peninsula History Conference*, 1982, 81; Mrs. S.C. Tolan, "Christian Warner – A Methodist Pioneer," *Ontario History, Proceedings and Records* 37 (1945): 71–77; John C. Stevenson, *One Hundred Years of Methodism in Lundy's Lane* (Niagara Falls: Adviser Office, 1912), 4.

56 Moir, 87–88; Samuel D. Clark, *Church and Sect in Canada* (Toronto: Univ. of Toronto Press, 1948), 94.

57 Carroll, *Case*, 1:11. See also Simpson, intro.; Whitney Cross, *The Burned-over District: The Social and Intellectual History of Enthusiastic Religion in Western New York, 1800–1850* (Ithaca, NY: Cornell Univ. Press, 1950; New York: Harper & Row, 1965); McNairn, "Mission to Canada," 46; William Lamb, "William Losee: Ontario's Pioneer Methodist Missionary," UCA, *Bulletin* 21 (1969–70): 28.

58 "Darius Dunham," *Encyclopedia of World Methodism*, 1:729; Stevenson, 4; Carroll, *Case*, 1:12; Jesse Riley, *One Hundred and Fifty Years on Lundy's Lane* (Niagara Falls, 1944), 5.

59 Cornish, 1:31; Ormond Embleton, *Updating His Continuing Story at Stamford United Church* (n.p., c. 1977), 2; Carroll, *Case*, 1:109–110.

60 See, for instance, UCA, Joseph Gatchell Papers, MS Autobiography, 24–27; Stevens, *Life and Times of Nathan Bangs*, 41, 78–79; UCA, George Ferguson Papers, Journal, 55.

61 Riley, 8; Carroll, *Case*, 1:120–121.

62 Carroll, *Case*, 1:113. See also Margaret Betts, "From Butcher's Block to Cathedral: The Methodists in Kingston, 1798–1852" (MA, Queen's Univ., 1989).

63 Thomas Webster, *History of the Methodist Episcopal Church in Canada* (Hamilton: Canada Christian Advocate Office, 1870), 94; Carroll, *Case*, 1:47, 51, 56, 172; 2:58–59.

64 UCA, William Case biographical file; "William Case," DCB, 8:132–134, WMC, *Minutes of Annual Conference*, 1856, 330–331; Carroll, *Case*, 1:112, 2:132; Z. Paddock, *Memoir of Rev. Benjamin Paddock with Brief Notices of Early Ministerial Associates* (New York: Nelson & Phillips, 1875), 326–329.

65 Carroll, *Case*, 1:225–226, 285–288; 2:127, 312–315, 373. See also "Henry Ryan," DCB, 6:670–676; Carroll, *Past and Present*, 214–219; William Canniff, *The Settlement of Upper Canada* (Belleville: Mika, 1971 [Toronto: Dudley & Burns, 1869]), 295–299; Joseph Gatchell Papers, MS Autobiography, 29.

66 Canniff, 292–293; French, 42; extrapolated from Cornish, 1:35.

67 Moir, 91; Carroll, *Case*, 1:258–301; Joseph Gatchell Papers, MS Autobiography, 29; McNairn, "Mission to Canada," 60; Eula Lapp, *To Their Heirs Forever* (Belleville: Mika, 1977), 307–308.

68 Carroll, *Case*, 1:289, 301; Playter, 113.

69 French, *Parsons and Politics*, 68; McNairn, "American Contribution to Early Methodism in Canada," 83–84; Cornish, 1:31; Nathan Hatch, *The Democratization of American Christianity* (New Haven: Yale Univ. Press, 1989).

70 Moir, 189–190; Carroll, *Case*, 1:290–294; 2:10.

71 Henry H. Walsh, *The Christian Church in Canada* (Toronto: Ryerson Press, 1956), 139–141; Carroll, *Case*, 2:344–345.

72 William Pierce, *The Ecclesiastical Principles and Polity of the Wesleyan Methodists* (London: Hamilton, Adams, 1868), 757–758; Carroll, *Case*, 2:345.

73 WMSC, James Hallowell to Missionary Secretaries, May 26, 1812, with addendum, March 29, 1813; Carroll, *Case*, 1:282–283; 2:5–6; Carroll quotes Dr Luckey on Burch, "All his actions as well as words breathed the spirit of good will."

74 WMSC, Fifteen lay leaders (Montreal) to Missionary Secretaries, November 11, 1815. See also Russell Richey, "The Four Languages of Early American Methodism," CMHS, *Papers* 7 (1989): 158–160.

75 WMSC, Fifteen lay leaders (Montreal) to Missionary Secretaries, November 11, 1815. See also Carroll, *Case*, 1:178, 271; WMSC, John Hick to Missionary Secretaries, February 27, 1822. There was also a problem at Montreal over the refusal of the trustees to allow Burch to preach and in Halifax a generation earlier, when Marchington refused the Methodists permission to use his chapel. Later, difficulties would also appear in Belleville and York between the Wesleyans and the new Methodist Episcopal Church over control since local trustees technically owned the church property.

76 Carroll, *Case*, 1:321, 2:25; WMSC, John Strong to Missionary Committee, 1816.

77 WMSC, John Strong to Missionary Committee, June 13, 1815; ibid., John Strong to Rev. Blanchard, November 14, 1814; Arthur Kewley, "Henry Ryan," 4 (UCA, Henry Ryan biographical file).

78 Carroll, *Case*, 2:18–22, 75–76; WMCEBA, *Minutes of Annual Conference*, 1857, 5;
   WMSC, Richard Williams to Secretary of Conference, February 1816.

79 Drew University, General Conference Papers, William Black and William Bennett,
   Address to General Conference, May 19, 1816; WMSC, Henry Ryan to Missionary
   Committee, October 9, 1815; ibid., James Wood, Joseph Benson et al. to American
   General Conference, Baltimore, May 1816; ibid., William Bennett to Missionary
   Committee, April 2, 1816; UCAMA, William Black Papers, General Conference,
   USA, to Missionary Committee, May 22, 1816; Carroll, *Case*, 1:321; 2:31–33.

80 Drew University, Genesee Conference Papers, Darius Dunham to Genesee Conference, June 17, 1815. Carroll quotes Ryan as saying, "I have opposed them in life,
   and I will oppose them in death, and at the bar of God" (Carroll, *Case*, 2:36). Even
   Case had difficulties, however; see WMSC, William Case to Missionary Committee,
   January 10, 1817.

81 WMSC, John de Putron to Missionary Committee, November 1816; ibid., John
   de Putron to Missionary Committee, July 12, 1817; ibid., John de Putron to
   Missionary Committee, May 21, 1818; John Borland, quoted in Carroll, *Case*, 2:77;
   WMSC, James Booth to Missionary Committee, December 23, 1817.

82 WMSC, Richard Pope to Missionary Committee, April 8, 1818.

83 WMSC, James Gardner to Missionary Committee, August 10, 1816. See also ibid.,
   Richard Williams to Secretary of Conference, February 1816.

84 Carroll, *Case*, 2:179.

85 Extract of letter, Henry Pope to Missionary Committee, May 28, 1818, in *Methodist
   Magazine*, February 1819, 76–77. See also UCA, Henry Pope biographical file.

86 *Methodist Magazine*, February 1819, 76–7; WMSC, Missionaries in Canada to
   Missionary Committee, March 17, 1817; Arthur Kewley, "Mass Evangelism in Upper Canada before 1830" (ThD, Victoria University, 1960), 340.

87 Carroll, *Case*, 2:133. See also Genesee Conference Papers, "Report of Committee
   appointed to examine into the state of our Church in the Provinces of Canada,"
   submitted to 1817 Genesee Conference; ibid., "Report of the Committee to examine Report re state of Church in Canada," 1817; ibid., William Case and William
   Barlow, Address re state of work in Montreal; WMSC, Ninian Holmes to Missionary
   Committee, February 1, 1817; ibid., Henry Ryan to Missionary Society, March 8,
   1817; ibid., Bay of Quinte Circuit (MEC) to Missionary Committee, February 4,
   1817; UCA, George Ferguson Papers, Journal, 58.

88 WMSC, Edward Johnston to Missionary Committee, April 1818. Johnston's views
   were disavowed by the other British Wesleyan missionaries; see WMSC, James Booth
   to Missionary Committee, June 11, 1818.

89 Methodist Episcopal Church (US), *Journals of General Conferences, 1796–1836*,
   1820; Playter, 181; Webster, 152; Carroll, *Case*, 2:275–288; General Conference
   Papers, William McKendree to Methodist Episcopal Church in Lower Canada,
   October 16, 1820; ibid., Jabez Bunting to John Emory, August 26, 1820.

90 Carroll, *Case*, 2:200–201; Playter, 183; WMSC, Resolution of Committee to resolve
   disputes between American and British Methodism in Upper Canada, 1821.

91 Carroll, *Case*, 2:335.

92 Article in *Niagara Advance*, September 17, 1980, 5; WMSC, Thomas Catterick to
   Missionary Committee, September 13, 1820; ibid., Neil McLeod et al. to Missionary Committee, January 21, 1821; ibid., Fort Wellington members and trustees to

Missionary Secretaries, December 26, 1820; ibid., Kingston members and trustees to Missionary Secretaries, December 29, 1820; ibid., Robert Lusher to Missionary Secretaries, November 17, 1820; ibid., William Lunn to Missionary Secretaries, February 3, 1824; ibid., Joseph Stinson to Joseph Taylor, October 18, 1824; Carroll, *Case*, 2:200–201, 321.

93 Carroll, *Case*, 2:165–167, 283, 293–295.

CHAPTER THREE

1 Ralph Gabriel, "Evangelical Religion and Popular Romanticism in Early Nineteenth-Century America," *Church History* 29 (1950).

2 Theodore Runyon, "Wesley and 'Right Experience,'" CMHS, *Papers* 7 (1989): 62.

3 MEC, *Doctrines and Discipline* (1829), 51.

4 Northrop Frye, "Conclusion to a Literary History of Canada," in *The Bush Garden* (Toronto: Anansi Press, 1971), 225; G. Ramsay Cook, "Imagining a North American Garden," *Canadian Literature*, 1984, 12–16.

5 UCA, WMSC, Henry Pope to Missionary Secretaries, January 16, 1818.

6 Jacob Mountain to Henry Dundas, September 1794, in John Strachan, *Sermon on the Death of Bishop Mountain* (Kingston, 1826); quoted in George Playter, *The History of Methodism in Canada* (Toronto: Anson Green, 1862), 40–41.

7 Douglas McCalla, "The Loyalist Economy of Upper Canada, 1784–1806," *Histoire Sociale/Social History* 16 (1983): 280.

8 *The Minutes of the Annual Conferences of the Wesleyan Methodist Church in Canada, 1824–1845* (Toronto: Anson Green, 1846), intro., i.

9 William Canniff, *The Settlement of Upper Canada* (Belleville: Mika, 1971 [Toronto: Dudley & Burns, 1869]), 293.

10 Russell Richey, "Community, Fraternity and Order in Methodism," CMHS, *Papers* 4 (1984): 5.

11 *CG*, August 21, 1830, 314. See also *CCA*, April 28, 1846, 1.

12 *CG*, June 4, 1831, 118; Ernest J. Dick, "From Temperance to Prohibition in 19th Century Nova Scotia," *Dalhousie Review* 61 (1981): 513; Arthur Kewley, "Mass Evangelism in Upper Canada before 1830" (ThD, Victoria Univ., 1960), 323.

13 W. Reginald Ward, "Class, Denomination and the Development of the Connexional Frame of Mind in the Age of Bunting," CMHS, *Papers* 4 (1984).

14 See, for example, Elie Halévy, *History of the English People in the Nineteenth Century*; E.P. Thompson, *The Making of the English Working Class*; E.J. Hobsbawm, *Labouring Men*; and Bernard Semmel, *The Methodist Revolution*.

15 Ward, 6–7; Curtis Fahey, *In His Name: The Anglican Experience in Upper Canada, 1791–1854* (Ottawa: Carleton Univ. Press, 1991), 1; W. Reginald Ward, "The Religion of the People and the Problem of Control, 1790–1830," in G.J. Cumming and Derek Baker (eds.), *Popular Belief and Practice* (Cambridge: Univ. Press, 1972), 238. It should be noted that Ward goes on to say that denominational loyalties had re-emerged by the 1830s and that they formed the basis of political action during this latter period, acting as a counterpoise to class strife. In Upper Canada, Fahey also sees the emergence of a strong Anglican denominationalism to offset the growing power of the other denominations at about the same time.

16 John Carroll, *My Boy Life* (Toronto: Wm. Briggs, 1882), 247–248.

17 W.S. Pascoe, "In Memoriam – C. Barker," in Cephas Barker, *Notes by the Way* (Bowmanville: H.J. Nott, 1882), 98–9; see also Richard Shiels, "The Methodist Circuit Rider in the Second Great Awakening in New England," Wesleyan/ Holiness Conference, Asbury Seminary, 1989, 10.

18 *The Doctrines and Discipline of the Methodist Episcopal Church in America, with Explanatory Notes, by Thomas Coke and Francis Asbury* (Philadelphia, 1798; facsimile ed., Frederick Norwood, ed., Rutland: Academy Books, 1979), 157, notes. See also CG, January 2, 1833, 30.

19 MEC, *Minutes of Annual Conference*, 1824, 4.

20 CG, October 2, 1833, 186.

21 William Jessop to Daniel Fidler, January 15, 1795, in Goldwin French (ed.), "Daniel Fidler Papers," UCA, *Bulletin*, 12 (1959): 14. See also Richey, 3.

22 Elizabeth Muir, *Petticoats in the Pulpit: The Story of Early Nineteenth-Century Methodist Women Preachers in Upper Canada* (Toronto: United Church Publishing House, 1991); Marilyn F. Whiteley, "Modest, Unaffected and Fully Consecrated: Lady Evangelists in Canadian Methodism, 1884–1900," CMHS, *Papers* 6 (1987): 18–31.

23 Richey, 2.

24 Russell Richey, "The Four Languages of Early American Methodism," CMHS, *Papers* 7 (1989): 153–172.

25 William Westfall, *Two Worlds: The Protestant Culture of Nineteenth-Century Ontario* (Kingston: McGill-Queen's Univ. Press, 1989), 55.

26 UCA, George Abbs, "Sketches from an Itinerant's Scrapbook" (MS, 1892), 22, 24. See also UCA Seth Ryerson Papers, S.M. Phillips to Seth Ryerson, June 25, 1847; UCA Francis Coleman Papers, Diary, December 21, 1841; Jane A. Hopper, *Old-Time Primitive Methodism in Canada, 1829–1884* (Toronto: Wm. Briggs, 1904), 107–8. On humanity's natural depravity and the ineffectiveness of good works themselves, as well as the overarching concern with death, see Samuel Bromley, *Sinners Invited to Consider the Evidences of Their Own Natural Depravity* (London: Wilson, 1834); Robert Cooney, *The Judgement Seat of Christ: A Sermon* (Halifax: Wm. Cunnabell, 1838); and William Wilson, *The Warning Voice* (Halifax: Wm. Cunnabell, 1835).

27 UCA, Matthew Richey Papers, Cardiphonia, Matthew Richey to Augusta Richey (daughter), February 20, 1836. See also WMC, *Minutes of Annual Conference*, 1835, 99; UCA J. George Hodgins Papers, George Hodgins to John Shea, February 12, 1842; Samuel Watkins, "The Cause and Cure of Earthquakes: Methodists and the New Madrid Earthquakes, 1811–1812," *Methodist History* 30 (1992): 242–50.

28 UCA, William Blackstock Papers, Sermons, "Psalms 55:22." Egerton Ryerson also looked for conversion when he was ill; see Egerton Ryerson, *The Story of My Life*, ed. J.G. Hodgins (Toronto: Wm. Briggs, 1883), 38 (diary extract from February 12, 1825). See also Nels Ferre, "Fear, Duty and Love," *International Review of Missions*, 1948, 396.

29 Joseph Anderson to Daniel Fidler, April 9, 1794, in French (ed.), "Daniel Fidler Papers," UCA *Bulletin* 12 (1959): 12.

30 Matthew Richey Papers, Matthew Richey to his wife's aunt, April 15, 1825.

31 WMC, *Minutes of Annual Conference*, 1835, 89; ibid., 1834, 71; MEC, *Minutes of Annual Conference*, 1829, 24; N.P. Goldhawk, "The Methodist People in the Early

Victorian Age: Spirituality and Worship," in Rupert Davies et al. (eds.), *A History of the Methodist Church in Great Britain,* (London: Epworth Press, 1965–88), 3:123; John Carroll, *Case and His Cotemporaries* (Toronto: Samuel Rose, 1867–77), 5:251.

32 Matthew Richey Papers, Matthew Richey to Louisa Richey (wife), August 17, 1846. See also Carroll, *My Boy Life,* 258–259; UCA Duncan McColl Papers, Anne Anderson to Alexander Anderson, June 9, 1807.

33 WMC, *Minutes of Annual Conference,* 1835, 103; MEC, *Minutes of Annual Conference,* 1830, 38. See also Marguerite Van Die, *An Evangelical Mind: Nathanael Burwash and the Methodist Tradition in Canada, 1839–1918* (Kingston: McGill-Queen's Univ. Press, 1989), 20.

34 George Burns, *Prayers Adapted for Public Worship, the Domestic Altar* (Saint John: Cameron & Seeds, 1829), 177. See also CCA, April 2, 1873, 1.

35 Thomas Webster, *History of the Methodist Episcopal Church in Canada* (Hamilton: Canada Christian Advocate Office, 1870), 57.

36 MEC, *Minutes of Annual Conference,* 1824, 4; ibid., 1826, 13. See also WMC, *Minutes of Annual Conference,* 1836, 123, 125.

37 Webster, 57.

38 *Nova Scotia and New Brunswick Wesleyan Methodist Magazine,* March 1832, 41.

39 See, For instance, CCA, October 6, 1846, 4; also A. Harold Wood, "Our Heritage in Charles Wesley's Hymns," in James Udy and Eric Clancy (eds.), *Dig or Die* (Sydney, Australia: World Methodist Historical Society, 1981), 49.

40 Ryerson, 38.

41 CCA, April 2, 1873, 1.

42 CG, October 2, 1833, 186. See also ibid., September 11, 1830, 338.

43 WMC, *Minutes of Annual Conference,* 1863, 99.

44 "A Good Wife," CG, November 28, 1829, 13. See also ibid., October 2, 1833, 186; January 8, 1831, 32; December 4, 1830, 10; July 31, 1831, 153; CCA, January 8, 1846, 4.

45 "A Good Husband," CG, November 28, 1829, 13. See also ibid., November 23, 1831, 5–6; CCA, May 24, 1871, 1; Hopper, 74–77.

46 CCA, May 5, 1846, 1.

47 Van Die, 24. See also Carroll, *My Boy Life,* 247; E. Arthur Betts, *Bishop Black and His Preachers: The Story of Maritimes Methodism to 1825* (Halifax, 1974), 3; Carroll, *Case,* 2:306; Playter, 41; UCA, Stephen Rice Papers, Diary, 304; CG, November 20, 1830, 2; February 5, 1831, 49.

48 CG, August 13, 1831, 157.

49 Ibid., November 28, 1829, 13; CCA, September 15, 1846, 1; WMC, *Minutes of Annual Conference,* 1836, 132.

50 CG, August 20, 1831, 161. See also ibid., December 12, 1829, 32.

51 Ibid., November 28, 1829, 12. See also ibid., August 6, 1831, 156; December 4, 1830, 10; November 20, 1830, 2; February 5, 1831, 49; March 19, 1831, 73.

52 Ibid., January 5, 1881, 1.

53 CMM, 10 (1879): 87. See also WMC, *Minutes of Annual Conference,* 1835, 103; 1839, 217–218; 1852, 205.

54 *The Doctrines and Discipline of the Methodist Episcopal Church* (1798), 133–4; MEC, *Doctrines and Discipline* (1829), 37–38, 81–83.

55 Christine McInnes, *Window on the Past: The Story of the Halifax Wesleyan Female Benevolent Society* (n.p., 1966). See also Betts, 61; M.I. Campbell, *No Other Foundations: A History of Zoar Methodist Church, Halifax* (n.p.), 100–101.

56 *CG*, August 15, 1832, 158; January 30, 1833, 45; Allen Robertson, "'Give All You Can': Methodists and Charitable Causes in Nineteenth-Century Nova Scotia," in Charles Scobie and John W. Grant (eds.), *The Contribution of Methodism to Atlantic Canada* (Montreal: McGill-Queen's Univ. Press, 1992), 92–103.

57 *CG*, October 15, 1831, 193.

58 Ibid., August 27, 1831, 165. See also ibid., May 30, 1832, 114; *CCA*, October 30, 1846, 4; July 28, 1846, 3; March 26, 1846, 1–2; July 14, 1846, 2; May 12, 1846, 1; May 30, 1848, 89.

59 MEC, *Minutes of Annual Conference*, 1830, 35; *CG*, December 5, 1829, 22; March 20, 1830, 138; July 31, 1830, 295; August 21, 1830, 316; July 9, 1831, 140; August 6, 1831, 156; May 14, 1831, 106.

60 Montreal Temperance Society, *An Appeal to the Inhabitants of Lower Canada, on the Use of Ardent Spirits* (Montreal, 1828), 11; Webster, 238; MEC, *Doctrines and Discipline* (1829); Dick, 531; Rideau Circuit, Minutes of Quarterly Official Board, January 1831; Charles R. Wood, "The Historical Development of the Temperance Movement in Canada" (BD, Emmanuel College, Victoria University, 1958), 12–13; *CG*, May 21 1831, 111.

61 *CG*, December 5, 1829, 22. See also ibid., February 20, 1830, 110.

62 MEC, MS Minutes of Annual Conference, 1830, 35–36. See also *CG*, October 2, 1830, 365; Webster, 245.

63 *CG*, April 24, 1830, 181. See also ibid., February 20, 1830, 110; August 21, 1830, 316; December 7, 1831, 16; January 16, 1833, 38. Some groups in Upper Canada went so far as to advocate that farmers not grow and millers not grind grain for distillers; see *CG*, April 9, 1831, 86; November 31, 1831, 12.

64 Winthrop P. Bell, *A Genealogical Study* (Sackville: Tribune Press, 1962); *CG*, April 24, 1830, 181.

65 *CG*, July 3, 1830, 262; Carroll, *Case*, 3:481–482; Dick, 532.

66 *CG*, April 24, 1830, 182. See also ibid., July 3, 1830, 262; Wood, 11–14; MEC, MS Minutes of Annual Conference, 1830, 39.

67 *An Appeal to the Inhabitants of Lower Canada*, 11; *CG*, February 13, 1830, 100.

68 *CG*, June 5, 1830, 230; May 14, 1831, 106; May 28, 1831, 114.

69 *CCA*, October 20, 1846, 2; *CG*, February 12, 1831, 56; March 28, 1832, 78.

70 *CG*, December 7, 1831, 16.

CHAPTER FOUR

1 George Peck, *Early Methodism within the Bounds of Genesee Conference, 1788–1829* (New York: Carlton & Porter, 1860), 501; Methodist Episcopal Church (US), *Journals of General Conference, 1796–1836*, 1820, 214; Norman McNairn, "The American Contribution to Early Methodism in Canada, 1790–1840" (ThD, Iliff School of Theology, 1969), 114; Nathan Hatch, *The Democratization of American Christianity* (New Haven: Yale Univ. Press. 1989).

2 John Carroll, *Case and His Cotemporaries* (Toronto: Samuel Rose, 1867–77), 2:396–397, 465; UCA Gordon Schroeder, "Henry Ryan: Arrogant Demagogue or Canadian Churchman?" (unpub., 1977).

3 Carroll, *Case*, 2:472.

4 Methodist Episcopal Church (US), *Journals of General Conference*, 1796–1836, 1824, 294; Nathan Bangs, *A History of the Methodist Episcopal Church* (New York: T. Mason, 1839–41), 3:274–279; Frederick Norwood, "A Crisis of Leadership: The General Conference of 1792," *Methodist History* 28 (1990): 195–201.

5 UCA, WMSC, Petition from Elders, Preachers, Deacons, Elizabethtown, Upper Canada, June 16, 1824; Carroll, *Case*, 2:465–466.

6 Carroll, *Case*, 2:326–327, 465–473; George Playter, *The History of Methodism in Canada* (Toronto: Anson Green, 1862), 235.

7 John S. Moir, *The Church in the British Era* (Toronto: McGraw-Hill Ryerson, 1972), 113; Thomas Webster, *History of the Methodist Episcopal Church in Canada* (Hamilton: Canada Christian Advocate Office, 1870), 213–215, MEC, *Minutes of Annual Conference*, 1824, 4–5; MEC, MS Minutes of Annual Conference, 1824, n.p.; Carroll, *Case*, 2:493.

8 Carroll, *Case*, 3:4–5, 24, 34. See also MEC, MS Minutes of Annual Conference, 1824, n.p.; MEC, *Minutes of Annual Conference*, 1824, 3.

9 Playter, 244–245; MEC, MS Minutes of Annual Conference, 1825, n.p.; 1828, n.p.; UCA, Joseph Gatchell Papers, MS Autobiography, 36; Webster, 201; Schroeder, 59–60; Carroll, *Case*, 3: 212–213; MEC, *Proceedings of the Canada Conference in the Case of Henry Ryan* (Kingston: S. Miles, 1829); UCA, Arthur Kewley, "The Trial of Henry Ryan" (unpub.); MEC, *Minutes of Annual Conference*, 1827, 14–15.

10 UCA, George Ferguson Papers, Journal, 1828, 82–85; MEC, MS Minutes of Annual Conference, 1829, 10–13; Carroll, *Case*, 3:233–237, 244–254; Playter, 299, 321; UCA Peter Fisher Papers, "Some Jottings Along My Life's Journey," 4–6; UCA Egerton Ryerson Papers, William Case to John Ryerson, November 17, 1828; ibid., John Ryerson to Egerton Ryerson, January 2, 1829; ibid., William Smith to William Ryerson, March 2, 1829.

11 Egerton Ryerson Papers, John Ryerson to Egerton Ryerson, May 18, 1828. The move to have Conference elect, rather than bishops appoint, presiding elders failed. The Canada Conference also established a committee in 1828 to promote cordial relations with British and American Methodism; see Carroll, *Case*, 3:213–217.

12 Queen's Univ., Archives, Methodist Papers, Egerton Ryerson to Franklin Metcalf, March 4, 1828.

13 MEC, *Minutes of Annual Conference*, 1828, 20; 1830, 33; Carroll, *Case*, 3:217; Egerton Ryerson Papers, William Case to Egerton Ryerson, March 19, 1829.

14 George Ferguson Papers, Journal, 1828, 85; MEC, *Minutes of Annual Conference*, 1824, 2; 1828, 19–20; 1832, 47–49; W. Stewart Wallace, *The Ryerson Imprint* (Toronto: Ryerson Press, 1954), 9.

15 Nathanael Burwash, *The History of Victoria College* (Toronto: Victoria University, 1927), 4–7, 15–24, 43–58; Charles Bruce Sissons, *A History of Victoria University* (Toronto: Univ. of Toronto Press, 1952), 1–22; UCA, William Lamb, "Young Men from Upper Canada who attended Cazenovia Seminary" (unpub., 1983).

16 WMSC, William Lunn to Missionary Secretaries, February 3, 1824.

17 WMSC, Joseph Stinson to Joseph Taylor, September 23, 1824; ibid., Joseph Stinson to Joseph Taylor, October 18, 1824; ibid., Robert Alder to Missionary Secretaries, June 13, 1826.

18 John W. Grant, *A Profusion of Spires: Religion in Nineteenth-Century Ontario* (Toronto: Univ. of Toronto Press, 1988), 86; Gerald Craig, *Upper Canada: The Formative Years, 1784–1841* (Toronto: McClelland & Stewart, 1963).

19 Egerton Ryerson, *The Story of My Life*, ed. J.G. Hodgins (Toronto: Wm. Briggs, 1883), 102; Grant, 8; WMC, *Minutes of Annual Conferences, 1824–1845*, appendix, 399–402.

20 Graeme Patterson, "Early Compact Groups in the Politics of York," in David Keane and Colin Read (eds.), *Old Ontario: Essays in Honour of J.M.S. Careless* (Toronto: Dundurn Press, 1990); Alan Wilson, *The Clergy Reserves in Upper Canada: A Canadian Mortmain* (Toronto: Univ. of Toronto Press, 1968).

21 Ryerson, *The Story of My Life*, 95–106; Adam Townley, *Ten Letters on the Church and Church Establishments* (Toronto: Commercial Herald, 1839).

22 Carroll, *Case*, 3:47; WMSC, Robert Alder to George Morley, November 23, 1826; ibid., Joseph Stinson to Robert Alder, April 21, 1834.

23 Curtis Fahey, *In His Name: The Anglican Experience in Upper Canada, 1791–1854* (Ottawa: Carleton Univ. Press, 1991), 61; William Westfall, *Two Worlds: The Protestant Culture of Nineteenth-Century Ontario* (Kingston: McGill-Queen's Univ. Press, 1989), chap. 2; John S. Moir, "The Political Ideas of the *Christian Guardian*, 1829–1849" (MA, Univ. of Toronto, 1949), 11–12; WMSC, Robert Alder to John James, August 15, 1832; ibid., Robert Alder to (Br.) Parliamentary Committee on Canadian Affairs, June 28, 1828.

24 N.P. Goldhawk, "The Methodist People in the Early Victorian Age: Spirituality and Worship," in Rupert Davies et al. (eds.), *A History of the Methodist Church in Great Britain* (London: Epworth Press, 1965–88), 2:117. See also WMSC, Robert Alder to Missionary Secretaries, April 1, 1824; ibid., Robert Alder to George Morley, June 4, 1827; Robert Alder, *The Substance of a Sermon ... on the occasion of the Death of ... the Duke of York* (Montreal: Mower, 1827), 27; "Robert Alder," DCB, 10:3–5; Ralph Reed, "From Riots to Revivalism: The Gordon Riots of 1780," *Methodist History* 26 (1988); William Pierce, *The Ecclesiastical Principles and Polity of the Wesleyan Methodists* (London: Hamilton, Adams, 1868), 759.

25 WMSC, Wesleyan Methodist Missionary Society, Extract of Minutes, February 15, 1832.

26 CG, January 4, 1832, 30; January 18, 1832, 38; WMSC, Robert Alder to Sir John Colborne, 1830; ibid., E. MacMahon to James Townley, October 13, 1831, forwarded by Thomas Turner, October 26, 1831; ibid., Richard Watson to Lord Goderich, November 22, 1832; C.B. Sissons, *Egerton Ryerson: His Life and Letters* (Toronto: Clark, Irwin, 1937), 1:145–147; Moir, *The Church in the British Era*, 119–120; Goldwin S. French, *Parsons and Politics* (Toronto: Ryerson Press, 1962), 134.

27 WMSC, Wesleyan Methodist Missionary Society, Extract of Minutes, May 11, 1831.

28 Ibid., Missionary Society of the Methodist Episcopal Church in Upper Canada to Missionary Secretaries, October 14, 1831.

29 Ibid., Wesleyan Methodist Missionary Society, Extract of Minutes, February 15, 1832; May 11, 1831; ibid., John Ryerson to Missionary Secretaries, October 14, 1831; French, 134; Egerton Ryerson, *Canadian Methodism: Its Epochs and Characteristics* (Toronto: Wm. Briggs, 1882), 300.

30 Moir, *The Church in the British Era*, 120; French, 134; Samuel D. Clark, *Church and Sect in Canada* (Toronto: Univ. of Toronto Press, 1948), 203–204; WMSC, Kingston Quarterly Board to Missionary Secretaries, November 14, 1831.

31 Egerton Ryerson Papers, James Howard to Egerton Ryerson, December 11, 1828.

32 WMSC, Wesleyan Methodist Church, Minutes of General Committee, petition to British Parliament, June 19, 1828.

33 MEC, *Minutes of Annual Conference*, 1828, 20; Egerton Ryerson Papers, William Case to Egerton Ryerson, March 19, 1829; WMSC, John Ryerson to Missionary Secretaries, May 31, 1831; ibid., Egerton Ryerson to Richard Watson, October 19, 1831.

34 Egerton Ryerson Papers, George Ryerson to Egerton Ryerson, August 6, 1831; CG, November 30, 1831, 10; John W. Grant, *The Canadian Experience of Church Union* (London: Lutterworth Press, 1967), 13; French, 137; WMSC, MEC, Missionary Society, Extract of Minutes to Missionary Secretaries, July 2, 1832.

35 WMSC, Robert Alder to Richard Watson, July 16, 1832. See also ibid., Robert Alder to Upper Canada Conference in session, August 15, 1832.

36 WMSC, Robert Alder to Richard Watson, July 16, 1832; Robert Alder to Sir John Colborne, August 27, 1832, quoted in Thomas Webster, *The Union Considered and the Methodist Episcopal Church in Canada Defended* (Belleville: Victoria Chronicle, 1842), 11–12, 78–80. The abandonment of the episcopacy was contingent on it not detrimentally affecting the ownership of church property; See Carroll, *Case*, 3:354–363; MEC, *Minutes of Annual Conference*, 1832, 50–51.

37 WMC, *Minutes of Annual Conference*, 1833, 65. See also Elizabeth Cooper, "Religion, Politics and Money: The Methodist Union of 1832–1833," *Ontario History* 81 (1989).

38 WMC, *Minutes of Annual Conference*, 1833, 67. Carroll, *Case*, 3:404–411; G.G. Findlay and W.W. Holdsworth, *The History of the Wesleyan Methodist Missionary Society* (London: Epworth Press, 1921), 1:425: CG, October 16, 1833, 193–194; August 29, 1832, 167; March 16, 1833, 67; WMSC, Egerton Ryerson to Robert Alder, October 10, 1833.

39 French, 137; John Carroll, *The School of the Prophets* (Toronto: Burridge & Magurn, 1876), 185; CG, August 29, 1832, 167; WMSC, Egerton Ryerson to Missionary Secretaries, October 9, 1833.

40 WMSC, Wesleyan Methodist Missionary Society, Minutes, December 20, 1833. See also ibid., Thomas Turner to Missionary Secretaries, March 16, 1832.

41 WMSC, Robert Alder to Richard Watson, July 16, 1832. See also ibid., Robert Alder to John James, July 14, 1832; ibid., Joseph Stinson to Missionary Secretaries, November 13, 1833; CG, October 16, 1833, 194.

42 WMSC, Sir John Colborne to Robert Alder, July 14, 1832.

43 WMC, *Minutes of Annual Conference*, 1833, 55–56.

44 CG, May 15, 1832, 106; UCA, Benjamin Slight Papers, Journal, 1833; Carroll, *Case*, 3:394–395; George Cornish, *Cyclopaedia of Methodism in Canada* (Toronto: Methodist Book Room, 1881, 1905), 1:65, 82, 99; WMSC, Joseph Stinson to Robert Alder, December 31, 1833; ibid., Egerton Ryerson to Robert Alder, October 10, 1833; ibid., William Croscombe to John Hick, May 31, 1833; ibid., Robert Alder to Missionary Secretaries, May 19, 1834; Egerton Ryerson Papers, John Ryerson to Egerton Ryerson, November 7, 1833.

45 WMC, *Minutes of Annual Conference*, 1835, 102. See also WMSC, Joseph Stinson to Jabez Bunting, March 15, 1834; Clark, 297.

46 WMSC, Joseph Stinson to Robert Alder, April 21, 1834; ibid., Joseph Stinson to Robert Alder, November 11, 1833; ibid., Stewards (York) to Wesleyan Missionary Society, January 20, 1834.

47 WMSC, Wesleyan Missionary Society, Extract of Minutes, December 6, 1833; ibid., December 20, 1833; ibid., Joseph Stinson to Robert Alder, April 21, 1834; ibid., Letter of Censure and Inquiry, Jabez Bunting to William Croscombe, December 30, 1833; ibid., John Beecham to John Barry, April 25, 1834; ibid., Robert Alder to Jabez Bunting and John Beecham, May 19, 1834; ibid., Joseph Stinson to Jabez Bunting, March 15, 1834.

48 WMSC, Egerton Ryerson to James Richardson (with MS Minutes of Montreal District meeting), May 16, 1834; ibid., Egerton Ryerson to Robert Alder, May 21, 1834; ibid., Joseph Stinson to Joseph Taylor, June 4, 1834; Ibid., Egerton Ryerson to Robert Alder, July 10, 1834; ibid., Joseph Stinson to Robert Alder, September 16, 1834; ibid., Robert Alder to Committee of House of Commons (Br.), June 28, 1828.

49 WMSC, Egerton Ryerson to Robert Alder, October 10, 1833; ibid., Local preacher (Fenton), address re local preachers' rights, February 28, 1833; CCA, December 8, 1846, 2; UCA, Nelson Circuit, MEC, Minutes of Quarterly Meeting, January 1833; Webster, *Union Considered*, 46–49; Carroll, *Case*, 3:439–442.

50 *CG*, June 6, 1832, 118; March 6, 1833, 66; March 13, 1833, 70; April 10, 1833, 82; Webster, *Union Considered*, 32–33.

51 John Shearman, "A Local Response to the Union/Secession Crisis of 1834 in the Nelson Circuit," CMHS, *Papers* 6 (1987): 4–7; Henry H. Walsh, *The Christian Church in Canada* (Toronto: Ryerson Press, 1956), 180–181; Peter Fisher Papers, "Jottings," 30–45; *CG*, July 17, 1833, 142–143; July 24, 1833, 146–147.

52 WMSC, Egerton Ryerson to Robert Alder, August 23, 1832. See also ibid., Joseph Stinson to Missionary Secretaries, February 7, 1834.

53 *CG*, September 5, 1832, 170; March 27, 1833, 78; November 27, 1833, 10; WMSC, Egerton Ryerson to Robert Alder, July 10, 1834; Egerton Ryerson Papers, James Richardson to Egerton Ryerson, April 8, 1833.

54 Egerton Ryerson Papers, Edwy Ryerson to Egerton Ryerson, November 26, 1833. See also WMSC, Egerton Ryerson to Robert Alder, November 13, 1833; Egerton Ryerson Papers, John Ryerson to Egerton Ryerson, January 8, 1834; ibid., James Evans to Egerton Ryerson, December 3, 1833; French, 143; UCA Portraits and Letters of Presidents of the Canada Conference, Edmund Grindrod to Egerton Ryerson, March 4, 1834; ibid., George Marsden to Egerton Ryerson, September 4, 1834.

55 *CG*, October 16, 1833, 194; November 27, 1833, 10. See ibid., September 5, 1832, 170, for Richardson's opinion on right to intervene in political questions; also WMSC, Egerton Ryerson to Robert Alder, May 21, 1834; Egerton Ryerson Papers, John Ryerson to Egerton Ryerson, April 8, 1832; ibid., John Ryerson to Egerton Ryerson, November 7, 1833; ibid., John Ryerson to Egerton Ryerson, November 15, 1833.

56 Carroll, *The School of the Prophets*, 238; Joseph Gatchell Papers, MS Autobiography, 49; George Cornish, *Hand-book of Canadian Methodism* (Toronto: Wesleyan Book Room, 1867), 29; MEC, *Minutes of Niagara Conference*, 1863, 38–39; Carroll, *Case*,

1:255–263; 3:313–314, 447–450; UCA, John Reynolds Papers, Philip Roblin to John Reynolds, December 21, 1833; ibid., Philip Roblin to John Reynolds, February 20, 1834; UCA, John Reynolds biographical file; Cornish, *Cyclopaedia of Methodism*, 1:46–47.

57 Cornish, *Cyclopaedia of Methodism*, 1:130, 140; "James Richardson," *DCB*, 10:617; Carroll, *Case*, 4:3, 116–117, 155–156.

58 AO, Samuel Rose Papers, Samuel Rose to John Rose, December 16, 1835; WMC, *Minutes of Annual Conference*, 1834, 77. See also WMC, *Minutes of Annual Conference* 1836, 130; Carroll, *Case*, 4:21, 42–43.

59 Webster, *Union Considered*, 10–11, 14, 18, 20, 32–33, 53; CCA, February 19, 1852, 2; John Carroll, *A Needed Exposition on the Claims and Allegations of the Canadian Episcopals* (Toronto: Samuel Rose, 1877).

60 George Ferguson Papers, Journal, 92–93.

61 MEC, *Minutes of Annual Conference*, 1836, 3; 1843, 5; Carroll, *Case*, 4:100–101, 134–141, 400–403; CCA, February 19, 1852, 2; Webster, *Union Considered*, 41–45, 72–73, 82–120; *Methodist Chapel Property Case* (Toronto: Conference Office, 1837); Upper Canada Queen's Bench, *Reports*, old series, 5 (1837): 344–433.

62 Carroll, *Case*, 4:152, 184, 271; Portraits and Letters of Presidents of the Canada Conference, Joseph Stinson to Egerton Ryerson, November 2, 1838; Egerton Ryerson Papers, D.M. McMullen to Egerton Ryerson, June 7, 1839. Ironically, Ephraim Evans, who opposed the political use of the *Guardian*, was the only editor to condemn American slavery and the mistreatment of Canadian blacks.

63 WMC, *Minutes of Annual Conference*, 1837, 166. See also ibid., 1835, 96; Carroll, *Case*, 4:4, 299; Portraits and Letters of Presidents of the Canada Conference, Anson Green to Egerton Ryerson, July 26, 1837.

64 WMC, *Minutes of Annual Conference*, 1837, 166–167.

65 Ibid., 1838, 202; Carroll, *Case*, 4:199–200; Portraits and Letters of Presidents of the Canada Conference, Joseph Stinson to Egerton Ryerson, November 2, 1838.

66 Findlay and Holdsworth, 1:436–437; Carroll, *Case*, 4:237–245; Benjamin Slight Papers, Journal, June 12, 1839; WMC, *Minutes of Annual Conference*, 1839, 212.

67 Joseph Stinson and Matthew Richey to Hon. Poulett Thompson (Lord Sydenham), January 3, 1840, in Joseph Stinson and Matthew Richey, *A Plain Statement of Facts connected with the union and separation of the British and Canadian Conferences* (Toronto: R. Stanton, 1840), 44. See also Carroll, *Case*, 4:238; Missionary Secretary to Sir George Arthur, February 8, 1839, in *Documents Relating to the Recent Determination of the British Wesleyan Conference to Dissolve Official Union with the Provincial Conference of Upper Canada* (London: Mason, 1841), 66–7; "Matthew Richey," *DCB*, 11:733–735.

68 Egerton Ryerson to Lord Sydenham, January 17, 1840, in *A Plain Statement of Facts*, 36. See also Robert Alder to Lord John Russell, December 28, 1840, in *Documents relating to the Recent Determination*, appendix 1:49, 54–59.

69 Robert Alder to John Russell, April 29, 1840, in *Documents relating to the Recent Determination*, 1–3; ibid., December 28, 1840, appendix 1; Webster, *Union Considered*, 12–13.

70 Carroll, *Case*, 4:299; Missionary Committee to Canada Conference, April 29, 1840, in *Documents Relating to the Recent Determination*, 1; ibid., William Lord to Robert Alder, September 12, 1840, 65; WMSC, Egerton Ryerson to Robert Alder, May 21, 1834; CG, September 30, 1840, 195; Walsh, 214–215.

71 Findlay and Holdsworth, 1:439; UCA, John Douse Papers, John Douse to wife, June 15, 1840; WMC, *Minutes of Annual Conference*, 1840, 233.

72 Egerton Ryerson Papers, Egerton Ryerson to Lord John Russell, July 27, 1840; WMC, *Minutes of Annual Conference*, 1840, 241; Carroll, *Case*, 4:300.

73 Donald B. Smith, *Sacred Feathers: The Reverend Peter Jones (Kahkewaquonaby) and the Mississauga Indians* (Lincoln: Univ. of Nebraska Press, 1987), 152–153; WMC, *Minutes of Annual Conference*, Special Conference, October 1840, 245–302; Carroll, *Case*, 4:313, 321–324, 356, 377–381.

74 Carroll, *Case*, 4:324–343, WMC *Minutes of Annual Conference (Br.)*, 1841, 214.

75 WMC, *Minutes of Annual Conference*, 1840, 232; ibid., 1841, 266; Carroll, *Case*, 4: 295–297, 320, 327; George Ferguson Papers, Journal, 98, 106; MEC, *Minutes of Annual Conference*, 1840, 9.

76 WMSC, William Harvard to Robert Alder, April 19, 1843; Westfall, 166–174; Grant, *A Profusion of Spires*, 73, 114–116, 161, 167; W.W. Andrews, *The Catholic Apostolic Church* (1877); David Arthur, "Come Out of Babylon: A Study of Millerite Separatism and Denominationalism, 1840–1865" (PhD, Univ. of Rochester, 1970); Carroll, *Case*, 4:477; William Henry Draper, *Ten Letters on the Church and Church Establishments* (Toronto: Commercial Herald, 1839); Henry Esson, *A Plain and Popular Exposition on the Principles of Voluntaryism* (Toronto: J. Cleland, 1849); Thomas McCrie, *On Church Establishments* (Glasgow: Ogle, 1832); Douglas Morgan, "Adventism, Apocalyptic, and the Cause of Freedom," *Church History* 63 (1994): 235–249; WMC, *Minutes of Annual Conference*, 1837, 172.

77 CCA, June 16, 1846, 2; Carroll, *Case*, 4:396, 432–435; Egerton Ryerson, *The Story of My Life*, 395–396; Egerton Ryerson, *Sir Charles Metcalfe Defended against the Attacks of his Late Counsellors* (Toronto: British Colonist Office, 1844). In 1840 the clergy reserves were transferred to British jurisdiction.

78 WMSC, William Harvard to Robert Alder, April 19, 1843; Benjamin Slight Papers, Journal, 11, August 7, 1842; Egerton Ryerson Papers, Egerton Ryerson to John Scott, December 23, 1841; ibid., John Ryerson to Egerton Ryerson, June 24, 1845.

79 Carroll, *Case*, 4:407–408, 431–433, 449, 478–485; 5:2, 88–90; Portraits and Letters of Presidents of the Canada Conference, Anson Green to Jabez Bunting, July 12, 1847; ibid., Egerton Ryerson to Nathan Bangs, May 10, 1841.

80 WMC, *Minutes of Annual Conference*, 1847, 35–38; CCA September 1, 1846, 1; National Archives of Canada, RG 1 E5, v. 13, W. Badgeley and Henry Draper, legal opinion re grants to Methodists.

81 CCA, October 20, 1846, 2; December 22, 1846, 2; April 4, 1848, 2; Anson Green, *The Life and Times of the Rev. Anson Green* (Toronto: Methodist Book Room, 1877), 348; MEC, *Minutes of Annual Conference*, 1847, 28. The *Canada Christian Advocate* had been established in 1845, and the Episcopal Methodists had over two thousand adherents in Lower Canada in 1851

82 *Globe* (Toronto), August 14, 1852, 390. See also MEC, *Minutes of Annual Conference*, 1847, 28; WMC, *Minutes of Annual Conference*, 1850, 134, 137, AO, Shefford Circuit, Wesleyan Methodist Church, Minute Book, 1852–53.

83 WMC, *Minutes of Annual Conference*, 1854, 261; 1855, 239. The number of adherents is drawn from the census of 1852.

84 Green, 345; Michael Owen, "'Nurseries of the Church of God': British Wesleyan Missions in Rupert's Land, 1840–1854," CMHS, *Papers* 3 (1983).

CHAPTER FIVE

1 Harlan Douglass and Ernest Brunner, *The Protestant Church as a Social Institution* (New York: Russell & Russell, 1935), 33. See also WMC, *Minutes of Annual Conference*, 1835, 99; Thomas Acheson, "Methodism and the Problem of Methodist Identity in Nineteenth-Century New Brunswick," in Charles Scobie and John W. Grant (eds.), *The Contribution of Methodism to Atlantic Canada* (Montreal: McGill-Queen's Univ. Press, 1992), 107–126.

2 UCA, MS Minutes of the Annual Meeting of the Wesleyan Methodist Missionaries of Newfoundland, Nova Scotia, and New Brunswick Districts, 1827. All subsequent statistics in this section are from the same source for the appropriate year unless otherwise cited. All these statistics must be viewed with some suspicion, but they do help elaborate certain trends.

3 These district totals equal 11,890 members. However, the WMCEBA, *Minutes of Annual Conference*, 1855, reports 13,136 members. I cannot explain the discrepancy.

4 See for example, WMC (Br.), Minutes of Nova Scotia District, 1833, 157; 1835, 209; ibid., Special Meeting, July 1839, 336; 1846, n.p. Yarmouth circuit was badly divided in 1831 because of the arrival of a popular Baptist minister (see Minutes of Nova Scotia District, 1831, 115) and again in 1835, when an Anglican minister took over many Wesleyans.

5 Goldwin S. French, *Parsons and Politics* (Toronto: Ryerson Press, 1962), 198. French is somewhat more optimistic about increases in membership because of expansion into new areas of New Brunswick.

6 Minutes of Newfoundland District, 1843, 1854, n.p.

7 UCA, WMSC, Ephraim Evans to Missionary Secretaries, December 11, 1851.

8 Minutes of Nova Scotia District, 1827, 6.

9 French, 87; Minutes of Nova Scotia District, 1836, 259; G.G. Findlay and W.W. Holdsworth, *The History of the Wesleyan Methodist Missionary Society* (London: Epworth Press, 1921), 1:334.

10 Minutes of Nova Scotia District, 1832, 143; 1834, 197.

11 French, 88–90, 198.

12 William Brooks, "The Changing Character of Maritime Wesleyan Methodism, 1855–1883" (MA, Mount Allison University, 1965), 20, 35; French, 199–200. This desire to control local affairs frequently meant they wanted to be able to spend money, often irresponsibly, without having to report to the Missionary Committee. See, for example, WMSC, Enoch Wood to Robert Alder, July 16, 1842.

13 Minutes of Newfoundland District, 1824, n.p. A few examples may suffice: In New Brunswick district in 1827, the grant was £194, while the deficit was £234; in Nova Scotia district in 1839, £1,434 was budgeted and £2,874 spent; and finally in 1854, when the committee stopped covering deficits, the Nova Scotia districts spent £386 more than the combined total of local receipts and the missionary grant.

14 Minutes of Nova Scotia District, 1832, 143; 1836, n.p.; 1844, n.p.; Minutes of Newfoundland District, 1854, n.p.; WMSC, Robert Alder to Missionary Committee, January 13, 1823; ibid., Robert Alder to George Morley, June 4, 1823; ibid., Enoch Wood to Robert Alder, July 16, 1842; T. Watson Smith, *History of the Methodist*

*Church within the Territories embraced in the Late Conference of Eastern British America* (Halifax: Methodist Book Room, 1877, 1890), 2:435; Brooks, 50.

15 "The Wesleyan," *Encyclopedia of World Methodism*, 2:2522; Minutes of Nova Scotia District, 1833, 168–169; French, 92.

16 Minutes of Nova Scotia District, 1833, 168–169.

17 French, 92–93.

18 Ibid., 200.

19 Minutes of Nova Scotia District, 1833, 174–175, 186; French, 93–94; John G. Reid, *Mount Allison University: A History, to 1963* (Toronto: Univ. of Toronto Press, 1984), 1:4–5.

20 Minutes of Nova Scotia District, Special Meeting, July 1839, 337–338. See also David W. Johnson, *History of Methodism in Eastern British America* (Sackville: Tribune Printing, 1925), 365; French, 204; "Charles Allison," *DCB* 8:15–16.

21 Reid, 1:3–6, 21–23, 57–61; WMSC, Enoch Wood to Robert Alder, January 29, 1842; ibid., William Temple to Robert Alder, January 27, 1842; ibid., William Temple to Jabez Bunting, January 27, 1842; John G. Reid, "The Education of Women at Mount Allison, 1854–1914," *Acadiensis* 12 (1983): 4–10; "Humphrey Pickard," *DCB*, 11:687–688.

22 Minutes of Nova Scotia District, Special Meeting, July 1839, 339.

23 Minutes of Nova Scotia District, 1843; UCA, Portraits and Letters of Presidents of the Canada Conference, William Lord to James Matthewson, January 3, 1842.

24 WMSC, Enoch Wood to Missionary Secretaries, July 30, 1842.

25 WMSC, Ephraim Evans to Missionary Secretaries, December 11, 1851: "I am persuaded that the time is not very remote when, by the blessing of God, the District will be self-sustaining." Evans went on to request "a well digested proposal" for a separate conference. He reiterated his request a few months later; see WMSC, Ephraim Evans to Missionary Secretaries, February 4, 1852.

26 WMSC, Ephraim Evans to Missionary Secretaries, February 12, 1851. Between 1846 and 1849, the Nova Scotia district's deficit beyond missionary grants averaged £244 per year. In 1850 it was only £70, and Evans hoped to break even in 1851. He met with the district officials, "encouraging them in their efforts to promote the spiritual interests of the Societies, and of explaining and bringing into more efficient operation our financial economy." Nevertheless, he wanted to use any excess in the 1851 grants to pay off the £70 deficit from 1850 since it remained an embarrassment to the connexion. The British Conference deficit for 1855 was estimated at £38,779 (Brooks, 66).

27 Brooks, 60, 68–69.

28 Thomas Goldsmith, *A Manual of the Distinctive Features of the Polity of the Canadian Wesleyan Methodist New Connexion Church* (London, CW: Conference Office, 1859), 6.

29 "Methodist New Connexion," *Encyclopedia of World Methodism*, 2:1576–1577; "Alexander Kilham," ibid., 1:1333; "William Thom," ibid., 2:2335.

30 Goldsmith, 6; N. P. Goldhawk, "The Methodist People in the Early Victorian Age: Spirituality and Worship," in Rupert Davies et al. (eds.), *A History of the Methodist Church in Great Britain* (London: Epworth Press, 1965–88), 2:118.

31 UCA Albert Burnside, "The Canadian Wesleyan Methodist New Connexion Church, 1841–1874" (unpub., 1967), 6, 11; *Methodist New Connexion Magazine*, 6

(February 1838): 77; *Minutes of the 41st Annual Conference of the Methodist New Connexion*, 1837, 45.

32 "Methodist Protestant Church," *Encyclopedia of World Methodism*, 2:1578–1579. See also Methodist Episcopal Church, *Journal of General Conferences, 1796–1836*, 1820, 1824, 1828, 1832; Burnside, 14–17; William Williams, "Historical Sketch of the Methodist New Connexion Church in Canada," in *Centennial of Canadian Methodism* (Toronto: Wm. Briggs, 1891), 95–100.

33 John Carroll, *Case and His Cotemporaries* (Toronto: Samuel Rose, 1867–77), 4:294–295; Goldsmith, 10–12.

34 NCC, *Minutes of Annual Conference*, 1840, 15. See also WMSC, John Williams to Robert Alder, June 1832; Burnside, 28.

35 NCC, *Minutes of Annual Conferences, 1835–41*. The number of preachers listed were 1835, 63; 1836, 49; 1837, 39; 1838, 44; 1839, 39; 1840, 33. Among others, in 1836 Donald Frazer and Matthew Dunbar were expelled and A.K. McKenzie, the previous secretary, withdrew. In 1838 H.R. Smith, the previous secretary, withdrew and S. Bougnet was expelled. The following year I.N.D. West was expelled. In 1840, Abraham Crouter and John Sanderson were expelled, and Robert Earl, the preceding year's president, Moses Blackstock, president in 1837 and 1838, and Alexander Anderson withdrew. In 1841 Kennedy Creighton, previous secretary, and James Culham also withdrew. See *Canadian Wesleyan*, November 8, 1832 (one issue extant); Goldsmith, 9–10, 18; UCA, James Jackson biographical file; "James Jackson," *DCB*, 8:422–423; Burnside, 27.

36 Burnside, 1, 34, 40–45, 58.

37 NCC, *Minutes of the Annual Conference*, 1844, 7; Burnside, 30, 68. The church changed its name in 1863 to the Methodist New Connexion Church in Canada. Basically, this change involved dropping the term "Wesleyan," which had been offensive to the British church, but was a proud badge to the early Ryanites. By 1863 the reasons for its inclusion had been long forgotten. See Williams, 109; Carroll, *Case*, 4:484.

38 NCC, *Minutes of Annual Conference*, 1855, 7; 1846, 7–8; 1854, 11; William Westfall, "The Sacred and the Secular: Studies in the Cultural History of Protestant Ontario in the Victorian Period" (PhD, Univ. of Toronto, 1976), appendices; Neil Semple, "The Impact of Urbanization on the Methodist Church in Central Canada, 1854–1884" (PhD, Univ. of Toronto, 1979), 55–57; Burnside 46.

39 "Primitive Methodists," *Encyclopedia of World Methodism*, 2:1950–1952. Lorenzo Dow (1777–1834) was a Methodist preacher born in Connecticut who began preaching in 1794. He travelled to Britain in 1799, 1805, and 1818 introducing camp-meeting revivals to the country. Although his techniques were condemned by the Wesleyans, they gained him widespread fame and influence among sections of discontented Methodists.

40 John Hoover, "The Primitive Methodist Church in Canada, 1829–1884" (MA, Univ. of Western Ontario, 1970), 9; John Petty, *The History of the Primitive Methodist Connexion to 1859* (London: Conference Office, 1860), 3, 25; "Hugh Bourne," *Encyclopedia of World Methodism*, 1:307.

41 Petty, 4–5; "William Clowes," *Encyclopedia of World Methodism*, 1:526.

42 Robert Cade's speech to the Jubilee Meeting, Alice Street church, October 11, 1860 in *CJ*, October 20, 1860; Petty, 40.

43 Hoover, 16–20, 34; *Primitive Methodist Magazine*, January 1829, 25–27, 33; February 1829, 42–46, 56; May, 1831, 184–187; July 1838, 253–257; Elizabeth Muir, *Petticoats in the Pulpit: The Story of Early Nineteenth-Century Methodist Women Preachers in Upper Canada* (Toronto: United Church Publishing House, 1991), 36–41, 85–101.

44 Hoover, 18–28; Petty, 80–90; "Primitive Methodists," *Encyclopedia of World Methodism*, 2:1951.

45 Hoover 34–42. See also Petty, 254.

46 Petty, 252–254; Hoover, 76–82. Lawson moved to Brampton, where he opened a general store in 1834 and helped develop Primitive Methodism in the community. He later returned to Toronto and reopened his store there. Later still, he turned the Toronto store over to his son and moved permanently to Hamilton. Primitive Methodist strongholds followed his movements. Robert Walker gave considerable sums to the church. See Mrs R.P. Hopper, *Old-time Primitive Methodism in Canada* (Toronto: Wm. Briggs, 1904), 20, 44–46.

47 Hoover, 83–85.

48 UCA, Primitive Methodist Conference, Correspondence, William Summersides to William Clowes, September 1833; ibid., William Summersides to William Flesher, October 17, 1833; Hoover, 88–100.

49 Hoover, 103, 116; Primitive Methodist Conference, Correspondence, William Summersides to William Clowes, July 1, 1835; ibid., William Summersides to William Clowes, June 14, 1836; ibid., William Summersides to William Clowes, September 7, 1836; ibid., William Summersides to William Clowes, April 14, 1837.

50 Hoover, 118.

51 Robert Cade, "Primitive Methodism in Canada," address to Canadian Methodist Historical Society, 1906, 7.

52 Hoover, 131–132.

53 Ibid., 134–143; UCA, John Davison biographical file.

54 PMC, *Minutes of Annual Conference*, 1855, 3; Hoover, 144–160; *Evangelist*, March 1851, 37–38.

55 John Kent, "The Wesleyan Methodists to 1849," in *A History of the Methodist Church in Great Britain*, 2:214; "Bible Christians," *Encyclopedia of World Methodism*, 1:267.

56 William Luke, *The Bible Christians: Their Origin, Constitution, Doctrines and History* (London: Bible Christian Book Room, 1878), 1–5; John C. Wilkinson, "The Rise of the Other Methodist Traditions," in *A History of the Methodist Church in Great Britain*, 2:294–303; Albert Burnside, "The Bible Christians in Canada, 1832–1884" (ThD, Toronto Graduate School of Theological Studies, 1969), 4–12.

57 BCC (Br.), *Minutes of Annual Conference*, 1835, 11–13.

58 Burnside, "The Bible Christians in Canada," 13, 20–23; "Bible Christians," *Encyclopedia of World Methodism*, 1:267–268.

59 Luke, 6; Burnside, "The Bible Christians in Canada," 19.

60 Elizabeth Muir, "Methodist Women Preachers: An Overview," CMHS, *Papers* 7 (1987): 51–52; *Minutes of the First Conference of the Preachers in Connexion with William O'Bryan* (1819), 6–7; Muir, *Petticoats in the Pulpit*, 41–48; BCC (Br.), *Minutes of Annual Conference*, 1838.

61 Burnside, "The Bible Christians in Canada," 38, 46–48; Harris, *The Life of Frances Metherall and the History of the Bible Christian Church in Prince Edward Island*, (London: Bible Christian Book Room, 1883), 33–34.

62 Harris, 33–34; *Bible Christian Magazine*, October 1833, 67–69.

63 *Bible Christian Magazine*, April 1833, 68.

64 BCC (Br.), *Minutes of Annual Conference*, 1835, 8; *Bible Christian Magazine*, November 1835, 49–50; Burnside, "The Bible Christians in Canada," 68–69, 88.

65 BCC (Br.), *Minutes of Annual Conference*, 1849, "Missionary Society Reports," 21. See also Harris, 49, 54, 68.

66 Harris, 82.

67 George Webber, "Bible Christian Church," in *Centennial of Canadian Methodism*, 210; *Bible Christian Magazine*, June 1834, 110–112; May 1835, 73–75.

68 BCC, *Minutes of Annual Conference*, 1865, 13. See also MC, *Minutes of Toronto Conference*, 1890, 75; Burnside, "The Bible Christians in Canada" 103; *Bible Christian Magazine*, December 1853, 474–476; "Elizabeth Dart Eynon," DCB, 8:200–201; "Ann Vickery Robins," DCB, 8:908–909.

69 BCC, *A Digest of the Rules and Regulations of the People Denominated Bible Christians* (Cobourg: Bible Christian Book Room, 1866), 19.

70 Burnside, "The Bible Christians in Canada," 78, 88; *Bible Christian Magazine*, July 1849, 257–260.

71 Webber, 212–213; letter from Philip James to Missionary Committee, September 11, 1847, in *Bible Christian Magazine*, January 1848.

72 BCC (Br.), *Minutes of Annual Conference*, 1849, 18.

73 Burnside, "The Bible Christians in Canada," 141–151; BCC (Br.), *Minutes of Annual Conference*, 1849, 19.

74 BCC, *Digest of the Rules*, 78–79.

75 Harris, 35–41; Burnside, "The Bible Christians in Canada," 108–109; BCC, *Minutes of Annual Conference*, 1856, 7, 11–12.

76 Semple, 47–49, 52.

77 Russell Richey, "Community, Fraternity and Order in Methodism," CMHS, *Papers*, 4 (1984): 5. John Wesley opposed slavery and worked to promote better treatment of blacks.

78 Carol George, *Segregated Sabbaths: Richard Allen and the Rise of Independent Black Churches, 1760–1840* (New York: Oxford Univ. Press, 1973), 15–17; Lewis V. Baldwin, *"Invisible" Strands in African Methodism: A History of the African Union Methodist Protestant and Union American Methodist Episcopal Churches, 1805–1980* (Metuchen: Scarecrow Press, 1983), 11–16; David Bradley, *A History of the African Methodist Episcopal Zion Church* (Nashville: Parthenon Press, 1956), 43–50.

79 George, 72–74, 91; British Methodist Episcopal Church, *Doctrines and Discipline* (Toronto: Wm. Briggs, 1890), 12; UCA, Clayton Munro, "A Methodist Epic: An Historical Record of the Methodist Church in Bermuda" (unpub., 1949), 51–55.

80 George, 110–111, 118; C. Peter Riley (ed.), *The Black Abolitionist Papers*, vol. 2, *Canada, 1830–1865* (Chapel Hill: Univ. of North Carolina Press, 1985); John W. Grant, *A Profusion of Spires: Religion in Nineteenth-Century Ontario* (Toronto: Univ. of Toronto Press, 1988), 108, 166.

81 Allen P. Stouffer, *The Light of Nature and the Law of God: Antislavery in Ontario, 1833–1877* (Montreal: McGill-Queen's Univ. Press, 1992), chap. 3; *Evangelist*, February 1851, 28; Allan K. Miller, "The Roots of Black Methodism in Ontario and the Rise

of the African Methodist Episcopal Church in Canada West, 1830–1870" (ThM, Emmanuel College, Victoria University, 1985).

82 Minutes of Nova Scotia District, 1835, n.p.; 1842, n.p.

83 British Methodist Episcopal Church, *Doctrines and Discipline*, 11–12; Jonathan Walton, "Blacks in Buxton and Chatham, Ontario, 1830–1890" (PhD, Princeton Univ., 1979); Jason Silverman, "Unwelcome Guests: American Fugitive Slaves in Canada, 1830–1860" (PhD, Univ. of Kentucky, 1985); Robin Winks, *The Blacks in Canada. A History* (Montreal. McGill-Queen's Univ. Press, 1971), 240.

84 British Methodist Episcopal Church, *Doctrines and Discipline*, 12.

85 Minutes of Nova Scotia District, 1846, n.p.

## CHAPTER SIX

1 Richard Carwardine, *Transatlantic Revivalism: Popular Evangelicalism in Britain and America, 1790–1865* (Westport, Conn.: Greenwood Press, 1978), 10.

2 William McLoughlin, *Revivals, Awakenings and Reform: An Essay on Religion and Social Change, 1607–1977* (Chicago: Univ. of Chicago Press, 1978), 98, 101, 115. Orthodox Calvinism had been shocked by Jonathan Edwards's revivalism, but in the nineteenth century, Calvinism was further undermined by the learned speculations of Timothy Dwight, Lyman Beecher, and Nathaniel Taylor. "By grafting onto Covenant theology the doctrine of the moral nature of divine government, which required the consent of the human will to all that God provided or demanded; by locating depravity not in our natures as had Jonathan Edwards, but in our dispositions – our selfish wills – and by adopting Samuel Hopkins' idea that disinterested benevolence, or unselfish love toward God and other humans, was the sum of the Christian's duty, Taylor and Beecher transformed Calvinist dogma into a practical Arminianism, without having to jettison Calvinist verbiage" (Timothy L. Smith, "Holiness and Radicalism in Nineteenth-Century America," in Theodore Runyon, (ed.), *Sanctification and Liberation* (Nashville: Parthenon Press, 1977), 118).

  Calvinists rejected the type of antinomian or sinless perfectionism often appearing in some Unitarian and New Light movements or in extreme perfectionist revivals such as John Noyes's communistic experiment at Oneida, New York, and the adventist and Mormon developments (see Nancy Hardesty, *Women Called to Witness: Evangelical Feminism in the Nineteenth Century* [Nashville: Abingdon Press, 1984], 52–53). However, they could not resist the successful practices of Charles Grandison Finney. He went further even than Taylor or Beecher in stressing the role of the human will in achieving salvation. See also Keith Hardman, *Charles Grandison Finney, 1792–1875: Revivalist and Reformer* (Syracuse: Syracuse Univ. Press, 1987); Paul E. Johnson, *A Shopkeeper's Millennium: Society and Revivals in Rochester, New York, 1815–1837* (New York: Hill & Wang, 1978).

3 Charles Grandison Finney, *Lectures on Revivals of Religion* ([Boston, 1835]; Halifax, 1848), 2–3.

4 Timothy L. Smith, *Revivalism and Social Reform in Mid-Nineteenth-Century America* (Nashville: Abingdon Press, [1957] 1980); Sydney Mead, *The Nation with the Soul of a Church* (New York: Harper & Row, 1978); Russell E. Richey, "America as a

Religious Problem," *Quarterly Review*, 1982, 94–103; Russell E. Richey, "The Civil
Religion Debate," in Russell Richey and Donald G. Jones (eds.), *American Civil
Religion* (New York: Harper & Row, 1974).

5 James Edgar, "Revivals of Religion," in *Heralds of Zion* (Toronto: Thomas Cuttell &
Son, 1856), 5. See also Finney, 2–3; James Watson, *Helps to the Promotion of Revivals*
(New York: Carlton & Porter, 1856), 31–32, 82; UCA, Joseph Gatchell Papers, MS
Autobiography, 16.

6 Kirk Mariner, "William Penn Chandler and Revivalism in the East," *Methodist
History* 25 (1987): 135–146; Arthur Kewley, "Camp Meetings in Early Canadian
Methodism," CMHS, *Papers* 2, (1982).

7 Whitney Cross, *The Burned-over District: The Social and Intellectual History of Enthusiastic Religion in Western New York, 1800–1850* ([Ithaca: Cornell Univ. Press, 1950];
New York: Harper Torchbooks, 1965).

8 UCA, Portraits and Letters of Ministers at St James Street Methodist Church (Montreal), Samuel Coate to Joseph Benson, September 13, 1805.

9 George Rawlyk, *The Canada Fire: Radical Evangelicalism in British North America,
1775–1812* (Kingston: McGill-Queen's Univ. Press, 1994), 143–155; Arthur
Kewley, "Some Early Sites of Methodist Camp Meetings on the Niagara Peninsula,"
in *Proceedings of the Niagara Peninsula History Conference*, 1982, 74; Joseph Gatchell
Papers, MS Autobiography, 16; John Carroll, *Case and His Cotemporaries* (Toronto:
Samuel Rose, 1867–77), 1:113.

10 John Carroll, *Past and Present* (Toronto: Alfred Dredge, 1860), 62–63.

11 WMSC, James Booth to Robert Alder, November 25, 1835. See also John Kent,
"The Wesleyan Methodists to 1849," in Rupert Davies et al. (eds.), *A History of the
Methodist Church in Great Britain* (London: Epworth Press, 1965–88), 2:234–236;
John S. Moir, *The Church in the British Era* (Toronto: McGraw-Hill Ryerson, 1972),
41; E. Arthur Betts, *Bishop Black and His Preachers: The History of Maritime Methodism
to 1825* (Halifax, 1974), 69–70.

12 WMSC, James Booth to Robert Alder, November 25, 1835. See ibid., William
Harvard to Robert Alder, October 29, 1842; also UCA, Nathanael Burwash Papers,
MS Autobiography, re the influence of camp meetings on his father and grandpar-
ents on the Quebec side of the Ottawa River in 1836–37.

13 Kewley, "Some Early Sites," 74; WMC, *Minutes of Annual Conference*, 1846, 20.

14 *CG*, January 13, 1841, 46; April 2, 1856, 103; February 8, 1832, 50; February 23,
1841, 58; *Wesleyan* (Montreal), February 4, 1841, 113.

15 *CG*, September 10, 1831, 173.

16 W. Reginald Ward, "The Religion of the People and the Problem of Control,
1790–1830," in G.J. Cumming and Derek Baker (eds.), *Popular Belief and Practice*
(Cambridge: Univ. Press, 1972), 242; William Harvard, *Defence of Protracted Meetings*
([Quebec: Wm Neilson, 1839]; London: John Mason, 1841), 15; Kent, 223;
*Wesleyan* (Montreal), December 24, 1840, 89.

17 Arthur Kewley, "Mass Evangelism in Upper Canada before 1830" (ThD, Victoria
Univ., 1960), 2; John Webster Grant (ed.), *Salvation! Oh the Joyful Sound* (Toronto:
Oxford Univ. Press, 1967), intro., 15; WMC, *Minutes of Annual Conference*, 1846,
12–16; Finny, 15; UCA, Rideau Circuit Records, Minutes of Quarterly Board, June
1824, 5; Carroll, *Case*, 1:47–48; 2:474; George Playter, *The History of Methodism in
Canada* (Toronto: Anson Green, 1862), 160–163; *Wesleyan* (Nova Scotia), January,

February 1851; *Nova Scotia and New Brunswick Wesleyan Methodist Magazine*, March 1832, 59; *CG*, July 25, 1832, 145.

18 Russell Richey, "From Quarterly to Camp Meeting: A Reconsideration of Early American Methodism," *Methodist History* 28 (1985): 199, 203. See also W. Reginald Ward, "Class, Denomination and the Development of the Connexional Frame of Mind in the Age of Bunting," CMHS, *Papers* 4 (1984): 3–4; Russell Richey, "Community, Fraternity and Order in Methodism," CMHS, *Papers* 4 (1984): 4–5.

19 Kewley, "Mass Evangelism in Upper Canada," 3; Watson, 66.

20 J. Wesley Johnston, "Tongues of Fire," in Johnston, *The Baptism of Fire and other Sermons* (Toronto: Wm. Briggs, 1888), 28. See also *CG*, September 4, 1830, 330; Finney, 13–14.

21 Watson, 93. See also Kewley, "Mass Evangelism in Upper Canada," 4; Charles Hawkins, "The Law of Revivals," in Hawkins, *Sermons on the Christian Life* (Toronto: Wm. Briggs, 1880), 64; *CG*, December 4, 1830, 9; August 5, 1840, 162; February 7, 1855, 70; *CCA*, May 2, 1848, 2; Harvard, 7.

22 *CG*, April 4, 1832, 83. See also Robert Handy, "American Methodism and its Historical Frontier: Interpreting Methodism on the Western Frontier," *Methodist History* 22 (1984): 52.

23 *CG*, April 4, 1832, 82; Kewley, "Mass Evangelism in Upper Canada," 64; Ralph Gabriel, "Evangelical Religion and Popular Romanticism in Early Nineteenth-Century America," *Church History*, 1950, 39; Dorothy H. Farquharson, "Camp Meetings: Their History and Song," CMHS, *Papers* 5 (1986): 74–76.

24 *CG*, January 18, 1843, 50; *Wesleyan* (Montreal), December 24, 1840, 89; February 4, 1841, 113; *CCA*, March 26, 1846, 2; Carroll, *Case*, 1:15. For instance, in the Canadas, the Wesleyans declined by nearly two thousand members during the middle 1840s at least partially because of the loss of revival converts.

25 *CG*, December 4, 1830, 9; July 3, 1833, 135; July 11, 1838, 142; UCA, George Ferguson Papers, Journal, 87; Carroll, *Case*, 3:298; 4:92.

26 Kewley, "Mass Evangelism in Upper Canada," 5; Gerald Craig, *Upper Canada: The Formative Years, 1784–1841* (Toronto: McClelland & Stewart, 1963), 166; AO, James and Ogle Gowan Papers, Elizabeth Gowan to James Gowan, June 7, 1835; *CG*, July 17, 1844, 153.

27 Charles E. Jones, *Perfectionist Persuasion, The Holiness Movement and American Methodism, 1867–1936* (Metuchen, NJ: Scarecrow Press, 1974), 1; Alden Aikens, "Christian Perfection in Four Representative Canadian Methodists," CMHS, *Papers* 6 (1987): 32–45; *CCA*, July 18, 1848, 117; September 12, 1848, 149.

28 Carwardine, 104; "Lorenzo Dow," *Encyclopedia of World Methodism*, 1:711–712; Lorenzo Dow, *A History of Cosmopolite: or the Writings of Lorenzo Dow* (Cincinnati: Anderson, 1858), 19; Nathan Hatch, *The Democratization of American Christianity* (New Haven: Yale Univ. Press, 1989), 7, 128–135.

29 See "journal" and sermons in Dow, *History of Cosmopolite*; Lorenzo Dow, *The Eccentric Preacher* (Lowell, Mass.: E.A. Rice, 1841); Lorenzo Dow, *Vicissitudes in the Wilderness* (Norwich, Conn.: Faulkner, 1833).

30 Carroll, *Case*, 3:235–236; Dow, *History of Cosmopolite*, 210; Carwardine, 104.

31 "Charles G. Finney," *Schaaf-Herzog Encyclopaedia of Religious Knowledge*, 1:813–814; Hardman, *Charles Grandison Finney*; Mark Ellingsen, "Defining Evangelicalism: A Mainstream View," Wesleyan/Holiness Consultation, 1988, 23, 40; Carwardine,

13–14; Hardesty, 49–50; William McLoughlin, *Modern Revivalism, Charles G. Finney to Billy Graham* (New York: Ronald Press, 1959), 54–55, 84–91. See also Charles G. Finney, *Guide to the Saviour, or … Entire Holiness of the Heart and Life* (Oberlin: J. Fitch, 1849).

32 McLoughlin, *Modern Revivalism*, 84–121; Hardesty, 48–49. See also Finney, *Lectures on Revivals of Religion*.

33 McLoughlin, *Modern Revivalism*, 12–13.

34 Garth Rosell, "American Revivalism, 1835–1875," Wesleyan/ Holiness Consultation, 1988, 2–3.

35 Johnson, 3; Hardesty, 49–50; Watson, 31–32.

36 Hardesty, 56.

37 Charles E. White, "The Beauty of Holiness: The Career and Influence of Phoebe Palmer," *Methodist History* 25 (1987): 67–69; "Phoebe Palmer," *Encyclopedia of World Methodism*, 2:1852; Rosell, 5.

38 Smith, "Holiness and Radicalism," 116. See also White, 71; Jones, 3; "Holiness Movement," *Encyclopedia of World Methodism*, 1:1140–1141; Melvin Dieter, *The Holiness Revival of the Nineteenth Century* (Metuchen, NJ: Scarecrow Press, 1980), 38–44; Richard Wheatley, *The Life and Letters of Phoebe Palmer* (New York, 1876).

39 Hardesty, 57.

40 Jones, 4; White, 68–69. See, for instance, Phoebe Palmer, *The Way of Holiness, Present to My Christian Friend, and Faith and its Effects*, all reprinted in 1855 or 1856 by the Wesleyan Book Room in Toronto. The *Guide to Holiness* was widely distributed in British America after its founding in 1839.

41 Harvard, 15; *Wesleyan* (Montreal), December 24, 1840, 89; Carwardine, 107–110; James Caughey, *Earnest Christianity Illustrated*, ed. by Daniel Wise (Toronto: G.R. Sanderson, 3rd ed., 1857), 14–20; James Caughey, *Letters on Various Subjects* (London: Simkin, Marshall & Co., 1846), 1:30.

42 Caughey, *Earnest Christianity Illustrated*, 16; Caughey, *Letters*, 16. Harvard defended mass evangelism in his pamphlet *Defence of Protracted Meetings*, which was first published in Quebec City.

43 Caughey, *Earnest Christianity Illustrated*, 34–35.

44 *Wesleyan* (Montreal), February 4, 1841, 128; Caughey, *Letters*.

45 *Wesleyan* (Montreal), December 24, 1840, 89; April 1, 1841, 144; Caughey, *Earnest Christianity Illustrated*, 16; Caughey, *Letters*, 63; Carroll, *Case*, 4:343; UCA, Thomas Cosford Papers, Journal, 8; UCA, WMSC, Wm Wilson to Missionary Secretaries, January 21, 1843; ibid., Charles De Wolfe to Robert Alder, August 18, 1843; ibid., Wm Smith to Missionary Secretaries, November 13, 1843; ibid., Richard Knight to Missionary Secretaries, December 15, 1843.

46 *Wesleyan* (Montreal), February 4, 1841, 113. See also ibid., March 4, 1841, 128.

47 CCA, November 10, 1846, 2; John Hetherington, *The Whole Case Stated: Being Correspondence on the Case of the Rev. James Caughey* (Sheffield: Chaloner, 1846); Kent, 223; Ward, 242.

48 CG, July 20, 1853, 162. See also Peter Bush, "James Caughey, Phoebe and Walter Palmer and the Methodist Revival Experience in Canada West, 1850–1858" (MA, Queen's Univ., 1985); Carroll, *Case*, 5:134, 158–161.

49 CG, July 20, 1853, 162. See also William H. Pearson, *Recollection and Records of Toronto of Old* (Toronto: Wm. Briggs, 1914), 289.

50 *CG*, April 30, 1856, 119. See also Carroll, *Case*, 5:167–168; *CG*, March 26, 1856, 99. Peter Bush analyses the membership growth after the local revivals during the 1850s.

51 Nathanael Burwash Papers, MS Autobiography, chap. 1, 15–18. See also Marguerite Van Die, *An Evangelical Mind: Nathanael Burwash and the Methodist Tradition in Canada, 1839–1918* (Kingston: McGill-Queen's Univ. Press, 1989), 40. Significantly, Burwash never felt he achieved entire sanctification.

52 *CCA*, February 15, 1848, 29; July 18, 1848, 117; September 12, 1848, 149: Carroll, *Case*, 4:11; Alden Aikens, "Christian Perfection in Central-Canadian Methodism, 1828–1884" (PhD, McGill Univ., 1987); Robert Samms, "Revivalism in Central-Canadian Wesleyan Methodism, 1824–1860" (PhD, McGill Univ., 1984).

53 *Wesleyan* (Montreal), February 4, 1841, 113; *CG*, March 25, 1857, 98. Most of the contemporary Methodist literature defended revival converts, but some thoughtful critics recognized the shallowness of revivalism as opposed to the use of the regular means of grace. See Carroll, *Case*, 4:411; Harvard, 26–33.

54 Nathanael Burwash Papers, MS Autobiography, 16, 58; UCA, Henry Flesher Bland Papers, Diary, 1858, 36–37; *CG*, August 23, 1854, 180; Carroll, *Case*, 4:457–458; Bush, chap. 5; Marilyn Fardig Whiteley, "Modest, Unaffected and Fully Consecrated: Lady Evangelists in Canadian Methodism, 1884–1900," CMHS, *Papers* 6, (1987): 18–31.

55 UCAMa, Charles Ladner Papers, memoirs, 18. See also *CG*, July 22, 1857, 166.

56 Carwardine, 12; Smith, *Revivalism and Social Reform*, 67–68 (1980 rev. ed., 256); J. Edwin Orr, *The Fervent Prayer: The Worldwide Impact of the Great Awakening of 1858* (Chicago: Moody Press, 1974), 2–3.

57 Kewley, "Mass Evangelism in Upper Canada," 238.

58 Quoted in Carroll, *Case*, 5:22.

59 Smith, *Revivalism and Social Reform*, 8; See also McLoughlin, *Revivals, Awakenings and Reform*; Carwardine.

60 Dow, "On the Ministry," in *History of Cosmopolite*, 559. See also Rosell, 5.

61 Carroll, *Past and Present*, 87–88; Joseph Gatchell Papers, MS Autobiography, 13; *CG*, July 4, 1866, 105; Finney, 10; Kewley, "Mass Evangelism in Upper Canada," 2; William Westfall, *Two Worlds: The Protestant Culture of Nineteenth-Century Ontario* (Kingston: McGill-Queen's Univ. Press, 1989), 41–45, 55–63.

62 *CG*, July 3, 1833, 135; January 9, 1850, 248; July 4, 1866, 105; UCA, Samuel S. Nelles Papers, Diary, December 26, 1866; Hardesty, 9.

63 Victor Shepherd, "Calvin's Doctrine of Church, Ministry and Sacraments," UCA, *Bulletin* 29 (1983): 75; Carwardine, chap. 1; McLoughlin, *Modern Revivalism*, 7–8; Jerald C. Brauer, "Conversion: From Puritanism to Revivalism," *Journal of Religion*, 1978, 227–243; Jerald C. Brauer, "Revivalism and Millenarianism in America" in Joseph Ban and Paul Dekar (eds.), *In the Great Tradition: In Honour of Winthrop S. Hudson* (Valley Forge: Judson Press, 1982), 147.

64 John Wesley, "On Working Out Our Salvation," in *The Works of John Wesley* (London: 1811), 10: 79; Ole Borgen, "John Wesley and the Sacraments," CMHS, *Papers* 2 (1980): 2.

65 *CG*, October 18, 1843, 206; MEC, *Minutes of Annual Conference*, 1830, 36–37; Kewley, "Mass Evangelism in Upper Canada," 83.

66 Watson, 12–17. See also Finney, 12; *CCA*, November 7, 1848, 2; February 2, 1852, 2; *CG*, January 24, 1844, 54; May 31, 1854, 133; Wesleyan Missionary Society Auxiliary, Nova Scotia District, Annual Report, 1836, 8.

67 *CCA*, October 27, 1846, 2.

68 Richey, "From Quarterly to Camp Meeting," 201. See also *CCA*, March 2, 1846, 2; May 9, 1848, 72; George Rawlyk, *Wrapped up in God* (Burlington, Ont.: Welch, 1988), 98–113.

69 James W. May, "From Revival Movement to Denomination: A Reexamination of the Beginnings of American Methodism" (Ph D, Columbia Univ., 1962), 4.

70 Quoted in Kewley, "Some Early Sites of Methodist Camp Meetings," 79. See also Watson, 26.

71 William Westfall, "The End of the World: An Account of Time and Culture in Nineteenth-Century Protestant Ontario," *Religion/Culture, Canadian Issues* 7 (1985): 78–79; Westfall, *Two Worlds*, 166–177.

72 Ruth Alden Doan, "Perfectionism in the Adventist Tradition," Wesleyan/Holiness Consultation, 1988; "Advent," *Encyclopedia of World Methodism*, 1:52–55; Douglas Morgan, "Adventism, Apocalyptic, and the Cause of Liberty," *Church History* 63 (1994): 235–249.

73 Quoted in Carroll, *Case*, 3:141.

74 Harvard, 11; Wesley M. Gewehr, "Some Factors in the Expansion of Frontier Methodism, 1800–1811," *Journal of Religion* 8 (1928): 114; *CG*, August 29, 1832, 165.

75 Johnson, 8.

76 *CG*, July 25, 1832, 145; January 11, 1854, 54; *CCA*, February 15, 1848, 29; Johnson, 5–6; Hardesty, 45–46. A decline in revival meant to many a neglect of the poor.

77 Joseph E. Sanderson, *Suffering and Glory: A Sermon Preached at the Oakville Camp Meeting, 1857* (Toronto: Wesleyan Book Room, 1857), 14–15.

78 WMSC, A.W. McLeod to Missionary Secretaries, October 18, 1843; Carroll, *Case*, 3:191; 5:106–107; David W. Johnson, *History of Methodism in Eastern British America* (Sackville: Tribune Printing, 1925), 34.

CHAPTER SEVEN

1 *CG*, September 21, 1853, 197. See also ibid., May 28, 1834, 114.

2 WMC, *Minutes of Annual Conference*, 1855, 318–319; *CG*, November 4, 1835, 206; December 3, 1845, 26; March 11, 1857, 89.

3 John W. Grant, *Moon of Wintertime: Missionaries and the Indians of Canada in Encounter since 1534* (Toronto: Univ. of Toronto Press, 1984), 76–77.

4 Some Europeans were content to categorize native peoples as a separate, inferior race who could not and should not be treated as equals. This perception helped justify genocide. At the other extreme, some considered them "noble savages" living according to uncontaminated natural laws in a pristine environment. The Canadian Methodist missionary Conrad Van Dusen wrote, "Before it was polluted by the pernicious examples of others – the demoralizing and debasing influences of white men – the genuine North American pagan presents to the World the most noble specimen of the natural man that can be found." The native appeared to illustrate the popular misconception of Rousseau's ultimately perfectable man in harmony with nature, who was moving from primitive isolation to cosmopolitan civilization. See Conrad Van Dusen, *The Indian Chief* (London: Nichols, 1867), 1; Donald Smith, *Le Sauvage* (Ottawa: National Museum of Man, 1974).

5 Donald Smith, "The Mississauga, Peter Jones and the White Man" (PhD, Univ. of Toronto, 1975), 310–315.

6 Hope MacLean, "The Hidden Agenda: Methodist Attitudes to the Ojibwa and the Development of Indian Schooling in Upper Canada, 1821–1860" (MA, OISE, 1978), 73. See also Grant, 75.

7 George Playter, *The History of Methodism in Canada* (Toronto: Anson Green, 1862), 389–391; CG, March 19, 1834, 72; May 28, 1834, 114; August 31, 1842, 177; April 17, 1846, 101; May 6, 1846, 113; MEC, *Missionary Society Reports*, 1825, 12; MacLean, 25.

8 John Carroll, *Case and His Cotemporaries* (Toronto: Samuel Rose, 1867–77), 1:100–101; Playter, 74; Abel Stevens, *Life and Times of Nathan Bangs* (New York: Carlton & Porter, 1863), 110; UCA, Albert Burnside, "The Work of William Case, 1780–1855" (unpub.), 6–7, 22.

9 Donald Smith, *Sacred Feathers: The Rev. Peter Jones (Kahkewaquonaby) and the Mississauga Indians* (Lincoln: Univ. of Nebraska Press, 1987), 86–88; Curtis Fahey, *In His Name: The Anglican Experience in Upper Canada, 1791–1854* (Ottawa: Carleton Univ. Press, 1991), 39–41.

10 Grant, 68–69.

11 Smith, *Sacred Feathers*, 34–39.

12 Anthony Hall, "The Red Man's Burden: Land, Law and the Lord in the Indian Affairs of Upper Canada, 1791–1858" (PhD, Univ. of Toronto, 1984), 40–62.

13 Grant, 75; G.G. Findlay and W.W. Holdsworth, *The History of the Wesleyan Methodist Missionary Society* (London: Epworth Press, 1921), 1:498; CG, October 26, 1842, 2; April 9, 1845, 98.

14 Philip Smith, "Beothuks and Methodists," *Acadiensis* 15 (1986): 130–134; WMSC, Richard Knight to Missionary Secretaries, October 22, 1825; ibid., Thomas Hickson Journal, June-September 1824; ibid., George Ellidge to Missionary Secretaries, September 11, 1826; UCA, Minutes of Newfoundland District, 1845, n.p.

15 Smith, *Sacred Feathers*, 61.

16 WMSC, James Evans to Missionary Secretaries, 1836. See also Playter, 391; CG, March 11, 1835, 69; Maureen Haigh, "The Methodist Contribution to Indian Education in Upper Canada, 1824–1847" (MA, McGill Univ., 1976).

17 WMC, *Minutes of Annual Conference*, 1849, 108. See also Smith, *Sacred Feathers*, 69; Van Dusen, 5.

18 Grant, 75.

19 Findlay and Holdsworth, 1:452; MEC, *Missionary Society Reports*, 1825, 12–13; *New York Christian Advocate*, May 5, 1827, 137; Carroll, *Case*, 2:360; John W. Grant, "The Hunters Hunted: Methodists of Three Countries in Pursuit of the Indians of Canada," CMHS, *Papers* 4 (1984): 1.

20 Fahey, 39–41; Smith, *Sacred Feathers*, 49; John W. Grant, *A Profusion of Spires. Religion in Nineteenth-Century Ontario* (Toronto: Univ. of Toronto Press, 1988), 18–19; DCB, 4:lvi; "Thomas Davis," ibid., 6:758.

21 Carroll, *Case*, 2:401–403. See also Alvin Torry, *The Autobiography of Alvin Torry* (Auburn: Moses, 1865), 60, 67; Findlay and Holdsworth, 1:449–450.

22 William Case, *Jubilee Sermon* (1855), 16; Smith, *Sacred Feathers*, 52, 62, Torry, 77–82; "Thomas Davis," DCB, 6:758.

23 Playter, 217–218; Torry, 83; Carroll, *Case*, 2:409–411.

24 Smith, *Sacred Feathers*; "Peter Jones," DCB, 8:439–442.

25 Carroll, *Case*, 2:414. See also Smith, *Sacred Feathers*, 63–64.

26 Hall, 84; "William Case," DCB, 8:132–134.

27 Peter Jones, *History of the Ojebway Indians* (London: Bennett, 1861), 30; Carroll, *Case*, 4:64–73; CG, March 2, 1842, 75; Hall, 217–219; Elizabeth Graham, *Medicine Man to Missionary: Missionaries as Agents of Change among the Indians of Southern Ontario, 1784–1867* (Toronto: Peter Martin, 1975), 80–82.

28 MEC, *Missionary Society Reports*, 1825, 8–10.

29 MacLean, 66–70; Smith, *Sacred Feathers*, 77–79; Torry, 89; Graham, 83.

30 Constance Backhouse, *Petticoats and Prejudice: Women and Law in Nineteenth-Century Canada* (Toronto: Osgoode Society, 1991), 14; Smith, *Sacred Feathers*, 78; Graham, 82; Playter, 352.

31 Backhouse, 111; WMSC, James Evans to John Beecham, March 29, 1836.

32 Smith, "The Mississauga," 169–171; Grant, *Moon of Wintertime*, 110. Peter and John Jones adopted the name of their father. Peter Jacobs (Pahtahsega) and John Summerfield (Sahgahgewagahbaweh) were named after benevolent Methodists. Yellowhead, John Crane, and Henry Snake drew their names from translations of their native designations.

33 Burnside, 44–45; MacLean, 66–70; Graham, 68–71; Grant, *Moon of Wintertime*, 75.

34 Hall, 376; Graham, 1.

35 CG, February 17, 1847, 70; Smith, *Sacred Feathers*, 225–226; Hall, 60; Benjamin Slight, *Indian Researches; or Facts Concerning the North American Indians* (Montreal: J.E.L. Miller, 1844), 129.

36 Hall, 374.

37 Smith, *Sacred Feathers*, 90; Torry, 67, 94.

38 Grant, *Profusion of Spires*, 17–19; Graham, 86, 91.

39 Hall, 7–8, 221–230; Graham, 72.

40 Carroll, *Case*, 3:20; Smith, *Sacred Feathers*, 64–65.

41 WMSC, Peter Jones to Adam Townley, July 20, 1831.

42 Carroll, *Case*, 3:65, 20, 70–72. See also MEC, *Minutes of Annual Conference*, 1824, 2; 1825, 7.

43 Carroll, *Case*, 3:450–454; MEC, *Minutes of Annual Conference*, 1827, 13; 1829, 21; Playter, 276; MEC, *Missionary Society Reports*, 1830, 60; CG, December 4, 1830, 10.

44 Playter, 363; Smith, *Sacred Feathers*, 74–75; UCA, Joseph Gatchell Papers, MS Autobiography, 42; George Hammell, "Strawberries, Floating Islands and Rabbit Captains: Mythical Realities and European Contact in the Northeast during the Sixteenth and Seventeenth Centuries," *Journal of Canadian Studies* 21 (1986): 82–90; MacLean, 29–30.

45 *New York Christian Advocate*, May 5, 1827, 137; Smith, "The Mississauga," 300–301.

46 CG, June 5, 1830, 225; March 4, 1836, 70; Carroll, *Case*, 3:241, 474.

47 Playter, 341. See also Peter Jones, *Life and Journals of Kah-ke-wa-quo-na-by* (Toronto: Anson Green, 1860), 54; Smith, "The Mississauga," 166–167; Hall, 83–84, 96; CG, February 18, 1835, 58.

48 MEC, *Missionary Society Reports*, 1825, 7; Smith, *Sacred Feathers*, ix–xiv, Carroll, *Case*, 3:302–306; 4:168; Grant, "Hunters Hunted," 5; Hall, 63–64, 166–167; CG, March 4, 1836, 70; WMC, *Minutes of Annual Conference*, 1846, 17.

49 Smith, *Sacred Feathers*, 72–73, 99–104; Hall, 3–4, 99–100; Carroll, *Case*, 3:63; "Peregrine Maitland," DCB, 8:596.

50 *New York Christian Advocate*, May 12, 1827, 141; Smith, *Sacred Feathers*, 72, 81, 86.

51 MEC, *Minutes of Annual Conference*, 1826, 11; 1829, 25; *New York Christian Advocate*, February 24, 1827, 99; Smith, "The Mississauga," 8; Carroll, *Case*, 3:201–202.

52 Victoria University, Peter Jones Papers, Peter Jones to Samuel Martin, January 18, 1830; Smith, *Sacred Feathers*, 78–79; Playter, 346–349; Graham, 91.

53 UCA, Richard Boehme, "The Mission to Grape Island" (unpub.); William Canniff, *The Settlement of Upper Canada* (Belleville: Mika, 1971 [Toronto: Dudley & Burns, 1869]), 325–326; Playter, 292; Smith, "The Mississauga," 203–204; *New York Christian Advocate*, November 25, 1826, 46; March 31, 1827, 118; Case, 22.

54 WMC, *Minutes of Annual Conference*, 1837, 148; Carroll, *Case*, 4:128.

55 MEC, *Minutes of Annual Conference*, 1827, 15; *New York Christian Advocate*, May 5, 1827, 137.

56 Carroll, *Case*, 3:94–96; Case, 24–27; Smith, *Sacred Feathers*, 90–93; *New York Christian Advocate*, September 23, 1826, 10; April 7, 1827, 122; April 14, 1827, 126.

57 *New York Christian Advocate*, August 24, 1827, 201; Case, 27; Smith, *Sacred Feathers*, 94–95; MEC, *Minutes of the Annual Conference*, 1828, 18.

58 Hall, 290; Findlay and Holdsworth, 1:456; John Carroll, *Past and Present* (Toronto: Alfred Dredge, 1860), 59–60; Carroll, *Case*, 3:109, 110; 4:78–84; Jones, *History of the Ojebway*, 7–8; Jones, *Life and Journals*, 75; Playter, 249, 284; Smith, *Sacred Feathers*, 95–96.

59 Smith, "The Mississauga," 221; Hall, 97; WMSC, L. Mudge to Egerton Ryerson, July 16, 1830.

60 Hall, 3–4, 78–79, 104–105, 108–110.

61 Graham, 23; Smith, "The Mississauga," 221–223; Hall, 167.

62 Hall, 220, 111, 373. See also Smith, "The Mississauga," 225; MEC, *Missionary Society Reports*, 1830, 7–8. By the late 1830s most of these natives had moved to Rama or Manitoulin Island. In 1844 Chief Yellowhead and much of his band converted to the Anglican church. The Methodists condemned this ecclesiastical poaching.

63 Carroll, *Case*, 3:331–333, 471. See also Graham, 17.

64 WMSC, Solomon Waldron to Enoch Wood, September 29, 1847; Smith, *Sacred Feathers*, 89; CG, December 10, 1834, 18.

65 CG, February 6, 1839, 53. The Jesuits working on Walpole Island suffered a similar lack of initial success.

66 WMSC, Thomas Turner to Missionary Secretaries, November 29, 1831.

67 WMSC, James Evans to John Beecham, March 29, 1836. See also ibid., Thomas Turner to Robert Alder, September 27, 1832; ibid., Thomas Turner to Missionary Secretaries, January 5, 1833; ibid., Thomas Turner to Robert Alder, May 30, 1833; ibid., Thomas Turner to Missionary Secretaries, January 15, 1834.

68 "James Evans," DCB, 7:275–277; WMC, *Minutes of Annual Conference*, 1836, 119; WMSC, John Douse to Joseph Stinson, April 1, 1839; ibid., James Evans to John Beecham, March 29, 1836.

69 CG, January 7, 1835, 34. See also MEC, *Minutes of Annual Conference*, 1831, 42; WMC, *Minutes of Annual Conference*, 1840, 229.

70 Hall, 143–144; CG, March 30, 1836, 83; March 21, 1838, 78.

71 UCA, "James Evans' Tour of Lake Huron"; *CG*, September 7, 1836, 174; June 14, 1837, 126; October 23, 1839, 205; August 27, 1845, 179; Van Dusen, 61–70; Henry Bowden, *American Indians and Christian Missions* (Chicago: Univ. of Chicago Press, 1981), 164–178; Hall, 153.

72 WMSC, Peter Jones to John Beecham, February 16, 1836; ibid., James Evans to John Beecham, March 29, 1836; ibid., "Defence of Indian Rights in Upper Canada by Methodists," 1837; ibid., Petition to Lord Glenelg, 1837; *CG*, March 21, 1838, 78; April 4, 1838, 86; April 11, 1838, 90–91; April 18, 1838, 94; April 25, 1838, 98; May 30, 1838, 117; August 1, 1838, 154; Smith, *Sacred Feathers*, xi–xiv, 165, 174–178; Carroll, *Case*, 4:133, 161–172, 205; Jones, *Life and Journals*, 394, 405–408.

    Joseph Stinson, the Wesleyan Missionary superintendent after 1833, was not convinced that the removal to Manitoulin was a bad policy. Unlike Evans, he thought the land was good enough for native needs (*CG*, September 7, 1836, 174). Evans kept up his attack on government policy even after Bond Head's recall. While touring Lake Superior in December 1838, he sarcastically reported on a band of starving natives, "Here I found existing in all its luxuriance, the 'simple virtue' so much admired by Sir F. B. Head, which in his estimation, many of the Indians of U.C. have changed for the less admired virtues of Christianity" (*CG*, April 17, 1839, 97).

73 *CG*, July 18, 1838, 146; December 2, 1846, 27; January 12, 1848, 49; Van Dusen, 45–47; Findlay and Holdsworth, 1:465–466.

74 WMC, *Minutes of Annual Conference*, 1837, 160; Carroll, *Case*, 3:54; 4:265; MacLean, 129–131; Hall, 314, 368; Van Dusen, 5; *CG*, July 1, 1842, 142; May 6, 1846, 113; July 6, 1846, 150; Henry Baldwin, *Minutes of the General Council of Indian Chiefs and Principal Men, Orillia, 1846* (Montreal: Canada Gazette, 1846), 5–10.

75 *CG*, December 12, 1849, 236; February 19, 1845, 70; July 13, 1842, 150; WMSC, John Sunday to Robert Alder, April 7, 1841; ibid., John Sunday to Robert Alder, April 19, 1841; WMC, *Minutes of Annual Conference*, 1846, 17; 1837, 160; Grant, "Hunters Hunted," 9; Hall, 316; Case, 23; William Phinney, "William Case, Apostle to the Canadian Indians," CMHS, *Papers* 1 (1978).

76 *CG*, July 13, 1842, 150; August 23, 1848, 178; April 12, 1848, 102; July 25, 1849, 162; March 20, 1850, 288; WMC, *Minutes of Annual Conference*, 1846, 17; 1850, 138; 1852, 211–213; UCA, Elgee Joblin Papers, Scrapbooks on Residential Schools.

77 *CG*, May 12, 1858, 127; WMC, *Missionary Society Reports*, 1861–62, xviii.

78 *CG*, November 16, 1859, 182; September 21, 1853, 197; Hall, 240, 244; Fahey, 43–44; Graham, 47–48; Jones, *Life and Journals*, 165; Grant, *Moon of Wintertime*, 85–86; James R. Miller, *Skyscrapers Hide the Heavens: A History of Indian White Relations in Canada* (Toronto: Univ. of Toronto Press, 1989).

79 "James Evans' Tour of Lake Huron," 7. See also *CG*, December 10, 1834, 18; May 20, 1835, 110; September 7, 1836, 174; April 7, 1841, 94; John W. Grant, "Rendezvous at Manitowaning," UCA, *Bulletin* 28 (1978).

80 *CG*, January 22, 1834, 42; December 16, 1835, 22; February 22, 1837, 61; September 28, 1842, 194.

81 WMC, *Missionary Society Reports*, 1852, xviii–xix; 1857, xxv; Smith, "The Mississauga," 214.

82 *CG*, January 2, 1839, 34; April 17, 1839, 97; March 18, 1840, 81; July 1, 1840, 142; Carroll, *Case*, 4:219–227, 230.

83 Michael Owen, " 'Nurseries of the Church of God': British Wesleyan Missions in Rupert's Land, 1840–1854," CMHS, *Papers* 3 (1983): 4–6; Gerald Hutchinson, intro., in Hugh Dempsey (ed.), *The Rundle Journals, 1840–1848* (Calgary: Alberta Historical Society, 1977); "James Evans," DCB, 7: 275–276; WMSC, George Simpson to Robert Alder, April 15, 1850.

84 CG, November 23, 1842, 18; WMSC, Joseph Stinson to James Evans, March 27, 1840; ibid., Peter Jacobs to Missionary Society, June 18, 1841; ibid., Thomas Hurlburt to Robert Alder, January 11, 1841; "Robert Rundle," DCB, 12:931.

85 UCA, James Evans biographical file; Carroll, *Case*, 4:227; WMSC, James Evans to Ephraim Evans, May 12, 1840; Gerald Hutchinson, "James Evans' Last Year," UCA, *Bulletin* 26 (1977): 42–56; WMC, *Minutes of Annual Conference*, 1848, 56; Sylvia Van Kirk, *Many Tender Ties: Women in Fur-Trade Society in Western Canada, 1670–1870* (Winnipeg: Watson, 1980), 88.

86 Gerald Hutchinson, "Robert T. Rundle, 1811–1896," CMHS, *Papers* 1 (1978): 9; "Robert Rundle," DCB, 12:931–932; WMSC, George Simpson to James Evans, n.d.

87 John Long, "George Barnley, Wesleyan Methodism and the Fur Trade Company Families of James Bay," *Ontario History* 77 (1985): 43–45; WMSC, George Simpson to Robert Alder, November 8, 1847; UCA, George Barnley Papers, *Journal.*

88 "Abishabis," DCB, 7:1; WMSC, Extracts of Journal of William Mason, January 17, 1848.

89 CG, May 5, 1847, 115. See also Hutchinson, "Robert T. Rundle," 7.

90 WMSC, George Simpson to Robert Alder, April 15, 1850.

91 WMSC, Peter Jacobs to Missionary Society, December 14, 1847; UCA, Allen Salt Papers, Diary, September 4, 1854; September 19, 1854; February 17, 1855; "Peter Jacobs (Pahtahsega)," DCB, 11:660–661; CG, September 28, 1848, 194.

92 WMSC, William Mason to Missionary Secretaries, August 19, 1852. See also ibid., Extracts of Journal of William Mason, November 3, 1847; January 3, 1848; "Sophia Thomas," DCB, 9:784.

93 WMSC, Bishop Anderson to Robert Alder, October, 1853; ibid., Bishop Anderson to Enoch Wood, October 15, 1854; ibid., William Mason to Missionary Secretary, August 18, 1853; ibid., William Mason to Missionary Secretary, December 23, 1853; ibid., Enoch Wood to Missionary Secretary, December 29, 1853. Enoch Wood in Canada supervised the Methodist missions in the northwest beginning in 1851.

94 WMC, *Minutes of Annual Conference*, 1854, 258; 1855, 295; "Henry B. Steinhauer," DCB, 11:848–849.

95 Carroll, *Past and Present*, 301–304; WMC, *Minutes of Annual Conference*, 1854, 258; 1857, 394; "Thomas Hurlburt," DCB, 10:372–373; Smith, *Sacred Feathers*, 186–187; WMSC, Robert Brooking to Elijah Hoole, August 21, 1854; UCA, Robert Brooking biographical file.

96 Allen Salt Papers, Diary, July 7, 1855; J.E Nix, "City Meets Wilderness: Thomas Woolsey in Edmonton House and Rocky Mountains," CMHS, *Papers* 8 (1990), J.E. Nix, "John Maclean's Mission to the Blood Indians, 1880–1889" (MA, McGill University, 1977).

97 WMC, *Minutes of Annual Conference*, 1859, 27; Ebenezer Robson, *How Methodism Came to British Columbia* (Toronto: Methodist Missionary Society, 1904); John W. Grant, "Ephraim Evans," CMHS, *Papers* 8 (1990): 107–116.

CHAPTER EIGHT

1  *CJ*, September 5, 1873, 2; *CG*, June 13, 1877, 185; January 19, 1881, 23;
   October 5, 1881, 313; July 5, 1882, 212; February 18, 1885, 97; June 17, 1885,
   369; August 12, 1885, 501; MCC, *Minutes of Toronto Conference*, 1882, 161; MEC, *Journal of General Conference*, 1878, 89.
2  MC, *Journal of the United General Conference*, 1883, 120–121.
3  Late-nineteenth-century Methodists commonly used the term "heroic age" to
   describe earlier Canadian Methodism. Goldwin French, in *Parsons and Politics*
   (Toronto: Ryerson Press, 1962), and William Brooks, in "The Changing Character
   of Maritime Wesleyan Methodism, 1855–1883" (MA, Mount Allison Univ., 1965),
   pick up the term.
4  French, *Parsons and Politics*, 281.
5  All population statistics and numbers of adherents are drawn from the respective
   censuses. Percentages are computed from the same sources. "Large" urban centres
   are defined as over 5,000 in population.
6  R. Cole Harris and John Warkentin, *Canada before Confederation* (Toronto: Oxford
   Univ. Press, 1974), 69; Serge Courville and Norman Seguin, *Rural Life in Nineteenth-Century Quebec* (CHA Bulletin 47, Ottawa, 1989); Michael Behiels, *Quebec and
   the Question of Immigration: From Ethnocentrism to Ethnic Pluralism, 1900–1985* (CHA
   Ottawa: Bulletin 18, 1991), 3–6; Dale Postage and Ken McRoberts, *Quebec, Social
   Change and Political Crisis* (Toronto: McClelland & Stewart, 1980).
7  J. Warren Caldwell, "The Unification of Methodism in Canada, 1865–1884 ," UCA,
   *Bulletin* 19 (1967): 4. The pattern is illustrated by an analysis of the census data by
   county.
8  NCC, *Minutes of Annual Conference*, 1855, 11. The New Connexion represented 0.7
   per cent of the population of cities over 5,000 in 1851 in Canada West. Membership statistics are taken from the relevant conference and district minutes.
9  PMC, *Minutes of Special Conference*, 1875, 29; John Hoover, "The Primitive Methodist
   Church in Canada, 1829–1884" (MA, Univ. of Western Ontario, 1970), 179.
10 *CMM* 1 (1875): 187.
11 Albert Burnside, "The Bible Christians in Canada, 1832–1884" (ThD, Toronto
   Graduate School of Theological Studies, 1969), 206; BCC, *Minutes of Annual Conference*, 1869, 17; 1879, 28; 1882, 35; BCC, *Missionary Society Reports*, 1858, 12–13;
   1880, 10; 1881, 11; 1882, 12.
12 NCC, *Minutes of Annual Conference*, 1856, 10; Hoover, 159–160; PMC, *Minutes of
   Annual Conference*, 1871, 20; William Brooks, "The Primitive Methodists in the
   Northwest," *Saskatchewan History*, 1976, 30.
13 NCC, *Minutes of Annual Conference*, 1864, 36. See also ibid., 1871, 37; *Observer* (Bible
   Christian), January 17, 1872, 14.
14 PMC, *Minutes of Special Annual Conference*, 1875, 11.
15 *CJ*, March 10, 1865, 2.
16 BCC, *Minutes of Annual Conference*, 1872, 14.
17 Ibid., 1873, 21. See also UCA, Mary Ann Tyler, "Methodist Churches in Toronto"
   (unpub. research aid); NCC, *Minutes of Annual Conference*, 1870, 36.
18 NCC, *Minutes of Annual Conference*, 1859, 15.
19 BCC, *Missionary Society Reports*, 1867, 3.

20 BCC, *Minutes of Annual Conference,* 1872, 14–15; Charles Hawkins, "The Profit of Godliness," in Hawkins, *Sermons on the Christian Life* (Toronto: Wm. Briggs, 1880), 96; UCA, John G. Laird Papers, file 10, undated lecture. More positively, the combination of sacred and secular values developing from the urbane, middle-class church was remoulding the entire English-Canadian community. See William Westfall, *Two Worlds: The Protestant Culture of Nineteenth-Century Ontario* (Kingston: McGill-Queen's Univ. Press, 1989).

21 PMC, *Minutes of Annual Conference,* 1873, 9; *CMM,* 1 (1875): 186.

22 *Historical Census of the Canadas,* 1871 for 1851.

23 MEC, *Minutes of Bay of Quinte Conference,* 1855, 25; MEC, *Minutes of Niagara Conference,* 1852, 10.

24 UCA, Albert Carman Papers, Thomas Pickett to Albert Carman, December 28, 1880; MEC, *Minutes of Niagara Conference,* 1876, 8.

25 Albert Carman Papers, A.W. Edwards to Albert Carman, August 3, 1880. See also MEC, *Minutes of Bay of Quinte Conference,* 1878, 91.

26 Albert Carman Papers, R.M. Pope to Albert Carman, September 20, 1880.

27 Ibid., R.M. Pope to Albert Carman, December 10, 1880. See also ibid., Thomas Argue to Albert Carman, March 20, 1882.

28 MEC, *Minutes of Niagara Conference,* 1875, 16–17, 30–31; MEC, *Minutes of Bay of Quinte Conference,* 1879, 143; 1881, 16; MEC, *Minutes of Ontario Conference,* 1874, 48; MEC, *Journal of General Conference,* 1874, 24; Albert Carman Papers, Thomas Pickett to Albert Carman, December 28, 1880.

29 John W. Grant, "The Church and Canada's Self Awareness," *Canadian Journal of Theology* (1967): 159; Neil Semple, "The Impact of Urbanization on the Methodist Church in Central Canada, 1854–1884" (PhD, Univ. of Toronto, 1979).

30 WMC, *Minutes of Annual Conference,* 1859, 27, 83; 1869, 42; WMC, *Missionary Society Reports,* 1859–60, xxiii; 1860–61, xxvii; 1870–71, xv; CG, October 5, 1859, 158–159.

31 WMC, *Minutes of Annual Conference,* 1871, 114. See also WMC, *Missionary Society Reports,* 1853–54, xxiii.

32 CG, January 2, 1867, 2; August 2, 1882, 244; WMC, *Minutes of Annual Conference,* 1864, 90; anon., *Out of the Fold* (Toronto: Wesleyan Publishing House, 1871), 3; Stephen Bond, *Notes on Methodism,* 49–50.

33 WMC, *Minutes of Annual Conference,* 1868, 110.

34 WMC, *Missionary Society Reports,* 1869–70, li; 1868–69, lxii.

35 CG, September 20, 1876, 302.

36 WMC, Minutes of Stationing Committee, 1865; CG, October 8, 1856, 2; April 20, 1859, 63; June 19, 1861, 95; May 7, 1873, 149; January 5, 1876, 4; UCA, Toronto, Wesleyan Metropolitan Church, Minute Book, November 10, 1874; January 1875.

37 UCA, Henry Flesher Bland Papers, Diary, October 10, 1871, 95. Punshon served as president of Conference for five consecutive years between 1868 and 1873. See Frederick W. Macdonald, *The Life of William Morley Punshon* (London: Hodder & Stoughton, 1887).

38 MCC, *Journal of General Conference,* 1878, 94, 97–98, 101, 169; 1882, 141; WMC, *Minutes of Annual Conference,* 1861, 97; MCC, *Minutes of Montreal Conference,* 1879, 64; MCC, *Minutes of Toronto Conference,* 1880, 87; 1882, 146; CG, January 19, 1881, 23; Albert Carman Papers, R. McCormick to Albert Carman, December 9, 1881;

UCA MC, Board of Missions Papers, Alexander Sutherland Letterbooks, II, 95, Alexander Sutherland to George Cochrane, November 28, 1875; Anson Green, *The Life and Times of the Rev. Anson Green* (Toronto: Methodist Book Room, 1877), 384.

39 Thomas Webster, *The Union Considered and the Methodist Episcopal Church in Canada Defended* (Belleville: Victoria Chronicle, 1842); Thomas Webster, *History of the Methodist Episcopal Church in Canada* (Hamilton: Canada Christian Advocate Office, 1870); UCA Peter Fisher Papers, "Jottings"; Burnside, "The Bible Christians in Canada," 330–331; Albert Carman Papers, Philip Carman to Albert Carman, December 22, 1882.

40 *CG*, April 19, 1854, 107; WMC, *Minutes of Annual Conference*, 1858, 91; 1865, 75–77; BCC, *Minutes of Annual Conference*, 1865, 8; MEC, Minutes of Ontario Conference, 1866, 39–40; 1868, 46; MEC, *Minutes of Niagara Conference*, 1877, 15–16; UCA, Egerton Ryerson Papers, Egerton Ryerson to George Hodgins, January 4, 1866; Albert Carman Papers, John Carroll to Albert Carman, March 2, 1869.

41 MCC, *Journal of General Conference*, 1874, 13; Egerton Ryerson Papers, Egerton Ryerson to Oliver Mowat, October 17, 1874.

42 *Bible Christian Magazine* (British), 1883, 543. See also *Pleasant Hours*, January 27, 1883, 12; Hoover, 216.

43 Burnside, "The Bible Christians in Canada ," 323; MCC, *Minutes of Toronto Conference*, 1882, 161; MCC, *Journal of General Conference*, 1882, 161; MEC, *Journal of General Conference*, 1878, 78; *The First Canadian Christian Conference* (Toronto: Willard Tract Society, 1878), vi; *Proceedings of the Ecumenical Methodist Conference, 1881* (Hamilton: S.G. Stone, 1882).

44 Burkhard Kiesekamp, "Presbyterian and Methodist Divines: Their Case for a National Church in Canada, 1875–1900 ," *Studies in Religion* 2 (1973): 313–326; *CG*, June 13, 1877, 185; January 9, 1881, 23; UCA, Church Union Papers, Anglican/United Church.

45 *CJ*, September 15, 1873, 2; Egerton Ryerson Papers, Lemuel A. Wilmot to Egerton Ryerson, October 20, 1874.

46 Egerton Ryerson Papers, Morley Punshon to Egerton Ryerson, February 19, 1875; Hoover, 218; Peter Fisher Papers, "Jottings," 52–53; John Carroll, *A Needed Exposition on the Claims and allegations of the Canadian Episcopals* (Toronto: Samuel Rose, 1877).

47 *CMM*, 1 (1875): 549–550; 5 (1877): 372–373; BCC, *Minutes of Annual Conference*, 1875, 25; John Carroll, *A Humble Overture for Methodist Unification* (Toronto: S. Rose, 1876).

48 *Observer* (Bible Christian), July 23, 1873, 2; Hoover, 6–8.

49 MEC, *Minutes of Bay of Quinte Conference*, 1870, 72; MEC, MS Journal of General Conference, 1870, 202; MEC, *Journal of General Conference*, 1874, 41; 1878, 60, 123–124; 1882, 10. Pressure from the American Methodist church was also important (see *CG*, September 22, 1875, 297).

50 WMC, *Minutes of Annual Conference*, 1836, 138–139; 1845, 387; 1855, 307; 1856, 354–355; *CG*, March 22, 1854, 92; John Carroll, *Case and His Cotemporaries* (Toronto: Samuel Rose, 1867–77), 4:459; 5:109–111, 221; Henry Flesher Bland Papers, Diary, June 14, 1871.

51 WMC, *Minutes of Annual Conference,* 1873, 163–196; MCC, *Journal of General Conference,* 1878, 86.

52 Albert Carman Papers, William Graham to Albert Carman, November 18, 1881; *CG,* April 12, 1882, 119; MCC, *Journal of General Conference,* 1882, 240.

53 *CMM* 1 (1875): 15–16. See also *CG,* September 6, 1882, 284.

54 Herman Geissler, "The Laity in the United Church of Canada" (MTh, Toronto Graduate School of Theological Studies, 1960), 16; MEC, *Minutes of the Bay of Quinte Conference,* 1882, 20; *CG,* September 7, 1881, 284; March 22, 1882, 94.

55 Hoover, 6–8; Burnside, "The Bible Christians in Canada," 6–7; UCA, Albert Burnside, "The Canadian Wesleyan Methodist New Connexion Church, 1841–1874" (unpub., 1967), 5; *CMM* 16 (1882): 170–181.

56 UCA, Arthur Reynolds, "The Bishop in the Methodist Episcopal Church" (unpub.), 6; MEC, *Minutes of Annual Conference,* 1828, 17; WMC, *Minutes of Annual Conference,* 1833, 67; 1860, 75.

57 MCC, *Journal of General Conference,* 1878, 7–8.

58 *CMM* 16 (1882): 142. See also *CG,* August 30, 1882, 276–277; MCC, *Journal of General Conference* 1878, 133–134.

59 Albert Carman Papers, Addresses, "The Methodist Doctrine of the Episcopacy," 1883; UCA, John Alley (1799–1847), John Reynolds (1786–1857), Philander Smith (1769–1870), and James Richardson (1791–1875) biographical files.

60 UCA, Albert Carman biographical file; Albert Carman, *The Bishop's Address at the Opening of the General Conference* (1883).

61 *CG,* February 14, 1883, 52; Henry Flesher Bland Papers, Diary, May 28, 1883, 196; Albert Carman Papers, Philip Carman to Albert Carman, April 6, 1882; ibid., A. Cooper to Albert Carman, September 25, 1882; ibid., Thomas Webster to Albert Carman, September 27, 1882; ibid., Emerson Bristol to Albert Carman, October 5, 1882; ibid., Emerson Bristol and Thomas Webster, circular letter, January 31, 1884; ibid., James Webb to Albert Carman, January 18, 1884.

62 *CMM* 16 (1882): 137, 170–181; ibid., 17 (1883): 127; *CG,* September 20, 1882, 302.

63 Samuel Dwight Rice and Carman were elected general superintendents in 1883, but Rice died on December 15, 1884. At that time, the executive appointed John A. Williams as co–general superintendent, and the position was confirmed by the General Conference in 1886. However, Williams died in the fall of 1889, and Carman carried on alone until he was joined by Samuel Dwight Chown in 1910. Carman retired in 1914 and suffered an accident which hastened his death three years later. Chown remained the only general superintendent until 1925.

64 MEC, *Minutes of Niagara Conference,* 1877, 15–16; UCA, MCC, "1884 Union Vote by Circuit"; *Bible Christian Magazine,* 1883, 539–546; MC, *Journal of the United General Conference,* 1883, 18, 21–22, 25; BCC, *Minutes of Annual Conference,* 1883, 15; Hoover, 214; Burnside, "The Bible Christians in Canada," 359–360.

65 Harry Manning, "Changes in Evangelism within the Methodist Church in Canada, 1884–1925" (MA, Univ. of Toronto, 1975); Robert Chiles, *The Theological Transition in American Methodism* (New York: Abingdon Press, 1965), 136.

66 MC, *Journal of General Conference,* 1886, 273; Gwen Norman, *One Hundred Years in Japan, 1873–1973,* 2 vols. (Toronto: United Church, 1981); Alvyn Austin, *Saving*

*China: Canadian Missionaries to the Middle Kingdom* (Toronto: Univ. of Toronto Press, 1986).

67 James S. Woodsworth, *Strangers within Our Gates* (Toronto: Methodist Missionary Society, 1909); James S. Woodsworth, *My Neighbour* (Toronto: Methodist Missionary Society, 1911); UCA, John Thomas, "The Master's Vineyard: the Origins, Work and Growth of the Fred Victor Mission, 1896–1911" (unpub., 1980).

68 Douglas Wilson, *The Church Grows in Canada* (Toronto: Ryerson Press, 1966), 53; H.Richard Niebuhr, *The Social Sources of Denominationalism* (New York: 1957), 59–60; *CMM* 16 (1882): 137–148.

69 MEC, *Minutes of Bay of Quinte Conference,* 1847, 29; PMC, *Minutes of Annual Conference,* 1858, 13; BCC, *Minutes of Annual Conference,* 1867, 8; UCAMa M.R. Barkhouse, "*The Wesleyan:* Spokesman for Methodism in Eastern British America" (unpub., 1971).

70 *CMM* 1 (1875): 73. See also ibid., 4 (1876): 553–556.

71 *Canadian Methodist Quarterly* 1 (1889): masthead.

72 Lorne Pierce, *The House of Ryerson* (Toronto: Ryerson Press, 1954); W. Stewart Wallace, *The Ryerson Imprint* (Toronto: Ryerson Press, 1954).

73 MEC, *Minutes of Bay of Quinte Conference,* 1863, 54–55.

74 WMC, *Minutes of Annual Conference,* 1866, 93; MEC, *Minutes of Ontario Conference,* 1864, 10; MEC, *Minutes of Bay of Quinte Conference,* 1870, 67.

75 *CG,* February 19, 1873, 61. See also ibid., June 16, 1875, 190; *Milestones in Methodism: A History of Centenary–Queen's Square United Church, 1791–1966* (1967).

76 UCA, Nathanael Burwash Papers, MS Autobiography, chap. 9, 7; *CG,* June 6, 1866, 91; Nathanael Burwash, *Memorials of Edward and Lydia Jackson* (Toronto: S. Rose, 1876), 19; Sydney Ahlstrom, *A Religious History of the American People* (New Haven: Yale Univ. Press, 1973), 740.

77 *CG,* August 28, 1872, 277. See also ibid., September 20, 1876, 302; May 26, 1875, 166; MEC, *Minutes of Bay of Quinte Conference,* 1878, 90–91; Hoover, 181; Thomas Champion, *The Methodist Churches of Toronto* (Toronto: G.M. Rose, 1899).

78 *CG,* January 18, 1871, 10. See also ibid., July 31, 1870, 136; UCA, Henry Bland Papers, Diary, October 18, 1871, 96.

79 *CG* April 10, 1872, 116. See also Westfall, *Two Worlds,* chap. 5; William Westfall and Malcolm Thurlby, "Church Architecture and Urban Space: The Development of Ecclesiastical Forms in Nineteenth-Century Ontario," in David Keane and Colin Read (eds.), *Old Ontario: Essays in Honour of J.M.S. Careless* (Toronto: Dundurn Press, 1990), 118–147; John Ross Robertson, *Landmarks of Toronto* (Toronto: J.R. Robertson, 1904); Robert D. Cross, *The Church and the City* (Indianapolis: Bobs-Merrill, 1967), xvi.

80 WMC, *Minutes of Annual Conference,* 1842, 312; 1843, 337; 1872, 121; 1874, 115–116.

81 Marilyn Whiteley, "Conversion and Corrective Domesticity: The Misson of the Chinese Rescue Home," CMHS, *Papers* 8 (1990): 158–173; Rosemary Gagan, *A Sensitive Independence: Canadian Women Missionaries in Canada and the Orient, 1881–1925* (Montreal: McGill-Queen's Univ. Press, 1992).

82 John Thomas, "'A Pure and Popular Character': Case Studies in the Development of the Methodist 'Organizational' Church, 1884–1925" (PhD, York Univ., 1991), v, 9, 17, 53.

83  *CJ* March 9, 1883; March 16, 1883; April 6, 1883; April 27, 1883; *CCA*,
    November 7, 1860, 1; March 12, 1884, 4; *CG*, May 29, 1867, 86; July 14, 1875,
    217; *CMM* 4 (1876): 70–71, 148–155, 242–249,327–333, 417–421, 500–507; MC,
    *Minutes of Niagara Conference*, 1891, 64–65; 1893, 55–56; MEC, *Minutes of Bay of
    Quinte Conference*, 1879, 118; Benjamin Austin, *The Gospel to the Poor versus Pew Rents*
    (Toronto: Wm. Briggs, 1884); John Thomas, "The Christian Law of Living: The
    Institutionalization of Christian Stewardship in the Methodist Church, 1884–
    1925," CMHS, *Papers* 9 (1991): 109–128.
84  MC, *Minutes of Niagara Conference*, 1890, 71–72; 1891, 59; 1894, 73; MC, *Journal of
    General Conference*, 1886, 165; 1906, 294–295; Thomas, "The Christian Law of Liv-
    ing," 109–128.

CHAPTER NINE

1  *Observer* (Bible Christian), December 24, 1867, 2; CCA, February 13, 1884, 1;
   UCAMa, Charles Stewart Papers, Charles Stewart to Arthur Morton, December 25,
   1866; Phyllis Airhart, *Serving the Present Age: Revivalism, Progressivism, and the Methodist Tradition in Canada* (Montreal: McGill-Queen's Univ. Press, 1992), 36–37;
   Borden Parker Bowne, "The Immanence of God," in Thomas Langford, *Wesleyan
   Theology: A Sourcebook* (Durham, NC: Labyrinth Press, 1984), 157.
2  William Arthur, *May We Hope for a Great Revival* (Toronto: Wesleyan Book Room,
   1867), 67. See also William McLoughlin, *Revivals, Awakenings and Reform: An Essay
   on Religion and Social Change, 1607–1977* (Chicago: Univ. of Chicago Press, 1978).
3  *CG*, September 25, 1866, 154; June 3, 1869, 89; BCC, *Minutes of Annual Conference*,
   1883, 29; UCA, Samuel S. Nelles Papers, Sermons, May 9, 1858; H. Richard Niebuhr, *The Social Sources of Denominationalism* (New York, 1957), 63; Paul Carter, *The
   Spiritual Crisis of the Gilded Age* (Dekalb: Northern Illinois Univ. Press, 1971), 157.
4  UCA, Stephen Rice Papers, Diary, 5.
5  Neil Semple, "Samuel Sobieski Nelles and Victoria College, 1850–1887" (unpub.).
6  *CCA*, July 19, 1871, 1; *CG*, March 25, 1885, 85; Arthur Kewley, "Mass Evangelism in
   Upper Canada before 1830" (ThD, Victoria University, 1960), 4; Charles Hawkins,
   "The Law of Revivals," in Hawkins, *Sermons on the Christian Life* (Toronto: Wm.
   Briggs, 1880), 64.
7  Bowne, 154.
8  *CCA*, May 16, 1860, 4. See also ibid., June 25, 1873, 1; MEC, *Minutes of Niagara
   Conference*, 1845, 10; John Wesley, *The Appeals to Men of Reason and Religion*, in
   Gerald Cragg (ed.), *The Works of John Wesley* (Oxford: Clarendon Press, 1975), 11:
   intro., 25.
9  Samuel Nelles Papers, Sermons, March 10, 1859. See also *CJ*, November 17, 1882;
   *CG*, March 26, 1884, 102; April 1, 1885, 195.
10  *CJ*, March 16, 1883; *CG*, February 27, 1884, 68; *Wesleyan* (Halifax), March 7, 1884,
    5; *CMM*, 22 (1885): 375.
11  *CCA*, December 3, 1862, 2; December 17, 1862, 2; UCA, Henry Bland Papers,
    Diary 7a, 1858, 37; UCA, Albert Carman Papers, James Gray to Albert Carman,
    September 20, 1857; *CG*, August 23, 1854, 180; *CMM* 4 (1876): 251; Sam Jones,
    *Sam Jones and Sam Small in Toronto* (Toronto: Samuel Rose, 1886), 29; *Earnest
    Christianity* 1 (1873): 38; John Carroll, *Case and His Cotemporaries* (Toronto: Samuel

Rose, 1867–77), 5:134; Robert Boyd, *The Lives and Labours of Moody and Sankey* (Toronto: A.H. Hovey, 1876), intro.

12  UCA, Egerton Ryerson Papers, James Richardson to Egerton Ryerson, April 8, 1832; *CG*, April 23, 1883, 132.

13  MC, *Minutes of Newfoundland Conference*, 1895, 45–46. See also MC, *Minutes of Manitoba and North-West Conference*, 1896, 67–68; *CG*, March 12, 1884, 86; April 8, 1885, 209; *Newfoundland Methodist Monthly Greeting*, April 1913, 8–9.

14  WMC, *Minutes of Annual Conference*, 1870, 102.

15  BCC, *Minutes of Annual Conference*, 1861, 8. See also *Observer*, April 27, 1870; *CG*, April 9, 1884, 113; May 7, 1884, 145; PMC, *Minutes of Annual Conference*, 1877, 39; MC, *Minutes of Nova Scotia Conference*, 1897, 67–68; MC, *Minutes of London Conference*, 1892, 42–43; MC, *Minutes of Manitoba and North-West Conference*, 1892, 61–63; MC, *Minutes of Guelph Conference*, 1892, 42.

16  Kewley, 15; *CG*, May 9, 1849, 117; March 18, 1874, 86; BCC, *Minutes of Annual Conference*, 1866, 12–13; MC, *Minutes of Toronto Conference*, 1893, 56–58; MC, *Journal of General Conference*, 1902, 300–301; Hawkins, 57.

17  *CG*, February 17, 1855, 70; Kewley, 11; Charles Stewart Papers, Margery Johnson to Charles Stewart, April 10, 1862.

18  UCA, Samuel Dwight Chown Papers, MS "Story of My Life," 28–29.

19  *CG*, January 31, 1883, 36.

20  Albert Carman Papers, William Barnett to Albert Carman, October 3, 1881; *Earnest Christianity* 1 (1873): 210; *CG* March 23, 1870, 45; December 3, 1873, 390; WMC, *Minutes of Annual Conference*, 1868, 123.

21  *CG*, May 27, 1885, 332; February 2, 1872, 18; April 22, 1874, 124. The Reverend David Savage organized and trained bands of lay workers to assist in revival work, and they often specialized in bringing the penitent to a crisis of faith and beyond.

22  *CG*, December 2, 1885, 760.

23  Harriet Youmans, *Grimsby Park, Historical and Descriptive* (Toronto: Wm. Briggs, 1900), 59. See also *CG*, September 16, 1874, 293; *CMM* 8 (1878): 110–113.

24  MC, *Minutes of Hamilton Conference*, 1897, 74; 1896, 65; 1895, 56; *CG*, July 29, 1885, 469.

25  *CG*, July 19, 1882, 258. See also ibid., August 5, 1885, 484; August 12, 1885, 500.

26  Introduction by B.F. Austin, in, *Sermons by the Rev. Thomas DeWitt Talmage and others, St. Lawrence Central Camp Ground* (Ottawa: Loveday, 1878), 1–2; MEC, *Minutes of Bay of Quinte Conference*, 1878, 91. See also Randall Balmer, "From Frontier Phenomenon to Victorian Institution: The Methodist Camp Meeting in Ocean Grove, New Jersey," *Methodist History* 25 (1987): 194–200.

27  *Wesleyan* (Halifax), July 12, 1905. See also ibid., January 4, 1884; Margaret Ells, *Chapel Chimes: A History of the UCW & WMS at Berwick Camp* (1907), 1–2; S.C. Swallow, *Camp Meetings, Their Origin, History and Utility* (New York: Nelson & Phillips, 1879), 12; *CMM* 12 (1880): 277; 5 (1877): 373–374; 22 (1885): 127; *CG*, September 2, 1884, 548; July 30, 1879, 244; August 29, 1883, 276; MEC, *Minutes of Ontario Conference*, 1879, 84–85.

28  *CG*, July 4, 1866, 105; April 2, 1890, 218; Samuel Nelles Papers, Sermons, "Laws of the Spirit," n.d.; John Hoover, "The Primitive Methodist Church in Canada, 1829–1884" (MA, Univ. of Western Ontario, 1970), 177; Airhart, 91–93.

29 MEC, *Minutes of Bay of Quinte Conference*, 1866, 57; MC, *Minutes of Bay of Quinte Conference*, 1893, 58; *CG*, January 31, 1877, 36; March 14, 1877, 86; Henry Bland Papers, Diary, August 17, 1876; Airhart, 40–48.

30 MCC, *Minutes of Toronto Conference*, 1877, 68. See also MEC, *Minutes of Niagara Conference*, 1877, 119; MC, *Journal of General Conference*, 1890, 320; MC, *Minutes of Nova Scotia Conference*, 1891, 68; *CG*, September 1, 1901, 8.

31 *Newfoundland Methodist Monthly Greeting*, November 1912, 3. See also ibid., February 1913, 18–20; *CG*, February 4, 1885, 68; April 13, 1885, 229; December 9, 1885, 773; December 30, 1885, 821; MC, *Minutes of London Conference*, 1890, 43; MC, *Minutes of Guelph Conference*, 1893, 43–44; MC, *Minutes of Nova Scotia Conference*, 1890, 50–51; MC, *Minutes of British Columbia Conference*, 1892, 30; Stephen Rice Papers, Diary, January 30, 1896, 239.

32 WMC, *Minutes of Annual Conference*, 1872, 119; MCC, *Minutes of London Conference*, 1877, 124; MCC, *Minutes of Montreal Conference*, 1875, 53; MEC, *Journal of General Conference*, 1878, 62; MEC, *Minutes of Ontario Conference*, 1882, 20; *CG*, February 20, 1878, 57; Marilyn F. Whiteley, "Modest, Unaffected and Fully Consecrated: Lady Evangelists in Canadian Methodism, 1884–1900," CMHS, *Papers* 6 (1987).

33 *CG*, April 15, 1885, 229. See also ibid., February 18, 1885, 100; CMM 22 (1885): 375–376; MC, *Minutes of London Conference*, 1890, 43; MC, *Minutes of Niagara Conference*, 1893, 75–77.

34 Whiteley, 18–23; Elizabeth Muir, *Petticoats in the Pulpit: The Story of Early Nineteenth-Century Methodist Women Preachers in Upper Canada* (Toronto: United Church Publishing House, 1991).

35 UCA, Crossley Hunter Papers, scrapbook; UCA John E. Hunter biographical file; UCA, Hugh Crossley biographical file; Stephen Rice Papers, Diary, December 6, 1895, 236; *CG*, March 7, 1888, 147–148; David Johnson, *History of Methodism in Eastern British America* (Sackville: Tribune Printing, 1925), 359.

36 MC, *Minutes of Niagara Conference*, 1893, 77. See also MC, *Minutes of Guelph Conference*, 1893, 43–44; Joanne Carlson Brown, "So That Heart Purity Might Rule the Land," Bicentennial Consultation on Wesleyan Theology, Emory University, 1983, 9; Phoebe Palmer, "The Way of Holiness," in *Wesleyan Theology: A Sourcebook*, 86–90.

37 Brian Ross, "Ralph Cecil Horner: A Methodist Sectarian Deposed, 1887–1895," UCA, *Bulletin* 26 (1977): 94–103; MC, General Conference Papers, Court of Appeal Records.

38 UCA, William R. Young Papers, Sermons, "Doing One's Bit," n.d.; *CG*, September 11, 1901, 1; January 12, 1870, 6; November 29, 1876, 382; February 26, 1896, 138; October 5, 1910, 1; Jones, 24; Boyd, 244.

39 CMM, 24 (1886): 285.

40 MC, *Minutes of Nova Scotia Conference*, 1897, 67–68; *Newfoundland Methodist Monthly Greeting*, February 1913, 18–20; Neil Semple, "The Quest for the Kingdom: Aspects of Protestant Revivalism in Nineteenth-Century Ontario," in David Keane and Colin Read, eds., *Old Ontario: Essays in Honour of J.M.S. Careless* (Toronto: Dundurn Press, 1990) 113–114.

41 WMC, *Minutes of Annual Conference*, 1835, 101–102; CCA, April 30, 1884, 1; John Gilpin, "Heaven and How to Get There," in David Rogers (ed.), *Sermons by Minsters of the Guelph Conference* (Toronto: Wm. Briggs, 1886), 91; James Gray, "Introduction," in *Sermons by Ministers of the Guelph Conference*, xi; James Spencer, "The

Sufficiency of the Gospel Means of Grace," in Spencer, *Sermons by the Rev. James Spencer* (Toronto: Anson Green, 1864), 27.

42 *CG*, February 11, 1885, 81; May 6, 1885, 274; September 24, 1873, 308–309; MCC, *Minutes of Montreal Conference*, 1883, 108; MC, *Minutes of Toronto Conference*, 1896, 57; MC, *Minutes of New Brunswick and P.E.I. Conference*, 1896, 63.

43 Alexander Sutherland, *Counsels to Young Converts* (Toronto: Wesleyan Conference Office, 1871), 40.

44 MCC, *Minutes of London Conference*, 1875, 89; MEC, *Journal of General Conference*, 1878, 113; UCA, Lachlin Taylor Papers, Diary, July 23, 1865; MC, *Doctrines and Discipline*, 1890, paragraph 84.

45 MCC, *Minutes of Montreal Conference*, 1881, 55. See also UCA, Nathanael Burwash Papers, MS Autobiography, 52; Sutherland, 40–41; *CG*, March 1, 1854, 80; January 2, 1867, 2; *CJ*, March 23, 1883, 1; UCA Toronto, Adelaide Street Methodist Church, Minutes of Official Board, September 1867.

46 BCC, *Minutes of Annual Conference*, 1873, 12; *CG*, March 16, 1870, 43; March 18, 1885, 165.

47 Sutherland, 41. See also UCA, Thomas Cosford Papers, Journal, 50.

48 *CG*, October 28, 1885, 678; July 31, 1901, 2; April 17, 1872, 122; April 22, 1874, 125; *CCA*, April 30, 1884, 1; January 16, 1884, 2.

49 William Brooks, "The Changing Character of Maritime Wesleyan Methodism, 1855–1883" (MA, Mount Allison Univ., 1965), 31; Daniel Rupwate, "John Wesley's Covenant Theology," CMHS, *Papers* 9 (1991): 79–89.

50 MCC, *Journal of General Conference*, 1878, 31. See also WMC, *Doctrines and Discipline*, 1859, 92–93; Marion Jackson, "An Analysis of the Source of John Wesley's 'Directions for Renewing our Covenant with God,'" *Methodist History* 30 (1992): 176–184.

51 UCA, John G. Laird Papers, Addresses, n.d. (box 2, file 11); John Miley, *Treatise on Class Meetings* (Cincinnati: Swornstedt, 1854), 44; Jeremiah Chapman, *The Class Meeting* (Toronto: Wm. Briggs, 1882), 12; WMC, *Doctrines and Discipline*, 1859, 88; CMM 8 (1878): 465; Samuel Hunter, "Our Methodist Heritage," in W.J. Hunter (ed.), *Memorial Sermons and Addresses by the Late S.J. Hunter* (Toronto: Wm. Briggs, 1890), 288; Stephen Bond, *Church Membership* (Toronto: Wm. Briggs, 1882), 48–52; David Watson, "The Origins and Significance of the Early Class Meeting" (PhD, Duke University, 1978).

52 WMC, *Doctrines and Discipline*, 1859, 91. See also Bond, 49–50; John Atkinson, *The Class Leader* (Toronto: Samuel Rose, 1875), 84; Albert Burnside, "The Bible Christians in Canada, 1832–1884" (ThD, Toronto Graduate School of Theological Studies, 1969), 211.

53 John Carroll, *My Boy Life* (Toronto: Wm. Briggs, 1882), 251; William Morley Punshon, *Tabor; or the Class Meeting* (Toronto: Sanderson, 1855), 6–10; Chapman, 9.

54 Henry Bland Papers, Diary, 1860, 280; Miley, 32–33; Atkinson, 10–23; John Carroll, *The School of the Prophets* (Toronto: Burrage & Magurn, 1876), 32.

55 Burnside, 212; *CG*, March 25, 1885, 179.

56 MEC, *Minutes of Bay of Quinte Conference*, 1880, 16; MCC, *Minutes of Montreal Conference*, 1883, 71–72; *CG*, January 21, 1885, 34; MC, *Journal of General Conference*, 1918, 353.

57  Charles Hawkins, "Lukewarmness," in *Sermons on the Christian Life*, 179; BCC, *Minutes of Annual Conference*, 1871, 11; MCC, *Minutes of Montreal Conference*, 1875, 46; Albert Carman Papers, Leo Abbs to Albert Carman, November 15, 1881; CG, January 20, 1875, 15; February 24, 1874, 61; March 11, 1885, 147–148.

58  Egerton Ryerson Papers, Egerton Ryerson to Enoch Wood, January 2, 1854, 2.

59  Ibid., 3.

60  Carroll, *Case*, 5:170.

61  Egerton Ryerson, *The Story of My Life*, ed. J. George Hodgins (Toronto: Wm. Briggs, 1883), 481; Egerton Ryerson, *Scriptural rights of the Members of Christ's Visible Church* (Toronto: Brewer & McPhail, 1854), 12; Neil Semple, " 'The Nurture and Admonition of the Lord': Nineteenth-Century Canadian Methodism's Response to 'Childhood,' " *Histoire Sociale/Social History* 14 (1981).

62  WMC, *Minutes of Annual Conference*, 1854, 268. See also John Borland, *Dialogues Between Two Methodists* (Toronto: J. Dough, 1856); Spencer, 23; CG, May 31, 1854, 131; May 24, 1854, 130; February 14, 1855, 73; August 22, 1855, 181. The attack on Ryerson's position was led by James Spencer, the editor of the *Christian Guardian*, and John Borland.

63  Ryerson summarized his arguments in *Scriptural rights of the Members of Christ's Visible Church*. It was immediately countered by articles in the *Christian Guardian* and by Borland's *Dialogues Between Two Methodists*. John Miley's treatise on the subject was also widely circulated among Canadian Methodists in 1854. The following year, Henry Wilkinson, the chairman of the London District of the Wesleyan Methodist Church, explicitly answered Ryerson in *The Antidote to Dr. Ryerson's Scriptural rights* (London: Newcombe, 1855), and the Wesleyan Book Room republished William Morley Punshon's 1848 address to the British Conference as *Tabor; or the Class Meeting*.

64  Egerton Ryerson Papers, Egerton Ryerson to J. George Hodgins, November 8, 1855; WMC, *Minutes of Annual Conference*, 1856, 359.

65  CJ, November 10, 1865, 1; CG, January 29, 1873, 36; October 11, 1865, 161; *Observer*, July 23, 1873, 2; Jesse Hurlbut, *Our Church* (Toronto: Wm Briggs, 1903), 117.

66  CG, March 18, 1874, 84. See also CJ, March 30, 1883; WMC, *Minutes of Annual Conference*, 1873, 114.

67  MCC, *Minutes of Toronto Conference*, 1878, 81; MCC, *Minutes of Montreal Conference*, 1878, 57; MCC, *Journal of General Conference*, 1878, 119–126, 272; Henry Bland Papers, Diary 8, 352–353.

68  CG, April 5, 1882, 110; April 16, 1879, 126; January 21, 1885, 34; April 29, 1885, 259; March 21, 1888, 184; December 24, 1902, 2; *Wesleyan*, February 1, 1884, 6; CJ, February 16, 1883; *Rat Portage Methodist*, February 1, 1901, 1; MC, *Journal of General Conference*, 1890, 321; 1894, 243; 1902, 273; 1910, 317, 335–337, 412; MC, *Minutes of Nova Scotia Conference*, 1893, 51; MC, *Minutes of Newfoundland Conference*, 1894, 52–53; MC, *Minutes of Toronto Conference*, 1895, 51; MC, *Minutes of London Conference*, 1895, 70–71; MC, *Minutes of Montreal Conference*, 1891, 58–59; MC, *Minutes of Hamilton Conference*, 1896, 70–71.

69  Charles Hawkins, "The Profit of Godliness," in *Sermons on the Christian Life*, 91; MC, *Journal of General Conference*, 1910, 413; 1914, 59; CG, December 31, 1902, 2.

70  UCA, William Shannon Papers, Diary, 1854; Thomas Cosford Papers, Journal, 18–19.

71 John Carroll, *Past and Present* (Toronto: Alfred Dredge, 1860), 188–189; WMC, *Minutes of Annual Conference*, 1871, 8 (obituary of Stephen Brownell); CCA, May 2, 1848, 73.

72 Carroll, *School of the Prophets*, 64. See also W.S. Griffin, "Introduction," in *Sermons by the Rev. James Spencer*, 11–13; William Shannon Papers, Diary, 1854.

73 Sutherland, 42.

74 CG, January 23, 1856, 61. See also ibid., August 1, 1855, 170; *Earnest Christianity* 1 (1873): 266.

75 Henry Bland Papers, Diary, July 1, 1880, 75; Margaret Agar, "Antique Ontario," *In Americana* 34 (1940): 33.

76 WMC, *Minutes of Annual Conference*, 1870, 94; CG, May 23, 1883, 166; May 16, 1883, 158; January 16, 1895, 4; CCA, August 27, 1862, 2; Leonard Sweet, *The Minister's Wife* (Philadelphia: Temple Univ. Press, 1983); Goldwin S. French, "The People Called Methodists in Canada," in John W. Grant (ed.), *The Churches and the Canadian Experience* (Toronto: Ryerson Press, 1963), 76.

77 Egerton Ryerson Papers, Egerton Ryerson to J. George Hodgins, June 9, 1855; ibid., J. George Hodgins to Egerton Ryerson, June 11, 1855; CG, June 24, 1875, 150; WMC, Minutes of Stationing Committee, n.p.; Toronto, Wesleyan Metropolitan Church, Minutes of Quarterly Board, August 11, 1874; *Observer*, July 23, 1873, 2; PMC, *Minutes of Annual Conference*, 1873, 8; NCC, *Minutes of Annual Conference*, 1864, 19–20.

78 CG, January 17, 1883, 23; January 2, 1884, 6; Stephen Rice Papers, Diary, September 15, 1895, 73; MC, *Journal of General Conference*, 1894, 43; MC, *Minutes of Montreal Conference*, 1895, 73.

79 WMC, Minutes of Stationing Committee, 1865, n.p.; WMC, *Minutes of Annual Conference*, 1854, 271–272; Toronto, Adelaide Street Methodist Church, Quarterly Circuit Meeting, February 5, 1867; UCA, Donald Sutherland Papers, Correspondence, 1886–1887; CG, January 13, 1875, 9; January 2, 1884, 6; MCC, *Minutes of London Conference*, 1876, 57–58; 1877, 126.

80 CG, April 8, 1885, 213; May 14, 1902, 2; MC, *Journal of General Conference*, 1894, 285; 1898, 312; PMC, *Minutes of Annual Conference*, 1873, 7; CCA, January 16, 1884, 4; UCA, MCC, Board of Missions, Alexander Sutherland Letterbooks, II, Alexander Sutherland to George Cochrane, April 6, 1876, 203.

81 CG January 2, 1867, 1; January 12, 1870, 7; *Observer*, July 23, 1873, 2; MCC, *Minutes of Toronto Conference*, 1879, 98; MCC, *Minutes of London Conference*, 1877, 126.

82 CG, February 27, 1884, 71. See also ibid., April 11, 1900, 2; April 23, 1902, 5; March 27, 1895, 198–199; November 6, 1895, 4; December 11, 1901, 2; CJ, March 23, 1883; *Newfoundland Methodist Monthly Greeting*, January 1913, 14; MC, *Minutes of Newfoundland Conference*, 1898, 53–54; William Patterson, "The Doctrine of Ministry in the Methodist Church, Canada" (MTh, Emmanuel College, 1961).

83 CG, December 23, 1896, 818. See also CJ, March 9, 1883; *Newfoundland Methodist Monthly Greeting*, February 1913, 9; MC, *Minutes of Montreal Conference*, 1895, 73.

84 CG, January 14, 1885, 25; March 18, 1885, 162; April 1, 1885, 81; CCA, February 20, 1884, 1; CJ, April 27, 1883; *Rat Portage Methodist*, August 2, 1900, 2; UCA, George M. Young Papers, MS "This is My Story," 1897, n.p.

85 CG, August 21, 1861, 131; February 16, 1870, 1; March 23, 1870, 45; Sutherland, 42; John G. Laird Papers, n.d. (file 10).

86  *CG*, February 2, 1872, 18. See also ibid., December 28, 1870, 204; July 8, 1885, 424; June 24, 1885, 385; *Observer*, February 14, 1872, 2; BCC, *Minutes of Annual Conference*, 1874, 22.

87  *CJ*, February 19, 1875; *CG*, March 23, 1870, 46; April 6, 1870, 54; March 11, 1885, 152; April 23, 1902, 5; July 20, 1910, 19; *Observer*, January 16, 1878; MC, *Journal of General Conference*, 1910, 317–319.

88  George Jackson, *Old Methodism and New* (London: Hodder & Stoughton, 1903), 43.

### CHAPTER TEN

1  *CG*, January 25, 1832, 44; April 24, 1844, 105; *CCA*, December 31, 1873, 1; Alison Prentice, *The School Promoters: Education and Social Class in Mid-Nineteenth Century Upper Canada* (Toronto: McClelland & Stewart, 1977), 25; Robert Gidney and W.P.J. Millar, *Inventing Secondary Education: The Rise of the High School in Nineteenth-Century Ontario* (Montreal: McGill-Queen's Univ. Press, 1990), chap. 1; Egerton Ryerson, *First Lessons in Christian Morals; for Canadian Families and Schools* (Toronto: Copp, 1871).

2  *CG*, April 11, 1832, 85. See also *CCA*, May 23, 1848, 85.

3  UCA, Samuel Nelles Papers, Sermons, July 10, 1854. In 1882 Nelles wrote, "An intellect bereft of moral aim is bewildered and lost" (*CMM* 16 (1882): 122).

4  Thomas Arnold, "Inaugural Address on Appointment as Regius Professor of Modern History, 1841," in David Newsome, *Godliness and Good Living* (London: Murray, 1961), 2. See also *CG*, April 3, 1844, 94; *CCA*, January 14, 1857, 2; November 19, 1862, 1; George Webber, *The Pulpit the Age Needs* (Toronto: Wm. Briggs, 1886), 25; Neil Semple, " 'The Nurture and Admonition of the Lord': Nineteenth-Century Methodism's Response to 'Childhood,' " *Histoire Sociale/Social History* 14 (1981).

5  Samuel Nelles Papers, Random Thoughts, 1846–1849, n.d. See also *CG*, April 3, 1844, 94; Brian McKillop, *A Disciplined Intelligence: Critical Inquiry and Canadian Thought in the Victorian Era* (Montreal: McGill-Queen's Univ. Press, 1979), 19. In the 1870s, the Protestant churches in Ontario were deeply involved in retaining the Bible in the classroom and having clergy lead prayer and Bible study. Similar interests emerged in Newfoundland during the 1880s (Newfoundland, Methodist College, Minute Book, July 3, 1888; December 2, 1891).

6  Samuel Nelles Papers, Random Thoughts, "Methodism – A Germ," n.d. See also *CG*, June 7, 1843, 131.

7  *CG*, January 9, 1850, 248; WMC, *Minutes of Annual Conference*, 1860, 83; William Westfall, *Two Worlds: The Protestant Culture of Nineteenth-Century Ontario* (Kingston: McGill-Queen's Univ. Press, 1989), chap. 1.

8  *CG*, January 2, 1833, 30 31; December 5, 1829, 20–21, *CCA*, June 13, 1860, 4; *Journal of Education for Upper Canada*, 1848, 207, 215.

9  Albert Fiorino, "The Philosophical Roots of Egerton Ryerson's Ideas of Education" (PhD, Univ. of Toronto, 1975), 58, 141; Prentice, 14; Goldwin S. French, "Egerton Ryerson and the Methodist Model for Upper Canada," in Neil MacDonald and Alf Chaiton (eds.), *Egerton Ryerson and His Times* (Toronto: Macmillan, 1978), 45–58; Goldwin S. French, "Methodism and Education in the Atlantic Provinces," in Charles Scobie and John W. Grant (eds.), *The Contribution of Methodism to Atlantic*

*Canada* (Montreal: McGill-Queen's Univ. Press, 1992), 148; "Egerton Ryerson," *DCB*, 11:783–793; *Journal of Education for Upper Canada*, 1852, 145; Egerton Ryerson, *Report on a System of Public Elementary Instruction for Upper Canada* (1847).

10 French, "Methodism and Education in the Atlantic Provinces," 150–152; Judith Fingard, *The Anglican Design in Loyalist Nova Scotia* (London: SPCK, 1972), 151–152; T. Watson Smith, *History of the Methodist Church within the Territories embraced in the Late Conference of Eastern British America* (Halifax: Methodist Book Room, 1877, 1890), 2:385–386; John Reid, *Mount Allison University: A History, to 1963* (Toronto: Univ. of Toronto Press, 1984), 1:4–25.

11 UCANfld, Newfoundland, Department of Public Schools, *Reports*, 1876, 9–10; 1900, 5–6; Smith, 2:398–402. See also British Wesleyan Missionary Society, Correspondence, re early schools.

12 MEC, *Minutes of Annual Conference*, 1830, 34–35; Charles Bruce Sissons, *A History of Victoria University* (Toronto: Univ. of Toronto Press, 1952), 1–21; Nathanael Burwash, *The History of Victoria College* (Toronto: Victoria Univ. Press, 1927), 1–66.

13 MEC, *Minutes of Annual Conference*, 1830, 38. See also MEC, MS Minutes of Annual Conference, 1830, 35; WMC, *Minutes of Annual Conference*, 1835, 105; UCA, Egerton Ryerson Papers, Egerton Ryerson to John Stephenson, April 15, 1836; ibid., William Lord to Egerton Ryerson, May 31, 1836; ibid., Memorandum, June 28, 1836.

14 WMC, *Minutes of Annual Conference*, 1837, 172. See also MEC, MS Minutes of Annual Conference, 1831, 50; Sissons, 20.

15 UCAMa, Charles Allison Papers, Charles Allison to Alexander Campbell, March 27, 1845. See also ibid., William Temple to Charles Allison, January 25, 1843; UCA, WMSC, Charles Allison to William Temple, June 4, 1839; "Charles Allison," *DCB*, 8:15; Reid, 1: chap. 1.

16 John Carroll, *Case and His Cotemporaries* (Toronto: Samuel Rose, 1867–77), 4:369–370, 445; CCA July 21, 1846, 3; August 1, 1848, 126; WMC, *Minutes of Annual Conference*, 1848, 37; CG, May 3, 1843, 111; May 29, 1844, 126; Newfoundland, Methodist College, Minute Book, April 12, 1866; Marion Royce, *Landmarks in the Victorian Education of 'Young Ladies' under Methodist Church Auspices* (Toronto: OISE, 1977).

17 CMM 9 (1879): 399–403; George Cornish, *Cyclopaedia of Methodism in Canada* (Toronto: Methodist Book Room, 1881, 1905), 1:547–549.

18 MEC, *Minutes of Niagara Conference*, 1858, 11–12. See also CCA, December, 1, 1846, 2; October 3, 1848, 162; August 29, 1848, 142–143; August 1, 1848, 126.

19 UCA, Albert Carman Papers, Albert Carman to Philip Carman, February 27, 1858; ibid., Albert Carman to Philip Carman, May 8, 1858; ibid., Albert Carman to Philip Carman, September 23, 1858; ibid., Albert Carman to Philip Carman, November 19, 1858; ibid., Albert Carman to Philip Carman, January 28, 1858; CCA, January 29, 1862, 2; ibid., July 30, 1862, 4; Waldo Smith, *Albert College, 1857–1957* (Belleville, n.d.). Carman became bishop in 1874 but remained at Albert College until 1875.

20 Edwin Edwards, *The History of Alma College* (St. Thomas: College Board, 1927); CCA, July 5, 1871, 2; August 23, 1876, 2; July 30, 1862, 2.

21 CG, December 31, 1873, 420–421; Ontario Ladies College, *Vox Collegii, Centennial Edition, 1874–1974*, 7–15.

22 Raymond Archibald, *Historical Notes on the Education of Women at Mount Allison, 1854–1954* (Sackville: Mount Allison Univ., 1954); John G. Reid, "The Education of Women at Mount Allison, 1854–1914," *Acadiensis* 12 (1983): 3–33; J.T. Mellish, *Outlines of the History of Methodism in Charlottetown* (Charlottetown: Hazzard, 1888), 60.

23 Newfoundland, Methodist College, Minute Book, December 6, 1859 (clipping); August 1, 1869; April 19, 1870; April 15, 1874; March 31, 1871; April 14, 1886; August 24, 1892; June 4, 1902; Department of Public Schools, *Reports,* 1914, letter from superintendents of education to E.P. Morris, the premier, July 24, 1914.

24 UCABC, *The Calendar of Ryerson College,* 1926, 5; Robin Harris, *A History of Higher Education in Canada, 1663–1960* (Toronto: Univ. of Toronto Press, 1976), 262.

25 United Church, *Record of Proceedings,* 1926, 222–226; James Pitsula, *An Act of Faith: The Early Years of Regina College* (Regina: Canadian Plains Research Centre, 1988).

26 *Vox Collegii,* 18; Sissons, 27–30; Newfoundland, Methodist College, Minute Book, May 12, 1875.

27 *CCA,* May 30, 1848, 90. See also ibid., July 5, 1871, 2; Reid, "The Education of Women," 8.

28 MC, *Journal of General Conference,* 1886, 235. See also Gidney and Millar, 15–18; Albert Carman Papers, Albert Carman to Philip Carman, December 30, 1858; *CG,* March 12, 1884, 81.

29 *CCA,* May 30, 1848, 90.

30 Reid, "The Education of Women," 3, 9; Elsie Pomeroy, "Mary Electa Adams: A Pioneer Educator," *Ontario History* 41 (1949): 107–117; "Mary E. Adams," *DCB,* 12:9–10; Royce, part 3.

31 *CG,* April 29, 1840, 106; Sissons, 62.

32 Albert Carman Papers, Albert Carman to Philip Carman, January 6, 1858; *CCA,* July 5, 1871, 2; August 23, 1876, 2; Reid, "The Education of Women," 10; Newfoundland, Methodist College, Minute Book, 1859.

33 Samuel Nelles Papers, Addresses, "The Importance of Religion to Education," October, 1851; *CG,* January 9, 1850, 248; Alison Prentice, "Education and the Metaphor of the Family: The Upper Canadian Example," *History of Education Quarterly* 12 (1972).

34 McKillop, 17–21; Brian McKillop, "The Founders of Victoria," in Goldwin S. French and Gordon McLennan (eds.), *From Cobourg to Toronto: Victoria University in Retrospect* (Toronto: Chartres Books, 1989), 20; Brian McKillop, *Matters of Mind: The University in Ontario, 1791–1951* (Toronto: Univ. of Toronto Press, 1994), 14–15; John W. Grant, "Theological Education at Victoria," in *From Cobourg to Toronto,* 87; Egerton Ryerson Papers, Egerton Ryerson to J. George Hodgins, June 8, 1861.

35 Egerton Ryerson Papers, Samuel Nelles to Egerton Ryerson, September 21, 1846; ibid., John Ryerson to Egerton Ryerson, June 24, 1845; ibid., Egerton Ryerson to Dr. Olin, July 3, 1847; ibid., John Wilson to Egerton Ryerson, January 5, 1850; WMC, *Minutes of Annual Conference,* 1843, 351; Sissons, 66–70; Burwash, 5, 18, 23, 45, 62, 70, 81, 155.

36 WMC, *Minutes of Annual Conference,* 1850, 128; *CG,* September 25, 1850, 394; November 13, 1850, 18; January 16, 1850, 252; June 19, 1850, 340.

37 Samuel Nelles Papers, address on back of letter, November 12, 1859; Egerton Ryerson Papers, J. George Hodgins to Egerton Ryerson, September 26, 1857;

*CMM*, 12 (1880): 482–483; Neil Semple, "Samuel Sobicski Nelles and Victoria College, 1850–1887" (unpub.).

38  Samuel Nelles Papers, Egerton Ryerson to Samuel Nelles, April 21, 1854; ibid., John MacLaren to Samuel Nelles, October 5, 1883; ibid., Convocation Address, 1885; Egerton Ryerson Papers, Joseph Stinson to Egerton Ryerson, April 20, 1860; ibid., George Hodgins to Egerton Ryerson, September 26, 1857; WMC, *Minutes of Annual Conference*, 1852, 198; 1856, 47, 52; 1867, 94–95; 1868, 89; *CMM*, 24 (1886): 161; MC, *Journal of General Conference*, 1886, 161, 191–216; 1890, 214–216; 1894, 142–153; Sissons, 158–190; Semple, "Samuel Sobieski Nelles and Victoria College."

39  Arie Korteweg, "Dr. J.R. Jaques and Albert University, 1875–1885," CMHS, *Papers* 4 (1984); MEC, *Minutes of Bay of Quinte Conference*, 1868, 68–69; MEC, *Minutes of Niagara Conference*, 1868, 20; MC, *Journal of United General Conference*, 1883, 205–208; *CCA*, April 9, 1884, 4; January 16, 1884, 6; January 2, 1884, 4–5.

40  WMCEBA, *Minutes of Annual Conference*, 1859, 20; Reid, *Mount Allison University*, 1:79–80.

41  John Reid, "Mount Allison College: The Reluctant University," *Acadiensis* 10 (1980): 35–66: WMCEBA, *Minutes of Annual Conference*, 1874, 61; MCC, *Journal of General Conference*, 1882, 162–164.

42  *Wesleyan*, January 25, 1884, 4–5; February 15, 1884, 5; February 29, 1884, 4; March 14, 1884, 4–6; MCC, *Journal of General Conference*, 1882, 162–164; Reid, "The Reluctant University," 43.

43  *CG*, August 15, 1885, 516–517; August 19, 1885, 520; MC, *Journal of General Conference*, 1886, 31; 1883, 208; Alfred G. Bedford, *The University of Winnipeg: A History of the Founding Colleges* (Toronto: Univ. of Toronto Press, 1976), 24–55.

44  *Rat Portage Methodist*, September 2, 1901, 1; MC, *Journal of General Conference*, 1890, 237–240.

45  Morgan Dix, "The Education of Women for Her Work," in Benjamin Austin (ed.), *Woman; Her Character, Culture and Calling* (Brantford: The Book and Bible House, 1890), 450–451; Benjamin Austin, "The Higher Christian Education of Women: Its Mission and Its Methods," in *Woman; Her Character, Culture and Calling*, 372–381; *CCA*, October 8, 1873, 2; *Bible Christian Magazine*, 1883, 464–472.

46  Reid, "The Reluctant University," 42; Reid, "The Education of Women," 48; Chaviva Hosek, "Women at Victoria," in *From Cobourg to Toronto*, 55, 58.

47  WMC, *Doctrines and Discipline*, 1859, 57–59; MCC, *Doctrines and Discipline*, 1874, 57; John Carroll, *Past and Present* (Toronto: Alfred Dredge, 1860), 184; Adam Clarke, *A Letter to a Preacher* (London, 1800), 76; *CG*, April 15, 1896, 242; March 2, 1910, 29; Thomas Crompton, *Intellectual and Spiritual Progress* (Hamilton, 1856), 22; *Earnest Christianity* 2 (1874): 22, 196; H. Richard Niebuhr, *The Social Sources of Denominationalism* (New York, 1957), 30; John Carroll, *The School of the Prophets* (Toronto: Burrage & Magurn, 1876), 152; Reid, *Mount Allison University*, 1:109; Albert Carman Papers, Stephen Card to Albert Carman, October 16, 1862; UCA, Joseph Gatchell Papers, MS Autobiography, 25.

48  MEC, *Minutes of Annual Conference*, 1825, 8. See also John Davison, *An Address Delivered at the Ordination of Seven Ministers* (Toronto: Maclear, 1857), 17–18; UCA, Thomas Cosford Papers, Journal, 52; Robert Cooney, *The Autobiography of a Wesleyan Methodist Missionary* (Montreal: Pickup, 1856), 260; Albert Carman Papers, J.A.

Bloodsworth to Albert Carman, July 23, 1883; W. Morley Punshon, *Canada; Its Religious Prospects* (Toronto: Wesleyan Book Room, 1871), 9; W. Morley Punshon, *The Pulpit and the Pew* (London: James Clarke, 1869).

49 Samuel Nelles Papers, Addresses, n.d., 13. See also ibid., Addresses, October 20, 1848; ibid., Diary, December 26, 1866; *CG*, February 10, 1875, 45; WMCEBA, *Minutes of Annual Conference*, 1871, 114; MCC, *Journal of General Conference*, 1878, 181; Jesse Hurlbut, *Our Church* (Toronto: Wm. Briggs, 1903), 12; Charles Eby, *Methodism and the Missionary Problem* (Toronto: Wm. Briggs, 1886), 33.

50 Webber, 15. See also *CG*, January 14, 1885, 17; February 4, 1885, 65; MCC, *Minutes of London Conference*, 1876, 76; 1878, 82.

51 MCC, *Journal of General Conference*, 1882, 198; MCC, *Doctrines and Discipline*, 1874, 190–193; MEC, *Journal of General Conference*, 1878, 91.

52 MEC, *Minutes of Niagara Conference*, 1840, 10; MEC, *Minutes of Bay of Quinte Conference*, 1852, 21; WMC, *Minutes of Annual Conference*, 1857, 84; UCA, William Shannon Papers, Diary; Grant, 87; Carroll, *Past and Present*, 182–197.

53 Samuel Nelles Papers, Random Thoughts, "Plan of Labour, Toronto, 1848"; Henry Bland Papers, Diary 7a, 1859; UCAMa, Charles Stewart Papers, Diary, September 21, 1852.

54 Samuel Nelles Papers, John Maclean to Samuel Nelles, April 1, 1882.

55 Eby, 36; MEC, *Journal of General Conference*, 1878, 92.

56 MEC, *Minutes of Bay of Quinte Conference*, 1853, 25; BCC, *Minutes of Annual Conference*, 1860, 9–10; WMCEBA, *Minutes of Annual Conference*, 1868, 26; MCC, *Doctrines and Discipline*, 1874, 190–193; George Playter, *The History of Methodism in Canada* (Toronto: Anson Green, 1862), 260.

57 UCA, J. George Hodgins Papers, Samuel Nelles to George Hodgins, April 6, 1867. See also UCA, Thomas Darby Papers, Diary, 1892–1893, 70, 87; Russell Richey, "Evolving Patterns of Methodist Ministry," *Methodist History* 22 (1983): 32.

58 WMC, *Minutes of Annual Conference*, 1854, 277; 1855, 361; 1858, 76; 1862, 67; Carroll, *Case*, 4:394; WMCEBA, *Minutes of Annual Conference*, 1870, 28–29; Sissons, 474.

59 Smith, 14; Harris, 152; Grant, 91; Albert Burnside, "The Canadian Wesleyan Methodist New Connexion Church, 1841–1874" (unpub., 1967), 83–85; Albert Burnside, "The Contribution of Albert Carman to Albert College, Belleville and to the Methodist Episcopal Church in Canada, 1857–1884" (MTh, Toronto School of Theological Studies, 1962), 203; MEC, *Minutes of Bay of Quinte Conference*, 1878, 90; John Hoover, "The Primitive Methodist Church in Canada, 1829–1884" (MA, Univ. of Western Ontario, 1970), 199–200.

60 WMCEBA, *Minutes of Annual Conference*, 1860, 22; 1867, 21; 1871, 24; Reid, *Mount Allison University*, 1: 79–80, 106–110, 136–137, 282; 2:17–18, 68–70; Arthur Betts, *Pine Hill Divinity Hall, 1820–1970* (Halifax: Pine Hill, 1970), 34–35; J.W. Falconer and W.G. Watson, *A Brief History of Pine Hill Divinity Hall and the Theological Department of Mount Allison University* (Halifax, 1946), 34.

61 WMC, *Minutes of Annual Conference*, 1868, 116; F.W. MacDonald, *The Life of William Morley Punshon* (London: Hodder Stoughton, 1887), 355; Burwash, 235–240; Grant, 88.

62 UCAMo, Montreal, Wesleyan Theological College, Board of Governors, Minutes, 1872, 1–2, 16; 1878, 36; 1879, 39; 1882, 56; 1883, 71; 1887, 93; 1889, 100; 1898,

162–165; 1899, 185; Wesleyan Theological College, Senate Minutes, 1892, 26; 1893, 33; 1900, 88; MC, *Minutes of Montreal Conference*, 1899, 185; UCA, William Birks Papers, Scrapbook, *Montreal Witness*, April 2, 1913; ibid., *Montreal Herald*, February 15, 1913; March 5, 1913; CG, January 23, 1907, 22; Sissons, 145; Stanley Frost, *McGill University* (Montreal: McGill-Queen's Univ. Press, 1980–84), 2:286; Cyrus Macmillan, *McGill and Its Story, 1821–1921* (Toronto: Oxford Univ. Press, 1921), 234.

63  WMC, *Minutes of Annual Conference*, 1873, 115–116; Nathanael Burwash, *Memorials of the Life of Edward and Lydia Jackson* (Toronto: Samuel Rose, 1876); Sissons, 143–144, 221–222, 245–247, 265–270, 284–289; Burwash, *The History of Victoria College*, 418–419; CG, April 9, 1884, 119.

64  MC, *Minutes of Manitoba Conference*, 1884, 38; Bedford, 22–67; *The Calendar of Ryerson College*, 1926, 5–6.

65  Samuel Nelles Papers, Addresses, November, 1851. See also CMM 8 (1878): 69; Michael Gauvreau, "The Golden Age of the Church College: Mount Allison's Encounter with 'Modern Thought,' 1850–1900," in *The Contribution of Methodism to Atlantic Canada*, 180; Albert Carman Papers, Misc. Addresses, n.d. (box 25, file 171); Jon Roberts, *Darwinism and the Divine in America* (Madison, Wisconsin: Univ. of Wisconsin Press, 1988), 18–20.

66  Michael Gauvreau, *The Evangelical Century: College and Creed in English Canada from the Great Revival to the Great Depression* (Montreal: McGill-Queen's Univ. Press, 1991), 17, 38; Michael Gauvreau, "Baconianism, Darwinism, Fundamentalism: A Transatlantic Crisis of Faith," *Journal of Religious History* 13 (1985): 435; Carl Berger, *Science, God and Nature in Victorian Canada* (Toronto: Univ. of Toronto Press, 1983); CMM, 1 (1875): 174; Burwash, *The History of Victoria College*, 462–463; McKillop, "The Founders of Victoria," 17–22; Roberts, 239.

67  CG, September 19, 1855, 199; David Livingstone, *Darwin's Forgotten Defenders* (Grand Rapids: Eerdmans Press, 1987), 6–8, 13.

68  UCA, David Black Papers, Scrapbook, Toronto *Globe*, November 24, 1876, 1; George Douglas, *Discourses and Addresses* (Toronto: Wm. Briggs, 1894), 60–63; James Moore, *The Post-Darwinian Controversies* (London: Cambridge Univ. Press, 1979), 218; Leonard Elliott-Binns, *English Thought, 1860–1900* (London: Longmans, Green, 1956), 27; Herbert Spencer, *The Principles of Ethics* (New York: Appleton, 1898), 1:8–20; McKillop, *Matters of Mind*, 122. Spencer's work on ethics, biology, and sociology applied evolutionary principles to human affairs.

69  Moore, 15, 108, 307–311; Roberts, 16–17.

70  McKillop, *A Disciplined Intelligence*, 23; CMM 1 (1875): 174; Marguerite Van Die, *An Evangelical Mind: Nathanael Burwash and the Methodist Tradition in Canada, 1839–1918* (Kingston: McGill-Queen's Univ. Press, 1989), 105–107; Moore, 126; Livingstone, 37.

71  William R. Hutchison, "Introduction," in Hutchison (ed.), *American Protestant Thought; The Liberal Era* (New York: Harper & Row, 1968), 1–2; Henry Ward Beecher, "The Study of Human Nature," in *American Protestant Thought*, 38; Kenneth Cauthen, *The Impact of American Religious Liberalism* (New York: Harper & Row, 1962), 51–54, 57; McKillop, *Matters of Mind*, 217.

72  *Canadian Methodist Quarterly* 1 (1889): 167–169. See also Albert Knudson, "Henry Clay Sheldon – Theologian," in Thomas Langford, *Wesleyan Theology: A Sourcebook*

(Durham, NC: Labyrinth Press, 1984), 168; Livingstone, 3–4. See also William Paley, *Natural Theology* (London, 1802).

73 Borden Parker Bowne, "The Immanence of God," in *Wesleyan Theology: A Sourcebook*, 151–153, 157–159. See also Hutchison, 2; Alexander Allen, "The Continuity of Christian Thought," in *American Protestant Thought*, 57–58; Cauthen, 91–94; Livingstone, 45; Roberts, 20.

74 Cauthen, 55–57; Timothy Smith, intro., in Lyman Abbott, *Christianity and Social Problems* (New York: Johnson Reprint Corporation, 1970 [1896]), vi.

75 Hutchison, 2, 13–14, 23–24; Cauthen, 53–55, 85–87; Allen, 57; Knudson, 169. See also Walter Rauschenbusch, *Christianity and the Social Crisis* (New York: The Macmillan Co., 1907).

76 Hutchison, 1–2; David Swing, "A Religion of Words," in *American Protestant Thought*, 46–51; William Jewett Tucker, "The Fortune of My Generation," in *American Protestant Thought*, 18; Cauthen, 59; McKillop, *Matters of Mind*, 212–213.

77 Edward Burwash, *The New Theology* (New Westminster: Theological Union, 1909), 5. See also Gauvreau, *The Evangelical Century*, 125.

78 UCA, George Adams Papers, Lecture, "The Teaching of Enken," n.d., 7. See also UCA, William Henry Hincks Papers, Memoirs, 1:65; Samuel J. Hunter, "The Death of Moses," in Wm J. Hunter (ed.), *Memorial Sermons and Addresses by the Late Samuel James Hunter* (Toronto: Wm. Briggs, 1890), 106; Douglas, 279, 282, 307–308; Elliott-Binns, 28; George Boyle, "Higher Criticism and the Struggle for Academic Freedom in Canadian Methodism" (ThD, Victoria University, 1965), 21; Reid, *Mount Allison University*, 1:109–110, 222–228.

79 *CG*, March 28, 1883, 100; Paul Carter, *The Spiritual Crisis of the Gilded Age* (Dekalb, Ill.: North Illinois Univ. Press, 1971), 50–60; Bowne, 157; Moore, 224–227. See also John Fiske, *Excursions of an Evolutionist* (Boston: Houghton, Mifflin, 1883); John Fiske, *Darwinism and Other Essays* (Boston: Houghton, Mifflin, 1890); Henry Drummond, *The Ascent of Man* (London: Hodder & Stoughton, 1894).

80 *Canadian Methodist Quarterly* 2 (1890): 174–181; 4 (1892): 145–151; 5 (1893): 217–232; UCA, Nathanael Burwash Papers, Sermons, "All Scripture is Given by the Inspiration of God," 1881; Gauvreau, *The Evangelical Century*, 84.

81 Gauvreau, "The Taming of History: Reflections on the Canadian Encounter with Biblical Criticism, 1830–1900," *CHR* 65 (1984): 315; Milton Terry, "Methodism and Biblical Criticism," in *Wesleyan Theology: A Sourcebook*, 137–147; Elliott-Binns, 27; McKillop, *Matters of Mind*, 204.

82 Albert Carman Papers, "Alienation from God," November 19, 1873. See also ibid., "The Higher Criticism and the Lower Socialism," n.d.; James Graham, *Sin and Grace in Relation to God's Moral Government of Man* (Toronto: Wm. Briggs, 1883); *Wesleyan Sabbath School Magazine* 3 (1859): 147–151.

83 John Burwash, "The Limits of Religious Thought," in Samuel Phillips (ed.), *The Methodist Pulpit* (Toronto: Wm. Briggs, 1884), 181; Gauvreau, "The Golden Age of the Church College," 174; McKillop, *A Disciplined Intelligence*, 6.

84 Charles A. Briggs, "Orthodoxy," in *American Protestant Thought*, 28–34; Gauvreau, *The Evangelical Century*, 4, 7.

85 Samuel Nelles Papers, "Religion and Learning," November, 1857. See also ibid., "Spirit of Inquiry," April 20, 1843; ibid., "Free Thought," December 6, 1869; ibid., "New and Old," April, 1881; ibid., Diary, February 21, 1866; April 29, 1866; ibid.,

Correspondence, George Grant to Samuel Nelles, September 21, 1881; CMM 5 (1877): 107; 8 (1878): 370; MCC, *Minutes of London Conference*, 1876, 73; 1878, 82; Fred Dreyer, "Faith and Experience in the Thought of John Wesley," CMHS, *Papers* 3 (1983).

86 Nathanael Burwash, *Manual of Christian Theology on the Inductive Method* (London: Horace Marshall, 1900), 1:8–9. See also CMM 1 (1875): 136–138; 31 (1891): 93; Nathanael Burwash Papers, "Convocation Address, 1889"; Van Die, *An Evangelical Mind*, 89–113, 185–189; Albert Carman Papers, "Our Bacon," 8; Terry, 139.

87 George Workman, "Messianic Prophecy," *Canadian Methodist Quarterly* 2 (1890): 407–478. See also George Workman, *The Old Testament Vindicated* (Toronto: Wm. Briggs, 1897), 131–136; Samuel Nelles Papers, George Workman to Samuel Nelles, February 4, 1886; Tom Sinclair-Faulkner, "Theory Divided from Practice: The Introduction of Higher Criticism into Canadian Protestant Seminaries," *Studies in Religion* 10 (1981): 329.

88 Workman, *The Old Testament Vindicated*, 79–86; *Canadian Methodist Quarterly* 3 (1891): 407–454.

89 Albert Carman, *The Supernatural* (Toronto: L. Haynes, n.d.), 7; *Canadian Methodist Quarterly* 2 (1890): 174–181; 3 (1891): 1–24, 213–231; 4 (1892): 145–151; CMM 31 (1891): 93; Nathanael Burwash Papers, George Clark to Nathanael Burwash, September 16, 1890; ibid., "All Scripture is Given by Inspiration of God," 1881. During the Workman controversy, Burwash had "The Truth Shall Make You Free" (John 8:32) inscribed above the main entrance to the new Victoria University building in Toronto as a reminder of the need for uninhibited inquiry in the quest for Christ.

90 Nathanael Burwash, *Memorandum for the Committee on Education re Theological Teaching* (Toronto, 1910), 4–5.

91 Ibid., 6–7

92 UCA, Jackson-Carman Papers; Harry Manning, "Changes in Evangelism within the Methodist Church in Canada during the time of Carman and Chown, 1884–1925" (MA, Univ. of Toronto, 1975); Sissons, 233–239; Van Die, 111–112.

93 Burwash, *Manual of Christian Theology*, 1:23–24; Nathanael Burwash Papers, "The Poetical Book of the Old Testament," 1880; Cauthen, 66; Roberts, 117; Knudson, 169.

94 *Canadian Methodist Quarterly* 1 (1889): 94–95; CMM 4 (1876): 88; 2 (1875): 559. See also Stephen Chambers, "The *Canadian Methodist Magazine*: A Victorian Forum for New Scientific and Theological Ideas," UCA, *Bulletin* 30 (1983): 61–80; UCA, Lawrence Burkholder, "Canadian Methodism and Higher Criticism, 1860–1910" (unpub., 1976); Carter, 16.

95 *Canadian Methodist Quarterly* 1 (1889): 177; 3 (1891): 273; CMM 18 (1883): 278; CG July 26, 1882, 238.

96 Gauvreau, "The Taming of History," 316, 322; Hutchison, 23–24; George Workman, *Jesus the Man and Christ the Spirit* (New York: The Macmillan Co., 1928), 72–81; Richard Allen, "Salem Bland: the Young Preacher," UCA, *Bulletin* 26 (1977): 78–80, 84–85.

97 Reid, *Mount Allison University*, 1:227–228, 272–274; Sissons, 194–196; Gauvreau, "The Golden Age of the Church College," 180–181.

98 Gauvreau, "The Golden Age of the Church College," 170–171; *CMM* 7 (1878): 468–470; UCA, George Pidgeon Papers, "The Victorian Era," 1901; Elliott-Binns, 10; McKillop, *A Disciplined Intelligence*, 226; McKillop, *Matters of Mind*, 123, 204, 212.

99 The questioning of traditional beliefs by the young James S. Woodsworth was perhaps symptomatic of the theological confusion in twentieth-century Methodism. In 1902 and again in 1907, he attempted to resign from the Methodist ministry because he felt he could no longer subscribe to many of the central tenets of the Protestant church and many of Methodism's doctrinal standards. In reply, the committee established by Manitoba Conference to consider the latter resignation reported that nothing in Woodsworth's beliefs would require him to leave the ministry. If this was true, considering his declarations, little remained unassailable in Methodist theology. At the same time, Woodsworth was a well-known, intelligent, and respected son of the church who was obviously undergoing a serious crisis of faith, a common occurrence among Methodist preachers. The church leaders hoped that in time he would be able to accept the church's beliefs and should not be overly hasty in quitting the ministry (see Kenneth McNaught, *A Prophet in Politics: A Biography of J.S. Woodsworth* [Toronto: Univ. of Toronto Press, 1959], 20–21, 32–36).

### CHAPTER ELEVEN

1 MCC, *Journal of General Conference*, 1882, 264; George Emery, "Methodism on the Canadian Prairies, 1896–1914" (PhD, Univ. of British Columbia, 1970), 10–14; William Brooks, "Methodism in the Canadian West in the Nineteenth Century" (PhD, Univ. of Manitoba, 1972); Marilyn Barber, "Nationalism, Nativism and the Social Gospel," in Richard Allen (ed.), *The Social Gospel in Canada* (Ottawa: National Museum of Man, 1975), 190.

2 UCA, Enoch Wood biographical file; MEC, *Missionary Society Reports*, 1874, vii.

3 MCC, *Journal of General Conference*, 1878, 170; 1882, 140.

4 NCC, *Minutes of Annual Conference*, 1869, 19; 1874, 61; BCC, *Missionary Society Reports*, 1873–74, 22; 1879–80, 4; MC, *Journal of United General Conference*, 1883, 82–83, 210; PMC, *Minutes of Annual Conference*, 1860, 6; 1882, 6–8; PMC, *Missionary Society Reports*, 1873–74, 3; 1881–82, 48.

5 UCA, Albert Carman Papers, A.W. Edwards to Albert Carman, January 8, 1880; ibid., Fred Warne to Albert Carman, January 19, 1881; ibid., W.G. Hudgins to Albert Carman, September 12, 1881; ibid., D. Graham to Albert Carman, September 28, 1881; MEC, *Missionary Society Reports*, 1883, vi; 1874, vii; 1877, vii; MEC, *Minutes of Ontario Conference*, 1874, 48; MEC, *Journal of General Conference*, 1878, 128.

6 MEC, *Missionary Society Reports*, 1883, vii; MEC, *Journal of General Conference*, 1882, 70; Albert Carman Papers, R. Shorts to Albert Carman, April 12, 1880; ibid., A. Ferguson to Albert Carman, April 15, 1880; Albert Carman, *The Bishop's Address at the Opening of the General Conference* (1883), 15.

7 UCA, James Endicott, Charles Manning, Alexander Sutherland, Enoch Wood, and James Allen biographical files; MC, *Missionary Society Reports*, 1924–25, 4–5.

8 The statistics are drawn from the Methodist Church, *Missionary Society Reports*, for the respective years.

9 J.T. Gracey, "Women and Missions," in Benjamin Austin (ed.), *Woman; Her Character, Culture and Calling* (Brantford: The Book and Bible House, 1890), 165–166; Rosemary Gagan, *A Sensitive Independence: Canadian Methodist Women Missionaries in Canada and the Orient, 1881–1925* (Montreal: McGill-Queen's Univ. Press, 1992), 15–17; MCC, *Journal of General Conference, 1878*, 94, 220.

10 See MCC, *Woman's Missionary Society Reports, 1881–1882*; Rosemary Gagan, " 'Here I Am, Send Me': The Personnel of the WMS of the Methodist Church of Canada, 1881–1925," CMHS, *Papers* 4 (1985).

11 *Rat Portage Methodist,* March 1, 1901, 2; Woman's Missionary Society, British Columbia, *Diamond Jubilee of the Woman's Missionary Society in British Columbia, 1887–1947* (n.p.), 30–31; Wendy Mitchinson, "Canadian Women and Church Missionary Societies in the Nineteenth Century," *Atlantis,* 1977, 58–59; Gagan, *A Sensitive Independence,* 5; MC, *Woman's Missionary Society Reports,* 1889–90, 26; 1914–15, xl; 1924–25, lxv.

12 Albert Carman Papers, Mrs Carman's Addresses, "Mission Work and Women," 1886, 1–2. See also Isaac B. Aylesworth, "Woman as Missionary," in *Woman; Her Character,* 191–193.

13 Rosemary Gagan, "The Methodist Background of the Canadian WMS Missionaries," CMHS, *Papers* 7 (1989): 115–136.

14 CG, October 15, 1890, 664; *The First Annual Report of the Toronto Deaconess Home and Training School,* 1894–95, 15–16.

15 MC, *Journal of General Conference,* 1890, 321; CG, February 26, 1890, 136; October 15, 1890, 664; May 8, 1901, 3; Christopher Headon, "Women and Organized Religion in Mid and Late Nineteenth-Century Canada," *Journal of the Canadian Church Historical Society* 20 (1978): 3–18; Janet James, "Women in American Religious History," in Janet James (ed.), *Women in American Religion* (Philadelphia: Univ. of Pennsylvania Press, 1980), 18–19; John Thomas, "Servants of the Church: Canadian Methodist Deaconess Work, 1890–1926," CHR 65 (1984): 372.

16 *The First Annual Report of the Toronto Deaconess Home and Training School, 1894–95,* 7; Thomas, 371. See also CMMR 48 (1898): 117–122; UCA, Montreal Deaconess Board, Minutes, June 6, 1911.

17 Deaconess Society, National Training School, *Calendar,* 1911, 14. See also UCA, MC, Deaconess Society, General Board of Management, Executive Committee, Minutes, February 12, 1915, 151.

18 Deaconess Society, National Training School, *Calendar,* 1911, 23; United Church of Canada, *The First Fifty Years, 1895–1945* (Toronto: Woman's Missionary Society, 1945), 8; Thomas, 371.

19 Deaconess Society, National Training School, Report, 1904–05, 54; Thomas, 372–377.

20 *Western Methodist Times,* March 1906, 6. See also Ruth Brouwer, "The Canadian Methodist Church and Ecclesiastical Suffrage for Women, 1905–1914," CMHS, *Papers* 2 (1980); *The First Fifty Years,* 8.

21 MC, Deaconess Society, Report of Commission of Inquiry, March 1923, 4–5.

22 MC, *Missionary Society Reports,* 1893–94, i–iv.

23 UCA, Frederick C. Stephenson biographical file; CG, May 11, 1910, 13.

24 MC, *Journal of General Conference,* 1922, 274–275. See also MC, Board of Home Missions, Stephenson Papers, Annual Reports of YPFM, 1902–25.

25 MC, Board of Missions, James Endicott and J.H. Arnup Papers, Fred Hollinrake to James Endicott, October 6, 1911; ibid., Laymen's Missionary Movement, Minutes, August 4, 1910; August 3, 1911; ibid., T. Egerton Shore Papers, Eber Crummy to Egerton Shore, November 6, 1909; ibid., F.C. Stephenson Papers, Historical Sketches, "The LMM ," n.d.; MC, *Journal of General Conference*, 1910, 284; Margaret Prang, *N.W. Rowell: Ontario Nationalist* (Toronto: Univ. of Toronto Press, 1975), 68–69.

26 MC, Board of Missions, T. Egerton Shore Papers, George Williams to Egerton Shore, November 18, 1912; MC, Manitoba Conference, Laymen's Missionary Society, Minutes, June 6, 1917.

27 UCAMa, Thomas Allen Papers, Diary, August 4, 1867.

28 MC, *Missionary Society Reports*, 1885–86, lx; David W. Johnson, *History of Methodism in Eastern British America* (Sackville: Tribune Printing, 1925), 249; *CMM* 21 (1885): 164–176, 269–273, 336–340, 431–436, 518–524; 22 (1885): 63–67, 259–263, 365–367, 445–448, 542–547.

29 *Rat Portage Methodist*, October 1, 1901, 3.

30 *CG*, April 17, 1901, 8.

31 UCA, James Woodsworth biographical file.

32 John Webster Grant, "Ephraim Evans," CMHS, *Papers* 8 (1990): 107–114; WMC *Minutes of Annual Conference*, 1860, 26–27; Ebenezer Robson, *How Methodism Came to British Columbia* (Toronto: Methodist Missionary Society, 1904), 5.

33 WMC, *Minutes of Annual Conference*, 1861, 96–97. See also Robson, 8–9.

34 WMC, *Minutes of Annual Conference*, 1864, 30, 38; 1868, 45; WMC, *Missionary Society Reports*, 1866–67, xxx–xxxii; Robson, 13–14; Ivan Jesperson, "Missions to the Miners of Barkerville, 1860–1871" (BD, Univ. of British Columbia, 1968).

35 WMC, *Minutes of Annual Conference*, 1868, 33; 1871, 76; Robson, 14–16; MCC, *Missionary Society Reports*, 1874–75 to 1883–84; MC, *Missionary Society Reports*, 1884–85 to 1890–91.

36 MC, *Minutes of British Columbia Conference*, 1887, 1, 11; UCA, Cornelius Bryant and Charles Tate biographical files; UCABC, Charles M. Tate, "The Life and Missionary Activities of Rev. Charles Montgomery Tate, 1852–1933" (unpub. memoirs).

37 MC, *Missionary Society Reports*, 1885–86, xxxiv.

38 MC, Department of Evangelism and Social Service, "Report of the Rural Problem Committee, 1914"; John MacDougall, *Rural Life in Canada* (Toronto: Westminster Press, 1913); *Rural Survey, County of Huron, Ontario* (Toronto: Presbyterian & Methodist Churches, 1914); *Rural Survey, Swan River Valley, Manitoba* (Toronto: Presbyterian & Methodist Churches, 1914).

39 MC, *Missionary Society Reports*, 1907–08, 60; 1919–20, vii; UCA, Stephen Rice Papers, Diary, March 31, 1903, 335. Sixty-three of the one hundred and two students employed during the summer of 1907 in mission work were sent to serve in the northwest.

40 UCAMo, Montreal, Hochelaga Methodist Church Records, Official Quarterly Board, Minute Book, July 2, 1913; MC, *Missionary Society Reports*, 1885–86, xlii–xliii.

41 MC, Board of Missions, Correspondence, C.L. McIrvine to Charles Manning, January 10, 1921; MC, *Journal of General Conference*, 1902, 319.

42 WMC, *Missionary Society Reports*, 1854–55, xiii; 1868–69, xxxiv; MCC, *Missionary Society Reports*, 1874–75, xix, xxv; 1875–76, x; MC, *Missionary Society Reports*, 1885–86, xv, xx; 1924–25, 4; MC, *Woman's Missionary Society Reports*, 1925–26, x–xi.

43 WMC, *Missionary Society Reports*, 1854–55, xxi; 1869–70, xxxiv; MCC, *Journal of General Conference*, 1878, 166; Thomas Cosford Papers, Journal, 40; Benjamin Slight, *Indian Researches; or Facts Concerning the North American Indians* (Montreal: J.E.L. Miller, 1844), 126–130; William Henry Withrow, *Native Races of North America* (Toronto: Methodist Board of Missions, [1895]), 114; Thompson Ferrier, *Indian Education in the North-west,* (Toronto: Methodist Board of Missions, 1906).

44 Olivier Maurault, "Oka," in *Nos Messieurs* (Montreal: Editions du Zodiaque, 1937); MCC, *Minutes of Montreal Conference*, 1881, 13–14; WMC, Board of Missions, Enoch Wood Letterbooks, Enoch Wood to John Borland, December 30, 1869.

45 Armand Parent, *The Life of Armand Parent* (Toronto: Wm. Briggs, 1887), 199; John Borland, *The Seminary of St. Sulpice and the Indians of the Lake of Two Mountains* (Montreal: Gazette Printing, 1872); MCC, Board of Missions, Alexander Sutherland Letterbooks, v, Alexander Sutherland to John Borland, May 31, 1880; WMC, *Missionary Society Reports*, 1869–70, xxxiv; MCC, *Missionary Society Reports*, 1874–75, xlv; Albert Carman Papers, Petition from Governor in Council to Supreme Court of Canada [1904]; Protestant Defence Alliance of Canada, *The Indians of the Lake of Two Mountains* (Montreal: Witness Printing, n.d.); William Scott, *Report Relating to the Affairs of the Oka Indians* (Ottawa: MacLean, Roger & Co., 1883).

46 MC, *Missionary Society Reports*, 1883–84, xxx–xxxi; 1885–86, xxv; 1924–25, 4; Anthony Hall, "The Red Man's Burden: Land, Law and the Lord in the Indian Affairs of Upper Canada, 1791–1858" (PhD, Univ. of Toronto, 1984), 210.

47 UCA, Henry B. Steinhauer, Thomas Woolsey, Egerton Ryerson Young, and John Maclean biographical files; UCA, Thomas Woolsey Papers, Diary; J. Ernest Nix, "City Meets Wilderness: Thomas Woolsey in Edmonton House and Rocky Mountains, 1855–1864," CMHS, *Papers* 8 (1990): 189–201; J. Ernest Nix, "John Maclean's Mission to the Blood Indians, 1880–1889" (MA, McGill Univ., 1977); UCA, John Semmens Papers, MS, John Semmens, "Under Northern Lights," 22; Hugh Dempsey (ed.), *Heaven Is near the Rocky Mountains: The Journals and Letters of Thomas Woolsey, 1855–1869* (Calgary: Glenbow Museum, 1989).

48 "George M. McDougall," *DCB*, 10:471–472; UCA, John C. McDougall biographical file; John Maclean, *Vanguards of Canada* (Toronto: Methodist Church, 1918); J. Ernest Nix, "Pioneers, Patriots and Missionaries: An Appraisal of the Work of the Rev. George McDougall and Rev. John McDougall" (BD, Univ. of Alberta, 1954).

49 Alexander Morris, *The Treaties of Canada with the Indians of Manitoba and the North-West Territories* (Toronto: Willing & Williamson, 1880); George F. Stanley, *The Birth of Western Canada* (Toronto: Univ. of Toronto Press, 1960); John L. Taylor, "The Development of an Indian Policy for the Canadian Northwest" (PhD, Queen's Univ., 1975).

50 *CG*, April 8, 1885, 209. See also Ibid., January 28, 1885, 49; April 15, 1885, 228, 232; May 27, 1885, 323; December 23, 1885, 49; also MC, Board of Missions, Alexander Sutherland Letterbooks, correspondence with missionaries in the northwest, 1885–86; MC, *Minutes of Manitoba Conference*, 1886, 29.

51 UCABC, Ebenezer Robson Papers, Diaries; UCA, Ebenezer Robson and Ephraim Evans biographical files; B.C. Freeman, *The Indians of Queen Charlotte Islands* (Toronto: Missionary Society, n.d.): Charles M. Tate, *Our Indian Missions in British Columbia* (Toronto: Missionary Society, n.d.).

52 Thomas Crosby, *Up and Down the North Pacific Coast by Canoe and Mission Ship* (Toronto: Missionary Society, 1914); Thomas Crosby, *Among the An-ko-me-nums* (Toronto: Wm. Briggs, 1907); Emma Crosby, *How the Gospel Came to Fort Simpson* (Toronto: WMS, n.d.); Clarence Bolt, "The Conversion of the Port Simpson Tsimshian: Indian Control or Missionary Manipulation?" *B.C. Studies* 57 (1983): 38–43.

53 UCA, Thomas Crosby biographical file; MC, *Missionary Society Reports*, 1889–90, xxiii; MC, Board of Missions, Sutherland Letterbooks, Alexander Sutherland to Thomas Crosby, September 25, 1889; Mrs W.H. Graham, *Forty-Four Years' Effort of the WMS* (Toronto: WMS, 1925), 6–7; *Diamond Jubilee of the WMS in British Columbia*, 30–37; Archibald Greenway, "The Challenge of Port Simpson," (unpub., Union College, BC, 1955).

54 Oliver Howard, "Fire in the Belly," CMHS, *Papers* 8 (1990): 227; Crosby, *Up and Down the North Pacific Coast;* MC, *Missionary Society Reports*, 1924–25, 34.

55 UCABC, Robert C. Scott Papers, Chilliwack Record Book, 1878–1906; MC, *Missionary Society Reports*, 1895–96, xlii; UCABC, S.S. Osterhout, "Indian and Oriental Mission Fields, British Columbia" (unpub., 1929).

56 UCA, Dr R.W. Large, Dr H.C. Wrinch, and Dr Bolton biographical files; UCA local history files, Bella Bella, D.C. Darby, "Medical Missions, Bella Bella, B.C."; *Diamond Jubilee of the WMS in British Columbia*, 39; MC, *Missionary Society Reports*, 1924–25, 33.

57 Bolt, 46–56; MC, Board of Missions, Sutherland Letterbooks, Alexander Sutherland to Thomas Crosby, March 9, 1895.

58 MC, *Missionary Society Reports*, 1887–88, xvi; 1924–1925, 34; R. Whittington, *The British Columbia Indian and his Future* (Toronto: Methodist Board of Missions, 1906); anon., *The Conference of Friends of the Indians of British Columbia, Its Objects, Work and Needs* (Victoria: the Conference, [1910]).

59 *Vancouver Daily Province*, May 1, 1909; CG, July 31, 1901, 8; MC, *Missionary Society Reports*, 1895–96, xlii.

60 Halifax Wesleyan City Mission, *Annual Report*, 1872, 5. See also Wesleyan City Mission, Toronto, *Annual Report*, 1871; CG, November 3, 1869, 175; CMM 3 (1876): 277; 21 (1885): 376–377.

61 *Western Methodist Recorder*, April 1910, 4. See also *Western Methodist Bulletin*, December 1904, 4; John Macdonald, "The Maintenance of Home Missions among the most degraded Populations," *Proceedings of the Ecumenical Methodist Conference, London, 1881* (Hamilton: S.G. Stone, 1882), 413–419; Terry Copp, *The Anatomy of Poverty* (Toronto: McClelland & Stewart, 1975); Peter Goheen, *Victorian Toronto, 1850–1900* (Chicago: Univ. of Chicago Press, 1970).

62 UCABC, Turner Institute, *Annual Report*, 1917, 3–5; *Diamond Jubilee of the WMS in British Columbia*, 42; CG, June 5, 1907, 9–10; UCA, John Thomas, "Caesar's Household: The Methodist Social Union and Toronto Church Work, 1892–1926" (unpub., 1984), 1–53.

63 Margaret I. Campbell, *No Other Foundation: The Jost Mission of Halifax* (n.p.); *Newfoundland Methodist Monthly Greeting*, August 1912.

64 *Twenty-One Years of Mission Work in Toronto, 1886–1907: The Story of the Fred Victor Mission* (Toronto: Missionary Society, 1907); UCA, John Thomas, "The Master's Vineyard: The Origins, Work and Growth of the Fred Victor Mission" (unpub., 1980); Prang, 24; MC, *Minutes of Toronto Conference*, 1911, 60–61; Toronto Methodist Union, Missionary Committee, Minutes, June 13, 1913; April 7, 1914.

65 *CG*, March 6, 1907, 4; April 27, 1910, 4; MC, Board of Missions, Charles Manning Papers, J.S. Woodsworth to Charles Manning, December 23, 1907; ibid., Thomas Marshall to Charles Manning, January 19, 1909; ibid., W. Jackson to Charles Manning, November, 1909; ibid., Wellington Bridgeman to William Briggs, April 13, 1910; ibid., W.A. Cooke to James Allen, December 3, 1914; ibid., Marshall Hartley to Charles Manning, June 25, 1924; *Census of Canada*, 1901, 1:144–145; anon., *Immigration; Facts and Figures* (Ottawa: Ministry of the Interior, 1912), 3, 5, 7–8.

66 *CG*, January 16, 1907, 4; UCABC, William Lashley Hall Papers, Lashley Hall to Mr Stead, November 26, 1908.

67 UCABC, Vancouver Methodist Ministerial Association, Minutes, February 15, 1917; *CG* May 29, 1901, 4; December 25, 1907, 5; May 27, 1914, 4; July 1, 1914, 10–11; MC, Department of Evangelism and Social Service, *Report*, 1922, 69; 1924, 60; Prang, 57, 68–69; Donald Avery, *Dangerous Foreigners*, (Toronto: McClelland & Stewart, 1979); James S. Woodsworth, *Strangers within Our Gates* (Toronto: Missionary Society, 1909); James S. Woodsworth, *My Neighbour* (Toronto: Missionary Society, 1911); Mariana Valverde, *The Age of Light, Soap, and Water: Moral Reform in English Canada, 1885–1925* (Toronto: McClelland & Stewart, 1991), 17–19, 104–118, 132–134; *Immigration; Facts and Figures*, 7–8.

68 Edward B. Ryckman, *Our French Work* (Toronto: Board of Missions, 1906), 3–14; Harriet L. Platt, *The Story of the Years: A History of the Woman's Missionary Society of the Methodist Church, Canada, 1881–1906*, (Toronto: WMS, 1908), 1:83–84; Wesley T. Halpenny, *Our French Missions in Quebec* (Toronto: WMS, n.d.), 7; *CG*, April 25, 1885, 250; March 27, 1901, 2; UCAMo, French Methodist Church, Trustee Board, Minutes, April 14, 1881; WMC, *Minutes of Annual Conference*, 1856, 361.

69 Vancouver Methodist Ministerial Association, Minutes, September 28, 1914, George Hartwell, "Impressions of Our Oriental Work in B.C."; MC, Board of Missions, Oriental Committee, Minutes, January 23, 1911; MC, Board of Missions, Asiatic Committee, Western Section, Minutes, November 10, 1910; Canada, *Royal Commission on Chinese Immigration: Report and Evidence* (Ottawa, 1885); W. Peter Ward, "The Oriental Immigrant and Canada's Protestant Clergy," *B.C. Studies* (1974), 40–55; Karen Van Dieren, "The Response of the WMS to the Immigration of Asian Women, 1888–1942," in Barbara Latham (ed.), *Not Just Pin Money: Selected Essays on Women's Work in British Columbia* (Victoria: Camosun College, 1984), 79–87.

70 Van Dieren, 80–87; Marilyn F. Whiteley, "Conversion and Corrective Domesticity: The Mission of the Chinese Rescue Home," CMHS, *Papers* 8 (1990): 158–173.

71 MC, Board of Missions, Asiatic Committee, Minutes, November 10, 1910; MC, *Missionary Society Reports*, 1924–25, 64–65; 1904–05, xlviii-l; MC, Laymen's Missionary Movement Papers, Alexander Sutherland, "Our Duty to the Asiatics in Canada" (presented to Canada Missionary Congress, Toronto, 1909), 109–114; Charles Eby, "The True Inwardness of the Yellow Peril," *Empire Club Speeches, 1907–1908* (Toronto: Wm. Briggs, 1910), 43–53.

72 Tadashi Mitsui, "The Ministry of the United Church of Canada amongst Japanese Canadians in British Columbia" (STM, Union College, British Columbia, 1964), 6–11, 15–35; MC, Board of Missions, Asiatic Committee, Minutes, November 10, 1910.

73 Mitsui, 11–12; MC, WMS, Committee of Japanese Missions, Minutes, January 1911; MC, *Missionary Society Reports*, 1924–25, 29, 64–65; 1905–06, xlvi–li; 1906–07, lxxv–lxxx; MC, *Woman's Missionary Society Reports*, 1925–26, cliii–clxiv; 1896–97, lxvi–lxx; 1905–06, lxxxvii–lxxxix.

74 MC, *Missionary Society Reports*, 1898–99, c; 1899–1900, cvi; 1901–02, civ; 1906–07, cix; MC, Board of Missions, James Allen Papers, Charles Lawford to James Allen, March 20, 1908; ibid., R.E. Harrison to Charles Manning, July 26, 1911; ibid., W.A. Lewis to James Allen, May 5, 1911; *CG*, October 20, 1915, 8–9.

75 MC, *Missionary Society Reports*, 1924–25, 8, 11, 12, 15, 20, 24; MC, Board of Missions, James Allen Papers, H.R. Smith to James Allen, April 3, 1907; ibid., Charles Lawford to James Allen, November 9, 1911; *CG*, July 1, 1914, 10–11.

76 MC, Board of Missions, James Allen Papers, J.K. Smith to James Allen, January 3, 1913; Ibid., James S. Woodsworth to James Allen, May 21, 1907; MC, *Woman's Missionary Society Reports*, 1905–06, lxxxi.

77 MC, Department of Evangelism and Social Service, *Report*, 1916, 29; UCA, Robert Young Papers, Sermons, "Privilege-Reward."

78 Robert Harney and Harold Troper, *Immigrants: A Portrait of the Urban Experience, 1890–1930* (Toronto: Van Nostrand Reinhold Ltd., 1975), 48; Valverde, 105, 117; Enrico Cumbo, "Impediments to the Harvest: The Limitations of Methodist Proselytization of Toronto's Italian Immigrants, 1905–1925," in Mark McGowan and Brian Clarke (eds.), *Catholics at the "Gathering Place"* (Toronto: Canadian Catholic Historical Association, 1993), 155–176; MC, *Missionary Society Reports*, 1906–07, cxxiv–cxxx.

79 Toronto Methodist Union, Missionary Committee, Minutes, November 17, 1913; January 6, 1914; MC, Board of Missions, Italian Work, Correspondence, Missionary Secretary to P. DiFlorio, November 2, 1922; ibid., Italian Methodist Workers' Conference, May 8, 1923; MC, *Missionary Society Reports*, 1914–15, xx–xxiii; 1915–16, xxiv–xxvi.

80 MC, *Missionary Society Reports*, 1907–08, 76; 1909–10, 49–50; 1912–13, xxii; MC, Board of Missions, Montreal Italian Mission Report, August, 7, 1908; ibid., Italian Work, Correspondence, anon., to Missionary Secretary, 1917; Michael Catalano, *Italian Methodist Missions – What They Mean to Italians in Canada* (Toronto: Woman's Missionary Society, n.d.).

81 MC, *Missionary Society Reports*, 1899–1900, xcix; 1902–03, cviii; 1903–04, cviii; 1905–06, cx; 1906–07, cxiii–cxv; Mrs H.A. Lavell, *Canada's Immigration Problem, 1906–1916* (Toronto: Woman's Missionary Society, 1916); Kenneth McNaught, *A Prophet in Politics: A Biography of J.S. Woodsworth* (Toronto: Univ. of Toronto Press, 1959).

82 Graham, 11; MC, *Missionary Society Reports*, 1919–20, x; MC, Department of Evangelism and Social Service, *Report*, 1922, 69; *Western Methodist Bulletin*, December, 1904, 21–22; *CG* May 29, 1901, 4; December 25, 1907, 5; Bohdan Kordan and Peter Meluychy (eds.), *In the Shadow of the Rockies: Diary of the Castle Mountain Internment Camp, 1915–1917* (Edmonton: Canadian Institute of Ukrainian Studies Press, 1991).

83 *Western Methodist Times*, March, 1906, 4–5; MC, Board of Missions, James Allen Papers, J.K. Smith to James Allen, January 3, 1913; ibid., T.C. Buchanan to Charles Manning, April 10, 1919.

CHAPTER TWELVE

1　David W. Johnson, *History of Methodism in Eastern British America* (Sackville: Tribune Printing, 1925), 354–360; Paul Varg, "Motives in Protestant Missions, 1890–1917," *Church History* 23 (1954): 68–70; WMC, *Minutes of Annual Conference*, 1874, 146–147; G.A. Oddie, "India and Missionary Motives, 1850–1900," *Journal of Ecclesiastical History* 25 (1974): 61–74.

2　MCC, *Journal of General Conference*, 1878, 167; Varg, 71; William Hutchison, "Modernism and Missions: The Liberal Search for an Exportable Christianity, 1875–1935," in J.K. Fairbank (ed.), *The Missionary Enterprise in China and America* (Cambridge, Mass.: Harvard Univ. Press, 1974), 111–112; Hamish Ion, "Canadian Missionaries in Meiji Japan: The Japan Mission of the Methodist Church of Canada, 1873–1889" (MA, McGill Univ., 1972), 99; *Missionary Outlook*, June 1881, 71; UCA, Nathanael Burwash Papers, Charles Eby to Nathanael Burwash, November 28, 1895.

3　Varg, 75–81; MC, *Journal of General Conference*, 1902, 101–103; MC, *Woman's Missionary Society Reports*, 1904–05, xxxix; MC, *Missionary Society Reports*, 1904–05, xxxi–xxxv.

4　CG, September 1, 1875, 274. See also ibid., February 18, 1885, 97; March 18, 1885, 168; Varg, 72.

5　Charles Eby, *Christianity and Humanity* (Yokohama: Meiklejohn, 1883), 27; CG, February 13, 1884, 52; Hutchison, 122; Arthur Schlesinger, "The Missionary Enterprise and Theories of Imperialism," in *The Missionary Enterprise in China and America*, 336–373.

6　Hutchison, 113–117; UCA, Thomas Henry Williams, Robert Armstrong, and Cornelius John Bates biographical files.

7　Charles Eby, *Methodism and the Missionary Problem* (Toronto: Wm. Briggs, 1886), 38–39; UCA, Gwen Norman, *One Hundred Years in Japan, 1873–1973* (Toronto: United Church, 1981), 1:13; CG, February 9, 1910, 8; MC, Board of Missions, T. Egerton Shore Papers, Egerton Shore to J.E. Jenner, November 29, 1910.

8　Isaac B. Aylesworth, "Woman as Missionary," in Benjamin Austin (ed.), *Woman; Her Character, Culture and Calling* (Brantford: The Book and Bible House, 1890), 191–193. See also CG, May 19, 1880, 157; Harriet Platt, *The Story of the Years: A History of the Woman's Missionary Society, 1881–1906* (Toronto: WMS, 1908), 2:7; Patricia Hill, "Heathen Women's Friends: The Role of Methodist Episcopal Women in the Women's Foreign Mission Movement, 1869–1915," *Methodist History* 19 (1981): 151–154.

9　*Missionary Outlook*, October 1883, 156. See also Rosemary Gagan, *A Sensitive Independence: Canadian Methodist Women in Canada and the Orient, 1881–1925* (Montreal: McGill-Queen's Univ. Press, 1992), 4–9.

10　*Missionary Outlook*, May 1882, 71–72; March 1885, 42.

11　WMC, *Minutes of Annual Conference*, 1871, 93, 143; 1873, 142; WMC, *Missionary Society Reports*, 1872–73, ix; 1873–74, xxiv–xxvi; Gagan, 11; Ion, 10–12; UCA, William Morley Punshon biographical file.

12　MCC, Board of Missions, Sutherland Letterbooks, Alexander Sutherland to George Meacham, July 28, 1876. See also Norman, 1:84–88; Ion, 38, 118; *Missionary Notices*, March 1876, 90–91; September 1877, 241; February 1878, 278.

13 Ion, 240; *Missionary Notices,* February 1878, 280; MC, *Journal of General Conference,* 1898, 124–125; Norman, 1:319; Ken Adachi, *The Enemy that Never Was* (Toronto: McClelland and Stewart, 1976), 81–82. In 1894–95 Japan defeated China in a war over control of Korea and also gained concessions in Manchuria and control of the Liaodung Peninsula, including Port Arthur. The war marked the beginning of a policy of territorial expansion and the arrival of the military as a major factor in Japanese politics. However, Russia, with the support of Germany and France, forced Japan to withdraw from the Liaodung Peninsula in 1898 and occupied the area itself. In a brief, but decisive, war with Russia between 1904 and 1905, Japan forced Russia out and regained pre-eminence in the region.

14 MC, Board of Missions, Japan Mission Papers, extract of report, 1906; Gagan, map, xiii.

15 Ion, i, 27, 50–52, 61; Eby, *Methodism and the Missionary Problem,* 39; *Missionary Notices,* August 1878, 302; WMC, *Missionary Society Reports,* 1873–74, xxv–xxvi.

16 UCA, Davidson Macdonald biographical file; Ion, 51–61.

17 UCA, George Cochran biographical file; MC, *Minutes of Toronto Conference,* 1901, 16–17, Ion, 93, 111.

18 MCC, Board of Missions, Enoch Wood Letterbooks, Enoch Wood to Davidson Macdonald, October 25, 1875; ibid., Alexander Sutherland Letterbooks, Alexander Sutherland to George Cochran, November 25, 1875; UCA, George Meacham and Charles Eby biographical files; Ion, 13.

19 *Missionary Outlook,* August 1884, 115. See also ibid., June 1881, 71; Norman, 1:24; MCC, *Missionary Society Reports,* 1878–79, xxv–xxvii; MCC, *Journal of General Conference,* 1878, 167–168.

20 Ion, 171–174; Annie Stephenson, *One Hundred Years of Canadian Methodist Missions, 1824–1924* (Toronto: Methodist Missionary Society, 1925), 2:161, 171–174; Norman, 1:52.

21 Charles Eby, *The Forward Movement in Japan* (Toronto: Missionary Society, 1889), 8; Ion, 175–177, 186–187; Norman, 1:121–122; Stephenson, 2:175–177; Hamish Ion, "British and Canadian Missionaries in the Japanese Empire, 1905–1925" (PhD, Univ. of Sheffield, 1978), 265; MC, Board of Missions, Japan Mission Papers, Correspondence, F.A. Cassidy to Albert Carman, November 16, 1897; ibid., Alexander Sutherland Letterbooks, Arthur Borden to Alexander Sutherland, January 23, 1905.

22 MC, *Journal of General Conference,* 1886, 256; Ion, "Canadian Missionaries in Meiji Japan," 177–180.

23 Norman, 1:141–142, appendix; UCA, Daniel R. MacKenzie, Eber Crummy, and Cornelius John Bates biographical files; Ion, "British and Canadian Missionaries in the Japanese Empire," 99, 259; MC, Board of Missions, T. Egerton Shore Papers, W.G. Connolly to Egerton Shore, December 30, 1911.

24 Ion, "Canadian Missionaries in Meiji Japan," 146; Norman, 1:88, 100, 107; Davidson Macdonald biographical file; *Missionary Outlook,* October 1883, 146; MC Board of Missions, T. Egerton Shore Papers, Daniel R. MacKenzie to Egerton Shore, report, 1911.

25 Ion, "Canadian Missionaries in Meiji Japan," 144; MC, *Missionary Society Reports,* 1888–89, xxxii; MC, Board of Missions, Japan Mission Papers, Alexander Sutherland to Albert Carman, March 28, 1898.

26 Ion, "British and Canadian Missionaries in the Japanese Empire," 292; MC, Board of Missions, Japan Mission Papers, Daniel Norman to Egerton Shore, September 26, 1910; Cornelius John Bates biographical file.

27 Ion, "Canadian Missionaries in Meiji Japan," 107–108; MCC, *Journal of General Conference,* 1878, 224; MC of C, Board of Missions, Finance Committee, Minutes, November 24, 1878; ibid., Alexander Sutherland Letterbooks, Alexander Sutherland to Davidson Macdonald, November 8, 1882; MC, Board of Missions, Japan Mission Papers, Alexander Sutherland to Albert Carman, March 28, 1898.

28 Norman, 1:121, 168–170; UCA, Stephen Rice Papers, Diary, October 7, 1895; *CG,* February 6, 1895, 89.

29 MC, Board of Missions, Committee on Japan Affair, Minutes, October 4, 1895; ibid., Japan Mission Papers, Alexander Sutherland, "A Review of Certain Matters Connected with the Japan Mission," 1898, 41, 54–55; *CG,* August 14, 1895, 523.

30 Norman, 1:41.

31 Ion, "Canadian Missionaries in Meiji Japan," 102, 156–162, 178; MCC, Board of Missions, Japan Mission Papers, Enoch Wood to Davidson Macdonald, October 25, 1875; ibid., Daniel Norman to Albert Carman, January 14, 1899; ibid., Minutes of Japan District, April 2, 1888, 12; MCC, *Missionary Society Reports,* 1882–83, xxxii; *Missionary Outlook,* February 1883, 22.

32 Ion, "Canadian Missionaries in Meiji Japan," 177; MC, Board of Missions, T. Egerton Shore Papers, report, 1908; ibid., Japan Mission Papers, George Meacham to Albert Carman, June 7, 1898; *CG,* July 31, 1901, 4; *New Outlook,* September 20, 1933, 686.

33 MC, *Journal of General Conference,* 1886, 256; 1890, 262–268, 283; 1898, 124–125; Ion, "British and Canadian Missionaries in the Japanese Empire," 32; Eby, *Methodism and the Missionary Problem,* 29–30; Ion, "Canadian Missionaries in Meiji Japan," 137; *Missionary Outlook,* August 1884, 115.

34 MC, Board of Missions, Japan Mission Papers, George Meacham to Albert Carman, June 7, 1898. See also ibid., Alexander Sutherland to Albert Carman, March 28, 1898; ibid., T. Egerton Shore Papers, R.C. Armstrong to Egerton Shore, June 15, 1908; ibid., E.C. Hennigar to Egerton Shore, November 29, 1909.

35 MC, Board of Missions, Japan Mission Papers, Yoshiyasu Hiraiwa, circular letter, January 1898; ibid., Yoshiyasu Hiraiwa to Albert Carman, February 5, 1902; ibid., Yoshiyasu Hiraiwa to John Scott, February 17, 1902; *CG,* February 20, 1901, 9; MC, *Journal of General Conference,* 1898, 124–125; 1902, 107–108, 120–121.

36 *CG,* April 3, 1895, 213; May 15, 1895, 313.

37 *Missionary Outlook,* July 1895, 99.

38 MC, *Journal of General Conference,* 1906, 372–374; Norman, 1:90, 141–142; MC, Board of Missions, Alexander Sutherland Papers, Harper Coates to Alexander Sutherland, February 18, 1904; ibid., D.R. MacKenzie to Alexander Sutherland, June 6, 1904.

39 Ion, "Canadian Missionaries in Meiji Japan," 113, 182; MC, Board of Missions, Japan Mission Papers, Minutes, 1906–07; ibid., Harper Coates to Alexander Sutherland, January 6, 1909; ibid., Minutes, February, 10, 1914; "Yoitsu Honda," *Encyclopedia of World Methodism,* 1:1151.

40 UCA, Martha Cartmell biographical file; Norman, 1: appendix; Ion, "Canadian Missionaries in Meiji Japan," 153; *CG,* May 19, 1880, 157; *Missionary Outlook,* April 1891, 53.

41  Ion, "Canadian Missionaries in Meiji Japan," 149, 156; Katherine Ridout, "A
    Woman of Mission: The Religious and Cultural Odyssey of Agnes Wintemute
    Coates" *CHR* 82 (1990): 208–244; Norman, 1:67, 133–134, 393.

42  Norman, 1:74, 268–269; Martha Cartmell biographical file.

43  *Missionary Outlook,* November 1884, 176; *CG,* January 24, 1900, 2; Norman, 1:79–
    80, 124–125, 141; Ion, "British and Canadian Missionaries in the Japanese Em-
    pire," 258–259, 280; MC, Board of Missions, T. Egerton Shore Papers, Daniel
    Norman to Egerton Shore, May 27, 1911.

44  Ion, "Canadian Missionaries in Meiji Japan," 162; Norman, 1:78–80, 121, 168–
    175, 178; MC, WMS, Annual Meeting, Minutes, March 18, 1891; ibid., Japan Coun-
    cil, Minutes, July 13, 1892.

45  Gagan, 83–96; UCA, Thomas Large and Eliza Spencer Large biographical files;
    Norman, 1:173. "The home-coming of Mrs. Large (1890), though sad, accom-
    plished a great deal for our society. She bravely took her place in annual meetings
    and pleaded for Japan, the land of her adoption; the scarred face and maimed
    hand adding to the pathos of her appeal" (Platt, 1:27).

46  MC, Board of Missions, Japan Mission Papers, D.R. MacKenzie to Alexander Suth-
    erland, November 24, 1897; UCA, E.C. Hennigar biographical file; Norman, 1:64,
    184; Ridout, 226–233.

47  Ion, "British and Canadian Missionaries in the Japanese Empire," 71, 309; *Mission-
    ary Leaflet,* August 1894, 6–7; MC, WMS, Japan Council, Minutes, July 13, 1892;
    Norman, 1:79, 121.

48  Ion, "British and Canadian Missionaries in the Japanese Empire," 82–84, 175–179,
    328; MC, Board of Missions, Alexander Sutherland Papers, Robert Armstrong to
    Alexander Sutherland, July 1904; MC, *Journal of General Conference,* 1914, 200.

49  MC, Board of Missions, T. Egerton Shore Papers, Robert Armstrong to Egerton
    Shore, June 15, 1908. See also ibid., Japan Mission Papers, Yoshiyasu Hiraiwa to
    Alexander Sutherland, August 14, 1908.

50  Ion, "British and Canadian Missionaries in the Japanese Empire," 103; MC, Board
    of Missions, T. Egerton Shore Papers, Robert Armstrong to Egerton Shore,
    June 15, 1908.

51  MC, *Journal of General Conference,* 1910, 255; 1914, 197; MC, Board of Missions,
    Japan Mission Papers, Harper Coates to Alexander Sutherland, January 6, 1909;
    ibid., T. Egerton Shore Papers, E.C. Hennigar to Egerton Shore, November 29,
    1909; ibid., Egerton Shore to J.G. Brown, October 26, 1909; ibid., D.R. Mackenzie
    to Egerton Shore, February 2, 1913; Ion, "British and Canadian Missionaries in the
    Japanese Empire," 137–139; *CG,* February 9, 1910, 8; June 8, 1910, 8.

52  UCA, Harper Coates, Robert Armstrong, and Cornelius John Bates biographical
    files; Henry King, *The Moral and Religious Challenge of Our Times* (New York: Mac-
    millan, 1915), 348–360; Leslie G. Kilborn, *The Colossal Conceit of Missionaries*
    (Toronto: United Church, n.d.).

53  MC, *Missionary Society Reports,* 1890–91, ix.

54  *CG,* July 15, 1885, 435; MC, *Journal of General Conference,* 1890, 257; Alvyn Austin,
    *Saving China: Canadian Missionaries in the Middle Kingdom, 1888–1959* (Toronto:
    Univ. of Toronto Press, 1986), 1–7, 24.

55  UCA, Virgil C. Hart and Dr Leonora Howard King biographical files; Austin, 27,
    50–51. The spelling of Chinese place-names has changed several times over the

last century. I have followed the spelling commonly used by the Methodist missionaries themselves.

56 MC, *Missionary Society Reports,* 1892–93, xxxii; Austin, 50–51; MC, *Woman's Missionary Society Reports,* 1891–92, 6; Edward Wilson Wallace, *The Heart of Sz-Chuan* (Toronto: YPFM, [1903] 1905), 9–25.

57 MC, *Missionary Society Reports,* 1892–93, xxxii–xxxvi; Austin, 52–56.

58 MC, *Journal of General Conference,* 1894, 132. See also MC, *Missionary Society Reports,* 1893–94, xxx; MC, *Woman's Missionary Society Reports,* 1892–93, 24; 1893–94, v, xx; UCA, Omar Kilborn biographical file; Austin, 113.

59 MC, *Woman's Missionary Society Reports,* 1896–97, liv; MC, *Missionary Society Reports,* 1892–93, xxxv; Elizabeth Strachan, *The Story of the Years: A History of the Woman's Missionary Society, 1906–1916* (Toronto: Wm. Briggs, 1917), 197; Austin, 57, 119, 138.

60 MC, *Woman's Missionary Society Reports,* 1894–95, xxi–xxii; MC, *Missionary Society Reports,* 1894–95, xxxix; 1895–96, xxxiii; MC, Board of Missions, West China Papers, Alexander Sutherland to James Endicott, May 5, 1896.

61 MC, *Missionary Society Reports,* 1901–02, xxvi; MC, *Woman's Missionary Society Reports,* 1901–02, lxxiii–lxxvii; Austin, 63.

62 MC, Board of Missions, West China Papers, Richard Wolfendale to Egerton Shore, December 5, 1911. See also Austin, 117–122; UCA, Richard Orlando Jolliffe biographical file; MC, *Journal of General Conference,* 1918, 226; Bruce Lawrie, "Educational Missionaries in China: A Case Study of the Educational Enterprise of the Canadian Methodist Mission in Szechuan, West China, 1891–1925" (PhD, Univ. of Toronto, 1979).

63 MC, Board of Missions, West China Papers, D.S. Kern to James Endicott, January 12, 1922; MC, *Journal of General Conference,* 1922, 260; United Church, *Record of Proceedings,* 1926, 260, 297.

64 MC, *Missionary Society Reports,* 1895–96, xxxix; 1898–99, xxviii; MC, *Woman's Missionary Society Reports,* 1894–95, xxi–xxii; 1895–96, xix–xxii; MC, Board of Missions, West China Mission Council, Minutes, May 23, 1902; Strachan, 181.

65 MC, *Missionary Society Reports,* 1905–06, xxx; MC, *Woman's Missionary Society Reports,* 1903–04, xli; MC, *Journal of General Conference,* 1906, 55; John Foster, "The Imperialism of Righteousness: Canadian Protestant Missionaries and the Chinese Revolution" (PhD, Univ. of Toronto, 1977), 38–42, 49; MC, Board of Missions, Alexander Sutherland Papers, Egerton Shore to Wesley Kerr, May 8, 1908; ibid., West China Papers, Egerton Shore to Omar Kilborn, December 4, 1907.

66 MC, *Missionary Society Reports,* 1906–07, lii; 1907–08, 24–26; 1908–09, 17; 1909–10, 10–15; 1924–25, 86, MC, *Woman's Missionary Society Reports,* 1906–07, li–lx; 1925–26, xxxvi; MC, Board of Missions, West China Papers, James Endicott to William Mortimore, February 7, 1921; Kenneth Kowalski, "The West China Mission of the Methodist Church of Canada, 1891–1911" (MA, Univ. of Alberta, 1970), 166–172.

67 MC, Board of Missions, West China Papers, Omar Kilborn to Albert Carman, July 30, 1907; Finding Aid, West China Papers, intro.; MC, *Woman's Missionary Society Reports,* 1901–02, lxxiv–lxxvii.

68 MC, Board of Missions, West China Papers, R.B. McAmmond to Board of Missions, November 29, 1910. See also ibid., West China Mission Council, Minutes, March 29, 1904.

69 MC, Board of Missions, West China Papers, Report of the Seventh Annual Meeting of West China Educational Union, October 19, 1914. See also Bruce Lawrie, "E.W. Wallace and the Canadian Methodist Response to Chinese Educational Reform, 1906–1925," *Methodist History* 32 (1994): 187–194.

70 MC, *Woman's Missionary Society Reports*, 1895–96, xxxiii; MC, *Missionary Society Reports*, 1892–93, xxxii; MC, Board of Missions, West China Union University Papers, Rupert Carscallen to Egerton Shore, July 3, 1911; *Missionary Outlook*, October 1910, 233; Austin, 56.

71 MC, Board of Missions, West China Mission Council, Minutes, May 7, 1900; ibid., T. Egerton Shore Papers, Egerton Shore to Vincent Massey, February 23, 1912; ibid., West China Papers, Alexander Sutherland to Omar Kilborn, March 9, 1905; MC, *Missionary Society Reports*, 1909–10, 12–13; 1910–11, 8; 1914–15, xliv; 1918–19, xlix; Bruce Lawrie, "An Historical Overview of the Canadian Methodist Mission in West China, 1891–1925," CMHS, *Papers* 2 (1980): 8–9; Joseph Taylor, *History of West China Union University, 1910–1935* (Chengtu: Canadian Mission Press, 1936).

72 MC, *Missionary Society Reports*, 1917–18, xlv; 1924–25, 56; MC, Board of Missions, West China Union University Papers, William Mortimore to James Endicott, June 17, 1921; ibid., Rupert Carscallen to Egerton Shore, January 11, 1911; ibid., James Endicott to William Mortimore, October 24, 1921; ibid., Minutes of Board of Governors, West China Union University, November 1922.

73 MC, Board of Missions, West China Papers, Omar Kilborn to Frederick Stephenson, May 19, 1900; ibid., West China Mission Council, Minutes, May 1903; June 25, 1906; UCA, Percy Westaway biographical file; Austin, 57.

74 Quoted in Austin, 53. See also *Missionary Outlook*, January 1905, 3.

75 MC, *Missionary Society Reports*, 1918–19, xlix; 1924–25, 62; MC, *Journal of General Conference*, 1918, 256–257; MC, Board of Missions, West China Mission Council, Minutes, May 7, 1900; Strachan, 215; CG, January 22, 1919, 7–8; Karen Minden, "Missionaries, Medicine and Modernization: Canadian Medical Missionaries in Sichuan, 1925–1952" (PhD, York Univ., 1981), 141–146, 161, 168–185.

76 MC, Board of Missions, West China Mission Council, Minutes, April 1, 1904; MC, *Missionary Society Reports*, 1908–09, 17; MC, *Woman's Missionary Society Reports*, 1898–99, lxiii; CG, April 13, 1921, 12; *Missionary Outlook*, May 1910, 118.

77 MC, *Woman's Missionary Society Reports*, 1893–94, xix; MC, Board of Missions, West China Papers, Rupert Carscallen to Egerton Shore, July 3, 1911; ibid., West China Mission Council, Minutes, March 29, 1904; ibid., "Review of Mission Council Meetings," n.d. (box 6, file 48), 12–13.

78 Edward W. Wallace, *The New Life in China* (London: Council for Missionary Education, 1914), 78–79; MC, Board of Missions, West China Papers, William Mortimore to James Endicott, February 13, 1924; ibid., West China Mission Council, "Review of Mission Council Minutes," 14–22; MC, *Journal of General Conference*, 1922, 263; MC, *Missionary Society Reports*, 1892–93, xxxii; 1907–08, 24; 1908–09, 27; 1917–18, xlv; United Church, *Record of Proceedings*, 1926, 351.

79 MC, *Missionary Society Reports*, 1908–09, 22; 1917–18, li; MC, Board of Missions, West China Mission Council, Minutes, February 10, 1908; ibid., "Review of Mission Council Minutes," 23–25; CG, September 14, 1920, 21.

CHAPTER THIRTEEN

1  John Thomas, " 'The Christian Law of Living': The Institutionalization of Christian Stewardship in the Methodist Church," CMHS, *Papers* 9 (1991); John Thomas, " 'A Pure and Popular Character': Case Studies in the Development of the Methodist 'Organizational' Church, 1884–1925" (PhD, York Univ., 1991).

2  John Macdonald, *Business Success: What It Is and How to Secure It* (Toronto: Adam Stevenson, 1872); "John Macdonald," *DCB*, 11:551–552.

3  Hugh Johnston, *A Merchant Prince: Life of the Hon. John Macdonald* (Toronto: Wm. Briggs, 1893), 289–292; *CCA*, July 9, 1873, 1; January 30, 1884, 1; *CG*, February 13, 1884, 50; *Wesleyan*, March 28, 1884, 6.

4  "Lemuel A. Wilmot," *DCB*, 10:709–714; "Hart Massey," *DCB*, 12:700–708; T.W. Acheson, "The Social Origins of the Canadian Industrial Elite, 1880–1885," in David MacMillan (ed.), *Canadian Business History: Selected Studies* (Toronto: McClelland & Stewart, 1972), 145–167; Douglas D. Pond, *The History of Marysville, New Brunswick* (Fredericton: D.D.Pond, 1983), 148; Margaret Prang, *N.W. Rowell: Ontario Nationalist* (Toronto: Univ. of Toronto Press, 1975), 234–238; UCA, Local church histories, Winnipeg, Grace church; J. Fraser Perry, *They Gathered at the River* (Calgary: Northwest Printing Co., 1975).

5  Prang, 22–23, 116, 128–129, 156, 220.

6  Albert Carman, "Introduction," in Benjamin Austin, *The Gospel to the Poor versus Pew Rents* (Toronto: Wm. Briggs, 1884), vi. See also *CJ*, October 6, 1865.

7  *Observer*, March 2, 1870, 1; MEC, *Minutes of Niagara Conference*, 1848, 8. See also *CG*, January 18, 1871, 10.

8  *CMM* 15 (1882): 8–9; F.J. Jobson, "Chapel and School Architecture (1850)," in Rupert Davies et al. (eds.), *A History of the Methodist Church in Great Britain* (London: Epworth Press, 1965–88), 4:492–493; Thomas Champion, *The Methodist Churches of Toronto* (Toronto: G.M. Rose, 1899), 110; William Westfall and Malcolm Thurlby, "Church Architecture and Urban Space: The Development of Ecclesiastical Forms in Nineteenth-Century Ontario," in David Keane and Colin Read (eds.), *Old Ontario: Essays in Honour of J.M.S. Careless* (Toronto: Dundurn Press, 1990), 118–147; William Westfall, *Two Worlds: The Protestant Culture of Nineteenth-Century Ontario* (Kingston: McGill-Queen's Univ. Press, 1989), 126–158.

9  UCA, Local church histories, Toronto, Sherbourne Street church, excerpt from *Daily Mail*. See also *CG*, April 10, 1872, 116; July 31, 1870, 136; February 19, 1873, 61; June 6, 1866, 91; MEC, *Minutes of Bay of Quinte Conference*, 1878, 90–91; *Western Methodist Bulletin*, December 1904, 7.

10  Jobson, 491; *CG*, April 18, 1883, 124.

11  *CMM* 1 (1875): 189, 382; Jobson, 494; Westfall and Thurlby, 129–131.

12  *CAA*, December 10, 1873, 2. See also *CG*, December 14, 1910, 3; J. Wesley Johnston, "The Baptism of Fire," in Johnston, *The Baptism of Fire and Other Sermons* (Toronto: Wm. Briggs, 1888) 135.

13  *CCA*, January 1, 1862, 1. See also ibid., December 3, 1873, 1; February 20, 1884, 1; *Wesleyan*, January 11, 1884, 4; John Lanceley, *Domestic Sanctuary* (Hamilton: Spectator, 1878), 111.

14  *Observer*, April 17, 1878, 4; See also *Wesleyan*, February 28, 1884, 4.

15 Austin, 88–100; MEC, *Minutes of Bay of Quinte Conference*, 1879, 118; *CG*, July 14, 1875, 217.

16 William Casson, "Union with Christ," in David Rogers (ed.), *Sermons by Ministers of the Guelph Conference* (Toronto: Wm. Briggs, 1886), 71; *CG*, July 9, 1873, 220; Sydney Ahlstrom, *A Religious History of the American People* (New Haven: Yale Univ. Press, 1972), 740.

17 *CCA*, May 28, 1873, 1. See also UCA, A.J. Irwin Papers, Sermons, Mark 10: 21; UCA, William R. Young Papers, Sermons, "Religion and the Rich"; *CG*, May 17, 1882, 153; September 4, 1907, 5–6; James Spencer, "The Punishment of the Rich Man," in *Sermons by the Rev. James Spencer* (Toronto: Anson Green, 1864), 36.

18 William R. Young Papers, Sermons, "Is it Wrong to Make Money"; *CG*, April 23, 1884, 132; William Westfall, "The Sacred and the Secular: Studies in the Cultural History of Protestant Ontario in the Victorian Period" (PhD, Univ. of Toronto, 1976), 220.

19 *CCA*, May 3, 1871, 1; *Observer*, January 16, 1878, 1; Charles Hawkins, "Profit of Godliness," in Hawkins, *Sermons on the Christian Life* (Toronto: Wm. Briggs, 1880), 96; UCA, John G. Laird Papers (file 10), Lectures, n.d.; UCA, Albert Carman Papers, Lectures, "Free Salvation, Costly Religion," July 26, 1884.

20 Hart Massey, *Why Save Money?* quoted in John W. Grant, "The Impact of Christianity on Canadian Culture and Society, 1867–1967," *Theological Bulletin*, 1968, 47. See also *CG*, February 26, 1890, 130.

21 *CG*, May 8, 1895, 296; *Home and School*, February 17, 1883, 28; *Observer*, January 23, 1878, 1; July 16, 1873, 2; Thomas, "The Christian Law of Living"; MEC, *Minutes of Bay of Quinte Conference*, 1870, 73; 1871, 65; *CMM*, 7 (1878): 549.

22 *Canada Presbyterian*, July 19, 1878, 598; John Thompson, *The Lambs in the Fold: The Relation of Children to the Church* (Montreal: Wm. Drysdale, 1893), 29; Anthony Wohl (ed.), *The Victorian Family: Structure and Stresses* (London: Groom Helm, 1978), 9–10.

23 William J. Hunter, *Manhood Wrecked and Rescued* (Toronto: Wm. Briggs, 1894), 15, 80, 144; *CCA*, January 1, 1862, 1. See also Emily Miller, "The Woman and Home," in Benjamin Austin (ed.), *Woman; Her Character, Culture and Calling* (Brantford: The Book and Bible House, 1890), 127–130.

24 Donald Yacovone, "Home as Found," review of Steven Mintz, *A Prison of Expectations: The Family in Victorian Culture* (New York: New York Univ. Press, 1983), in *Reviews of American History*, 1983, 544; Mintz, 14–17.

25 MC, Department of Evangelism and Social Service, *Report*, 1915, 5. This change is illustrated in such works as John Laing, *The Family; God's Appointed Institution* (Dundas: J. Somerville, 1878); John Lanceley, *Domestic Sanctuary* (Hamilton: Spectator, 1878); and Hugh Dobson, *The Christian Family* (Toronto: United Church, 1940).

26 O.H. Warren, "Woman in Social Structure," in *Woman; Her Character*, 402–403; *CCA*, July 5, 1871, 4.

27 *CCA*, January 4, 1848, 5. See also *CG*, April 29, 1914, 6; June 26, 1895, 406; May 19, 1920, 4; MC, Department of Evangelism and Social Service, *Report*, 1913, 44; 1911, 36.

28 James Snell, "The White Life for Two: The Defence of Marriage and Sexual Morality in Canada, 1890–1914," *Histoire Sociale/Social History* 16 (1983): 112, 116,

120–121. See also MC, Department of Evangelism and Social Service, *Report*, 1922, 86; W. Peter Ward, "Unwed Motherhood in Nineteenth-Century English Canada," CHA, *Historical Papers* (1981): 34–56; Rebecca Veinott, "Child Custody and Divorce: A Nova Scotia Study, 1866–1910," in Philip Gerard and Jim Phillips (eds.), *Essays in the History of Canadian Law, III, Nova Scotia* (Toronto: Osgoode Society, 1990), 273–302.

29 MC, Department of Evangelism and Social Service, *Report*, 1915, 6; 1916, 41; Constance Backhouse, *Petticoats and Prejudice: Woman and Law in Nineteenth-Century Canada* (Toronto: Osgoode Society, 1991).

30 MC, Department of Evangelism and Social Service, *Report*, 1913, 42–44; Ibid., 1920, 44; MC, *Minutes of Bay of Quinte Conference*, 1922, 77; CG, August 5, 1914, 28.

31 CG, January 2, 1895, 8. See also ibid., January 2, 1884, 1; CCA, January 18, 1871, 4.

32 CCA, January 1, 1873, 1. See also CG, February 20, 1895, 118.

33 CG, January 2, 1895, 8.

34 Ibid., January 2, 1895, 8. See also ibid., March 4, 1885, 130; April 8, 1885, 212; Benjamin Austin, "The Higher Education of Women," in *Woman; Her Character*, 380.

35 Ruth Brouwer, "The Methodist Church and the 'Woman Question,' 1902–1914," (unpub., 1976), 91; UCA, Toronto, Carlton Street church, Minutes of Ladies' Aid Society; Toronto, Sherbourne Street church, Minutes of King's Daughters; Montreal, St James Street church, Minutes of Dorcas Society; Ruth Bordin, *Women and Temperance: The Quest for Power and Liberty, 1873–1900* (Philadephia: Temple Univ. Press, 1981); CG, April 3, 1895, 214; July 31, 1901, 12; April 15, 1914, 5; *Rat Portage Methodist*, March 15, 1900, 2.

36 *Wesleyan*, November 15, 1905, 4. See also CG, April 18, 1883, 124; John Thomas, "Servants of the Church: Canadian Methodist Deaconess Work, 1890–1926," CHR, 65 (1984): 371–395; Marilyn Fardig Whiteley, "Modest, Unaffected and Fully Consecrated: Lady Evangelists in Canadian Methodism, 1884–1900," CMHS, *Papers* 6 (1987): 18–31.

37 CG, March 20, 1907, 3; Carol Lee Bacchi, *Liberation Deferred? The Ideas of English-Canadian Suffragists, 1877–1918* (Toronto: Univ. of Toronto Press, 1983), 58–59; Rosemary Ruether and Eleanor McLaughlin (eds.), *Women of Spirit: Female Leadership in the Jewish and Christian Tradition* (New York: Simon & Schuster, 1979), intro., 19, 26.

38 MC, Department of Evangelism and Social Service, *Report*, 1914, 31. See also CG, June 4, 1884, 182; *Rat Portage Methodist*, April 1, 1902, 1.

39 UCAMan, Manitoba Laymen's Association, Minutes, June 14, 1922; June 11, 1918; Austin, *The Gospel to the Poor*, 88; Ronald Huff, "Social Christian Clergymen and Feminism during the Progressive Era, 1890–1920" (PhD, Union Theological Seminary, 1978), 161.

40 Burkhard Kiesekamp, "Presbyterian and Methodist Divines: Their Case for a National Church in Canada, 1875–1900," *Studies in Religion* 2 (1973): 316–322; Rousas John Rushdooney, *The Messianic Character of American Education* (Nutley, NJ: Craig Press, 1963), 93; Paul Rutherford, *A Victorian Authority: The Daily Press in Late Nineteenth-Century Canada* (Toronto: Univ. of Toronto Press, 1982), 4; Brian McKillop, *Matters of Mind: The University in Ontario, 1791–1951* (Toronto: Univ. of Toronto Press, 1994), 206.

41 UCA, Samuel Dwight Chown Papers, Sermons, "The Right Hand of the Most High," n.d., 10. See also George Marsden (ed.), *The Fundamentals; A Testimony to Truth* (New York: Garland Press, 1988); McKillop, 204. At the most extreme, liberal Methodists such as Benjamin Austin applied scientific inquiry, especially through the study of psychic phenomena, to attempt to understand the spiritual afterlife. He, and a remarkably large number of other Canadians, ended by substituting spiritualism for orthodox Christianity as the best means of discovering humanity's present and future destiny. See Benjamin Austin, *The Mission of Spiritualism and Original Poems* (Toronto: Austin Publishing Co., 1902), 3–15; Benjamin Austin, *The A.B.C. of Spiritualism* (Los Angeles: Austin Publishing Co., 1920), 1, 5, 8; and Benjamin Austin, *The Heresy Trial of B. F. Austin* (Toronto: Sermon Publishing Co., 1899), 1–5.

42 Thomas Voaden, *Christ's Coming Again … A Refutation of Premillenial Views* (Toronto: McClelland & Stewart, 1918), 230–247; *CG*, July 31, 1901, 9.

43 *Western Methodist Bulletin*, May, 1905, 3; *Assiniboia Church Advocate*, March 15, 1905, 8; *CG*, September 14, 1910, 18–21.

44 *CG*, January 30, 1884, 36; MC, Department of Evangelism and Social Service, *Report*, 1916, 72; Standish Meacham, "The Evangelical Inheritance," *Journal of British Studies* 3 (1963): 88–104.

45 *CG*, April 23, 1890, 264; MC, Manitoba Laymen's Association, Minutes, June 11, 1919.

46 UCA, MC, Heresy trials, Nelson Burns, Ralph Horner, and others; Neil Semple, "Ontario's Religious Hegemony: The Creation of the National Methodist Church," *Ontario History* 77 (1985): 19–42.

47 Richard Allen, "The Background of the Social Gospel in Canada," in Allen (ed.), *The Social Gospel in Canada* (Ottawa: National Museum of Man, 1975), 2–34; Richard Allen, *The Social Passion: Religion and Social Reform in Canada: 1914–1928* (Toronto: Univ. of Toronto Press, 1971).

48 *Wesleyan Mirror* 11 (1922): 17; *CG*, May 11, 1910, 27; Richard Allen, "Salem Bland and the Spirituality of the Social Gospel: Winnipeg and the West, 1903–1913," in Dennis Butcher et al. (eds.), *Prairie Spirit* (Winnipeg: Univ. of Manitoba Press, 1985), 217–232; Richard Allen, "Salem Bland: the Young Preacher," UCA, *Bulletin*, 26 (1977): 75–93; Kenneth McNaught, *A Prophet in Politics: A Biography of J.S. Woodsworth* (Toronto: Univ. of Toronto Press, 1959).

49 *Wesleyan Mirror* 11 (1922): 18. See also MC, Department of Evangelism and Social Service, *Report*, 1915, 70; J.B. Silcox, *The Church in Vital Relation to Christ* (Winnipeg, 1912), 14–15.

50 MC, Department of Evangelism and Social Service, *Report*, 1916, 27; *CG*, August 3, 1910, 19; September 14, 1910, 18; UCA, Robert B. Cumming Papers, Sermons, July 19, 1925.

51 *CG*, January 9, 1901, 2; January 14, 1914, 28–29.

52 Allen, "The Background of the Social Gospel in Canada," 28–29; *CG*, April 2, 1890, 216; August 3, 1910, 19; March 11, 1914, 7; Kiesekamp, 323; MC, *Journal of General Conference*, 1898, 321.

53 *Western Methodist Recorder*, May 1905, 3; *CG*, May 27, 1914, 8–9; May 11, 1910, 27; April 29, 1914, 9–10; UCABC, British Columbia Laymen's Association, Minutes, May 16, 1910.

54 MC, Department of Evangelism and Social Service, *Report*, 1914, 44. See also MC, *Journal of General Conference*, 1902, 175–177; 1906, 275–277.

55 CG, January 23, 1907, 5; *Western Methodist Times*, January 1906, 6–8; MC, *Journal of General Conference*, 1906, 274–275.

56 Allen, *The Social Passion*, 35–62; Vera Fast, "The Labour Church in Winnipeg," in *Prairie Spirit*, 233–249.

57 Phyllis Airhart, *Serving the Present Age: Revivalism, Progressivism, and the Methodist Tradition in Canada* (Montreal: McGill-Queen's Univ. Press, 1992); Samuel Dwight Chown Papers, Sermons, "The Right Hand of the Most High," n.d.; MC, Department of Evangelism and Social Service, *Report*, 1916, 30; MC, *Journal of General Conference*, 1906, 268, 274; Michael Bliss, *A Canadian Millionaire: The Life and Business Times of Sir Joseph Flavelle, 1858–1939* (Toronto: Macmillan Press, 1978), 90–94.

58 Samuel Dwight Chown Papers, Sermons, September 1914, John 6:63. See also MC, *Journal of General Conference*, 1910, 415.

59 MC, *Journal of General Conference*, 1918, 341. See also MC, *Minutes of Guelph Conference*, 1890, 49; MC, Department of Evangelism and Social Service, *Report*, 1914, 46; 1915, 9; *Newfoundland Methodist Monthly Greeting*, August 1912, 8; Ian Manson, "Ernest Thomas and the Theology of the Social Gospel," CMHS, *Papers* 9 (1991): 51–64; David R. Elliott, "Hugh Wesley Dobson (1879–1956): Regenerator of Society," CMHS, *Papers* 9 (1991): 27–40.

60 Gene Homel, "James Simpson and the Origins of Canadian Social Democracy" (PhD, Univ. of Toronto, 1978), 716–721; CG, February 13, 1884, 52; February 12, 1890, 104; January 16, 1895, 33; June 12, 1895, 418; September 14, 1910, 18; *Columbian Methodist Recorder*, October 1899, 5; CMM 29 (1894): 550–554; UCA, Ernest Thomas biographical file.

61 CG, August 24, 1910, 5–6. See also William R. Young Papers, Sermons, "Our Heritage, Our Duty," July 11, 1907; George Webber, "Nature and Duty of Giving," in Samuel Phillips (ed.), *The Methodist Pulpit* (Toronto: Wm. Briggs, 1884).

62 G.F. Gibson, "The Business Man in the Church," in E.A. Davis (ed.), *Commemorative Review of the … Churches in British Columbia* (Vancouver: Joseph Lee, 1925), 158. See also J.A. Macdonald, "The Business Man and the Churches," in J. Castell Hopkins (ed.), *Empire Club Speeches* (Toronto: Wm. Briggs, 1910), 169–177; John Thomas, "The Christian Law of Living"; CG, September 14, 1910, 18; Allen, "The Background of the Social Gospel in Canada," 17.

63 CG, October 28, 1914, 22–24. See also ibid., July 3, 1895, 419; March 2, 1910, 5; May 27, 1914, 9; *Western Methodist Recorder*, May 1905, 6.

64 Voaden, 269. See also CG, July 24, 1895, 468; May 8, 1901, 3; *Western Methodist Times*, January 1906, 8.

65 See Hunter, *Manhood Wrecked and Rescued*; MC, Department of Evangelism and Social Service, *Report*, 1911, 31; 1916, 38; Beatrice Brigden, "One Woman's Campaign for Social Purity and Social Reform," in *The Social Gospel in Canada*, 36–62; Mariana Valverde, *The Age of Light, Soap and Water: Moral Reform in English Canada, 1885–1925* (Toronto: McClelland & Stewart, 1991).

66 C.S. Clark, *Of Toronto the Good* (Toronto: Toronto Publishing Co., 1898), 84–89; James Gray, *Red Lights on the Prairies* (Scarborough: New American Library, 1973); Social Service Council of Canada, Minutes of Annual Meeting, 1914, 4, 10; Lori

Rotenburg, "The Wayward Worker: Toronto's Prostitutes at the Turn of the Century," in Janice Acton (ed.), *Women at Work* (Toronto: Women's Educational Press, 1974), 33, 49; Judy Bedford, "Prostitution in Calgary, 1905–1914," *Alberta History* 29 (1981): 1–11; Deborah Nilsen, "The 'Social Evil': Prostitution in Vancouver, 1900–1925," in Barbara Latham (ed.), *In Her Own Right: Selected Essays on Women's History in British Columbia*, (Vancouver: Camosun College, 1980).

67  MC, *Journal of General Conference*, 1898, 321; MC, Department of Evangelism and Social Service, *Report*, 1920, 77; CG, May 25, 1910, 19; CMM, 40 (1894): 17–24.

68  MC, Department of Evangelism and Social Service, *Report*, 1923, 56, 60; 1920, 77; 1916, 37; CG, September 18, 1907, 8–9; October 26, 1910, 7; August 5, 1914, 13–14; MC, *Minutes of Toronto Conference*, 1898, 67.

69  *Columbian Methodist Recorder*, August 1900, 12; CCA, March 26, 1884, 1; *Pioneer*, March 6, 1914, 4; CG, January 2, 1907, 5; December 31, 1890, 840; October 30, 1901, 10; December 25, 1895, 871; MC, *Journal of General Conference*, 1914, 264–265.

70  MC, *Journal of General Conference*, 1898, 323; Paul Rutherford, "Tomorrow's Metropolis: The Urban Reform Movement in Canada, 1880–1920," CHA, *Historical Papers*, 1971, 203–224; Walter Van Nus, "The Plan Makers and the City: Architects, Engineers, Surveyors and Urban Planning in Canada, 1890–1939" (PhD, Univ. of Toronto, 1975).

71  CG, April 13, 1910, 18–21; April 29, 1914, 4; January 21, 1914, 5; MC, *Journal of General Conference*, 1918, 341–343.

72  CCA, November 28, 1860, 1; November 26, 1873, 1; CG, March 7, 1883, 76.

73  CJ, March 9, 1883, 5. See also H.V. Nelles and Christopher Armstrong, *The Revenge of the Methodist Bicycle Company* (Toronto: Peter Martin, 1977), 49–103; CG, December 3, 1890, 771; January 23, 1907, 5; UCABC, T.C. Darby Papers, Diary, 1892–93, 62; CMM, 32 (1890): 82–84.

74  CG, March 13, 1907, 4; *Newfoundland Methodist Monthly Greeting*, September 1913, 4; MC, *Minutes of British Columbia Conference*, 1892, 28; Paul Laverdure, "Canada's Sunday: The Presbyterian Contribution, 1875–1950 ," The Canadian Society of Presbyterian History, *Papers*, 1988, 1–30.

75  MC, *Minutes of Nova Scotia Conference*, 1899, 78; 1894, 61; *Sunday School Banner*, June 1893, 2; William Magney, "The Methodist Church and the National Gospel, 1884–1914," UCA, *Bulletin* 20 (1968): 89.

76  *Pioneer*, July 4, 1913, 3. See also Margaret Strople, "Prohibition and Movements of Social Reform in Nova Scotia, 1894–1920" (MA, Dalhousie Univ., 1975), chap. 2; Ruth Spence, *Prohibition in Canada* (Toronto: Dominion Alliance, 1919).

77  *Pioneer*, November 7, 1902, 2; December 27, 1912, 2; CMM 23 (1886): 280–281.

78  *Pioneer*, September 5, 1913, 8. See also ibid., July 11, 1913, 4; May 1, 1914, 4; CCA, September 27, 1871, 1; CG, December 4, 1901, 5; MC, *Minutes of Newfoundland Conference*, 1900, 58; Enest J. Dick, "From Temperance to Prohibition in 19th Century Nova Scotia," *Dalhousie Review* 61 (1981): 530–552; Prang, 33; *Newfoundland Methodist Monthly Greeting*, July 1912, 18; *Canadian Annual Review*, 1914, 572, 596; MC, *Journal of General Conference*, 1914, 253–261; Doris Miller, "Unfermented Wine on the Lord's Table: Origins and Implementation in Nineteenth Century Canadian Methodism," *Methodist History* 29 (1990): 3–13.

79  MC, *Minutes of Manitoba and North-West Conference*, 1898, 79; UCA, Stephen Rice Papers, Diary, January 21, 1888, 105; CG, August 3, 1910, 18.

80 *Wesleyan*, October 4, 1905, 4; January 25, 1905, 1; *Rat Portage Methodist*, January 1, 1902, 1; Prang, 234; *CG*, March 16, 1921, 6; May 13, 1914, 5; *Newfoundland Methodist Monthly Greeting*, October 1913, 9–10; *Pioneer*, September 12, 1902, 1.

81 MC, Army and Navy Board, Correspondence, Jean Stevenson to Board, October 1916; R. Craig Brown and G. Ramsay Cook, *Canada, 1896–1921: A Nation Transformed* (Toronto: McClelland & Stewart, 1974); Michael Bliss, "The Methodist Church and World War I," *CHR*, 49 (1968): 213–233.

82 *CG*, January 1, 1919, 20; November 30, 1921, 6; *Columbian Methodist Recorder*, September, 1900, 10–11; John H. Thompson, "The Voice of Moderation: The Defeat of Prohibition in Manitoba," in Susan M. Trofimenkoff (ed.), *The Twenties in Western Canada* (Ottawa: National Museum of Man, 1972), 170–190; Allen, *The Social Passion*, 264–283; MC, Department of Evangelism and Social Service, *Report*, 1923, 34.

CHAPTER FOURTEEN

1 Philippe Aries, *Centuries of Childhood: A Social History of Family Life*, trans. Robert Baldick (London: Jonathon Cape, 1962); Peter Slater, *Children in the New England Mind* (Hamden, Conn.: Archon Books, 1977); Philip Greven, *The Protestant Temperament* (New York: Alfred A. Knopf, 1977); Joseph Kett, "Adolescence and Youth in Nineteenth-Century America," in Theodore Rabb and Robert Rotberg (eds.), *The Family in History* (New York: M.I.T. Press, 1971); Peter Coveney, *The Image of Childhood* (Baltimore: Penguin Books, [1957] 1967).

2 Neil Semple, " 'The Nurture and Admonition of the Lord': Nineteenth-Century Canadian Methodism's Response to 'Childhood,'" *Histoire Sociale/Social History* 14 (1981): 157–175; Neil Sutherland, *Children in English Canadian Society* (Toronto: Univ. of Toronto Press, 1976), 21.

3 Alison Prentice, *The School Promoters: Education and Social Change in Mid-Nineteenth Century Upper Canada* (Toronto: McClelland & Stewart, 1977), 33; Egerton Ryerson, *Scriptural rights of the Members of Christ's Visible Church* (Toronto: Brewer & McPhail, 1854), 10–12; Egerton Ryerson, *First Lessons in Christian Morals; for Canadian Families and Schools* (Toronto: Copp, 1871).

4 Thomas Langford, "John Wesley's Doctrine of Justification by Faith," *CMHS, Papers* 1 (1978): 1–4; *Evangelical Witness*, April 16, 1873, 5.

5 John Marshall, *Scriptural Answer to a Pamphlet by A. Sutherland, on the Moral Status of Children* (Halifax: Nova Scotia Printing Co., 1877), 6, 10, 12; Nathanael Burwash, *The Relation of Children to The Fall, The Atonement and The Church* (Toronto: Wm. Briggs, 1882), 8, 14, 18–19; *CG*, July 5, 1882, 214; *CCA*, July 18, 1860, 1; UCA, Thomas Allen Papers, Diary, March 11, 1871; MEC, *Minutes of Bay of Quinte Conference*, 1866, 58.

6 Henry F. Bland, *Universal Childhood Drawn to Christ* (Toronto: Wm. Briggs, 1882), 10, 13; Alexander Sutherland, *The Moral Status of Children* (Toronto: Bell, 1876), 12–13, 21; Ryerson, *Scriptural rights*; Isaac Brock Aylesworth, "God's Eternal Purpose," in David Rogers (ed.), *Sermons by Ministers of the Guelph Conference* (Toronto: Wm. Briggs, 1886), 47, 54; *CG*, July 25, 1883, 236; July 29, 1885, 467; *CCA*, August 9, 1871, 2; August 16, 1871, 2; March 5, 1873, 1.

7 Marshall, 9; Albert Carman, "The Church of God," in Benjamin Austin (ed.), *The Methodist Episcopal Church Pulpit* (Toronto: Hunter & Rose, 1879), 21; *CCA*,

January 22, 1846, 3; January 11, 1860, 1; January 1, 1862, 4; UCA James Allen Papers, Sermons, 2 Peter 3:18.

8  *Bible Christian Magazine* 16 (1883): 72; UCAMa, Charles H. Paisley Papers, Diary, December 6, 1867.

9  WMC, *Doctrines and Discipline*, 1873, 69; MC, *Doctrines and Discipline*, 1884, 37.

10  WMC, *Minutes of Annual Conference*, 1853, 230–231.

11  Thomas Langford, "John Wesley's Doctrine of the Church, the Ministry and the Sacraments," CMHS, *Papers* 1 (1978): 11; Albert Outler (ed.), *John Wesley* (New York: Oxford Univ. Press, 1964), 323; Edward H. Dewart, *The Children of the Church* (Toronto: Guardian Office, 1861), 7–8; Sutherland, 12; CG, June 17, 1874, 190; December 5, 1883, 380; Burwash, 7.

12  Marshall, 5; Stephen Bond, *Church Membership* (Toronto: Wm. Briggs, 1882), 14.

13  Sutherland, 5, 12.

14  Bland, 12. See also CG, June 17, 1874, 190; July 5, 1882, 214; July 25, 1883, 236; *Observer*, November 5, 1867, 1; November 19, 1867, 1; CCA, August 9, 1871, 2; August 16, 1871, 2; John Carroll, *Reasons for Methodist Belief and Practice Relative to Water Baptism* (Toronto: Wesleyan Office, 1870), 30.

15  Ryerson, *Scriptural rights*, 12. See also CG, April 4, 1866, 54; MCC, *Minutes of Montreal Conference*, 1880, 62; UCA Henry Bland Papers, Diary, June 26, 1880, 74; MEC, *Minutes of Ontario Conference*, 1880, 36; MC, *Journal of General Conference*, 1886, 269–270; John Carroll, *The Stripling Preacher* (Toronto: Anson Green, 1852), 29; CG, March 26, 1879, 100; March 9, 1881, 78; *Observer*, January 21, 1874, 2; UCA, William Shannon Papers, Diary, August 1, 1854.

16  John Thompson, *The Lambs in the Fold: The Relation of Children to the Church* (Montreal: Wm. Drysdale, 1893), 29; James George, *The Sabbath School of the Fireside* (Kingston: James Creighton, 1859), 1; John Laing, *The Family; God's Appointed Institution* (Dundas: J. Somerville, 1878), 6; Sutherland, 3; Ryerson, *Scriptural rights*, 10; Conrad Van Dusen, *The Successful Young Evangelist* (Toronto: Dredge, 1870), 12; CG, October 22, 1890, 680; James Allen Papers, Sermons, John 13:12–16.

17  Robert Lynn and Elliot Wright, *The Big Little School: Sunday Child of American Protestantism* (New York: Harper & Row, 1971); Jack Seymour, *From Sunday School to Church School: Continuities in Protestant Church Education in the United States, 1860–1929* (Washington: Univ. Press of America, 1982), viii–xi; Allan Greer, "The Sunday Schools of Upper Canada," *Ontario History* 67 (1975): 169; William L. Brown, "The Sunday School Movement in the Methodist Church in Canada, 1875–1925" (MTh, Toronto Graduate School of Theological Studies, 1959).

18  Thomas Laqueur, *Religion and Respectability: Sunday Schools and Working Class Culture, 1780–1850* (New Haven: Yale University Press, 1976), x–xii, CMM 25 (1887) 142; *The Encyclopedia of Sunday Schools and Religious Education* (1915), 3:857–860.

19  CG, July 5, 1843, 146. See also WMC, *Minutes of Annual Conference*, 1857, 56; John James, *The Sunday School Teacher's Guide* (Montreal: Campbell & Becket, 1841), 30; Alison Prentice and Susan Houston (eds.), *Family, School and Society in Nineteenth Century Canada* (Toronto: Oxford Univ. Press, 1975), 69; *The Encyclopedia of Sunday Schools*, 3: 1149; Lynn and Wright, 12–13; Brown, 86; *Wesleyan Sabbath School Magazine*, 1868, 145; UCA, Hamilton, Sunday School Report, II, May 6, 1847; June 9, 1860; Toronto, Alice Street Primitive Methodist Church, Sunday School Teachers Minutes, Rules, I, 2–3.

20 Lynn and Wright, 31; wmc, *Minutes of Annual Conference*, 1835, 104; 1837, 159; 1869, 89; *cmmr* 48 (1898): 459.

21 James, 34, 53; uca, Toronto, Metropolitan Methodist church, Wesleyan Methodist Sunday School Society, Minutes, i, June 6, 1838; Hamilton, Sunday School Society, Teachers' Minutes, iii, April 27, 1858; wmc, *Minutes of Annual Conference*, 1868, 109; Laqueur, 59–60; William Alcott, *The Sunday School as it Should Be* (London: 1867), 18; Stephen Tyng, *Forty Years Experience in Sunday Schools* (New York: Sheldon, 1860), 63, 158.

22 uca, Bronte, Ontario, Sabbath School Constitution, May 12, 1845. See also W.A. Ross, *Fifty Years of Progress in Organized Sunday School Work in the Maritime Provinces* (Saint John: 1921), 3; Lynn and Wright, 10; Greer, 173.

23 Greer, 176, 179; Brown, 12, 17, 108; Toronto Sabbath School Association, *Sayings and Doings of the Toronto Sabbath-School Workers* (Toronto: Christian Guardian, 1871), 21; wmc, *Minutes of Annual Conference*, 1835, 109; 1842, 322; wmceba, *Minutes of Annual Conference*, 1862, 42; Robert Cooney, *The Autobiography of a Wesleyan Methodist Missionary* (Montreal: Pickup, 1856), 273; mc, Board of Sunday Schools and Young People's Societies, Report of General Secretary, 1915.

24 wmc, *Minutes of Annual Conference*, 1854, 267. See also ibid., 1842, 321–322; 1852, 36; 1861, 62; 1864, 69–70; mec, *Minutes of Bay of Quinte Conference*, 1852, 21; 1865, 64; bcc, *Minutes of Annual Conference*, 1867, 1; wmceba, *Minutes of Annual Conference*, 1866, 28–29; *Sunday School Banner*, November 1883, 3; Prentice and Houston, 128; William Shannon Papers, Diary, August 1, 1855. In Upper Canada and to a lesser extent in the Maritimes, the interdenominational Sunday schools received support from the government, but this money was used almost exclusively by the Anglican church leaders to promote Church of England doctrines. This situation encouraged the Methodists to establish their own schools.

25 wmc, *Minutes of Annual Conference*, 1848, 71; 1842, 322. See also ibid., 1857, 63–64; bcc, *Minutes of Annual Conference*, 1877, 21; Greer, 176.

26 *Sunday School Banner*, October 1893, ii. See also cg, July 6, 1885, 419; mec, *Minutes of Bay of Quinte Conference*, 1868, 66; pmc, *Minutes of Annual Conference*, 1861, 158; *cmm* 25 (1887): 43–45; Alexander Sutherland, *Counsels to Young Converts* (Toronto: Wesleyan Conference Office, 1871), 21; mc, General Board of Sunday Schools, Report, "Systematic Evangelism in the Sunday School," 1887, 2–6.

27 John Carroll, *Case and His Cotemporaries* (Toronto; Samuel Rose, 1867–77), 3:256; mec, *Minutes of Annual Conference*, 1829, 28–29; wmc, *Minutes of Annual Conference*, 1835, 95; 1837, 159; 1844, 365; 1853, 231–232; 1864, 69; wmceba, *Minutes of Annual Conference*, 1857, 20; 1862, 42; 1866, 28–29; Montreal Methodist Sunday School Association, Minutes, April 6, 1886; *Sayings and Doings*, 32; Brown, 10; Toronto, Metropolitan Methodist church, Wesleyan Methodist Sunday School Society, Minutes, i, 1836. In 1844 the Wesleyans hoped denominational Sunday schools would help combat the rising influence of the Mormons and Millerites.

28 wmc, *Minutes of Annual Conference*, 1869, 90–91; 1870, 86; *Observer*, February 14, 1883, 6; bcc, *Minutes of Annual Conference*, 1877, 21; *Wesleyan*, March 28, 1884, 4; mcc, *Journal of General Conference*, 1874, 230–231.

29 The statistics are drawn from the *Minutes of Annual Conference* of the Methodist connexions for the years indicated before 1884. Totals for the Bible Christians are only

estimated because the connexion included a number of circuits in the United
States until 1884. After that year the statistics come from the Methodist Church,
*Journal of General Conference*, or the Board of Sunday Schools and Young People's
Societies.

30 MC; *Journal of United General Conference*, 1883, 139–146; MC, *Journal of General Conference*, 1890, 302–309; 1902, 285–288.

31 MC, *Journal of General Conference*, 1910, 297–303; 1914, 237–246, 413–425; 1918, 267–273; 1922, 310–314; MC, Board of Sunday Schools and Young People's Societies, Minutes, September 12, 1917; January 16, 1918; September 18, 1921; MC, Board of Religious Education, Minutes, August 15, 1923; MC, Board of Publications, Journal of Book Committee, Minutes, May 5, 1921; CG, May 6, 1914, 8; Patricia Dirks, " 'Getting a Grip on Harry': Canada's Methodists Respond to the 'Big Boy' Problem," CMHS, *Papers* 7 (1989): 67–82.

32 James, 45. See also MEC, *Minutes of Ontario Conference*, 1880, 36; CG, November 10, 1880, 358; *Sunday School Banner*, January 1869, 11; WMC, *Minutes of Annual Conference*, 1866, 93; 1868, 109; *Observer*, June 21, 1874, 2. The great success the revivalist Edward Payson Hammond was having in converting children during the period also appeared to confirm both their ability to be converted and the necessity of emphasizing this work.

33 WMC, *Minutes of Annual Conference*, 1863, 73; 1871, 107; MCC, *Journal of General Conference*, 1878, 249; Brown, 151.

34 Neil Semple, "The Impact of Urbanization on the Methodist Church in Central Canada, 1854–1884" (PhD, Univ. of Toronto, 1979), 252–301; James Allen Papers, Sermons, 2 Peter 3: 18, 5–6.

35 WMC, *Minutes of Annual Conference*, 1835, 104; 1843, 349; 1852, 36; 1855, 45; 1863, 73; MCC, *Journal of General Conference*, 1878, 250; MC, *Journal of General Conference*, 1898, 202; 1918, 433; *Home and School*, May 12, 1883, 79; MC, Board of Sunday Schools and Epworth Leagues, Minute Book, September 15, 1891.

36 Sunday School Union of Canada, Report, 1829, 16; *Sayings and Doings*, 21. See also Maritime Sabbath School Convention, *Proceedings*, 1872, 11–13; *Sunday School Banner*, April 1873, 77; July 1873, 150; CCA, May 28, 1884, 3.

37 James Middlemiss, *Christian Instruction in the Public Schools of Ontario* (Toronto: Wm. Briggs, 1901), 232–233. See also *Newfoundland Methodist Monthly Greeting*, November 1912, 5–6; G. Stanley Hall, *Adolescence: Its Psychology* (New York: Appleton, 1904), 451; G. Stanley Hall, "The Moral and Religious Training of Children and Adolescents," *Pedagogy Seminar* 1 (1891): 196–210; Toronto, Metropolitan church, Sunday School Committee, Report, June 3, 1840.

38 *CMM*, 25 (1887): 449; *A Short History of the International Lesson System* (American Sunday School Union, 1902), 11–15; MCC, *Journal of General Conference*, 1878, 250; WMCEBA, *Minutes of Annual Conference*, 1874, 32–33; Maritime Provinces Sunday School Convention, *Proceedings*, 1872, 21; MEC, *Minutes of Ontario Conference*, 1874, 16; Presbyterian Church in Canada, *Acts and Proceedings*, 1875–76, 228.

39 *Sunday School Banner*, October 1893, 2–3. See also Lynn and Wright, 64–67.

40 *Sunday School Banner*, April 1873, 75. See also MC, *Journal of General Conference*, 1898, 202.

41 CG, January 5, 1883, 8; WMC, Committee on Sunday Schools, Minutes, June 4, 1873, 3; ibid., Report, 1873, 9–10; MC, *Journal of General Conference*, 1902, 295.

42 *A Short History of the International Lesson System*, 21; MC, Committee on Sunday Schools, Minute Book, September 15, 1891, 114.

43 Harold Rugg, *American Life and The School Curriculum* (Boston: Ginn, 1936), 92; *CG*, May 7, 1884, 146; December 28, 1910, 9–10.

44 Hall, *Adolescence*, 300; UCA, George Pidgeon Papers, Sermons, "Spiritual Infancy," October 1919; Semple, " 'The Nurture and Admonition of the Lord,' " 158–170. Granville Stanley Hall was an internationally renowned educator who is perhaps best remembered for his early championing of Sigmund Freud. His writings reflect a great satisfaction in finding in sexuality a systematic principle into which to fit his pedagogical ideas. As well as his interest in physical change, he mirrored John Fiske's emphasis on moral evolution as the means of understanding human development.

45 Hall, *Adolescence*, 346–347; Robert Stamp, "James L. Hughes, Proponent of the New Education," in Robert Patterson (ed.), *Profiles of Canadian Educators* (Toronto: Heath, 1974), 200.

46 Hall, *Adolescence*, 295, 357; Alison Prentice, "The American Example," in J.D. Wilson, R. Stamp, and L.-P. Audet (eds.), *Canadian Education: A History* (Scarborough: Prentice-Hall, 1970), 52.

47 Presbyterian Church in Canada, *Acts and Proceedings*, 1876–77, appendix, civ. See also *CG*, May 7, 1884, 146.

48 *CG*, May 6, 1914, 8; Dirks, " 'Getting a Grip on Harry,' " 67–82.

49 Hall, *Adolescence*, 287–88, 301, 313, 346–358; *CCA*, May 21, 1873, 1; Neil Semple, "Canadian Protestants' Perception of Childhood and the Function of Education," address to Canadian History of Education Association, 1982.

50 Prentice, "The American Example," 42; Rousas John Rushdooney, *The Messianic Character of American Education* (Nutley, NJ: Craig Press, 1963), 56–57.

51 Rugg, 40, 89–90; Patterson, 189–190; Stamp, 195–196; Hall, *Adolescence*, 357; *CG*, October 30, 1907, 10.

52 Rushdooney, 96. See also Rugg, 40; Stamp, 195–196; Hall, *Adolescence*, 322, 357, 384.

53 *The Encyclopedia of Sunday Schools*, 1:215; Hall, *Adolescence*, 451.

54 Prentice and Houston, 55. See also *Columbian Methodist Recorder*, March 1900, 4.

55 MC, *Journal of General Conference*, 1902, 286, 294; 1914, 238; 1918., 269; 1922, 310–314.

56 *CMMR*, 47 (1898): 458–459; MC, *Journal of General Conference*, 1902, 297. In 1902 there were 11,814 listed in the home department.

57 Ryerson, *First Lessons in Christian Morals*, 25. See also James, 35–78; *CMM* 25 (1887): 45; *Sunday School Banner*, November 1893, 4.

58 UCA, Toronto Sabbath School Association, Annual Report, May 1844; 1853; ibid., Second Teacher's Institute, Proceedings, 1871, 8–9; *CMM* 25 (1887): 446; MC, *Minutes of Toronto Conference*, 1894, 65; *CG*, January 8, 1890, 24; T.W. Acheson, "The Social Origins of the Canadian Industrial Elite, 1880–1885," in David MacMillian (ed.), *Canadian Business History: Selected Studies* (Toronto: McClelland & Stewart, 1972), 160.

59 *CCA*, February 18, 1857, 2; *Sunday School Banner*, January 1873, 9; MEC, *Minutes of Niagara Conference*, 1878, 20; MEC, *Minutes of Ontario Conference*, 1879, 83; MEC, *Minutes of Bay of Quinte Conference*, 1882, 30; UCAMa, Halifax Wesleyan Sunday

School Association, Report, 1861; *The Encyclopedia of Sunday Schools*, 1:207–210; Seymour, 63; MCC, *Journal of General Conference*, 1878, 254; *CMM* 8 (1878): 1–12; *British American Presbyterian,* July 14, 1876, 3; MC, Board of Sunday Schools and Epworth Leagues, Minutes, July 18, 1893; Theodore Morrison, *Chautauqua, a Center for Education, Religion and the Arts in America* (Chicago: Univ. Chicago Press, 1974).

60 MC, *Journal of General Conference,* 1902, 295; *Wesleyan,* August 30, 1905, 2; November 1, 1905, 4; *Western Methodist Bulletin,* April 1905, 5; *CG,* May 8, 1901, 13; MC, Board of Sunday Schools and Epworth Leagues, Minutes, March 31–April 1, 1909; April 1, 1910; July 4, 1910; Report, 1914, 157–158; Seymour, viii; Brown, 132–145.

61 *Sunday School Banner,* October 1883, 290. See also WMC, *Minutes of Annual Conference,* 1845, 384; 1847, 30; 1868, 82; MCC, Board of Publications, Minutes, November 12, 1880; *Home and School,* January 6, 1883.

62 William H. Withrow, "Methodist Literature and Methodist Sunday Schools," in *Centennial of Canadian Methodism* (Toronto: Wm. Briggs, 1891), 282–283. See also MC, Board of Publications, Journal of Book Committee, Report, November 5, 1884.

63 MC, *Journal of General Conference,* 1902, 206–207; 1906, 184–186; 1918, 274–275; *Adult Class,* April 1909; MC, Board of Publications, Journal of Book Committee, Report, May 7, 1919.

64 WMC, *Minutes of Annual Conference,* 1864, 69–70; MC, *Journal of General Conference,* 1894, 194–195; UCA, Peel County Sunday School Association, Convention Proceedings, 1902, 8–9.

65 George Henderson, *Early Saint John Methodism* (Saint John: George Day, 1890), 153; WMC, *Minutes of Annual Conference,* 1864, 70; MCC, *Journal of General Conference,* 1882, 230; *Pleasant Hours,* January 13, 1883, 4; *Home and School,* April 28, 1883, 69; March 17, 1883, 47; November 24, 1883, 188; *Western Methodist Recorder,* September 6, 1905, 3.

66 *CCA,* January 15, 1862, 4; September 3, 1862, 4; June 13, 1860, 3; December 24, 1862, 4; January 4, 1871, 4; February 2, 1884, 1; *Wesleyan Sabbath School Magazine,* every issue; *Sunday School Banner,* February 1869, 10; June 1873, 125–126; Tyng, 186; James, 34.

67 *Wesleyan,* February 1, 1884, 2; *Observer,* January 3, 1883, 3; William J. Hunter, *Manhood Wrecked and Rescued* (Toronto: Wm. Briggs, 1894).

68 WMC, *Minutes of Annual Conference,* 1861, 61; Wesleyan Methodist Sabbath School Committee, Minute Book, June 10, 1873, 6; July 18, 1893, 136; August 29, 1893.

69 *CCA,* February 25, 1857, 4–5; *Sunday School Banner,* January 1869, 2, 5; CJ, March 30, 1883, 4; MCC, *Journal of General Conference,* 1882, 235; MC, *Doctrines and Discipline,* 1890, 128; MC, Board of Religious Education, Minutes, January 1924.

70 Hall, *Adolescence,* 429. See also UCAMa, Charlottetown Methodist church, Sunday School Report, 1903–04, 10.

71 David MacLeod, "The Live Vaccine: The YMCA and Male Adolescence in the United States and Canada, 1870–1920," *Histoire Sociale/Social History* 11 (1978): 5–25; Patricia Dirks, "Beyond Family and School: An Analysis of the Changing Place of Protestant Churches in the Lives of Canada's Youth, 1900–1918," (unpub., 1983); *Western Methodist Recorder,* February, 1905 5; *CG,* February 5, 1890, 88; March 30, 1910, 5.

72 *Wesleyan*, January 4, 1905, 4; Frederick Norwood, *The Story of American Methodism* (Nashville: Abingdon Press, 1974), 305; *CG*, January 30, 1901, 2.

73 MC, *Journal of General Conference*, 1894, 197–198. See also "The Epworth League," *Encyclopedia of World Methodism*, 1:783–784; "John Heyl Vincent," ibid., 2:2429–2430.

74 *CMM* 31 (1890): 238, 241. See also *CG*, January 1, 1890, 3; February 5, 1890, 88; October 22, 1890, 676; November 12, 1890, 728; August 21, 1895, 532; MC, *Journal of General Conference*, 1890, 306–307.

75 S.T. Bartlett, *A Brief History of the Epworth League of the Board of Sunday Schools* (Toronto: Methodist Church, 1912); *CG*, March 6, 1895, 162; MC, *Minutes of Newfoundland Conference*, 1900, 72.

76 MC, *Journal of General Conference*, 1898, 256–257; 1914, 413; UCA, Fredrick C. Stephenson biographical file; *CG*, May 11, 1910, 13, 17; MC, *Journal of General Conference*, 1906, 387–396.

77 *Sunday School Banner*, June 1893, 2; MC, *Minutes of Niagara Conference*, 1893, 59; MC, Board of Sunday Schools and Epworth Leagues, Minutes, July 18, 1893; *CG*, March 20, 1895, 177; MC, *Journal of General Conference*, 1894, 197–198; 1910, 467.

78 *CMM* 34 (1891): 155–156; *CG*, May 8, 1895, 295; MC, *Journal of General Conference*, 1894, 203, 207.

79 MC, *Journal of General Conference*, 1894, 199, 203; 1898, 207; *Epworth Herald*, July 31, 1897, 7.

80 Bartlett, 2–8; MC, *Journal of General Conference*, 1906, 256; 1914, 360–361.

81 MC, *Journal of General Conference*, 1922, 398–408; Ruth Brouwer, "The Canadian Methodist Church and Ecclesiastical Suffrage for Women, 1902–1914," CMHS, *Papers* 2 (1981): 31; Dirks, "'Getting a Grip on Harry,'" 74–79; Young People's League, *Constitution*, 1922.

82 MC, Board of Sunday Schools and Young People's Societies, Minutes, September 12, 1917; September 8, 1921; MC, *Journal of General Conference*, 1918, 274; MC, Board of Religious Education, Report, April 1923; MC, Department of Evangelism and Social Service, address by Ernest Thomas, 1920; *CG*, February 20, 1895, 113; October 30, 1907, 10; March 25, 1914, 7; Margaret Beattie, *A Brief History of the Student Christian Movement in Canada, 1921–1974* (Toronto: SCM, 1975); Herbert Gray, *The Ferment of Thought in the Canadian Universities* (Toronto: SCM, 1923).

CHAPTER FIFTEEN

1 MC, *Journal of General Conference*, 1898, 324–325, 348. See also *CG*, February 13, 1901, 3; John Webster Grant, *The Church in the Canadian Era* (Toronto: McGraw-Hill Ryerson, 1972), 91–133.

2 MC, *Journal of General Conference*, 1898, 265; 1902, 320; *CG*, January 9, 1901, 1; April 17, 1901, 8; Michael Bliss, *A Canadian Millionaire: The Life and Business Times of Sir Joseph Flavelle, 1858–1939* (Toronto: Macmillan Press, 1978), 53–60, 142.

3 J.S. Ross, *A Catechism of the 20th Century Thanksgiving Fund* (Guelph, 1899), 2, 8; MC, *Journal of General Conference*, 1902, 320; 1906, 266–267; Phyllis Airhart, *Serving the Present Age: Revivalism, Progressivism, and the Methodist Tradition in Canada* (Montreal: McGill-Queen's Univ. Press, 1992), 132–134.

4 *Census of Canada*, 1901, 1:144–145; *Census of Canada*, 1921, 1:3, 568–569; MC, *Journal of General Conference*, 1902, 159.

5 MC, *Journal of General Conference*, 1914, 182. See also ibid., 1906, 268; *CG* June 12, 1912, 19.

6 MC, *Journal of General Conference*, 1906, 274; 1914, 324–325; 1910, 415; *CMM* 32 (1890): 367.

7 MC, *Journal of General Conference*, 1910, 317–318; John Thomas, "'A Pure and Popular Character': Case Studies in the Development of the Methodist 'Organizational' Church, 1884–1925" (PhD, York Univ., 1991), 40.

8 *CG* June 12, 1912, 19; MC, *Journal of General Conference*, 1898, 325; 1906, 174; 1914, 181, 265; Airhart, 129–130.

9 *CG*, February 13, 1901, 3; June 3, 1925, 4; UCA, Samuel Dwight Chown Papers, Sermons, "The Right Hand of the Most High," n.d., 10; Airhart, 135–136; Michael Gauvreau, *The Evangelical Century: College and Creed in English Canada from the Great Revival to the Great Depression* (Montreal: McGill-Queen's Univ. Press, 1991), 11; Kenneth Brown, "John Wesley – Post or Premillennialist?," *Methodist History* 28 (1989): 33–41.

10 Thomas, 40–45; MC, *Journal of General Conference*, 1898, 336–337; 1902, 172–173; *CG*, May 1, 1901, 1.

11 *CG*, January 9, 1901, 22; January 21, 1925, 14; MC, *Journal of General Conference*, 1902, 228, 265; 1914, 149, 168; 1922, 207.

12 MC, *Journal of General Conference*, 1902, 228–229, 243, 254; 1910, 310; 1914, 150; Brian McKillop, *Matters of Mind: The University in Ontario, 1791–1951* (Toronto: Univ. of Toronto Press, 1994), 123, 204.

13 MC, *Journal of General Conference*, 1902, 238, 243; 1914, 148, 156; John Reid, *Mount Allison University: A History, to 1963* (Toronto: Univ. of Toronto Press, 1984), 1:200–258; Charles Bruce Sissons, *A History of Victoria University* (Toronto: Univ. of Toronto Press, 1952), 224–225, 240, 259; Alfred G. Bedford, *The University of Winnipeg: A History of the Founding Colleges* (Toronto: Univ. of Toronto Press, 1976), 44–54.

14 MC, *Journal of General Conference*, 1906, 130, 277; 1910, 411; 1914, 145–147; Bedford, 61–62; John W. Grant, "Theological Education at Victoria," in Goldwin S. French and Gordon McLennan (eds.), *From Cobourg to Toronto: Victoria University in Retrospect* (Toronto: Chartres Books, 1989), 90–91.

15 MC, *Journal of General Conference*, 1918, 216; Bedford, 55; United Church, *Record of Proceedings*, 1925, 152; Cyrus Macmillan, *McGill and Its Story, 1821–1921* (Toronto: Oxford Univ. Press, 1921), 234; UCA, William Birks Papers, Scrapbook, *Montreal Witness*, April 2, 1913; Kenneth Cousland, *The Founding of Emmanuel College of Victoria University in the University of Toronto* (Toronto, 1978); Sissons, 265–270, 284–289.

16 MC, *Journal of General Conference*, 1902, 237, 242, 252–253; 1918, 192; UCA, Massey Family biographical file; Thomas, 39; Bliss, 142–143; Neil Semple, "Federation and the New 'Old Vic,'" in "Addresses Marking the Centenary of 'Old Vic,'" (unpub., 1992).

17 MC, *Journal of General Conference*, 1918, 191; 1922, 207; United Church, *Record of Proceedings*, 1925, 192–193; Reid, 2:3–15; Bedford, 54.

18 United Church, *Record of Proceedings*, 1925, 174; MC, *Journal of General Conference*, 1902, 204; 1918, 165; MC, Board of Publication Papers; W. Stewart Wallace, *The*

*Ryerson Imprint* (Toronto: Ryerson Press, 1954); Lorne Pierce, *The House of Ryerson* (Toronto: Ryerson Press, 1954), 21–32.

19 *CG*, January 2, 1918, 8; October 28, 1914, 22–24; May 12, 1915, 9; April 12, 1916, 2; MC, *Journal of General Conference,* 1906, 221; 1914, 405; MC, Board of Missions, Japan Mission Papers, James Endicott to D.R. MacKenzie, August 11, 1914; MC, Army and Navy Board, Report to Methodist General Conference, 1918, 7; UCA, William Robert Young Papers, Sermons, "Our Lord Jesus Christ Who Died for Us"; Michael Bliss, "The Methodist Church and World War I," CHR 49 (1968): 213.

20 *CG*, September 16, 1914, 5–6; August 2, 1916, 6; January 31, 1917, 11; March 30, 1918, 9.

21 Samuel Dwight Chown Papers, Address, 1915; UCA, George F. Salton Papers, Sermons, October 31, 1915. See also Bliss, "The Methodist Church and World War I," 215; *CG*, November 11, 1914, 26–27; October 4, 1916, 5.

22 MC, *Journal of General Conference,* 1914, 405–406.

23 *CG*, May 26, 1915, 5; October 3, 1917, 5; September 23, 1914, 8; Samuel Dwight Chown Papers, Sermons, "War Sermon, 1915"; ibid., "Some Gains in this War," 1916; ibid., "The Glory, Glamour and Gloom of War," n.d.

24 *CG*, January 27, 1915, 2, 5–6; February 3, 1915, 30; December 15, 1915, 5; January 5, 1916, 5; January 26, 1916, 5; September 6, 1916, 8–9.

25 Bliss, "The Methodist Church and World War I," 213. See also David Marshall, "Methodism Embattled: A Reconsideration of the Methodist Church and World War I," address to Canadian Methodist Historical Society, 1982, 6; UCA, Finding Aid 22, MC, Army and Navy Board Papers, intro.

26 *CG*, July 14, 1915, 2. See also UCA, Samuel Dwight Chown and T. Albert Moore biographical files.

27 *CG*, August 4, 1915, 5. See also ibid., November 24, 1915, 2; December 15, 1915, 6; MC, Army and Navy Board, First Annual Report, 1916.

28 MC, Army and Navy Board, circular letter, December 22, 1915; ibid., circular letter re militia enlistment results by denomination, September 27, 1916; ibid., Report to General Conference, 1918; ibid., Wesley Elliott to T. Albert Moore, October 16, 1916; *CG*, May 19, 1915, 25; January 19, 1916, 5; November 1, 1916, 11–12; C.A. Sharpe, "Enlistment in the Canadian Expeditionary Force, 1914–1918: A Regional Analysis," *Journal of Canadian Studies* 18 (1983–84): 15–29.

29 MC, Army and Navy Board, K. Kingston to T. Albert Moore, October 4, 1916; Barbara Wilson (ed.), *Ontario and the First World War, 1914–1918: A Collection of Documents* (Toronto: Univ. of Toronto Press, 1977), xxi, xxix; R. Craig Brown and G. Ramsay Cook, *Canada, 1896–1921: A Nation Transformed* (Toronto: McClelland & Stewart, 1974), 250–274.

30 MC, Army and Navy Board, Irwin Beatty to T. Albert Moore, March 17, 1916. See also ibid., T. Albert Moore to Irwin Beatty, March 24, 1916; Marshall, 1; Bliss, "The Methodist Church and World War I," 217; MC, *Journal of General Conference,* 1914, 286; 1918, 140–141; *CG*, July 19, 1916, 28; March 29, 1916, 28.

31 MC, Army and Navy Board, W.L. Lawrence to Samuel Dwight Chown, April 15, 1916. See also ibid., Samuel Dwight Chown to W.L. Lawrence, April 22, 1916.

32 Marshall, 1–6, 17; *CG*, May 5, 1915, 26; *The Message of the Canadian Chaplains Overseas Military Forces to the Churches in Canada* ([1918])

33 Samuel Dwight Chown biographical file, clipping, Toronto *Globe,* December 4, 1917. See also *CG,* October 11, 1916, 5; May 23, 1917, 5; MC, Army and Navy Board, First Annual Report, 1916; Samuel Dwight Chown Papers, S.D. Chown to Toronto *Globe,* September 14, 1916; Brown and Cook, 250–274.

34 *CG,* January 9, 1915, 22; April 12, 1916, 5; November 29, 1916, 5–6; October 10, 1917, 6; October 17, 1917, 6; Bliss, "The Methodist Church and World War I," 220–221; MC, Army and Navy Board, T. Albert Moore to Robert Borden, June 14, 1917.

35 MC, Army and Navy Board, T. Albert Moore to C.A. Williams, August 1916. See also ibid., Report from C.A. Williams to T. Albert Moore, August 1916; ibid., copy of sermon, W.B. Caswell, February 29, 1916; ibid., E. Farnsworth to T. Albert Moore, November 27, 1916.

36 MC, Army and Navy Board, J. Putnam to T. Albert Moore, September 29, 1916. See also *CG,* October 25, 1916, 5; January 23, 1918, 18–19.

37 *CG,* July 28, 1915, 30; January 26, 1916, 5; MC, *Journal of General Conference,* 1918, 342–344; Wilson, xl–xli.

38 Bliss, "The Methodist Church and World War I," 225–227; Marshall, 7; MC, Department of Evangelism and Social Service, *Report,* 1915, 21; MC, Army and Navy Board, T. Albert Moore to Robert Borden, October 26, 1914; ibid., October, 1916, circular letter from Jean Stevenson; ibid., Alexander Elliot to T. Albert Moore, November 7, 1916; *CG,* June 9, 1915, 5; January 26, 1916, 5; UCA, Hugh Dobson Papers, box A3, files M–N, including *Public Health Regulations in Britain* (1916); MC, Board of Evangelism and Social Service, "The Prevalence of Venereal Disease in Canada" (1917); National Council of Women, *Special Report on Control of Venereal Diseases* (Winnipeg, 1917), 3; W.H. Hattie, "Some Medico-Sociological Problems Arising Out of the War," *Public Health Journal,* October 1917, 254–259; F. S. Patch, "The Military Aspect of the Venereal Disease Problem in Canada," *Public Health Journal,* November 1917, 301–303.

39 Bliss, "The Methodist Church and World War I," 219; Samuel Dwight Chown Papers, "War Address," 1915; *CG,* July 28, 1915, 30; January 9, 1916, 5; April 19, 1916, 13; May 17, 1916, 6; November 22, 1916, 4; Wilson, xxxix, xl.

40 John H. Thompson, "'The Beginning of Our Regeneration': The Great War and Western Canadian Reform Movements," CHA, *Historical Papers,* 1972, 228–232; E.R. Forbes, "Prohibition and the Social Gospel in Nova Scotia," *Acadiensis,* 1971, reprinted in S.D. Clark, J.P. Grayson, and L.M. Grayson (eds.), *Prophecy and Protest: Social Movements in Twentieth-Century Canada* (Toronto: Gage, 1975), 74–75; Ruth Spence, *Prohibition in Canada* (Toronto: Dominion Alliance, 1919), 341–492; *CG* June 9, 1915, 5; November 10, 1915, 7; January 26, 1916, 5; *Canadian Annual Review,* 1914, 643; Samuel Dwight Chown Papers, Temperance Address, 1915; William Ivens, *The Last Great War* (Toronto: Dept. of Evangelism and Social Service, 1915).

41 Charles Stacey (ed.), *Historical Documents of Canada,* vol. 5, *The Arts of War and Peace, 1914–1945* (Toronto: Macmillan of Canada, 1972), 583–585; MC, *Journal of General Conference,* 1914, 263, 1918, 342–345; *CG,* August 5, 1914, 28; March 31, 1915, 16–17; November 17, 1915, 8; January 26, 1916, 5; November 22, 1916, 4; *Western Methodist Recorder,* April 1915, 7; MC, Department of Evangelism and Social Service, Social Workers' Report, 1916, 121; ibid., *Report,* 1917, 53; ibid., T. Albert Moore to Beatrice Brigden, January 23, 1915.

42 Marshall, 1, 19; *CG*, January 27, 1915, 5–6; May 5, 1915, 26.

43 *CG*, January 9, 1915, 22; October 6, 1915, 5; November 11, 1914, 26–27; March 1, 1916, 27; July 19, 1916, 26–27; MC, Army and Navy Board, K. Kingston to T. Albert Moore, October 4, 1916; Richard Allen, *The Social Passion: Religion and Social Reform in Canada, 1914–1928* (Toronto: Univ. of Toronto Press, 1971), 47–50; Kenneth McNaught, *A Prophet in Politics: A Biography of J.S. Woodsworth* (Toronto: Univ. of Toronto Press, 1959), 66–78.

44 Ramsay Cook, "Francis Marion Beynon and the Crisis of Christian Reformism," in Ramsay Cook and Carl Berger (eds.), *The West and the Nation* (Toronto: McClelland & Stewart, 1976), 196; Richard Allen, "The Social Gospel as the Religion of the Agrarian Revolt," in *The West and the Nation*, 174; MC, Department of Evangelism and Social Service, *Report*, 1916, 63; 1917, 54; 1918, 39; 1919, 57; *CG* February 5, 1919, 4; March 3, 1919, 5; July 14, 1920, 5.

45 Salem Bland, *The New Christianity, or the Religion of the New Age* (Toronto: Ryerson Press, 1920); Allen, *The Social Passion*, 75–76, 81–92; James S. Woodsworth, *The First Story of the Labour Church* (Winnipeg: Labour Church, [1920]); Cook, "Francis Marion Beynon," 192; *CG* September 1, 1920, 7.

46 MC, *Journal of General Conference*, 1922, 295–301; United Church, *Record of Proceedings*, 1925, 192–193; *CG*, June 10, 1925, 7.

47 *CG*, December 31, 1919, 15; June 13, 1921, 6; November 30, 1921, 6; MC, Department of Evangelism and Social Service, *Report*, 1920, 42; 1921, 88; 1923, 66, 84.

48 MC, Department of Evangelism and Social Service, *Report*, 1920, 15. See also *CG*, December 3, 1924, 17.

49 MC, Department of Evangelism and Social Service, *Report*, 1915, 43. See also MC, Army and Navy Board, *The Christian Men's Federation* (n.d.); ibid., Samuel Dwight Chown, "Report on Overseas Commission," 1917; ibid., Report to General Conference, 1918, 9; *CG* July 8, 1914, 16; September 16, 1914, 4; August 11, 1915, 5; July 5, 1916, 8–9; September 6, 1916, 8–9; October 3, 1917, 5; October 9, 1918, 10; November 6, 1918, 8–11.

50 MC, Department of Evangelism and Social Service, *Report*, 1914, 56–57; *CG*, January 14, 1925, 20; Margaret Prang, *N.W. Rowell: Ontario Nationalist* (Toronto: Univ. of Toronto Press, 1975), 271.

51 Gene Homel, "James Simpson and the Origins of Canadian Social Democracy" (PhD, Univ. of Toronto, 1978), 85–86, 396–397, 715; MC, Department of Evangelism and Social Service, *Report*, 1915, 53; 1918, 74; *CG*, March 3, 1919, 5.

52 MC, Army and Navy Board, Report to General Conference, 1918, 5–7; MC, Department of Evangelism and Social Service, *Report*, 1916, 40; 1919, 26; MC, *Journal of General Conference*, 1918, 341–342; 1914, 402–409; 1902, 175–178; 1906, 274–283; 1910, 408–411.

53 MC, Department of Evangelism and Social Service, *Report*, 1919, 28; ibid., Beatrice Brigden to T. Albert Moore, November 11, 1918; Hugh Dobson Papers, box A3, re Venereal Diseases, Food and Public Health.

54 MC, Army and Navy Board, Louis Moffit to Board, March 11, 1916; ibid., Minutes, November 22, 1918, 3; *CG*, September 27, 1915, 7; July 12, 1916, 6; MC, Department of Evangelism and Social Service, *Report*, 1922, 91.

55 *CG*, December 3, 1924, 5, 18; January 7, 1925, 6; *Telegram* (Toronto), August 13, 1925; Samuel Dwight Chown Papers, Sermons, "And He Shall Judge between the

Nations," [1919]; ibid., "The Abolition of War," [1926]; UCA, Robert Cumming Papers, Sermons, January 4, 1925; MC, Department of Evangelism and Social Service, *Report*, 1922, 61, 98; 1923, 88; 1924, 17, 75.

56 *Western Methodist Recorder,* May, 1915, 3–4; MC, Department of Evangelism and Social Service, *Report*, 1918, 23; 1920, 53.

57 MC, Department of Evangelism and Social Service, *Report*, 1917, 40; CG, April 29, 1914, 17–18; MC, *Journal of General Conference*, 1918, 341–342; Allen, "The Social Gospel as the Religion of the Agrarian Revolt," 174–175; William L. Morton, *The Progressive Party in Canada* (Toronto: Univ. of Toronto Press, 1950); William Irvine, *The Farmers in Politics* (Toronto: McClelland & Stewart, reprint, 1976).

58 Ian McKay, "Strikes in the Maritimes, 1901–1914," *Acadiensis* 13 (1983): 3–46; CG, January 2, 1907, 5; February 9, 1910, 4; July 8, 1914, 16; *Winnipeg Free Press Evening Bulletin,* November 1, 1920; Prang, 270–271; MC, Department of Evangelism and Social Service, *Report*, 1917, 54; 1918, 39; 1919, 57, 75; 1921, 22.

59 MC, *Journal of General Conference,* 1918, 341–342; MC, Department of Evangelism and Social Service, *Report*, 1915, 53, 84; 1916, 40, 63; CG, October 13, 1915, 5; October 28, 1918, 4; March 10, 1920, 7; August 25, 1920, 7; September 5, 1920, 8.

60 CG, January 1, 1919, 5; September 5, 1920, 8; December 29, 1920, 8; February 23, 1921, 6; May 11, 1921, 8; September 28, 1921, 4, 6; MC, Department of Evangelism and Social Service, *Report*, 1922, 91.

61 McNaught, 99–131; J.E. Rea (ed.), *The Winnipeg General Strike* (Toronto: Holt, Rinehart and Winston, 1973), 1–11; David Bercuson, "The Winnipeg General Strike, Collective Bargaining, and the One Big Union Issue," *CHR* 51 (1970): 164–176; MC, Department of Evangelism and Social Service, Beatrice Brigden to T. Albert Moore, July 26, 1919; CG, February 5, 1919, 19; May 21, 1919, 3; May 28, 1919, 18; June 4, 1919, 4, 14; UCA, Ernest Thomas biographical file.

62 Prang, 298–301; MC, Department of Evangelism and Social Service, *Report*, 1919, 66, 69; 1922, 74; CG, January 1, 1919, 19–20; June 11, 1919, 3; July 30, 1919, 8; July 7, 1920, 7; July 14, 1920, 5; August 25, 1920, 7.

63 MC, Board of Publication Papers, Strike Committee Report, May 5, 1921; ibid., Andrew Gerrard to Samuel Fallis, May 8, 1922; MC, Department of Evangelism and Social Service, *Report*, 1921, 22; MC, *Journal of General Conference*, 1922, 318.

64 MC, *Journal of General Conference,* 1918, 221; 1922, 226; CG December 3, 1924, 7; UCA, Margaret Addison biographical file; Chaviva Hosek, "Women at Victoria," in *From Cobourg to Toronto,* 58.

65 Elsinore Macpherson, "Survey of Women Graduates" (MA, Univ. of Toronto, 1920); Wilson, 101–124; CG, September 17, 1902, 5; Ruth Brouwer, "The Canadian Methodist Church and Ecclesiastical Suffrage for Women, 1905–1914," CMHS, *Papers* 2 (1977).

CHAPTER SIXTEEN

1 John W. Grant, *The Canadian Experience of Church Union* (London: Lutterworth Press, 1967), 29–30; John W. Grant, *The Church in the Canadian Era* (Toronto: McGraw-Hill Ryerson, 1972), 105–110; CMM 30 (1889): 88; CG, February 14, 1906, 20; September 19, 1906, 9.

2 *The First Canadian Christian Conference* (Toronto: Willard Press, 1878), vi; Evangelical Alliance, *Constitution* (Cornwall: Standard Press, 1890), 1. See also *The Canadian Congregational Year Book*, 1904–05, 82; William Mann, "The Canadian Church
Union, 1925," in Nils Ehrenstrom and Walter Meulder (eds.), *Institutionalism and
Church Unity* (New York: Association Press, 1963), 177.

3 CCA, March 8, 1871, 2.

4 UCA, Nathanael Burwash Papers, Charles Eby to Nathanael Burwash,
November 28, 1895. See also *The Canadian Congregational Yearbook*, 1874–75, 13;
1904–05, 79; "John Cook," DCB, 12:211.

5 Neil Semple, "Ontario's Religious Hegemony: The Creation of the National
Methodist Church," *Ontario History* 77 (1985): 19–42; Burkhard Kiesekamp, "Presbyterian and Methodist Divines: Their Case for a National Church in Canada,
1875–1900," *Studies in Religion* 2 (1973): 314; Mann, 176; Presbyterian Church in
Canada, *Acts and Proceedings*, 1887, 27; MC, *Journal of General Conference*, 1890, 172.

6 Brian P. Clarke, *Piety and Nationalism* (Montreal: McGill-Queen's Univ. Press,
1993), 3, 43, 66, 70, 219; Jacques Monet, "French-Canadian Nationalism and the
Challenge of Ultramontanism," CHA, *Historical Papers*, 1966, 41–55.

7 John S. Moir, *Enduring Witness. A History of the Presbyterian Church in Canada* (Tor-
onto: Bryant Press, 1975), 198; Roy Dalton, *The Jesuits' Estates Question, 1760–1888*
(Toronto: Univ. of Toronto Press, 1968), 147–165; James Watt, "Anti-Catholic
Nativism in Canada: The Protestant Protective Association," CHR 48 (1967): 45–
58; CMM 22 (1885): 560–561; MC, *Minutes of Montreal Conference*, 1885, 78; CG,
September 25, 1907, 4.

8 See UCA, Finding Aid 174, Anglican/United Church Union Papers, intro.; MC,
*Journal of General Conference*, 1886, 114–115; CG, May 1, 1889, 280; September 18,
1889, 600; December 11, 1889, 792–793; CMM 30 (1889): 87–89.

9 MC, *Journal of General Conference*, 1890, 172–174; 1894, 311; CG, January 9, 1901,
10; Presbyterian Church in Canada, *Acts and Proceedings*, 1890, 59–60, appendix
18, i; UCA, Anglican/United Church Union Papers, box 1, files 1–4; George Bond,
*The Methodist Point of View as to Union with the Anglican Church* (Halifax, 1914).

10 CG, January 16, 1885, 20; April 26, 1911, 6; MC, *Journal of General Conference*, 1890,
172; 1894, 310–311; 1898, 336.

11 MC, *Journal of General Conference*, 1890, 174; 1894, 95, 311; 1898, 337; CG,
January 9, 1901, 9; February 13, 1901, 3.

12 UCA, John Wood Papers, W.N. Allworth to John Wood, January 30, 1888; Mann,
173–176; *Census of Canada*, 1901, 1:144–145; Grant, *The Canadian Experience of
Church Union*, 19; MC, *Journal of General Conference*, 1902, 172–173; Presbyterian
Church in Canada, *Acts and Proceedings*, 1903, 51, 264; *The Canadian Congregational
Year Book*, 1903–04, 42; CG, February 4, 1903, 7; March 25, 1903, 4; April 8, 1903, 8.

13 Moir, 197–200; *Report of First Conference … on Church Union, 1904* (Toronto, 1905);
MC, *Journal of General Conference*, 1906, 160, 305–314; CG, March 9, 1904, 6;
June 22, 1904, 5; November 28, 1906, 7; December 26, 1906, 9.

14 E. Lloyd Morrow, *Church Union in Canada* (Toronto: Thomas Allen, 1923), 22;
Moir, 202; CG, September 26, 1906, 12; MC, *Journal of General Conference*, 1906,
311; *Basis of Union* (Toronto: United Church of Canada, 1925), 23–24. For a
review of committees' work, see UCA, Church Union Collection, Finding Aid 24,
intro.

15 Alfred Gandier, *The Doctrinal Basis of Union* (Toronto: Ryerson Press, 1926), 4; *CG*, February 4, 1903, 7; April 25, 1906, 19; June 27, 1906, 5; *Proceedings of the Third Conference of the Joint Committee on Church Union* (Toronto, 1907); *Basis of Union* (1925); Grant, *The Canadian Experience of Church Union*, 32–33; Claris Edwin Silcox, *Church Union in Canada; Its Causes and Consequences* (New York: Institute of Social Research, 1933), 130–134; UCA, Samuel Dwight Chown Papers, Addresses, "The Contribution of Methodism to Christian Unity," November 1916, 1–3.

16 Silcox, 159; *CG*, February 14, 1906, 8; May 30, 1906, 19; Morrow, appendix 5, "The *Basis of Union* (1914)," 322–330; *Basis of Union* (1925).

17 Moir, 200–202; Grant, *The Canadian Experience of Church Union*, 21.

18 UCA, T. Egerton Shore Papers, Egerton Shore to Lawson Caesar, February 2, 1912. See also UCA, Melvyn Matthew Bennett Papers, Melvyn Bennett to fiancée, February 19, 1899; *Newfoundland Methodist Monthly Greeting*, July 1911, 13; *CG*, April 19, 1911, 18; January 24, 1912, 8; Mary Vipond, "Canadian National Consciousness and the Formation of The United Church of Canada," UCA, *Bulletin* 24 (1975): 5; Allan Farris, "The Fathers of 1925," in Presbyterian Church, Centennial Committee (ed.), *Enkindled by the Word: Essays on Presbyterianism in Canada* (Toronto: Presbyterian Publications, 1966), 61; Morrow, 49–50.

19 *CG*, April 27, 1904, 6. See also ibid., May 1, 1901, 1; February 13, 1901, 3; February 14, 1906, 4; March 21, 1906, 5; May 19, 1909, 24; Samuel Dwight Chown Papers, Sermons, "That They All May Be One," January 1912; ibid., New Year's Address to Methodist Church, December 1924.

20 MC, Department of Evangelism and Social Service, *Report*, 1923, 36. See also ibid., 1924, 26; Twila Buttimer, " 'Great Expectations': The Maritime Methodist Church and Church Union, 1925" (MA, Univ. of New Brunswick, 1980), 69, 96–97; Morrow, 14, 53; Vipond, 13–14; *CG*, March 9, 1904, 6; August 10, 1904, 18; December 9, 1908, 7; June 7, 1911, 19; January 24, 1912, 8; January 28, 1925, 5, 22.

21 *CG*, February 13, 1901, 3; January 28, 1903, 7; April 20, 1903, 9; March 9, 1904, 6; Feburary 14, 1906, 8; MC, *Journal of General Conference*, 1906, 283; 1910, 310.

22 Grant, *The Canadian Experience of Church Union*, 36; Nathanael Burwash Papers, Charles Eby to Nathanael Burwash, November 28, 1895; Mann, 178; Kiesekamp, 313–316; Buttimer, 18; *CG*, February 26, 1908, 9; January 25, 1911, 21.

23 MC, *Journal of General Conference*, 1902, 172. See also *CG*, March 9, 1904, 6; April 6, 1904, 5.

24 *CG*, March 21, 1906, 5. See also ibid., March 2, 1910, 29; Feburary 14, 1906, 8; January 31, 1912, 13–15, 31; Grant, *The Canadian Experience of Church Union*, 25; Keith Clifford, "The Interpreters of the United Church of Canada," *Church History* 46 (1977): 208; Buttimer, 5; Mann, 183; Samuel Dwight Chown Papers, Addresses, "The Celebration of Two Hundredth Anniversary of John Wesley being Appointed a Fellow of Lincoln College," March 27, 1926.

25 *CG*, January 17, 1912, 9; August 8, 1906, 25. See also ibid., September 25, 1907, 4; April 26, 1911, 7; Vipond, 7–8; Mann, 189.

26 *CG*, January 28, 1903, 7; Kiesekamp, 320; Neil Semple, "The Quest for the Kingdom: Aspects of Protestant Revivalism in Nineteenth-Century Ontario," in David Keane and Colin Read (eds.), *Old Ontario: Essays in Honour of J.M.S. Careless* (Toronto: Dundurn Press, 1990), 112–114; Semple, "Ontario's Religious

Hegemony," 33–38; Mann, 190; Phyllis Airhart, *Serving the Present Age: Revivalism, Progressivism, and the Methodist Tradition in Canada* (Montreal: McGill-Queen's Univ. Press, 1992), 123–141.

27 Samuel Dwight Chown Paper, Correspondence, Open Letter to Methodist Church, November 1921. See also John Kent, "The Methodist Union in Britain, 1932," in *Institutionalism and Church Unity*, 195–220; J.L Allen, "The Methodist Union in the United States," in *Institutionalism and Church Unity*, 275–299; *CG*, June 10, 1903, 5; July 15, 1903, 8; January 24, 1906, 2; February 21, 1906, 3; February 28, 1906, 6; March 21, 1906, 5; September 19, 1906, 49; MC, *Journal of General Conference*, 1906, 69.

28 *CG*, February 14, 1906, 21; April 11, 1906, 7; January 25, 1911, 21; February 15, 1911, 22; June 7, 1911, 19; *Newfoundland Methodist Monthly Greeting*, May 1911, 9; William L. Brown, "The Sunday School Movement in the Methodist Church in Canada, 1875–1925" (MTh, Toronto Graduate School of Theological Studies, 1959), 112.

29 Grant, *The Canadian Experience of Church Union*, 24; Mann, 171–172, 183–185; Vipond, 5; Clifford, 208; N. Keith Clifford, "Church Union and Western Canada," in Dennis Butcher et al. (eds.), *Prairie Spirit* (Winnipeg: Univ. of Manitoba Press, 1985), 283–288; *CG*, January 16, 1901, 1; January 29, 1903, 7; April 20, 1904, 9; March 21, 1906, 5; February 26, 1908, 9; March 25, 1908, 26.

30 T. Egerton Shore Papers, Egerton Shore to Lawson Caesar, February 2, 1912; Morrow, 61; Silcox, 158; *CG*, March 21, 1906, 5; May 21, 1906, 5.

31 Margret Prang, *N.W. Rowell: Ontario Nationalist* (Toronto: Univ. of Toronto Press, 1975), 402–407; Michael Bliss, *A Canadian Millionaire: The Life and Business Times of Sir Joseph Flavelle, 1858–1939* (Toronto: Macmillan Press, 1978), 453–454; Mann, 189; Bond, 9; MC, *Journal of General Conference*, 1902, 176–177; John Thomas, "'A Pure and Popular Character': Case Studies in the Development of the Methodist 'Organizational' Church, 1884–1925" (PhD, York Univ. 1991), 39–47; *CG*, January 9, 1901, 9.

32 *Basis of Union*, 3.

33 Grant, *The Canadian Experience of Church Union*, 8–9; Vipond, 11–20; Mann, 189; Morrow, 14; Kiesekamp, 314, 317; Moir, 197–198; Clifford, "The Interpreters of Church Union," 207; *CG*, February 14, 1906, 20; October 7, 1911, 5; July 19, 1911, 19.

34 Buttimer, 42; *CG*, June 29, 1904, 10; March 21, 1906, 10; May 4, 1910, 24; June 15, 1910, 22; August 2, 1911, 22.

35 *Newfoundland Methodist Monthly Greeting*, July 1911, 13. See also *CG*, August 8, 1906, 9; May 18, 1910, 17; Church Union Collection, Methodist Papers, box 3, file 6, George Washington, "Why as a Methodist I Cannot Accept the *Basis of Union*"; ibid., John Staples to General Conference, August 12, 1910.

36 Silcox, 185; *CG*, April 4, 1906, 15; September 5, 1906, 16.

37 MC, *Journal of General Conference*, 1910, 316–318; 1914, 181; *CG*, June 29, 1904, 10; January 15, 1908, 8.

38 *CG*, January 15, 1908, 8; May 19, 1909, 24; June 1, 1910, 26.

39 *CG*, July 24, 1907, 8; August 14, 1907, 7; August 28, 1907, 8; September 11, 1907, 24–25; May 4, 1910, 24; March 8, 1911, 18; "Doctrine," in *Basis of Union*.

40 *CG*, June 29, 1904, 10; July 20, 1904, 29; April 4, 1906, 15; August 8, 1906, 9; March 16, 1910, 2; March 30, 1910, 21; April 6, 1910, 23; May 4, 1910, 24.

41  *CG*, July 20, 1904, 29. See also ibid., May 18, 1910, 17; March 4, 1910, 24; March 30, 1910, 21–22; May 25, 1910, 29, 35.

42  *CG*, February 5, 1908, 8. See also ibid., April 8, 1903, 8; August 6, 1906, 9; June 8, 1910, 17; July 5, 1911, 25–26; April 26, 1911, 20–21; Farris, 60–62; Morrow, addendum 2, 435–444.

43  *CG*, April 4, 1906, 15. See also ibid., March 21, 1906, 10; December 3, 1924, 17.

44  Ibid., August 8, 1906, 9; July 20, 1904, 29; Ibid., August 28, 1907, 9; June 15, 1910, 22.

45  Silcox, 185; *CG*, July 20, 1904, 29; March 21, 1906, 10; August 8, 1906, 9; April 26, 1911, 18–19; May 18, 1910, 17.

46  *Newfoundland Methodist Monthly Greeting*, February 1912, 5; *CG*, January 16, 1901, 2.

47  *CG*, December 16, 1908, 5; *The Canadian Congregational Yearbook*, 1907–08, 31; 1909–10, 42–44; 1910–11, 31–32, 76–77; 1912–13, 37–39; MC, *Journal of General Conference*, 1910, 167; Morrow, 26.

48  *The Canadian Congregational Yearbook*, 1911–12, 38; MC, *Journal of General Conference*, 1910, 100; Church Union Collection, Methodist Papers, box 5, files 89–119.

49  David W. Johnson, *History of Methodism in Eastern British America* (Sackville: Tribune Printing, 1925), 401; Buttimer, 48; Mann, 178; *CG*, February 14, 1912, 3; April 24, 1912, 21.

50  Presbyterian Church in Canada, *Acts and Proceedings*, 1912, 300. See also ibid., 1909, 39, 42; 1910, 29–30, 38–39, 43; 1911, 71; N. Keith Clifford, *Resistance to Church Union in Canada, 1904–1939* (Vancouver: Univ. of British Columbia Press, 1985); Samuel Dwight Chown, *The Story of Church Union in Canada* (Toronto: Ryerson Press, 1930); *Documents approved by the General Assembly of the Presbyterian Church in Canada as a Basis of Union* (Toronto: Murray Printing Co., 1912), 1–2.

51  Presbyterian Church in Canada, *Acts and Proceedings*, 1912, 330–333; Johnson, 397–400.

52  Presbyterian Church in Canada, *Acts and Proceedings*, 1913, 305. See also *The Union Movement in Australia* (1903); James Udy, "Wesley Heritage in the Formation of the Uniting Church in Australia," in James Udy and Eric Clancy (eds.), *Dig or Die* (Sydney: WMHS, 1981).

53  Morrow, 57–61; Moir 203; Mann, 179; Farris, 60–62; *CG*, April 5, 1911, 9–10; Presbyterian Church in Canada, *Acts and Proceedings*, 1914, 335–343; UCA, Ephraim Scott biographical file; Prang, 403–405.

54  James Cameron, "The Garden Distressed: Church Union and Dissent on Prince Edward Island, 1904–1947" (PhD, Queen's University, 1989), iii, xxvii–xxxix. See also *CG*, April 6, 1904, 5; May 25, 1904, 19.

55  Mann, 179; Clifford, "Church Union and Western Canada," 291; *CG*, April 5, 1911, 9–10; Presbyterian Church in Canada, *Acts and Proceedings*, 1913, 315; 1914, 336; UCA, John MacKay biographical file.

56  *CG*, January 10, 1912, 17; April 24, 1912, 5–6, 9–10; Presbyterian Church in Canada, *Acts and Proceedings*, 1913, 304.

57  *Census of Canada*, 1921, 1:568–569; *CG*, February 14, 1906, 8, 20.

58  Presbyterian Church in Canada, *Acts and Proceedings*, 1914, 50; 1915, 295.

59  Mann, 174; Presbyterian Church in Canada, *Acts and Proceedings*, 1916, 379–382.

60  Church Union Collection, Co-operation and Local Union Papers, "Historical Sketch of the Movement for Co-operation" (1917), 1–3; ibid., *Co-operation and*

*Union* (Toronto: Joint Committee on Church Union, 1923), 1–21; ibid., Provincial Files, Manitoba, Charles Manning to J.A. Doyle, May 13, 1922; Brown, 117; Mann, 181; MC, *Journal of General Conference*, 1902, 124–125; 1914, 261–262; UCA, MC, Department of Evangelism and Social Service, *Report*, 1916, 15; 1923, 36; Silcox, 158, 231.

61 MC, *Journal of General Conference*, 1914, 219; MC, Department of Evangelism and Social Service, *Report*, 1922, 36; *Co-operation and Union*, 3; Mann, 180–181; Silcox, 215–221; Presbyterian Church in Canada, *Acts and Proceedings*, 1913, 301; CG, April 5, 1911, 7; August 6, 1913, 19; June 3, 1914, 22; July 1, 1914, 8; June 28, 1916, 2; January 10, 1917, 2; April 25, 1917, 14.

62 Church Union Collection, Co-operation and Local Union Papers, "Changes in Union," January 23, 1923; *Co-operation and Union*, 3; Presbyterian Church in Canada, *Acts and Proceedings*, 1921, 49–50; Silcox, 74.

63 MC, Army and Navy Board, E.I. Hart, "What Canadian Churches Have Done to Win the War" (1918), 7; ibid., *A War-Time Programme for the Local Church* (Toronto: Army and Navy Board, n.d.), 1–2; Moir, 204–205; Morrow, 178; Silcox, 179; Edmund H. Oliver, *Organic Union of the Presbyterian, Methodist and Congregational Churches in the Dominion of Canada* (Toronto: Presbyterian Union Committee, 1923); Presbyterian Church in Canada, *Acts and Proceedings*, 1921, 46; 1923, 29–66, 82.

64 Silcox, 246; Church Union Collection, Bureau of Literature and Information; UCA, Finding Aid 24, Introduction to Church Union Papers, Bureau of Literature and Information; United Church, *Record of Proceedings*, 1925, 75; Presbyterian Church in Canada, *Acts and Proceedings*, 1925, 33.

65 Presbyterian Church in Canada, *Acts and Proceedings*, 1921, 58. See also ibid., 1924, 38, 54, 62–63; 1925, 33.

66 George Pidgeon, *The Church Union Situation in Canada* ([1924]), 18.

67 Gershom W. Mason, *The Legislative Struggle for Church Union* (Toronto: Ryerson Press, 1956), 1–36, 47–49, 140–159; Silcox, 259–268; Church Union Collection, Law and Legislation Papers; Presbyterian Church in Canada, *Acts and Proceedings*, 1924, 42; United Church, *Record of Proceedings*, 1925, 67; John W. Grant, *George Pidgeon: A Biography* (Toronto: Ryerson Press, 1962), 99.

68 Prang, 402–407; Mason, 36–46, 50–139; United Church, *Record of Proceedings*, 1925, 74–75; CG, December 3, 1924, 4; January 21, 1925, 4.

69 Church Union Collection, Dominion Property Commission; Clifford, "Church Union and Western Canada," 290–295.

70 General Commission on Church Union, *Plan of Union and By-Laws* (Toronto: 1972), 12. See also United Church, *Record of Proceedings*, 1925, 74–75; CG, December 24, 1924, 5; Neil Semple, *The United Church of Canada: The First Sixty Years* (Toronto: United Church, 1985), 1–2.

EPILOGUE

1 S.T. Kimbrough, *Charles Wesley, The Meaning of His Hymns Today* (Nashville: The Upper Room Press, 1987), 11.

2 For a discussion on the conflict between science and religion and the effect of liberal theology and the social gospel in promoting secularism in Canada, see Brian McKillop, *A Disciplined Intelligence;* Ramsay Cook, *The Regenerators;* David

Marshall, *Secularizing the Faith;* and Michael Gauvreau, *The Evangelical Century.* For a broader perspective on these questions, see Owen Chadwick, *The Secularization of the European Mind;* George Marsden, *Fundamentalism and American Culture;* James Moore, *The Post-Darwinian Controversies;* John H. Brooke, *Science and Religion: Some Historical Perspectives;* and Bryan Wilson, *Contemporary Transformations of Religion.*

3  *Canadian Evangel,* Historical Final Issue, Spring 1969, 1–32; UCA, Evangelical United Brethren Papers; MC, *Journal of General Conference,* 1914, 277–279; Howard Brox, "The Beginnings of the Evangelical United Brethren in Upper Canada," CMHS, *Papers* 10 (1995).

4  Donald Dayton, "The Holiness Churches: A Significant Ethical Tradition," *Christian Century,* February 26, 1975, 197; Charles Jones, *Guide to the Study of the Holiness Movement* (Metuchen: Scarecrow Press, 1974); Melvin Dieter, "Hanna among the Methodists: A Quaker Woman in the Methodist Holiness Revival," CMHS, *Papers* 7 (1989): 99–114.

5  Wayne Kleinsteuber, *More than a Memory: The Renewal of Methodism in Canada* (Mississauga: Light & Life Press, 1984); Dayton, 200.

6  Ralph Horner, *Pentecost* (Toronto: Wm. Briggs, 1891); Ralph Horner, *The Feast of 1905* (1905); Ralph Horner, *The Doctrines of the Standard Church of America* (Brockville: Standard Book Room, n.d.), 13; Alden Aikens, "The Legacy of John Wesley in The Church of the Nazarene in Canada," CMHS, *Papers* 9 (1991): 5–25; Gerald Hobbs, "Stepchildren of John Wesley: the Gospel Workers Church of Canada," CMHS, *Papers* 8 (1990): 174–188.

7  Gordon Moyles, *The Blood and Fire: A History of the Salvation Army in the Dominion, 1882–1976* (Toronto: Peter Martin, 1977); Phyllis Airhart, *Serving the Present Age: Revivalism, Progressivism, and the Methodist Tradition in Canada* (Montreal: McGill-Queen's Univ. Press, 1992), 72–75; Victor Shepherd, "From New Connexion Methodist to William Booth," CMHS, *Papers* 9 (1991): 91–107; Richard Allen, *The Social Passion: Religion and Social Reform in Canada, 1914–1928* (Toronto: Univ. of Toronto Press, 1971), 81–86.

8  United Church, *Record of Proceedings,* 1925, 5–6. See also CG, January 28, 1925, 5.

9  United Church, *Record of Proceedings,* 1946, 163–166; 1956, 180–193; 1984, 474; 1986, 180–183.

10  John Webster Grant, "And are we yet alive?" CMHS, *Papers* 8 (1990): 105.

11  Louis Benson, *The English Hymn* (Richmond: John Knox Press, 1915), 246; Samuel P. Rose, *The Genius of Methodism* (Toronto: Ryerson Press, 1923), 3; James Udy, "Wesley Heritage in the Formation of the Uniting Church in Australia," in James Udy and Eric Clancy (eds.), *Dig or Die* (Sydney: WMHS, 1981), 194; Victor Shepherd, "John Wesley: A Parent to be Honoured" (address, London, Ontario, 1984), 4; Gerald Hobbs, "Methodism in The United Church of Canada," CMHS, *Papers* 8 (1990): 89–95.

12  William R. Hutchison, "Introduction," in Hutchison (ed.), *American Protestant Thought: The Liberal Era* (New York: Harper & Row, 1968), 1–14; David Marshall, *Secularizing the Faith: Canadian Protestant Clergy and the Crisis of Belief, 1850–1940* (Toronto: Univ. of Toronto Press, 1992), 228–248; *Christianizing the Social Order* (Toronto: Board of Evangelism and Social Service, 1934); *New Outlook,* February 8, 1933, 1; United Church, *Record of Proceedings,* 1938, 174–182.

13 Walter M. Horton, "The Decline of Liberalism," in *American Protestant Thought: The Liberal Era*, 190–196; Rosemary Keller, "Vocational Journey and Vocational Identity in the Life and Work of Georgia Harkness," CMHS, *Papers* 7 (1989): 137–151; David R. Elliott, "Hugh Wesley Dobson (1879–1956): Regenerator of Society," CMHS, *Papers* 9 (1991): 27–40; Ian Manson, "Ernest Thomas and the Theology of the Methodist Social Gospel," CMHS, *Papers* 9 (1991): 51–64.

14 Udy, 197, 178, 189.

15 Edward Jackman, "The Interaction Between John Wesley and the Roman Catholic Church," CMHS, *Papers* 9 (1991): 41–49; William R. Cannon, "John Wesley and the Catholic Tradition," CMHS, *Papers* 2 (1980); Albert Outler, "John Wesley's Interests in the Early Fathers of the Church," CMHS, *Papers* 2 (1980).

16 Theodore Runyon, "What Is Methodism's Theological Contribution Today?" Bicentennial Consultation on Wesleyan Theology, Emory University, 1983, 3–15; United Church, *Record of Proceedings*, 1984, 344–346; 1986, 180–183.

17 United Church, *Record of Proceedings*, 1946, 238–246; 1980, 703–713, 942–943; Neil Semple, *The United Church of Canada: The First Sixty Years* (Toronto: United Church, 1985), 1–16; Glenn Lucas, "Wesley Heritage in the United Church of Canada," in *Dig or Die*, 149; A.J. Armstrong and David Goa, "Praise and The Prophetic: Methodist Resonances in United Church Worship," CMHS, *Papers* 10 (1995).

18 United Church, *Record of Proceedings*, 1936, 288–290; 1982, 315–321; 1984, 341–349, 352–354, 450–455; 1988, 316; Clifford Elliott, *Journey into Understanding* (Toronto: Ryerson Press, 1962).

19 United Church, *Record of Proceedings*, 1936, 14, 224; 1982, 370–375; 1986, 439–519; Shirley Davy (ed.), *Women, Work and Worship in the United Church of Canada* (Toronto: United Church, 1983).

# Index